Frommer's®
Belize

My Belize

by Eliot Greenspan

WITH THE LONGEST BARRIER REEF IN THE WESTERN HEMISPHERE, THE highest density population of the New World's largest cat, and one of the most extensive known Maya ceremonial cities of the classic period, Belize is positive proof of that popular cliché: *Good things come in small packages.*

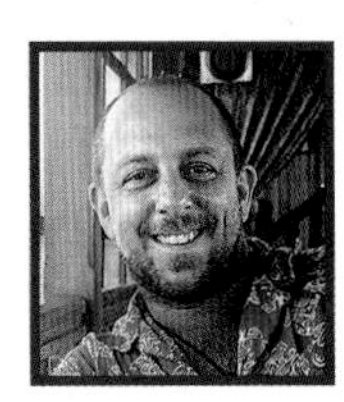

The whale shark, the ocean's biggest fish, congregates off of Gladden Spit at regular intervals, and more than 600 species of birds are either migrants or residents in this tiny country.

The Belize barrier reef provides endless opportunities for world-class scuba diving and snorkeling, from the Blue Hole to the touristy feeding spot known as Shark-Ray Alley. Inland adventure hounds can stalk a wild jaguar or climb towering Maya temples.

Belize is a polyglot's paradise. It was first settled by the Maya and later colonized by the British. The unique Garifuna people were banished to exile in Belize several hundred years ago, and Mexican, Guatemalan, Chinese, East Indian, and German Mennonite settlers have joined the mix.

The photos here capture some of my favorite Belizean images and experiences. But don't leave your camera at home . . . I'm sure you'll have plenty of your own.

© Vicki Smith/AP Photo

© SIME s.a.s/eStock Photo

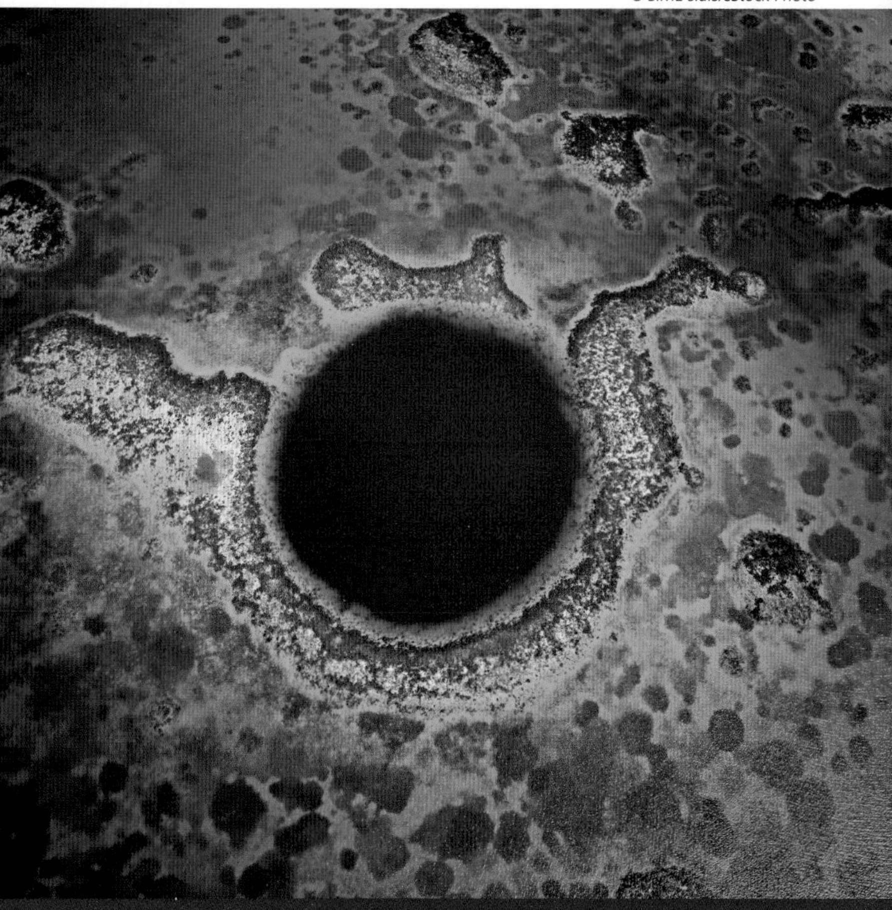

CHICKEN DROP (left) It ain't Vegas, *baby,* but I think that gambling by betting on the number where a chicken will poop is far more fun than plopping down coins on roulette at the Bellagio. Beware: The winner cleans up, both by raking in the winnings and wiping up the droppings.

THE BLUE HOLE (above) Jacques Cousteau loved the Blue Hole. At nearly 1,000 feet in diameter, this mid-ocean sinkhole drops almost perfectly straight down for some 400 feet. The Blue Hole sits almost in the center of Lighthouse Reef Atoll, one of Belize's three stunning atolls.

First page: top, © Gavin Hellier/Robert Harding Travel/PhotoLibrary; bottom, © NHPA/Photoshot

HAWKSBILL SEA TURTLE (left) The Belize barrier reef offers up a bounty of colorful corals and critters for snorkelers and scuba divers alike. Here, a solitary Hawksbill sea turtle swims past some coral and soft sponges.

WHALE SHARK (above) In addition to being a living psychedelic artwork, the whale shark is the largest fish in the sea. They can reach up to 40 feet in length and almost 20 feet in width. Gentle, slow-moving filter-feeders, whale sharks regularly gather to gorge themselves at Gladden Spit, off of Placencia, for several days on either side of the full moon between April and June (and, to a lesser extent, up until August).

© Jim West/Alamy

GARIFUNA DRUMMER (left) The Garifuna, or Garinagu, people are descendents of intermixed escaped African slaves and Carib Indians. In the late 18th century, the British colonial authorities left several thousand Garifuna abandoned along the desolate coast, somewhere between northern Honduras and Belize. Since then, their unique culture, language, dance, and song have survived, relatively intact and unchanged.

CARACOL (below) In a country with only a handful of elevators, Maya ruins remain the tallest man-made structures to be found, and the temples at Caracol are the tallest of these. You'll have to climb to the top on your own, but the view is worth it.

© Dan Hallman/Photodisc/Alamy

© Alain Le Garsmeur/Corbis

MENNONITE COMMUNITY (above) While the Garifuna, Maya, Creole, Mestizo, and descendents of British colonizers are the main ethnic groups you'll find in Belize, don't be surprised to come upon a group of Mennonites traveling down some Belizean highway or byway in their traditional horse-drawn buggy.

SAN PEDRO FESTIVAL (right) San Pedro on Ambergris Caye is the place to go in Belize for Carnival. The San Pedrenos pull out all the stops, with a series of concerts, parades, and public parties.

© JC Cuellar/Tony Rath Photography/drr.net

SMOOTH SAILING Sure, speedboats will get you there quicker, but nothing beats the peace, quiet, and romance of exploring the Belizean cayes in a sailboat. The crystal-clear waters, calm seas, and isolated anchorages around Ambergris Caye, Caye Caulker, and Placencia make them excellent spots for sailing and snorkeling. *© Mira/Alamy*

Frommer's®

Belize

3rd Edition

by Eliot Greenspan

Here's what the critics say about Frommer's:

"Amazingly easy to use. Very portable, very complete."
—**BOOKLIST**

"Detailed, accurate, and easy-to-read information for all price ranges."
—**GLAMOUR MAGAZINE**

"Hotel information is close to encyclopedic."
—**DES MOINES SUNDAY REGISTER**

"Frommer's Guides have a way of giving you a real feel for a place."
—**KNIGHT RIDDER NEWSPAPERS**

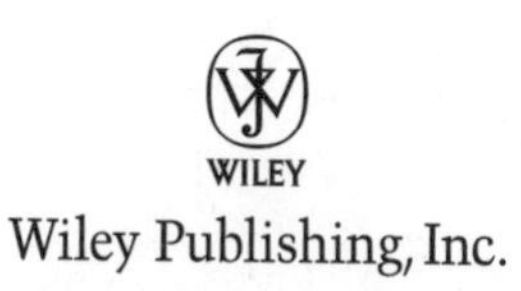

Wiley Publishing, Inc.

Published by:

WILEY PUBLISHING, INC.

111 River St.
Hoboken, NJ 07030-5774

ISBN 978-0-470-28779-8

Editor: mcd editorial with Anuja Madar
Production Editor: Suzanna R. Thompson
Cartographer: Andrew Murphy
Photo Editor: Richard Fox
Production by Wiley Indianapolis Composition Services

Front cover photo: Snorkeling in the Caribbean
Back cover photo: Traversing caves on the Caves Branch River

For information on our other products and services or to obtain technical support, please contact our Customer Care Department within the U.S. at 800/762-2974, outside the U.S. at 317/572-3993 or fax 317/572-4002.

Wiley also publishes its books in a variety of electronic formats. Some content that appears in print may not be available in electronic formats.

Manufactured in the United States of America

5 4 3 2 1

CONTENTS

4 SUGGESTED BELIZE ITINERARIES 60

5 THE ACTIVE VACATION PLANNER 70

6 BELIZE CITY 86

7 THE NORTHERN CAYES & ATOLLS 112

8 SOUTHERN BELIZE 155

LIST OF MAPS

ABOUT THE AUTHOR

Eliot Greenspan is a poet, journalist, musician and travel writer who took his backpack and typewriter the length of Mesoamerica before settling in Costa Rica in 1992. Since then, he has worked steadily as a travel writer, freelance journalist, and translator, and has continued his travels in the region. In addition to this book, he is the author of *Frommer's Guatemala, Frommer's Costa Rica, Frommer's Ecuador,* and *Costa Rica For Dummies,* as well as the chapter on Venezuela in *Frommer's South America,* and is co-author of *Frommer's Cuba.* He is also the author of *The Tico Times Restaurant Guide to Costa Rica* and the poetry collection *Map of You, Map of Me.*

ACKNOWLEDGMENTS

I'd like to tip my hat and extend my thanks to Myka Carroll and Anuja Madar. I'd also like to thank Erin Z. Weaver for her assistance with the wildlife guide.

—Eliot Greenspan

AN INVITATION TO THE READER

In researching this book, we discovered many wonderful places—hotels, restaurants, shops, and more. We're sure you'll find others. Please tell us about them, so we can share the information with your fellow travelers in upcoming editions. If you were disappointed with a recommendation, we'd love to know that, too. Please write to:

Frommer's Belize, 3rd Edition
Wiley Publishing, Inc. • 111 River St. • Hoboken, NJ 07030-5774

AN ADDITIONAL NOTE

Please be advised that travel information is subject to change at any time—and this is especially true of prices. We therefore suggest that you write or call ahead for confirmation when making your travel plans. The authors, editors, and publisher cannot be held responsible for the experiences of readers while traveling. Your safety is important to us, however, so we encourage you to stay alert and be aware of your surroundings. Keep a close eye on cameras, purses, and wallets, all favorite targets of thieves and pickpockets.

FROMMER'S STAR RATINGS, ICONS & ABBREVIATIONS

Every hotel, restaurant, and attraction listing in this guide has been ranked for quality, value, service, amenities, and special features using a **star-rating system.** In country, state, and regional guides, we also rate towns and regions to help you narrow down your choices and budget your time accordingly. Hotels and restaurants are rated on a scale of zero (recommended) to three stars (exceptional). Attractions, shopping, nightlife, towns, and regions are rated according to the following scale: zero stars (recommended), one star (highly recommended), two stars (very highly recommended), and three stars (must-see).

In addition to the star-rating system, we also use **seven feature icons** that point you to the great deals, in-the-know advice, and unique experiences that separate travelers from tourists. Throughout the book, look for:

Finds	Special finds—those places only insiders know about
Fun Facts	Fun facts—details that make travelers more informed and their trips more fun
Kids	Best bets for kids, and advice for the whole family
Moments	Special moments—those experiences that memories are made of
Overrated	Places or experiences not worth your time or money
Tips	Insider tips—great ways to save time and money
Value	Great values—where to get the best deals

The following **abbreviations** are used for credit cards:

AE	American Express	DISC	Discover	V	Visa
DC	Diners Club	MC	MasterCard		

FROMMERS.COM

Now that you have this guidebook to help you plan a great trip, visit our website at **www.frommers.com** for additional travel information on more than 4,000 destinations. We update features regularly to give you instant access to the most current trip-planning information available. At Frommers.com, you'll find scoops on the best airfares, lodging rates, and car rental bargains. You can even book your travel online through our reliable travel booking partners. Other popular features include:

- Online updates of our most popular guidebooks
- Vacation sweepstakes and contest giveaways
- Newsletters highlighting the hottest travel trends
- Podcasts, interactive maps, and up-to-the-minute events listings
- Opinionated blog entries by Arthur Frommer himself
- Online travel message boards with featured travel discussions

What's New in Belize

PLANNING YOUR TRIP **Astrum Helicopters** (© **222-5100;** www.astrumhelicopters.com) is a new company with modern four- and six-passenger helicopters available for charter tours and transfers all over the country.

Based in Placencia, **Goss Chocolate** (www.gosschocolate.com) makes organic dark and milk chocolate bars that are available in gift shops and supermarkets around the country. These bars are delicious and make great gifts.

BELIZE CITY After many years in the downtown business district, Jambel's Jerk Pit has moved to 164 Newtown Barracks Rd., near the Princess Hotel & Casino. The restaurant is now called **Jambel's Jerk Pit Too** (© **223-1966**).

The folks at the Belize Zoo have begun to try to attract more overnight visitors, re-christening their few rooms and dormitories as the **Belize Zoo Jungle Lodge** (© **220-8003**).

See chapter 6 for more information.

NORTHERN CAYES & ATOLLS **Cayo Espanto** (© **888/666-4282** in the U.S. and Canada; www.aprivateisland.com) has added one more luxurious villa and updated their interior decor and linens.

Jambel's Jerk Pit (© **226-3515**) has moved to a new location, right on Barrier Reef Drive in the center of San Pedro.

Forget about golf carts, scooters, and bicycles: If you want a unique means of transport on Ambergris Caye, check in with the folks at **Segway of Belize** (© **226-3344;** www.segwayofbelize.com).

Over on Caye Caulker, **Kitexplorer** (© **602-9297;** www.kitexplorer.com) is a new operation offering classes and rentals for those looking to either or both kitesurfing and sailboarding. Or, if you're looking for more mellow pursuits, you can check in with **Great Island Yoga** (© **660-0411;** www.greatislandyoga.com).

For eats on Caye Caulker, it's worth stopping in at **Agave** (© **226-0403**), an excellent restaurant with a chill ambience and creative menu. Also, be aware that the longstanding **Rasta Pasta Rainforest Café** (© **206-0356**) has moved to a new location on the southern end of Front Street.

See chapter 7 for complete coverage.

SOUTHERN BELIZE The small Garífuna village of Hopkins now has an excellent Indian restaurant, **Taste of India** (© **660-0971**).

In Placencia, **Turtle Inn** (© **800/746-3743;** www.turtleinn.com) has added six new cabins, a new swimming pool, and a new outdoor grill restaurant.

The **Placencia Village Square** is a new shopping center located just across from the soccer field; it now houses the Placencia Information Center and Tutti Frutti ice cream shop, as well as several other stores. Right next door is the rebuilt and renewed **Purple Space Monkey** (© **523-4094**).

Creating a taste sensation in Placencia, **The French Connection** (© **523-3656**) has kicked up the ante on fine dining in this little beach town.

Finally, for nightlife in Placencia, there's the new **D'Eclipse Entertainment Club** (© **523-3288**), offering live music, DJs, and karaoke in an air-conditioned space near the airstrip.

Down in Punta Gorda, the former El Pescador South is now **Machaca Hill Lodge** (© **722-0050;** www.machacahill.com). The old Titanic Bar has become the **Deja View Café** for breakfast and lunch, and the **Reef Bar** (✆ **702-0154**) for dinner and drinks.

See chapter 8 for more information.

NORTHERN BELIZE Up in Corozal, the **Mirador Hotel** (✆ **442-0189;** www.mirador.bz) is a new high-rise option—four stories is considered a high-rise in Corozal—set right on the waterfront in the center of town.

See chapter 9 for more information.

CAYO DISTRICT & WESTERN BELIZE The United States has moved its embassy from Belize City to a large new building in the capital city of Belmopan.

In March 2008, two massive rocks collapsed the ceiling near the entrance to **St. Herman's Cave.** At present, the cave is closed, and at press time it's unclear if and when it will be reopened.

The folks at **Jaguar Paw** (✆ **824-2023;** www.jaguarpaw.com) have opened the first zip-line canopy tour operation in the country.

Blancaneaux Lodge (✆ **800/746-3743** in the U.S., or 824-3878 in Belize; www.blancaneaux.com) now has two new honeymoon villas and one exclusive "Enchanted Cottage"; all include a private plunge pool and butler service. They have also added a midsize outdoor pool and a new intimate restaurant specializing in Guatemalan cuisine.

See chapter 10.

TIKAL & GUATEMALA'S PETEN At the time of this writing, the exchange rate was 7.38 Guatemalan quetzales to the U.S. dollar and 14.09 quetzales to the British pound.

See chapter 11 for complete coverage.

1 The Best of Belize

Belize proves the cliché that big things come in small packages. This tiny Central American country has the longest continuous barrier reef in the Western Hemisphere; the largest known Classic Mayan city, Caracol; and the highest concentration per square mile of the largest new-world cat, the jaguar. It also has one of the most extensive and easily accessible cave systems for amateur and experienced spelunkers alike, as well as a nearly endless supply of some of the world's best snorkeling and scuba-diving opportunities. Depending on your personal preferences, you can choose to stay in an intimate and luxurious hotel, an isolated nature lodge in the heart of the Mundo Maya, or a tent on your own desert island. Or you can sample all three. The best part about all these world-class places and experiences is that Belize's compact size makes it easy to sample a wide range of them in a short period of time. The lists below should help you zero in on a few personal bests of your own.

1 THE BEST PURELY BELIZEAN EXPERIENCES

- **Betting on a Chicken Drop:** A chicken drop is a sort of poor man's version of roulette, and much more fun. Numbers are painted on a grid and bets are placed. Then, a chicken is set loose on a wire mesh screen suspended over the grid. The winner is chosen by the chicken's first "drop." In addition to any monetary winnings, the "winner" often must clean the grid. You'll find a chicken drop held every Wednesday night at the Pier Lounge on Ambergris Caye. See "Ambergris Caye" in chapter 7.
- **Drinking a Cool Seaweed Shake:** Made from dried natural seaweed, blended with both condensed and evaporated milk, cinnamon, nutmeg, vanilla, and some ice, this drink is surprisingly refreshing and tasty. You can get these drinks at several beach destinations around Belize, but Placencia seems to be the home of the seaweed shake. See "Placencia" in chapter 8.
- **Staying with a Maya Family:** It certainly isn't going to be like a night at the Four Seasons, but if you're looking for a real cultural exchange experience, you should consider actually staying with a traditional Maya family. **The Maya Village Homestay Network** (© **722-2470;** demdatsdoin@btl.net) can organize this for you. See "Punta Gorda & the Toledo District" in chapter 8.
- **Spending the Night in a Maya Ceremonial City:** An intimate and rather luxurious nature lodge, **Chan Chich Lodge** (© **800/343-8009** in the U.S., or 223-4419 in Belize; www.chanchich.com) is built right on the site of a minor Mayan ceremonial city. The hills just outside your private cabin are unexcavated residences and pyramids. Ruins and basic excavations dot the grounds, and the surrounding rainforests are rich in bird and animal life. See p. 213.

The Best of Belize

THE BEST OF NATURAL BELIZE

The Atolls **10**
Caves **15**
The Cayes and Barrier Reef **9**
Cockscomb Basin Wildlife Sanctuary and Cockscomb Basin Forest Reserve **18**
Crooked Tree Wildlife Sanctuary **5**
Río Bravo Conservation Area **2**
Río On Pools **16**

THE BEST DIVING & SNORKELING

Caye Caulker **8**
Gladden Spit **21**
Glover's Reef Atoll **20**
Shark-Ray Alley and Hol Chan Marine Reserve **7**
Turneffe Island and Lighthouse Reef Atolls **10**

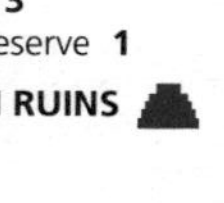
THE BEST BIRD-WATCHING
Caracol 17
Cockscomb Basin Forest Reserve 18
Crooked Tree Wildlife Sanctuary 5
Half Moon Caye National Monument 11
Man-O-War Caye 19
New River Lagoon 3
Shipstern Nature Reserve 1
THE BEST MAYAN RUINS
Altun Ha 6
Caracol 17
El Pilar 12
Lamanai 4
Tikal 14
Xunantunich 13
KEY TO ABBREVIATIONS
AR Archaeological Reserve
FR Forest Reserve
MR Marine Reserve
NP National Park
NM Natural Monument
NR Nature Reserve
PR Private Reserve
WS Wildlife Sanctuary
Reef
Marine Reserve boundary
Xunantunich
San Ignacio
San Antonio
Tapir Mountain NR
Blue Hole NP
Hummingbird Hwy.
Gales Point
Mullins River
Half Moon Caye NM
CAYO
Sibun FR
Middlesex
Grants Works FR
Dangriga
Vaca FR
Mountain Pine Ridge FR
Sittee River FR
Mayflower Bocawina NP
Hopkins Village
Victoria Peak NM
STANN CREEK
Caracol AR
Caracol
Chiquibul FR
Chiquibul NP
Cockscomb Basin WS
MAYA MOUNTAINS
Maya Mountain FR
Southern Hwy.
Mango Creek FR
Maya Beach
Placencia
South Water Caye MR
Glover's Reef Atoll
Glover's Reef MR
CARIBBEAN SEA
Bladen NR
Swasey Bladen FR
Deep River FR
Monkey River
Columbia River FR
Monkey Caye FR
Laughing Bird Caye NP
Payne's Creek NP
TOLEDO
San Antonio
Big Falls
Machaca Creek FR
Port Honduras MR
Sapodilla Cayes MR
Blue Creek
Agua Caliente Luha WS
Punta Gorda
Gulf of Honduras
Temash-Sarstoon NP
Barranco
Bahia de Amatique
Sarstoon River
GUATEMALA

- **The Cayes & Barrier Reef:** Running the entire length of the country's coastline, the Belize Barrier Reef is the second longest continuous barrier reef in the world. Here you will find some of the best snorkeling opportunities and scuba-diving sites in the world. Moreover, the barrier reef is lined with hundreds and hundreds of small islands, or cayes. Most are uninhabited. These cayes range in size from tiny patches of sand or mangrove smaller than a football field to the larger and more developed vacation destination islands of Caye Caulker and Ambergris Caye. Whether you want the hustle and bustle of the latter, the deserted isle feel of a smaller or even private caye, or something in between, your choices are many and uniformly inviting. See chapters 7 and 8.
- **The Atolls:** Belize's three mid-ocean atolls are arguably more spectacular than the barrier reef and its many cayes. Unique formations of small islands and reef surrounding a mid-ocean saltwater lagoon, atolls are an isolated and stunning phenomena. Belize has three of them: Turneffe Island, Lighthouse Reef, and Glover's Reef. These atolls are very sparsely developed, and any visit here will be imbued with a sense of adventure, isolation, and romance. See "The Outer Atolls" in chapter 7 and "Dangriga" in chapter 8.
- **Cockscomb Basin Wildlife Sanctuary & Cockscomb Basin Forest Reserve** (Southern Belize): This is a huge protected area comprised of rugged, forested mountains. The sanctuary was designed to protect and help researchers study the largest new-world cat, the jaguar. The park is also home to Belize's other four wildcat species, as well as Baird's tapirs, coati-mundis, tayra, kinkajous, deer, peccaries, anteaters, and armadillos, as well as some 300 species of birds. Inside the park you'll also find Victoria Peak, the country's highest mountain. See "Dangriga" in chapter 8.
- **Crooked Tree Wildlife Sanctuary** (Northern Belize): This preserve is a swampy lowland that is home to over 250 resident species of birds and serves as a resting spot for scores of migratory species. It is also the principal nesting site of the endangered jabiru stork, the largest bird in the Americas. The sanctuary is an excellent place to spot other wildlife as well, including crocodiles, iguanas, coati-mundi, and howler monkeys. The best way to explore Crooked Tree is by paddling around the network of lagoons in a dugout canoe. See "En Route North: Crooked Tree Wildlife Sanctuary" in chapter 9.
- **Río Bravo Conservation Area** (Northern Belize): This massive mixed tract of virgin forest, sustainable-yield managed forest, and recovering reforestation areas is home to nearly 400 bird species and over 200 species of tropical trees. It also supports a healthy population of most of the new-world cat species, and is one of the best areas in the Americas to try your luck in spotting a jaguar. The Río Bravo Conservation Area is also home to La Milpa, an ongoing excavation of a major Mayan ceremonial city. See "Going West: Río Bravo Conservation Area, La Milpa & Chan Chich" in chapter 9.
- **Caves** (Cayo District and Western Belize): Belize has an extensive network of caves, which were considered by the ancient Maya to be a mystical portal between the world of the living and the underworld of spirits and the dead. They called this mystical realm Xibalba. In almost every explored cave in Belize, some evidence of use by the Mayans has been uncovered. Fire pits, campsites, burial mounds, and ritual altars have all

been found. Numerous pieces of pottery and abundant skeletons, bones, and artifacts have also been encountered. These caves are relatively easily accessible and you should not leave Belize without at least one foray into Xibalba. See chapter 10.

- **Río on Pools** (Cayo District and Western Belize): This series of flowing falls and pools is somewhat reminiscent of Ocho Ríos in Jamaica. While the views and swimming are fine at the base of the falls, it's worth the hike upstream to even better views and numerous pools flowing between big rocks, which are perfect for sunbathing. This place can get crowded on weekends, when locals come for family picnics and getaways. See "Mountain Pine Ridge & Caracol" in chapter 10.

3 THE BEST DIVING & SNORKELING

Belize is rightly considered one of the top scuba diving and snorkeling destinations on the planet. The Belize Barrier Reef, second only to Australia's Great Barrier Reef, runs the length of its coastline, and the country has three open-ocean atolls. Diving and snorkeling are superb all along the barrier reef; the following are just a few of the truly standout sites and dives.

- **Shark-Ray Alley & Hol Chan Marine Reserve** (Northern Cayes and Atolls): These two very popular snorkeling sites are threatened with overcrowding but still live up to their billing. Shark-Ray Alley guarantees a very close encounter with schools of large stingrays and nurse sharks. The experience provides a substantial adrenaline rush for all but the most nonchalant and veteran divers. Hol Chan Marine Reserve is an excellent snorkeling destination comprised of a narrow channel cutting through a rich and well-maintained shallow coral reef. See "Ambergris Caye" in chapter 7.
- **Caye Caulker** (Northern Cayes and Atolls): If you're looking for a relaxed vacation spot to serve as a base for some good snorkeling, you can't do much better than Caye Caulker, which has some excellent and easily accessible snorkeling sites. It's also much less developed and less crowded than its more popular neighbor, Ambergris Caye. Many of the dive sites are a very short boat ride from shore. See "Caye Caulker" in chapter 7.
- **Turneffe Island & Lighthouse Reef Atolls** (Northern Cayes and Atolls): For many divers coming to Belize, these spots are the holy grail, and justifiably so. Both of these mid-ocean atoll formations feature nearly endless opportunities for world-class wall, drift, and coral-garden diving. As a cherry to top this cake, this is also where you'll find the Blue Hole. A host of dive operators all across Belize offer day trips to dive these sites, although these usually involve a 90-minute to 3-hour ride each way. Alternatively, you can stay at one of the very few lodges out here, or take a vacation on a live-aboard dive boat. See "The Outer Atolls" in chapter 7.
- **Glover's Reef Atoll** (Southern Belize): Glover's Reef is the third of Belize's mid-ocean atolls. The diving here is spectacular and underexploited. Unlike the Turneffe Island and Lighthouse Reef atolls, far fewer day-trippers visit the dive sites around Glover's Reef Atoll. The best way to really take advantage of the diving and snorkeling is to stay out here, and for this, **Glover's Atoll Resort** (**© 520-5016;** www.glovers.com.bz) is your best option. See "Dangriga" in chapter 8.
- **Gladden Spit** (Southern Belize): More or less due east of Placencia, Gladden Spit is a world-renowned spot for diving

with massive whale sharks. This mid-ocean site is the natural spawning ground for a variety of marine species. Whale sharks come regularly to feed on the energetically rich and very plentiful reproductive effluence. Whale-shark sightings are fairly common here from late March through June, and to a lesser extent from August to October and in December and January. Since the sharks tend to feed and cruise close to the surface, snorkelers and divers alike can enjoy the spectacle. See "Placencia" in chapter 8.

4 THE BEST NONDIVING ADVENTURES

- **Chartering a Sailboat for Some Isolated Island Explorations:** The protected waters, steady gentle trade winds, and hundreds of isolated islands and anchorages make Belize an ideal place for bareboat charters. Given the shallow draft, increased interior space, and reduced drag, a multihull is your best bet. **The Moorings** (© **888/952-8420** in the U.S. and Canada, or 523-3351; www.moorings.com) and **TMM** (© **800/633-0155** in the U.S., or 226-3026; www.sailtmm.com) are two large-scale charter companies with operations on Ambergris Caye and in Placencia. See "Ambergris Caye" in chapter 7 and "Placencia" in chapter 8.
- **Fly-Fishing for Bonefish, Permit & Tarpon on the Outer Atoll Flats:** Belize is a world-class fishing destination, and while offshore fishing for bigger game is possible, the real draw here is fly-fishing for feisty and world-record size bonefish, permit, and tarpon (actually, the tarpon get as big as most deep-sea game). **Turneffe Flats** (© **888/512-8812** in the U.S.; www.tflats.com) is an excellent fishing operation located on Turneffe Island Atoll. See "The Outer Atolls" in chapter 7.
- **Kayaking & Camping around Glover's Reef Atoll:** The relatively calm protected waters of the atoll and manageable distances between islands make this a perfect place to explore under your own power, paddling a one- or two-person sea kayak. Both **Island Expeditions** (© **800/667-1630** or 604/452-3212 in the U.S.; www.islandexpeditions.com) and **Slickrock Adventures** (© **800/390-5715** or 435/259-4225 in the U.S.; www.slickrock.com) run various adventurous multiday kayak tours to small camps and lodges on private isolated cayes of Glover's Reef Atoll. See "Dangriga" in chapter 8.
- **Riding an Inner Tube through the Caves Branch River Cave System** (Cayo District and Western Belize): This is certainly the most popular and probably the easiest way to explore Belize's vast network of caves. You strap on a battery-powered headlamp, climb into the center of an inflated car inner tube, and gently float through a series of limestone caves, your headlamp illuminating the stalactites and the occasional bat. The entire sensation is eerie and slightly claustrophobic, but fun nonetheless—especially if you go with a small group on a day when the caves are not crowded. See "Belmopan" in chapter 10.
- **Canoeing, Kayaking, or Inner Tubing on the Macal or Mopan Rivers** (Western Belize): These two rivers converge around the city of San Ignacio, in the Cayo District. Upstream from town on either river are ample opportunities for paddling or floating. Depending on the water level and the section you choose, this can range from a lazy canoe or inner-tube paddle to a Class III kayak

trip over rushing rapids. Any of the hotels in the Cayo District can help you organize one of these adventures. See "San Ignacio" in chapter 10.

- **Horseback Riding through the Cayo District** (Western Belize): The Cayo District is a perfect area to explore on horseback. Rides can be combined with visits to jungle waterfalls and swimming holes, as well as nearby Mayan ruins. **Mountain Equestrian Trails** (✆ **669-1124;** www.metbelize.com) has one of the better stables and horse-riding operations in the Cayo District. See "San Ignacio" and "Mountain Pine Ridge & Caracol" in chapter 10.

5 THE BEST DAY HIKES & NATURE WALKS

- **Cockscomb Basin Forest Reserve** (Southern Belize): This large forest reserve has an excellent network of well-maintained trails. The Cockscomb Basin Forest Reserve—in addition to being the only dedicated reserve designed to protect the endangered jaguar—is also home to an amazing array of tropical flora and fauna. Truly adventurous hikers can arrange to climb Belize's tallest mountain, Victoria Peak, which is found inside this reserve. See "Dangriga" in chapter 8.
- **Guanacaste National Park** (Cayo District and Western Belize): This small national park is located right on the side of the Western Highway, about 3.2km (2 miles) north of Belmopan. The gentle trails and easy accessibility here make this an excellent choice for an introduction to tropical forests. There are nearly 3.2km (2 miles) of well-marked and well-maintained trails in the park, with several benches for sitting and observing wildlife. The park is bordered on the west by Roaring Creek and on the north by the Belize River. See "Belmopan" in chapter 10.
- **Blue Hole National Park** (Cayo District and Western Belize): This hike combines a pleasant 2.4km (1.5-mile) hike through dense primary and secondary tropical forest and a refreshing dip in the park's beautiful namesake swimming hole, or cenote. If you hire a guide, you can actually hike for several miles more inside the stunning **Crystalline Cave.** See "Belmopan" in chapter 10.
- **Tikal National Park** (Tikal, Guatemala): In addition to being one of the best excavated and preserved ancient Mayan cities, Tikal offers an extensive trail network running through dense tropical rainforest. Howler and spider monkeys clamor overhead, and parrots squawk through the canopy. You can see a wealth of tropical fauna here, as you slowly wander from plaza to plaza and pyramid to pyramid. See "Tikal" in chapter 11.

6 THE BEST BIRD-WATCHING

Belize is home to some 618 species of resident and migratory birds. With varied ecosystems ranging from coastal mangroves and swamps; to isolated barrier-reef cayes; to dense tropical rainforest and clear, open savannahs, Belize is a wonderful destination for avid bird-watchers and amateurs alike.

- **Half Moon Caye National Monument** (Northern Cayes and Atolls): This isolated wildlife and marine reserve is a major nesting site for the red-footed booby. Thousands of these birds can be spotted on the island at any one time, an amazing sight. In addition, you can also spot a wide range of resident and migratory sea birds here. See "The Outer Atolls" in chapter 7.

- **Man-O-War Caye** (Southern Belize): This small caye is a government-monitored bird sanctuary and major nesting site for the magnificent frigate, or man-o-war. Circling the island in a small boat, you'll see hundreds of these large seabirds roosting on and hovering above the tiny caye. In addition to the frigates, the island also is home to a large community of brown boobies. See "Dangriga" in chapter 8.
- **Cockscomb Basin Forest Reserve** (Southern Belize): In addition to its jaguar reserve, the Cockscomb Basin Forest Reserve is home to a large number of tropical forest–dwelling bird species. This is one of the best sites in Belize to spot the large and loud scarlet macaw, as well as several toucan species and the imposing king vulture. See "Dangriga" in chapter 8.
- **Crooked Tree Wildlife Sanctuary** (Northern Belize): This rich wetland is perhaps the top bird-watching site in Belize. Home to hundreds of resident and migrant species, it is one of the best spots to see the giant and rare jabiru stork, especially during the dry season. You can spot various heron and kingfisher species here, as well as the yellow-lored parrot and Yucatán jay. See "En Route North: Crooked Tree Wildlife Sanctuary" in chapter 9.
- **New River Lagoon** (Northern Belize): This wide-open lagoon is reached via the winding and narrow New River, and branches off into a network of narrow canals, streams, and marshlands, the perfect and preferred habitat for a wide range of bird species. Common species sighted include the black-collared hawk, northern jacana, and purple gallinule. You can combine a bird-watching trip here with a visit to the Lamanai Mayan ruin, which also has wonderful opportunities for bird-watching all along its trails and from the peaks of its pyramids. See "The Submerged Crocodile: Lamanai" in chapter 9.
- **Shipstern Nature Reserve** (Northern Belize): Covering some 8,903 hectares (22,000 acres), including several distinct ecosystems, Shipstern Nature Reserve is home to over 250 bird species. You can explore the area on foot, as well as in little dugout canoes and flat-bottomed boats. See "Corozal Town" in chapter 9.
- **Caracol** (Cayo District and Western Belize): Also a major Mayan ruin, Caracol and its surrounding forest are prime bird-watching destinations. The area is replete with numerous tropical forest species, including such beauties as the keel-billed motmot, violaceous trogon, ocellated turkey, crested guan, and great curassow. Some visitors have even spotted the harpy eagle here. See "Mountain Pine Ridge & Caracol" in chapter 10.

7 THE BEST MAYAN RUINS

- **Altun Ha** (Northern Belize): One of the most easily accessible Mayan ruins from Belize City, Altun Ha is a small yet well-preserved site featuring two large central plazas surrounded by midsized pyramids and mounds. Only a few of the most imposing temples, tombs, and pyramids have been uncovered and rebuilt; hundreds more lie under the jungle foliage. Many jade, pearl, and obsidian artifacts have been discovered here, including the unique jade-head sculpture of **Kinich Ahau** (the Mayan sun god), the largest carved jade piece from the Mayan era. See "Along the Old Northern Highway: Altun Ha & Maruba Resort Jungle Spa" in chapter 9.

- **Lamanai** (Northern Belize): One of the more interesting and picturesque Mayan ruins in Belize, Lamanai features three large pyramids, a couple of residential areas, various restored stelae, and open plazas, as well as a small and unique ball court. Moreover, the ruins of two 16th-century Spanish churches are nearby. The site is set on the banks of the New River Lagoon. Since it was still occupied by the Maya when the Spanish arrived, Lamanai is one of the few sites in Belize to retain its traditional name. See "The Submerged Crocodile: Lamanai" in chapter 9.
- **Xunantunich** (Cayo District and Western Belize): Xunantunich is an impressive, well-excavated, and easily accessible Mayan site, close to San Ignacio. Xunantunich was a thriving Mayan city during the Classic Period, from about A.D. 600 to 900. You'll find carved stelae and one very tall main pyramid here. To reach the ruins, you must cross the Mopan River aboard a tiny hand-cranked car-ferry in the village of San José Succotz. See "San Ignacio" in chapter 10.
- **El Pilar** (Cayo District and Western Belize): El Pilar just may be the most underappreciated major Mayan city in Mesoamerica. The site is huge, with over 25 known plazas, covering some 40 hectares (100 acres) that straddle the Belize and Guatemala border. Excavation and exploration here are in their early stages, and I actually think that, in time, El Pilar will join the ranks of Caracol and Tikal as one of the major Classic Mayan sites of this region. See "San Ignacio" in chapter 10.
- **Caracol** (Cayo District and Western Belize): Caracol (www.caracol.org) is the largest known Mayan archaeological site in Belize, and one of the great Mayan city-states of the Classic era. Located deep within the Chiquibil Forest Reserve, the ruins are not nearly as well excavated as those at Tikal, Xunantunich, or any number of other sites. However, this is part of Caracol's charm. The main pyramid here, **Caana** or "Sky Palace," stands some 41m (136 ft.) high; it is the tallest Mayan building in Belize and still the tallest man-made structure in the country. See "Mountain Pine Ridge & Caracol" in chapter 10.
- **Tikal:** Just over the Belizean border in neighboring Guatemala, **Tikal** is the grandest of the surviving Classic Mayan cities. Tikal is far more extensively excavated than any ruins in Belize. The pyramids here are some of the most perfect examples of ceremonial architecture in the Mayan world. The peaks of several temples poke through the dense rainforest canopy. Toucans and parrots fly about, and the loudest noise you'll hear is the guttural call of howler monkeys. In its heyday, the city probably covered as much as 65 sq. km (25 sq. miles) and supported a population of over 100,000. See "Tikal" in chapter 11.

8 THE BEST VIEWS

- The **Blue Hole** is probably best experienced and viewed from above. A perfectly round sinkhole measuring some 305m (1,000 ft.) across in the middle of the Lighthouse Reef Atoll lagoon, the Blue Hole appears as a deep, dark blue circle in a sea of shimmering turquoise. The best way to get this bird's-eye view with **Astrum Helicopters** (✆ **222-5100;** www.astrumhelicopters.com). See chapters 3 and 7 for more information.
- Try watching the **sun rise over the New River Lagoon** from a hammock strung on the front porch of your veranda at the **Lamanai Outpost Lodge** (✆ **800/733-7864** in the U.S., or 672-2000 in

Belize; www.lamanai.com). It is a view you'll always treasure. The view is lovely throughout the day, but it's worth waking up early for. See chapter 9.

- Although the **main temple at Cerros** is a just a diminutive 21m (70 ft.) tall, it offers excellent views across Corozal Bay. Moreover, this is an easy climb for most, and far easier than the climbs to the tops of most other major Mayan ceremonial pyramids. See chapter 9.
- The main pyramid at Xunantunich, **El Castillo,** rises to 39m (127 ft.). It's a steep climb, but the view from the top is worth it. On a clear day, you'll be able to make out the twin border towns of Benque Viejo, Belize, and Melchor de Menchos, Guatemala. See chapter 10.
- Poking their heads over the dense rainforest canopy, the **pyramids of Tikal** offer some of the best views to be found in all of Central America. Temple IV is the tallest and the preferred platform for enjoying this view, but Temple II just off the Great Plaza is really just as good. Get here early, or stay late, to enjoy the views without the hustle and bustle of busloads of tourists. See chapter 11.

9 THE BEST DESTINATIONS FOR FAMILIES

- **Belize Zoo** (near Belize City): The Belize Zoo (✆ **220-8003;** www.belizezoo.org) houses over 125 animals, all native Belizean species. It is considered a national treasure and a model for the possibilities of a conservation-based zoo. The zoo itself is wonderfully laid out, on meandering trails with large and well-maintained enclosures for the animals. See "What to See & Do" in chapter 6.
- **Old Belize** (Belize City): Old Belize (✆ **222-4286;** www.oldbelize.com) is part museum, part playground, part beach, and part adventure attraction. There's something here for everyone, and plenty for the kids. It's easy to spend several hours, if not a whole day here. See p. 103.
- **Ambergris Caye** (Northern Cayes and Atolls): Ambergris Caye is the most developed of Belize's beach and diving destinations. As such, it has the greatest selection of hotels and activities, many of them either geared towards or just plain great for kids. From snorkeling to paragliding to touring the island on golf carts and visiting the Butterfly Jungle, there's plenty to keep families and kids of all ages occupied here. **Xanadu Island Resort** (✆ **226-2814;** www.xanaduresort-belize.com) and **Captain Morgan's Retreat** (✆ **888/653-9090** or 307/587-8914 in the U.S., or 226-2207 in Belize; www.belizevacation.com) are two good choices for families. See "Ambergris Caye" in chapter 7.
- **Jaguar Reef Lodge** (Hopkins Village, Southern Belize; ✆ **800/289-5756** in the U.S., or 520-7040 in Belize; www.jaguarreef.com): This intimate beachfront resort has a range of amenities and activities that will make parents happy and keep kids occupied. In addition to the pool and long beach, this place has sea kayaks and mountain bikes, and an extensive menu of daily tours and activities. See p. 112.
- **The Inn at Robert's Grove** (Placencia, Southern Belize; ✆ **800/565-9757** in the U.S., or 523-3565 in Belize; www.robertsgrove.com): This is another small beach resort that is well suited for families. As at Jaguar Reef, there's a wide enough range of activities available here to keep families active and interested for a full vacation. What makes this place slightly trump Jaguar Reef are its two swimming pools and two private cayes. See p. 182.

- **Cayo District** (Western Belize): The Cayo District is the heart of Belize's Mayan world, as well as its prime ecotourism destination. Between a full plate of active adventure activities and a steady diet of Mayan ruins and ancient burial caves, families will find this a great place to spend time in Belize. **Chaa Creek** (✆ **824-2037;** www.chaacreek.com) is not only extremely comfortable for families, but they also have their own butterfly breeding project and natural history museum on-site. And if parents need a little pampering, they also have an excellent spa. See chapter 10.
- **Caves Branch** (Cayo District and Western Belize): You'll be heroes in your kids' eyes after you take them inner-tubing through the dark and spooky network of limestone caves traversed by the slow-moving Caves Branch River. Families looking for some creature comfort would be wise to choose **Jaguar Paw** (✆ **877/624-3770** in the U.S., or 820-2023; www.jaguarpaw.com), while those with a real hankering for adventure should head to **Ian Anderson's Caves Branch** (✆ **822-2800;** www.cavesbranch.com). See "Belmopan" in chapter 10.

10 THE BEST LUXURY HOTELS & RESORTS

- **Radisson Fort George Hotel & Marina** (Belize City; ✆ **800/333-3333** in the U.S. or 223-3333 in Belize; www.radisson.com): This is the top business-class and luxury hotel in Belize City. This oceanfront hotel is located in the quiet Fort George neighborhood, out by the lighthouse, just a block from the cruise-ship tourist village. The hotel has an excellent swimming pool, a well-equipped gym, several restaurants and bars, and easy access to the best Belize City has to offer. See p. 95.
- **The Great House** (Belize City; ✆ **223-3400;** www.greathousebelize.com): Housed in an old wooden mansion a half-block from the lighthouse, this place offers up plush, well-equipped rooms, with an intimate and elegant vibe. Try for one of the top-floor rooms, with great views over the harbor and city. See p. 95.
- **Victoria House** (Ambergris Caye; ✆ **800/247-5159** or 713/344-2340 in the U.S., or 226-2067; www.victoria-house.com): Casual elegance and attentive service await you at this Ambergris Caye resort. A varied collection of rooms, suites, and villas is spread around an expansive piece of land planted with lush tropical gardens. The hotel also has one of the best restaurants in the country, as well as a wonderful patch of soft white-sand beach. See p. 129.
- **Cayo Espanto** (just off the coast of Ambergris Caye; ✆ **888/666-4282** in the U.S. and Canada; www.aprivateisland.com): What could be more decadent and luxurious than staying in a private villa, with a private swimming pool, a private dock, and a personal butler, on an almost private island? (There are six villas here, although you can rent out the whole island if you like.) This place pulls out all the stops, providing all the modern conveniences and pampering possible on a desert-island getaway. See p. 131.
- **Turtle Inn** (Placencia; ✆ **800/746-3743** in the U.S., or 824-4912; www.turtleinn.com): Building on the experience gained from his Blancaneaux Lodge, and building upon the ruins of a hotel destroyed by Hurricane Iris, director Francis Ford Coppola has upped the ante on high-end hotels in

Belize. The individual villas here are the most beautiful and luxurious in Belize. The hotel is set right on an excellent stretch of beach, and the service and dining are top-notch. See p. 183.

- **Machaca Hill Lodge** (Punta Gorda; ✆ **722-0050;** www.machacahill.com): This is by far the most luxurious option around Punta Gorda, and one of the nicer rain forest lodges in the country. This place features a series of large and plush individual cabins set on a thickly forested hillside. See p. 196.
- **Maruba Resort Jungle Spa** (off the Old Northern Hwy.; ✆ **800/627-8227** in the U.S., or 225-5555; fax 225-5506; www.maruba-belize.com): This small resort and spa is set in a patch of lush forest and flowering gardens. The whole operation is an eclectic orgy designed to please the eyes and all other senses. The individual villas here are spectacular. A wide range of spa treatments is available, and excellently and professionally done. Don't miss out on their signature Mood Mud Massage, perhaps one of the few massage experiences for which you'll want to bring a camera. See p. 202.
- **Chaa Creek** (off the road to Benque Viejo, Cayo District; ✆ **824-2037;** www.chaacreek.com): A pioneer nature lodge in Belize, this collection of individual and duplex cottages was also a pioneer in the whole concept of rustic luxury. Cool terra-cotta tile floors, varnished wood, thatched roofs, and beautiful Guatemalan textiles and handicrafts are elegantly yet simply combined. The property is set on a steep hillside over the lovely Macal River. Service is very friendly and personable, and the lodge provides easy access to a wealth of natural adventures and ancient Mayan wonders. See p. 245.
- **Blancaneaux Lodge** (Mountain Pine Ridge Reserve, Cayo District; ✆ **800/746-3743** in the U.S., or 824-4912; www.blancaneaux.com): Francis Ford Coppola's first Belizean mountain retreat remains one of the most elegant and luxurious nature lodges in the country. The hotel is set on a steep pine-forested hillside, overlooking the Privassion River and a series of gentle falls. The individual cabanas are all spacious, are beautifully decorated, and feature a private balcony or deck designed to take in the excellent views. The hotel recently added a wonderful riverside spa facility. See p. 254.
- **La Lancha Resort** (Lago Petén Itzá, Petén; ✆ **800/746-3743** in the U.S., or ✆/fax 502/7928-8331 in Guatemala; www.lalanchavillage.com): Set on a steep, high hillside overlooking the lake, this is the plushest option close to the amazing ruins of Tikal. Another of Francis Ford Coppola's regional resorts, the rooms here are once again decorated with style, featuring furniture and artwork from around the world. The food is also excellent. See p. 274.

11 THE BEST MODERATELY PRICED HOTELS

- **San Pedro Holiday Hotel** (Ambergris Caye; ✆ **226-2014;** www.sanpedro holiday.com): This brilliantly white three-building complex with painted purple and pink trim sits in the center of San Pedro town. This was the first hotel on Ambergris Caye when Celi McCorkle opened it over 40 years ago, and it's still one of the best. Grab a room with an oceanview balcony and you'll be in tropical vacation heaven. See p. 128.
- **Tides Beach Resort** (Ambergris Caye; ✆ **226-2283;** www.ambergriscaye.com/tides): Every room comes with either a private or shared balcony or veranda

overlooking the Caribbean Sea. The hotel and its in-house dive shop are run by the very friendly and highly respected local couple of Patojo and Sabrina Paz. See p. 128.

- **Seaside Cabanas** (Caye Caulker; ✆ **226-0498;** www.seasidecabanas.com): This place offers up comfy rooms, a fabulous location, and a complete range of amenities, all at a great price. Located in the heart of downtown Caye Caulker, it also boasts one of the few pools on the island. See p. 146.
- **Blue Crab Resort** (Seine Bight Village; ✆ **523-3544;** www.bluecrabbeach.com): Simple, comfortable, and cool rooms located on a beautiful and isolated patch of beach make this a wonderful option. Throw in an excellent restaurant serving eclectic international fare, and you've got the makings of a perfect getaway. This place is located just a little bit north of the traditional Garífuna village of Seine Bight. See p. 184.
- **Coral House Inn** (Punta Gorda; ✆ **722-2878;** www.coralhouseinn.net): By far the best option in the town of Punta Gorda itself, this little bed-and-breakfast is set right on the edge of the ocean. The hotel offers neat rooms, a refreshing pool, and free Wi-Fi access throughout its rooms and grounds. See p. 197.
- **Cahal Pech Village Resort** (San Ignacio, Cayo District; ✆ **888/790-5264** in the U.S. and Canada; or 824-3740 in Belize; www.cahalpech.com): With a commanding hillside perch, this collection of individual cabins and hotel rooms is an excellent option in the San Ignacio area. The resort is located just beyond the entrance to the Cahal Pech Mayan ruins, and a whole host of tours and activities can be arranged here. See p. 242.
- **Black Rock Jungle River Lodge** (Cayo District; ✆ **824-2529;** www.blackrocklodge.com): Located down a long dirt road on the edge of a cliff overlooking the Macal River, this place offers up all the benefits and amenities of a top-notch ecolodge at very reasonable rates. See p. 247.

12 THE BEST BUDGET HOTELS

- **Belcove Hotel** (Belize City; ✆ **227-3054;** www.belcove.com): This budget hotel is set on the banks of Haulover Creek, just a block from the Swing Bridge and the heart of downtown Belize City. The old wooden building is in funky shape, but the river-view balconies are one of my favorite spots in all of Belize to sit and read a book, or watch the sporadic action on the river and streets below. See p. 97.
- **Ruby's** (Ambergris Caye; ✆ **226-2063;** www.ambergriscaye.com/rubys): Located right on the waterfront in the center of San Pedro, most of the rooms here overlook the ocean, and the best ones come with a balcony. This is one of the older and more historic hotels on the island, and you just can't do much better on Ambergris Caye for this price. See p. 128.
- **De Real Macaw** (Caye Caulker; ✆ **226-0459;** www.derealmacaw.biz): This small compound on Front Street in Caye Caulker is a great bargain. The hotel is close to all the action, and the rooms are clean, cool, and comfortable. Plenty of trees strung with hammocks make this a great place for a well-deserved tropical siesta. See p. 147.
- **Tree Tops Guest House** (Caye Caulker; ✆ **226-0240;** www.treetopsbelize.com): While the best rooms here actually fall into the moderately priced category

(and are some of the best rooms on Caye Caulker), the whole place offers such good value for your money that it's getting a listing in this category. The budget rooms here continue to set the standard on Caye Caulker, and the service is friendly, knowledgeable, and attentive. See p. 147.

- **Tipple Tree Beya** (Hopkins Village; ©/fax **520-7006;** http://tippletree.net): There are just five simple rooms at this friendly hostel-like option at the southern end of Hopkins Village. However, if the rooms are full, you can also camp. The hotel sits on a lovely section of beach, and is within easy walking distance of the small Garífuna village of Hopkins. See p. 174.
- **Jungle Jeanie's by the Sea** (Hopkins Village; © **523-7047;** www.junglebythesea.com): Located at the southern end of this small traditional Garífuna fishing village, the individual wooden cabins are just steps from the ocean on a beautiful patch of beach. See p. 174.
- **Tradewinds** (Placencia; © **523-3122;** www.placencia.com): Set on a curving spit of sand at the southern edge of Placencia, the individual cabins here are so close to the water's edge that I worry it's only a matter of time before the ocean reclaims them. But if you get here soon enough and land one of them, you'll likely never want to leave. Each has a private front porch strung with a hammock, where you can swing and listen to the lapping waves. See p. 186.
- **Mirador Hotel** (Corozal Town; © **442-0189;** www.mirador.bz): While the large concrete building is a bit imposing and lacking in warmth, you can't beat the view or location of this new downtown hotel. And the price is pretty right as well. See p. 221.
- **Midas Tropical Resort** (San Ignacio, Cayo District; © **824-3172;** www.midasbelize.com): Sure you can stay in San Ignacio for a little less, but this collection of cottages and cabins is just a half-mile or so from downtown, right on the banks of the Macal River. You can also camp here. The whole thing has the feel of an isolated nature lodge, at a fraction of the cost. See p. 243.
- **Hotel Santana** (Flores, Petén, Guatemala; ©/fax **502/7867-5123** or 7867-5193; www.santanapeten.com): This lakefront hotel is the best budget choice on the island of Flores. In fact, it might just be the best hotel on the island itself, regardless of price. See p. 284.

13 THE BEST RESTAURANTS

- **Harbour View** (Belize City; © **223-6420**): Set on the water's edge overlooking the juncture of Haulover Creek and the Caribbean Sea, this is the most creative and elegant restaurant in Belize City. Fresh seafood and local staples are cooked with fusion flare and some Asian accents. If the weather's right and you land one of the outdoor tables on the wraparound veranda, you'll enjoy the finest dining experience available in the city. See p. 99.
- **Wet Lizard** (Belize City; © **223-5973**): Much less formal than the Harbour View mentioned above, this often-rowdy little restaurant and bar still serves up excellent fresh seafood and burgers, in an open-air setting overlooking the Swing Bridge and Belize Harbor. This is a great place to savor some late-afternoon conch fritters and a refreshing drink. See p. 99.
- **Elvi's Kitchen** (San Pedro, Ambergris Caye; © **226-2176;** www.elviskitchen.com): Elvia Staines has come a long way

since she began selling hamburgers out of a takeout window over 30 years ago. Today her friendly and very popular restaurant oozes island charm. The restaurant is a thatched, screened-in building with picnic tables, with a large flamboyant tree growing up through the roof and a floor of crushed shells and sand. No visit to Ambergris Caye is complete without a meal here. See p. 134.

- **Palmilla** (Ambergris Caye; ✆ **226-2067**): This is easily the most elegant and finest dining to be had on Ambergris Caye, if not in all of Belize. The atmosphere is island formal, meaning relaxed yet refined at the same time, and the chefs here prepare the freshest of local ingredients with a creative blend of techniques, spices, and cuisines from around the world. When the weather's nice, you can dine under the stars by candlelight. See p. 134.
- **Casa Picasso** (Ambergris Caye; ✆ **226-4507**): Located on the back side of San Pedro, this hyper-hip place serves up a broad menu of creative tapas-size items. There are almost as many martini concoctions and an ample dessert menu to choose from as well. See p. 134.
- **Rojo Lounge** (Ambergris Caye; ✆ **226-4012**): The folks at Azul Resort, an isolated little place on Northern Ambergris Caye, serve up very creative and well-prepared fusion cuisine in a relaxed and inviting open-air ambience. The menu features some of the more creative fusion items to be had—no mean feat, given the competition—and there are also nightly specials. See p. 136.
- **Habaneros** (Caye Caulker; ✆ **226-0487**): Featuring a creative menu with influences from various Caribbean and Asian cuisines, this is a perennial must-visit restaurant on Caye Caulker. Be sure to grab one of the outdoor tables on the wraparound porch. See p. 149.
- **Rasta Pasta Rainforest Café** (Caye Caulker; ✆ **206-0356**): Sure there are fancier places on Caye Caulker, but this long-standing and perennially popular option offers up a wide and eclectic menu, huge portions, and excellent service. What's more, the food is delicious and there are some top-notch vegetarian selections. See p. 149.
- **The French Connection** (Placencia; ✆ **523-3656**): This new place has been the buzz in Placencia, and they've already outgrown their first location. At once elegant and relaxed, the food here is a creative take on contemporary bistro fare. See p. 187.
- **Marian's Bayview** (Punta Gorda; ✆ **722-0129**): The ambience and decor here are basic—at best. But the mix of Indian and Belizean cuisine is some of the most spectacular in southern Belize. The small menu changes regularly, but always includes some of Marian's expertly prepared spicy East Indian fare. See p. 199.
- **Café Sol** (San Ignacio; ✆ **824-2166**): Not only does this place serve up some of the best food in San Ignacio, it's also my favorite place to hang out for a while after enjoying a meal. See p. 244.
- **La Luna** (Flores, Guatemala; ✆ **502/7926-3346**): If you find yourself in Flores, Guatemala, be sure to seek out this hip little restaurant. The eclectic decor varies from room to room, but like the food, it is consistently creative and tasteful. See p. 285.

14 THE BEST AFTER-DARK FUN

Belize doesn't really have all that much in the way of nightlife. The capital city is small and relatively quiet by most international standards. In both the capital and throughout the rest of the country, you'd be hard-pressed to find a truly notable bar or club. Still, some unique after-dark destinations and activities are out there, and should not be missed.

- **Stargazing:** This is one of my favorite nighttime activities, but it is especially rewarding when there is no (or little) ambient light. Given its sparse development and low population density, Belize offers a wealth of opportunities for some truly spectacular stargazing. Your best spots are the isolated beach getaways of Belize's three mid-ocean atolls, but you can also enjoy the astronomical splendor from any number of deserted beaches or rural mountain getaways.
- **Night Diving:** If you've come to Belize to scuba dive, you should definitely try a night dive. Many creatures are nocturnal, and the reefs here come alive at night. Moreover, the brilliant colors of the coral and sea life really shine under the strong glare of an underwater light, and there's something truly eerie about the experience. All of the major dive destinations and resorts offer night diving. See chapter 5 and the destination chapters for more details.
- **Riverside Tavern** (Belize City; ✆ **223-5640**): Featuring excellent steaks, fresh fish, and bar food, this place is a local favorite. There are TV screens for sporting events, and always an interesting mix of locals, expatriates, and tourists alike. See p. 101.
- **Barefoot Iguana** (Ambergris Caye; ✆ **226-2927**): This cavernous bar features everything from hot local DJs to mud-wrestling to sporting events shown on a giant screen. The two-story hangar-sized space is hung with faux jungle plants and foliage, and it has quickly become the most happening nightspot in San Pedro. See "Ambergris Caye" in chapter 7.
- **Barefoot Beach Bar** (Placencia; ✆ **523-3515**): Located on the beachfront, just off the central sidewalk, this casual outdoor spot is the best place in Placencia to enjoy some live music or a simple drink with friends in a totally tropical setting, befitting the place. See "Placencia" in chapter 8.
- **Moon Rise at Tikal:** Watching the full moon rise from the top of Temple IV in Tikal is one of the highlights of my many travels to this region. You'll have to stay at one of the hotels on-site to do this, and you may even have to persuade or bribe a park guard. You'll also have to time your visit with the moon phase. But if all these things come together, you're in for a memorable and awe-inspiring evening. See "Tikal" in chapter 11.

15 THE BEST WEBSITES ABOUT BELIZE

- **Latin American Network Information Center** (http://lanic.utexas.edu/la/ca/belize): Hosted by the University of Texas Latin American Studies Department, this site houses a vast collection of information about Belize. This is hands-down the best one-stop shop for Web browsing on the country, with helpful links to a wide range of tourism and general-information sites.
- **Belize by Naturalight** (www.belizenet.com): This is probably the single best collection of links to Belize's individual hotels, restaurants, and attractions. The site also boasts links to the various regions and destinations within Belize, as well as links to most other major and important websites on the country.
- **The Belize Forums** (www.belizeforum.com): These are active and informative

forums on living in and traveling around Belize. Several regular posters are quite knowledgeable, and are generous with that knowledge.

- **Belize News** (www.belizenews.com): This site provides access to all of Belize's major online news sources, including all the major weekly print newspapers.
- **Belize Kriol** (www.kriol.org.bz): If you want to know about Belize's Kriol (Creole) culture, this is the place to go. The site includes pages on Kriol history, culture, and language. There's a handy spelling guide and Kriol dictionary here as well.
- **The Toucan Trail** (www.toucantrail.com): This is an excellent site geared towards budget travelers, with extensive links and comprehensive information.
- **Belize Tourist Board** (www.travelbelize.org): This is the official site of the Belize Tourist Board. It has its fair share of information and links, although you'll probably end up being directed to one of the other sites mentioned earlier.

2

Belize in Depth

"You'd betta Belize it!" goes the common local exclamation. But before you can Belize it, you better know a little bit about this little bitty country. Belize is the second youngest nation in the Western Hemisphere, having been granted independence from Britain in 1981. It's also a decidedly sparsely populated country, with just under 300,000 citizens and no large cities. Belize is the only country in Central America where English is the official and predominant language.

Originally a major part of the ancient Mayan empire, Belize was next settled by pirates and then colonized by the British, using slave labor. The descendants of each of these groups are woven into the historical lore and cultural fabric of modern Belize. Add to the mix the independent Garífuna people, who settled along the remote southern shore in the early part of the 19th century, and the more recent waves of Mexican, Chinese, and East Indian immigrants, and you have an idea of the cultural meld that constitutes this unique Central American country. Surprisingly, Belizeans of all cultural stripes tend to get along a lot better and with far fewer outward and untoward shows of racism than citizens of most other nations. This is a small country. The sense of community is strong and, even in the big city, people tend to know their neighbors and almost everyone is somehow related.

Tourism is the fastest growing segment of the economy, and the country offers a wide range of attractions for visitors, from sun-'n'-fun beach vacations to active adventures and ecotourism explorations. This chapter will help you get acquainted with the history, people, culture, and natural environment of this small yet very diverse and exciting Central American nation.

1 BELIZE TODAY

Belize is a developing nation, limited by a small economy, a tiny industrial base, a huge trade deficit, widespread unemployment, and a historic dependence on foreign aid. These problems have only been compounded since independence. Sugar, bananas, and citrus are the principal cash crops, though seafood exports also help. However, thanks to a modest oil find in 2005, crude oil is currently the country's number one export. Tourism is also a promising and important source of income, and this is sure to continue. Increasingly, Belizeans whose fathers and grandfathers were farmers or fishermen find themselves hotel owners, tour guides, waiters, and cleaning personnel.

Belize has a population of some 297,000, roughly half of whom live in one of the six major towns or cities, with the rest living in rural areas or small villages. About 45% of the population is considered mestizo, descendants of mixed Spanish, Mexican, and/or Mayan blood. Making up 30% of the population are the Creoles, predominantly black descendants of slaves and the early British colonists. Belize's three Mayan tribes—Yucatec, Mopan, and Kekchi—make up around 10% of the population. The Garífuna

Speaking of Tongues

English is the official language of Belize, but a traveler will most likely run across a wide range of languages. Three centuries of colonization have given the Queen's English some foothold here; however, a large percentage of the local population, particularly black Creoles, speak a Creole English that is downright unintelligible to most English-speaking visitors. In recent years there have been attempts to standardize and record the Creole dialect, and you may see it written out on billboards and in newspapers. *How Fi Rite Bileez Kriol (How To Write Belize Creole),* is a helpful pamphlet that can sometimes be found at local bookstores and gift shops, and an excellent and entertaining reference if you want to take a stab at Creole.

Moreover, this is still Central America, and Spanish is widely spoken in Belize, especially in the northern and western regions near the borders with Mexico and Guatemala. If that's not enough, Belize has three relatively homogenous ethnic groups, the Garífunas and the Kekchi and Mopan Mayas, each of whom has a distinct language. Finally, rounding out this polyglot pastiche, you may also hear some Chinese, Arabic, Hindi, or even the archaic German used by the country's small Mennonite community.

Check out appendix B for some useful terms and phrases in Creole and Spanish.

constitute approximately 6.5% of the population, while a mix of whites of British descent, Mennonites, Chinese, and East Indians fill out the rest.

In general, the pace of life and business is slow in Belize. You'll seldom find people rushing down the sidewalks or dirt streets. There are only four major highways in the country, and traffic is never heavy. In fact, all of these highways actually have speed bumps along their length, as they pass through the many roadside towns and villages.

Belize held its first parliamentary elections in 1984. Since then, power has ping-ponged back and forth between the United Democratic Party (UDP) and the People's United Party (PUP). The former is a more conservative, free-market oriented party, while the latter champions a more liberal, social-democratic agenda. In the August 1998 elections, PUP won 26 of the 29 parliamentary seats, while the UDP managed to win just 3. However, by 2005 discontent with the PUP over tax increases and money mismanagement had grown widespread, and there were some public demonstrations and disturbances. The UDP pummeled them in the 2006 municipal elections, and again in the 2008 national elections, electing Dean Barrow as the country's first black prime minister and maintaining a strong majority of parliamentary seats.

2 LOOKING BACK AT BELIZE

EARLY HISTORY

Before the arrival of the first Europeans, this was the land of the ancient Mayas. Although most people think of Mexico's Mayan cities in the Yucatán and Guatemala's Tikal when they think of *El Mundo*

Belize by Any Other Name

There's some debate as to the origin of the name "Belize." Some claim it is the timeworn corruption of the name Wallace, one of the early buccaneer captains to set anchor here. Others claim it comes from the Mayan word *beliz,* which translates as "muddy water."

Maya, or the Maya World, ongoing archaeological discoveries show that what is today known as Belize was once a major part of the Mayan Empire. River and coastal trade routes connected dozens of cities and small towns throughout this region to each other and to the major ceremonial and trading cities of Mexico and Guatemala. Caracol, a Maya ruin in the Cayo District of western Belize, is a huge ceremonial city that defeated Tikal in battle in A.D. 562. Other sites, like Lamanai, Altun Ha, and Xunantunich, were thriving ceremonial and trade centers, with impressive ruins and artifacts. Moreover, ongoing excavations at sites like Pilar and La Milpa may eventually reveal other cities and ceremonial sites of equal or greater importance.

One of the earliest known Mayan cities in Mesoamerica, Cuello, is located just outside of Orange Walk Town and has been dated to B.C. 2000 or earlier. Mayan history is often divided into several distinct periods: Archaic (10,000–2000 B.C.), Pre-Classic (2000 B.C.–A.D. 250), Classic (A.D. 250–900), and Post-Classic (900–1540). Within this timeline, the Classic Period itself is often divided into Early, Middle, Late, and Terminal stages. At the height of development, as many as two million Maya may have inhabited the region that is today known as Belize. No one knows for sure what led to the decline of the Classic Maya, but somewhere around A.D. 900 their society entered a severe and rapid decline. Famine, warfare, deforestation, and religious prophecy have all been sited as possible causes. Nevertheless, Belize is somewhat unique in that it had several major ceremonial or trading cities still occupied by Maya when the first Spanish conquistadors arrived.

SPANISH ATTEMPTS AT CONQUEST

Christopher Columbus sailed past the Belize coast in 1502, and even named the Bay of Honduras, but he never anchored or set foot ashore here, and the Spanish never had much success in colonizing Belize. In fact, they met with fierce resistance from the remaining Maya. Part of their problem may have come from Gonzalo Guerrero, a Spanish sailor who was shipwrecked off the coast of Belize and the Yucatán in the early years of the 16th century. Originally pressed into slavery, Guerrero eventually married the daughter of a Mayan ruler, and became an important warrior and military advisor in the Maya battles with the Spanish.

To be sure, the Spanish led various attacks and attempts at conquest and control of the territory that is present-day Belize. Many of these were brutal and deadly. They were also able to set up some missionary outposts, most notably those near Lamanai, where travelers today can still see the ruins of these early Spanish churches. Nevertheless, by the mid-1600s, the Spanish had been militarily forced to abandon all permanent settlements and attempts at colonialism in Belize, concentrating their efforts on more productive regions around Central and South America and the Caribbean Sea.

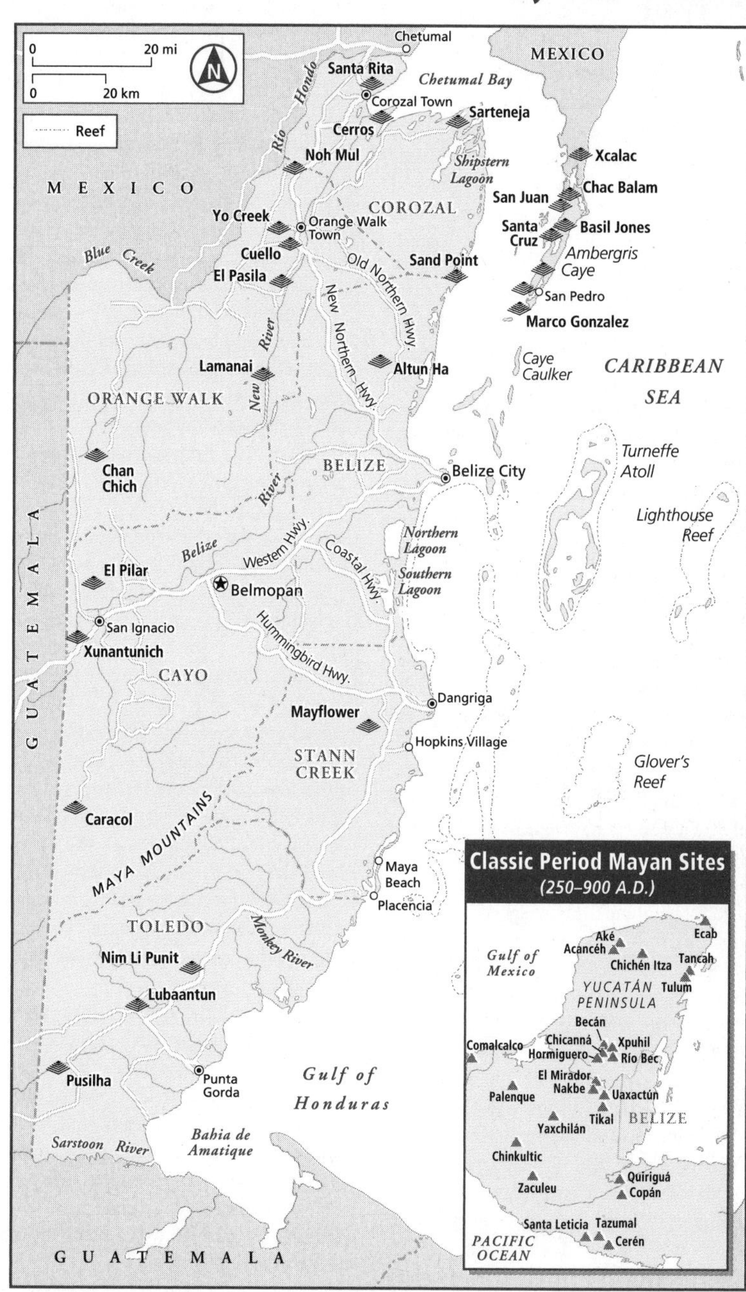
0 20 mi
0 20 km
N
Reef
MEXICO
M E X I C O
Chetumal
Santa Rita
Chetumal Bay
Corozal Town
Sarteneja
Cerros
Río Hondo
Noh Mul
Shipstern Lagoon
Xcalac
Chac Balam
San Juan
COROZAL
Yo Creek
Orange Walk Town
Santa Cruz
Basil Jones
Cuello
Sand Point
Ambergris Caye
El Pasila
Old Northern Hwy.
San Pedro
Blue Creek
Marco Gonzalez
New River
New Northern Hwy.
Lamanai
Altun Ha
Caye Caulker
CARIBBEAN SEA
ORANGE WALK
Turneffe Atoll
Chan Chich
BELIZE
Belize City
Belize River
Lighthouse Reef
Northern Lagoon
Western Hwy.
Coastal Hwy.
El Pilar
Southern Lagoon
Belmopan
San Ignacio
Hummingbird Hwy.
Xunantunich
CAYO
G U A T E M A L A
Dangriga
Mayflower
Hopkins Village
STANN CREEK
Glover's Reef
Caracol
MAYA MOUNTAINS
Maya Beach
Placencia
TOLEDO
Monkey River
Nim Li Punit
Lubaantun
Pusilha
Punta Gorda
Gulf of Honduras
Sarstoon River
Bahia de Amatique
G U A T E M A L A
Classic Period Mayan Sites
(250–900 A.D.)
Gulf of Mexico
Aké
Acancéh
Ecab
Chichén Itza
Tancah
YUCATÁN PENINSULA
Tulum
Becán
Comalcalco
Chicanná
Xpuhil
Hormiguero
Río Bec
El Mirador
Nakbe
Uaxactún
Palenque
Yaxchilán
Tikal
BELIZE
Chinkultic
Quiriguá
Zaculeu
Copán
Santa Leticia
Tazumal
Cerén
PACIFIC OCEAN

THE BRITISH ARE COMING

Belize likes to play up the fact that it was founded by pirates and buccaneers, and indeed, these unsavory characters were among the first to make this region their base of operations. Many of these pirates and buccaneers used the Belize coastline and its protected anchorages as hideouts and bases following their attacks on Spanish fleets transporting gold and silver treasures from their more productive colonies.

By the mid–17th century, British loggers were settling along the coast and making their way up the rivers and streams in search of mahogany for shipbuilding and other types of wood for making dyes. Proud and independent, these early settlers called themselves "Baymen" (after the Bay of Honduras). Politically, the Baymen treaded a delicate balance between being faithful British subjects and fiercely independent settlers.

Throughout this period and into the 18th century, the Spanish launched regular attacks on pirate bases and Baymen settlements in Belize. Spanish attacks devastated early settlements in Belize in 1679, 1717, 1730, and 1754, although after the dust cleared and the Spanish fleet moved on, the Baymen would always return. As the attacks increased in intensity, the Baymen sought more and more support from the British. In 1763, Spain and Britain signed the Treaty of Paris, which granted Britain official rights to log in Belize, but maintained Spanish sovereignty. Still, in 1779, Spain attacked the principal Belizean settlement on St. George's Caye, capturing 140 British and Baymen settlers and 250 slaves and shipping them off into custody on Cuba.

Diplomatic and military give and take between Spain and Britain ensued until 1798, when the Baymen won a decisive military victory over a larger Spanish fleet, again just off the shores of St. George's Caye. The Battle of St. George's Caye effectively ended all Spanish involvement and claim to Belize, and it solidified Belize's standing within the British Empire.

In 1862, with more or less the same borders it has today, Belize was formally declared the colony of British Honduras (after functioning as a colony for the previous century). This small colonial outpost became a major source of hardwood and dyewood for the still-expanding British Empire. The forests were exploited, and agriculture was never really encouraged. The British wanted their colony to remain dependent on the mother country, so virtually all the necessities of life were imported. Few roads were built, and the country remained unexplored and undeveloped, with a tiny population mostly clustered along the coast.

Throughout the 18th and 19th centuries, African slaves were brought to British Honduras. The slave period was marked by several revolts and uprisings. Black Caribs, today known as Garífuna, also migrated here from the Bay Islands of Honduras, although they originally hailed from the Caribbean island of St. Vincent. Beginning in the early 1800s, the Garífuna established their own villages and culture along the southern coast, predominantly in the towns of Dangriga and Punta Gorda. The Abolition Act of 1833 abolished slavery throughout the British Empire, and former Belizean slaves and Garífuna villagers slowly began to integrate into the economic and cultural life of this budding colony.

During the mid–19th century, many Mexican and Guatemalan refugees of the bloody Caste Wars fled across the borders into British Honduras and founded such towns as Corozal Town and Benque Viejo. A century later, further waves of Guatemalan, Salvadoran, and Honduran refugees, who were fleeing civil wars and right-wing death squads, immigrated to Belize during the 1970s and '80s.

Moments **Place Your Bet**

Whether or not you're the gambling type, you'll want to wager a few bucks on a **chicken drop.** This very loose variation on roulette involves wagering on a number written on a wooden board. Above the board is a wire cage. Once all the bets are in, a chicken is placed in the cage, and the number where the chicken's poop lands wins the pot. The "lucky" winner, however, usually must clean up the board before collecting. There's a chicken drop every Wednesday night at 6pm at the **Pier Lounge** (p. 136) at the Spindrift Hotel.

FROM INDEPENDENCE TO THE PRESENT

In the early 1960s, groundwork was laid by the People's United Party (PUP) for granting British Honduras independence. In 1973, the country's name was officially changed to Belize. Although the 1964 constitution granted self-government to the British colony, it was not until September 21, 1981, that Belize finally gained its true independence, making it Central America's newest nation. The delay was primarily due to Guatemala's claim on the territory. Guatemala actually sent troops into the border Petén Province several times during the 1970s. Fearful of an invasion by Guatemalan forces, the British delayed granting full independence until an agreement could be reached with Guatemala. Although to this day no final agreement has actually been inked, tensions cooled enough to allow for the granting of full sovereignty in 1981. British troops officially pulled out of Belize in 1994. The British legacy in Belize is a relatively stable government with a parliamentary system and regular elections that are contested by two major parties and several smaller parties. The country is still a member of the Commonwealth.

It was big news when oil was discovered near the Mennonite community of Spanish Lookout in 2005. It has quickly become the country's number one export, with international crude prices helping substantially on that front. The country currently exports a little over 5 million barrels of oil a month.

3 THE LAY OF THE LAND

Belize is a narrow strip of land on the Caribbean coast of Central America, located due south of Mexico's Yucatán Peninsula. It covers an area of just under 23,210 sq. km (9,000 sq. miles), about the same size as the state of Massachusetts, and is bordered on the west and south by Guatemala and on the east by the Caribbean Sea. Offshore from mainland Belize are hundreds of tiny islands, known as cayes (pronounced "keys"), which rise from the world's second-longest barrier reef, which extends for more than 298km (185 miles) along the Belizean coast. From the broad, flat coastal plains, Belize rises to form the **Maya Mountains,** mountain peaks of more than 914m (3,000 ft.) and the source of the many rivers that wind through the country. For centuries these rivers were the principal means of transportation within Belize. Moreover, most of these mountains are limestone karst formations, which has left them coursed with caves, caverns, and underground rivers.

Even though much of Belize's primary forest and tropical hardwoods were harvested throughout the past 3 centuries, population density has always been extremely low, and the forest reclaims ground quickly. Though Belize lacks much true primary tropical rainforest, it does possess large expanses of tropical moist and lowland secondary rainforest, as well as mangrove, swamp, and even highland pine forests. In fact, nearly 65% of Belize is uninhabited, while over 20% of the country and its offshore reefs are considered protected land, private reserve, or marine reserve. The combination of a low level of human population and conscious conservation efforts has been a boon for a wide range of flora and fauna.

FLORA & FAUNA

At least 618 species of migratory and resident bird species have been identified in Belize, including the massive jabiru stork, the scarlet macaw, and the keel-billed toucan. Belize is also home to the densest concentration of jaguars on the planet. Revered by the ancient Maya and feared by most jungle dwellers, the jaguar is the largest new-world cat, and can reach over 1.8m (6 ft.) in length and weigh over 113 kilograms (250 lb.). The **Cockscomb Basin Wildlife Sanctuary** (p. 168) was created as the world's only jaguar preserve.

In addition to the jaguar, Belizean forests are home to four other wild cats, the puma, ocelot, margay, and jaguarundi, as well as such quintessential jungle dwellers as howler monkeys, green iguanas, and boa constrictors. The tapir is the country's national animal. Also called a mountain cow, the tapir is docile, curious, and entirely vegetarian. Still, these wild creatures stand nearly 1.5m (5 ft.) tall and can weigh over 227 kilograms (500 lb.).

Bird-watchers will want to visit several of Belize's lowland and offshore sanctuaries, including **Crooked Tree Wildlife Sanctuary** (p. 204), the **Shipstern Nature Reserve** (p. 218), **Río Bravo Conservation Area** (p. 212), and the **Half Moon Caye National Monument** (p. 153).

Off Belize's coast, the barrier reef is a world all its own. Though the cayes are little more than low, flat coral and limestone outcroppings, the myriad of underwater flora and fauna here is truly astounding. Colorful angelfish, parrotfish, and triggerfish feed on the multicolored coral. Giant sponges provide homes and feeding grounds for hundreds of smaller fish and delicate coral shrimp. Under the rocks and caverns dwell lobsters, moray eels, and octopuses. Larger predators like sharks and barracudas cruise the reefs for their plentiful prey, while manta and spotted eagle rays glide gracefully over the sand bottoms and conch thrive in the sea grass. The **Gladden Spit** area, off the coast from Placencia, is quickly being recognized as one of the world's top spots to snorkel and dive with giant whale sharks, while Belize's three mid-ocean atolls are wonderlands for a wide range of nature-loving adventurers and travelers.

Although it might seem strange to think of it, the cayes also support a unique and endangered forest environment, the **littoral forest,** as well as rich **mangroves.** These saltwater-tolerant environments are major breeding and life-support grounds for a broad range of fauna.

See "Tips on Health, Safety & Etiquette in the Wilderness" in chapter 5 for additional tips on enjoying Belize's natural wonders, and appendix C for more information on the fauna and flora of Belize.

4 ART & ARCHITECTURE

With its tiny population and relative isolation from the outside world, Belize lacks the vibrant cultural scene found in larger, more cosmopolitan countries. Still, if you poke around, you'll find some respectable local music, literature, art, and architecture to enjoy. For current information about the arts and what might be happening while you're in Belize, contact the **Belize Arts Council** (**© 227-2110**), which is housed in the Bliss Institute for the Performing Arts (p. 102) in Belize City.

ARCHITECTURE

Only a few colonial buildings of any interest survive in Belize City. Most of the rest have succumbed to the ravages of time or were destroyed in the major hurricanes of 1931 and 1961. The most prominent survivors are the brick **St. John's Cathedral** and the downtown **Paslow Building,** which houses the city's main post office. **Clapboard houses** built on stilts are the most typical architectural feature, and quite a few of these buildings, often painted in the pastel colors that are so popular throughout the Caribbean, can be seen in Belize City and in small towns around the country, but most commonly along the coast and out on the cayes.

If you're looking for classic monumental architecture, however, you're in luck. Stone fares better than wood in these parts. The two tallest structures in Belize remain the Mayan pyramids at **Caracol** and **Xunantunich.** Moreover, the country is dotted with lesser sites, and one almost entirely unexcavated city, **Pilar,** which might prove to be the largest Classic-era Mayan city in the region. For those looking to see perhaps the finest example of Classic Mayan ceremonial architecture, a trip to neighboring Guatemala and the ruins at **Tikal** are a must.

ART

Belizean artists range from folk artists and artisans working in a variety of forms, materials, and traditions to modern painters, sculptors, and ceramicists producing beautiful representational and abstract works.

Out in the western Cayo district, the traditional Mayan arts are kept alive by several talented artisans working in carved slate bas-reliefs. Of these, the **García sisters,** who run a gallery and small museum in the Mountain Pine Ridge area, are the prime proponents.

Perhaps the most vibrant place to look for modern art is Dangriga, where Garífuna painters like **Benjamín Nicholas** and **Pen Cayetano** have produced wonderful bodies of work depicting local life in a simple style. **Walter Castillo** is another excellent modern painter.

Several galleries in Belize City and San Pedro carry a wide range of locally produced art; see chapters 6 and 7 respectively for more information.

5 BELIZE IN BOOKS, FILM & MUSIC

LITERATURE

Belize doesn't have a strong literary tradition. However, most gift shops and bookstores around the country have a small collection of locally produced short stories, poetry, fiction, and nonfiction. In recent years, there has been a trend to resuscitate and transcribe the traditional Mayan and Garífuna tales and folklore, along with the publication of modern pieces of fiction and nonfiction either set in Belize or written by Belizeans.

Recommended Books

For a good, comprehensive look at the country's history, check out ***Understanding Belize: A Historical Guide*** (Harbour Publishing, 2006), by Alan Twigg. For a more first-hand, somewhat opinionated and local take on the subject, you could turn to Assad Shoman's ***Thirteen Chapters of a History of Belize*** (Angelus Press, 2000).

If you're more interested in a mix of modern history and the environment, don't miss ***The Last Flight of the Scarlet Macaw*** ★★ (Random House, 2008), by Bruce Barcott, which tells the story of Sharon Matola's fight to stop the Chalillo dam on the Macal River. Matola is the founder and director of the Belize Zoo, and the dam destroyed important habitat of the fragile and endangered Belizean macaw population. The book is far more interesting and better written than the above description might lead you to believe.

To prepare your eyes for possible sensory overload when you arrive in Belize, you may want to get your hands on a copy of Thor Janson's coffee table book of photography, ***Belize: Land of the Free by the Carib Sea*** ★★ (Bowen and Bowen Ltd., 2000). This book is chock-full of beautiful photos of Belizean countryside, wildlife, local festivities, and people.

If the wildlife and nature pictures in Janson's book move you and leave you anxious to see the real deal, there are a slew of books dedicated to observing the wonders of Belizean flora and fauna. Updated and reissued in 2004, Les Beletsky's ***Belize and Northern Guatemala: The Ecotravellers' Wildlife Guide*** ★★ (Natural World Academic Press, 2004), which features descriptions and color plates of most of the commonly spotted mammals, birds, amphibians, reptiles, fish, and corals, is probably the best all-around field guide for first-timers and armchair naturalists. Those with more specific interests in, say, birds, butterflies or ocean species, can find any number of more specific field guides.

Jaguar: One Man's Struggle to Establish the World's First Jaguar Preserve (Island Press, 2000), by Alan Rabinowitz, is an account of the author's time in Belize studying and working to protect jaguars. As you might have already guessed from the title, Rabinowitz was a major force in the establishment of the world's first jaguar preserve in the Cockscomb Basin Wildlife Sanctuary.

Maya-philes will want to have some reference material handy when visiting the many Belizean ruins. ***The Maya*** ★ (Thames and Hudson, 2005), by Michael D. Coe, is a good primer on the history of this advanced and enigmatic culture. As is ***Chronicle of the Maya Kings and Queens*** (Thames and Hudson, 2005), by Simon Martin and Nicolai Grube. However, I find ***A Forest of Kings: The Untold Story of the Ancient Maya*** ★★ (Harper Perennial, 1992), by David Freidel and Linda Schele, to be a better read, and one that gives a good feel for what life might have been like in the Mayan world. To delve into the intricacy and reasoning behind the Mayan aesthetic legacy, check out Mary Ellen Miller's book, ***Maya Art and Architecture*** (Thames and Hudson, 1999). Anabel Ford has published a helpful pamphlet/book entitled ***The Ancient Maya of Belize: Their Society and Sites*** that is available at many bookstores and gift shops in Belize.

There is also a host of excellent books on the Maya and Tikal. ***Tikal: An Illustrated History of the Ancient Maya Capital*** ★, by John Montgomery (Hippocrene Books, 2001), is a good place to start. ***The Lords of Tikal: Rulers of an Ancient Maya City*** (Thames & Hudson, 2000), by Peter D. Harrison et al., is another similar option.

The history of Ix Chel Farm is chronicled in ***Sastun: My Apprenticeship with a Maya Healer*** ★ (HarperOne, 1995), by

Rosita Arvigo, who spent years studying with Mayan bush doctor Don Elijio Panti. If this book on Belizean natural medicine doesn't satisfy your shamanistic tendencies, don't fret; there are several additional books on the subject. Check out ***One Hundred Healing Herbs Of Belize*** (Lotus Press, 1993), by Arvigo and Michael Balick; or ***Rainforest Home Remedies: The Maya Way to Heal Your Body and Replenish Your Soul*** ★ (HarperOne, 2001), by Rosita Arvigo and Nadine Epstein.

Belize, A Novel ★ (BookSurge Publishing, 2008), by Carlos Ledson Miller, is a lively novel covering 4 decades of life in a family, beginning with the disastrous consequences and events of Hurricane Hattie.

If you're bringing along the little ones, or even if you're leaving them behind but want to share a little bit of Mayan culture with them, look for Pat Mora's beautifully illustrated book ***The Night the Moon Fell: A Maya Myth*** ★ (Groundwood Books, 2000). Or, for a handy little picture book filled with photographs of Mayan daily life, check out ***Hands of the Maya: Villagers at Work and Play*** (Henry Holt & Company, 2002), by Rachel Crandell. Older children and adults alike should read ***Beka Lamb*** ★ (Heinemann, 1986), by Zee Edgell; it is a beautiful coming-of-age story by one of Belize's most prolific modern fiction writers.

FILM

Although it wasn't a box-office hit, you might want to rent a copy of *The Mosquito Coast* (1986), which was filmed in Belize. Starring Harrison Ford and River Phoenix and directed by Peter Weir, the film is about an inventor who relocates his family to the Central American jungle. Other films shot in Belize include *Dogs of War* (1980), which features Christopher Walken, and *Heart of Darkness* (1994), with John Malkovich.

MUSIC

The most distinctive and popular form of Belizean music you will come across is **Punta** and **Punta Rock.** Punta is similar to many Afro-Caribbean and Afro-pop music forms, blending traditional rhythms and drumming patterns with modern electronic instruments (Punta is usually more rootsy and acoustic than Punta Rock, which features electric guitars and keyboards). Pen Cayetano is often credited as being the founder of Punta Rock; you will find his discs and cassettes for sale throughout Belize, as well as those by his successors Andy Palacio, the Garífuna Kids, Travesia Band, Peter Flores (aka Titiman), and Chico Ramos. Punta music is usually sung in the Garífuna dialect, although the latest incarnations feature lyrics in English and even Spanish. Dancing to Punta and Punta Rock is sensuous and close, often settling into a firm butt-to-groin grind.

Paranda is another modern yet more traditional offshoot of Garífuna music and culture. Featuring acoustic guitars and rhythm ensembles, paranda is a lively, syncopated musical form. Paul "Nabby" Nabor is a popular paranda artist. A similar and rootsy form of contemporary folk music that comes from the Kriol tradition is known as **brukdown.**

In northern and western Belize, near the Mexican and Guatemalan borders, the local **mestizo** musical forms reflect their Spanish roots with marimba bands and Spanish-language folk songs influenced by the mariachi and ranchero traditions.

There is very little in the way of a club or live music scene in Belize. However, at the hotels in the southern Garífuna region, you are likely to be treated to a performance of traditional Garífuna drumming and dance, and at a few clubs around Belize City, San Pedro, and other popular tourist destinations you should be able to find various rock, reggae, and Punta Rock bands playing.

Palacio R.I.P.

On January 19, 2008, Andy Palacio died. Perhaps the best known and most popular proponent of Punta music, he was just 48. In addition to his musical fame, Palacio, who was born in the southern village of Barranco, was a tireless prominent proponent of all facets of Garífuna culture. His final album, *Wátina,* was released in 2007 to critical acclaim and was awarded the prestigious WOMEX award for World Music.

The best online sources I've found for Belizean music are www.stonetreerecords.com and www.calabashmusic.com. I'd avoid the various vendors selling bootleg cassettes and CDs on the side of the road, since the quality can be sketchy, and the artists don't receive a dime.

6 CONCH FRITTERS, STEW FISH & BELIKIN: BELIZEAN FOOD & DRINK

While it is hard to pin down any truly distinctive Belizean cuisine, what you will find in Belize is a mix of Caribbean, Mexican, African, Spanish, and Mayan culinary influences. You'll also find burgers, pizzas, Chinese food, and even Indian restaurants.

Belize's strongest suit is its **seafood.** Fresh fish, lobster, shrimp, and conch are widely available, especially in the beach and island destinations. Belize has historically been a major exporter of lobster, but overharvesting has caused the population to decline. It is still readily available and relatively inexpensive, but there is a lobster season, from June 15 to February 14.

Rice and beans is a major staple, often served as an accompaniment to almost any main dish. A slight difference is to be inferred between "rice and beans," which are usually cooked (sometimes in coconut milk) and served together, and "beans and rice," which are usually cooked and served separately. Belizeans tend to use a small red bean, but black beans are sometimes used.

Aside from rice and beans, if there were such a thing as a national dish it would be **stew chicken** and its close cousins stew beef and stew fish. These Kriol-based recipes are dark stews that get their color from a broad mix of spices, as well as red *recado,* which is made from annatto seed or achiote. A similar and related stew commonly found around Belize is **chimole,** which is sometimes called black gumbo.

Perhaps the most distinctive element of Belizean cuisine and dining is **Marie Sharp's Hot Sauce.** Almost no dining table is complete without a bottle of Marie Sharp's. The original Marie Sharp's is a very spicy sauce made from a base of habanero peppers, carrots, and onions. Currently, Marie Sharp's has a wide range of different hot sauces, jams, and chutneys. If you have a hankering for the hot stuff, you will find that your options aren't confined to Marie Sharp's. In many restaurants, you will often see a jar of habanero peppers and onions marinating in simple white vinegar. Marie Sharp's original sauce was named **Melinda's;** however, she no longer has anything to do with Melinda's (it's not even made in Belize anymore). One other local hot sauce you might see is **Lizette's,** which is also quite good.

A new local product to look out for is homemade organic chocolate, which you'll see in supermarkets and gift shops around the country under the label **Goss Chocolate** (www.gosschocolate.com).

MEALS & DINING CUSTOMS

Belizeans tend to eat three meals a day, in similar fashion and hours to North Americans. Breakfasts tend to be served between 6:30 and 9am; lunch between noon and 2pm; and dinner between 6 and 10pm. Most meals and dining experiences are quite informal. In fact, there are only a few restaurants in the entire country that could be considered semiformal, and none require a jacket or tie, although you could certainly wear them.

Food

BREAKFAST The typical breakfast in Belize is quite simple, usually anchored by some scrambled eggs and refried red or black beans. However, instead of toast, you will often have a choice of tortillas, **johnnycakes,** or **fry jacks** to accompany them. A johnnycake is a semidry, baked, round flour biscuit, served with butter or stuffed with ham and/or cheese. Fry jacks are a similar batter and shape, but deep-fried, and either served as is or dusted with confectioner's sugar. The most common tortillas served in Belize are corn tortillas.

APPETIZERS **Conch fritters** are by far the country's most popular and tastiest appetizer. These deep-fried balls of flour batter and chopped conch meat are on most bar and restaurant menus in the country, particularly on the cayes and along the coast. Try some.

SANDWICHES & SNACKS Belize's light menus show a heavy Mexican and American influence. Many simple eateries and roadside carts will feature simple tacos, tamales (also called *dukunu*), or **garnaches.** The latter, a fried corn tortilla topped with beans, cheese, or shredded meat or chicken, would probably be considered a tostada by many. Popular stuffed pastries include meat pies and ***panades,*** small, deep-fried empanadas.

You can also get traditional sandwiches, often served on sliced white bread, as well as American-style burgers. I personally recommend looking for fish, shrimp, or conch burgers, which are available at most beach and island destinations.

MEAT, POULTRY & WILD GAME Belizeans also eat a fair amount of meat and poultry, as well as some more interesting game. Because Belize only recently began to raise its own beef, the country relied for a long time on wild game. Some of the more interesting game items you might see on a Belizean menu include **gibnut** (paca) and **iguana.** The gibnut is a large rodent, *Agouti paca,* which some say tastes like rabbit, although I find it a bit gamier. Iguana is frequently called "bamboo chicken," and it does actually taste a bit like chicken. Occasionally, you may also come across wild boar, armadillo, or some other forest-dwelling creature.

Another popular wild animal found in restaurants is the **sea turtle,** endangered all over the world, including in Belize. It's not yet illegal to sell sea turtle within Belize, but international agreements prohibit its export. Please don't order turtle steak, turtle soup, or turtle eggs. In fact, I'm a little hesitant to recommend the eating of wild game at all. So far, there's no reliable data on the impact that the hunting of wild game has had or could have, but there is reason for concern. Belize is struggling to preserve its natural environment, and as long as people order wild game, it will continue to show up on menus. Exceptions would be any farm-raised wild animals, like iguanas. When harvested from commercial "iguana farms," this wild game actually has the potential to mix sustainable yield with modern conservation.

Fun Facts The Queen's Rat

The gibnut is often called "The Queen's Rat" or "The Royal Rat" because Queen Elizabeth was served gibnut during a visit here. Headlines in London read "Queen eats rat."

SEAFOOD Seafood is the basic staple of most of the country's coastal and island destinations. It is fresh and plentiful. Shrimp, conch, lobster (in season), and a variety of fish are almost always on the menu. You're best off sticking to simple preparations, either grilled or fried. My favorite fishes are grouper, snapper, and dorado (or mahimahi). You will also come across barracuda, shark, and marlin. You'll rarely find **snook** on the menu, and if so, you should definitely try this delicate white fish.

If you are in a Garífuna region, you should not miss the chance to try ***hudut,*** a fish stew or whole fish preparation served in a coconut-milk broth, often accompanied by mashed, fried green plantains. ***Sere*** is a very similar Kriol dish that seems more like a traditional fish or seafood stew, but again, based on a coconut-milk broth.

Ceviche, a cold marinade of fish, conch, and/or shrimp "cooked" in lime juice and seasoned, is a great treat for lunch or as an appetizer.

VEGETABLES On the whole, you'll find vegetables surprisingly lacking in Belizean meals. Fresh garden salads are rare and hard to come by. A lack of fresh ingredients makes other vegetable dishes and sides almost as uncommon. Most restaurant meals come accompanied by a simple slaw of grated cabbage, or a potato or beet salad.

FRUITS Belize has a wealth of delicious tropical fruits. The most common are mangoes (the season begins in May), papayas, pineapples, melons, and bananas. Other fruits you might find include the **fruit of the cashew tree,** which has orange or yellow glossy skin, and **carambola** (star fruit), a tart fruit whose cross-sections form perfect stars.

DESSERTS Belize doesn't have a very extravagant or refined dessert culture. After all, the country was colonized by the British, not the French. However, you can usually find homemade coconut pie, chocolate pie, or bread pudding on most menus. Flan, an egg-and-condensed-milk custard imported from Mexico, is also popular.

Drink

BEVERAGES Most major brands of soft drinks are available, as are fresh lime juice (limeade) and orange juice. You're in the tropics, so expect to find fresh shakes made with papaya, pineapple, or mango.

One of the most unique drinks you're likely to sample anywhere is a **seaweed shake,** a cooling concoction made of dried seaweed, evaporated and condensed milk, cinnamon, and nutmeg, and blended with ice. Seaweed shakes are sometimes kicked up with a shot of rum or brandy.

WATER Much of the drinking water in Belize is **rainwater.** People use the roofs of their houses to collect water in a cistern, which supplies them for the year. Tap water isn't generally considered safe to drink, even in most cities and popular tourist towns. The water in Belize City and San Ignacio is relatively safe to drink, but travelers often get a touch of diarrhea whenever they hit a foreign country, so always play it safe. Ask for bottled drinking water at your hotel, and whenever you can, pick up a bottle of spring or purified water (available in most markets) to have handy.

BEER, WINE & LIQUOR The Belize Brewing Company's **Belikin** beer is the national beer of Belize. It comes in several varieties, including Belikin Lager, Belikin Premium, and Belikin Stout. The recipes and original brew masters all came from Germany. Both the lager and premium are full-bodied, hearty beers. The Belikin brewery also bottles a **locally produced Guinness Stout,** as thick and rich as its brand name demands.

As you'll find throughout the Caribbean, rum is the liquor of choice in Belize. There are several brands and distilleries producing rum in Belize. Probably the finest Belizean rum is the 5-year-aged **Prestige.** One of the most popular brands you'll come across is **1 Barrel,** which has a hint of vanilla, and is slightly sweet for my taste.

Belize doesn't produce any traditional wines of note. The climate and soil are not very well suited for growing the right kinds of grapes. On Ambergris Caye, the **Rendezvous Restaurant & Winery** (p. 135) does in fact import grape juice for the purpose of producing and bottling their own wines, although they are really more of a novelty than a delicacy.

Several different **fruit wines** are produced in Belize using native fruits, including pineapple and even banana. These wines are very sweet and are more a novelty than anything else. In remote parts of the country, you'll find homemade fruit wines that are a bit like hard cider.

3

Planning Your Trip to Belize

Belize offers a wealth of vacation options, ranging from sun-and-fun beach time, to dedicated scuba diving or fishing trips, to themed vacations exploring the ancient Mayan culture and archaeology. Moreover, given the compact size of the country, it's very possible to cover a lot of ground in a short time, and to mix and match these options. Whatever your interests, this chapter (as well as chapter 5) will provide you with all the tools and information necessary to plan and book your trip.

1 VISITOR INFORMATION

The **Belize Tourism Board,** at 64 Regent St. (P.O. Box 325) in Belize City, will mail you a basic information packet, which you can order on their website at **www.travelbelize.org**. Alternatively, folks in the United States and Canada can call the Belize Tourism Board toll free at ✆ **800/624-0286.** Travelers from the United Kingdom, Australia, and New Zealand will have to rely primarily on the website, or dial direct to Belize (✆ **227-2430**), as the Belize Tourism Board does not have offices or a toll-free number in these countries.

In addition to the official website, you'll be able to find a wealth of Web-based information on Belize with a few clicks of your mouse. See "The Best Websites About Belize" in chapter 1 for some helpful suggestions on where to begin your online search.

2 ENTRY REQUIREMENTS & CUSTOMS

ENTRY REQUIREMENTS

A current passport, valid through your departure date, is required for entry into Belize. Driver's licenses and birth certificates are not valid travel documents. In some cases you may be asked to show an onward or return plane ticket.

Visas

No visas are required for citizens of the United States, the European community (including Ireland), Great Britain, South Africa, Australia, or New Zealand. Nationals of certain other countries do need a visa or consular permission to enter Belize. For a current list, see the Belize Tourism Board website (www.travelbelize.org) or call the nearest Belizean consulate or embassy.

Tourists are permitted a maximum stay of 30 days. The **Belize Department of Immigration and Nationality** in Belmopan (✆ **822-2423**) will sometimes grant an extension of up to three months. These extensions are handled on a case-by-case basis and cost BZ$100 (US$50/£27) per month.

If you have additional travel or visa questions about Belize, you can contact any of the following Belizean embassies or consulates: in the **United States** or **Canada,** 2535

Cut to the Front of the Airport Security Line as a Registered Traveler

In 2003, the **Transportation Security Administration (TSA;** www.tsa.gov) approved a pilot program to help ease the time spent in line for airport security screenings. In exchange for information and a fee, persons can be pre-screened as registered travelers, granting them a front-of-the-line position when they fly. The program is run through private firms—the largest and most well-known is Steven Brill's **Clear** (www.flyclear.com), and it works like this: Travelers complete an online application providing specific points of personal information including name, addresses for the previous five years, birth date, social security number, driver's license number, and a valid credit card (you're not charged the **$99 fee** until your application is approved). Print out the completed form and take it, along with proper ID, with you to an "enrollment station" (these can be found in over 20 participating airports and in a growing number of American Express offices around the country, for example). It's at this point where it gets seemingly sci-fi. At the enrollment station, a Clear representative will record your biometrics necessary for clearance; in this case, your fingerprints and your irises will be digitally recorded.

Once your application has been screened against no-fly lists, outstanding warrants, and other security measures, you'll be issued a clear plastic card that holds a chip containing your information. Each time you fly through participating airports (and the numbers are steadily growing), go to the Clear Pass station located next to the standard TSA screening line. Here you'll insert your card into a slot and place your finger on a scanner to read your print—when the information matches up, you're cleared to cut to the front of the security line. You'll still have to follow all the procedures of the day like removing your shoes and walking through the X-ray machine, but Clear promises to cut 30 minutes off your wait time at the airport.

On a personal note: Each time I've used my Clear Pass, my travel companions are still waiting to go through security while I'm already sitting down, reading the paper and sipping my overpriced smoothie. Granted, registered traveler programs are not for the infrequent traveler, but for those of us who fly on a regular basis, it's a perk I'm willing to pay for.

—David A. Lytle

Massachusetts Ave. NW, Washington, DC 20008 (✆ **202/332-9636;** www.embassyofbelize.org); in **Great Britain,** Belize High Commission, 22 Harcourt House, 45 Crawford Pl., London, W1H 4LP (✆ **020/7723-3603**); and in **Australia,** 5/1 Oliver Rd., Roseville NSW (✆ **02/9905-8144**). There is no Belizean embassy or consulate in New Zealand.

For information on how to get a passport, go to "Passports" in the "Fast Facts" section of appendix A—the websites listed provide downloadable passport applications as well as the current fees for processing passport applications. For an up-to-date, country-by-country listing of passport requirements around the world, go to the "Foreign Entry Requirement"

Web page of the U.S. State Department at **http://travel.state.gov**.

Medical Requirements

No shots or inoculations are required to enter Belize.

For more on medical concerns and recommendations, see "Health," p. 46.

CUSTOMS

What You Can Bring into Belize

Visitors to Belize may bring with them any and all reasonable goods and belongings for personal use during their stay. Cameras, computers, and electronic equipment, as well as fishing and diving gear for personal use, are permitted duty free. Customs officials in Belize seldom check arriving tourists' luggage.

What You Can Take Home from Belize

It is expressly illegal to take out any pre-Columbian artifact from Belize, whether you bought it, you discovered it, or it was given to you. Do not traffic in Maya artifacts.

U.S. Citizens: For specifics on what you can bring back and the corresponding fees, download the invaluable free pamphlet *Know Before You Go* at **www.cbp.gov** (click on "Travel," and then click on "Know Before You Go! Online Brochure"). Or contact the **U.S. Customs & Border Protection (CBP),** 1300 Pennsylvania Ave. NW, Washington, DC 20229 (© **877/287-8667**) and request the pamphlet.

Canadian Citizens: For a clear summary of Canadian rules, write for the booklet *I Declare,* issued by the **Canada Border Services Agency** (© **800/461-9999** in Canada, or 204/983-3500; www.cbsa-asfc.gc.ca).

U.K. Citizens: For information, contact **HM Customs & Excise** at © **0845/010-9000** (from outside the U.K., 020/8929-0152), or consult their website at www.hmce.gov.uk.

Australian Citizens: A helpful brochure available from Australian consulates or Customs offices is *Know Before You Go.* For more information, call the **Australian Customs Service** at © **1300/363-263,** or log on to www.customs.gov.au.

New Zealand Citizens: Most questions are answered in a free pamphlet available at New Zealand consulates and Customs offices: *New Zealand Customs Guide for Travellers, Notice no. 4.* For more information, contact **New Zealand Customs,** The Customhouse, 17–21 Whitmore St., Box 2218, Wellington (© **04/473-6099** or 0800/428-786; www.customs.govt.nz).

3 WHEN TO GO

Belize's high season for tourism runs from late November to late April, which coincides almost perfectly with the chill of winter in the United States, Canada, and Great Britain. The high season is also the dry season. If you want some unadulterated time on a tropical beach and a little less rain during your rainforest experience, this is the time to visit. During this period (and especially around the Christmas and Easter holidays), the tourism industry operates at full tilt—prices are higher, attractions are more crowded, and reservations need to be made in advance.

The weather in Belize is subtropical and generally similar to that of southern Florida. The average daytime temperature on the coast and cayes is around 80°F (27°C), although it can get considerably warmer during the day during the summer months. During the winter months, when northern cold fronts extend their grip south, it can get downright nippy. In fact, from late December to February, "northers" can hit the coastal and caye areas hard, and hang around for between 3 and 5 days, putting a severe crimp in any beach vacation. The best months for guaranteed sun and fun are March through May.

The rainy season runs from June to mid-November, while the hurricane season runs from July to October, with the most active months being August, September, and October. For the most part, the rainy season is characterized by a dependable and short-lived afternoon shower. However, the amount of rainfall varies considerably with the regions. In the south, there may be more than 150 inches of rain per year, while in the north, it rarely rains more than 50 inches per year. Usually there is also a brief dry period in mid-August, known as the *mauger.* If you're skittish about rain and hurricanes, don't come to Belize between late August and mid-October, the height of both the rainy and hurricane seasons. However, if you do come, you should be able to land some good bargains.

The Cayo District and other inland destinations tend to be slightly cooler than the coastal and caye destinations, although since there is generally little elevation gain, the differences tend to be slight.

Average Monthly Temperatures & Rainfall in Belize

	Jan	Feb	Mar	Apr	May	Jun	Jul	Aug	Sep	Oct	Nov	Dec
Temp (°F)	73	76	78	80	82	82	82	82	81	79	75	74
Temp (°C)	23	24	26	27	28	28	28	28	27	26	24	23
Days of Rain	12	6	4	5	7	13	15	14	15	16	12	14

PUBLIC HOLIDAYS

Official holidays in Belize include **January 1** (New Year's Day), **March 9** (Baron Bliss Day), Good Friday, Holy Saturday, Easter Sunday, Easter Monday, **May 1** (Labour Day), **May 24** (Commonwealth Day), **September 10** (St. George's Caye Day), **September 21** (Independence Day), **October 12** (Pan American Day), **November 19** (Garífuna Settlement Day), **December 25** (Christmas Day), **December 26** (Boxing Day), and **December 31** (New Year's Eve).

Government offices and banks are closed on official holidays, transportation services are reduced, and stores and markets may also close.

BELIZE CALENDAR OF EVENTS

Some of the events listed here might be considered more of a community celebration or tradition than an event—there's not, for instance, a Deer Dance Festival PR Committee that readily dispenses information. If I haven't listed a contact number, your best bet is to call the **Belize Tourism Board** at ✆ **800/624-0286** in the U.S. and Canada, or 227-2430 in Belize, or visit www.travelbelize.org for additional information.

For an exhaustive list of events beyond those listed here, check http://events.frommers.com, where you'll find a searchable, up-to-the-minute roster of what's happening in cities all over the world.

JANUARY

Krem New Year's Cycling Classic. This New Year's Day road race starts in Corozal Town and ends in Belize City. The competitors are mostly Belizean, although Guatemalan and Mexican teams occasionally enter. The winners usually take around 3½ to 4 hours to cross the finish line; crowds usually form at the start and finish points. January 1.

FEBRUARY

International Billfish Tournament. Hosted by the Radisson Fort George Hotel and Marina (✆ **800/333-3333**

in the U.S., or 223-3333; www.radisson.com), this multiday event features cash prizes. Early February.

Carnival. Nationwide celebrations during the week before Lent. Larger towns have parades and dance competitions. In San Pedro, watch out for getting "painted."

March

La Ruta Maya Belize River Challenge. This 4-day canoe race begins in San Ignacio in the Cayo District and ends at the Swing Bridge in Belize City. For more details, visit www.larutamayabelize.com. March 6 to 9.

Baron Bliss Day. The day is marked with nationwide celebrations of Belize's benefactor. The greatest festivities are held in Belize City, which hosts a regatta, as well as horse and foot races. March 9.

May

Labour Day. After a national address by the prime minister or minister of labour (carried on all local radio and television stations), the rest of Labour Day is filled with street celebrations, regattas, and horse races. May 1.

Cashew Festival, Crooked Tree Village. Celebrating the cashew harvest, this weekend celebration features local booths selling everything possible under the sun made with this coveted nut, including cashew wine and cashew jelly. Live music and general revelry accompany the celebrations. First weekend in May.

National Agriculture & Trade Show, Belmopan. This national fair is geared towards farmers, cattle ranchers, large-scale agro-business, and buyers, but it's still an interesting event to tour or visit if you're in the country at the time. Mid-May.

Toledo Cacao Fest, Punta Gorda. Chocolate lovers should head to southern Belize in late May for this festival. In addition to food and desserts, there are concerts, games, parades and tour activities planned. For exact dates, see www.toledochocolate.com.

June

Día de San Pedro, San Pedro, Ambergris Caye. This is a 3-day celebration of the island's patron saint, Saint Peter, or San Pedro. Boats are blessed, and there are parades and processions. June 27 to 29.

Lobster Festival, Placencia. During this extended weekend celebration of the opening of lobster season, this beach town pulls out all the stops. There's plenty of lobster to be had in a variety of preparations, at temporary outdoor stalls and restaurants around town. There are also concerts and dancing and an arts fair. Check www.placencia.com for the latest details. Late June.

July

Lobster Festival, Caye Caulker. Not to be outdone by Placencia, Caye Caulker also puts on a long weekend celebration of the start of lobster season. Food, music, and dancing are all served up in hearty portions around town. Early July.

August

Costa Maya Festival, San Pedro, Ambergris Caye. This is perhaps the largest festival in the country. Drawing participants from the neighboring countries of El Salvador, Mexico, Guatemala, and Honduras, this celebration features a steady stream of live concert performances, street parades, beauty pageants, and water shows and activities. Early August.

Deer Dance Festival, San Antonio, Toledo District. This 9-day Mayan festival is celebrated in the small Mayan village of San Antonio. Highlights include costumed and dance performances. Late August to early September.

September

Independence Day. Patriotic parades and official celebrations are mixed with street parties, beauty pageants, and open-air concerts. September 21.

October

Pan American Day. Formerly known as Columbus Day, this day now celebrates mestizo and Mayan culture with parades, street fairs, and concerts. October 12.

November

Garífuna Settlement Day. The greatest Garífuna celebration occurs in Dangriga, where Garífunas from across Belize and throughout the region gather to commemorate their arrival from St. Vincent in 1832. Street parades, religious ceremonies, and dance and drumming performances are all part of the celebrations throughout the southern coastal zone. November 19.

December

Boxing Day. While Christmas Day is predominantly for the family in Belize, Boxing Day is a chance to continue the celebration with friends, neighbors, and strangers. Dances, concerts, horse races, and general festivities are put on around the country. December 26.

4 GETTING THERE & GETTING AROUND

GETTING THERE

By Plane

Belize City's **Philip S. W. Goldson International Airport** (airport code BZE) is serviced by several airlines out of major U.S. hubs. **American Airlines, Continental, Delta, Grupo Taca,** and **US Airways** all have regular direct service to Belize. Flying time from Miami is just over 2 hours.

There are no direct flights to Belize from Europe, Australia, New Zealand, mainland Asia, or Africa. From Canada, the only direct flights are seasonal winter charters. To get to Belize from any of these points of origin, you will have to connect through one of the U.S. hubs.

For additional help in booking your air travel to Belize, please turn to appendix A.

Getting into Town from the Airport

The **Philip S. W. Goldson International Airport** is located 16km (10 miles) northwest of the city on the Northern Highway. There is no public bus service or shuttle van service. However, taxis are there to meet every flight. A taxi into town will cost BZ$50 to BZ$60 (US$25–US$30/£13–£16). See p. 91 for more info.

Long-Haul Flights: How to Stay Comfortable

- Your choice of airline and airplane will definitely affect your leg room. Find more details about U.S. airlines at **www.seatguru.com**. For international airlines, the research firm Skytrax has posted a list of average seat pitches at **www.airlinequality.com**.
- Emergency exit seats and bulkhead seats typically have the most legroom. Emergency exit seats are usually left unassigned until the day of a flight (to ensure that someone able-bodied fills the seats); it's worth checking in online at home (if the airline offers that option) or getting to the ticket counter early to snag one of these spots for a long flight. Many passengers find that bulkhead seating offers more legroom, but keep in mind that bulkhead seats have no storage space on the floor in front of you.

- To have two seats for yourself in a three-seat row, try for an aisle seat in a center section toward the back of coach. If you're traveling with a companion, book an aisle and a window seat. Middle seats are usually booked last, so chances are good you'll end up with three seats to yourselves. And in the event that a third passenger is assigned the middle seat, he or she will probably be more than happy to trade for a window or an aisle.
- To sleep, avoid the last row of any section or the row in front of an emergency exit, as these seats are the least likely to recline. Avoid seats near highly trafficked toilet areas. Avoid seats in the back of many jets—these can be narrower than those in the rest of coach. Or reserve a window seat so you can rest your head and avoid being bumped in the aisle.
- Get up, walk around, and stretch every 60 to 90 minutes to keep your blood flowing. This helps avoid **deep vein thrombosis,** or "economy-class syndrome." See the box "Avoiding 'Economy-Class Syndrome,'" p. 47.
- Drink water before, during, and after your flight to combat the lack of humidity in airplane cabins. Avoid caffeine and alcohol, which will dehydrate you.

BY CRUISE SHIP

As many as one million tourists stop in Belize as part of a cruise itinerary per year. All ships call at Belize City and offer a wide range of day-tour options around the country. Cruise lines that offer stops in Belize as part of their Caribbean and Panama Canal routes include **Crystal Cruises** (✆ 888/722-0021; www.crystalcruises.com), **Celebrity Cruises** (✆ 800/647-2251; www.celebritycruises.com), **Holland America** (✆ 877/932-4259; www.hollandamerica.com), **Norwegian Cruise Lines** (✆ 866/234-7350; www.ncl.com), **Princess** (✆ 800/774-6237; www.princess.com), **Royal Caribbean** (✆ 866/562-7625; www.rccl.com), **Radisson Seven Seas Cruises** (✆ 877/505-5370; www.rssc.com), and **Seabourn Yachts** (✆ 800/929-9391; www.seabourn.com). It might pay off to book through a travel agency that specializes in cruises; these companies buy in bulk and stay on top of the latest specials and promotions. Try either the **Cruise Company** (✆ 800/289-5505; www.thecruisecompany.com) or **World Wide Cruises** (✆ 800/882-9000; www.wwcruises.com).

GETTING AROUND

By Plane

Traveling around Belize by commuter airline is common, easy, and relatively economical. Two local commuter airlines serve all the major tourist destinations around Belize. The carriers are **Maya Island Air** (✆ **223-1140;** www.mayaairways.com) and **Tropic Air** (✆ **800/422-3435** in the U.S. or Canada, or 226-2012 in Belize; www.tropicair.com). Both operate out of both the **Philip S. W. Goldson International Airport** and the Belize City **Municipal Airport.** In both cases, flights are considerably less expensive into and out of the Municipal Airport. See the destination chapters for specific details on schedules and costs.

By Car

There are only four major roads in Belize: the Northern, Western, Southern, and Hummingbird highways. All are just two-lane affairs, and all actually have speed bumps as they pass through various towns and villages along their way. Belize is only 113 km or so (70 miles) wide, and around 402km (250 miles) long. Renting a car is an excellent way to see the country. If you are going to the Mountain Pine Ridge area of the Cayo District, or to the Gallon Jug or Lamanai areas, you will certainly need a four-wheel-drive vehicle. However, if you're just visiting the major towns and cities of San Ignacio, Placencia, Corozal, or Punta Gorda, you'll probably be fine in a standard sedan. That said, it's always nice to have the extra clearance and off-road ability of a four-wheel-drive vehicle, particularly during the rainy season (June through mid-Nov).

Among the major international agencies operating in Belize are Avis, Budget, Hertz, and Thrifty. **Crystal Auto Rental** (✆ **800/777-7777** toll-free in Belize or 223-1600; www.crystal-belize.com) is a local company, with an excellent fleet and good prices. For a complete list of car rental agencies and their contact information, see appendix A, as well as the "Getting Around" sections of other major tourist-destination chapters.

Prices run between BZ$120 and BZ$240 (US$60–US$120/£32–£64) per day for a late-model compact to a compact SUV, including insurance. Most of the rental companies above have a 25-year-old minimum age requirement for renting, although Crystal Auto Rental will rent to 21- to 24-year-olds, but with twice the deductible.

Often included in the price, car-rental insurance runs about BZ$24 to BZ$40 (US$12–US$20/£6.35–£11) per day with an average deductible of around BZ$1,500 (US$750/£398), although sometimes for a few extra dollars per day you can get no-fault, no-deductible coverage.

Before driving off with a rental car, be sure that you inspect the exterior and point out to the rental-company representative every tiny scratch, dent, tear, or any other damage.

Note: It's sometimes cheaper to reserve a car in your home country than to book when you arrive in Belize. If you know you'll be renting a car, it's always wise to reserve it well in advance for the high season, as the rental fleet can't match demand.

MAPS There are so few roads in Belize that you will probably be fine using the maps in this book, or the free maps given out at the airport or by your car rental agency. If you really want a more detailed map, the Belize map produced by the **International Travel Maps and Books** (www.itmb.com) is a good option. You can get this and other maps at many bookstores and gift shops in Belize, if you are unable to buy it in advance either online or at a bookstore near you. Alternatively, you can pick up a copy of Emory King's *Driver's Guide to Beautiful Belize* (Tropical Books, 2003).

GASOLINE Gas stations can be found in all the major towns and tourist destinations. At press time, a gallon of premium or "super" unleaded gas cost BZ$10 (US$5/£2.65).

DRIVING RULES A current foreign driver's license is valid for the time you are in Belize. Despite having been a British colony and current member of the Commonwealth, cars drive on the right-hand

Road Distances from Belize City

Belmopan	84km (52 miles)
Benque Viejo	130km (81 miles)
Corozal Town	138km (86 miles)
Dangriga	116km (72 miles)
Orange Walk Town	89km (55 miles)
Placencia	241km (150 miles)
Punta Gorda	330km (205 miles)
San Ignacio	116km (72 miles)

Car-Rental Tips

While it's preferable to use the coverage provided by your home auto-insurance policy or credit card, check carefully to see if the coverage really holds in Belize. Many policies exclude four-wheel-drive vehicles and off-road driving—but good portions of Belize can in fact be considered off road. While it's possible at some car-rental agencies to waive the insurance charges, you will have to pay all damages before leaving the country if you're in an accident. If you do take the insurance, you can expect a deductible of between US$750 and US$1,500 (£398–£795). At some agencies, you can buy additional insurance to lower the deductible.

side of the road, just as in the United States. Seatbelt use is mandatory in Belize, and failure to comply carries a fine. One odd driving law in Belize is that drivers wishing to make a left-hand turn while traveling along any of the country's "highways" must first pull over to the right-hand shoulder until all oncoming and following traffic has cleared.

RENTER'S INSURANCE Even if you hold **your own car-insurance policy** at home, coverage doesn't always extend abroad. Be sure to find out whether you'll be covered in Belize, whether your policy extends to all persons who will be driving the rental car, how much liability is covered in case an outside party is injured in an accident, and whether the *type* of vehicle you are renting is included under your contract.

Most **major credit cards** provide some degree of coverage as well—provided that they were used to pay for the rental. Again, terms vary widely, so be sure to call your credit card company directly before you rent. Usually, if you are **uninsured** or are **driving abroad,** your credit card provides primary coverage as long as you decline the rental agency's insurance. This means that the credit card will cover damage or theft of a rental car for the full cost of the vehicle. If you already have insurance, your credit card will provide secondary coverage, which basically covers your deductible. *Credit cards will not cover liability* or the cost of injury to an outside party and/or damage to an outside party's vehicle.

If you do not hold an insurance policy, you might seriously want to consider purchasing additional liability insurance from your rental company. Be sure to check the terms, however. Some rental agencies cover liability only if the renter is not at fault; even then, the rental company's obligation varies by location.

The basic insurance coverage offered by most car-rental companies, known as **Loss/Damage Waiver (LDW)** or **Collision Damage Waiver (CDW),** can cost as much as $20 (£11) per day. It usually covers the full value of the vehicle, with no deductible if an outside party causes an accident or other damage to the rental car. Liability coverage varies according to the company policy. If you are at fault in an accident, however, you will be covered for the full replacement value of the car, but not for liability. Most rental companies require a police report to process claims, but your private insurer will not be notified of the accident.

BREAKDOWNS Be warned that emergency services, both vehicular and medical, are extremely limited in Belize, and their availability is directly related to the remoteness of your location at the time of breakdown. You'll find service stations spread over the entire length of the major highways, and a fair number of these of these have tow trucks and mechanics. The major towns of Belize City, Belmopan, Orange Walk, Corozal, Dangriga, Punta Gorda and San Ignacio all have hospitals, and most other moderately sized cities and tourist destinations have some sort of clinic or health-services provider.

Note: It should go without saying, but you cannot rent a car on or drive to any of the cayes or outer atolls.

By Bus

Belize has an extensive network of commuter buses serving all of the major villages and towns and tourist destinations in the country. However, this system is used primarily by Belizeans. The buses tend to be a bit antiquated, and buyouts and bankruptcies within the industry have left the status of the local bus network in a state of confusion and limbo. See the destination chapters for specific details on schedules and costs, and be sure to check in advance, or as soon as you arrive, as schedules (and costs) do change regularly.

By Boat

While it's possible to fly to a few of the outer cayes, most travel between mainland Belize and the cayes and atolls is done by high-speed launch. There are regular water taxis between Belize City and Ambergris Caye, Caye Caulker, Caye Chapel, and St. George's Caye. Hotels and resorts on the other islands all either have their own boats, or can arrange transport for you. See the destination chapters for specific details on how to get to the cayes and atolls by boat.

By Helicopter

Astrum Helicopters ★ (**✆ 222-5100;** www.astrumhelicopters.com) is a new company with a small fleet of sleek and modern helicopters. They will take you to just about any destination in Belize, including remote lodges, islands and atolls. They will also take you out on sightseeing tours. Rates run between BZ$2,400 (US$1,200/£636) and BZ$3,750 (US$3,200/£1,696), depending upon the distance and number of passengers.

5 MONEY & COSTS

It's always advisable to bring money in a variety of forms on a vacation: a mix of cash, credit cards, debit cards, and, occasionally, traveler's checks.

CURRENCY

The Belize dollar, abbreviated BZ$, is the official currency of Belize. It is pegged to the U.S. dollar at a ratio of 2 Belize dollars to 1 U.S. dollar. Both currencies are acceptable at almost any business or establishment around the country. As long as you have U.S. dollars or U.S. dollar-based traveler's checks, it is entirely unnecessary to change for Belize dollars in advance of your trip. However, travelers from Canada, Europe, Australia, and New Zealand will want to change a sufficient amount of their home currency to U.S. dollars before traveling. To check the very latest exchange rates before you leave home, point your browser to **www.xe.com/ucc**.

Once you are in Belize, the change you receive will most likely be in Belize dollars, although it is not uncommon for it to be a mix of both currencies. However, do try to have some small-denomination bills for paying taxis, modest meal tabs, and tips.

The branch of the **Belize Bank** (**✆ 225-2107**) at the international airport is only open Monday through Friday from 8:30am to 4pm. If you are flying out on a weekend, or outside of these hours, be sure

The Belize Dollar, the U.S. Dollar, the Euro, & the British Pound

BZ$	US$	Euro €	UK£
1.00	0.50	0.34	0.27
2.00	1.00	0.67	0.53
5.00	2.50	1.68	1.33
10.00	5.00	3.35	2.65
20.00	10.00	6.70	5.30
25.00	12.50	8.38	6.63
50.00	25.00	16.75	13.25
100.00	50.00	33.50	26.50
200.00	100.00	67.00	53.00
500.00	250.00	167.50	132.50
1,000.00	500.00	335.00	265.00
2,000.00	1,000.00	670.00	530.00
5,000.00	2,500.00	1,675.00	1,325.00

to spend or exchange any Belize dollars beforehand.

Tip: Be careful to note whether or not the price you are being quoted is in Belize or U.S. dollars. Many hotels, restaurants, and tour operators actually quote in U.S. dollars. If in doubt, ask. At a two-to-one ratio, the difference can be substantial.

ATMS

The easiest and best way to get cash away from home is from an ATM (automated teller machine), sometimes referred to as a "cash machine," or a "cashpoint." The **Cirrus** (✆ **800/424-7787;** www.mastercard.com) and **PLUS** (✆ **800/843-7587;** www.visa.com) networks span the globe; look at the back of your bank card to see which network you're on, then call or check online for ATM locations at your destination. Be sure you know your personal identification number (PIN) and daily withdrawal limit before you depart.

Note: Many banks impose a fee every time you use a card at another bank's ATM, and that fee can be higher for international transactions (up to $5/£2.65 or more) than for domestic ones (where they're rarely more than $2/£1.05). In addition, the bank from which you withdraw cash may charge its own fee. For international withdrawal fees, ask your bank.

Note: Banks that are members of the **Global ATM Alliance** charge no transaction fees for cash withdrawals at other Alliance member ATMs; these include Bank of America, Scotiabank (Canada, Caribbean, and Mexico), Barclays (U.K. and parts of Africa), Deutsche Bank (Germany, Poland, Spain, and Italy), and BNP Paribas (France). Scotiabank has branches in Belize.

It's probably a good idea to change your PIN to a four-digit PIN. While many ATM machines in Belize will accept five- and six-digit PINs, some will only accept four-digit PINs.

Currently, in Belize, you will only find internationally accessible ATMs in major cities or towns and tourist destinations, including Belize City, San Pedro, Caye Caulker, Placencia, Punta Gorda, San Ignacio, Belmopan, Dangriga, and Corozal

What Things Cost in Belize	BZ$	US$
Taxi from the airport to Belize City	50.00–60.00	25.00–30.00
Local taxi ride	6.00–14.00	3.00–7.00
Water taxi ride to Ambergris Caye	20.00	10.00
One-way flight to San Pedro from Municipal Airport	63.00	31.50
One-way flight to San Pedro from International Airport	114.00	57.00
Double room, expensive	250.00–400.00	125.00–200.00
Double room, moderate	120.00–250.00	60.00–125.00
Double room, inexpensive	50.00–120.00	25.00–60.00
Dinner for one without wine, expensive	80.00	40.00
Dinner for one without wine, moderate	40.00	20.00
Dinner for one, inexpensive	16.00	8.00
Bottle of Belikin beer	3.00–5.00	1.50–2.50
Bottle of Coca-Cola	1.50	0.75
Cup of coffee	1.00	0.50
Gallon of premium gas	10.00	5.00
Admission to most national parks	10.00	5.00
Admission to Belize Zoo	16.00	8.00
Two-tank dive with equipment	150.00–240.00	75.00–120.00
Exit tax	70.00	35.00

Town. It's wise to bring some spending cash, and charge the rest of your bills. Try not to rely on your ATM card for an emergency cash bailout.

CREDIT CARDS

Credit cards are another safe way to carry money. They also provide a convenient record of all your expenses, and they generally offer relatively good exchange rates. You can withdraw cash advances from your credit cards at banks or ATMs, but high fees make credit card cash advances a pricey way to get cash. Keep in mind that you'll pay interest from the moment of your withdrawal, even if you pay your monthly bills on time. Also, note that many banks now assess a 1% to 3% "transaction fee" on **all** charges you incur abroad (whether you're using the local currency or your native currency).

Most major credit cards are accepted in Belize, although MasterCard and Visa are much more widely accepted than American Express, especially by smaller hotels, restaurants, and tour operators. While there are some exceptions, Diners Club and Discover are rarely accepted around Belize.

Some credit card companies recommend that you notify them of any impending trip abroad so that they don't become suspicious when the card is used numerous times in a foreign destination and block your charges. Even if you don't call your credit card company in advance, you can always call the card's toll-free emergency number (see "Lost & Found" in appendix A) if a charge is refused—a good reason to carry the phone number with you. But perhaps the most important lesson here is to carry more than one card with you on your trip; a card might not work for any number of reasons, so having a backup is the smart way to go.

Telephone Access Charges

I supply local toll-free access numbers to the major international phone carriers on the inside front cover of this guide, but make sure you know what the charges are for your particular international long-distance provider. Be careful about using these numbers if you're not on a specific plan. If you don't have an international calling plan, only charge calls to your credit card as a very last resort, as these calls are usually exorbitantly expensive. If you are making direct-dial international calls from your hotel, always find out what the charges are in advance. A good option is to buy a local international calling card, which will be billed at approximately BZ$1 (US50¢/25p) per minute for calls to the U.S., or BZ$1.40 (US70¢/35p) per minute for calls to much of the rest of the world.

TRAVELER'S CHECKS

Given widespread acceptance of credit cards and growing prevalence of ATM machines, traveler's checks are becoming pretty anachronistic. Still, traveler's checks are accepted at most hotels in Belize, but less frequently at restaurants. You can buy traveler's checks at most banks. They are offered in denominations of $20, $50, $100, $500, and sometimes $1,000. Generally, you'll pay a service charge ranging from 1% to 4%.

The most popular traveler's checks are offered by **American Express** (✆ **800/807-6233,** or ✆ 800/221-7282 for cardholders—this number accepts collect calls, offers service in several foreign languages, and exempts Amex gold and platinum cardholders from the 1% fee); **Visa** (✆ **800/732-1322;** AAA members can obtain Visa checks for a $9.95 fee for checks up to $1,500 at most AAA offices or by calling ✆ **866/339-3378**); and **MasterCard** (✆ **800/223-9920**).

Be sure to keep a record of the traveler's checks' serial numbers separate from your checks in the event that they are stolen or lost. You'll get a refund faster if you know the numbers.

Another option is the new prepaid traveler's check cards, reloadable cards that work much like debit cards but aren't linked to your checking account. The **American Express Travelers Cheque Card,** for example, requires a minimum deposit, sets a maximum balance, and has a one-time issuance fee of US$14.95. You can withdraw money from an ATM (for a fee of US$2.50 per transaction, not including bank fees), and the funds can be purchased in dollars, euros, or pounds. If you lose the card, your available funds will be refunded within 24 hours.

IF YOUR WALLET IS LOST OR STOLEN

For tips and telephone numbers to call if your wallet is stolen or lost, go to "Lost & Found" in the "Fast Facts" of appendix A.

6 HEALTH

STAYING HEALTHY

The only major modern hospitals in Belize are located in Belize City, although there are smaller hospitals or clinics in every major town or city. In general, you should bring any prescription drugs you will need with you, although there are reasonably

Avoiding "Economy-Class Syndrome"

Deep vein thrombosis, or as it's know in the world of flying, "economy-class syndrome," is a blood clot that develops in a deep vein. It's a potentially deadly condition that can be caused by sitting in cramped conditions—such as an airplane cabin—for too long. During a flight (especially a long-haul flight), get up, walk around, and stretch your legs every 60 to 90 minutes to keep your blood flowing. Other preventative measures include frequent flexing of the legs while sitting, drinking lots of water, and avoiding alcohol and sleeping pills. If you have a history of deep vein thrombosis, heart disease, or another condition that puts you at high risk, some experts recommend wearing compression stockings or taking anticoagulants when you fly; always ask your physician about the best course for you. Symptoms of deep vein thrombosis include leg pain or swelling, or even shortness of breath.

well-stocked pharmacies in most major towns and tourist destinations.

General Availability of Healthcare

There are two major hospitals in Belize City: **Belize Medical Associates,** 5791 St. Thomas Kings Park (✆ **223-0303;** www.belizemedical.com), a modern, 24-hour private hospital, with emergency care and numerous private-practice physicians; and the city's main public hospital, the **Karl Heusner Memorial Hospital** on Princess Margaret Drive (✆ **223-1548**), which is also open 24 hours and has a wide range of facilities and services.

Most of the other towns and major tourist destinations either have a small hospital or a local health clinic, in addition to private-practice doctors. Any foreign consulate can provide a list of area doctors. If you get sick, consider asking your hotel concierge or front desk staff to recommend a local doctor—even his or her own. We list **additional emergency numbers** in the "Fast Facts" section of appendix A, and I've listed hospitals and emergency numbers under "Fast Facts" in the regional destination chapters.

Before You Go

If you suffer from a chronic illness, consult your doctor before your departure. For conditions like epilepsy, diabetes, or heart problems, wear a **MedicAlert identification tag** (✆ **888/633-4298;** www.medicalert.org), which will immediately alert doctors to your condition and give them access to your records through MedicAlert's 24-hour hot line.

Pack **prescription medications** in your carry-on luggage, and carry prescription medications in their original containers, with pharmacy labels—otherwise they won't make it through airport security. Also bring along copies of your prescriptions in case you lose your pills or run out. Carry the generic name of prescription medicines, in case a local pharmacist is unfamiliar with the brand name. Don't forget an extra pair of contact lenses or prescription glasses.

If you worry about getting sick away from home, consider purchasing **medical travel insurance** and carry your ID card in your purse or wallet. In most cases, your existing health plan will provide the coverage you need.

Common Ailments

TROPICAL ILLNESSES None of the major tropical illnesses are epidemic in Belize, and your chance of contracting any serious tropical disease in the country is slim. However, several mosquito-borne illnesses are present, particularly malaria and dengue.

Although **malaria** is found in Belize, it's far from epidemic. It is most common along the coastal lowlands, as well as in some of the more remote southern inland communities. Malaria prophylaxes are available, but several have side effects, and others are of questionable effectiveness. Consult your doctor as to what is currently considered the best preventive treatment for malaria. Be sure to ask whether a recommended drug will cause you to be hypersensitive to the sun—it would be a shame to come down here for the beaches and then have to hide under an umbrella the whole time. Because malaria-carrying mosquitoes usually come out at night, you should do as much as possible to avoid being bitten after dark. If you are in a malarial area, wear long pants and long sleeves, use insect repellent, and either sleep under a mosquito net or burn mosquito coils (similar to incense but with a pesticide).

Of greater concern may be **dengue fever,** which has had periodic outbreaks in Latin America since the mid-1990s. Dengue fever is somewhat similar to malaria and is spread by an aggressive daytime mosquito. This mosquito seems to be most common in lowland urban areas, and Belize City and Dangriga have been the hardest hit cities in Belize. Dengue is also known as "bone-break fever," because it is usually accompanied by severe body aches. The first infection with dengue fever will make you very sick but should cause no serious damage. However, a second infection with a different strain of the dengue virus can lead to internal hemorrhaging and may be life-threatening. As with malaria, your best protection is to not get bitten. Use plenty of repellent, and wear light long-sleeved shirts and long pants, especially on bird-watching tours or nature hikes.

Many people are convinced that taking B-complex vitamins daily will help prevent mosquitoes from biting you. I don't think the American Medical Association has endorsed this idea yet, but I've run across it in enough places to think there may be something to it.

Belize has been relatively free from the **cholera** epidemic that has spread through much of Latin America in recent years. This is largely due to an extensive public-awareness campaign that has promoted good hygiene and increased sanitation. Your chances of contracting cholera while you're here are very slight.

DIETARY RED FLAGS Even though the water around Belize is generally safe, particularly in most of the popular tourist destinations, and even if you're careful to buy and drink only bottled water, you still may encounter some intestinal difficulties. Most of this is just due to tender northern stomachs coming into contact with slightly more aggressive Latin American intestinal flora. In extreme cases of diarrhea or intestinal discomfort, it's worth taking a stool sample to a lab for analysis. The results will usually pinpoint the amoebic or parasitic culprit, which can then be readily treated with available over-the-counter medicines.

If you have any strict dietary restrictions, be it for health, religious, or ethical reasons, be sure to check with your hotel in advance to ensure that you don't starve while on vacation.

BUGS, BITES & OTHER WILDLIFE CONCERNS Although Belize has Africanized bees (the notorious "killer bees" of fact and fable) and several species of venomous snakes, your chances of being bitten are minimal, especially if you refrain from sticking your hands into hives or under rocks in the forest. If you know that you're allergic to bee stings, consult your doctor before traveling.

Snake sightings, much less snakebites, are very rare. Moreover, the majority of snakes in Belize are nonpoisonous. If you do encounter a snake, stay calm, don't make any sudden movements, and do not try to handle it. If you're bitten, seek medical attention immediately—don't try to bleed the area of the wound or suck the poison out.

Scorpions, black widow spiders, tarantulas, bullet ants, and other biting insects can all be found in Belize. In general, they are not nearly the danger or nuisance most visitors fear. (If you're a serious arachnophobe, stick to the beach resorts.) You should be fine if you watch where you stick your hands; in addition, you might want to shake out your clothes and shoes before putting them on to avoid any painful surprises.

The most prevalent and annoying biting insect you are likely to encounter, especially on the cayes and along the coast, are sand flies or "no-see-ems." These tiny biting bugs leave a raised and itchy welt, but otherwise are of no significant danger. Sand flies and no-see-ems tend to be most active around sunrise and sunset, or on overcast days. Your best protection is to wear light long-sleeved shirts and long pants when these bugs are biting.

TROPICAL SUN Limit your exposure to the sun, especially during the first few days of your trip and, thereafter, from 11am to 2pm. Use a sunscreen with a high protection factor and apply it liberally. Remember that children need more protection than adults do.

Also, drink plenty of water and other fluids to avoid dehydration.

What to Do If You Get Sick Away from Home

Your hotel will be your best resource if you fall ill while traveling in Belize. Most hotels will be able to refer you to a local doctor, clinic, or hospital.

For travel abroad, you may have to pay all medical costs up front and be reimbursed later. Medicare and Medicaid do not provide coverage for medical costs outside the U.S. Before leaving home, find out what medical services your health insurance covers. To protect yourself, consider buying medical travel insurance (see "Insurance," in the "Fast Facts" section of appendix).

Very few health insurance plans pay for medical evacuation back to the U.S. (which can cost US$10,000 and up). A number of companies offer medical evacuation services anywhere in the world. If you're ever hospitalized more than 150 miles from home, **MedjetAssist** (✆ **800/527-7478;** www.medjetassistance.com) will pick you up and fly you to the hospital of your choice virtually anywhere in the world in a medically equipped and staffed aircraft 24 hours day, 7 days a week. Annual memberships are US$225 individual, US$350 family; you can also purchase short-term memberships.

We list **additional emergency numbers** in the "Fast Facts" section of appendix A as well as in the "Fast Facts" sections of the chapters on major towns and tourist destinations.

7 SAFETY

Belize City itself has a somewhat deserved reputation for being a dangerous city for travelers, especially after dark, and especially in neighborhoods off the beaten path. See "Safety" in "Fast Facts: Belize City" in chapter 6 for more details. That said, if you use basic common sense and take standard precautions, you should have no problems staying safe in Belize.

Despite a seemingly relaxed and open drug culture at some of the popular beach and caye destinations, visitors should be very careful. Drugs, including marijuana, are strictly illegal, even in small quantities, and the laws are applied firmly to foreigners.

8 SPECIALIZED TRAVEL RESOURCES

TRAVELERS WITH DISABILITIES

Most disabilities shouldn't stop anyone from traveling. There are more options and resources out there than ever before. However, in general, there are relatively few handicapped-accessible buildings or transport vehicles in Belize. A very few hotels offer wheelchair-accessible accommodations, and there are no public buses, commuter airlines, or water taxis thus equipped. In short, it's relatively difficult for a person with disabilities to get around in Belize.

Access-Able Travel Source (✆ **303/232-2979;** www.access-able.com) has a comprehensive database of travel agents around the world with experience in accessible travel; destination-specific access information; and links to such resources as service animals, equipment rentals, and access guides.

Many travel agencies offer customized tours and itineraries for travelers with disabilities. Among them are **Flying Wheels Travel** (✆ **507/451-5005;** www.flyingwheelstravel.com) and **Accessible Journeys** (✆ **800/846-4537** or 610/521-0339; www.disabilitytravel.com).

Flying with Disability (www.flying-with-disability.org) is a comprehensive information source on airplane travel. **Avis Rent a Car** (✆ **888/879-4273**) has an "Avis Access" program that offers services for customers with special travel needs. These include specially outfitted vehicles with swivel seats, spinner knobs, and hand controls; mobility scooter rentals; and accessible bus service. Be sure to reserve well in advance.

Also check out the quarterly magazine ***Emerging Horizons*** (www.emerginghorizons.com), available by subscription ($16.95 year in the U.S.; $21.95 outside U.S.).

The "Accessible Travel" link at **Mobility-Advisor.com** (www.mobility-advisor.com) offers a variety of travel resources to persons with disabilities.

British travelers should contact **Holiday Care** (✆ **0845/124-9971** in U.K. only; www.holidaycare.org.uk) to access a wide range of travel information and resources for the elderly and people with disabilities.

For more on organizations that offer resources to travelers with disabilities, go to **www.frommers.com**.

GAY & LESBIAN TRAVELERS

Belize is a small, socially conservative, provincial country where public displays of same-sex affection are rare and considered somewhat shocking. In fact, homosexual sodomy is still illegal and even occasionally prosecuted here. There is virtually no open gay or lesbian bar or club scene in Belize City or any of the major tourist destinations. Gay and lesbian travelers should choose their hotels with care, and be discreet in most public areas and situations.

Gay.com Travel (✆ **800/929-2268** or 415/644-8044; www.gay.com/travel or www.outandabout.com) is an excellent online successor to the popular ***Out & About*** print magazine. It provides regularly updated information about gay-owned, gay-oriented, and gay-friendly lodging, dining, sightseeing, nightlife, and shopping establishments in every important destination worldwide. British travelers should click on the "Travel" link at **www.uk.gay.com** for advice and gay-friendly trip ideas.

The Canadian website **GayTraveler** (www.gaytraveler.ca) offers ideas and advice for gay travel all over the world.

The following travel guides are available at many bookstores, or you can order them from any online bookseller: ***Spartacus International Gay Guide, 35th Edition*** (Bruno Gmünder Verlag; www.spartacusworld.com/gayguide) and the ***Damron*** guides (www.damron.com), with separate, annual books for gay men and lesbians.

For more gay and lesbian travel resources, visit **www.frommers.com**.

SENIOR TRAVEL

Members of **AARP** (formerly known as the American Association of Retired Persons), 601 E St. NW, Washington, DC 20049 (✆ **888/687-2277;** www.aarp.org), get discounts on hotels, airfares, and car rentals. AARP offers members a wide range of benefits, including *AARP: The Magazine* and a monthly newsletter. Anyone over 50 can join.

Many reliable agencies and organizations target the 50-plus market. **Elderhostel** (✆ **800/454-5768;** www.elderhostel.org) arranges worldwide study programs for those ages 55 and older. **ElderTreks** (✆ **800/741-7956** or 416/558-5000 outside North America; www.eldertreks.com) offers small-group tours to off-the-beaten-path or adventure-travel locations, restricted to travelers 50 and older. Both of the above-mentioned companies have periodic trips Belize.

Due to its temperate climate, stable government, low cost of living, and friendly retiree incentive program, Belize is popular with retirees from North America. The country's retirement and incentive program is run by the **Belize Tourism Board** (✆ **800/624-0286** in the U.S. and Canada, or 227-2430 in Belize). They have a website dedicated to the subject at www.belizeretirement.org.

Frommers.com offers more information and resources on travel for seniors.

FAMILY TRAVEL

If you have enough trouble getting your kids out of the house in the morning, dragging them thousands of miles away may seem like an insurmountable challenge. But family travel can be immensely rewarding, giving you new ways of seeing the world through smaller pairs of eyes.

Hotels in Belize often give discounts for children under 12 years old, and children under 3 or 4 years old are usually allowed to stay for free. Discounts for children and the cutoff ages vary according to the hotel, but in general, don't assume that your kids can stay in your room for free.

Many hotels, particularly on the cayes, offer rooms equipped with kitchenettes or full kitchen facilities. These can be a real money-saver for those traveling with children, and I've listed many of these accommodations in the destination chapters that follow.

Hotels offering regular, dependable babysitting service are few and far between. If you will need babysitting, make sure your hotel offers it before you make your reservation.

To locate accommodations, restaurants, and attractions that are particularly kid-friendly, refer to the "Kids" icon throughout this guide, and check out "The Best Destinations for Families" in chapter 1.

Recommended family travel websites include **Family Travel Forum** (www.familytravelforum.com), **Family Travel Network** (www.familytravelnetwork.com), **Traveling Internationally with Your Kids** (www.travelwithyourkids.com), and **Family Travel Files** (www.thefamilytravelfiles.com).

For a list of more family-friendly travel resources, turn to the experts at Frommers.com.

STUDENT TRAVEL

Check out the **International Student Travel Confederation (ISTC)** (www.istc.org) website for comprehensive travel services information and details on how to get an **International Student Identity Card (ISIC),** which qualifies students for substantial savings on rail passes, plane tickets, entrance fees, and more. It also provides students with basic health and life insurance and a 24-hour helpline. The card is valid for a maximum of 18 months. You can apply for the card online or in person at **STA Travel** (✆ **800/781-4040** in North America; ✆ 132-782 in Australia; ✆ 0871/230-0040 in the U.K.; www.statravel.com), the biggest student travel agency in the world; check out the website to locate STA Travel offices worldwide. If you're no longer a student but are still under 26, you can get an **International Youth Travel Card (IYTC)** from the same people, which entitles you to some discounts. **Travel CUTS** (✆ **800/592-2887;** www.travelcuts.com) offers similar services for both Canadians and U.S. residents. Irish students may prefer to turn to **USIT** (✆ **01/602-1904;** www.usit.ie), an Ireland-based specialist in student, youth, and independent travel.

9 SUSTAINABLE TOURISM

Sustainable tourism is conscientious travel. It means being careful with the environments you explore, and respecting the communities you visit. Two overlapping components of sustainable travel are **ecotourism** and **ethical tourism. The International Ecotourism Society (TIES)** defines ecotourism as responsible travel to natural areas that conserves the environment and improves the well-being of local people. TIES suggests that ecotourists follow these principles:

- Minimize environmental impact.
- Build environmental and cultural awareness and respect.
- Provide positive experiences for both visitors and hosts.
- Provide direct financial benefits for conservation and for local people.
- Raise sensitivity to host countries' political, environmental, and social climates.
- Support international human rights and labor agreements.

You can find some eco-friendly travel tips and statistics, as well as touring companies and associations—listed by destination under "Travel Choice"—at the **TIES** website, www.ecotourism.org. Also check out **Ecotravel.com,** which lets you search for sustainable touring companies in several categories (water-based, land-based, spiritually oriented, and so on).

Belize is a major ecotourism destination. While much of the focus of ecotourism is about reducing impacts on the natural environment, ethical tourism concentrates on ways to preserve and enhance local economies and communities, regardless of location. You can embrace ethical tourism by staying at a locally owned hotel or shopping at a store that employs local workers and sells locally produced goods.

Responsible Travel (www.responsibletravel.com) is a great source of sustainable travel ideas; the site is run by a spokesperson for ethical tourism in the travel industry. **Sustainable Travel International** (www.sustainabletravelinternational.org) promotes ethical tourism practices, and manages an extensive directory of sustainable properties and tour operators around the world.

In the U.K., **Tourism Concern** (www.tourismconcern.org.uk) works to reduce social and environmental problems connected to tourism. The **Association of Independent Tour Operators (AITO)**

It's Easy Being Green

Here are a few simple ways you can help conserve fuel and energy when you travel:

- Each time you take a flight or drive a car, greenhouse gases are released into the atmosphere. You can help neutralize this danger to the planet through "carbon offsetting"—paying someone to invest your money in programs that reduce your greenhouse gas emissions by the same amount you've added. Before buying carbon offset credits, just make sure that you're using a reputable company, one with a proven program that invests in renewable energy. Reliable carbon offset companies include **Carbonfund** (www.carbonfund.org), **TerraPass** (www.terrapass.org), and **Carbon Neutral** (www.carbonneutral.org).
- Whenever possible, choose nonstop flights; they generally require less fuel than indirect flights that stop and take off again. Try to fly during the day—some scientists estimate that nighttime flights are twice as harmful to the environment. And pack light—each 15 pounds of luggage on a 5,000-mile flight adds up to 50 pounds of carbon dioxide emitted.
- Where you stay during your travels can have a major environmental impact. To determine the green credentials of a property, ask about trash disposal and recycling, water conservation, and energy use; also question if sustainable materials were used in the construction of the property. The website **www.greenhotels.com** recommends green-rated member hotels around the world that fulfill the company's stringent environmental requirements. Also consult **www.environmentallyfriendlyhotels.com** for more green accommodations ratings.
- At hotels, request that your sheets and towels not be changed daily. (Many hotels already have programs like this in place.) Turn off the lights and air-conditioner (or heater) when you leave your room.
- Use public transport where possible—trains, buses and even taxis are more energy-efficient forms of transport than driving. Even better is to walk or cycle; you'll produce zero emissions and stay fit and healthy on your travels.
- If renting a car is necessary, ask the rental agent for a hybrid, or rent the most fuel-efficient car available. You'll use less gas and save money at the tank.
- Eat at locally owned and operated restaurants that use produce grown in the area. This contributes to the local economy and cuts down on greenhouse gas emissions by supporting restaurants where the food is not flown or trucked in across long distances. Visit **Sustain Lane** (www.sustainlane.org) to find sustainable eating and drinking choices around the U.S.; also check out **www.eatwellguide.org** for tips on eating sustainably in the U.S. and Canada.

Frommers.com: The Complete Travel Resource

Planning a trip or just returned? Head to **Frommers.com,** voted Best Travel Site by *PC Magazine*. We think you'll find our site indispensable before, during and after your travels—with expert advice and tips; independent reviews of hotels, restaurants, attractions, and preferred shopping and nightlife venues; vacation giveaways; and an online booking tool. We publish the complete contents of over 135 travel guides in our **Destinations** section, covering over 4,000 places worldwide. Each weekday, we publish original articles that report on **Deals and News** via our free **Frommers.com Newsletters.** What's more, **Arthur Frommer** himself blogs 5 days a week, with frank opinions about the state of travel in the modern world. We're betting you'll find our **Events** listings an invaluable resource; it's an up-to-the-minute roster of what's happening in cities everywhere—including concerts, festivals, lectures, and more. We've also added weekly **podcasts, interactive maps,** and hundreds of new images across the site. Finally, don't forget to visit our **Message Boards,** where you can join in conversations with thousands of fellow Frommer's travelers and post your trip report once you return.

(www.aito.co.uk) is a group of specialist operators leading the field in making holidays sustainable.

Several of the tour operators listed in the "Organized Adventure Trips" in chapter 5 (p. 70) have trips specifically geared towards ecotourists. You might also focus on specific lodges that have an ecotourism bent, such as **Chan Chich Lodge** (p. 213), **Lamanai Outpost Lodge** (p. 212), **Chaa Creek** (p. 245), **The Lodge at Big Falls** (p. 196), and **Ian Anderson's Caves Branch** (p. 231).

Volunteer travel has become increasingly popular among those who want to venture beyond the standard group-tour experience to learn languages, interact with locals, and make a positive difference while on vacation. Volunteer travel usually doesn't require special skills—just a willingness to work hard—and programs vary in length from a few days to a number of weeks. Some programs provide free housing and food, but many require volunteers to pay for travel expenses, which can add up quickly.

For general info on volunteer travel, visit **www.volunteerabroad.org** and **www.idealist.org**. Specific volunteer options in Belize are listed under "Ecologically Oriented Volunteer & Study Programs" in chapter 5.

Before you commit to a volunteer program, it's important to make sure any money you're giving is truly going back to the local community, and that the work you'll be doing will be a good fit for you. **Volunteer International** (www.volunteerinternational.org) has a helpful list of questions to ask to determine the intentions and the nature of a volunteer program.

Animal-Rights Issues

Although there are currently no swim-with-the-dolphin attractions or tours in Belize, I wouldn't be surprised if someone opened one soon. For information about the ethics of swimming with dolphins, visit the **Whale and Dolphin Conservation Society** (www.wdcs.org). For information on animal-friendly issues throughout the world, visit **Tread Lightly** (www.treadlightly.org).

10 PACKAGES FOR THE INDEPENDENT TRAVELER

Package tours are simply a way to buy the airfare, accommodations, and other elements of your trip (such as car rentals, airport transfers, and sometimes even activities) at the same time and often at discounted prices.

One good source of package deals is the airlines themselves. Most major airlines offer air/land packages, including **American Airlines Vacations** (✆ 800/321-2121; www.aavacations.com), **Delta Vacations** (✆ 800/654-6559; www.deltavacations.com), **Continental Airlines Vacations** (✆ 800/301-3800; www.covacations.com), and **United Vacations** (✆ 888/854-3899; www.unitedvacations.com). Several big **online travel agencies**—Expedia, Travelocity, Orbitz, Site59, and Lastminute.com—also do a brisk business in packages.

Travel packages are also listed in the travel section of your local Sunday newspaper. Or check ads in national travel magazines such as *Budget Travel Magazine, Travel + Leisure, National Geographic Traveler,* and *Condé Nast Traveler.*

For more information on package tours and for tips on booking your trip, see Frommers.com.

11 ESCORTED GENERAL-INTEREST TOURS

Escorted tours are structured group tours with a group leader. The price usually includes everything from airfare to hotels, meals, tours, admission costs, and local transportation.

Despite the fact that escorted tours require big deposits and predetermine hotels, restaurants, and itineraries, many people derive security and peace of mind from the structure they offer. Escorted tours—whether they're navigated by bus, motor coach, train, or boat—let travelers sit back and enjoy the trip without having to drive or worry about details. They take

Ask Before You Go

Before you invest in a package deal or an escorted tour:

- Always ask about the **cancellation policy.** Can you get your money back? Is there a deposit required?
- Ask about the **accommodations choices and prices** for each. Then look up the hotels' reviews in a Frommer's guide and check their rates online for your specific dates of travel. Also find out what types of rooms are offered.
- Request a complete **schedule.** (Escorted tours only)
- Ask about the **size** and demographics of the group. (Escorted tours only)
- Discuss what is included in the **price** (transportation, meals, tips, airport transfers, and the like). (Escorted tours only)
- Finally, look for **hidden expenses.** Ask whether airport departure fees and taxes, for example, are included in the total cost—they rarely are.

you to the maximum number of sights in the minimum amount of time with the least amount of hassle. They're particularly convenient for people with limited mobility, and they can be a great way to make new friends.

On the downside, you'll have little opportunity for serendipitous interactions with locals. The tours can be jam-packed with activities, leaving little room for individual sightseeing, whim, or adventure—plus they often focus on the heavily touristed sites, so you miss out on many a lesser-known gem.

You'll find a list of reputable escorted general interest and "soft adventure" tour operators in chapter 5. For more information on escorted general-interest tours, visit Frommers.com.

12 STAYING CONNECTED

TELEPHONES

Belize has a standardized seven-digit phone numbering system. There are no city or area codes to dial from within Belize.

To call Belize:

1. Dial the international access code: 011 from the U.S.; 00 from the U.K., Ireland, or New Zealand; or 0011 from Australia.
2. Dial the country code: 501.
3. Dial the number.

To make international calls: To make international calls from Belize, first dial 00 and then the country code (U.S. or Canada 1, U.K. 44, Ireland 353, Australia 61, New Zealand 64). Next dial the area code and number. For example, if you wanted to call the British Embassy in Washington, D.C., you would dial ✆ 00-1-202-588-7800.

For directory assistance: Dial ✆ **113** if you're looking for a number inside Belize, and for numbers to all other countries dial ✆ **115** and (for a charge) an operator will connect you to an international directory assistance operator.

For operator assistance: If you need operator assistance in making a call, dial ✆ **115,** whether you're trying to make a local or an international call.

Toll-free numbers: Numbers beginning with 0800 and 800 within Belize country are toll-free, but calling a 1-800 number in the States from Belize is not toll-free. In fact, it costs the same as an overseas call.

CELLPHONES

The three letters that define much of the world's wireless capabilities are **GSM** (Global System for Mobile Communications), a big, seamless network that makes for easy cross-border cellphone use throughout Europe and dozens of other countries worldwide. If your cellphone is on a GSM system, and you have a world-capable multiband phone such as many Sony Ericsson, Motorola, or Samsung models, you can make and receive calls across civilized areas around much of the globe. Just call your wireless operator and ask for "international roaming" to be activated on your account. Unfortunately, per-minute charges can be high—usually US$1.50 to US$3.50 (80p–£1.85) in Belize.

For many, **renting** a phone is a good idea. (Even worldphone owners will have to rent new phones if they're traveling to non-GSM regions, such as Japan or Korea.) While you can rent a phone from any number of overseas sites, including kiosks at airports and at car-rental agencies, we suggest renting the phone before you leave home. North Americans can rent one before leaving home from **InTouch USA** (✆ **800/872-7626;** www.intouchglobal.com) or **RoadPost** (✆ **888/290-1606** or 905/272-5665; www.roadpost.com). InTouch will also, for free, advise you on whether your existing phone will work overseas; simply call ✆ **703/222-7161**

Online Traveler's Toolbox

Veteran travelers usually carry some essential items to make their trips easier. Following is a selection of handy online tools to bookmark and use.

- **Airplane Food** (www.airlinemeals.net)
- **Airplane Seating** (www.seatguru.com or www.airlinequality.com)
- **Maps** (www.mapquest.com)
- **Time and Date** (www.timeanddate.com)
- **Travel Warnings** (http://travel.state.gov, www.fco.gov.uk/travel, www.voyage.gc.ca, or www.smarttraveller.gov.au)
- **Universal Currency Converter** (www.xe.com/ucc)
- **Visa ATM Locator** (www.visa.com); **MasterCard ATM Locator** (www.mastercard.com)
- **Weather** (www.intellicast.com or www.weather.com)

between 9am and 4pm EST, or go to **http://intouchglobal.com/travel.htm**.

Belize Telecommunications Limited (BTL) and their cellular division **DigiCell** (© **227-2017;** www.digicell.bz) have a virtual monopoly on cellular service in Belize. Luckily, DigiCell does have affordable packages for SIM card activation. If you have an unlocked 1900MHz GSM phone, they sell local prepaid SIM cards in various denominations, although the initial activation costs BZ$54 (US$27/£14), including BZ$10 (US$5/£2.65) of calls. You can buy subsequent minutes in the form of scratch-off cards in a variety of denominations. Calls anywhere within Belize are BZ65¢ (US30¢/15p), and you are not charged for incoming calls. The SIM chips and calling cards are sold at their desk at the airport or at one of their many outlets around Belize. Their website also has information on setting up your home phone for roaming in Belize. But be careful, the rates are quite high.

VOICE-OVER INTERNET PROTOCOL (VOIP)

If you have Web access while traveling, consider a broadband-based telephone service (in technical terms, **Voice-over Internet Protocol,** or **VoIP**) such as Skype (www.skype.com) or Vonage (www.vonage.com), which allow you to make free international calls from your laptop or in a cybercafe. Neither service requires the people you're calling to also have that service (though there are fees if they do not). Check the websites for details.

INTERNET/E-MAIL

Without Your Own Computer

In Belize, you'll readily find cybercafes in most major destinations. Many of the more upscale, isolated nature lodges also provide guest connectivity in one form or another. To search for cybercafes in Belize check **www.cybercaptive.com** and **www.cybercafe.com**.

For more help locating cybercafes and other establishments where you can go for internet access, please see "Internet Access" in the "Fast Facts" section of appendix A.

With Your Own Computer

More and more hotels, cafes, and retailers in Belize are signing on as Wi-Fi (wireless fidelity) "hotspots." Mac owners have their own networking technology: Apple AirPort. iPass providers (see below) also give you access to a few hundred wireless hotel lobby setups. To locate other hotspots that provide **free wireless networks** in cities around the world, go to **www.personaltelco.net/index.cgi/WirelessCommunities**.

For dial-up access, most business-class hotels throughout the world offer dataports for laptop modems, and a few thousand hotels in the U.S. and Europe now offer free high-speed Internet access. In addition, major Internet Service Providers (ISPs) have **local access numbers** around the world, allowing you to go online by placing a local call. The **iPass** network also has dial-up numbers around the world. You'll have to sign up with an iPass provider, who will then tell you how to set up your computer for your destination(s). For a list of iPass providers, go to www.ipass.com and click on "Individuals Buy Now." One solid provider is **i2roam** (✆ **866/811-6209** or 920/235-0475; www.i2roam.com).

Wherever you go, bring a **connection kit** of the right power and phone adapters, a spare phone cord, and a spare Ethernet network cable—or find out whether your hotel supplies them to guests. Electricity in Belize is 110-volt AC, and most outlets are either two- or three-prong U.S.-style outlets.

13 TIPS ON ACCOMMODATIONS

Belize has no truly large-scale resorts or hotels. While the Radisson and Best Western chains have one property each in Belize City, there are no other chain hotels in Belize. Upscale travelers looking for over-the-top luxury have very few options here. True budget hounds will also find slim pickings, especially in the beach and caye destinations. What the country does have is a host of intimate and interesting **small to midsize hotels** and **small resorts.** Most of these are quite comfortable and reasonably priced by most international standards, although nowhere near as inexpensive as neighboring Mexico.

Belize is a noted ecotourism and bird-watching destination, and there are small nature-oriented **ecolodges** across the inland portion of the country. These lodges offer opportunities to see wildlife (including sloths, monkeys, and hundreds of species of birds) and learn about tropical forests. They range from spartan facilities catering primarily to scientific researchers to luxury accommodations that are among the finest in the country.

At the more popular beach and resort destinations, specifically Ambergris Caye, Caye Caulker, and Placencia, you might want to look into renting a **condo** or efficiency unit, especially for longer stays.

Throughout this book, I've separated hotel listings into several broad categories: **Very Expensive,** $200 (£106) and up; **Expensive,** $126 to $199 (£67–£105); **Moderate,** $61 to $125 (£32–£66); and

Speak Up

If you are booking directly with your hotel (either by phone, fax, or e-mail), remember that most hotels are accustomed to paying as much as 20% in commission to agents and wholesalers. It never hurts to ask if they will pass some of that on to you. Don't be afraid to bargain.

Inexpensive, under $60 (£32) for a double. *Rates given in this book do not include the 9% hotel tax.* This tax will add to the cost of your room, so do factor it in.

One item you're likely to want to bring with you is a beach towel. Your hotel might not provide one at all, and even if it does, it might be awfully thin.

For tips on surfing for hotel deals online, visit Frommers.com.

14 TIPS ON DINING

Belizean cuisine is a mix of Caribbean, Mexican, African, Spanish, and Mayan culinary influences. Belize's strongest suit is its **seafood.** Fresh fish, lobster, shrimp, and conch are widely available, especially at the beach and island destinations. **Rice and beans** are another major staple, served as an accompaniment to almost any main dish. Often the rice and beans are cooked together, with a touch of coconut milk.

Belizeans tend to eat three meals a day, in similar fashion and hours to North Americans. Breakfasts tend to be served between 6:30am and 9am; lunch between noon and 2pm; and dinner between 6 and 10pm. Most meals and dining experiences are quite informal. In fact, there are only a few restaurants in the entire country that could be considered semiformal, and none require a jacket or tie, although you could certainly wear them.

I have separated restaurant listings throughout this book into three price categories based on the average cost per person of a meal, including tax and service charge. The categories are **Expensive,** more than $25 (£13); **Moderate,** $10 to $25 (£5.30–£13); and **Inexpensive,** less than $10 (£5.30). (Note, however, that individual items in the listings—entrees, for instance—do not include the sales or service taxes.) Keep in mind that there is an additional 10% GST tax, and a 10% service charge is often added on. Belizeans rarely tip, but that doesn't mean you shouldn't. If the service is particularly good and attentive, you should probably leave a little extra.

For a more detailed discussion of Belizean cuisine and dining, see "Conch Fritters, Stew Fish & Belikin: Belizean Food & Drink" in chapter 2.

4

Suggested Belize Itineraries

Don't be fooled by its size—there's a lot to see and do in Belize. And the fact that the country is so small makes it easy to see and do a lot in a short time. Still, many visitors simply come for a solid week of rest and relaxation, fishing and/or scuba diving at a beach or island resort, without ever getting to know the rest of the country. The following itineraries are meant to serve as rough outlines to help you structure your time and get a taste of some of the country's must-see destinations. Other options include specialized itineraries focused on a particular interest or activity. Bird-watchers could design an itinerary that visits a series of prime bird-watching sites. Cave enthusiasts and spelunkers could design a trip to take in several of Belize's caves.

1 THE REGIONS IN BRIEF

BELIZE CITY Belize City is a modest-size coastal port city located at the mouth of the Belize River. Although it's no longer the official governmental seat, Belize City remains the most important city—culturally, economically, and historically—in the country. It is also Belize's transportation hub, with the only international airport, an active municipal airport, a cruise-ship dock, and all the major bus-line and water-taxi terminals. Still, Belize City is of limited interest to most visitors, who quickly seek the more provincial and pastoral charms of the country's various tourist destinations and resorts. Belize City has a reputation as a rough and violent urban center, and visitors should exercise caution and stick to the most popular tourist areas of this small city.

THE NORTHERN CAYES & ATOLLS This is Belize's primary tourist zone and attraction. Hundreds of palm-swept offshore islands lie between the coast of the mainland and the protection of the 298km (185-mile) Belize Barrier Reef. The reef, easily visible from many of the cayes, offers some of the world's most exciting snorkeling, scuba diving, and fishing. The most developed cayes here, Ambergris Caye and Caye Caulker, have numerous hotels and small resorts, while some of the less developed cayes maintain the feel of fairy-tale desert isles. In addition to the many cayes, there are two open-ocean atolls here, Turneffe Island Atoll and Lighthouse Reef Atoll. Each of these unique rings of coral, limestone, and mangrove cayes surrounds a central, protected saltwater lagoon.

For those whose main sport is catching rays, not fish, it should be mentioned that the cayes, and Belize in general, lack wide, sandy beaches. Although the water is as warm and clear blue as it's touted to be, most of your sunbathing will be on docks, deck chairs, or imported patches of sand fronting a sea wall or sea-grass patch of shallow ocean. Also, note that there are still no large-scale all-inclusive resorts like those found throughout much of the rest of the Caribbean.

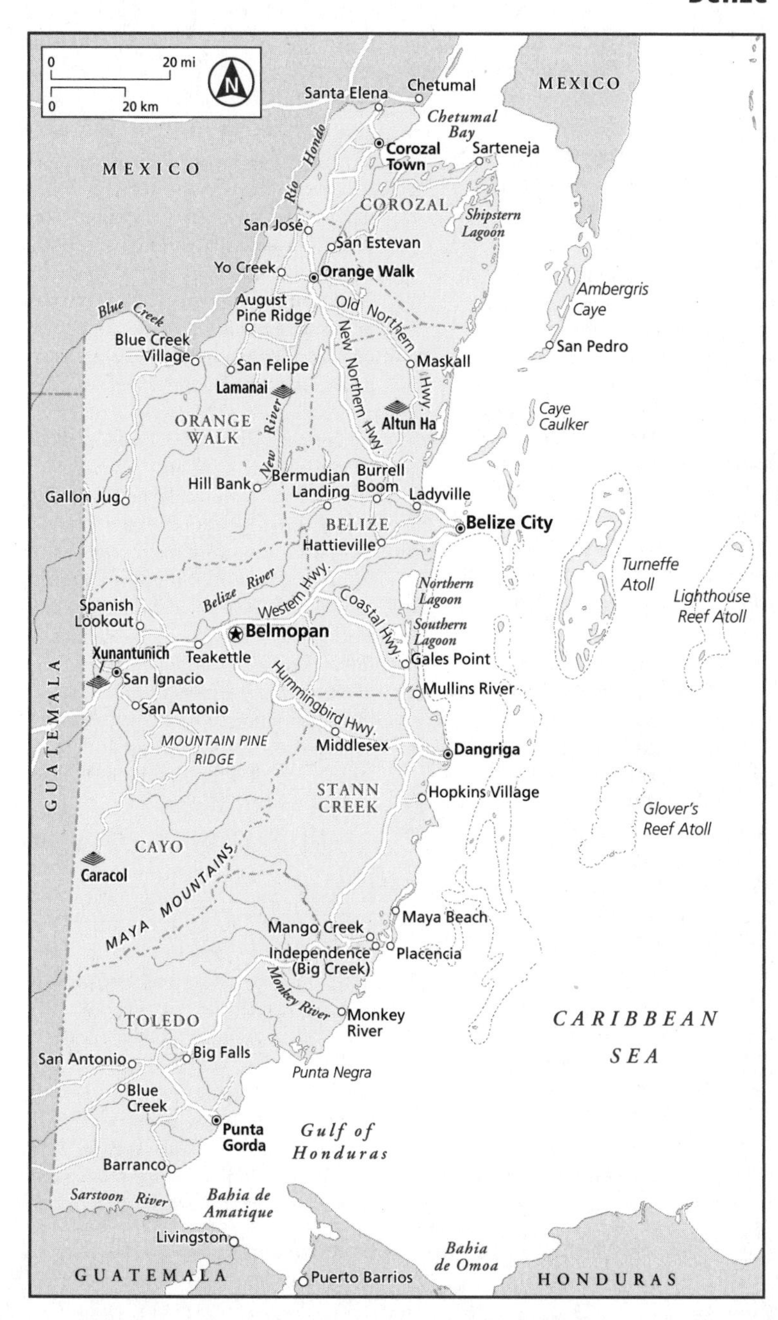
0
20 mi
0
20 km
N
MEXICO
Santa Elena
Chetumal
MEXICO
Chetumal Bay
Rio Hondo
Corozal Town
Sarteneja
COROZAL
Shipstern Lagoon
San José
San Estevan
Yo Creek
Orange Walk
Ambergris Caye
August Pine Ridge
Old Northern Hwy.
New Northern Hwy.
Blue Creek
Blue Creek Village
San Felipe
Maskall
San Pedro
Lamanai
Altun Ha
Caye Caulker
ORANGE WALK
New River
Hill Bank
Bermudian Landing
Burrell Boom
Ladyville
Gallon Jug
BELIZE
Belize City
Hattieville
Turneffe Atoll
Belize River
Western Hwy.
Coastal Hwy.
Northern Lagoon
Lighthouse Reef Atoll
Spanish Lookout
Belmopan
Southern Lagoon
Xunantunich
Teakettle
Gales Point
San Ignacio
Hummingbird Hwy.
Mullins River
San Antonio
MOUNTAIN PINE RIDGE
Middlesex
Dangriga
GUATEMALA
STANN CREEK
Hopkins Village
Glover's Reef Atoll
CAYO
Caracol
MAYA MOUNTAINS
Maya Beach
Mango Creek
Independence (Big Creek)
Placencia
Monkey River
Monkey River
TOLEDO
CARIBBEAN SEA
San Antonio
Big Falls
Punta Negra
Blue Creek
Punta Gorda
Gulf of Honduras
Barranco
Sarstoon River
Bahia de Amatique
Livingston
Bahia de Omoa
GUATEMALA
Puerto Barrios
HONDURAS

SOUTHERN BELIZE Southern Belize encompasses two major districts, Stann Creek and Toledo. The former includes the Cockscomb Basin Wildlife Sanctuary and the coastal towns of Dangriga, Hopkins Village, and Placencia. Dangriga is the country's major center of Garífuna culture, and Placencia boasts what is arguably the country's best beach. Farther south, the Toledo District is Belize's final frontier. The inland hills and jungles are home to numerous Kekchi and Mopan Mayan villages. Hidden in these hills are some lesser known and less visited Mayan ruins, including Lubaantun and Nim Li Punit. The Toledo District is also emerging as an ecotourism destination, with the country's richest, wettest, and most undisturbed rainforests. Off the shores of southern Belize lie more cayes and yet another mid-ocean atoll, Glover's Reef Atoll. The cayes down here get far less traffic and attention than those to the north, and they are perfect for anyone looking for all of the same attractions, but fewer crowds.

NORTHERN BELIZE Anchored on the south by Belize City, this is the country's business and agricultural heartland. Towards the north lie Orange Walk Town and Corozal Town. Both of these small cities have a strong Spanish feel and influence, having been settled largely by refugees from Mexico's Caste War. The Maya also lived here, and their memories live on at the ruins of Altun Ha, Lamanai, Cerros, and Santa Rita, all in this zone. This is a land that was once submerged and is still primarily swamp and mangrove. Where the land is cleared and settled, sugar cane is the main cash crop, although bananas, citrus fruits, and pineapples are also grown. Towards the western section of this region lies the Río Bravo Conservation Area, a massive tract of virgin forest, sustainable-yield managed forest, and recovering reforestation areas. Northern Belize has some of the country's premier isolated nature lodges, as well as some of the prime destinations for bird-watchers, including the Shipstern Nature Reserve and Crooked Tree Wildlife Sanctuary.

THE CAYO DISTRICT & WESTERN BELIZE This mountainous district near the Guatemalan border has become Belize's second most popular destination. Here you'll find some of Belize's most beautiful countryside and most fascinating natural and man-made sights. The limestone mountains of this region are dotted with numerous caves, sinkholes, jagged peaks, underground rivers, and waterfalls. There are clear-flowing aboveground rivers that are excellent for swimming and canoeing, as well as mile after mile of unexplored forest full of wild animals and hundreds of bird species. Adventurers, nature lovers, and bird-watchers will definitely want to spend some time in the Cayo District. This is also where you'll find Belize's largest and most impressive Mayan ruins. In the remote Mountain Pine Ridge section of the Cayo District lies Caracol, one of the largest known Classic Maya cities ever uncovered. Closer to the main town of San Ignacio, you'll find Xunantunich, Pilar, and the smaller Cahal Pech.

TIKAL & GUATEMALA'S PETEN Just over Belize's western border lies Guatemala's Petén province, a massive and remote area of primary forest and perhaps Mesoamerica's most spectacular Maya ruin, Tikal. The level of preservation, restoration, and rich rainforest setting make Tikal one of the true wonders of the world, and an enchanting stop for anyone even remotely interested in the ancient Maya or archaeology. The surrounding jungles and small Guatemalan villages are easily accessible from Belize and allow travelers the chance to add yet another unique adventure to any itinerary.

2 BELIZE IN 1 WEEK

The timing is tight, but this itinerary packs a trio of Belize's best destinations into 1 week. It allows for a chance to visit a major Maya ruin, snorkel on the barrier reef, ride an inner tube on an underground river, and relax a bit on the beach.

Day ❶: Arrive & Head to Placencia

Arrive into **Belize City** and grab a quick connecting flight to **Placencia ★★**. Spend the afternoon strolling along the beach and the town's famous sidewalk. Head back to the sidewalk after dark, and enjoy some time mingling with locals and tourists alike at the **Barefoot Beach Bar ★** (p. 189).

Day ❷: Way Down upon the Monkey River

Take a tour on the **Monkey River ★** (p. 181), where you're sure to see a rich array of wildlife. In the afternoon you can treat yourself to a spa treatment, get some snorkeling in, or try a seaweed shake. For dinner, head to the **French Connection ★★★** (p. 187).

Day ❸: Cayo Calling

Fly back to Belize City and pick up a rental car for the drive to the **Cayo District ★★**. Stop at the **Belize Zoo ★★** (p. 105) or for a cave tubing adventure near Jaguar Paw en route. Settle into one of the hotels in San Ignacio or one of the lodges located out on the way to Benque Viejo. If there's time, take an afternoon tour to the ruins at **Xunantunich ★★** (p. 236).

Day ❹: Climbing Caana

Wake up very early and head to the Mayan ruins at **Caracol ★★** (p. 253), stopping at the **Río on Pools ★★** and Río Frío Cave (p. 252) on your way back to San Ignacio.

Days ❺ & ❻: Fly to the Cayes

Head for the cayes. Choose between **Caye Caulker ★★★**, with its intimate funky charm, or **Ambergris Caye ★★**, with its wide choice of hotels, resorts, and restaurants. A whole range of activities and adventures awaits you here. Be sure to try the snorkel trip to **Hol Chan Marine Reserve ★★** and **Shark-Ray Alley ★★** (p. 121). You can also just chill in the sun and sand.

Day ❼: Going Home

Return to **Belize City** in time for your international connection. If you have time, stop off at the **Belize Tourism Village** (p. 103) to do some last minute shopping before you go.

3 BELIZE IN 2 WEEKS

If you have 2 weeks, you'll be able to hit all the highlights mentioned above, as well as some others, including a side trip to the ruins of Tikal, in neighboring Guatemala. And, you can do all this at a slightly more relaxed pace to boot.

Day ❶: Arrive & Head to Placencia

Arrive into **Belize City** and grab a quick connecting flight to **Placencia ★★**. Spend the afternoon strolling along the beach and the town's famous sidewalk. Head back to the sidewalk after dark, and enjoy some time mingling with locals and tourists alike at the **Barefoot Beach Bar ★** (p. 189).

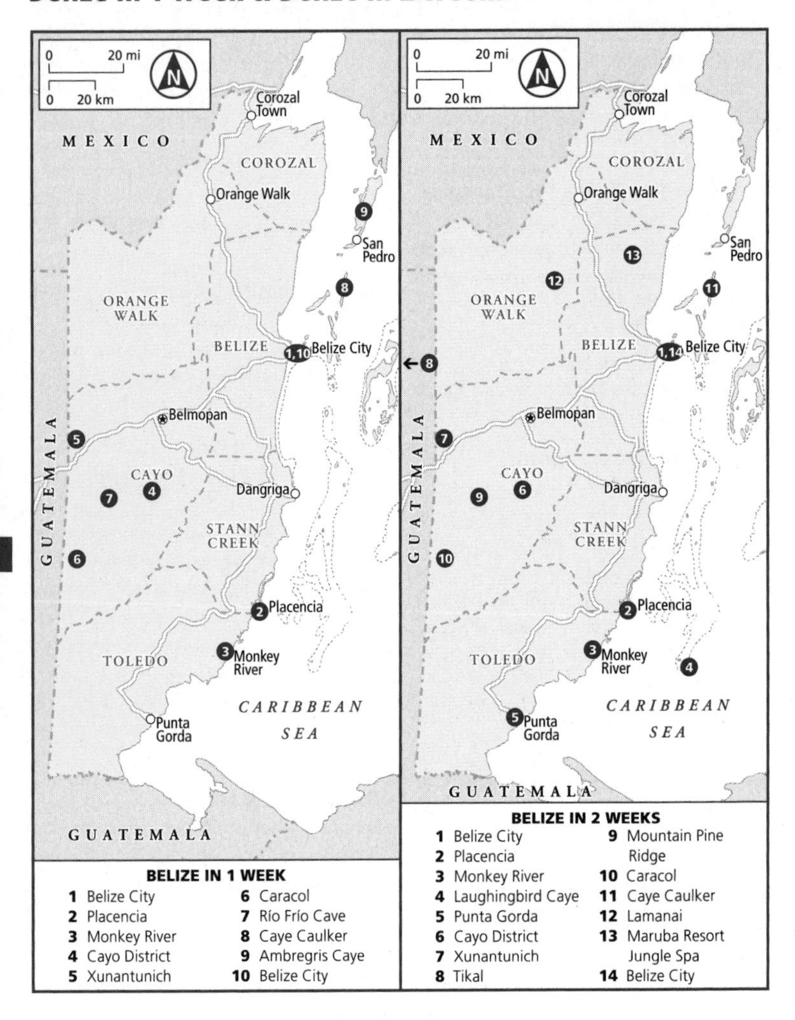

Day 2: Way Down upon the Monkey River

Take a tour on the **Monkey River** ★ (p. 181), where you're sure to see a rich array of wildlife. In the afternoon you can treat yourself to a spa treatment, and try a seaweed shake. For dinner, head to the **French Connection** ★★★ (p. 187).

Day 3: Get Wet & Wild

Take a snorkel trip to **Laughing Bird Caye** ★★ (p. 179) and enjoy a picnic lunch on this tiny little gem of an island. In the afternoon, visit the small Garífuna village of Seine Bight.

Day 4: Punta Gorda

Fly down to the remote town of **Punta Gorda** in the far southern reaches of

Belize. Get there in time to head out into the nearby mountains, where you'll find several small Mayan villages. Visit the village of San Antonio, and then head on to **Blue Creek** ★★ (p. 194), where you'll find a beautiful swimming hole in a forested river that flows out from a jungle cave. The **Reef Bar** ★ and **Earth Runnins' Café** ★ are two great places for dinner and drinks. They're pretty close to each other, so you could choose whichever one strikes your fancy, or enjoy some time at both.

Days ❺ & ❻: Cayo Calling

Fly back to Belize City and pick up a rental car for the drive to the **Cayo District** ★★. Stop at the **Belize Zoo** ★★ (p. 105) or for a cave tubing adventure near Jaguar Paw en route. Settle into one of the hotels in San Ignacio or one of the lodges located out on the way to Benque Viejo. If you have time, take an afternoon tour to the ruins at **Xunantunich** ★★ (p. 236). If you didn't visit Xunantunich the previous afternoon, you'll want to stop in on day 6. You'll also want to check out the **Belize Botanic Gardens** ★★ (p. 239) or the nearby **Chaa Creek Natural History Museum and Rainforest Medicine Trail** ★ (p. 240). If you're hardy, you can visit both.

Days ❼ & ❽: Tikal Time

Take a 2-day/1-night trip to **Tikal** ★★★ (p. 258). Stay at one of the lodges right at the ruins. Get an early start in order to beat the crowds and because the ruins here are so extensive. Make sure you set aside plenty of time to explore the amazing ruins here, but also schedule some time to enjoy the quaint little island city of Flores. Return to Belize in the afternoon, and head to the **Mountain Pine Ridge** ★★ area, staying either at **Blancaneaux Lodge** ★★★ (p. 254) or **Five Sisters Lodge** ★ (p. 254).

Day ❾: Climb Caana

Visit the ruins at **Caracol** ★★ (p. 253) and climb to the top of the tallest man-made structure in Belize. Stop at the Rio Frio Cave and **Río on Pools** ★★ (p. 252) on your way back from the ruins.

Days ❿, ⓫ & ⓬: Go Slow on Caye Caulker

It's time to head to funky **Caye Caulker** ★★★. Be sure to try the snorkel trip to **Hol Chan Marine Reserve** ★★ and **Shark-Ray Alley** ★★ (p. 121) while you're in the area. If you haven't gotten your fill of Mayan ruins, you can do a day trip to **Lamanai** ★★ (p. 210). Any extra time you have you can use to chill in the sun and sand.

Days ⓭ & ⓮: Massage Your Muscles with Mud

Finish your trip off with some decadent pampering at the **Maruba Resort Jungle Spa** ★★ (p. 202), before heading home from **Belize City.**

4 BELIZE FOR FAMILIES

Belize doesn't have any large resorts with well-staffed children's programs. Nor will you find many activities or attractions specifically geared for the very young. Still, this English-speaking country is a great destination for families, especially if your children have an adventurous streak.

Day ❶: Head for Hopkins

Arrive into **Belize City** and head straight to **Hopkins Village** ★★★. Settle into a comfortable suite at **Jaguar Reef Lodge** ★★ (p. 172).

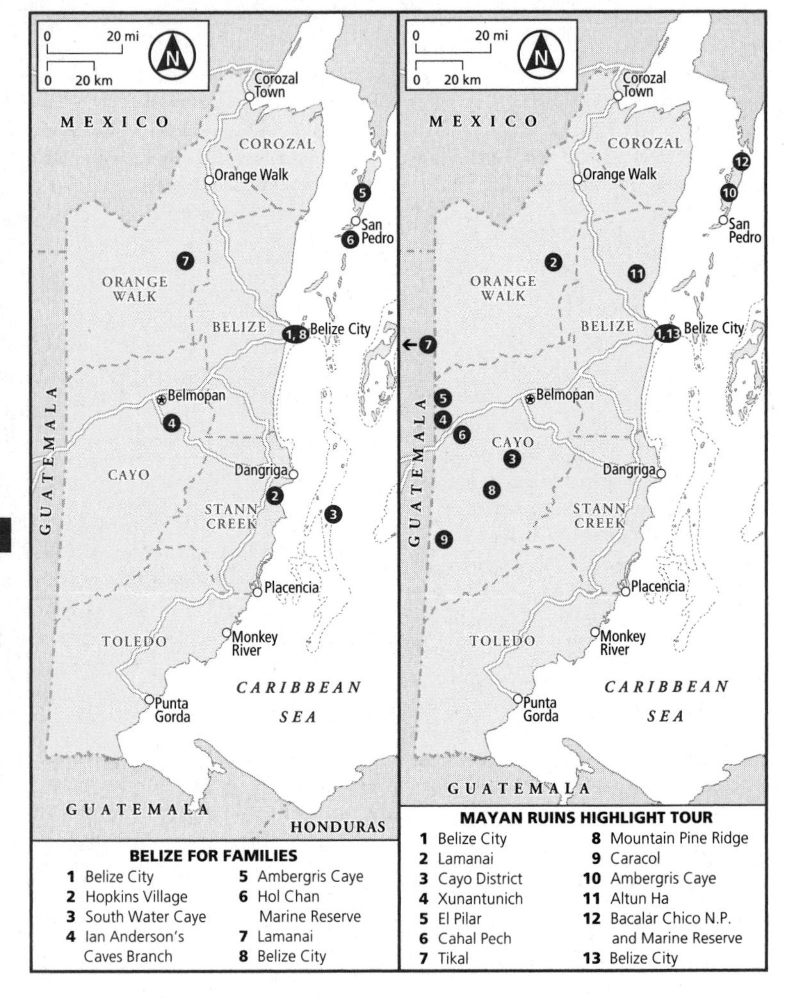

Day 2: Go Garífuna

Sign up for a class in traditional Garífuna drumming and dancing at the **Lebeha Drumming Center** ★ (p. 171). When you and yours aren't banging a drum, take advantage of the resort's ample facilities and activity options.

Days 3 & 4: A Nearly Deserted Island

Head out to **South Water Caye** ★★. The island here is tiny, and the kids will no doubt fantasize about being stranded on a deserted island. The waters here are extremely calm and protected by the barrier reef, which lies just offshore. This is a great place to introduce the family to snorkeling, and to head out in individual or tandem kayaks.

Days 5 & 6: Into the Dark

On your way up north, stop off at **Ian Anderson's Caves Branch** ★ (p. 231). Accommodations range from quite rustic to almost luxurious. The folks here also offer adventure options that range from cushy to hard core. Most revolve around the surrounding forest and the area's namesake river, which runs through a series of underground caves.

Days 7, 8 & 9: Sun & Fun in San Pedro

Head for **Ambergris Caye** ★★, with its wide choice of hotels, resorts, and restaurants. A whole range of activities and adventures available for the family are here. Be sure to schedule in a snorkel trip to **Hol Chan Marine Reserve** ★★ (p. 121) and **Shark-Ray Alley** ★★ (p. 121). More adventurous members of the family can try parasailing or windsurfing. Reserve 1 day for a visit to the Mayan ruins at **Lamanai** ★★ (p. 210). You'll also want to visit the **Butterfly Jungle** (p. 123). Fly right from San Pedro to the international airport in **Belize City** in time for your return flight home.

5 MAYAN RUINS HIGHLIGHTS

Belize boasts dozens of known Mayan ruins of varying sizes and in varying states of excavation and exploration. The following itinerary hits most of the major ruins, and even allows you some time to visit the cayes. You could easily add on a side trip to the northern or southern zones, where there are several lesser-known ruins.

Day 1: The Sleeping Crocodile

Arrive into **Belize City** and head straight to **Lamanai,** staying right next door to the ancient Mayan city at the **Lamanai Outpost Lodge** ★ (p. 212). You'll probably arrive in the afternoon. Save the ruins for the next day, but take a boat tour on the New River Lagoon around sunset, and you'll see a host of bird species, and perhaps a real crocodile or two.

Days 2 & 3: Life in Ruins

Spend the morning exploring the **Lamanai ruins** ★★ (p. 210). Get there early before the tour groups arrive, and enjoy the peace and quiet of the site. Have lunch at the hotel and then head over to **Chan Chich Lodge** ★★ (p. 213). Settle into your room here, which is set on the central plaza of a Mayan ruin. Spend the following day exploring the ruins at and around Chan Chich. If you have time, head over to nearby **La Milpa** (p. 213), a large site with an active and ongoing excavation.

Days 4 & 5: Cayo Calling

Head to the **Cayo District** ★★ and stay at one of the lodges in San Ignacio or on the way to Benque Viejo. It might be tight, but in your time here you can visit the ruins of **Xunantunich** ★★ (p. 236), **El Pilar** ★★ (p. 249), and **Cahal Pech** ★ (p. 236), as well as the Mayan ceremonial burial cave at **Chechem Ha** ★ (p. 238).

Day 6: Tikal Time

Take a 2-day/1-night trip to **Tikal** ★★★ (p. 258). Stay at one of the lodges right at the ruins. Get an early start in order to beat the crowds and because the ruins here are so extensive. Make sure you set aside plenty of time to explore the amazing ruins here, but also schedule some time to enjoy the quaint little island city of Flores.

Return to Belize in the afternoon, and head to the **Mountain Pine Ridge ★★** area (p. 250), staying either at **Blancaneaux Lodge ★★★** (p. 254) or **Five Sisters Lodge ★** (p. 254).

Day 7: Caracol

Visit the ruins at **Caracol ★★** (p. 253). Stop at the Río Frío Cave and **Río on Pools ★★** (p. 252) on your way back from the ruins.

Days 8 & 9: Enjoying the Cayes

Unwind for a couple of days on **Ambergris Caye ★★**. If you didn't get to visit **Altun Ha ★** (p. 201) during your inland stint, you can easily visit as a day tour by boat and minivan from here. You can also arrange boat trips to the tiny ruins of Chac Balam in the **Bacalar Chico National Park & Marine Reserve ★** (p. 220) or to **Cerros** (p. 218) outside Corozal.

Day 10: Heading Home

Return to **Belize City** in time for your international connection.

6 BELIZE CITY IN 1 DAY

While most tourists seek to avoid Belize City entirely—and I pretty much advise as much in this book—if you plan properly, Belize City can actually serve well as a good base if you only have a few days in the country.

Day 1: Getting to Know the City

Begin your day early at the **Fort George Lighthouse** and **Baron Bliss Memorial,** and follow the walking tour outlined on p. 103. When you reach the **Commercial Center,** be sure to stop in for a coffee and some fry jacks at **Big Daddy's Diner** (2nd floor, Commercial Center, Booth 54; ✆ **227-0932**); see p. 100. After you finish the walking tour, take a taxi out to **Old Belize ★** (Western Hwy., Mile 5; ✆ **222-4286**), an attraction that offers a peek into various facets of the natural, cultural, and political history of the country. Have lunch at the ocean-side open-air restaurant here. See p. 103.

WET LIZARD ★
Have a sunset drink and some conch fritters at the **Wet Lizard,** 1 Fort St. (✆ **223-5973**). This might just hold you over for the night. See p. 99.

After night falls, head to the **Radisson Fort George Hotel ★** (p. 95) and see if there's any live music at their poolside Stonegrill Restaurant & Bar. Even if music isn't on the agenda, this remains one of the main gathering spots for locals and tourists alike. If the food at the Wet Lizard doesn't hold you over, grab something to eat at the restaurant here, or head for a more elegant meal at the **Harbour View ★★** (p. 99).

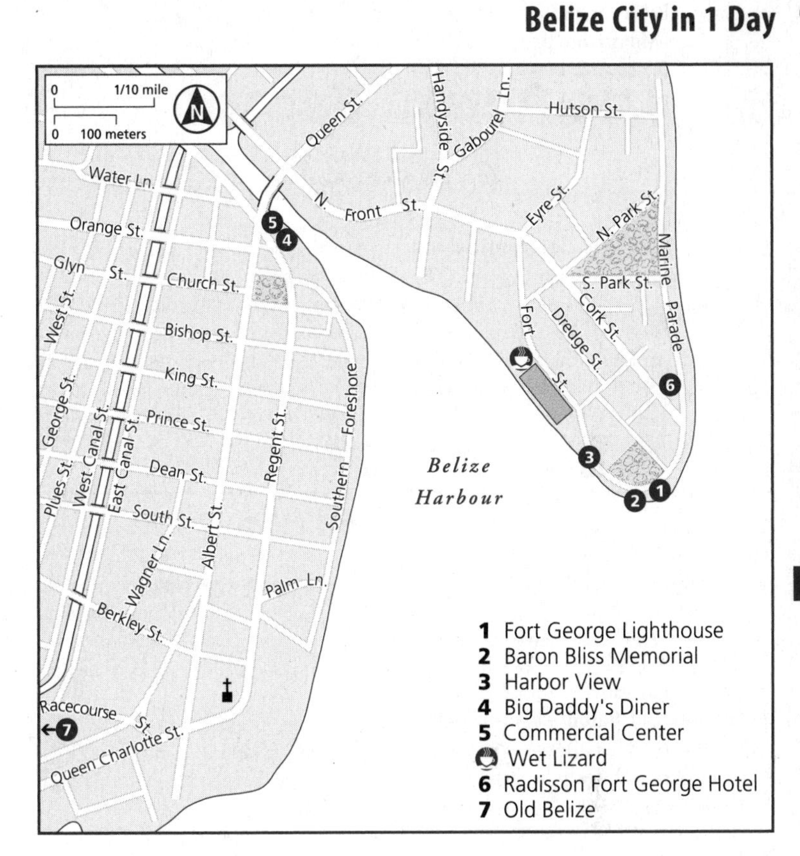
0 1/10 mile
0 100 meters
N
Water Ln.
Orange St.
Glyn St.
Church St.
West St.
Bishop St.
King St.
George St.
West Canal St.
East Canal St.
Prince St.
Dean St.
Plues St.
South St.
Wagner Ln.
Albert St.
Regent St.
Southern Foreshore
Palm Ln.
Berkley St.
Racecourse St.
Queen Charlotte St.
Queen St.
Handyside St.
Gabourel Ln.
Hutson St.
N. Front St.
Eyre St.
N. Park St.
Marine Parade
S. Park St.
Cork St.
Fort St.
Dredge St.
Belize Harbour
1 Fort George Lighthouse
2 Baron Bliss Memorial
3 Harbor View
4 Big Daddy's Diner
5 Commercial Center
Wet Lizard
6 Radisson Fort George Hotel
7 Old Belize

5

The Active Vacation Planner

Belize is fantastic destination for the active and adventurous traveler. The range of available sport and tour options is wide; the quality of the adventures and local tour operators is high; and the fact that the country is so compact allows you to mix and match. Whether your interests are scuba diving, snorkeling, fishing, sailing, spelunking, mountain biking, horseback riding, or bird-watching, Belize has some fabulous terrain and opportunities that are perfect for you. I hope that the following chapter, combined with the regional and destination chapters that follow it, will help you design and enjoy your dream vacation.

1 ORGANIZED ADVENTURE TRIPS

Because many travelers have limited time and resources, organized ecotourism or adventure-travel packages are a popular and efficient way of combining several activities. Bird-watching, cave-exploring, and hiking can be teamed with, say, visits to classical Mayan ruins and a few days on an outlying caye for snorkeling and diving, sea kayaking, and more bird-watching.

Traveling with a group on an organized trip has several advantages over traveling independently. Your accommodations and transportation are arranged, and most (if not all) of your meals are included in the cost of a package. If your tour operator has a reasonable amount of experience and a decent track record, you should proceed to each of your destinations quickly without the snags and long delays that those traveling on their own can occasionally face. You'll also have the opportunity to meet like-minded souls who are interested in nature and active sports. Of course, you'll pay more for the convenience of having all your arrangements handled in advance.

In the best cases, group size is kept small (10–20 people), and the tours are conducted by knowledgeable guides who are either naturalists or biologists. Be sure to ask about difficulty levels when you're choosing a tour. While most companies offer "soft adventure" packages that those in moderately good (but not phenomenal) shape can handle, others focus on more hard-core activities geared toward only seasoned athletes or adventure travelers.

NORTH AMERICA–BASED TOUR OPERATORS

These agencies and operators specialize in well-organized and coordinated tours that cover your entire stay. Many travelers prefer to have everything arranged and confirmed before arriving in Belize, and this is a good idea for first-timers and during the high season. ***Note:*** Most of these operators are not cheap, with 10-day tours generally costing in the neighborhood of US$2,000 to US$3,500 (£1,060–£1,855) per person, not including airfare to Belize.

Bike Hike Adventures (✆ **888/805-0061** or 604/731-2442; www.bikehike.com) is a Canada-based company specializing in multiday, multiadventure tours for small groups. They have several different offerings in Belize. Their 9-day tour will have you horseback riding, mountain biking, cave tubing, and either snorkeling or diving. The cost is around US$2,500 (£1,325) per person, not including airfare to Belize.

International Expeditions ★ (✆ **800/633-4734** or 205/428-1700; www.ietravel.com) specializes in independent programs and natural history group tours. They run a regular 9-day tour to Belize and Tikal that takes in several of the major Mayan sites and tropical ecosystems, while staying in top-end lodges. The cost is US$3,900 (£2,067) per person, not including airfare to Belize.

Island Expeditions ★★ (✆ **800/667-1630** or 604/452-3212; www.islandexpeditions.com) runs various adventurous multiday land and sea tours around Belize. Kayaking the atolls is one of their strong suits, but they also combine this with inland adventures. These trips usually involve some island camping. Prices run around US$1,800 (£954) for a 7-day trip, not including airfare to Belize.

Journeys International (✆ **800/255-8735** or 734/665-4407; www.journeys-intl.com) offers small-group natural history and adventure packages around Belize, including trips especially geared towards families. Their 9-day family trip costs US$3,250 (£1,723) per adult and US$2,295 to US$2,895 (£1,216–£1,534) per child. Airfare to Belize is extra.

Slickrock Adventures ★★ (✆ **800/390-5715** or 435/259-4225; www.slickrock.com) offers a variety of multiday land and sea tours around Belize. They specialize in a sea-kayak and dive extravaganza based out of their camp and lodge on the private Long Caye in Glover's Reef atoll. A full week with these folks, not including international airfare, costs around US$1,975 (£1,047).

U.K.-BASED TOUR OPERATORS

Imaginative Traveller (✆ **0845/077-8802;** www.imaginative-traveller.com) is a good-value operator specializing in budget student, group, and family travel. Their offerings in Belize focus on the entire Mundo Maya, and usually also take in parts of southern Mexico and Guatemala. These trips range in duration from 9 to 31 days.

Journey Latin America ★ (✆ **020/8747-8315;** www.journeylatinamerica.co.uk) is a large British operator specializing in Latin American travel. They offer a range of escorted tours around Latin America, including a few that touch down in Belize. They also design custom itineraries, and often have excellent deals on airfare.

BELIZE-BASED TOUR OPERATORS

Because many U.S.-based companies subcontract portions of their tours to established Belizean companies, some travelers like to set up their tours directly with these companies, thereby cutting out the middleman. While that means these packages are often less expensive than those offered by U.S. companies, it doesn't mean they are cheap. You're still paying for the convenience of having all your arrangements handled for you.

There are scores of tour agencies in Belize City and at all of the major tourist destinations around the country that offer a plethora of adventure options. These agencies, and the tour desks at most hotels, can arrange everything from cave tubing to Mayan ruins tours to scuba diving and snorkeling. While it's generally quite easy to arrange most of these popular tours and adventures at the spur of the moment during your vacation, some are offered only when there are enough interested people or on set dates. If you have a very specialized tour or activity in mind, it pays to contact the hotel you will be staying at or a few of the companies listed here before you leave home to find out what they might be doing when you arrive.

Belize Trips ★★ (✆ **610-1923** or 223-0376; www.belize-trips.com) is the place to come to set up a custom tour. Owner and longtime resident Katie Valk is extremely knowledgeable, friendly, and responsive.

Destination Belize ★ (✆ **523-4018;** www.destinationsbelize.com) is an excellent Belize-based company specializing in creating custom itineraries and tours.

Discovery Expeditions (✆ **223-0748;** www.discoverybelize.com) is a long-standing and well-respected Belizean company with a broad offering of soft adventure and natural history tours.

S & L Travel & Tours ★ (✆ **227-7593;** www.sltravelbelize.com) is one of the original tour operators in Belize, with nearly 30 years of experience in both adventure and regular tours. It's still one of the best, with excellent on-staff guides and a good working relationship with all the hotels.

2 ACTIVITIES A TO Z

Each listing in this section describes the best places to practice a particular sport or activity and lists tour operators and outfitters. If you want to focus on only one active sport during your time in Belize, these companies are your best bets for quality equipment and knowledgeable service.

Adventure activities by their very nature carry certain risks. In the past couple of years there have been several deaths and dozens of relatively minor injuries in activities ranging from mountain biking to white-water rafting to canopy tours. I try to list only the most reputable and safest of companies. However, if you ever have any doubt as to the safety of the guide, equipment, or activity, it's better to be safe than sorry. Moreover, know your limits and abilities and don't try to exceed them.

BIKING

Belize is not a major biking destination. In fact, there are only four or so major paved roads in the entire country—the Northern, Western, Southern, and Hummingbird highways. Except for the wild Maya Mountains and Mountain Pine Ridge areas, the country is almost entirely flat. It would be possible to tour Belize's major mainland destinations on a touring bike, but the heat and humidity are often oppressive, and those few highways get plenty of traffic and generally don't have very wide shoulders.

The options are slightly more appealing for mountain bikers and off-track riders, however. Fat-tire explorations are relatively new and underexploited in Belize. Just about every major hotel in the Cayo District and the southern zone has mountain bikes for guest use or rental, or can hook you up with a local rental company. These bikes are fine for day trips and nontechnical riding. However, if you plan to do any serious biking, you might consider bringing your own rig, as quality mountain bike rentals are still a rarity in Belize. The **Mountain Pine Ridge Forest Reserve** and the area around it win my vote as the best place for mountain biking in Belize. The scenery's great, with primary and secondary forests, waterfalls, and plenty of trails. Truly hearty bikers can make it all the way to Caracol. See "Mountain Pine Ridge & Caracol" in chapter 10 for details.

BIRD-WATCHING

With some 618 recorded species of resident and migrant birds identified throughout the country, and a wide variety of ecosystems and habitats, Belize abounds with great bird-watching sites. Even amateur bird-watchers should have little trouble checking off upwards of 100 species in a week's worth of watching.

Lodges with the best bird-watching include **Chan Chich Lodge** (p. 213), near Gallon Jug; **Lamanai Outpost Lodge** (p. 212) on the New River Lagoon; **Chaa Creek** (p. 245), **duPlooy's** (p. 247), or any of the nature lodges outside of San Ignacio; **Blancaneaux Lodge** (p. 254) or any of the lodges in the Mountain Pine Ridge area; **Lighthouse Reef Resort** (p. 152) on the Lighthouse Reef Atoll; **Pook's Hill** (p. 232) outside of Belmopan; and **The Lodge at Big Falls** (p. 196) in the Toledo District.

Some of the best parks and reserves for serious birders are **Cockscomb Basin Forest Reserve** ★, for scarlet macaws and a host of primary forest dwellers; **Shipstern Nature Reserve** ★★, for scores of different sea and shore birds; **Crooked Tree Wildlife Sanctuary** ★★★, for large varieties of wading birds, including the jabiru stork; **Man-O-War Caye** ★★, a major nesting site for the magnificent frigate; **Caracol** Mayan ruins and the **Chiquibil National Park** ★★, for many different resident and migratory forest species; **Half Moon Caye,** for the vast nesting flocks of red-footed boobies; and the **Río Bravo Conservation Area** ★★, for ocellated turkeys and trogons. You'll also find excellent bird-watching in neighboring Guatemala's **Petén** ★★ province and around the **Tikal** ★★ area.

Bird-watchers staying on Ambergris Caye should certainly head to the **Bacalar Chico National Park & Marine Preserve.**

Tour Operators

Sierra Club ★ (✆ **415/977-5588;** www.sierraclub.org) leads at least one 10-day trip each year to Belize, often with a side trip to Guatemala. The focus is on bird-watching and natural history, but you'll also visit several Mayan ruins and spend some time on Caye Caulker. The cost is between US$2,300 and US$3,700 (£1,219–£1,961) per person, not including airfare to Belize.

Victor Emanuel Nature Tours ★★ (✆ **800/328-8368** or 512/328-5221 in the U.S.; www.ventbird.com) is a very well-respected small-group tour operator specializing in bird-watching trips, and a pioneer of the genre in Belize. These tours focus primarily on the area around Chan Chich Lodge and Crooked Tree Wildlife Sanctuary, two of the country's prime bird-watching destinations. Their 10-day trip costs US$4,275 (£2,266) and is limited to 10 participants.

Wings ★ (✆ **888/293-6443** or 520/320-9868; www.wingsbirds.com) is also a specialty bird-watching travel operator with more than 28 years of experience in the field.

Tips A Bird-Watcher's Bible

Any serious bird-watcher will want to pick up a copy of ***Birds of Belize*** (University of Texas Press) by H. Lee Jones. Published in January 2004, this dedicated guide to the birds of Belize was long overdue. The book is wonderfully illustrated by Dana Gardener, and includes 574 species of birds.

Its 7-day Belize trip is based at the remote and luxurious Chan Chich Lodge and costs around US$3,800 (£2,014), not including airfare. Trip size is limited to eight people.

A Belizean Birding Company

In addition to the operator listed below, the **Belize Audubon Society** (✆ **223-4985;** www.belizeaudubon.org) is an active and informative organization worth contacting.

Paradise Expeditions ★ (✆ **824-2772;** www.birdinginbelize.com) specializes in bird-watching trips and adventures. Based in San Ignacio in the Cayo District, these folks offer small-group package tours and personalized guided and unguided itineraries to a selection of the top birding spots and lodges in Belize and western Tikal. A 7-day/6-night tour costs around US$1,295 (£686) per person.

CAVING

Belize is an excellent destination for spelunking. Whether you're passionate about cave exploration or you've never been underground in the dark, you should not leave Belize without venturing into one or more of its vast cave systems. The ancient Mayans believed caves to be a mystical portal between the world of the living and the underworld of spirits and the dead. They called this mystical realm Xibalba. In almost every explored cave in Belize, some evidence of use by the Mayans has been uncovered. Fire pits, campsites, burial mounds, and ritual altars have all been found. Numerous pieces of pottery, as well as skeletons, bones, and religious artifacts have also been encountered.

The aptly named **Caves Branch region** ★★, just outside of Belmopan, is a prime (and certainly the most popular place) to go caving. The cave tube trips here, including the spectacular **Crystal Cave** ★★, are excellent introductions to the underworld. There are also several great caves for exploring in the Cayo District, including the **Barton Creek Cave** ★ and **Chechem Ha** ★. Perhaps the most adventurous and rewarding cave to explore is **Actun Tunichil Muknal** ★★. For more information, see chapter 10.

Tour Operators

The premier cave adventure operator in Belize is **Ian Anderson's Caves Branch** ★★, Hummingbird Highway, Mile Marker 41½ (✆ **822-2800;** www.cavesbranch.com). The company has a lovely forested setting at a far upstream entrance to the Caves Branch River, and a wide variety of cave tours and explorations are offered; most full-day trips run from US$75 to US$155 (£40–£82).

Jaguar Paw ★★, Western Highway, Mile Marker 37 (✆ **877/624-3770** or 820-2023; www.jaguarpaw.com), is a very comfortable lodge located at the prime entry and takeout point for the popular cave tubing tours. They are also basically at the entrance to the Crystal Cave, and the owners here have been instrumental in efforts to explore and preserve this amazing cave. A half-day at Crystal Cave or cave tubing costs US$45 (£24), a full day US$75 (£40).

CRUISING

Belize is blessed with some wonderful cruising grounds. Steady yet gentle trade winds, combined with protected internal passages and innumerable isolated islands and anchorages, make this a perfect place to explore by boat. Cruising options in Belize range from bareboat charters of modern catamarans and monohulls to funky converted Belizean fishing sloops pressed into the snorkel-and-sunset cruise market. Belize is also a major port of call for many Caribbean cruise lines. For information on the major cruise lines that ply the waters of Belize, see "By Cruise Ship" under "Getting There" in chapter 3.

Virtually any section of Belize's coast and its outlying cayes and barrier reef are perfect for sailing. At nearly every beach or dive destination, it is possible to get out on the water for a cruise. Given the choice, I'd say the more remote and isolated cayes of southern Belize are the best places to venture out to sea. The two operations listed below are by far your best bets for bareboat cruising.

Yacht Outfitters

With operations in both Placencia and Ambergris Caye, **TMM** ★ (✆ **800/633-0155** in the U.S., or 226-3026; www.sailtmm.com) offers mostly catamarans, with the option for either bareboat or crewed chartering.

The Moorings ★ (✆ **888/952-8420** in the U.S. and Canada, or 523-3351; www.moorings.com) has its main base in Placencia. They offer bareboat and crewed charters on both monohull and catamaran yachts.

Depending on the season and boat size, rates for a bareboat run between US$2,000 and US$7,000 (£1,060–£3,710) per week, and crewed charters cost from US$3,000 to US$9,000 (£1,590–£4,770) per week.

FISHING

Any angler worth his or her saltwater fly rod already knows that Belize is a world-class fishing destination. Fly-fishing on the flats for permit, tarpon, and bonefish is the main draw, and the fish are excellent all up and down the coast and on the saltwater flats the length of the barrier reef. Bonefish- and permit-fishing is good year-round, while tarpon are best sought from April to November, with July and August being the best months. The southern zone around Punta Gorda and Placencia is prime fishing grounds for permit, while the coastal mangroves and rivers are excellent spots to land lively snook.

Just beyond the barrier reef, anglers can land snapper, barracuda, jack, and grouper, while those who head further out can stalk sailfish and marlin.

Action Belize (✆ **888/383-6319** in the U.S., or 223-2987 in Belize; www.actionbelize.com) is a Belize City–based operation offering a vast array of package and custom tour options. They are especially good with fishing itineraries, and even have their own boats and captains. A 7-day/6-night trip with 4 full days of fishing costs US$1,359 (£720) per person, double occupancy. A full day of fishing starts at US$150 (£80) per person for cruise-ship passengers and independent travelers.

Fishing Lodges

El Pescador ★ (Ambergris Caye; ✆ **800/242-2017** in the U.S. and Canada, or 226-2398; www.elpescador.com) is a luxury lodge on the northern end of Ambergris Caye, specializing in fishing packages. They have excellent guides and boats.

Turneffe Flats ★ (Turneffe Island Atoll; ✆ **888/512-8812** in the U.S.; www.tflats.com) is a beautiful fishing lodge with a privileged position right on the ring of the Turneffe Island Atoll and its extensive mid-ocean lagoon and open-water flats. See p. 153 for a complete review.

GOLF

Belize is not one of the world's great golfing destinations; in fact, it's not a golf destination at all. But Belize does boast one beautiful oceanfront course that takes up almost an entire private little island. While relatively flat, the par-72 course features plenty of water and sand hazards, and an unmatched number of oceanfront holes. The steady trade winds often come into play here, so be prepared. However, there are never any crowds or waits on the course.

Caye Chapel Island Resort ★★ (✆ **800/901-8938** in the U.S. and Canada, or 226-8250 in Belize; www.cayechapel.com), has luxury condominium units and private villas, as well as a marina, a pool, and tennis facilities. Rates run between BZ$600 and BZ$2,400 (US$300–US$1,200/£159–£636), with unlimited golf included. Players not staying on the island can play with an advance reservation. Rates for a full day of unlimited golfing, including carts, club rental, and use of the resort's pool and beach area cost BZ$300 (US$150/£80) per person.

HORSEBACK RIDING

Although Belize is very sparsely populated, and much of it is ideal for exploring on the back of a horse, horseback riding is still a relatively undeveloped sport. The best place to grab a mount and explore is the Mountain Pine Ridge Forest Reserve, and the best outfitter to tour with here is **Mountain Equestrian Trails** (✆ **669-1124;** www.metbelize.com). A half-day trip including lunch costs BZ$122 (US$61/£32) per person; a full-day trip costs BZ$166 (US$83/£44). Even if you're not staying here, most of the lodges in this area also offer horseback riding. For more information on riding in this region, see chapter 10.

A Montana Cowboy in Central Belize

Banana Bank Lodge ★, Western Highway, Mile Marker 47½ (✆ **820-2020;** www.bananabank.com), is a rustic riverside lodge owned by a former cowboy from Montana. Horseback riding is a major attraction here, so avid riders will feel right at home. For more information on this hotel, see p. 231.

KAYAKING & CANOEING

Belize lacks the major white water necessary for serious rapid enthusiasts. Most of the rivers here are rated Class I, II, or III. Still, many of these rivers are quite well suited for gentle canoe explorations and less technical kayaking adventures. The Macal and Mopan rivers in the Cayo District are perfect for these types of adventures, and most of the hotels and tour operators in the area offer a range of these types of tours. See chapter 10 for more information.

However, sea kayaking in Belize is excellent. The relatively calm waters and protection provided by the barrier reef and mid-ocean atoll lagoons, combined with a string of small, relatively closely spread cayes, makes this a perfect place to tour and explore by sea kayak. **Glover's Reef Atoll** is probably the most popular and best place for a sea kayak adventure; see "Dangriga" in chapter 8 for more information.

Outfitters

Island Expeditions ★★ (✆ **800/667-1630** or 604/452-3212 in the U.S.; www.islandexpeditions.com) run various multiday kayaking tours to the outer atolls, Glover's Reef Atoll, and the coral islands along the southern stretch of Belize's barrier reef. An 8-day/7-night excursion runs US$1,500 to US$2,000 (£795–£1,060).

Slickrock Adventures ★★ (✆ **800/390-5715** or 435/259-4225 in the U.S.; www.slickrock.com) specializes in multiday kayak tours around Glover's Reef Atoll, and they even have their own rustically comfortable base camp and lodge on a private caye here. An 8-day/7-night trip costs US$1,975 (£1,047) per person.

SCUBA DIVING & SNORKELING

Belize is one of the world's top spots for scuba diving and snorkeling. I've said it before, and I'll probably say it again, but Belize has the second longest barrier reef in the world,

When a Package Isn't a Deal

While it's often tempting to purchase all-inclusive dive packages before coming to Belize, this limits your flexibility. For example, if the weather and water are really rough, you're already committed, even though you might prefer taking an inland tour to a Mayan ruin instead of a rough dive.

as well as three spectacular mid-ocean atolls. The diving and snorkeling all along this reef and at the atolls are world-class. In general, the reef is in very healthy shape and the water quality and visibility are consistently excellent.

Amateur or casual divers and snorkelers should really be happy almost anywhere in Belize, and every major beach and island destination has easy access to some fabulous dive and snorkel sites. Truly dedicated divers will probably want to head to one of the outer atolls. **Glover's Reef ★★**, **Turneffe Island ★★**, and **Lighthouse Reef atolls ★★** all offer outstanding diving opportunities. The Blue Hole and several other sites on Lighthouse Reef Atoll make it the top choice for scuba divers, amongst a crowded field. **Shark-Ray Alley ★★** and **Hol Chan Marine Reserve ★★** are two deservedly popular snorkel spots just off of Ambergris Caye, although overpopularity and overcrowding are threatening the experience there. And finally, only just becoming known to cognoscenti, the **Gladden Spit ★★** area, off the coast from Placencia, is one of the top spots on the planet to snorkel or dive with giant whale sharks.

There are several dedicated dive resorts around Belize. Another option for hard-core divers is to stay on a live-aboard dive boat. These midsize vessels usually carry from between 10 to 20 divers in private staterooms. The boats feature fully equipped dive operations and a host of amenities. One of the advantages here is that you get to hit several of the top reef and atoll sites in a weeklong vacation.

Information on snorkeling, scuba diving, and local operators is in each of the destination chapters that follow. Almost every beach resort in Belize, as well as most hotels in Belize City, either has its own dive shop and operation or can hook you up with a local crew. Below are listed a couple of live-aboard operations, and a couple of the best dedicated dive resorts in Belize.

Note: While many of the beach and island hotels and all of the dive shops in Belize have snorkeling and diving gear for rent, you might consider bringing your own. If nothing else, bring your own mask. A good, properly fitting mask is the single most important factor in predicting the success of a dive outing. Faces come in all sizes and shapes, and I really recommend finding a mask that gives you a perfect fit. Fins are a lesser concern, as most operators should have fins to fit your feet. As for your own snorkel, well, in this day and age, I think you should want your own. If you plan on going out snorkeling or diving more than a few times, the investment will more than pay for itself.

Live-Aboard Dive Boats

Aggressor Fleet ★★ (✆ **800/348-2628** or 985/385-2628 in the U.S.; www.aggressor.com) has the 34m (110-ft.) *Aggressor III,* a comfortable dive boat with deluxe staterooms. Rates cost around US$2,300 to US$2,900 per week (£1,219–£1,537).

Peter Hughes Diving ★★ (✆ **800/932-6237** or 305/669-9391 in the U.S.; www.peterhughes.com) runs the *Sundancer II,* a 42m (138-ft.) yacht with 10 staterooms. Rates range from US$2,200 to US$2,400 per week (£1,166–£1,272).

Tips Capturing It on Film

No longer is underwater photography and video the exclusive realm of professionals with very expensive equipment. Generic and custom waterproof housings can be purchased for most modern digital still and video cameras. However, if you don't own your own underwater camera or casing, you might want to bring one or more cheap, disposable waterproof or underwater cameras. Alternatively, many dive shops will rent professional or semiprofessional underwater still and video cameras for about US$20 to US$40 (£11–£21) per day.

Tip: Both boats are very comfortable and well equipped, with full dive and photo-lab operations, rental equipment, attentive service, and plenty of deck and lounge areas. Each boat has one or two master staterooms with a queen-size bed for couples. The *Aggressor III* features TVs and VCRs in every stateroom, and even has a hot tub on the upper deck. Couples will probably prefer the *Aggressor III*'s wider lower bunk of their staggered quasi-bunk bed arrangement, while buddies traveling together may be more comfortable with the two separate single beds in the standard staterooms on the *Sundancer II.*

Diving Resorts & Outfitters

In addition to the folks listed below, check the listings at specific beach and island destinations in the regional chapters, particularly those in Placencia, Ambergris Caye, Caye Caulker, and the outer cayes and atolls.

Hamanasi ★★ (✆ **877/552-3483** in the U.S., or 520-7073; www.hamanasi.com) is an excellent dive resort located on a beautiful patch of beach south of Hopkins Village. The location grants good access to a wide range of dive sites, including the outer atolls. See p. 172 for a complete review.

SPAS & RETREATS

So far the trend towards destination spas and yoga or tai chi retreats hasn't caught on in Belize. In fact, there are no true dedicated destination spas or retreats in the country yet. However, the two places listed below do a pretty good job at what they do.

Primarily a nature lodge and ecotourism resort, **Chaa Creek** ★★, off the road to Benque Viejo in the Cayo District (✆ **824-2037;** www.chaacreek.com), has a very nice full-service day spa offering a wide range of body and skin treatments. Multiday packages are available and can be designed to give the feel of a full-destination spa experience. See p. 245 for a complete review of the resort.

Maruba Resort Jungle Spa ★★ (✆ **800/627-8227** in the U.S., or 225-5555 in Belize; fax 225-5506; www.maruba-spa.com) is a true spa, offering a wide range of treatments and packages. Their various massages, mud and exfoliating treatments, and the general sense of sensual overload and pampering, are all top-notch. But aside from horseback riding options, they don't really offer any of the classes or active exercise programs that you would expect at a destination spa. For more information, see "Along the Old Northern Highway: Altun Ha & Maruba Resort Jungle Spa" in chapter 9.

WINDSURFING & KITESURFING

Its steady trade winds and calm waters make Belize a great place for beginning and intermediate windsurfers, and a good place to learn how to kiteboard. More advanced boardsailers would probably want more extreme conditions, but this is a great place to learn and perfect your skills. That said, this is still a relatively minor activity in Belize. Your best bet for either of these activities is to check in with the folks at **Sail Sports Belize** (✆ **226-4488;** www.sailsportsbelize.com) on Ambergris Caye, or **Kitexplorer** (✆ **602-9297;** www.kitexplorer.com) on Caye Caulker. Both offer top-notch equipment rentals and lessons in both sports.

3 BELIZE'S TOP PARKS & BIORESERVES

Belize has a broad mix of national parks, forest reserves, marine reserves, natural monuments, wildlife sanctuaries, archaeological reserves, and private reserves. All told, more than one-fifth of the country's landmass and much of its offshore waters are, to some extent, protected areas. In fact, the entire Belize Barrier Reef was declared a World Heritage Site by UNESCO in 1996.

Most of the national parks charge a BZ$10 (US$5/£2.65) per-person per-day fee for any foreigner, although some have begun charging slightly more and a few slightly less. Belizeans and foreign residents often pay less. At parks where camping is allowed, an additional charge of around BZ$4 (US$2/£1.05) per person per day is usually charged. Fees at private reserves vary, but are similar to those listed above.

The following section is not a complete listing of all of Belize's national parks, protected areas, and private reserves, but rather a selective list of those parks that are of greatest interest and accessibility. They're the most popular, but they're also among the best. You'll find detailed information about food and lodging options near each of the individual parks in the regional chapters that follow.

NORTHERN CAYES & ATOLLS

BACALAR CHICO NATIONAL PARK & MARINE RESERVE This is one of the newest additions to Belize's national park system. In addition to being home to scores of bird, animal, and plant species (many of which are endemic), the park also features several ancient Mayan ceremonial and trading sites. Nearly 200 species of birds have been spotted here, and the park allegedly contains all five wildcat species found in Belize, including the jaguar. The park is only accessible by boat, but once you get here, there are several trails. **Location:** On the far northern end of Ambergris Caye. For more details, see "Ambergris Caye" in chapter 7.

HALF MOON CAYE NATIONAL MONUMENT This is a combined land and marine reserve. Half Moon Caye itself is the principal nesting ground for the red-footed booby, as well as for both hawksbill and loggerhead turtles. There is a visitor center here, and overnight camping is permitted with prior arrangement. **Location:** On the southern tip of the Lighthouse Reef Atoll. For more information, see "The Outer Atolls" in chapter 7.

HOL CHAN MARINE RESERVE *Hol chan* is a Mayan term meaning "little channel," which is exactly what you'll find here—a narrow channel cutting through the shallow coral reef. The reserve covers 7.8 sq. km (3 sq. miles) and is divided into three zones: the reef, the sea-grass beds, and the mangroves. The walls of the channel are popular with divers, and the shallower areas are frequented by snorkelers. Some of the exciting residents of the area are large green moray eels, stingrays, and nurse sharks (harmless). **Location:** 6.4km (4 miles) southeast of San Pedro on Ambergris Caye. For more details, see "Ambergris Caye" in chapter 7.

SOUTHERN BELIZE

COCKSCOMB BASIN WILDLIFE SANCTUARY The world's first jaguar reserve, this place covers nearly 389 sq. km (150 sq. miles) of rugged, forested mountains and has the greatest density of jaguars on the planet. Other resident mammals include tapirs, otters, coati-mundis, tayra, kinkajous, deer, peccaries, anteaters, armadillos, and four other species of wild cats, as well as nearly 300 species of birds. The sanctuary is part of the even larger Cockscomb Basin Forest Reserve. Trails inside the park range from gentle and short to quite arduous and long. During the dry season, you can even climb Victoria Peak here, which, at 1,122m (3,681 ft.), is the country's highest mountain. **Location:** 10km (6 miles) west of the Southern Highway, at a turnoff 32km (20 miles) south of Dangriga. For more information, see "Dangriga" in chapter 8.

FIVE BLUES LAKE NATIONAL PARK The main attraction here is a stunning cenote, whose various hues of blue give the park its name. All around the park lie forested lands and beautiful karst hill formations. **Location:** Mile Marker 32 on the Hummingbird Highway. For more information, see "Dangriga" in chapter 8.

GLOVER'S REEF ATOLL MARINE RESERVE This stunning and isolated mid-ocean coral formation features an oval-shaped central lagoon nearly 35km (22 miles) long. The steep-walled reefs here offer some of the best wall diving anywhere in the Caribbean. The entire atoll was declared a World Heritage Site by the United Nations. **Location:** 121km (75 miles) southeast of Belize City; 45km (28 miles) east of Dangriga. For more information, see "Dangriga" in chapter 8.

NORTHERN BELIZE

CROOKED TREE WILDLIFE SANCTUARY This swampy lowland is home to over 250 resident species of birds and serves as a resting spot for scores of migratory species. During a visit here, you are sure to spot any number of interesting water birds. However, the sanctuary was established primarily to protect Belize's main nesting site of the endangered jabiru stork, the largest bird in the Western Hemisphere. Crocodiles, iguanas, coati-mundi, and howler monkeys are all frequently sighted. There are six major lagoons here connected by a series of creeks, rivers, and wetlands. The best way to explore the preserve is by dugout canoe. **Location:** 53km (33 miles) northwest of Belize City. For more information, see "En Route North: Crooked Tree Wildlife Sanctuary" in chapter 9.

RIO BRAVO CONSERVATION AREA This 105,218-hectare (260,000-acre) tract is a mix of virgin forest, sustainable-yield managed forest, and recovering reforestation areas. The land is home to nearly 400 bird species and over 200 species of tropical trees. It also supports a healthy population of most of the new-world cat species, and is one of the best areas in the Americas for spotting a jaguar, even better than Cockscomb Basin. La Milpa, one of Belize's largest known Mayan sites, is located within this reserve, and Río Bravo is bordered by some 101,171 hectares (250,000 acres) of private reserve at Chan Chich, as well as the Kalakmul Reserve in Mexico and the Maya Biosphere Reserve in Guatemala, making it part of a massive regional biological and archaeological protected area. **Location:** 89km (55 miles) southwest of Orange Walk Town. For more information, see "Going West: Río Bravo Conservation Area, La Milpa & Chan Chich" in chapter 9.

SHIPSTERN NATURE RESERVE The 8,903 hectares (22,000 acres) of this reserve protect a variety of distinct ecosystems and a wealth of flora and fauna. Shipstern Nature Reserve is home to over 250 bird species, and its mangroves, lagoons, and flat wetlands offer some of the best bird-watching sites in Belize. The lagoons and wetlands here are

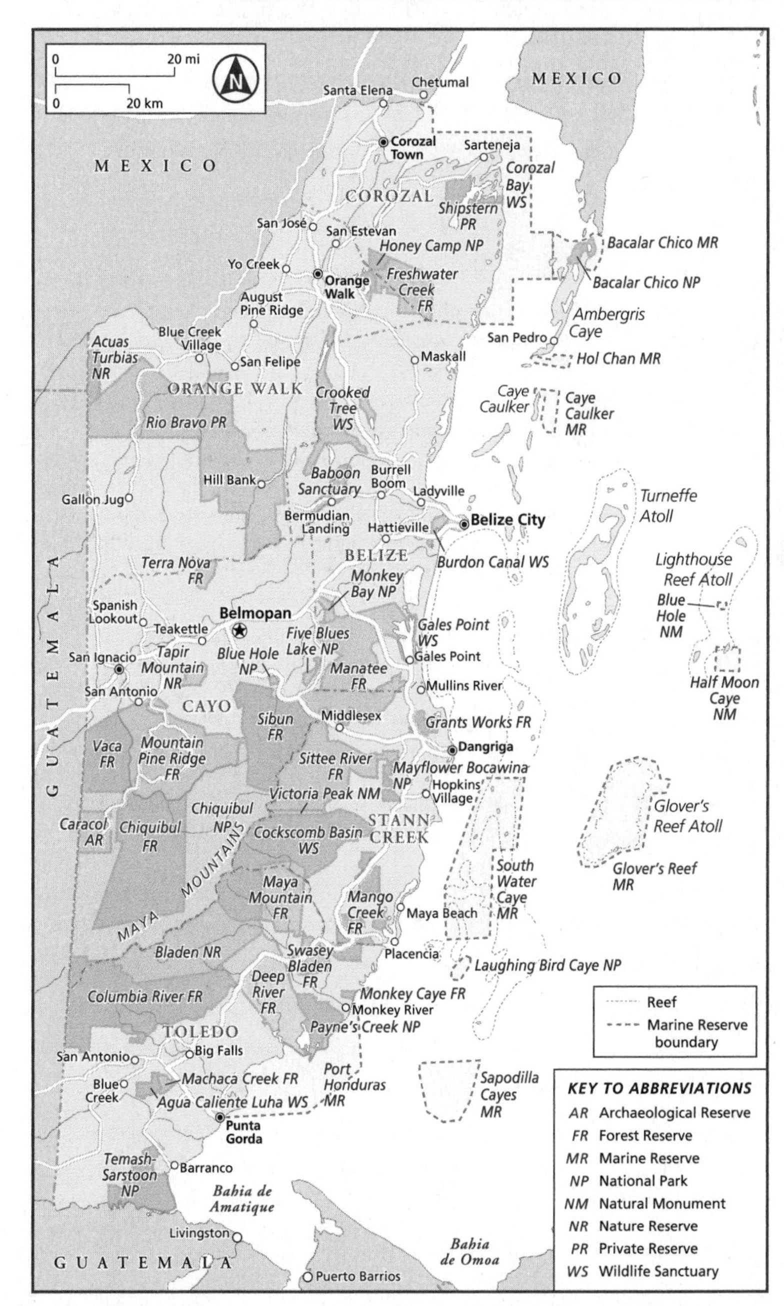
0 20 mi
0 20 km
N
MEXICO
MEXICO
Santa Elena
Chetumal
Corozal Town
Sarteneja
Corozal Bay WS
COROZAL
Shipstern PR
San José
San Estevan
Honey Camp NP
Bacalar Chico MR
Bacalar Chico NP
Yo Creek
Orange Walk
Freshwater Creek FR
August Pine Ridge
Ambergris Caye
San Pedro
Blue Creek Village
Acuas Turbias NR
San Felipe
Maskall
Hol Chan MR
ORANGE WALK
Crooked Tree WS
Caye Caulker
Caye Caulker MR
Rio Bravo PR
Hill Bank
Baboon Sanctuary
Burrell Boom
Ladyville
Turneffe Atoll
Gallon Jug
Bermudian Landing
Hattieville
Belize City
Burdon Canal WS
BELIZE
Lighthouse Reef Atoll
Terra Nova FR
Monkey Bay NP
Blue Hole NM
Spanish Lookout
Belmopan
Teakettle
Five Blues Lake NP
Gales Point WS
Gales Point
San Ignacio
Tapir Mountain NR
Blue Hole NP
Manatee FR
Mullins River
San Antonio
CAYO
Half Moon Caye NM
Sibun FR
Middlesex
Grants Works FR
Vaca FR
Mountain Pine Ridge FR
Dangriga
Sittee River FR
Mayflower Bocawina NP
Hopkins Village
Victoria Peak NM
Glover's Reef Atoll
Chiquibul NP
Caracol AR
Chiquibul FR
Cockscomb Basin WS
STANN CREEK
MAYA MOUNTAINS
South Water Caye MR
Glover's Reef MR
Maya Mountain FR
Mango Creek FR
Maya Beach
Placencia
Bladen NR
Swasey Bladen FR
Laughing Bird Caye NP
Deep River FR
Columbia River FR
Monkey Caye FR
Monkey River
Reef
Marine Reserve boundary
TOLEDO
Payne's Creek NP
San Antonio
Big Falls
Port Honduras MR
Sapodilla Cayes MR
Blue Creek
Machaca Creek FR
Agua Caliente Luha WS
Punta Gorda
Temash-Sarstoon NP
Barranco
Bahia de Amatique
Livingston
Bahia de Omoa
GUATEMALA
GUATEMALA
Puerto Barrios
KEY TO ABBREVIATIONS
AR Archaeological Reserve
FR Forest Reserve
MR Marine Reserve
NP National Park
NM Natural Monument
NR Nature Reserve
PR Private Reserve
WS Wildlife Sanctuary

home to manatees and Morelet's crocodiles. The reserve also has lowland tropical dry forest unique to Belize, as well as a butterfly-breeding project. **Location:** 60km (37 miles) north of Orange Walk Town. For more information, see "Corozal Town" in chapter 9.

THE CAYO DISTRICT & WESTERN BELIZE

BLUE HOLE NATIONAL PARK This park gets its name from a crystal-clear pool, or cenote, formed in a collapsed cavern. A short, well-marked trail leads to the main attraction here. Dense jungle surrounds a small natural pool of deep turquoise. This park also features **St. Herman's Cave,** one of the largest and—at one time—most easily accessible caves in Belize. The trail that connects the cenote and the cave passes through lush and beautiful primary and secondary tropical forests that are rich in flora and fauna. However, as of press time, St. Herman's Cave has been blocked by a massive rock collapse, and there's no indication if and when it may be cleared and re-opened. **Location:** 19km (12 miles) south of Belmopan on the Hummingbird Highway. For more information, see "Belmopan" in chapter 10.

CARACOL ARCHAEOLOGICAL RESERVE Caracol is the largest known Mayan archaeological site in Belize, and one of the great Mayan city-states of the Classic era. So far three main plazas with numerous structures and two ball courts have been excavated. Caracol is located deep within the **Chiquibil Forest Reserve,** which is a largely undeveloped tract of primary and secondary tropical rain and pine forests. The bird-watching here is excellent. **Location:** 80km (50 miles) from the Western Highway at a turnoff just south of San Ignacio. For more information, see "Mountain Pine Ridge & Caracol" in chapter 10.

GUANACASTE NATIONAL PARK This 20-hectare (50-acre) park is named for a huge old guanacaste, or tubroos, tree that is found within the park. There are nearly 3.2km (2 miles) of well-marked and well-maintained trails in the park. The park is bordered on the west by Roaring Creek and on the north by the Belize River. Among the animals you might see are more than 120 species of birds, large iguanas, armadillos, kinkajous, deer, agoutis (large rodents that are a favorite game meat in Belize), and jaguarundis (small jungle cats). **Location:** 3.2km (2 miles) north of Belmopan, where the Hummingbird Highway turns off the Western Highway. For more information, see "Belmopan" in chapter 10.

MONKEY BAY The combined Monkey Bay Wildlife Sanctuary and Monkey Bay Nature Reserve represent over 1,344 hectares (3,320 acres) of private, protected reserve of forest and wetlands. Over 250 species of birds have been recorded here so far, and the number is growing. There are hiking trails, as well as canoe tours on the Sibun River. **Location:** 50km (31 miles) west of Belize City, just off the Western Highway. For more information, see "Belmopan" in chapter 10.

TIKAL, GUATEMALA

TIKAL NATIONAL PARK While it's obviously not in Belize, the close proximity and convenient access have earned this spectacular Guatemalan national park and ancient Mayan ceremonial city a place on this list and in this book. Surrounded by dense, virgin tropical rainforest, the Tikal ruins are perhaps the most spectacularly preserved and restored Mayan ruins yet uncovered. **Location:** 100km (62 miles) northwest of the Belize border; 64km (40 miles) north of Flores. For more information, see "Tikal" in chapter 11.

4 TIPS ON HEALTH, SAFETY & ETIQUETTE IN THE WILDERNESS

Much of what is discussed below is common sense. For more detailed information, see "Health & Safety" in chapter 3.

TAKING CARE

While most tours are safe, there are risks involved in any adventurous activity. Know and respect your own physical limits before undertaking any strenuous activity. Be prepared for extremes in temperature and rainfall and for wide fluctuations in weather. A sunny morning hike can quickly become a cold and wet ordeal, so it's usually a good idea to carry along some form of rain gear when hiking in the rainforest, or to have a dry change of clothing waiting at the end of the trail. Make sure to bring along plenty of sunscreen when you're not going to be covered by the forest canopy.

If you do any backcountry packing or camping, remember that it really *is* a jungle out there. Don't go poking under rocks or fallen branches. Snakebites are very rare, but don't do anything to increase the odds. If you do encounter a snake, stay calm, don't make any sudden movements, and *do not* try to handle it. Also, avoid swimming in major rivers unless a guide or local operator can vouch for their safety. Though white-water sections and stretches in mountainous areas are generally pretty safe, most mangrove canals and river mouths in Belize support healthy crocodile and caiman populations.

Bugs and bug bites will probably be your greatest health concern in Belize, and even they aren't as big a problem as you might expect. Mostly bugs are an inconvenience, although mosquitoes can carry malaria or dengue (see "Health," in chapter 3, for more information). A strong repellent and proper clothing will minimize both the danger and inconvenience; you may also want to bring along some cortisone or Benadryl cream to soothe itching. At the beaches, you'll probably be bitten by sand fleas, or "no-see-ems." These nearly invisible insects leave an irritating welt. Try not to scratch, as this can lead to open sores and infections. No-see-ems are most active at sunrise and sunset, so you might want to cover up or avoid the beaches at these times.

And remember: Whenever you enter and enjoy nature, you should tread lightly and try not to disturb the natural environment. There's a popular slogan well known to most campers that certainly applies here: "Leave nothing but footprints, take nothing but memories." If you must take home a souvenir, take photos. Do not cut or uproot plants or flowers. Pack out everything you pack in, and *please* do not litter.

SEARCHING FOR WILDLIFE

Animals in the forests are predominantly nocturnal. When they are active in the daytime, they are usually elusive and on the watch for predators. Birds are easier to spot in clearings or secondary forests than they are in primary forests. Unless you have lots of experience in the tropics, your best hope for enjoying a walk through the jungle lies in employing a trained and knowledgeable guide. (By the way, if it's been raining a lot and the trails are muddy, a good pair of rubber boots comes in handy. These are usually provided by the lodges or at the sites, where necessary.)

Here are a few helpful hints:

- **Listen.** Pay attention to rustling in the leaves; whether it's monkeys up above or pizotes on the ground, you're most likely to hear an animal before seeing one.

- **Keep quiet.** Noise will scare off animals and prevent you from hearing their movements and calls.
- **Don't try too hard.** Soften your focus and allow your peripheral vision to take over. This way you can catch glimpses of motion and then focus in on the prey.
- **Bring your own binoculars.** It's also a good idea to practice a little first to get the hang of them. It would be a shame to be fiddling around and staring into space while everyone else in your group oohs and aahs over a trogon or honeycreeper.
- **Dress appropriately.** You'll have a hard time focusing your binoculars if you're busy swatting mosquitoes. Light, long pants and long-sleeved shirts are your best bet. Comfortable hiking boots are a real boon, except where heavy rubber boots are necessary. Avoid loud colors; the better you blend in with your surroundings, the better your chances are of spotting wildlife.
- **Be patient.** The jungle isn't on a schedule. However, your best shots at seeing forest fauna are in the very early-morning and late-afternoon hours.
- **Read up.** Familiarize yourself with what you're most likely to see. Most lodges and hotels have a copy of ***Birds of Belize*** (University of Texas Press, 2004) by H. Lee Jones, and other wildlife field guides, although it's always best to have your own. A good all-around book to have is Les Beletsky's ***Belize and Northern Guatemala: The Ecotravellers' Wildlife Guide*** ★ (Natural World Academic Press, 2004).

5 ECOLOGICALLY ORIENTED VOLUNTEER & STUDY PROGRAMS

Below are some institutions and organizations that are working on ecology and sustainable development projects.

Cornerstone Foundation ★★ (✆ **678-9909;** www.cornerstonefoundationbelize.org), based in San Ignacio in the Cayo District, is an excellent and effective nonreligious, nongovernmental peace organization with a variety of volunteer and cultural exchange program opportunities. Programs range from AIDS education to literacy campaigns to renewable resource development and use. Overall, costs are pretty low, and reflect the costs of basic food, lodging, and travel in country, with some extra going to support the organization and its work.

Earthwatch Institute ★ (✆ **800/776-0188;** www.earthwatch.org) organizes volunteers to go on research trips to help scientists collect data and conduct field experiments in a number of scientific fields and a wide range of settings. Current expeditions to Belize focus on the study and field research on manatees. Fees for food and lodging average around US$2,700 (£1,431) for a 9-day expedition, excluding airfare.

Habitat for Humanity International ★ (✆ **800/422-4828** in the U.S. and Canada, or 227-6818 in Belize; www.habitat.org) is a nonprofit, nondenominational Christian volunteer organization, specializing in building individual housing for needy folks around the world. Habitat has an independent chapter in Belize and sometimes runs organized Global Village programs here. It usually costs between US$1,200 and US$1,600 (£636–£848) per person for a 2-week program, including room, board, and in-country transportation (but not airfare to Belize).

International Zoological Expeditions ★★ (✆ **800/548-5843;** www.ize2belize.com) has two research and educational facilities in Belize, on South Water Caye and in

Blue Creek Village. IZE organizes and administers a variety of educational and vacation trips to these two stations, for both school groups and individuals. A 10-day program usually costs about US$1,250 to US$1,800 (£663–£954).

Maya Research Program at Blue Creek ★ (✆ **817/831-9011** in the U.S.; www.mayaresearchprogram.org) runs volunteer and educational programs at an ongoing Mayan archaeological dig. Two-week sessions allow participants to literally dig in and take part in the excavation of a Mayan ruin. The cost is US$1,450 (£769) for the 2-week program; discounts are available for students and longer stays.

Monkey Bay Wildlife Sanctuary ★ (✆ **820-3032;** www.monkeybaybelize.org) is a private reserve and environmental education center that specializes in hosting study-abroad student groups. They also run their own in-house educational programs and can arrange a variety of volunteer stays and programs, including homestays with local Belizean families. See "Belmopan" in chapter 10 for complete details.

Toledo Institute for Development and Environment ★ (✆ **722-2274;** www.tidebelize.org) is a small, grassroots environmental and ecotourism organization working on sustainable development and ecological protection issues in the Toledo District. Contact them directly if you are interested in volunteering.

6

Belize City

Long ago stripped of its status as the country's capital, Belize City remains Belize's business, transportation, and cultural hub. Sooner or later you'll probably have to spend some time here, unless you do all your in-country traveling by air or have a very precisely planned itinerary. In fact, since the country itself is so small, Belize City makes a good base for a host of interesting day trips to most of the country's major destinations and attractions.

With a population of some 71,000, Belize City is surrounded on three sides by water, and at high tide it is nearly swamped. It's a strange, dense warren of narrow streets and canals (the latter being little more than open sewers, and pretty pungent in hot weather), modern stores, dilapidated shacks, and quaint wooden mansions, coexisting in a seemingly chaotic jumble.

The city was originally settled by the ancient Mayans, who lived up and down the coast here. By the mid-1600s, pirates were using the current site of Belize City as a hideout and provisioning spot. Soon after, the British arrived and set up a logging base here, fueled by slave labor. Logs were harvested inland and floated down the Belize River for milling and shipping. This logging base soon became a colonial settlement and the seat of Britain's colonial empire on the Central American isthmus. Belize City itself is said to sit on a foundation of wood chips, discarded ship's ballast, and empty rum bottles.

Belize City has historically been beset by tragedy. The entire population abandoned the city and moved to St. George's Caye in 1779 following a Spanish attack. The Baymen, as the British settlers called themselves, returned and resettled the city in 1784. Massive fires razed much of the city in 1804, 1806, and 1856. Deadly hurricanes inflicted heavy damage in 1931 and 1961. Between these events, the residents endured smallpox, yellow fever, and cholera epidemics. Belize City had been declared the capital of British Honduras in 1892, but after Hurricane Hattie struck in 1961, the country's capital was relocated inland to Belmopan.

Despite a reputation for crime and violence, periodic devastation from passing hurricanes, and the loss of its capital status, Belize City remains the urban heart and soul of Belize. Most visitors treat Belize City merely as a transition point and transportation hub. This is probably what you'll want to do too. But if you've got a day or two to burn on a layover here, Belize City is a good place to walk around, admire the fleet of working wooden fish sloops, do some craft and souvenir shopping, and stock up on Marie Sharp's Hot Sauce to bring home with you.

1 ORIENTATION

ARRIVING

By Plane

All international flights into Belize land at the **Philip S. W. Goldson International Airport** (© **225-2045**; www.pgiabelize.com; airport code BZE), which is located 16km

(10 miles) northwest of the city on the Northern Highway. See chapter 3 for details about airlines that service Belize City.

In the baggage claim area, there's an information booth maintained by the **Belize Tourist Board.** This booth supplies maps and brochures, and will often make a call for you if you need a hotel or car-rental reservation. Inside the international departure terminal is a branch of **Belize Bank** (✆ **225-2107**), open daily from 8:30am to 4pm. Across the parking lot, you'll find car-rental and tour-agency desks, open daily from 8am to 9:30pm. A taxi into town will cost BZ$50 to BZ$60 (US$25–US$30/£13–£16).

If you fly in from somewhere else in Belize, you'll probably land at the **Municipal Airport** (airport code TZA), which is on the edge of town. A taxi from here costs just BZ$10 (US$5/£2.65). There's no bank or any other services at the Municipal Airport, although most car-rental agencies can arrange to have a car there for you. See p. 91 for taxi info.

There is no direct bus service to either airport.

By Car

There are only two highways into Belize City: the Northern Highway, which leads to the Mexican border (166km/103 miles away), and the Western Highway, which leads to the Guatemalan border (132km/82 miles away). Both are well marked and in good driving condition. If you arrive by car from the north, stay on the road into town, paying close attention to one-way streets, and you'll end up at the Swing Bridge. If you're arriving on the Western Highway, stay on it after it becomes Cemetery Road, and you'll end up at the intersection with Albert Street, a block away from the Swing Bridge.

By Bus

If you arrive in town by bus, you'll probably end up at the main **bus terminal** on West Collet Canal Street. This is an easy walk to downtown, but it is not recommended after dark. A taxi from the bus station to any hotel in town will cost around BZ$8 (US$4/£2); see p. 91 for taxi info.

VISITOR INFORMATION

The **Belize Tourist Board** (✆ **800/624-0686** toll-free in the U.S. and Canada, or 227-2430 in Belize; www.travelbelize.org) has its main office at 64 Regent Street, in the heart of the business district of Belize City. If you missed their desk at the airport, they have another information desk here with regional brochures, basic maps, and a score of hotel and tour fliers; the office is open Monday through Friday from 8am to 5pm. Local travel agencies are another good source of information. Two in Belize City to try are **Discovery Expeditions,** 5916 Manatee Dr., Buttonwood Bay (✆ **223-0748;** www.discoverybelize.com) and **S&L Travel and Tours,** 91 N. Front St. (✆ **227-7593;** www.sltravelbelize.com).

CITY LAYOUT

Belize City is surrounded on three sides by water, with Haulover Creek dividing the city in two. The Swing Bridge, near the mouth of Haulover Creek, is the main route between the two halves of the city, as well as the city's principal landmark. At the south end of the bridge is Market Square and the start of Regent Street and Albert Street. This is where you'll find most of Belize City's shops and offices. To the west and east of these two major roads is a grid of smaller roads lined with dilapidated wooden houses. On the north side of the bridge and to the right is the Fort George area. From the southern side of the city, Cemetery Road heads out of town to the west and becomes the Western Highway, while

Belize City

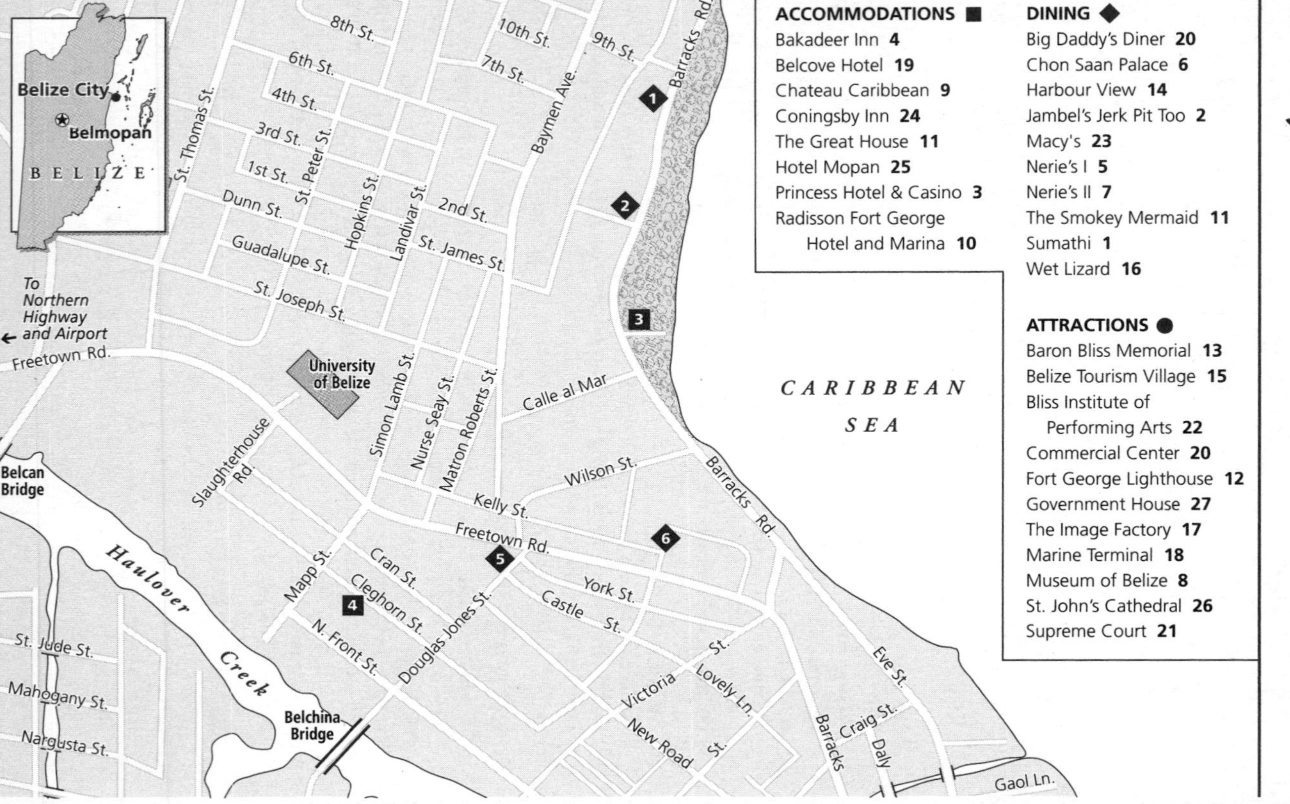
ACCOMMODATIONS ■
Bakadeer Inn 4
Belcove Hotel 19
Chateau Caribbean 9
Coningsby Inn 24
The Great House 11
Hotel Mopan 25
Princess Hotel & Casino 3
Radisson Fort George Hotel and Marina 10
DINING ◆
Big Daddy's Diner 20
Chon Saan Palace 6
Harbour View 14
Jambel's Jerk Pit Too 2
Macy's 23
Nerie's I 5
Nerie's II 7
The Smokey Mermaid 11
Sumathi 1
Wet Lizard 16
ATTRACTIONS ●
Baron Bliss Memorial 13
Belize Tourism Village 15
Bliss Institute of Performing Arts 22
Commercial Center 20
Fort George Lighthouse 12
Government House 27
The Image Factory 17
Marine Terminal 18
Museum of Belize 8
St. John's Cathedral 26
Supreme Court 21
CARIBBEAN SEA
Belize City
Belmopan
BELIZE
To Northern Highway and Airport
Freetown Rd.
University of Belize
Belcan Bridge
Belchina Bridge
Haulover Creek
8th St.
10th St.
9th St.
6th St.
7th St.
4th St.
3rd St.
1st St.
Dunn St.
Guadalupe St.
St. Joseph St.
St. Thomas St.
St. Peter St.
Hopkins St.
Landivar St.
2nd St.
St. James St.
Baymen Ave.
Barracks Rd.
Simon Lamb St.
Nurse Seay St.
Matron Roberts St.
Calle al Mar
Slaughterhouse Rd.
Wilson St.
Kelly St.
Freetown Rd.
Mapp St.
Cran St.
Cleghorn St.
N. Front St.
Douglas Jones St.
York St.
Castle St.
Victoria St.
Lovely Ln.
New Road St.
Eve St.
Craig St.
Daly
Barracks
Gaol Ln.
St. Jude St.
Mahogany St.
Nargusta St.

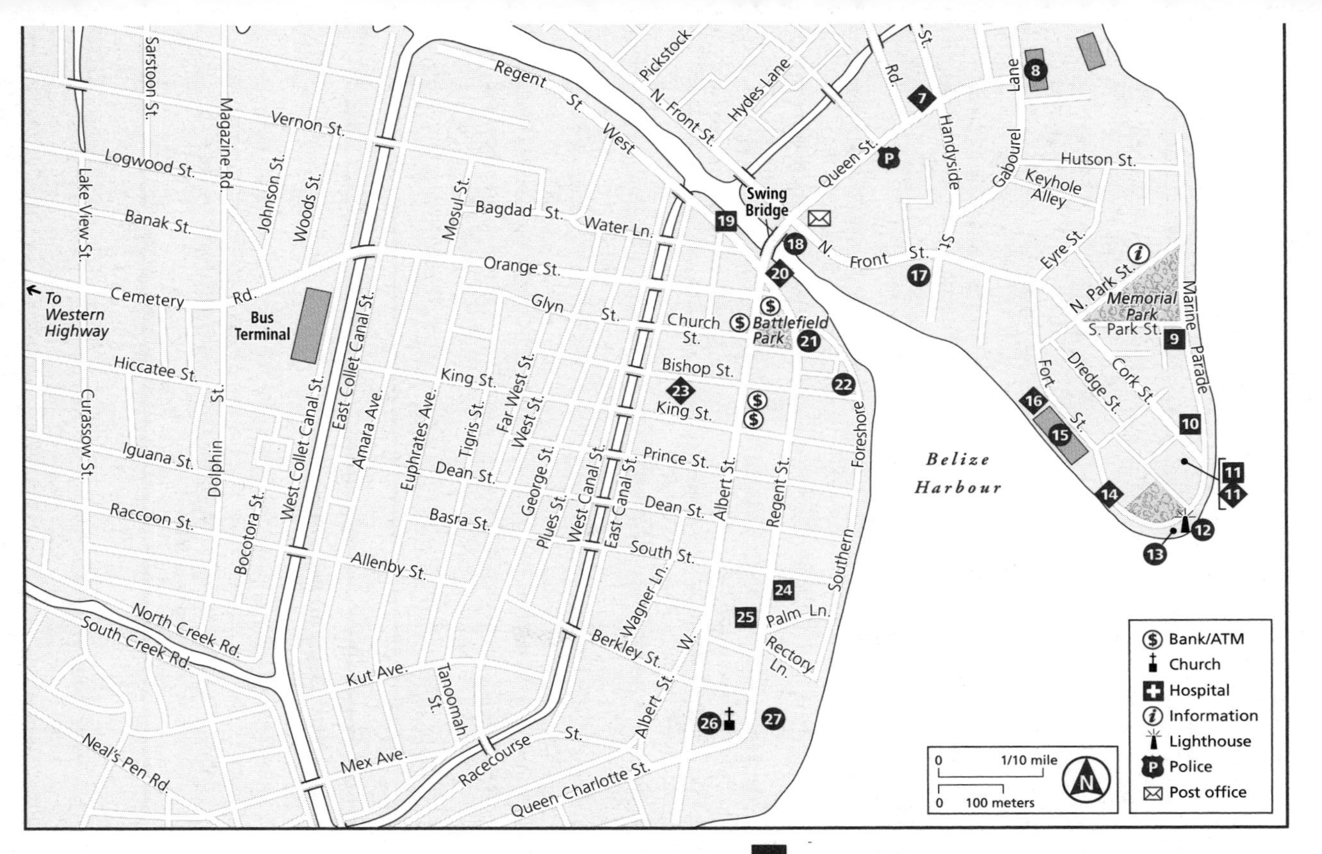
Belize Harbour
Swing Bridge
Bus Terminal
Memorial Park
Battlefield Park
To Western Highway
Regent St.
West St.
N. Front St.
Pickstock
Hydes Lane
Queen St.
Handyside St.
Gabourel Lane
Hutson St.
Keyhole Alley
Eyre St.
N. Park St.
S. Park St.
Marine Parade
Cork St.
Dredge St.
Fort St.
Rd.
Sarstoon St.
Magazine Rd.
Vernon St.
Logwood St.
Johnson St.
Woods St.
Lake View St.
Banak St.
Mosul St.
Bagdad St.
Water Ln.
Orange St.
Cemetery Rd.
Glyn St.
Church St.
Bishop St.
King St.
Prince St.
Dean St.
South St.
Albert St.
Regent St.
Foreshore
Southern
Palm Ln.
Rectory Ln.
Hiccatee St.
Curassow St.
Iguana St.
Dolphin St.
Raccoon St.
Bocotora St.
West Collet Canal St.
East Collet Canal St.
Amara Ave.
Euphrates Ave.
Tigris St.
Far West St.
West St.
George St.
Plues St.
West Canal St.
East Canal St.
Basra St.
Allenby St.
Wagner Ln.
W. Albert St.
Berkley St.
North Creek Rd.
South Creek Rd.
Kut Ave.
Tanoomah St.
Mex Ave.
Racecourse St.
Queen Charlotte St.
Neal's Pen Rd.
0 1/10 mile
0 100 meters
N
Bank/ATM
Church
Hospital
Information
Lighthouse
Police
Post office

from the northern side of the city, Freetown Road becomes Haulover Road and then the Northern Highway.

THE NEIGHBORHOODS IN BRIEF

North Side

Fort George Anchored by the Fort George Lighthouse and Radisson Fort George Hotel & Marina at the eastern tip of the city, the Fort George neighborhood encompasses the area south of Queen Street, beginning at the northern side of the Swing Bridge, until it ends at Gabourel Lane. This neighborhood is easily the most upscale and picturesque in Belize City, with stately houses and mansions, generally kept in good repair. Most of the best hotels in the city are located here. It also includes the small triangular Memorial Park and the Belize Tourism Village, as well as the lovely seaside Marine Promenade. The area was originally an island, but was deliberately connected to the mainland with landfill. This area should probably be your first choice for a stay in Belize City.

Barracks Road Located a mile or so north of downtown, Barracks Road runs along the Caribbean Sea for a good stretch before curving inland and becoming Princess Margaret Drive. This is where you'll find the Princess Hotel & Casino, as well as a couple of good restaurants. Much of the land on either side of Barracks Road is set aside as public park land, while just inland is an area that is made up mostly of modern middle-class homes. While not within easy walking distance of downtown, it's just a very short taxi ride away. The seaside setting and parks make this a relaxing option for those wanting to avoid the bustle of downtown.

South Side

Business District Belize City's downtown business district runs from the south end of the Swing Bridge between East Canal Street and Southern Foreshore Road to the aptly named South Street. In addition to a busy mix of banks and businesses, this area is home to a host of inexpensive hotels, as well as the Supreme Court and the Bliss Institute. Just south of this area, you will find the old Government House and St. John's Cathedral. This is a good option for budget travelers, but those with a little more money to spend will probably head across the river to the Fort George neighborhood.

Fun Facts Hauled Over Haulover

Haulover Creek is actually just what locals call the final few miles of the Belize River, before it joins the Caribbean Sea. It got its name as an outgrowth of common usage, as this is the area where goods and cattle used to be "hauled over" by early settlers, before a bridge was built.

2 GETTING AROUND

BY FOOT

Belize City's downtown hub is compact and easy to navigate on foot. However, the city has a rather nasty reputation for being unsafe for visitors, and you'd be wise to stick to the busiest sections of downtown and obvious tourist districts. You can easily walk the entire Fort George neighborhood, as well as the compact business area just south of the Swing Bridge. If you need to venture any further, take a taxi. Be careful when you walk, as sidewalks are often in bad shape and sometimes quite narrow. And don't walk anywhere at night, except perhaps around the downtown hub of budget hotels and restaurants and the Fort George area.

BY TAXI

Taxis are plentiful and relatively inexpensive. A ride anywhere in the city should cost between BZ$6 and BZ$14 (US$3–US$7/£1.60–£3.70). There's no standardized look or color to taxis in Belize. Many are old, gas-guzzling American models, although newer Japanese sedans are starting to appear more frequently. Most taxis are clearly marked in some form or other, usually with a roof ornament. Very few taxis use meters, so be sure to negotiate your fare in advance. If you need to call a cab, ask at your hotel or try **Belize Marine Terminal Land Taxi Association** (✆ 223-5850), **Cinderella Plaza Taxi Stand** (✆ 203-3340), **Taxi Garage Services** (✆ 227-3031), or **Majestic Taxi** (✆ 203-4465).

BY CAR

You shouldn't need to navigate Belize City in a car. If you do find yourself driving around Belize City, go slowly, as pedestrians can appear out of nowhere, and pay attention to the general flow of traffic and the wealth of one-way streets. Despite being members of a former British colony, Belizeans drive on the right-hand side of the road, and road distances are listed in miles.

Most rental car agencies are based at the Philip S. W. Goldson International Airport, although a couple have offices downtown or at the Municipal Airport, and almost all will arrange to deliver and pick up your vehicle at any Belize City hotel. The most reputable rental car agencies in Belize include: **Avis** (✆ **225-2629;** www.avis.com), **Budget** (✆ **223-2435;** www.budget-belize.com), **Crystal Auto Rental** ★ (✆ **0800/777-7777** toll-free in Belize, or 223-1600; www.crystal-belize.com), **Hertz** (✆ **223-5396;** www.hertz.com), and **Thrifty** (✆ **207-1271;** www.thrifty.com). Prices run between BZ$120 and BZ$240 (US$60–US$120/£32–£64) per day for a late-model compact to a compact SUV, including insurance. For more information on renting a car in Belize, see chapter 3.

BY BUS

While Belize has an extensive network of bus connections to most cities and rural destinations, there is no metropolitan bus system in Belize City.

Fast Facts Belize City

Airport See "Arriving," above.

American Express American Express Travel Services is represented in Belize by **Belize Global Travel Services Ltd.,** 41 Albert St. (✆ **227-7185;** www.belizeglobal.bz), which can issue traveler's checks and replacement cards, and provide other standard services. They are open Monday through Friday from 8am to noon and 1 to 5pm, and on Saturday from 8am to noon. To report lost or stolen Amex credit card or traveler's checks within Belize, call the local number above, or call collect to ✆ **336/393-1111** in the U.S.

Babysitters Your hotel front desk is your best bet for finding a babysitter.

Bookstores Bibliophiles will be disappointed in Belize. You'd be best off purchasing any specific reading material, either for pleasure or research, before arriving in the country. Many gift shops carry a small selection of locally produced fiction and poetry, as well as guidebooks and maps. One decent bookstore in Belize City was **The Book Center,** 4 Church St. (✆ **227-7457**). However, it was destroyed in a fire in March 2008, and at press time it was still unclear if, when, and where it might re-open.

Camera Repair Although your chances of having any serious repair work done are slim, your best bet for camera repair is the **Belize Photo Lab,** at the corner of North Front St. and Queen St. (✆ **223-5682**).

Car Rentals See "Getting Around," above.

Cellphones **DigiCell** (✆ **227-2017;** www.digicell.bz) has a booth at the airport. If you have an unlocked 1900MHz GSM phone, they'll sell you a local prepaid SIM chip with a local number. The chip and initial activation costs BZ$54 (US$27/£14), including BZ$10 (US$5/£2.65) of calls. You can buy subsequent minutes in the form of scratch-off cards in a variety of denominations. The SIM chips and calling cards are sold at their desk at the airport or at one of their many outlets around Belize. Their website also has information on setting up your home phone for roaming in Belize. But be careful, the rates are quite high.

Currency Exchange Most banks will exchange money for a small service charge. It is virtually unnecessary to exchange U.S. dollars for Belize dollars while in Belize, as U.S. dollars are universally accepted at the official 2-to-1 exchange rate. The exception to this is upon leaving the country, when you will want to convert your remaining Belize dollars. There is a branch of **Belize Bank** (✆ **225-2107**) at the international airport, open Monday through Friday from 8:30am to 4pm. If you are flying out on a weekend, or outside of these hours, be sure to exchange any Belize dollars beforehand.

Dentists Call your embassy, which will have a list of recommended dentists, or ask at your hotel.

Doctors Contact your embassy for information on doctors in Belize City, or see "Hospitals," below.

Drugstores There are a handful of pharmacies around Belize City. In downtown, try **Brodie James & Co. Ltd.,** Regent Street (✆ **227-7070**); it's open Monday through Friday from 8am to 6pm and Saturday from 9am to 2pm. Perhaps the best stocked pharmacy can be found at **Belize Medical Associates,** 5791 St. Thomas Kings Park (✆ **223-0303;** www.belizemedical.com); it's open Monday through Friday from 8am to 7pm and Saturday from 8am to 1pm, and it makes emergency deliveries at any hour.

Embassies & Consulates See "Fast Facts" in appendix A.

Emergencies In case of any emergency, dial ✆ **90** from anywhere in Belize City. This will connect you to the police, fire department, and ambulance central switchboard. You can also call ✆ **911.**

Express Mail Services Several international courier and express-mail services have offices in Belize City, including **DHL,** 38 New Rd. (✆ **223-4350;** www.dhl.com); **FedEx,** 1 Mapp St. (✆ **224-5221;** www.fedex.com); and **Mail Boxes Etc.,** 166 N. Front St. (✆ **227-6046;** www.mbe.com). All can arrange pickup and delivery services to any hotel in town. ***Note:*** Despite what you may be told, packages sent overnight to U.S. addresses tend to take 3 to 4 days to reach their destination.

Eyeglasses The **Hoy Eye Center** is a small nationwide chain of opticians and eyeglass stores. Their Belize City branch (✆ **223-0994**) is located at the corner of St. Thomas and St. Joseph streets.

Hospitals **Belize Medical Associates,** 5791 St. Thomas Kings Park (✆ **223-0303;** www.belizemedical.com), is a modern, 24-hour private hospital, with emergency care and numerous private-practice physicians. The city's main public hospital, the **Karl Heusner Memorial Hospital,** Princess Margaret Drive (✆ **223-1548**), is also open 24 hours and has a wide range of facilities and services.

Internet Access Internet cafes are becoming increasingly common in Belize City. Rates run between BZ$2 and BZ$10 (US$1–US$5/55p–£2.65) per hour. Most hotels listed in this chapter either have Wi-Fi or a small business center with Internet connections. You can find also Internet cafes scattered around the principal business and tourist districts of Belize City. Alternatively, **BTL** (✆ **0800/112-4636;** www.btl.net), the state Internet monopoly, sells prepaid cards in denominations of BZ$10 (US$5/£2.65), BZ$25 (US$13/£6.90), and BZ$50 (US$25/£13) for connecting your laptop to the Web via a local phone call. Some knowledge of configuring your computer's dial-up connection is necessary, and be sure to factor in the phone charge if calling from a hotel. The cards are only good for 30 days. In addition, you can buy a 24-hour period of Wi-Fi access from BTL for BZ$34 (US$17/£9), which will work at a number of hot spots around the city.

Laundry & Dry Cleaning Most folks rely on their hotel's laundry and dry cleaning services, although these can be expensive. Alternatively, you can try the **C.A. Coin Laundromat,** 114 Barrack Rd. (✆ **203-3063**), **Belize Dry Cleaners & Laundromat,** 3 Dolphin St. (✆ **227-3396**), or **Southside Coin Laundromat,** 6 Neal's Pen Rd. (✆ **207-0301**).

Maps The **Belize Tourist Board** (✆ **227-2430**) can provide you with good maps to both the city and country at either their kiosk at the international airport, or at their main office at Mile 3½ of the Northern Highway. Also, most gift shops sell maps of the country.

Newspapers & Magazines Belize has no daily newspaper. There are four primary weeklies: *Amandala,* the *Reporter, Belize Times,* and the *Guardian.* Most come out on Friday, and all are relatively similar in terms of content, although with some differing and usually obvious political leanings. A couple, most notably *Amandala* and the *Reporter,* actually publish twice weekly. *Belize First* is a periodic book-style magazine aimed at the tourist trade.

Photographic Needs While I recommend bringing as much film as you foresee needing and waiting until you return home to develop it, if you'd rather not wait, your best bet is the **Belize Photo Lab,** at the corner of North Front St. and Queen St. (✆ **223-5682**).

Police The main Belize City station is at 9 Queen St.; the Tourist Police is a division of the small force. Dial ✆ **90** or **911** in the case of emergency. You can also call ✆ **227-2222.**

Post Office The main post office (✆ **227-2201**) is located at the corner of Queen and North Front streets, across from the Swing Bridge. It costs BZ$.80 (US40¢/20p) to send a letter to the United States, and BZ$1 (US50¢/25p) to send a letter to Europe. Postcards to the same destinations cost BZ$.40 (US20¢/11p) and BZ$.50 (US25¢/15p) respectively.

Restrooms There are very few public restrooms in Belize City. The only ones I know of are located at the little cruise-ship tourist village on Fort Street in the Fort George neighborhood. However, if you're not a cruise-ship passenger, you must leave an ID at the gate and get a guest pass. Most hotels and restaurants will let travelers use their facilities, although they are happiest about providing the service to clients.

Safety Belize City has a reputation for being a rough and dangerous city. While things have improved somewhat in recent years, the reputation was earned for a reason. Tourist police do patrol the busiest tourist areas during the day and early evenings. Still, while most populous downtown areas and tourist attractions are quite safe during the daytime, travelers are strongly advised to not walk around very much at night, except in the best-lit and most popular sections of downtown. Basic common sense and street smarts are to be employed. Don't wear flashy jewelry or wave wads of cash around. Be aware of your surroundings, and avoid any people and places that make you feel uncomfortable.

Rental cars generally stick out and they are easily spotted by thieves, who know that such cars are likely to be full of expensive camera equipment, money, and other valuables. Don't ever leave anything of value in an unattended parked car.

Taxes There is a US$35 departure tax that must be paid in cash (either in U.S. or Belize dollars) at the international airport upon departure; the land exit fee is US$19. There is a 9% hotel tax added on to all hotel bills, and there is a 10% GST tax on all goods and services. A 10% service charge is sometimes added on to restaurant bills. Take this into account when deciding how much to tip (if the service is really good, an extra 5%–10% is fine).

Taxis See "Getting Around," above.

Time Zone Belize City is on Central Standard Time, 6 hours behind Greenwich Mean Time. Belize does not observe daylight saving time.

Useful Telephone Numbers For directory assistance, call ✆ **113;** for an international operator, call ✆ **115;** for the exact time, date, and temperature, call ✆ **121.**

Water The water in Belize City is ostensibly safe to drink. However, many travelers react adversely to water in foreign countries, so it's probably best to drink bottled water during your visit to Belize.

Weather The weather in Belize City is subtropical, and generally similar to that of southern Florida. The average daytime temperature is around 80°F (27°C), although it can get considerably warmer during the summer months, while during the winter months, when northern cold fronts extend their grip south, it can get downright nippy. For more details, see "When to Go" in chapter 3.

3 WHERE TO STAY

Belize City is small, and your options on where to stay are limited, especially for a capital city. The most picturesque and safest neighborhood by far is the area around the Fort George Lighthouse. Here you'll find most of the city's best shopping, dining, and accommodations. Still, since the city is so compact, and it's not really recommended to walk around anywhere at night, you're best off choosing a hotel that best meets your needs, style, and budget. There are really only three large, modern hotels in town, and they're all listed below. If your tastes tend towards smaller, more intimate lodgings, there are several good options in different price ranges to choose from.

When getting a price quote from or negotiating with a hotel in Belize, be careful to be clear whether or not you are being quoted a price in Belize or U.S. dollars. There is a 9% tax on all hotel stays in Belize, which isn't included in the rates listed below.

FORT GEORGE

Expensive

The Great House ★★ (Finds This stately, colonial-style, small hotel is aptly named. Set a block from the water, near the Fort George lighthouse, this three-story converted mansion was originally built in 1927. It has been well maintained and restored. All rooms are on either the second or third floor, and there are no elevators, if that is an issue for you. The rooms on the top floor are my favorites, with high ceilings, wood floors, and a large, shared wraparound veranda. In fact, there are wraparound verandas on both the second and third floors. While the rooms vary in size, most are very spacious; room no. 1 is one of the largest. Room no. 8 is the smallest room, but it just may have the best view. Throughout the building you'll find a mix of wicker, neo-colonial, and locally made modern wood furniture.

13 Cork St. (opposite the Radisson Fort George), Belize City. ✆ **223-3400.** Fax 223-3444. www.greathousebelize.com. 16 units. BZ$300 (US$150/£80) double. AE, DISC, MC, V. Free parking. **Amenities:** Restaurant; lounge; concierge; tour desk; small shopping arcade; laundry service; nonsmoking rooms. *In room:* A/C, TV, dataport, Wi-Fi, fridge, coffeemaker, hair dryer, safe.

Radisson Fort George Hotel & Marina ★ (Kids This is Belize City's best business-class and luxury hotel, although that's not necessarily saying a whole lot. The hotel is located in the quiet Fort George neighborhood fronting the ocean, out by the lighthouse, just 1 block from the cruise-ship tourist village. The best rooms here are located in the six-story Club Tower; those on the higher floors have the best views. All are spacious and relatively modern, and feature marble floors and plush furnishings. The Club Tower also has one junior suite on each floor. The Colonial rooms, all of which are nonsmoking, are also large and comfortable. Rooms on the ground floor come with a small, private, garden terrace, while some of those on the higher floors offer enticing ocean views. The least expensive and least attractive rooms here are the misnamed "Villas," which are located in a separate building across the street from the principal facility. While these rooms are slated for a complete remodel, I still think it's best to splurge a little for the better Club Tower or Colonial rooms. The poolside bar here is one of the more popular spots in town, and often features live music. The hotel also features a full-service marina and dive shop.

2 Marine Parade, Belize City. ✆ **800/333-3333** in the U.S., or 223-3333 in Belize. Fax 227-3820. www.radisson.com. 102 units. BZ$278–BZ$348 (US$139–US$174/£74–£92) double. Rates slightly lower in the off season. AE, DISC, MC, V. Free parking. **Amenities:** 3 restaurants; 2 bars; lounge; 2 midsize outdoor pools; small gym; concierge; tour desk; room service (6am–10:30pm); babysitting; laundry service; nonsmoking rooms. *In room:* A/C, TV, dataport, Wi-Fi, minibar, coffeemaker, hair dryer.

Moderate

Chateau Caribbean This midsize hotel is housed in an old wooden mansion set facing the sea. The rooms here are all carpeted, with double beds, modern furnishings, and cable TV. The third-floor deluxe rooms are somewhat misnamed; while they are huge and have excellent ocean views from their private balconies, I find them a bit threadbare and barren, with too much empty space. The second-floor dining room serves good, moderately priced meals of Belizean, Chinese, and international cuisine, with a wonderful view of the ocean. Some recent paint and upkeep have cheered things up here, although it's mostly cosmetic, and I still believe the hotel needs a major overhaul.

6 Marine Parade (P.O. Box 947), Belize City. ✆ **223-0800.** Fax 223-0900. www.chateaucaribbean.com. 21 units. BZ$178 (US$89/£47) double; BZ$218 (US$109/£58) deluxe. AE, MC, V. Free parking. **Amenities:** Restaurant; tour desk; laundry service. *In room:* A/C, TV, dataport.

BARRACKS ROAD

Moderate

Princess Hotel & Casino This is the largest hotel in Belize City, and the only one with a resort feel to it. The massive lobby area lets out into the hotel's casino, two movie theaters, a shopping arcade, an eight-lane bowling alley, a salon, and various restaurants and bars. The hotel is set right on the water's edge a little bit north of downtown and is built as one, long, six-story structure so that every room has an ocean view. The rooms are all large and come with either one king bed or two full-size beds, a working desk, large bathrooms, and bathrobes. The junior suites are a little bit larger and have private oceanfront balconies. The casino here is definitely one of the prime nightlife attractions in the country, although it feels increasingly seedy as the years go by. The Princess also has a full-service marina and dive shop. The Radisson is definitely more elegant and better maintained, but the Princess does have a bit more in the way of facilities and nightlife.

Barracks Rd., Belize City. ✆ **888/790-4264** in the U.S., or 223-0638 in Belize. Fax 223-3148. www.princessbelize.com. 181 units. BZ$240 (US$120/£64) double; BZ$300–BZ$600 (US$150–US$300/£80–£159) suite; BZ$1,000 (US$500/£265) presidential suite. Rates include breakfast buffet. AE, DISC, MC, V. Free parking. **Amenities:** 2 restaurants; 2 bars; lounge; large outdoor pool; fitness center; concierge; tour desk; salon; limited room service (7am–9pm); in-room massage; laundry service; nonsmoking rooms. *In room:* A/C, TV, dataport, hair dryer, safe.

BUSINESS DISTRICT

Inexpensive

Belcove Hotel *Finds* This funky canal-front hotel is my preferred budget choice in town. You just can't beat the charm of grabbing a seat on one of the upstairs balconies overlooking Haulover Creek and the Swing Bridge, especially at these prices. Sure, the rooms are simple and very basic, but they are neatly kept with shiny, varnished wood floors, while the old wooden building is kept in fresh yellow paint with blood-red trim, yet still feels weathered and historic. These folks also offer airport transfers at a better rate than the local taxis.

9 Regent St., Belize City. ✆ **227-3054.** Fax 227-5248. www.belcove.com. 12 units. BZ$64–BZ$104 (US$32–US$52/£17–£28) double. MC, V. Free street parking. *In room:* No phone.

Coningsby Inn *Value* Housed in a converted old home towards the western end of Regent Street, the rooms here are compact and rather nondescript. Still, they are clean and comfortable. I prefer those on the second floor, although don't choose one of these for the view, which is over an abandoned lot. I would definitely recommend a splurge for one of the air-conditioned rooms. There's a convivial hostel-like vibe to this operation, and the second-floor bar and lounge area is the social hub of the joint.

76 Regent St., Belize City. ✆ **227-1566.** Fax 227-3726. www.coningsby-inn.com. 10 units. BZ$100 (US$50/£27) double without A/C; BZ$120 (US$60/£32) double with A/C. MC, V. Free street parking. **Amenities:** Bar; tour desk; laundry service. *In room:* TV.

Hotel Mopan Located a block or so from the water towards the western end of Regent Street, this longstanding and humble little hotel is a good option in downtown Belize City. The rooms are clean and comfortable, and most of them have air-conditioning. It's definitely worth the slight splurge—I'd say it's necessary—for one of the air-conditioned rooms. Those on the third floor are the best, with the end units, nos. 301 and 304, the best of these. There's no true restaurant here, but breakfast is served in the large first-floor dining room and common area, which also serves as the social hub of the hotel throughout the day, and as a bar at night.

55 Regent St., Belize City. ✆ **227-7351.** Fax 227-5383. www.hotelmopan.com. 12 units. BZ$90–BZ$150 (US$45–US$75/£24–£40) double. MC, V. Free street parking. **Amenities:** Bar; tour desk; laundry service. *In room:* TV, free Wi-Fi, no phone.

AROUND TOWN

In addition to the places listed below, **D'Nest Inn** ★ (✆ **223-5416;** www.dnestinn.com) is a cute, well-run little bed-and-breakfast located about 4.8km (3 miles) outside of downtown, just off the Northern Highway.

Expensive

Best Western Belize Biltmore Plaza Located on the northern outskirts of the city, this chain hotel is simple and straightforward, but it lacks any sense of Caribbean or colonial charm. It's a decent choice if you want to be a little closer to the airport and avoid the crowds and commotion of downtown. The rooms are contemporary and comfortable, with tile floors and heavy wood furnishings. All face the hotel's central courtyard and pool area. As at the Radisson and Princess hotels, the bar here is a popular meeting place for locals, after work and on weekends.

Northern Hwy., Mile Marker 3½, Belize City. ✆ **800/698-2915** in the U.S. and Canada, or 223-2302 in Belize. Fax 223-2301. www.belizebiltmore.com. 75 units. BZ$240–BZ$320 (US$120–US$160/£64–£85) double. AE, MC, V. Free parking. **Amenities:** Restaurant; 2 bars; small outdoor pool; small gym; tour desk; limited room service (6:30am–10pm); laundry service; nonsmoking rooms. *In room:* A/C, TV, Wi-Fi, hair dryer, coffeemaker, safe.

Inexpensive

Bakadeer Inn Built in 1990, this hotel has a pleasant pseudo-Tudor exterior, although inside there's little in the way of old-world charm or character. Still, the rooms are well-kept and have cable TV. The rooms on the first floor are tiled, while those on the second floor are carpeted; I prefer the former, as the latter can get a tad musty at times. The hotel is located several blocks north of the downtown hub, in a somewhat quiet residential area. There's secure parking here, and if you don't have a car, a taxi to the city center should cost you around BZ$8 (US$4/£2.10).

74 Cleghorn St. (P.O. Box 512), Belize City. ✆ **223-0659.** www.bakadeerinn.com. 12 units. BZ$100–BZ$120 (US$50–US$60/£27–£32) double. MC, V. Free parking. **Amenities:** Nonsmoking rooms. *In room:* A/C, TV, fridge.

NEAR THE AIRPORT

The airport is located just 16km (10 miles) north of downtown Belize City, a 15- to 20-minute drive, depending on traffic. The area around the airport is decidedly undeveloped and of little interest to visitors. Few international flights arrive late enough or leave early enough to necessitate a stay near the airport. If you really want to stay just a stone's throw away from the airport, try the **Global Village Hotel** (✆ **225-2555;** fax 220-3000; globalhotel@btl.net). While large and modern, this place has virtually no atmosphere or life of its own, and there's not much else nearby either. I really recommend you take the short taxi ride into Belize City, or stay at one of the places listed below.

In addition to the place listed below, the **Belize River Lodge** (✆ **888/275-4843** in the U.S. and Canada, or 225-2002 in Belize; www.belizeriverlodge.com) is an upscale fishing lodge located on the banks of the Belize River, just a few miles from the airport, while the **Black Orchid Resort** (✆ **866/437-1301** in the U.S. and Canada, or 225-9158 in Belize; www.blackorchidresort.com) is a small resort hotel, also on the banks of the Belize River near the town of Burrell Boom.

Moderate

Villa Boscardi ★ This small and elegant bed-and-breakfast is the plushest lodging you'll find near the airport. Housed in a converted private home, the rooms here are spacious and decorated with a sense of style. Most have interesting artwork and headboard treatments over the beds. The best room here is actually a detached cottage. The hotel is located on the northern outskirts of Belize City, in a quiet neighborhood, just a block or so from the water.

6043 Manatee Dr., Buttonwood Bay, Belize City. ✆/fax **223-1691.** www.villaboscardi.com. 6 units. BZ$154 double (US$72–US$79/£38–£42). Rates include full breakfast. AE, MC, V. Free parking. **Amenities:** Tour desk; massage; laundry service; free Wi-Fi. *In room:* A/C, TV.

4 WHERE TO DINE

Despite its small size, Belize City actually has an excellent and varied selection of dining options open to visitors. While Belizean cuisine and fresh seafood are most common, you can also get excellent Chinese, Indian, and other international fare at restaurants around the city.

Note: When the cruise ships are in town, the restaurants in the Fort George area can get extremely crowded, especially for lunch.

FORT GEORGE

In addition to the places listed below, you can get good burgers and bar food at the **Bayman's Tavern** at the Radisson Fort George Hotel.

Expensive

Harbour View ★★ INTERNATIONAL This is probably the most expensive and creative restaurant in town. The menu here features some fusion touches you won't find at other Belize City restaurants. I like the Parasol of Reddened Shrimp, which are coated in an Asian-style sweet and pungent glaze and served atop a rice palau. Another excellent choice is the Picasso Pork Tenderloin, which comes with a delicious jalapeño relish. You can also get thick cuts of steak and a host of other dishes. The main dining room is a second-floor space with large picture windows opening onto Belize Harbour. However, when the weather's right, I recommend grabbing one of the outdoor tables on the wooden wraparound veranda, which will put you even closer to the water. There's often live jazz music in the evenings. During the day, they feature a more modest menu with a selection of salads and sandwiches.

Fort St., next to the Belize Tourism Village. ✆ **223-6420.** Reservations recommended. Main courses BZ$32–BZ$80 (US$16–US$40/£8.50–£21). AE, DISC, MC, V. Mon–Fri 11:30am–3pm; daily 5–11pm.

Moderate

The Smokey Mermaid ★ INTERNATIONAL I love the open-air brick courtyard setting of this semi-elegant yet relaxed restaurant. There are a couple of raised decks and gazebos and a few fountains, spread out amongst heavy wooden tables and chairs under broad canvas umbrellas in the shade of large seagrape and mango trees and a wealth of other lushly planted ferns and flowers. An equally pleasant choice for breakfast, lunch, or dinner, the menu here ranges from Jamaican jerk pork to shrimp thermidor to chicken Kiev. I recommend the yuca-crusted catch of the day. The desserts here are excellent, with their signature sweet being the Decadent Ecstasy, a chocolate-coconut pie swimming in ice cream, nuts, and chocolate sauce.

13 Cork St., in The Great House. ✆ **223-4722.** Reservations recommended. Main courses BZ$24–BZ$72 (US$12–US$36/£6.35–£19). AE, MC, V. Daily 6:30am–10pm.

Inexpensive

Le Petit Café ★ COFFEEHOUSE This place does a brisk business for breakfast, especially amongst local workers. A variety of both sweet and savory baked goods are available, as well as a wide range of coffee drinks. Most of the seating is in an open-air courtyard, under shade trees and flower-covered trellises. If you come for lunch, or even dinner, you're not bound to wash things down with a caffeinated brew; they have a small wine list. At press time, this place is slated for a remodeling and expansion, with the addition of some indoor seats.

2 Marine Parade, at the Radisson Fort George Hotel. ✆ **223-3333.** Reservations not accepted. Main courses BZ$4–BZ$16 (US$2–US$8/£1.05–£4.25). AE, MC, V. Daily 6am–8pm.

Wet Lizard ★ Finds BELIZEAN Boasting a prime setting on a second-floor covered deck overlooking the Swing Bridge and Belize City's little harbor, this raucous restaurant is one of the most popular spots in town. The menu here is simple, with an emphasis on sandwiches, burgers, and American-style bar food. Start things off with some coconut shrimp, conch fritters, or fried calamari, before tackling one of the hearty sandwiches or wraps. You can also get tacos, nachos, fajitas, and quesadillas, as well as a daily special or two. If you like sweets, save room for the banana chimichanga. The best seats here are the small tables and high stools ringing the railing and overlooking the water. Everything is painted in bright primary colors, and the walls are quickly being covered with graffiti and signatures from guests. The practice is actually encouraged, so be sure to ask for a magic marker and add to the wall art. When the cruise ships are in town, this place is overrun and even serves a separate menu, so be sure to ask for their full menu.

1 Fort St. ✆ **223-5973.** Reservations not accepted. Main courses BZ$10–BZ$24 (US$5–US$12/£2.65–£6.35). AE, MC, V. Tues–Sat 11am–9:30pm.

BARRACKS ROAD

Moderate

Jambel's Jerk Pit Too ★ CARIBBEAN/BELIZEAN With a new location, on Barracks Road, this simple, long-standing restaurant continues to serve up spicy curries and jerk concoctions, alongside local specialties. The coconut curry chicken is excellent, and there are several vegetarian options. Still, the spicy Jamaican jerk is the signature here, and you can get it served over fish, shrimp, chicken, or conch. The restaurant is housed in a two-story converted home located across the street from the water just a little way north of the Princess Hotel. The walls are painted lavender, and there are large picture windows overlooking the BTL park and harbor. When the weather's cooperative, try to grab a seat on their outdoor patio-balcony.

164 Newtown Barracks Rd. ✆ **223-1966.** Main courses BZ$12–BZ$30 (US$6–US$15/£3.20–£7.95). AE, MC, V. Daily 10am–10pm.

Sumathi ★ INDIAN Despite the very spartan decor, this is the best Indian restaurant in town. Located just up the road from the Princess Hotel, the restaurant is housed on the bottom floor of a rundown and hurricane-damaged three-story concrete monster. The menu features a wide selection of northern Indian and tandoori specialties. If you're familiar with Indian cuisine, you won't be disappointed here. And if you like it hot and spicy, you're in the right place. This is also an excellent option for vegetarians, who probably won't find as broad a selection to fit their dietary needs in any other restaurant in the city.

190 Newtown Barracks Rd. ✆ **223-1172.** Main courses BZ$10–BZ$28 (US$5–US$14/£2.65–£7.40). MC, V. Tues–Sun 11am–11pm.

BUSINESS DISTRICT

In addition to the places listed below, **Nerie's,** which has two locations (124 Freetown Rd., ✆ **224-5199;** and at the corner of Queen and Daly sts., ✆ **223-4028**) is another simple restaurant specializing in Belizean cuisine, and it's very popular with locals.

Inexpensive

Big Daddy's Diner BELIZEAN Located in the two-story concrete Belize City market, just over the Swing Bridge, Big Daddy's is a clean and comfortable cafeteria-style restaurant. A breakfast here of scrambled eggs and fry jacks is filling and inexpensive. For lunch there are always several salads, rice dishes, vegetables, and main courses to choose from, and the portions are large. There are great views of the sailboats in the river from the restaurant's big windows.

2nd floor, Commercial Center, Booth 54. ✆ **227-0932.** Main courses BZ$8–BZ$20 (US$4–US$10/£2.10–£5.30). MC, V. Mon–Sat 7am–5pm.

Macy's Finds BELIZEAN For authentic Belizean cooking and a down-home funky vibe, you can't beat this tiny local place. The food is good, the service is friendly, the prices are right, and the dining room is cool and cozy. Order a fish filet with rice and beans, or curried chicken, or be more daring and try one of their daily wild-game chalkboard specials, which could feature anything from armadillo and deer to wild pig or gibnut. Macy's no longer serves turtle or other endangered species, and there seem to be fewer wild game options than there were in the past. There are only five tables, and each is set with a plastic tablecloth and plastic place mat, under a strategically placed overhead fan.

18 Bishop St. ✆ **207-3419.** Main courses BZ$10–BZ$30 (US$5–US$15/£2.65–£7.95). No credit cards. Mon–Sat 11:30am–9pm.

AROUND TOWN

Moderate

Chon Saan Palace ★ CHINESE If you're in the mood for Chinese food in Belize City, you can't do better than this local favorite. The room and the menu are immense. You'll find plenty of chow mein and Cantonese dishes, but there's also a substantial Szechuan section and a show-stopping sizzling steak that comes hissing and screaming to your table. If you're primed for seafood, you'll love the large fish tanks stocked with live lobster (in season), shrimp, and the daily catch. This is a great place to come with a group, as there are plenty of large, round tables with built-in Lazy Susans, just perfect for sharing food and a good time. Don't take the easy way out and head to the more conveniently located New Chon Saan Palace—it's worth the short taxi ride to eat at the original.

1 Kelly St. ✆ **223-3008.** Main courses BZ$10–BZ$36 (US$5–US$18/£2.65–£9.55). MC, V. Mon–Sat 11am–3pm and 5–11:30pm (Fri–Sat until midnight or later); Sun 5–11pm.

Riverside Tavern ★★ INTERNATIONAL One of the most popular spots in Belize City, this large place has both indoor and outdoor seating on a spot overlooking Haulover Creek. The restaurant also specializes in hefty steaks and delicious ribs. But you can also get seared tuna, grilled snapper, coconut shrimp, or jerk shrimp. The lunch menu features pizzas, pastas, sandwiches, and rolls. The burgers here are rightly famous and served for both lunch and dinner. There are TVs showing sporting events, and at times this place can get quite boisterous. There's actually a bit of a dress code here: Shorts, sleeveless shirts, and sandals are discouraged after dark.

2 Mapp St. ✆ **223-5640.** Lunch BZ$15–BZ$36 (US$7.50–US$18/£4–£9.55); dinner main courses BZ$22–BZ$55 (US$11–US$23/£5.85–£12). DISC, MC, V. Tues–Wed 11am–midnight; Thurs–Fri 11am–2am; Sat noon–2am; Sun noon–midnight.

Sibun Bite Bar & Grill ★ Kids BELIZEAN/INTERNATIONAL What this restaurant lacks in creativity and fancy fare, they make up for in portion size. The servings are huge. There's an emphasis on fried foods here—chicken and shrimp are favorites. But you can also get pizzas, burritos, burgers, hot dogs, and buffalo wings. The best seats are on the long, open-air deck fronting the lagoon here. This is a great spot for lunch. It's also a great spot to bring the kids, as it's part of the Old Belize complex, with an attached museum, beach, and children's play area.

Western Hwy., Mile 5. ✆ **222-4286.** www.oldbelize.com. Main courses BZ$12–BZ$50 (US$6–US$25/£3.20–£13). AE, MC, V. Sun–Thurs 11am–9pm; Fri–Sat 11am–10pm.

5 WHAT TO SEE & DO

There really isn't much reason to take a guided tour of Belize City. The downtown center is extremely compact and lends itself very easily to self-directed exploration. There are only a handful of interesting attractions, and all are within easy walking distance of the central Swing Bridge. Below you'll find reviews of the most interesting attractions, as well as a walking tour of the city.

If you really feel the need for a guided tour of the city, ask at your hotel desk for a recommendation, or call **Discovery Expeditions** (✆ **223-0748;** www.discoverybelize.com) or **S & L Travel and Tours** (✆ **227-7593;** www.sltravelbelize.com). A half-day city tour should cost around BZ$80 to BZ$100 (US$40–US$50/£21–£27) per person, but can easily be combined with a visit to one of the several popular nearby attractions. All the above companies offer a whole range of day trips and combinations to the attractions close to the city and even further afield (see "Attractions Outside Belize City," below, and "Side Trips from Belize City," later in this chapter).

THE TOP ATTRACTIONS

Belize City is very light on true attractions. The museums mentioned below are quite quaint and provincial by most international standards, although they are worth a visit if you are spending a day getting to know the city, residents, and local history.

Bliss Institute of Performing Arts ★ Totally rebuilt and reopened in 2005, the Bliss Institute is a busy little complex that is the cultural heart of Belize City. Housing a performing arts space, rehearsal halls, a cafeteria, the National Institute of the Arts, and a couple of gallery spaces, this is the place to check for live theater, dance, and music performances while you're in town. It's also a good place to stop and see if there's an interesting exhibit of art or photography. The main building's circular design takes advantage of the complex's setting, with large picture windows overlooking the Belize Harbour. The gallery spaces are fairly small, so you will only need about a half-hour, possibly less, to tour the institute.

Southern Foreshore, between Church and Bishop sts. ✆ **227-2110.** Free admission. Mon–Sat 8:30am–5pm.

The Image Factory ★ This is Belize City's top art gallery. With a large stable of local and regional artists to choose from, this non-profit gallery and arts organization has regularly rotating exhibitions, as well as a semi-permanent collection of art, photography, sculpture, and craft works.

91 North Front St. ✆ **223-4093.** www.imagefactory.bz. Free admission. Mon–Fri 9am–5pm.

Museum of Belize Housed in what was once "Her Majesty's Prison," this museum features a collection of historical documents, photographs, currency, stamps, and other artifacts, as well as exhibits of Mayan pottery and archaeological finds. Although somewhat small, the collection of Mayan ceramic, jade, and both ornamental and functional pieces is worth the price of admission. There are also traveling exhibits, and a room featuring attractively mounted insects from Belize. Just so you won't forget the building's history, a prison cell has been restored to its original condition. The museum takes up the two floors of this historic old brick building. Plan on spending between 1 and 2 hours here.

Gabourel Lane, in front of the Central Bank building. ✆ **223-4524.** Admission BZ$10 (US$5/£2.65) for adults, BZ$4 (US$2/£1) for students, free for children. Mon–Fri 9am–5pm.

Fun Facts Swingin'

The Swing Bridge officially opens twice a day, at 6am and 5:30pm Monday through Saturday, to let tall masted sailboats pass through. However, if there's no demand, it doesn't open. When it does, the entire process takes around 20 minutes, and in addition to being a minor spectacle, it is a major traffic hassle.

Old Belize ★★ Kids This attraction aims at providing a comprehensive experience of the natural, cultural, and political history of Belize, with exhibits recreating everything from a rainforest, to a Mayan ceremonial cave, to a logging camp, to a Garífuna home. Admission includes a 45-minute guided tour, but you'll probably want to stay longer to explore some exhibits on your own, visit the gift shop, or eat at the restaurant here (p. 101). There's even a pretty decent little beach here, with a waterslide and children's playground area, and separate zip-line cable adventure. Plan on spending between 1 and 2 hours here—more if you're going to eat or hang out at the beach. While certainly touristy, if you only have a limited amount of time in Belize City, or the country in general, this place does give a good overview.

Western Hwy., Mile 5. ✆ **222-4286.** www.oldbelize.com. Admission to full-access package BZ$30 (US$15/£7.95) adults, BZ$15 (US$7.50/£4) for children 6–12; just to museum BZ$5 (US$2.50/£1.40) adults, BZ$3 (US$1.50/80p) children. Tues–Sat 8am–4pm; Sun–Mon 10am–4pm.

St. John's Cathedral ★ This old brick church is the oldest Anglican cathedral in Central America, and the oldest standing structure in Belize. Built in 1812 by slaves using bricks brought over as ballast, it is also the only Anglican church outside of England where kings have been crowned—during the 1800s four Mosquito Indian kings held their coronation ceremonies here.

At the corner of Albert and Regent sts. ✆ **227-2137.** Free admission. Daily 8:30am–5pm.

A WALKING TOUR

The following walking tour covers both the north and south sides of Belize City, which together comprise the entire historic downtown center. For most of its length, you'll be either right on the water or just a block or two away. As described, the walking tour should take you anywhere from 2 to 4 hours, depending on how much time you take visiting the various attractions. The only major attraction not right on the route below is the Museum of Belize, although it's only a 4-block detour east from the Swing Bridge. The route laid out on this walking tour is pretty safe during daylight hours, but should not be attempted after dark.

Begin your stroll at the **Fort George Lighthouse** and **Baron Bliss Memorial,** out on the northeastern tip of the city. A small slate stone marks the grave of Henry Edward Ernest Victor Bliss (see "Baron Bliss" on p. 104). After soaking up the view of the Caribbean and some fresh sea air, head towards downtown on Fort Street. On your left, you'll find the **Belize Tourism Village** (✆ **223-2767**), which was built to accommodate the rising tide of cruise-ship passengers. Stop in and shop, or just browse the variety of local and regional arts and crafts. ***Note:*** If you're not a cruise-ship passenger, you'll have to leave a photo ID at the gate in exchange for a temporary pass to visit the shops and restaurants here.

Baron Bliss

Henry Edward Ernest Victor Bliss, the fourth Baron Bliss of the Kingdom of Portugal, anchored his yacht, *Sea King,* off of Belize City on January 14, 1926. Within 2 months, the baron would be dead, never having set foot on Belizean soil. Nonetheless, the eccentric Baron Bliss is this tiny country's most beloved benefactor. His time spent anchored in Belize Harbour was enough to convince him to rewrite his will and leave a large chunk of his estate—nearly $2 million at the time—to the country of Belize (then known as British Honduras). The trust he set up stipulated that the principal could never be touched, and only the interest was to be used. The ongoing bequest has funded numerous public works projects around the country, and today it's hard to miss the baron's legacy. There's the Baron Bliss Memorial, Baron Bliss Nursing School, Bliss Institute, and the Bliss (Fort George) Lighthouse. Every year on March 9, a large regatta is held in Belize Harbour in honor of the baron.

As you continue, Fort Street becomes North Front Street. Just north of the Belize Tourism Village you'll find **Fine Arts** (p. 108) and **The Image Factory** (p. 102), by far the two best galleries and fine arts gift shops in the country. Just before reaching the Swing Bridge, you'll pass a busy section of street that includes the vacant lot that once housed the famous **Paslow Building.** Thomas Paslow was a 19th-century Bayman who was a feared and hated slave owner and figured prominently in the 1878 Battle of St. George's Caye. The old wooden Paslow Building was burned down in a 2002 fire. Across the street, you'll find the **Maritime Terminal.**

Now, cross the **Swing Bridge** and head south. On your left is the **Commercial Center.** Wander through the stalls of fresh vegetables, butcher shops, and fish stands. You'll also find some gift shops and souvenir stands here.

The **Supreme Court building,** off the small **Battlefield Park** (or Market Square) just a block south of the Swing Bridge, is a real prize of English colonial architecture with the city's only clock tower. Walk around the four sides and see if any are accurately telling the time.

Down at the southern end of Regent Street, you'll find the **Government House** and **St. John's Cathedral** (p. 103), also known by its more officious-sounding moniker, the Anglican Cathedral of St. John the Baptist. Both of these buildings were constructed with slave labor in the early 19th century, and they remain the most prominent reminders of the 3 centuries of British colonial presence here. The Government House has been converted into a **House of Culture** (✆ **227-3050**), with the mission of encouraging and sponsoring local participation in the arts, music, and dance.

For your return to downtown, head towards the water and come back on the Southern Foreshore Road, stopping in at the **Bliss Institute** (p. 102) to see if there's an interesting exhibit on display or a performance scheduled for later in the evening.

ATTRACTIONS OUTSIDE BELIZE CITY

The attractions listed below are within an hour of Belize City; both can be reached by public transportation. In addition, the Mayan ruins of **Altun Ha** ★ and **Lamanai** ★★

and the **Crooked Tree Wildlife Sanctuary** ★ are all easily accessible from Belize City. All are popularly sold as day tours, often in various mix-and-match combinations. If you're interested in visiting one or more of these attractions as part of an organized tour, ask at your hotel, or call **Action Belize** (✆ 223-2987; www.actionbelize.com), **Discovery Expeditions** (✆ 223-0748; www.discoverybelize.com), or **S & L Travel and Tours** (✆ 227-7593; www.sltravelbelize.com). Prices range from about BZ$100 to BZ$280 (US$50–US$140/£27–£74) per person, depending on the tour, means of transportation, and the attraction(s) visited. Tours, especially those to Altun Ha and Crooked Tree, are often combined with lunch and an optional spa treatment at Maruba Resort Jungle Spa. For more information on Altun Ha, Lamanai, Crooked Tree Wildlife Sanctuary, and Maruba Resort Jungle Spa, see chapter 9.

BELIZE ZOO ★★ Founded in 1983 as part of a last-ditch and improvised effort to keep and care for a host of wild animals that were being used in a documentary film shoot, the **Belize Zoo,** Western Highway, Mile Marker 29 (✆ **220-8003;** www.belizezoo.org), is a national treasure. Gentle paths wind through some 12 hectares (29 acres) of land, where the zoo houses over 125 animals, all native Belizean species. According to their own promotional materials, "The zoo keeps animals which were either orphaned, born at the zoo, rehabilitated animals, or sent to the Belize Zoo as gifts from other zoological institutions."

Walking around the zoo, you'll see several species of Belizean cats, April the tapir, and other wild animals in idealized natural surroundings. The animals here are some of the liveliest and happiest looking that I've ever seen in a zoo. It's obvious that they're well cared for. All the exhibits have informative hand-painted signs accompanying them. It's best to visit early in the morning or close to closing time, when the animals are at their most active and the Belizean sun is at its least oppressive.

The entrance is a couple of hundred yards in from the Western Highway. Any bus traveling between Belize City and Belmopan or San Ignacio will drop you off at the zoo entrance. Admission is BZ$16 (US$8/£4.25) for adults and BZ$8 (US$4/£2.10) for children, and the zoo is open daily from 8am to 5pm.

Adjacent to the zoo is a sister project, the **Belize Zoo Jungle Lodge** (✆ **220-8003**). Set on 34 hectares (84 acres) of untouched savannah, the center has a nature trail, observation platform, classroom, and some simple guest rooms. An overnight stay here costs between BZ$60 and BZ$144 (US$30–US$72/£16–£38) per person, including hotel taxes, breakfast, and dinner. While most of the beds here are in dormitory-style rooms, a couple of private cabins are definitely worth the extra dollars. Folks who stay here can take a nocturnal tour of the zoo for BZ$30 (US$15/£7.95).

COMMUNITY BABOON SANCTUARY ★ There aren't really baboons in Belize; this is just the local name for the black howler monkeys who reside in this innovative sanctuary. The sanctuary is a community program run by local landowners in eight villages to preserve the local population of these vociferous primates. The howlers found here are an endangered endemic subspecies found only in Belize. There's a visitor's center (✆ **220-2181**) and natural history museum in the village of Bermudian Landing, and it is here that you pay your BZ$10 (US$5/£2.65) admission fee, which includes a short guided hike. If you want a longer guided hike, you should hire one of the many local guides for a modest fee. The preserve stretches for some 32km (20 miles) along the Belize River, and there are several trails that wind through farmland and secondary forest. You will undoubtedly hear the whooping and barking of the howler monkeys as they make their way through the treetops feeding on fruits, flowers, and leaves. In addition to the nearly

1,500 howler monkeys that make their home in the sanctuary, there are also numerous other bird and mammal species to be spotted here. With your guide's help, you should be able to spot the monkeys and, if you're lucky, any combination of peccaries, anteaters, pacas, and coati-mundi. Bring binoculars if you have them.

At the visitor's center, you can also hire a canoe for a leisurely paddle and float on the Belize River. The cost is around BZ$50 (US$25/£13) per person. Finally, the several small villages that comprise the conservation project are wonderful examples of rural Creole villages. Be sure to visit one or two, stroll around, talk to the residents, and see what kind of craftwork and food you can find. In each village, there are families that rent out simple rooms. Ask at the museum and information center, or reserve in advance via their website at **www.howlermonkeys.org**.

Bermudian Landing village, site of the sanctuary's visitor center, is about 32km (20 miles) west of Belize City. If you are driving, head north on the Northern Highway and watch for the Burrel Boom Road turnoff. Buses to Bermudian Landing leave Belize City several times a day. Call the sanctuary's visitor's center (see above) for current schedule and departure point. The one-way fare is BZ$5 (US$2.50/£1.35).

6 OUTDOOR ACTIVITIES

Due to the crime, chaos, and often oppressive heat and humidity, you'll probably want to get out of the city, or on to the water, before undertaking anything too strenuous. But if you want to brave the elements, there are a few outdoor activities for you to try in and around Belize City. See chapter 5 for more info on adventure sports in Belize.

CAVING The **Caves Branch ★★★** region is about a 50- to 90-minute drive from Belize City, depending on where you enter the cave systems. Several tour operators offer a variety of hiking and tubing trips through an extensive network of caves here. I recommend hiking because it allows more time for close examination of the formations and Mayan relics than tubing. The **Crystal Cave,** located adjacent to the Jaguar Paw Jungle Resort, is one of the more spectacular caves you will ever visit, with numerous stalactites, stalagmites, and pillars encrusted with the glimmering quartz crystals that give the cave its name. The **Caves Branch River** is a slow, meandering river that should probably be called a creek. Nevertheless, it passes through a series of long caves, making it perfect for a slow float on an inner tube through a dark and mysterious world. Most tour operators and tour desks in Belize City can arrange these trips, or you can call **Jaguar Paw Jungle Resort** (**✆ 820-2023;** www.jaguarpaw.com) or **Ian Anderson's Caves Branch Adventure Company** (**✆ 822-2800;** www.cavesbranch.com) directly. See "Belmopan" in chapter 10 for more information on the Caves Branch region.

FISHING While most serious fishermen head to one of the cayes or southern Belize destinations, it's possible to line up fishing charters out of Belize City. The marinas at the **Radisson Fort George Hotel & Marina** (**✆ 223-3333**), **Old Belize** (**✆ 222-4129**) and **Princess Hotel & Casino** (**✆ 223-2670**) all have regular sport charter fleets and can arrange a variety of options. You could also check in with the folks at the **Belize River Lodge** (**✆ 225-2002;** www.belizeriverlodge.com). Expect to pay around US$1,200 to US$1,800 (£636–£954) per day for a boat that can accommodate up to four fishermen.

GOLF & TENNIS Your options are limited if you want to play golf or tennis in Belize. There's only one regulation golf course in Belize and it's located on Caye Chapel, a little island in the middle of the Caribbean Sea. Luckily, Caye Chapel is only a 30-minute water taxi ride or an even shorter commuter flight from Belize City. The course at the **Caye Chapel Island Resort** (✆ **226-8250;** www.cayechapel.com) is flat and often very windy. Still it's rather gorgeous, with stunning views, plenty of water and sand hazards, and the ocean bordering the entire length of many holes. Nonguests on Caye Chapel can play the course with advance reservations only. The rate is US$150 (£80) per person per day for unlimited golf, cart, clubs, and use of the resort's pools and beach.

There are no public tennis courts in Belize City, and none of the major hotels have courts.

JOGGING Belize City is not very amenable to jogging. If you must run, you could try a loop around the Fort George neighborhood, hugging the coast from the Fort George Lighthouse to Memorial Park, then heading to Fort Street, which will bring you back to the lighthouse. It's best to jog very early, before there's much street traffic and before it gets too hot. Another nice stretch for jogging is on the sidewalk and parks that line Barracks Road where it fronts the sea.

SAILING The waters off Belize Harbour are theoretically perfect for day sailing excursions, although currently no one is consistently offering this option. The two main charter companies, **The Moorings** and **TMM Charters,** are both based outside of Belize City, the former in Placencia, the latter in both Placencia and San Pedro. However, if you're interested in trying to line up a day sail, ask at your hotel desk or check in with the marinas at the **Radisson Fort George Hotel & Marina** (✆ **223-3333**), **Old Belize** (✆ **222-4129**), and **Princess Hotel & Casino** (✆ **223-2670**). See chapters 7 and 8 for details on longer charter options.

SCUBA DIVING & SNORKELING The Belize Barrier Reef lies just off the coast from Belize City. It's a short boat ride to some excellent scuba diving and snorkeling. While most serious divers chose to stay out on one of the cayes for really close proximity to the reefs, it is still possible to visit any number of excellent sites on day trips from Belize City, including the Blue Hole and Turneffe and Lighthouse atolls. Check in with **Hugh Parkey's Belize Dive Connection** (✆ **223-5086;** www.belizediving.com).

SPAS & GYMS **Best Western Belize Biltmore Plaza** (p. 97) and **Princess Hotel & Casino** (p. 96) have small gym facilities and offer basic spa services. However, neither of these hotels allows nonguests use of their facilities.

If your hotel doesn't offer massage and you want some pampering, check in with the folks at **Oltsil Day Spa** (✆ **223-7722;** oltsil@yahoo.com), which is located on Barracks Road about 2 blocks south of the Princess Hotel & Casino.

SWIMMING A few of the higher-end hotels in Belize City have pools. Of these, **Radisson Fort George Hotel & Marina** (✆ **223-3333**), is your best bet, allowing nonguests to use their pool facilities for BZ$10 (US$5/£2.65) per day.

Alternatively, you can head out to the **Cucumber Beach** ★ at Old Belize (p. 103). The beach here has both an open-water section and an enclosed, and hence calmer, lagoon. There's also a waterslide and children's playground, as well as chaise lounges and palm-thatch shade shelters. Admission is BZ$5 (US$2.50/£1.35) for beach access, and BZ$10 (US$5/£2.65) for both the beach and waterslide privileges. Children are half-price.

7 SHOPPING

You won't be bowled over by shopping options here in Belize City, and very few people come to Belize specifically to shop. You will find a modest handicraft industry, with different specialties produced by the country's various ethnic communities. The Creole populations of the coastal area and outer cayes specialize in coral and shell jewelry, as well as woodcarvings with maritime (dolphins, turtles, and ships) themes. The Belizean Mayan population produces replicas of ancient petroglyphs and different modern designs on varying sized pieces of slate. Finally, the Garífuna peoples of the southern coastal villages are known for their small dolls.

My favorite gift item in Belize continues to be **Marie Sharp's Hot Sauce ★★**, which comes in several heat gradations, as well as some new flavors. The original blend of habanero peppers, carrots, and vinegar is one of my all-time favorite hot sauces. The company also produces mango chutney and an assortment of pepper jams. You can pick up Marie Sharp products at any supermarket and most gift shops; I recommend you stick to the supermarkets, though, to avoid price gouging. In addition to Marie Sharp's, Lizette's brand of hot sauces is also a good bet.

Please do not buy any kind of sea-turtle products (including jewelry); wild birds; lizard, snake, or cat skins; corals; or orchids (except those grown commercially). No matter how unique, beautiful, insignificant, or inexpensive it may seem, your purchase will directly contribute to the further hunting of endangered species.

THE SHOPPING SCENE

Most shops in the downtown district are open Monday through Saturday from about 8am to 6pm. Some shops close for lunch, while others remain open (it's just the luck of the draw for shoppers). Since the cruise ships are such a big market for local merchants, many adjust their hours to specifically coincide with cruise-ship traffic and their particular shore times.

SHOPPING A TO Z

Art

Fine Arts ★★ This is the best gallery and gift shop I've found in Belize. They have a large selection of original art works in a variety of styles, formats, and sizes. Browse primitivist works by Walter Castillo and Pen Cayetano, alongside more modern abstract pieces, traditional still lifes, and colorful representations of Belize's marine, natural, and human life. 1 Fort St., next to the Belize Tourism Village. ✆ **223-7773.** www.fineartsbelize.com.

The Image Factory Shop ★ Attached to the excellent gallery and exhibition space of the same name, this shop offers up prints, paintings, photographs, and craft pieces by prominent Belizean and regional artists, as well as books, music CDs, and more traditional souvenir items. 91 North Front Street. ✆ **223-4093.** www.imagefactory.bz,

Handicrafts & Souvenirs

By far the largest selection of gift shops and souvenir stands can be found at the **Belize Tourism Village** (8 Fort St.; ✆ 223-2767).

In addition to housing the best collections of fine art for sale in the city, **Fine Arts** and **The Image Factory Shop** (see "Art," above) also feature some of the best handicrafts and handmade jewelry. The quality and selection are a definite step above what you'll find at most other gift shops and tourist traps in town, and around the country.

Belize Handicrafts & Gift Center This place features the wooden sculptures of Stephen Okeke. Okeke works in both large and small formats, in one-off and commissioned designs. He carves wood directly, but also puts out limited editions of molded pieces made from a combination of sawdust and resin. The gallery also carries a wide selection of mass-produced wooden sculptures and craft items, as well as a smaller collection of assorted local crafts and jewelry, books, and of course hot sauces. 24 Albert Street. ✆ **227-0565.**

Go-Tees ★ This longstanding design and production company has moved to a larger facility and shop on the northern outskirts of the city. The shop and factory produces and carries an extensive collection of T-shirts, visored hats, and local textiles. They also sell a range of handmade jewelry, Guatemalan textiles, Mexican hammocks, and Belizean crafts. 6238 Park Ave., Buttonwood Bay. ✆ **223-4660.** www.gotees.net.

National Handicraft Center This place still houses a wide selection of local and regional crafts and souvenirs all under one roof, but it's no longer the main game in town. In fact, it's lost a lot of its luster and traffic to the Belize Tourism Village. Still, you'll find a decent selection of Mayan stone carvings, coconut shell jewelry, and wooden knickknacks, as well as some oil paintings, prints, and a small selection of books. Moreover, the prices here are slightly better than those at the Belize Tourism Village, and if you see something you really like, you might even be able to bargain for it. 2 S. Park St. ✆ **223-3636.**

Jewelry

Coral is a very delicate, rapidly disappearing living organism that grows very slowly; please avoid buying coral jewelry, as it just feeds demand and inevitably leads to the destruction of the spectacular Belizean reefs.

Maya Jade ★ This place bills itself as a museum and gallery, and while there is a whole room of museum-style displays explaining the history of Mesoamerican Mayan jade use and artistry, this is nonetheless predominantly a retail operation. That said, the small selection here includes some very well done necklaces and earrings that you won't find elsewhere. 8 Fort St. ✆ **203-1222.**

Liquor

Your best bet for liquor shopping is at local supermarkets, or the duty-free shop at the airport. There are several brands of Belizean rum available; the most popular is **One Barrel,** which has a hint of coconut and vanilla. Other brands produce some more heavily flavored coconut rums. The **Prestige** brand aged rum is pretty good, if you're looking for a straight, dry rum. Belize doesn't produce any wines or other spirits of note, although you may want to pick up a bottle of locally produced wine, or cashew wine, for the sake of novelty.

Markets

The only real market of note is the **Commercial Center** located just over the Swing Bridge, on the southern side of the city. This two-story modern concrete structure houses a mix of stalls and enclosed storefronts. The first floor is predominantly devoted to fresh produce, fish stalls, and butcher shops, but you'll also find stands selling flowers, fresh herbs, and some souvenir shops. There are more souvenir shops and some restaurants, including Big Daddy's, on the second floor. The Commercial Center is open daily from 7:30am to 5pm.

Music

Punta Rock is the most Belizean of music styles. A close cousin to soca and calypso, Punta is upbeat dance music. Popular proponents include Andy Palacios, Chico Ramos, Pen Cayetano, the Garífuna Kids, Travesia Band, and Peter Flores (aka Titiman). For a taste of traditional Creole folk music, try to track down a copy of *Mr. Peters' Boom & Chime.* You also might be able to find some traditional Garífuna music, which tends to be ceremonial dance music, very similar to traditional West African music.

The best place to find Belizean music is a gift shop. Still, these are very hit or miss. Check at the **Belize Tourism Village** (p. 104). You might also try online music stores; two good sources are **www.stonetreerecords.com** and **www.calabashmusic.com**. I'd avoid the various vendors selling bootleg cassettes and CDs on the side of the road, since the quality can be sketchy, and the artists don't receive a dime.

8 BELIZE CITY AFTER DARK

Again, Belize City is a small, provincial city in an underdeveloped country, so don't expect to find a raging nightlife scene. The most popular nightspots—for both locals and visitors alike—are the bars at the few high-end hotels in town.

THE PERFORMING ARTS

It's really the luck of the draw as to whether or not you can catch a concert, theater piece, or dance performance—they are the exception, not the norm. To find out if anything is happening, ask at your hotel, read the local papers, or check in with the **Bliss Institute** (© **227-2110**).

THE BAR SCENE

The bar and club scene in Belize City is rather lackluster. The most happening bar in town is the **Riverside Tavern** ★ (p. 101). This is especially true on weekends, and whenever there's an important soccer, basketball, or cricket match on.

Travelers and locals alike also tend to frequent the bars at the major hotels and tourist traps. The liveliest of these are the bars at the **Radisson Fort George Hotel & Marina** (p. 95), the **Best Western Belize Biltmore Plaza** (p. 97), and the **Princess Hotel & Casino** (p. 96), all of which often have a live band on weekend nights. Of these, I prefer the **Club Calypso** ★ (© **223-2670**), an open-air affair built over the water at the Princess Hotel & Casino, although it's sort of a crapshoot as to which bar will be hopping on any given night.

CASINOS

For gaming, the **Princess Hotel & Casino** (p. 96) is the only game in town, and the casino here is large, modern, and well equipped. While it's not on the scale of Vegas or Atlantic City, the casino is certainly respectable, with enough gaming tables, slots, and other attractions to make most casual gamblers quite happy to drop a few dollars.

9 SIDE TRIPS FROM BELIZE CITY

Given the fact that Belize is so small, it is possible to visit any of the country's major tourist destinations and attractions as a side trip from Belize City. Most are easily reached in less than 2 hours by car, bus, or boat taxi. Other attractions are accessible by short commuter flights. All in all, you can visit almost any destination or attraction described in this book as a day trip, except for the far southern zone.

For a listing of active adventures that make good day trips, see "Outdoor Activities," earlier in this chapter; for a description of the most popular attractions within close proximity to Belize City, see "What to See & Do," earlier in this chapter. Other possible destinations for side trips out of Belize City include **Caye Caulker** and **Ambergris Caye,** dive excursions to the nearby reefs, and even to the more isolated dive destinations like the **Blue Hole** and the **Lighthouse** and **Turneffe atolls ★★**. You can also visit the Mayan ruins of **Altun Ha, Lamanai, Xunantunich, Cahal Pech,** and even **Caracol** and **Tikal.** All of the popular side-trip destinations out of Belize City are discussed in more depth in "What to See & Do," earlier in this chapter, or in the subsequent destination chapters.

Most hotels can arrange any of the day trips suggested above. In addition, you can check in with **Discovery Expeditions** (**© 223-0748;** www.discoverybelize.com) or **S & L Travel and Tours** (**© 227-7593;** www.sltravelbelize.com). ***Note:*** Most of the tours and activities mentioned here and in "Outdoor Activities," earlier in this chapter, are also sold to visiting cruise-ship passengers. When the cruise ships are in town, a cave tubing adventure, snorkel trip to Hol Chan Marine Reserve and Shark-Ray Alley, or a visit to either Altun Ha or Lamanai ruins can be a mob scene. It's often possible to avoid these crowds by starting your tour or activity very early, or in the late afternoon. If you are organizing your tour or activity with a local operator, mention that you want to avoid the cruise-ship groups, if at all possible.

7

The Northern Cayes & Atolls

The cayes (pronounced "keys") are series of small islands strung along the length of the Belize Barrier Reef, set amidst waters that are at once crystal clear and brilliantly turquoise. Seen firsthand, there's something truly mesmerizing and almost unbelievable about the clarity and color of this water. But as they say around here: "You betta Belize it."

With the reef providing protection from the open ocean, the cayes are literally islands of tranquillity in a calm blue sea. Aside from sunbathing and slow strolling, scuba diving, snorkeling, and fishing are the main attractions in the cayes. They are all world class. From the bustling miniresorts of **Ambergris Caye** to the funky Rastafarian charm of tiny **Caye Caulker** to the deserted-isle feel of the **Turneffe Islands** and **Lighthouse Reef atolls ★★**, it's the idyllic combination of sun and sea, as well as adventure and relaxation, that attract and captivate most visitors to Belize. Most of the cayes are small enough to walk from one end to the other in under 20 minutes. On others, it won't take you nearly as long.

Jacques Cousteau put Belize on the diving map back in 1971, with his explorations of the **Blue Hole.** The country has almost 322km (200 miles) of continuous barrier reefs and visibility of up to 61m (200 ft.) on some days. It's hard to open a diving magazine without finding an article on diving in Belize. For those sticking a little closer to the surface, the snorkeling is just as rewarding, with **Hol Chan Marine Reserve** and **Shark-Ray Alley** considered two of the best snorkeling experiences on the planet.

On the plentiful flats found inside the reefs and up in nearby estuaries, anglers find action with tarpon, snook, permit, and feisty bonefish. There's more tarpon as well as giant snapper and grouper found along the reefs, while out on the open ocean the tackle and game get bigger, with marlin, sailfish, tuna, and wahoo as the principal prey.

1 AMBERGRIS CAYE ★★

58km (36 miles) N of Belize City; 64km (40 miles) SE of Corozal Town

San Pedro is Belize's principal sun-and-fun destination. The compact "downtown" area is a jumble of small hotels, souvenir shops, restaurants, dive shops, and tour agencies. Though San Pedro continues to attract primarily scuba divers and fishermen, it is today popular with a wide range of folks who like the slow-paced atmosphere, including an increasing number of snowbirds, expatriates, and retirees. While certainly not akin to big city traffic, golf carts and automobiles are proliferating on Ambergris Caye and constantly force pedestrians and bicycle riders to the sides of the road. In fact, the ongoing boom here has actually led to gridlock. During the busy parts of the day, the downtown area of San Pedro is a jumble of golf carts, cars, bicycles, and pedestrians all moving at a rather slow pace. As a separate byproduct of the boom, wooden Caribbean houses are giving way to concrete and cinder-block buildings, and even a small strip mall or two.

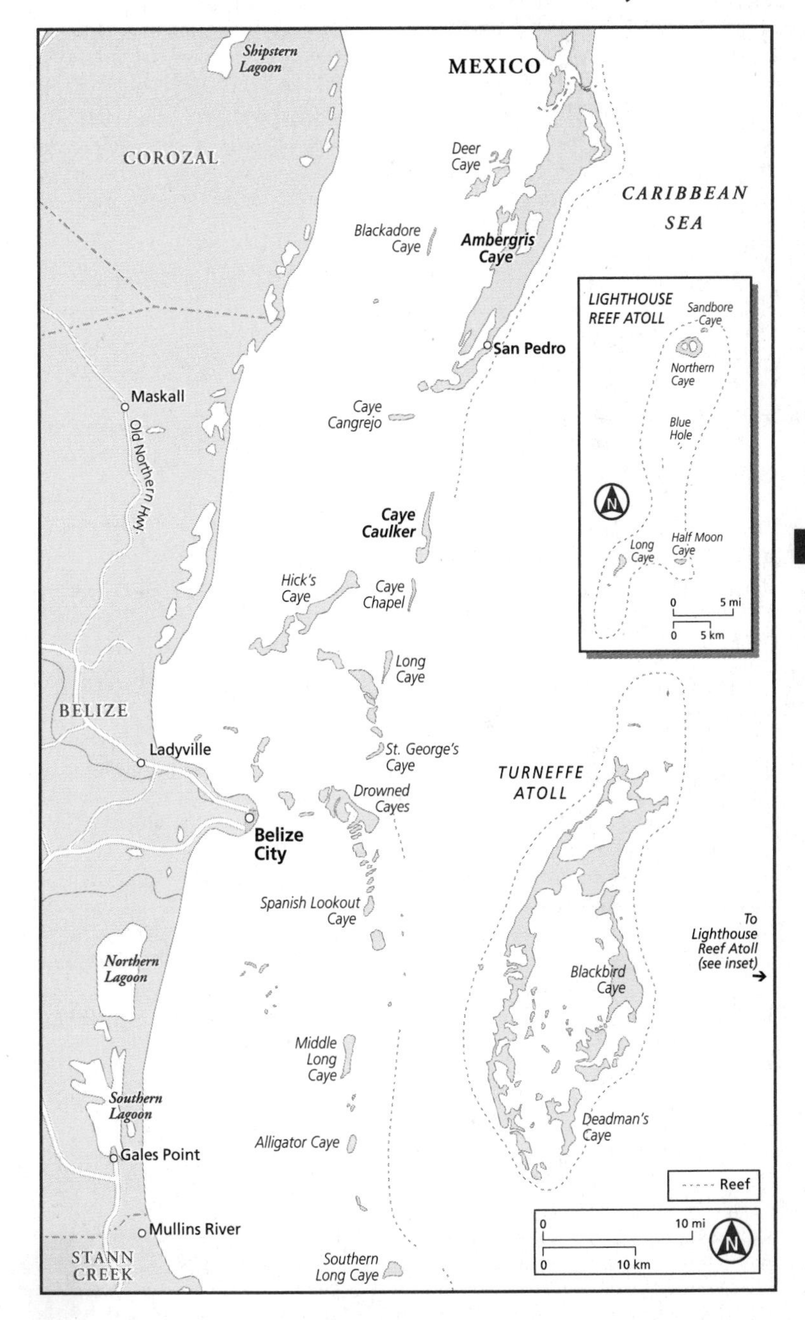
Shipstern Lagoon
MEXICO
COROZAL
Deer Caye
CARIBBEAN SEA
Blackadore Caye
Ambergris Caye
LIGHTHOUSE REEF ATOLL
Sandbore Caye
Northern Caye
Blue Hole
Long Caye
Half Moon Caye
0 5 mi
0 5 km
San Pedro
Maskall
Old Northern Hwy.
Caye Cangrejo
Caye Caulker
Hick's Caye
Caye Chapel
Long Caye
BELIZE
Ladyville
St. George's Caye
TURNEFFE ATOLL
Drowned Cayes
Belize City
Spanish Lookout Caye
To Lighthouse Reef Atoll (see inset)
Northern Lagoon
Blackbird Caye
Middle Long Caye
Southern Lagoon
Deadman's Caye
Alligator Caye
Gales Point
Reef
Mullins River
0 10 mi
0 10 km
STANN CREEK
Southern Long Caye

Development has reached both ends of Ambergris Caye, and steady construction appears destined to fill in the blanks from north to south. Still, for the time being, most of the resorts located north or south of San Pedro are isolated and tranquil retreats, set on the shores of crystal-clear waters.

Long before the British settled Belize, and long before the sun-seeking vacationers and zealous reef divers discovered Ambergris Caye, the Maya were here. In fact, the Maya created Ambergris Caye when they cut a channel through the long thin peninsula that extended down from what is now Mexico. The channel was cut to facilitate coastal trading and avoid the dangerous barrier reef that begins not too far north of San Pedro. Ambergris Caye is 40km (25 miles) long and only .8km (1/2 mile) wide at its widest point.

Despite the fact that much of the island is seasonally flooded mangrove forest, and despite laws prohibiting the cutting of mangroves, developers continue to clear cut and fill this marginal land. Indiscriminate cutting of the mangroves is already having an adverse effect on the nearby barrier reef: Without the mangroves to filter the water and slow the impact of waves, silt is formed and carried out to the reef, where it settles and kills the coral. There is still spectacular diving to be had just off the shore here, but local operators and long-term residents claim to have noticed a difference and are expressing concern.

ESSENTIALS

Getting There & Departing

You've got two options for getting to and from Ambergris Caye: sea or air. The trip is usually beautiful by either means. When the weather's rough, it's bumpy both ways, although it's certainly quicker by air, and you're more likely to get wet in the boat.

BY PLANE There are dozens of daily flights between Belize City and San Pedro Airport (airport code SPR) on Ambergris Caye. Flights leave from both Philip S. W. Goldson International Airport and Municipal Airport roughly every half-hour. Most stop en route at Caye Caulker to drop off and pick up passengers, and at Caye Chapel when there is demand. If you're coming in on an international flight and heading straight for San Pedro, you should book a flight from the international airport. If you're already in Belize City or in transit around the country, it's cheaper to fly from the Municipal Airport, which is also closer to downtown, and quicker and cheaper to reach by taxi. During the high season, and whenever possible, it's best to have a reservation. However, you can usually just show up at the airport and get a seat on a flight within an hour.

Both **Maya Island Air** (**© 223-1140** in Belize City, or 226-2435 in San Pedro; www.mayaairways.com) and **Tropic Air** (**© 800/422-3435** in the U.S. or Canada, 226-2012 in Belize; www.tropicair.com) have 11 flights daily between Goldson International Airport and San Pedro Airport, and they both follow the same schedule. The flights depart every hour beginning at 7:40am, with the last flight at 5:40pm. Flight time is around 15 minutes; the fare is BZ$114 (US$57/£30) each way. These flights actually originate at the Belize City Municipal Airport 10 minutes earlier. From the Municipal Airport, the fare is just BZ$63 (US$32/£17) each way. These flights take around 30 minutes, because they stop en route to pick up passengers at the international airport, and then at Caye Caulker to drop off passengers. When you're ready to leave, flights from San Pedro to Belize City run from 7am to 5pm. Most of these flights stop first at Caye Caulker and then at the international airport before continuing on to the Municipal Airport.

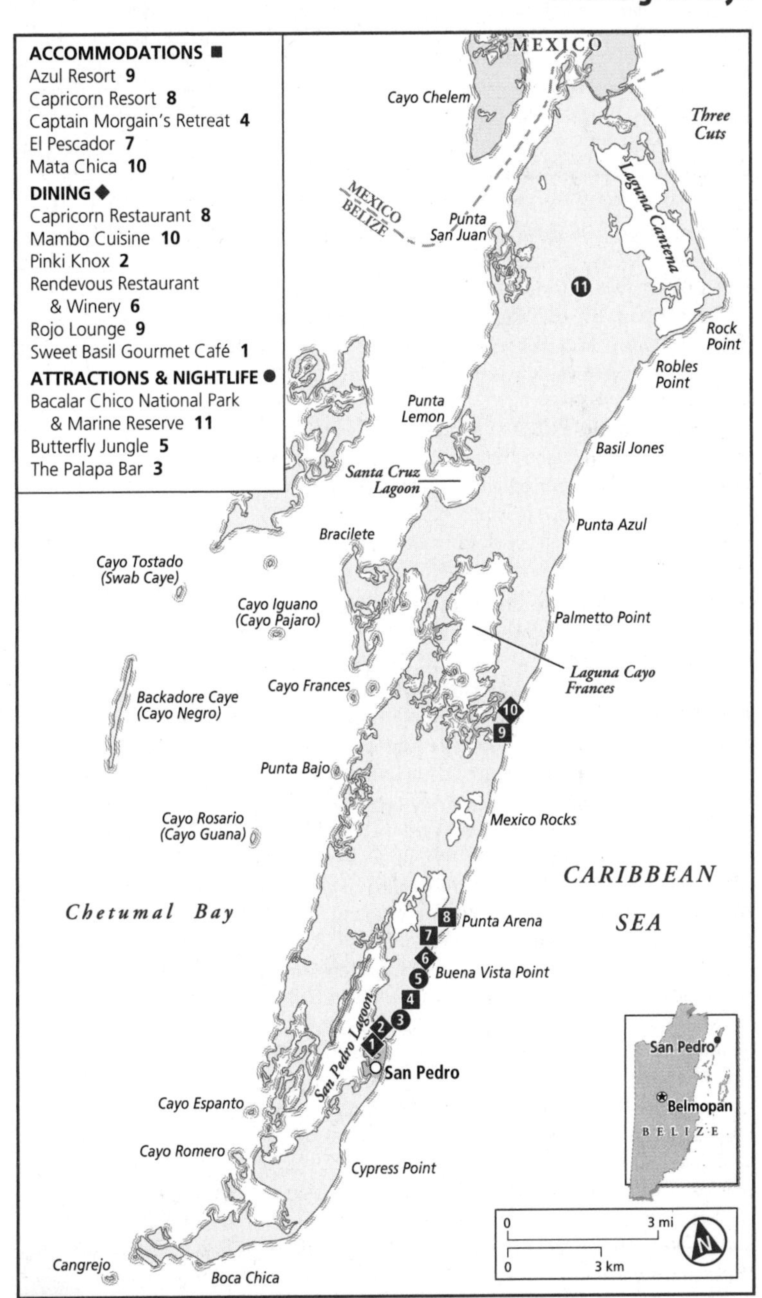
ACCOMMODATIONS ■
Azul Resort 9
Capricorn Resort 8
Captain Morgain's Retreat 4
El Pescador 7
Mata Chica 10
DINING ◆
Capricorn Restaurant 8
Mambo Cuisine 10
Pinki Knox 2
Rendevous Restaurant & Winery 6
Rojo Lounge 9
Sweet Basil Gourmet Café 1
ATTRACTIONS & NIGHTLIFE ●
Bacalar Chico National Park & Marine Reserve 11
Butterfly Jungle 5
The Palapa Bar 3
MEXICO
Cayo Chelem
Three Cuts
Laguna Cantena
MEXICO
BELIZE
Punta San Juan
Rock Point
Robles Point
Punta Lemon
Basil Jones
Santa Cruz Lagoon
Punta Azul
Bracilete
Cayo Tostado (Swab Caye)
Cayo Iguano (Cayo Pajaro)
Palmetto Point
Laguna Cayo Frances
Cayo Frances
Backadore Caye (Cayo Negro)
Punta Bajo
Mexico Rocks
Cayo Rosario (Cayo Guana)
CARIBBEAN SEA
Chetumal Bay
Punta Arena
Buena Vista Point
San Pedro Lagoon
San Pedro
Cayo Espanto
Cayo Romero
Cypress Point
Cangrejo
Boca Chica
San Pedro
Belmopan
BELIZE
0
3 mi
0
3 km
N

Tips Add It Up

Because a taxi into Belize City from the international airport costs BZ$50 to BZ$60 (US$25–US$30/£13–£16), and the boat to Ambergris Caye costs BZ$20 to BZ$30 (US$10–US$15/£5.30–£7.95), it is only slightly more expensive to fly if you are heading directly to the cayes after arriving on an international flight.

Almost any of the above Tropic Air and Maya Island Air flights can be used to commute between Caye Caulker and San Pedro. Flight duration is just 10 minutes, and the fare is BZ$63 (US$32/£17) each way.

Tropic Air has five daily flights between Corozal Town and San Pedro, leaving Corozal Town at 7:30, 9:30, and 11:30am, and at 1:30, 3:30, and 5:30pm. Flights from San Pedro to Corozal Town leave at 7, 9, and 11am, and at 1, 3, and 5pm. The fare is BZ$86 (US$43/£23) each way.

Maya Island Air (✆ **223-1140** in Belize City, or 422-2333 in Corozal; www.mayaairways.com) has daily flights between Corozal and San Pedro, leaving San Pedro at 7am, 10am, 2pm, and 4:30pm, and returning at 7:30 and 10:30am, and 2:30 and 5pm. Flight duration is 25 minutes. The fare is BZ$82 (US$41/£22) each way.

Connections to and from all the other major destinations in Belize can be made via the municipal and international airports in Belize City.

BY BOAT Regularly scheduled boats ply the route between Belize City and Ambergris Caye. All leave from somewhere near the Swing Bridge. Most boats leave directly from the **Marine Terminal,** which is located right on North Front Street just over the Swing Bridge; and the boats are associated with the **Caye Caulker Water Taxi Association** (✆ **223-5752;** www.cayecaulkerwatertaxi.com). Most are open speedboats with one or two very powerful engines. Most carry between 20 and 30 passengers, and make the trip in about 75 minutes. Almost all of these boats drop off and pick up passengers in Caye Caulker on their way, and on St. George's Caye and/or Caye Chapel when there's demand. If you're going to Ambergris from Caye Caulker, or either St. George's Caye or Caye Chapel, these boats will pick you up. Find out at the Marine Terminal just where and when they stop. The schedule is subject to change, but boats for Ambergris Caye leave the Marine Terminal roughly every 90 minutes beginning at 8am, with the last boat leaving at 4:30pm. The fare is BZ$20 (US$10/£5.30) one-way, BZ$40 (US$20/£11) round-trip between Belize City and Ambergris Caye; and BZ$15 (US$7.50/£4) one-way between Caye Caulker and San Pedro. (See "Two Small Cayes on the Way" on p. 151 for more details about St. George's Caye and Caye Chapel.)

It is possible to purchase a seat in advance by visiting the Marine Terminal personally. This is a good idea in the high season, although in most cases, you'll need to purchase the ticket in cash upfront. Some Belize City hotels provide this service or can get you a confirmed reservation by phone.

In addition to the Caye Caulker Water Taxi Association, the ***Triple J*** (✆ **223-3464**) leaves from Courthouse pier near the Marine Terminal every day at 8 and 10:30am, noon, and 3 and 4:40pm, returning from the Texaco dock on Ambergris Caye at 7, 8, and 10:30am, and 1, 2:30, and 3:30pm. The rates for the ***Triple J*** are similar to those listed above.

All the boats dock on Shark's Pier, near the center of town.

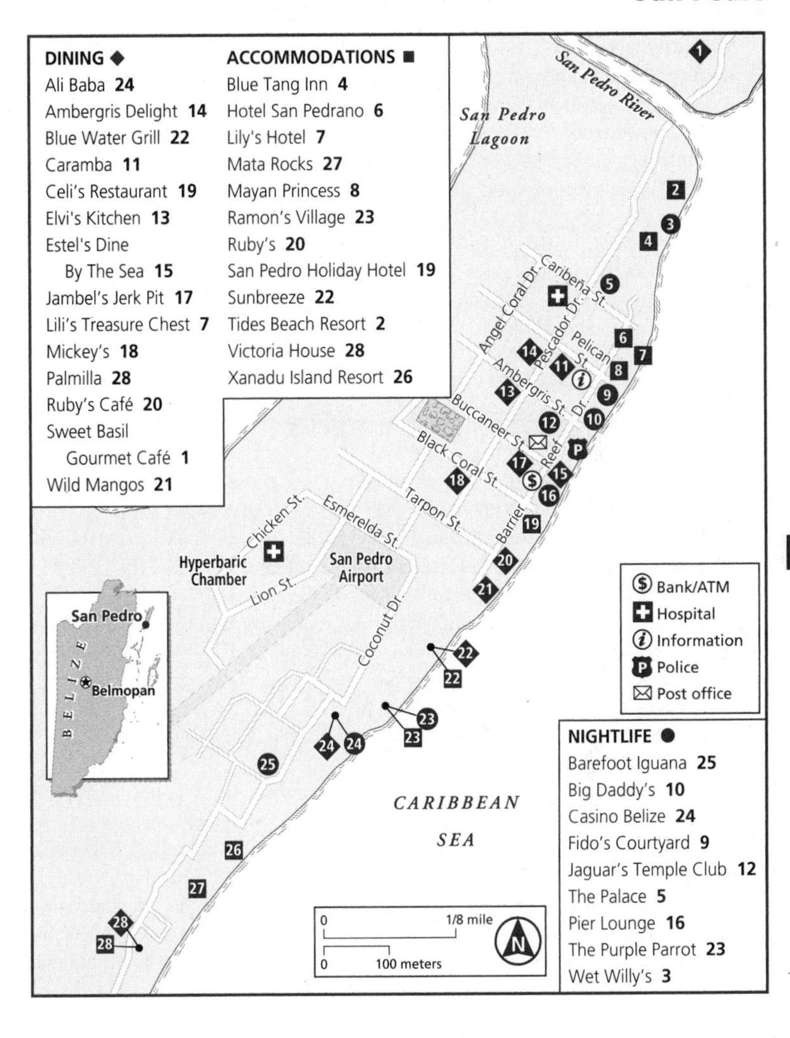

Getting Around

The downtown section of San Pedro is easily navigated by foot. Some of the hotels located on the northern or southern ends of the island can be quite isolated, however.

Most hotels arrange pickup and drop off for guests, whether they are arriving or departing by air or sea. Taxis are waiting for all flights that arrive at the airport, and are available for most trips around the island. If your hotel can't call you one, try **Amber Isle Taxi** (**© 226-4060**), **Felix Taxi** (**© 226-2041**), or **Island Taxi** (**© 226-3125**). Fares run between BZ$4 and BZ$15 (US$2–US$7.50/£1.05–£4) for most rides.

Ubiquitous golf carts are available for rent from several outlets on the island. Rates run around BZ$120 to BZ$160 (US$60–US$80/£32–£42) per day for a four-seat cart, and

International Costa Maya Festival

Begun as the San Pedro Sea & Air Festival, the annual **International Costa Maya Festival★★** is the largest public celebration on Ambergris Caye, even larger and more popular than Carnival. Celebrated from Thursday to Sunday in early August, the festival offers a steady stream of live concert performances, street parades, beauty pageants, and water shows and activities. When the festivities reinvented themselves several years ago, they had been transformed into a regional affair, honoring and inviting the peoples from around the Mayan world. Performers, participants, and festival-goers come from around Belize, as well as from Mexico, Honduras, El Salvador, and Guatemala, the five countries that comprise the Mundo Maya. San Pedro's football field is converted into the fairgrounds, and a large stage is set up at one end. Food stalls and arts and crafts booths are set up as well. Admission to most events is free, and a party atmosphere envelops the entire island.

BZ$160 to BZ$240 (US$80–US$120/£42–£64) for a six-seat cart. Hourly rates are between BZ$20 and BZ$40 (US$10–US$20/£5.30–£11). One of the largest and most dependable outfits is **Moncho's Rental** (✆ **226-3262;** www.monchosrentals.com). Other dependable options include **Cholo's Golf Cart Rental** (✆ **226-2406**) and **Ultimate Cart Rental** (✆ **226-3326;** www.ultimaterentalsbelize.com).

For a more distinctive ride around town, head to **Segway of Belize** (✆ **226-3344;** www.segwayofbelize.com). Rates run between BZ$56 and BZ$70 (US$28–US$35/£15–£19) per hour, and include free delivery to your hotel.

You can also rent scooters. **Island Scooters** (✆ **226-4152**) has a couple of stands and outlets around the island. A scooter should run you around BZ$90 to BZ$120 (US$45–US$60/£24–£32) per day.

I personally think the best way to get around is on a bicycle. Most hotels have their own bikes, either available for free or a small rental fee. If your hotel doesn't have a bike, call or head to **Joe's Bike Rental** on the south end of Pescador Drive (✆ **226-4371**). Rates run around BZ$20 to BZ$30 (US$10–US$15/£5.30–£7.95) per day.

Depending on where your hotel is located, a water taxi may just be your best means for commuting between your accommodations and the restaurants and shops of San Pedro. **San Pedro Water Taxi** (✆ **226-2194**) and **Island Ferry** (✆ **226-3231**) both run regularly scheduled launches that cover the length of the island, cruising just offshore from north to south and vice versa. The launches are in radio contact with all the hotels and restaurants, and they stop to pick up and discharge passengers as needed. Rates run around BZ$10 to BZ$40 (US$5–US$20/£2.65–£11) per person for a jaunt, depending on the length of the ride. Chartered water taxis are also available, and usually charge around BZ$80 to BZ$240 (US$40–US$120/£21–£64) depending on the length of the ride and size of your group.

Orientation

San Pedro (the only town on the island of Ambergris Caye) is just three streets wide. The streets, from seaside to lagoonside, are Barrier Reef Drive (Front St.), Pescador Drive (Middle St.), and Angel Coral Street (Back St.). The airport is at the south end of the busy little downtown. The island stretches both north and south of San Pedro. Less than a mile north of San Pedro there is a small channel, or cut, dividing the island in two. The northern section of the island is much less developed, and is where you will find more of the higher-end isolated resorts.

A bridge connects the north and southern sections of Ambergris Caye. Pedestrians and bicycles can cross the bridge for free, but golf carts and other vehicles must pay a toll of BZ$5 (US$2.50/£1.35) each way.

FAST FACTS For the local **police,** dial ✆ **911,** or 226-2022; for the **fire department,** dial ✆ **226-2372.** In the case of a medical emergency, call the **San Pedro Health Clinic** (✆ **226-2536**).

Atlantic Bank (✆ **226-3527**) and **Belize Bank** (✆ **226-2482**) are both located on Barrier Reef Drive in downtown San Pedro. The **post office** (✆ **226-2250**) is located on Barrier Reef Drive; it's open Monday through Friday from 8am to noon and from 1 to 5pm. There are plenty of Internet cafes on the island, and most hotels provide connections. One of the best and longest standing Internet cafes on the island is **Caribbean Connection Internet Café** (✆ **226-2573**), at 55 Barrier Reef Drive.

Most hotels also provide laundry service, but pricing varies widely, so ask first. **Nellie's Laundromat** (✆ **226-2454**) is located on Pescador Drive toward the south end of town. They charge around BZ$15 (US$7.50/£4) per load, and they even offer pickup and delivery service.

WHAT TO SEE & DO

Before you book your vacation, you should be aware that there really isn't any beach to speak of on Ambergris Caye: There is a narrow strip of sand for much of the length of the island, where the land meets the sea, but even at low tide it isn't wide enough for you to unroll a beach towel on in most places. Try walking north or south from town along the water to find a more secluded spot where you can sit and stare out to sea. Otherwise, the beachfront hotels create their own beaches by building retaining walls and filling them in with sand. You'll find the best of these at the resorts on the northern part of the island, and at Victoria House.

Likewise, swimming is not what you might expect. For 100 yards or more out from shore, the bottom is covered with sea grass. In a smart move that prioritizes the environment over tourism, the local and national government has decided to protect the sea grass, which supports a wealth of aquatic life. Beneath the grass is a layer of spongy roots and organic matter topped with a thin layer of white sand. Walking on this spongy sand is somewhat unnerving; there's always the possibility of a sea urchin or stingray lurking, and it's easy to trip and stumble. Swimming is best off the piers, and many of the hotels here have built long piers out into the sea, with steps down into the water, and usually a roped-off little swimming area. Beyond this, good swimming can be had from boats anchored out in the turquoise waters between the shore and the reef, or by taking a kayak offshore a little ways.

Take Care

There is a lot of boat traffic (some of it quite fast and furious) running up and down the coast of Ambergris Caye, so do not try to swim or snorkel from shore out to the reef. Unfortunately, over the years, more than one swimmer or snorkeler has been run over by a speeding motorboat.

Scuba Diving & Snorkeling

So why do people bother to come here if there is no beach and you can't go swimming right off the shore? They come for the spectacular coral reef, turquoise waters, and seemingly endless visibility. Less than a quarter-mile offshore is the longest coral reef in the Western Hemisphere. The Belize Barrier Reef is second only to Australia's Great Barrier Reef. Snorkeling, scuba diving, and fishing are the main draws here. All are consistently spectacular.

Within a 10- to 20-minute boat ride from the piers lie scores of **world-class dive sites★★**, including **Mexico Rocks, Mata Rocks, Tackle Box, Tres Cocos, Esmeralda, Cypress Tunnel,** and **Rocky Point.** A day's diving will almost always feature a mix of steep wall drops and coral caverns and tunnels. You'll see brilliant coral and sponge formations, as well as a wealth of colorful marine life. On good dives, you might see schools of spotted eagle rays, watch an octopus slither amongst the coral and rocks, or have the chance to swim face to face with a sea turtle. Nurse sharks, moray eels, and large barracuda are also commonly sighted.

There are scores of dive operators in San Pedro, and almost every hotel can arrange a dive trip, either because they have their own dive shop or they subcontract out. Rates are pretty standardized, but you should be able to get deals on multiday, multidive packages. While it's often tempting to purchase all-inclusive dive packages before coming to Belize, this limits your flexibility; for example, if the weather and water are really rough, you're already committed, although you might prefer taking an inland tour to a Mayan ruin over a rough dive.

For reliable scuba-diving service and reasonable rates, contact **Amigos del Mar** (© 226-2706; www.amigosdive.com), **Aqua Dives** (© 800/641-2994 in the U.S. and Canada, or 226-3415; www.aquadives.com), **Ecologic Divers** (© 226-4118; www.ecologicdivers.com), or **Patojo's Scuba Center ★** (© 226-2283; patojos@btl.net). Most of these companies, as well as the individual resorts, charge BZ$100 to BZ$140 (US$50–US$70/£27–£37) for a two-tank dive, with equipment rental running around BZ$30 to BZ$60 (US$15–US$30/£7.95–£16) for a complete package, and BZ$16 to BZ$24 (US$8–US$12/£4.25–£6.35) for a mask, snorkel, and fins.

For more adventurous and truly top-rate diving, you'll probably want to head out to the **Turneffe Island Atoll★★**, **Lighthouse Reef★★**, and **Blue Hole★★**. For more information on these sites, see section 2, later in this chapter. Most of the dive operations on the island offer this trip, or will subcontract it out. It's about a 2- to 3-hour ride each way (in a fast boat) over sometimes rough seas. You'll definitely want to choose a seaworthy, speedy, and comfortable boat. Most day trips out to Turneffe Island or Lighthouse Reef and Blue Hole run around BZ$280 to BZ$500 (US$140–US$250/£74–£133) per person, including transportation, two or three dives, and tanks and weights, as well as lunch and snacks. All the above-mentioned operators offer day and multiday trips to the outer atoll islands and reefs. Prices average around BZ$600 to BZ$900 (US$300–US$450/£159–£239) for a 2-day trip, BZ$800 to BZ$1,200 (US$400–US$600/£212–£318) for a 3-day trip.

If you've always dreamed of learning to scuba dive and plan on spending any time on Ambergris Caye, you should consider taking a course here. Resort courses will give you a great 1-day introduction into the world of scuba diving, including a very controlled shallow-water boat dive. These courses cost BZ$280 to BZ$360 (US$140–US$180/£74–£95). In 3 to 4 days, however, you can get your full open-water certification. These

The Perfect Plunge

If you're hesitant to take a tank plunge, don't miss a chance to at least snorkel. There's good snorkeling all along the protected side of the barrier reef, but some of the best is at **Shark-Ray Alley ★★** and **Hol Chan Marine Reserve ★★**, which are about 6.4km (4 miles) southeast of San Pedro. Shark-Ray Alley provides a nice adrenaline rush for all but the most nonchalant and experienced divers. Here you'll be able to snorkel above and between schools of nurse sharks and stingrays. *Hol chan* is a Mayan term meaning "little channel," which is exactly what you'll find here—a narrow channel cutting through the shallow coral reef. The walls of the channel are popular with divers, and the shallower areas are frequented by snorkelers. Some of the exciting residents of the area are large, green moray eels; stingrays; and nurse sharks (harmless). The reserve covers 13 sq. km (5 sq. miles) and is divided into three zones: the reef, the seagrass beds, and the mangroves. Most combination trips to Shark-Ray Alley and Hol Chan Marine Reserve last about 2½ to 3 hours, and cost around BZ$60 to BZ$100 (US$30–US$50/£16–£27). There is a BZ$20 (US$10/£5.30) park fee for visiting Hol Chan, which may or may not be included in the price of boat excursions to the reserve.

courses run between BZ$700 and BZ$1,000 (US$350–US$500/£186–£265), including all equipment rentals, class materials, and the processing of your certification, as well as four open-water and reef dives. All of the above-mentioned dive centers, as well as many of the individual resorts here, offer these courses.

There are a host of boats offering snorkeling trips, and most of the above dive operators also offer snorkel trips and equipment rental. Trips to other sites range in price from BZ$30 to BZ$60 (US$15–US$30/£7.95–£16) for short jaunts to half-day outings, and BZ$100 to BZ$140 (US$50–US$70/£27–£37) for full-day trips. One of the operators who specializes in snorkeling trips here is the very personable Alfonse Graniel and his launch ***Li'l Alfonse*** (**© 226-2992;** lilalfonse@btl.net). Snorkel gear is available from most of the above operators and at several other sites around town. A full set of mask, fins, and snorkel will usually cost BZ$16 to BZ$24 (US$8–US$12/£4.25–£6.35) per person per day.

Tip: Hol Chan and Shark-Ray Alley are extremely popular. If you really want to enjoy them, try to find a boat leaving San Pedro at or before 8am, and head first to Shark-Ray Alley. Most boats dive Hol Chan first, and this is the best way to get a dive with the greatest concentration of nurse sharks and stingrays. By all means, avoid snorkeling or diving these sites at times when the cruise ships are running excursions there. Alternatively, you may want to consider visiting a different snorkeling site, such as Mexico Rocks Coral Gardens, Tres Cocos, or Mata Rocks, where the snorkeling is just as good, if not better, and you're more likely to have the place to yourself.

COMBINING SNORKELING WITH MANATEE VIEWING Another trip that has recently become popular is a day trip to see manatees and do some snorkeling at remote cayes. These trips include a leisurely tour of manatee feeding sites on the way to the

Rough Seas

The Belize Barrier Reef acts like a giant sea wall. Given the prevailing trade winds, the waters on the inside of the reef are almost always quite calm. However, a quick jaunt outside the reef can bring you into often steep and agitated seas. Most snorkeling trips stick to the smooth waters inside the reef, while scuba trips almost always head for the deeper water on the outside. Always ask about current conditions and where you will be going before you sign up for a trip, and know your abilities and reaction to rough water before venturing out.

isolated Goff's and Sergeant's cayes, which are little more than football field–size patches of sand, with a few palm trees. These trips include all transportation, lunch on one of the cayes, and several snorkeling stops, and cost around BZ$120 to BZ$200 (US$60–US$100/£32–£53). Most hotels and tour agencies in town offer this trip; or check with **Sea-Rious Adventures** (✆ **226-4202**).

GLASS-BOTTOM BOATS If you really don't want to take a plunge of any sort, you can still get a good view of the reef and its undersea wonders aboard a glass-bottom boat. There are a few glass-bottom boats working Ambergris Caye. Most hotels and tour agencies on the island can book them for you, or you can contact the ***Reef Runner*** (✆ **226-2180**) directly. Rates run between BZ$50 and BZ$80 (US$25–US$40/£13–£21) depending on the length of the tour, and whether or not a meal or drink is involved. Most of the glass-bottom boat tours allow time for a snorkeling break as well.

Sailing

The crystal-clear waters, calm seas, and isolated anchorages and snorkeling spots all around Ambergris Caye make this an excellent place to go out for a sail. Your options range from crewed yachts and bareboat charters for multiday adventures to day cruises and sunset sails. A day cruise, including lunch, drinks, and snorkeling gear, should run between BZ$200 to BZ$320 (US$100–US$160/£53–£85) per person. Most hotels and tour operators around town can hook you up with a day sail or sunset cruise.

Although not a true sailboat, the ***Winnie Estelle*** (✆ **226-2394;** winnie_estelle@yahoo.com), a 20m (66-ft.) motor-sailer operated by Captain Roberto Smith, does a day cruise to Caye Caulker with several snorkel stops for BZ$110 (US$55/£29). There's a lunch stop on Caye Caulker, where you can dine at the restaurant of your choice, on your own account, while snacks and drinks are included on the cruise. This boat can also be chartered for longer trips to the outer atolls, or to southern cayes.

If you're looking for a longer and more adventurous time on the high seas, **TMM** (✆ **800/633-0155** in the U.S., or 226-3026 in Belize; www.sailtmm.com) is a large-scale charter company with operations on Ambergris Caye. Options include monohulls, catamarans, and trimarans of varying sizes. Given the shallow draft, increased interior space, and reduced drag, a multihull is your best bet. All of the boats are well equipped and seaworthy. Rates for a weeklong charter run between BZ$3,600 and BZ$18,000 (US$1,800–US$9,000/£954–£4,770), depending on the size of the boat, and whether or not you charter it bareboat or with a crew.

Fishing

Sport fishing for tarpon, permit, and bonefish is among the best in the world around these cayes and reefs, and over the years a few record catches have been made. If you prefer deep-sea fishing, there's plenty of tuna, dolphin, and marlin to be had beyond the reefs. **Fishing San Pedro** (© **607-9967;** www.fishingsanpedro.com), **The Rock** (© **226-3200;** www.belizefishfinder.com), and **Excalibur Tours** (© **226-3235**) all have respectable guides and equipment. A half-day reef trolling, casting, or fly-fishing for bonefish or tarpon runs around BZ$300 to BZ$500 (US$150–US$250/£80–£133), a full day BZ$400 to BZ$800 (US$200–US$400/£106–£212). Deep-sea trolling for larger game costs between BZ$800 and BZ$1,200 (US$400–US$600/£212–£318) for a half-day, and between BZ$1,600 and BZ$2,400 (US$800–US$1,200/£424–£636) for a full day. These prices are per boat for two to four fishermen and usually include drinks, tackle, and lunch.

Hard-core fishermen might want to check out one of the dedicated fishing lodges, like **El Pescador★** (© **800/242-2017** in the U.S. and Canada, or 226-2398; www.elpescador.com) on Ambergris Caye, or **Turneffe Flats★★** (© **888/512-8812** in the U.S., or 220-4046; www.tflats.com) out on the Turneffe Island Atoll.

Windsurfing, Parasailing & Watercraft

Ambergris Caye is a good place for beginning and intermediate windsurfers. The nearly constant 15- to 20-knot trade winds are perfect for learning on and easy cruising. The protected waters provide some chop, but are generally pretty gentle on beginning board sailors. If you're looking to do some windsurfing, or to try the latest adrenaline boost of kiteboarding, your best bet is to check in with the folks at **Sail Sports Belize** (© **226-4488;** www.sailsportsbelize.com). Sail board rentals run around BZ$44 to BZ$54 (US$22–US$27/£12–£14) per hour, or BZ$144 to BZ$164 (US$72–US$82/£38–£43) per day. Kite board rentals run BZ$120 (US$60/£32) for a half-day, and BZ$180 (US$90/£48) for a full day. Weekly rates are also available. These folks also rent out several types of small sailboats for cruising around close to shore.

Most resort hotels here have their own collection of all or some of the abovementioned watercraft. Rates run around BZ$40 to BZ$70 (US$20–US$35/£11–£19) per hour for a Hobie Cat, small sailboat, or wind surfer; and BZ$60 to BZ$80 (US$30–US$40/£16–£21) per hour for a jet ski. If not, **Sail Sports Belize** (see above) is your best bet.

Fun on Dry Land

Butterfly Garden

Located about 7.2km (4½ miles) north of the bridge, **Butterfly Jungle★** (© **226-2911;** www.butterflyjungle.bz) is a pleasant little attraction with a butterfly breeding program and covered butterfly enclosure. A visit here includes an informative tour and explanation of the butterfly life cycle, as well as a visit to the enclosure, where anywhere from 15 to 30 species may be in flight at any one time. This place is open daily 10am to 5pm, and admission is BZ$20 (US$10/£5.30) for adults, free for children under 12.

Spas, Fitness & Bodywork

While there are no full-scale resort spas or high-end facilities on Ambergris Caye, you can certainly get sore muscles soothed and a wide array of pampering treatments at a series of day spas and independent massage-therapy storefronts. The best of these includes **The Art of Touch,** at the entrance to the Sunbreeze Hotel (© **226-3357;** www.touchbelize.com), and **Asia Garden Day Spa★** (© **226-4072;** www.asiangardendayspa.com), across from Ramon's Village. Rates run around BZ$140 to BZ$200 (US$70–US$100/£37–£53) for an hour-long massage.

If you want to work out, there's a modest health club and gym at the **San Pedro Family Fitness Club** (see below). These folks also offer aerobic, Pilates, Tae Bo, and yoga classes.

Tennis

This is very far from a tennis destination, and very few hotels have courts. You'll find two lit courts at the **San Pedro Family Fitness Club,** on the west side of San Pedro (✆ **226-2683**). You'll want to play early in the morning or late in the afternoon or evening, as it's just too hot to play tennis most days during the heat of the day. This place is a bargain: BZ$30 (US$15/£7.95) gets you a full-day pass and access to all their facilities.

Golf

There's no golf on Ambergris Caye, but guests here can arrange to play the course on nearby **Caye Chapel ★** (✆ **226-8250;** www.cayechapel.com). The course is almost entirely flat, but it features a lot of water and sand hazards, as well as some stunning views. Rates for a full day of unlimited golfing, including carts, club rental, and use of the resort's pool and beach area run BZ$300 (US$150/£80) per person. Reservations are absolutely necessary. Transportation can be arranged by air, chartered water taxi, or regularly scheduled water taxi.

For a less challenging trip around the links, families might want to head to **San Pedro Family Fitness Club** (✆ **226-2683**), which has a basic minigolf course of thin carpeting over hard concrete. A round will run you just BZ$5 (US$2.50/£1.35).

Other Attractions

Bacalar Chico National Park & Marine Reserve

Occupying the northern end of Ambergris Caye and its surrounding waters, **Bacalar Chico National Park & Marine Reserve ★** (✆ **605-1633**) is one of the newest additions to Belize's national park system. In addition to being home to scores of bird, animal, and plant species (many of which are endemic), the park also features several ancient Mayan ceremonial and trading sites. The ranger station is, in fact, located at the diminutive Chac Balam ruins. Bacalar Chico is the name of the channel cut 1,500 years ago by the Maya to facilitate coastal trading. Just across the channel is Mexico. Nearly 200 species of birds have been spotted here, and the park allegedly contains all five wildcat species found in Belize, including the jaguar—although your odds of seeing a cat are remote at best. However, you've got decent odds of seeing a crocodile or wild deer, and of course numerous bird species. The park is only accessible by boat. All of the local tour outfits offer half- and full-day trips to Bacalar Chico. Depending on your needs, these trips usually provide a mix of bird- and nature-watching, snorkeling, and Mayan ruin explorations. Specialist guides can be hired around San Pedro, if you want to focus primarily on any one of these pursuits. Admission to the park is BZ$10 (US$5/£2.65).

Excursions Farther Afield

If you've been on the island for a while or just want to see more of Belize, a host of tour operators on Ambergris Caye offer excursions to all of the major attractions and destinations around the country, including Altun Ha, Lamanai, Xunantunich, Mountain Pine Ridge, and even Tikal. You can also go cave tubing in the Caves Branch region. Most of these tours involve a flight in a small charter plane.

Gonna Wash That Paint Right Out of My Hair

A modest version of the traditional Caribbean Carnival or Mardi Gras is celebrated in San Pedro—with an odd twist—over the weekend preceding Ash Wednesday and the period of Lent. Sure, there are colorful and lively *comparsa* parades, with marching drum bands and costumed dancers. But, over the years a tradition of painting has developed. This tradition predates paintball by decades. In times past, this was a fun and frivolous game between roaming bands of local residents using flour-based homemade "paints." Tourists were usually asked before being painted and their demurrals respected. Over the years, however, the painting fever has skyrocketed and gotten more aggressive: Fresh eggs and the occasional oil-based paint were introduced as weapons, and tourists are now often painted despite pleas to the contrary. It's definitely fun and a good way to meet some locals. If you get to a shower relatively quickly, it'll wash off without much hassle. Still, if you go out during Carnival, expect to get painted, and dress accordingly.

One of the most popular day trips is to the Mayan ruins at Altun Ha. This is also one of the most economical, as it doesn't require a flight. This begins on a powerful little boat that will whisk you over to the mainland. You'll then take a taxi to the ruins and have lunch before returning to San Pedro. Most operators offering the Altun Ha trip include a lunch stop at Maruba Resort (p. 202), with the option of adding on a decadent jungle spa treatment. Prices for these trips run around BZ$140 to BZ$200 (US$70–US$100/£37–£53). A similar trip by boat and land is offered to the ruins at Lamanai.

For trips involving a flight, prices range from BZ$200 to BZ$400 (US$100–US$200/£53–£106) per person, depending on the distance traveled and number of activities and attractions crammed into 1 day. Most hotels on the island can book these tours, or you can contact **Excalibur Tours** (✆ **226-3235**), **SEAduced** (✆ **226-2254;** www.seaducedbybelize.com), or **Sea-Rious Adventures** (✆ **226-4202**).

For detailed descriptions of these various destinations and attractions, see the respective regional chapters in this book.

SHOPPING

Most of the shopping on Ambergris Caye is typical tourist fare. You'll see tons of T-shirts and tank tops, with dive logos and silk-screen prints of the Blue Hole. Beyond this, the best buy on the island is handmade jewelry sold by local Belizean artisans from makeshift display stands along Barrier Reef Drive. I'd be wary of black coral jewelry, though. Black coral is extremely beautiful, but as with every endangered resource, increased demand just leads to increased harvesting of a slow-growing coral.

Inside Fido's Courtyard at **Belizean Arts** ★ (✆ **226-3019;** www.belizeanarts.com), you'll find the island's best collection of original paintings and crafts. Of special note are the prints and paintings of co-owner Walter Castillo, a Nicaraguan-born artist whose simple, but bold, style captures the Caribbean color and rhythm of Belize.

Another shop at Fido's Courtyard worth checking out is **Ambar** ★★ (✆ **226-3101**). The owner and artisan here sells handmade jewelry, with a specialty in amber. The stuff here is a significant cut above the wares you'll find in most other souvenir shops and street stands.

You can find some interesting locally made casual wear at **Isla Bonita Designs,** North Barrier Reef Drive (✆ **226-4258;** www.islabonitadesigns.com).

To get your fill of jade, head to the small **Ambergris Maya Jade & History Museum,** Barrier Reef Drive (✆ **226-3311**), which has a nice collection of jade artifacts and jewelry, and really functions as the draw to get folks into their retail store.

Finally, if you just need some reading material for the beach blanket or hammock, head to **Barefoot Books** (✆ **226-3563**), with a large selection of new and used books, right on Pescador Drive.

WHERE TO STAY

In San Pedro

There's a score of hotel options right in the heart of San Pedro town. Most are geared towards budget travelers, although a few of these are quite comfortable and charming. Most of the more upscale resorts are located a little bit further north or south of town. See below for these options.

Tip: Almost every hotel on Ambergris Caye, and certainly all of the resorts, offers scuba packages. If you plan to do a lot of diving, this is the way to go, as these packages can sometimes provide substantial savings over paying as you go. However, you can also buy dive packages from many of the individual dive operators, either in advance or upon arrival on the caye.

Expensive

In addition to the places below, the **Mayan Princess** (✆ **226-2778;** www.mayan princesshotel.com) is a large, contemporary resort with comfortable rooms and plenty of services and amenities, set in the heart of town.

Blue Tang Inn ★ This intimate option features all-suite accommodations. Housed in a three-story plantation-style building, the rooms are modern, comfortable, and spacious, and all feature a kitchenette, dining area, and living area with a fold-out futon, making them an excellent option for families and extended stays. The prized rooms here are the third-floor oceanfront suites, which feature king beds, wood floors, arched ceilings, and Jacuzzi bathtubs. However, all rooms are up to snuff. The hotel is located right on the waterfront, just north of the heart of downtown San Pedro. While there is no restaurant here, they do serve a complimentary continental breakfast. And if you choose to skip cooking on your own, a score of restaurants is just a few steps away.

Sand Piper St. (Box 231), San Pedro, Ambergris Caye. ✆ **866/881-1020** in the U.S. and Canada, or 226-2326 in Belize. Fax 226-2358. www.bluetanginn.com. 14 units. BZ$300–BZ$420 (US$150–US$210/£80–£111) double. Rate includes continental breakfast and San Pedro airport transfers. Rates lower in the off season; higher during peak periods. AE, MC, V. **Amenities:** Small outdoor pool; tour desk; laundry service. *In room:* A/C, TV, free Wi-Fi, kitchenette, no phone.

Ramon's Village ★ This place is one of the original resorts on Ambergris Caye, and it's grown over the years. The handiwork of local son Ramón Núñez, this place is appropriately named, as there is a small-village feel to the collection of thatch-roofed bungalows and suites. At the center of the complex is a small but inviting free-form pool, surrounded by palm trees and flowering plants. Rooms vary a bit in size, and are classified as beachfront, seaside, and garden view, with the beachfront units having the best unobstructed views of the water. Some of the older units are a bit dark and too close to the road and airstrip for my taste. All are clean, modern, and comfortable, with colorful-print bedspreads and dark-varnished wood trim. Most have a private or shared balcony with a sitting chair or hammock. There are a few suites, which are larger and provide more room to roam and relax. Room nos. 58 and 61 are large second-floor suites set right near the edge of the sea. A few open-air thatch palapas are spread around the grounds and hung with hammocks.

Ramon's has one of the longer and prettier beaches to be found in San Pedro, as well as a very long dock jutting into the sea, and a wide range of watersports equipment and activities to choose from. This place also manages Steve & Becky's Cute Little Hotel, which is across the street slightly inland, but allows guests to use all of the facilities at Ramon's.

Coconut Dr. (southern edge of town), San Pedro, Ambergris Caye. ✆ **800/624-4215** or 601/649-1990 in the U.S., or 226-2067 in Belize. Fax 226-2214. www.ramons.com. 60 units. BZ$290–BZ$370 (US$145–US$185/£77–£98) double; BZ$430–BZ$800 (US$215–US$400/£114–£212) suite. Rates slightly higher during peak weeks; lower in the off season. AE, MC, V. **Amenities:** Restaurant; bar; small outdoor pool; full-service dive shop; watersports equipment rental; bike and golf cart rental; tour desk; limited room service (6:30am–10pm); laundry service. *In room:* A/C, hairdryer, no phone.

Sunbreeze ★★ For my money, this is the best hotel right in San Pedro. This two-story seafront hotel is built in a horseshoe around a simple garden area, with a small pool at its core. The superior rooms are all spacious, recently remodeled, and nonsmoking. The standard rooms have slightly small bathrooms, but are otherwise quite acceptable. The five deluxe units feature Jacuzzi tubs, and the best views. Room no. 225 is the best of the bunch, a corner deluxe unit, with a large balcony facing the Caribbean Sea. On the other end of the horseshoe, no. 201 is the best standard room in the house. This hotel is very ideally located in the center of town, with its own dive operation and a small arcade of shops. The hotel's Blue Water Grill (p. 132) serves excellent international fare. One of the nicest features here is a covered open-air hammock area built over the restaurant and bar. The hotel is directly across from the airstrip, and quite convenient if you are arriving and departing by air.

Coconut Dr. (P.O. Box 14) San Pedro, Ambergris Caye. ✆ **800/688-0191** in the U.S., or 226-2191 in Belize. Fax 226-2346. www.sunbreeze.net. 42 units. BZ$306–BZ$372 (US$153–US$186/£81–£99) double; BZ$340 (US$170/£90) deluxe. Rates lower in the off season. AE, MC, V. **Amenities:** Restaurant; bar; small outdoor pool; full-service dive shop; watersports equipment rental; bike rental; tour desk; limited room service (7am–9:30pm); laundry service; nonsmoking rooms. *In room:* A/C, TV.

Moderate

Lily's Hotel Lily's is on the beach, toward the north end of Front Street. While this was one of the pioneering budget options on the island, it's received regular remodeling and upgrades over the years. In fact, it's actually nudged itself right out of the budget price range, although for Ambergris Caye these are arguably reasonable rates for a waterfront room. Get your money's worth by watching the sun rise every morning and listening to the waves lap at your doorstep after the sun sets.

The rooms are simple yet well maintained and feature air-conditioning, minifridges, and modern furnishings. Not all of the rooms here have a water view—be sure to ask for one. The best rooms are those on the second floor, enjoying a wonderful seaview shared veranda. Those on the ground floor also have ocean views, although you need to be prepared for a fair amount of pedestrian traffic, as they are set right on the island's main pedestrian and bicycle thoroughfare. There's a relaxed vibe throughout the operation here, and you'll definitely enjoy the lounge chairs set on the sand for the guests' use.

On the beach, San Pedro, Ambergris Caye. ✆ **800/345-9786** in the U.S. and Canada, or 206-2059 in Belize. Fax 226-2623. www.ambergriscaye.com/lilys. 10 units. BZ$130–BZ$150 (US$65–US$75/£34–£40) double. MC, V. **Amenities:** Restaurant; bar; tour desk; laundry service. *In room:* A/C, minifridge, no phone.

San Pedro Holiday Hotel ★ *Finds* You can't miss this brilliantly white three-building complex with painted purple and pink trim in the center of town. Every room comes with air-conditioning, and most have excellent ocean views and small refrigerators. Get a room on the second floor and you'll have a wonderful balcony—you won't want to leave. Celi McCorkle opened this hotel over 40 years ago, the first on the island, and it's continued to keep pace with the times and tourism boom. A full-service dive shop, a popular bar and restaurant, and a small gift shop round out the amenities. The whole operation has a festive and lively air to it. This hotel lacks some of the amenities of other options in this price range—there's no swimming pool and not all rooms have televisions—but it makes up for that with its funky island vibe and friendly service.

Barrier Reef Dr. (P.O. Box 61), San Pedro, Ambergris Caye. ✆ **226-2014.** Fax 226-2295. www.sanpedroholiday.com. 17 units. BZ$220–BZ$250 (US$110–US$125/£58–£66) double; BZ$350 (US$175/£93) apt. AE, MC, V. **Amenities:** 2 restaurants; bar; full-service dive shop; watersports equipment rental; bike rental; tour desk; laundry service. *In room:* A/C, no phone.

Tides Beach Resort ★ *Finds* With its wood construction, gingerbread trim, and faded paint, this three-story oceanfront hotel has a worn and weathered feel, although in fact it's not that old. The hotel and sister dive operation are owned and operated by the highly respected and personable local couple of Patojo and Sabrina Paz. All of the rooms are oceanfront, and have either a shared or small private veranda or balcony. They feature polished wood floors, simple furnishings, and either two double beds or one king bed. Patojo runs one of the better dive operations on the island, and this place is popular with scuba divers and dive groups. This hotel is located on the north end of San Pedro town.

Boca del Río Dr., San Pedro, Ambergris Caye. ✆ **226-2283.** Fax 226-3797. www.ambergriscaye.com/tides. 12 units. BZ$200–BZ$260 (US$100–US$130/£53–£69) double. Rates include full breakfast. AE, MC, V. **Amenities:** Bar; full-service dive shop; watersports equipment rental; bike and golf cart rental; tour desk; laundry service. *In room:* A/C, minifridge, no phone.

Inexpensive

There are quite a few budget options on Ambergris Caye, and almost all of them are concentrated in the compact downtown area of San Pedro. True budget hounds should just walk around and see who's got the best room for the best price. I list a couple of my personal favorites below.

Hotel San Pedrano Although few of the rooms here have ocean views, they are pretty close to the beach and do have varnished wooden floors, a single bed and a double bed in every room, and clean bathrooms with tubs. A few of the rooms even have air-conditioning. The best views can be enjoyed from the wide veranda that looks out over the rooftops of adjacent buildings, a great place to gather with fellow travelers or simply sit and read a book.

Barrier Reef Dr. (P.O. Box 131), San Pedro, Ambergris Caye. ✆ **226-2054.** Fax 226-2274. sanpedrano@btl.net. 7 units. BZ$50–BZ$80 double (US$25–US$40/£13–£21). Add BZ$20 (US$10/£5.30) for A/C. AE, MC, V. **Amenities:** Tour desk; laundry service. *In room:* No phone.

Ruby's *Value* Walking towards the ocean and into town from the airstrip, one of the first things you'll see is a three-story whitewashed building, with blood-red gingerbread trim. Most of the rooms at Ruby's overlook the water. The best ones have air-conditioning and a private balcony overlooking the sea. The floors are wooden, the rooms are simply furnished with a couple of beds and little else, and the showers and bathrooms are clean. You can't beat the location at this price in San Pedro. Downstairs you'll find Ruby's Deli, which is a good place for breakfast or a casual midday meal. These folks also have a separate hotel on the lagoon side of the island, with clean, spacious, simple rooms at even lower prices. After years of mixed messages, it seems like the owners here have settled on spelling Ruby's with a "y" and not "ie" at the end.

Barrier Reef Dr. (P.O. Box 56), San Pedro, Ambergris Caye. ✆ **226-2063.** Fax 226-2434. www.ambergriscaye.com/rubys. 21 units. BZ$80–BZ$120 (US$40–US$60/£21–£32) double. MC, V. **Amenities:** Restaurant; tour desk; laundry service. *In room:* No phone.

South of San Pedro

Expensive

Mata Rocks ★ Finds The blinding white paint and angular architecture of this intimate hotel conjure up images of the Greek isles. All of the rooms here have at least a partial ocean view. The best is no. 53, a second-floor unit fronting the sea, with a large private balcony. There are 6 suites and 11 standard rooms. All are clean, modern, and cheery. The suites come with a fully equipped kitchenette, king bed and sofa bed, and small sitting area. At the center of the hotel is a small free-form pool that is fed via a small artificial "stream," which is in turn fed by a small fountain. Purple and lavender Adirondack chairs provide splashes of color. There is an intimate and relaxed air about the whole operation. A complimentary continental breakfast buffet is served in the open-air beachfront palapa bar, as are snacks and light lunches. This place is located about 2.4km (1½ miles) south of San Pedro town.

Oceanfront, southern end of Ambergris Caye. ✆ **888/628-2757** in the U.S. and Canada, or 226-2336 in Belize. Fax 226-2349. www.matarocks.com. 17 units. BZ$270–BZ$290 (US$135–US$145/£72–£77) double; BZ$350–BZ$380 (US$175–US$190/£93–£101) suite. Rates include continental breakfast. Rates lower in the off season; higher during peak periods. AE, MC, V. **Amenities:** Bar; small outdoor pool; complimentary bike use; tour desk; laundry service; free Wi-Fi. *In room:* A/C, TV, minifridge, no phone.

Victoria House ★★★ Finds This elegant and exclusive island retreat features a varied collection of rooms, suites, and villas. Everything is done with a refined sense of style and attention to detail. The resort is set on an expansive piece of land a couple of miles south of San Pedro, with lush tropical gardens and a surprisingly good section of soft white sand fronting it. The plantation rooms and suites are spread through several buildings, and there's a string of individual casitas aligned around a grassy lawn facing the sea. These latter feature high-pitched thatch roofs, tile floors, and wide French doors letting out on to a private balcony. The newer villas and suites are large and well equipped, with flatscreen televisions and plush furnishings. Some have kitchenettes, and others are duplex units that can be joined or rented separately. Service is attentive yet understated. A full range of tours and activities is offered, and the Palmilla restaurant here (p. 134) is one of the finest on the island.

Beachfront, 3.2km (2 miles) south of San Pedro (P.O. Box 22, San Pedro), Ambergris Caye. ✆ **800/247-5159** or 713/344-2340 in the U.S., or 226-2067 in Belize. www.victoria-house.com. 42 units. BZ$360 (US$180/£95) double; BZ$596–BZ$620 (US$298–US$310/£158–£164) casita or plantation room; BZ$750–BZ$1,316 (US$375–US$658/£199–£349) suite; BZ$1,330–BZ$3,500 (US$665–US$1,750/£352–£928) villa. Rates higher during peak weeks; lower in the off season. AE, MC, V. **Amenities:** Restaurant; bar; 2 midsize outdoor pools; full-service dive shop; watersports equipment rental; golf cart rental; free bicycles for guests; tour desk; laundry service; free Wi-Fi. *In room:* A/C, safe, no phone.

Xanadu Island Resort ★ (Kids The two- and three-story thatch-roof buildings of this small resort are of sturdy construction, and are promoted as being hurricane-proof. They are set in a semicircle around a central pool area. All of the units here are quite large and loaded with amenities. In fact, all are classified as suites, although most have the feel of independent apartments or condo units. This isn't a bad thing, and it makes this a good choice for extended stays and for families. Each unit features a full kitchen or a kitchen and spacious living room. Each comes with a private balcony or front porch. There are single-bedroom as well as two- and three-bedroom units available. The resort has a long pier jutting into the ocean, with a wonderful swimming platform at the end. There's no restaurant here, but several are within close proximity, and the town of San Pedro is just 1.6km (1 mile) away.

Oceanfront (P.O. Box 109, San Pedro Town), southern end of Ambergris Caye. ✆ **226-2814.** Fax 226-3409. www.xanaduresort-belize.com. 19 units. BZ$380–BZ$540 (US$190–US$270/£101–£143) double; BZ$540–BZ$800 (US$270–US$400/£143–£212) 2-bedroom; BZ$800–BZ$1,300 (US$400–US$650/£212–£345) 3-bedroom. Rates slightly lower in the off season; slightly higher during peak periods. AE, MC, V. **Amenities:** Small outdoor pool; complimentary bike use; tour desk; laundry service. *In room:* A/C, TV, dataport, free Wi-Fi, kitchenette, coffeemaker, hair dryer, safe.

On North Ambergris Caye

This is where you'll find most of the larger, more isolated, and more upscale resorts on Ambergris Caye. If you stay here, you will have to rely on your hotel or on the local water taxis to get to and from San Pedro town.

In addition to the hotels listed below, **El Pescador**★ (✆ **800/242-2017** in the U.S. and Canada, or 226-2398; www.elpescador.com) is a lovely and luxurious resort primarily geared towards hard-core fishermen and women.

Very Expensive

Azul Resort ★★ There are only two large villas at this new luxury option on the north end of the island. Each is a two-bedroom, two-bathroom affair fronting the sea and sharing a large outdoor pool. The decor features stylish bamboo furniture, king-size beds, Egyptian cotton linens, and various contemporary accents. There's a flatscreen television in the spacious living room, and each villa comes with a fully stocked kitchen featuring top-line appliances, such as a Viking range and fancy espresso machine. My favorite feature here is the massive open-air rooftop patio with fantastic views, a private Jacuzzi hot tub, and a couple of shade-giving gazebos. There's also a smaller wraparound balcony off the second-floor loft bedroom. Each villa has personal concierge services. During most of the year, a 7-night stay is required. The restaurant here, Rojo Lounge (p. 136) is one of the best on the island.

Oceanfront, northern end of Ambergris Caye. ✆ **226-4012.** Fax 220-5058. www.azulbelize.com. 2 units. BZ$3,990 (US$1,995/£1,057) double. Rates include all meals and snacks, and transfers to and from San Pedro airport. Rates slightly lower in the off season. AE, MC, V. **Amenities:** Restaurant; bar; outdoor pool; complimentary bicycle and kayak use; tour desk; room service (8am–10pm), laundry service; nonsmoking rooms; free Wi-Fi. *In room:* A/C, TV, full kitchen, minibar, coffeemaker, hairdryer, safe, Jacuzzi.

Capricorn Resort ★ (Finds There are just three individual cabins at this intimate little hotel. Each cabin features high-vaulted ceilings, a large tile shower, and a private front deck with a hammock. The walls are painted bold primary colors, and artistic touches—in the form of local, Guatemalan, and other ethnic arts and crafts—abound. The cabins come with either one queen bed or two full beds; all come with mosquito netting. The restaurant here is excellent.

Oceanfront (P.O. Box 247, San Pedro), 4km (2½ miles) north of the cut on northern end of Ambergris Caye. ✆ **226-2809.** Fax 226-5091. www.capricornresort.net. 3 units. BZ$490 (US$245/£130) double. Rates include full breakfast and transfers to and from San Pedro airport. Rates lower in the off season. AE, MC, V. **Amenities:** Restaurant; bar; complimentary kayak use; tour desk; limited room service (8am–9pm); laundry service. *In room:* A/C, no phone.

Captain Morgan's Retreat ★★ (Kids Captain Morgan's is a large, lively, and well-equipped resort on a long and lovely section of beach. The rooms are either individual beachfront casitas, or one- or two-bedroom villas set in a series of two-story units. All feature thatch roofs and wood construction, as well as attractive Guatemalan bedspreads and varnished wood furnishings. Every room comes with a private balcony or veranda, and all are modern, comfortable, and plenty spacious. I prefer the casitas, which are named after famous pirate captains, for their sense of privacy, although if you want more space and amenities, choose one of the second-floor villas. The villas all come with a fully equipped kitchenette. Comfortable lounge chairs and hammocks are spread along the beach and in shady spots on the grounds, and a host of aquatic and land-based activities and tours are offered.

Oceanfront, 4.8km (3 miles) north of the cut on northern end of Ambergris Caye. ✆ **888/653-9090** or 307/587-8914 in the U.S., or 226-2207 in Belize. Fax 226-4171. www.belizevacation.com. 26 units. BZ$398 (US$199/£105) casita; BZ$498 (US$249/£132) 1-bedroom villa; BZ$840 (US$420/£223) 2-bedroom villa. Rates lower in the off season; higher during peak periods. AE, MC, V. **Amenities:** Restaurant; 2 bars; lounge; 2 outdoor pools; spa services; full-service dive shop; watersports equipment rental; complimentary bike use; tour desk; laundry service; free Wi-Fi. *In room:* A/C, minifridge, safe.

Mata Chica ★★ This is one of the more northern resorts on Ambergris Caye, and in many ways, the hippest. There's a sense of rustic luxury throughout. Artistic details abound, with an eclectic mix of fabrics, sculptures, ceramics, and paintings from around the world. Every room here is actually a private bungalow or villa, and all can be considered junior suites or better. My favorites are the casitas, which are the closest to the ocean and feature a large sitting area, a king bed on a raised platform, and an interior garden shower. The four bungalows are listed as having sea views, but they are set back a bit, and that view is mostly a glimpse through foliage and the gaps between the casitas. Set back even further, but set high on raised stilts, are two very large villas, and one immense mansion. The latter is over 465 sq. m (5,000 sq. ft.), and features three bedrooms, a full kitchen, three full bathrooms, a huge living room, and ample deck areas and views. There's a little outdoor pool surrounded by shady palm trees, in addition to a large outdoor Jacuzzi. There's also a small spa, with a full list of treatments and cures, as well as a full-service tour desk. The hotel has a martini/Internet bar, as well as an excellent restaurant, Mambo (p. 135).

Oceanfront, northern end of Ambergris Caye. ✆ **223-0002** reservations, or 220-5010 at the hotel. Fax 220-5012. www.matachica.com. 14 units. BZ$560–BZ$830 (US$280–US$415/£148–£220) double; BZ$1,450–BZ$2,090 (US$725–US$1,045/£384–£554) villa. Rates include continental breakfast and transfers to and from San Pedro airport. Rates slightly lower in the off season. AE, MC, V. **Amenities:** Restaurant; bar; small outdoor pool; Jacuzzi; small spa; complimentary kayak use; tour desk; laundry service; free Wi-Fi. *In room:* A/C, coffeemaker, no phone.

An Island of Your Own

Cayo Espanto ★★★ (Finds Whether you're a bona fide member of the jet set or you just want to feel like one, this is the place for you in Belize. Six individual bungalows are spread across this private island. Each bungalow is luxurious and elegantly appointed and set on the edge of the Caribbean Sea, and each comes with a private butler. All but one of the bungalows has a private plunge pool, and all have a private pier jutting out into the ocean. All have wide French doors and windows that open onto private decks and verandas and stunning views. A couple of the bungalows are set up to accommodate two couples or a small family. There's no restaurant or common lounge area here. All meals are served in your villa, or out on your own private deck or dock area. Service is very attentive and pampering, and the food is excellent. A minimum stay of 5 nights is required most of the year; it gets bumped up to a solid week during peak periods, although this is somewhat negotiable, depending upon demand. You can also rent the entire island. Cayo Espanto is located just off the western tip of Ambergris Caye.

Cayo Espanto. ✆ **888/666-4282** in the U.S. and Canada. www.aprivateisland.com. 6 units BZ$2,390–BZ$4,590 (US$1,195–US$2,295/£633–£1,216) double. Rates include 3 meals, all drinks (except wine and champagne), all nonmotorized watersports equipment usage, and transportation to and from San Pedro during daylight hours. Rates slightly higher during peak weeks. AE, MC, V. **Amenities:** 5 small outdoor pools; small exercise room; spa services; full-service dive operation; tour desk; room service (7am–10pm); laundry service. *In room:* A/C, TV, free Wi-Fi, minifridge, coffeemaker, hair dryer, safe.

WHERE TO DINE

In San Pedro

Seafood is, of course, the most popular food on the island, and there's plenty of it around all year. However, please keep in mind that there are seasons for lobster and conch (because sea turtles are endangered, never order turtle). Officially, lobster season runs from July 15 to February 14, while conch is available from October 1 to June 30. Local restaurants and fishery officials have struck a deal to allow lobster to be served in the off season. Supposedly this is lobster caught and frozen during the open season, and not while they are mating in the formerly closed season.

If you're staying for an extended period of time, or have a room equipped with a kitchenette, you'll find several good markets around town. The largest, most modern, and best stocked of these is **Island Supermarket** (✆ **226-2972**), located on Coconut Drive.

Finally, since it doesn't fit into any of the following locations, you might want to try **Blue Lotus** (✆ **610-2583**), which serves up Indian-inspired fusion cuisine on an open air spot over the water across the lagoon from downtown San Pedro. Call for a reservation, and they'll provide free water taxi service.

Expensive

Blue Water Grill ★★ INTERNATIONAL/ASIAN This hotel restaurant has a broad and extensive menu, as well as a lovely setting overlooking the ocean and piers from the waterfront in the heart of San Pedro. While there's a good selection of pizzas, pastas, and such hearty dishes as grilled beef tenderloin with a Creole mustard and black-pepper sauce; or chicken breasts served with fresh herbs, walnuts, and blue cheese, the real reason to come here is for their inspired Asian fare. Start things off with crispy coconut-battered shrimp sticks with a sweet and spicy black-bean dipping sauce. For a main course, I recommend the Japanese spiced grouper with a sesame vinaigrette, or the massive surf and turf. These folks also have sushi nights every Tuesday and Thursday. If you come for sushi, be sure to try their spicy scallop hand roll.

At the Sunbreeze hotel, on the waterfront. ✆ **226-3347.** www.bluewatergrillbelize.com. Reservations recommended. Main courses BZ$30–BZ$54 (US$15–US$27/£7.95–£14). AE, MC, V. Daily 7–10:30am, 11:30am–2:30pm, and 6–9:30pm.

Moderate

Celi's Restaurant ★ SEAFOOD/BELIZEAN This simple restaurant serves dependable local fare in a cheery setting. You can either dine indoors, or with your feet in the sand in the restaurant's screened-in outdoor dining area. Stick to the seafood, which is plentiful, reasonably priced, and expertly prepared. Freshly caught fish, shrimp, and conch are prepared in a variety of sauces, and lobster and stone crabs are offered seasonally. For dessert, be sure to try some of Celi's Caye Lime Pie. The neighboring Celi's Deli is a good choice for sandwiches and light meals, especially if you're planning a picnic on some deserted beach or caye. On Wednesday nights they have a popular beach barbecue.

On the beach at the San Pedro Holiday Hotel. ✆ **226-2014.** Reservations recommended. Main courses BZ$18–BZ$32 (US$9–US$16/£4.75–£8.50); burgers and sandwiches BZ$14–BZ$16 (US$7–US$8/£3.70–£4.25); lobster priced according to size and market. AE, MC, V. Daily 11am–2pm and 5:30–9pm.

Wild Mangos ★★ INTERNATIONAL/FUSION After establishing a reputation at Palmilla, and winning the Taste of Belize competition twice, chef Amy Knox has set up shop at this down-home open-air joint. The best seats are those on the outdoor, covered wooden deck, although if those are taken, there are a few tables in the indoor dining room and at the bar. The menu is fairly broad and almost endlessly creative. Start things off with the Fire and Ice Ceviche, sushi-grade chunks of raw tuna marinated in a coconut milk broth spiced with fresh chiles. For a main course I like the bacon-wrapped shrimp grilled with a rum glaze, or the Conchinita Pibil, a traditional Mayan pork dish slow cooked in banana leaves. There are often nightly specials, and the desserts are delectable. There's also a somewhat more streamlined lunch menu featuring excellent sandwiches, wraps, tacos, and burritos, as well as salads and other treats.

On the beach, just north of the Sunbreeze Hotel. ✆ **226-2859.** Reservations recommended. Main courses BZ$27–BZ$52 (US$14–US$26/£7.40–£14). AE, MC, V. Mon–Sat noon–9pm.

Inexpensive

In addition to the places below, **Jambel's Jerk Pit** (✆ **226-3515**) is located right on Barrier Reef Drive, and serves up the same excellent Caribbean fare you'll find at its sister restaurant in Belize City (p. 100). **Ruby's Cafe** and **Celi's Deli,** on the ground floors of Ruby's hotel (p. 128) and the San Pedro Holiday Hotel (p. 128) respectively, are good places to pick up a light meal, and both specialize in fresh-baked breads and pastries, and sandwiches to go.

Other dependable options include **Micky's** (✆ **226-2223**), which is a popular local joint, **Caramba** (✆ **226-4321**), which serves a mix of Belizean, Mexican, and Caribbean fare, and **Ali Baba** (✆ **226-4042**), which specializes in Middle Eastern cuisine. For a seafront seat in the sand, it's hard to beat **Lily's Treasure Chest** (✆ **226-2650**), which is great for breakfast, lunch or dinner.

Ambergris Delight ★ Finds BELIZEAN Located a block north of Elvi's (see below), Ambergris Delight is popular with locals and offers excellent and inexpensive seafood, burgers, and even some vegetarian plates. A big blackboard serves as the menu and includes occasional specials such as conch soup or crab claws. The pizzas here are also excellent. If you've been out fishing, these folks will cook up your catch for you. The ambience is down home and funky. A television over the bar usually has news programming or even some sports. Ambergris Delight also delivers.

35 Pescador Dr., San Pedro. ✆ **226-2464.** Reservations recommended. Main courses BZ$14–BZ$36 (US$7–US$18/£3.70–£9.55); burgers and sandwiches BZ$8–BZ$16 (US$4–US$8/£2.10–£4.25); lobster priced according to size and market. MC, V. Wed–Mon 6am–2pm and 6–10pm.

Elvi's Kitchen ★★ Finds BELIZEAN/SEAFOOD/INTERNATIONAL Local legend Elvia Staines began selling burgers out of a takeout window in 1974. Today, Elvi's is arguably the most popular and renowned restaurant on Ambergris Caye, with a word-of-mouth reputation built on the happy bellies of thousands of diners. Even after having enlarged the dining room, they still can't keep up with the dinner crowds that flock here for the lively ambience, substantial servings, fresh ingredients, and food cooked to order. The restaurant is a thatched, screened-in building with picnic tables, a large flamboyant tree growing up through the roof, and a floor of crushed shells and sand. You can get everything from Belizean stewed chicken to shrimp in watermelon sauce. For lunch, there are still burgers, including traditional beef burgers, although I prefer the shrimp and fish burgers. There's live music every night, with Caribbean night on Thursday, Mayan night on Friday, and Mexican night on Saturday. Food specials complement the musical selections.

Pescador Dr., San Pedro. ✆ **226-2176.** www.elviskitchen.com. Reservations recommended. Main courses BZ$16–BZ$50 (US$8–US$25/£4.25–£13); fresh fish, seafood, and lobster priced according to market. AE, MC, V. Mon–Sat 11am–2pm and 5:30–10pm.

Estel's Dine By the Sea ★ SEAFOOD/INTERNATIONAL If you want to dine right by the water, it's hard to get much closer than Estel's. This casual place has a sand floor with heavy wooden tables and plastic chairs inside the main dining room, and a sand terrace outside with pure plastic patio furniture. A broad range of memorabilia and antiques line the walls, and there's a piano in one corner. This is a popular place to start your day, with excellent huevos rancheros and breakfast burritos. The dinner menu features plenty of fresh seafood and fish simply prepared, as well as a host of Mexican and Belizean standards. Hosts Charles and Estella Worthington are usually on hand—they live upstairs. In general, it's a mellow scene, with great music on the stereo and occasional live performances.

Barrier Reef Dr., San Pedro. ✆ **226-2019.** Main courses BZ$10–BZ$44 (US$5–US$22/£2.65–£12). MC, V. Wed–Mon 6am–9pm.

South of San Pedro

Very Expensive

Palmilla ★★ Finds INTERNATIONAL/FUSION This continues to be one of the most elegant and refined dining experiences to be had on Ambergris Caye. The chef here always takes the freshest of local ingredients and prepares them with a creative blend of techniques and spices, influenced by a range of cuisines from around the world. The menu changes regularly, but might include cashew-crusted grouper or a pecan-crusted chicken breast. You can choose a table in the formal dining room, with its orgy of white linens, walls, and orchids, or dine alfresco by candlelight at one of the heavy wooden tables on the outdoor poolside deck. Save room for dessert, as the molten chocolate cake and rum-soaked bread pudding are both to die for.

At Victoria House, south of downtown San Pedro. ✆ **226-2067.** Reservations recommended. Main courses BZ$48–BZ$64 (US$24–US$32/£13–£17). AE, MC, V. Daily 6:30–9pm.

Moderate

Casa Picasso ★★★ INTERNATIONAL/TAPAS Housed on the ground floor of a converted residential house, this stylish place is probably the hippest little restaurant in San Pedro. The odd angles of the walls gave rise to its name, and some creative decor and eclectic music give it a comfortable and captivating ambience. The menu features a wide selection of tapas, both traditional and more modern choices. I particularly recommend the mini crab cakes with a chili-lime dipping sauce, as well as the chicken marinated in sangria and served with an orange-raisin-walnut salsa. If you want heartier fare, there are several pasta dishes to choose from. Casa Picasso advertises the widest selection of desserts on the island, and I definitely recommend saving room for their flourless chocolate cake. They also have an extensive list of creative martinis and coffee drinks, as well as a good selection of French, Italian, Chilean, and South African wines.

Sting Ray St., south of town on lagoon side of island. ✆ **226-4507.** Reservations recommended. Tapas BZ$14–BZ$24 (US$7–US$12/£3.70–£6.35); main courses BZ$28–BZ$32 (US$14–US$16/£7.40–£8.50). MC, V. Mon–Sat 5:30–10pm.

On North Ambergris Caye

Despite its relative isolation, the northern section of Ambergris Caye has perhaps the island's greatest concentration of truly excellent eateries. If you're staying in San Pedro or on the southern half of the island, you'll need to take a water taxi. Most of these restaurants will be able to arrange this for you, usually at a reduced rate from the going fare.

In addition to the places listed below, I've been hearing good reports about another new contemporary fusion-style restaurant, with a heavy Pacific Rim influence, called **Pinki Knox** (✆ **622-6991**), located a little bit north of the bridge.

Expensive

Capricorn Restaurant ★ INTERNATIONAL/SEAFOOD Grab one of the outdoor tables here on the wraparound seafront veranda of this boutique hotel's little restaurant. If these are all filled, don't despair, as you'll also be able to watch the water through the wide windows of the small dining room, which are almost always thrown open. Start things off with some fresh ceviche or some peel-and-eat shrimp. Be sure to ask about the nightly specials. For a main, I like the crab cakes made with local Stone Crab claws, although this can also be ordered as an appetizer. There's always fresh fish, and conch, stone crabs, scallops, or lobster depending on season and availability, as well as a handful of steak, chicken, and pork entrees.

At Capricorn Hotel, on northern end of Ambergris Caye. ✆ **226-2809.** Reservations recommended. Main courses BZ$40–BZ$75 (US$20–US$38/£1–£20). AE, MC, V. Thurs–Tues 8am–10am, 11:30am–2pm, and 6–9pm.

Mambo ★★ FUSION/INTERNATIONAL The eclectic menu here touches on a wide range of world cuisines. From the seared scallops in Jamaican jerk sauce to the filet mignon with blue-cheese crust drizzled with an orange-balsamic reduction, the food and presentation here are top-notch. I also enjoyed the mango-and-ginger-glazed pork chops, while the warm chocolate soufflé was perhaps the best dessert I tasted in Belize. The restaurant features an excellent and extensive wine list. And for those who want to keep on enjoying the finer things in life after dinner, these folks also offer a selection of Cuban cigars and cognacs. Service is attentive and professional, and the ambience is elegant without being stuffy.

At Mata Chica, on the northern end of Ambergris Caye. ✆ **220-5010.** Reservations required. Main courses BZ$32–BZ$60 (US$16–US$30/£8.50–£16). AE, MC, V. Daily noon–2:30pm and 6–10pm.

Rendezvous Restaurant & Winery ★★ THAI This refined restaurant serves excellent French-influenced Thai cuisine. You'll find Thai classics, such as pad Thai and Larb Nua, a delicious cold beef salad, right alongside *laksa,* a Malaysian version of bouillabaisse. There's a relaxed semiformal air to the whole operation, which is decorated with floral patterned tablecloths, subdued lighting, and cushioned rattan chairs. They vint a few wine varieties right on-site, with imported grape juices. Unfortunately, I find these to be pretty immature and thin; you'd do much better to buy an imported bottle off their more traditional wine list.

4½ miles (7km) north of cut, on the northern section of Ambergris Caye. ✆ **226-3426.** Reservations recommended. Main courses BZ$38–BZ$62 (US$19–US$31/£10–£16). MC, V. Daily 11:30am–2pm and 6–9pm.

Rojo Lounge ★★★ Finds FUSION This newer restaurant has quickly won over the hearts and taste buds of locals and tourists alike. Self-taught chef and owner Jeff Spiegel and his partner Vivian Yu have created an elegant and ultra-hip open-air restaurant. There are traditional chairs, as well as couch and plush chair seating, on a broad open deck facing the sea. The lighting and decor are very red, hence, the name—Rojo. It's always wise to try the nightly specials, but whatever you do, don't miss the chorizo, shitake, and shrimp pot stickers. The guava-glazed baby back ribs are also spectacular. If you're more interested in seafood, there are both crab and grouper cakes, or you could have some homemade conch sausage on a fresh pizza. This place has an extensive wine list, as well as an immense and fabulously stocked bar.

At Azul Resort, on the northern section of Ambergris Caye. ✆ **226-4012.** Reservations required. Main courses BZ$34–BZ$68 (US$17–US$34/£9–£18). MC, V. Tues–Sat 6–9pm.

Moderate

Sweet Basil Gourmet Café ★ INTERNATIONAL This breezy, two-story wood-frame house with a bright paint job and gingerbread trim is a great spot for lunch or dinner. A wide range of specialty items and imported goods, from cheeses to olives to deli meats, is used to create an extensive menu of interesting salads, sandwiches, and pasta dishes. The burgers are especially good. A selection of more substantial dinner options is also offered daily. While there's seating on the first floor, you'll definitely want to grab a seat on the open-air second-floor veranda, with views to both the lagoon and the Caribbean Sea.

Just across the cut, on the northern section of Ambergris Caye. ✆ **226-2113.** Reservations recommended during high season. Sandwiches BZ$20–BZ$32 (US$10–US$16/£5.30–£8.50); main courses BZ$30–BZ$38 (US$15–US$19/£7.95–£10); lobster priced according to market. AE, MC, V. Wed–Mon 11am–9pm.

AMBERGRIS CAYE AFTER DARK

Ambergris Caye is a popular beach and dive destination, and as such it supports a fairly active nightlife and late-night bar scene. I recommend starting things off at one of the beachside bars such as the **Pier Lounge** (✆ **226-2002**) at the Spindrift Hotel, or a bar built out over the water like **Wet Willy's ★** (✆ **226-4136**), located off the center of town, or **The Palapa Bar★** (✆ **226-3111;** www.palapabarandgrill.com), located about 1.6km (1 mile) north of the cut on the northern half of the island. Two other popular choices are **Fido's Courtyard** (✆ **226-2056**), which has live music every night of the week, and **The Purple Parrot** (✆ **226-2071**) in Ramon's Village, which claims to be a favorite haunt of Jimmy Buffet.

If you're looking for a dance club and late-night action, your best bets are the two traditional San Pedro discos, **Jaguar's Temple Club** (no phone) and **Big Daddy's** (no phone), which are within a stone's throw of each other on Barrier Reef Drive, near the basketball court and the church. Just south of downtown on Coconut Drive, you might try the huge **Barefoot Iguana ★** (✆ **226-2927**), which features everything from hot new DJs to mud wrestling to sporting events shown on a giant screen.

If you're the betting type looking for a bit more action than the chicken drop, try **The Palace** (✆ **226-3570**), at the corner of Caribeña and Pescador Drive, or the new, **Casino Belize** ★ (✆ **226-2777**), at the Belize Yacht Club, just south of the airstrip. Casino Belize is by far the much larger and swankier of the two.

2 CAYE CAULKER ★★★

32km (20 miles) N of Belize City; 16km (10 miles) S of Ambergris Caye

It's sad to say, but Caye Caulker is no longer the secret hideaway of a handful of happy hippie backers and a few chosen cognoscenti. That said, this remains the epitome of a small, isolated, and laid-back Caribbean getaway. Unlike neighboring San Pedro, you won't find any gridlock traffic here, or be constantly run off the road by cars and golf carts. In fact, golf-cart traffic is still relatively light, with flip flops and bicycles fulfilling most of the transportation needs. Let's hope it stays that way. Still, Caye Caulker has begun to experience some of the effects of the amazing boom going on just to the north on Ambergris Caye. There's more and more development on either end of the island, and the long-neglected northern section of Caye Caulker—across the Split—is even starting to be developed.

ESSENTIALS

Getting There & Departing

As with Ambergris Caye, you've got two options for getting to and from Caye Caulker: sea or air. When the weather's rough, it's bumpy both ways, although it's certainly quicker by air, and you're more likely to get wet in the boat.

BY PLANE There are dozens of daily flights between Belize City and Caye Caulker Airport (CUK). Flights leave from both Philip S. W. Goldson International Airport and Municipal Airport roughly every half-hour. Most will stop en route at Caye Chapel Airport (CYC), when there is demand. If you're coming in on an international flight and heading straight for Caye Caulker, you should book a flight from the international airport. If you're already in Belize City or in transit around the country, it's cheaper to fly from the Municipal Airport, which is also closer to downtown, and quicker and cheaper to reach by taxi. During the high season, and whenever possible, it's best to have a reservation. However, you can usually just show up at the airport and get a seat on a flight within an hour.

Both **Maya Island Air** (✆ **223-1140** in Belize City, or 226-2435 in San Pedro; www.mayaairways.com) and **Tropic Air** (✆ **800/422-3435** in the U.S. and Canada, or 226-2012 in Belize; www.tropicair.com) have 11 flights daily between Goldson International Airport and Caye Caulker, and they both follow the same schedule. The flights depart every hour beginning at 7:40am, with the last flight at 5:40pm. Flight time is around 15 minutes; the fare is BZ$114 (US$57/£30) each way. These flights actually originate at the Belize City Municipal Airport 10 minutes earlier. From the Municipal Airport, the fare is just BZ$63 (US$32/£17) each way. These flights take around 20 minutes, because they stop en route to pick up passengers at the international airport. When you're ready to leave, flights from San Pedro to Belize City run from 7:10am to 5:10pm. Most of these flights stop first at the international airport, before continuing on to the Municipal Airport.

Fun Facts What's in a Name?

The Spanish called this little island "Cayo Hicaco." *Hicaco* is Spanish for the coco plum palm. Some say the name comes from the fact that ships used to be caulked in the shallow calm waters off the back side of this island, hence Caye Caulker. However, a third theory purports that the island appears as Caye Corker on several early British maps. This line of reasoning claims that early sailors and pirates stopped to fill and then "cork" their water bottles with the abundant fresh water found here.

Almost all of the above flights originating in Belize City continue on to San Pedro on Ambergris Caye. Similarly, almost all the return flights originate in San Pedro. The flight between the two islands takes 10 minutes, and the fare is BZ$63 (US$32/£17) each way.

Connections to and from all the other major destinations in Belize can be made via the municipal and international airports in Belize City.

BY BOAT Regularly scheduled boats ply the route between Belize City and Caye Caulker. All leave from somewhere near the Swing Bridge, and the majority leave directly from the **Marine Terminal,** which is located right on North Front Street just over the Swing Bridge; these boats are associated with the **Caye Caulker Water Taxi Association** (✆ **226-0992;** www.cayecaulkerwatertaxi.com). Most are open speedboats with one or two very powerful engines, and carry between 20 and 30 passengers, making the trip in about 45 minutes. Almost all of these boats stop to drop off and pick up passengers on St. George's Caye or Caye Chapel, when there's demand. If you're going to Ambergris, St. George's, or Caye Chapel from Caye Caulker, these boats all continue on and will take you there. Find out on Caye Caulker just where and when they stop. The schedule is subject to change, but boats for Caye Caulker leave the Marine Terminal roughly every 90 minutes beginning at 8am, with the last boat leaving at 4:30pm. The fare is BZ$20 (US$10/£5.30) one-way, BZ$40 (US$20/£11) round-trip between Belize City and Caye Caulker; and BZ$15 (US$7.50/£4) one-way between Caye Caulker and San Pedro. (See "Two Small Cayes on the Way" on p. 151 for more details about St. George's Caye and Caye Chapel.)

In addition to the Caye Caulker Water Taxi Association, the ***Triple J*** (✆ **223-3464**) leaves from Courthouse pier near the Marine Terminal every day at 8 and 10:30am, noon, and 3 and 4:40pm, returning from the Texaco dock on Ambergris Caye at 7:30, 8:30, and 11am, and 1:30, 3, and 4pm. The rates for the ***Triple J*** are similar to those listed above.

It is possible to purchase a seat in advance by visiting the Marine Terminal personally. This is a good idea in the high season, although in most cases you'll need to purchase the ticket in cash, upfront. Some Belize City hotels provide this service, or they can get you a confirmed reservation by phone.

Getting Around

Caye Caulker is small. You can easily walk from one end of the island to the other in around 20 minutes. If you want to cover more ground quickly, a bicycle is your best bet. Many hotels have their own for guests to use free of charge or for a slight rental fee. If

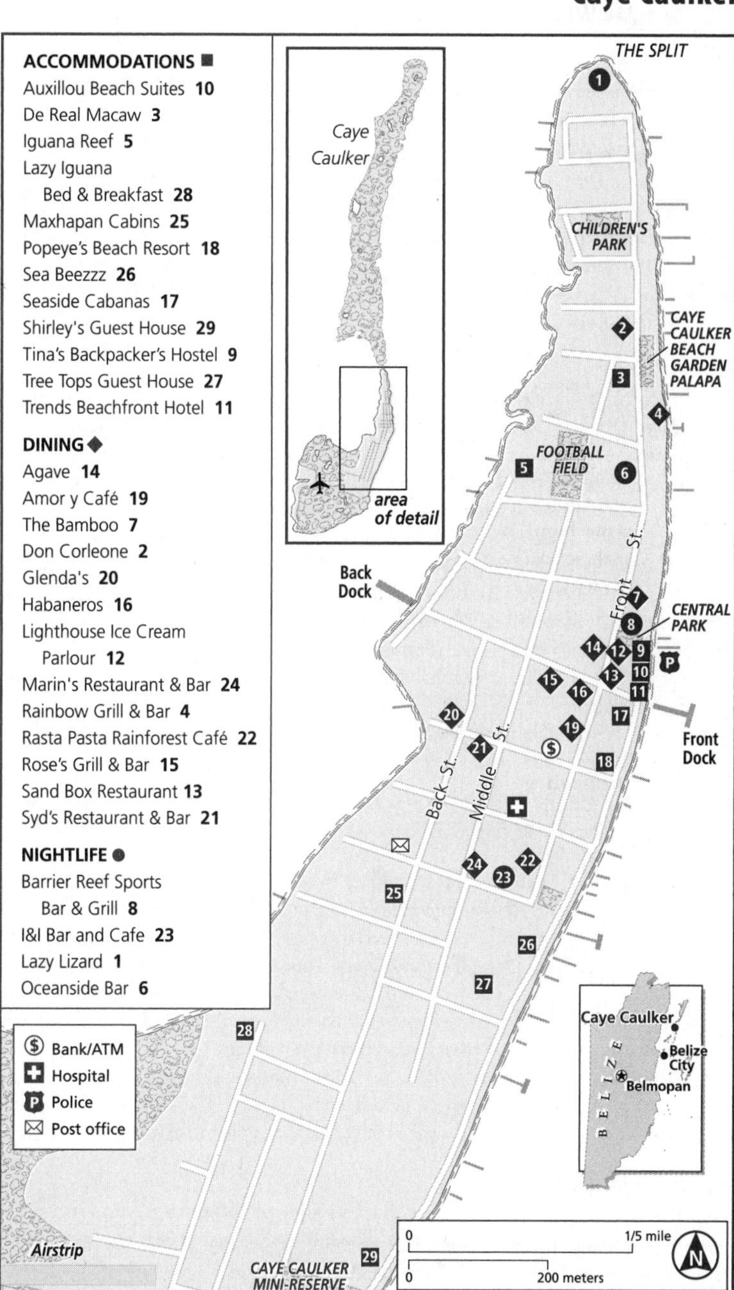
ACCOMMODATIONS
Auxillou Beach Suites 10
De Real Macaw 3
Iguana Reef 5
Lazy Iguana
Bed & Breakfast 28
Maxhapan Cabins 25
Popeye's Beach Resort 18
Sea Beezzz 26
Seaside Cabanas 17
Shirley's Guest House 29
Tina's Backpacker's Hostel 9
Tree Tops Guest House 27
Trends Beachfront Hotel 11
DINING
Agave 14
Amor y Café 19
The Bamboo 7
Don Corleone 2
Glenda's 20
Habaneros 16
Lighthouse Ice Cream
Parlour 12
Marin's Restaurant & Bar 24
Rainbow Grill & Bar 4
Rasta Pasta Rainforest Café 22
Rose's Grill & Bar 15
Sand Box Restaurant 13
Syd's Restaurant & Bar 21
NIGHTLIFE
Barrier Reef Sports
Bar & Grill 8
I&I Bar and Cafe 23
Lazy Lizard 1
Oceanside Bar 6
Bank/ATM
Hospital
Police
Post office
Caye Caulker
area of detail
THE SPLIT
CHILDREN'S PARK
CAYE CAULKER BEACH GARDEN PALAPA
FOOTBALL FIELD
Back Dock
Front St.
CENTRAL PARK
Front Dock
Back St.
Middle St.
Airstrip
CAYE CAULKER MINI-RESERVE
Caye Caulker
Belize City
Belmopan
BELIZE
0
1/5 mile
0
200 meters
N

Slow Ride

The unofficial, yet almost universal, motto on Caye Caulker is "Go Slow."

not, you can rent a bicycle in town. There are several places on Front Street that rent bicycles. Rates run around BZ$20 to BZ$30 (US$10–US$15/£5.30–£7.95) per day.

While I think it's really unnecessary, you can also rent a golf cart from **Caye Caulker Golf Rentals** (**✆ 226-0237**), **C & N Golf Carts** (**✆ 226-0252**), or **Jasmine Cart Rentals** (**✆ 206-0212**). Rates run around BZ$120 to BZ$160 (US$60–US$80/£32–£42) per day for a four-seat cart. Hourly rates are between BZ$20 and BZ$40 (US$10–US$20/£5.30–£11).

Orientation

Most boats dock at the pier jutting off Front Street at a spot called Front Bridge—so named because this is the front side of the island facing the reef (east). The town extends north and south from here. As you debark, if you kept walking straight ahead, you'd soon come to the western side of the island and the Back Bridge or dock, where some of the boats dock. Caye Caulker consists of two or three main north–south sand roads, a few cross streets, and numerous paths. The closest street to the water on the east side of the island is Front Street. The next street in is called either Middle Street or Hicaco Avenue, and the next street to the west is called alternately Back Street or Langosta Avenue. The small Caye Caulker airstrip is located on the southern outskirts of the town. At the north end of town you'll find the Split or Cut, the town's prime swimming and sunbathing spot.

Much of Caye Caulker is uninhabited. The small town and inhabited sections are quite concentrated.

Though Caye Caulker is still a relatively safe place, it is not advisable to leave money or valuables in your hotel room, except in a safe.

FAST FACTS For the local **police,** dial **✆ 911,** or 226-2022; for the **fire department,** dial **✆ 226-0353.** In the case of a medical emergency, call the **Caye Caulker Health Clinic** (**✆ 226-0166**).

Atlantic Bank (**✆ 226-0207**) is located on Back Street, near the center of the island, and has an ATM that accepts international credit and debit cards. The **post office** (**✆ 226-2325**) is also located on Back Street; it's open Monday through Friday from 8am to noon and from 1 to 5pm. There are several **Internet cafes** on the island; just walk along Front Street and find one with an open terminal. I like **Caye Caulker Cyber Café,** which serves drinks—and even has a popular happy hour with reduced rates on drinks and Internet usage. They also have a good book-swap library.

Most hotels provide laundry service, but pricing varies widely, so ask first. There are several coin-operated and full service **laundromats** on Caye Caulker, all in the central downtown area. Almost all of these are a better deal than going with your hotel's service.

WHAT TO SEE & DO

The main activities on Caye Caulker itself are strolling up and down the sand streets, and swimming and sunbathing off the docks. The most popular spot is at the north end of the island by the **Split★**. The Split was formed in 1961 when Hurricane Hattie literally split the island in two. You'll find the water's edge rimmed with a nice wooden dock, and there's even a decent little patch of beach and a roped-off swimming area. The water is very calm by the Split, making it a good place to practice if you're an inexperienced snorkeler. Take care when swimming off the docks here. The split is an active channel with regular boat traffic. At least one swimmer was killed by a boat, so stick to designated swimming areas, away from obvious boat channels. Also, when the tides are running strong, there's quite a bit of current through the split, and it's easy to get dragged along for a few hundred yards or so. If you do get caught in this current, treat it like any riptide: Don't panic, and swim diagonally across the current to get out of it.

Aside from the Split, and as on Ambergris Caye, there is not much beach to speak of on the rest of the island. There is a narrow strip of sand for much of the length of the island, where the land meets the sea, but even at low tide it isn't wide enough for you to unroll a beach towel on in most places. In fact, along most of its length this is a small bike and footpath that is probably the busiest thoroughfare on Caye Caulker. Just off the coast, for 100 yards or more out from shore, the bottom is covered with sea grass. Beneath the grass is a layer of spongy roots and organic matter topped with a thin layer of white sand. Walking on this spongy sand is somewhat unnerving, as you might encounter a sea urchin or stingray, and it's easy to trip and stumble.

Several of the hotels have built long piers out into the sea, with steps down into the water, and swimming is best here. Beyond this, some of the best swimming can be had from boats anchored out in the turquoise waters between the shore and the reef, or by taking a kayak offshore a little ways.

As on Ambergris Caye, snorkeling, scuba diving, and fishing are the main draws here. All are excellent.

On & Under the Water

Scuba Diving & Snorkeling ★★★

There's excellent diving and snorkeling close to Caye Caulker. Within a 5- to 20-minute boat ride from the pier lie some world-class dive sites, including **Caye Caulker North Cut, Coral Gardens, Pyramid Flats, Sponge Avenue,** and **Amigos Wreck.** As on Ambergris Caye, a day's diving here will almost always feature a mix of steep wall drops and coral caverns and tunnels. In addition, in Caye Caulker you can dive on the wreck of a 15m (50-ft.) boat, and amongst huge canyons of coral. You'll see brilliant coral and sponge formations, as well as a wealth of colorful marine life. The wreck and canyons are prime spots to spot giant grouper, and rays and turtles are fairly common here as well.

There are several dependable dive operators on Caye Caulker. Rates are pretty standardized, and you should be able to get deals on multiday, multidive packages. The best dive operations on the island are **Belize Diving Services** ★ (✆ 226-0143; www.belizedivingservice.com), **Big Fish Dive Center** (✆ 226-0450; www.bigfishdivebelize.com), and **Frenchie's Diving** (✆ 226-0234; www.frenchiesdivingbelize.com). All of these operators charge BZ$100 to BZ$160 (US$50–US$80/£27–£42) for a local two-tank dive, with equipment rental running around BZ$50 (US$25/£13) for a complete package, and BZ$12 to BZ$20 (US$6–US$10/£3.20–£5.30) for a mask, snorkel, and fins.

For more adventurous diving, you'll probably want to head out to the **Turneffe Island Atoll** ★★, **Lighthouse Reef** ★★, and **Blue Hole.** All of the dive operations on Caye Caulker offer this trip or will subcontract it out. It's about a 2- to 3-hour ride each way—depending upon the speed of your boat—over sometimes rough seas. Most day trips out to Turneffe Island or Lighthouse Reef and Blue Hole run around BZ$300 to BZ$400 (US$150–US$200/£80–£106) per person, including transportation, two or three dives,

Chocolate & the Manatees

Sure you can get candy bars and cakes and a whole host of products derived from the fruit of the cacao tree here. But on Caye Caulker, when someone mentions "Chocolate," they are almost inevitably referring to pioneering guide and boat captain Lionel "Chocolate" Heredia. Chocolate began his career as a fisherman, but he soon dedicated himself to the fledgling business of taxiing folks by speedboat back and forth between Belize City and Caye Caulker. This business soon expanded to include guided tours, snorkeling outings, and fishing adventures. Chocolate was also probably the first guide to introduce the popular day trip to see manatees and do some snorkeling at remote cayes. He and his wife, Annie, also led the battle to protect these gentle sea mammals and their feeding grounds, finally seeing the dedication of the Swallow Caye Manatee Reserve (www.swallowcayemanatees.org) in 1999.

Chocolate (✆ **226-0151;** chocolateseashore@gmail.com) still leads manatee and snorkel tours. These tours begin with a stop at the manatee-feeding site on Swallow Caye, before heading to either Goff's or Sergeant's cayes, which are little more than football field–size patches of sand with a few palm trees. The afternoons are usually spent snorkeling in the clear waters off these cayes, and lunching on the sand. These trips, which are also offered by most other tour operators on the island, include all transportation, lunch on one of the cayes, and several snorkel stops, and cost between BZ$120 and BZ$160 (US$60–US$80/£30–£40) per person.

tanks, and weights, as well as lunch and snacks. For more information on these dive sites, see section 3, later in this chapter.

Caye Caulker is another excellent place to learn how to scuba dive. Resort courses will give you an excellent 1-day introduction into the world of scuba diving, including a very controlled shallow-water boat dive. These courses cost BZ$200 to BZ$300 (US$100–US$150/£53–£80). In 3 to 4 days, however, you can get your full open-water certification. These courses cost between BZ$600 and BZ$800 (US$300–US$400/£159–£212), including all equipment rentals, class materials, and the processing of your certification, as well as four open-water and reef dives. All of the above-mentioned dive operations offer these courses.

There are a host of boats on Caye Caulker offering snorkeling trips, and most of the above dive operators also offer snorkeling trips and equipment rental. Snorkeling tours range in price from BZ$30 to BZ$60 (US$15–US$30/£7.95–£16) for short jaunts to half-day outings, and BZ$100 to BZ$160 (US$50–US$80/£27–£42) for full-day trips—a bit more if you want to jump on a trip all the way out to the Blue Hole. A full set of mask, fins, and snorkel will usually cost from BZ$12 to BZ$20 (US$6–US$10/£3.20–£5.30) per person per day.

All of the Caye Caulker dive and snorkel operators offer trips to **Shark-Ray Alley★★** and **Hol Chan Marine Reserve★★**. These trips cost between BZ$90 and BZ$240 (US$45–US$120/£24–£64) per person, depending on whether it is a snorkel or scuba dive trip, how long the tour lasts, and whether or not there is a stop on Ambergris Caye.

Many of these include a stop for lunch and a quick walk around town in San Pedro. See "What to See & Do" in section 1, earlier in this chapter, for more information and a detailed description of Shark-Ray Alley and Hol Chan Marine Reserve.

One of my favorite options for snorkelers is a day-cruise to Shark-Ray Alley and Hol Chan with **Raggamuffin Tours** ★ (✆ **226-0348;** www.raggamuffintours.com) aboard a classic wooden Belizean sloop. The trip makes three distinct snorkel stops, and includes lunch on board the boat, snorkeling gear, and the park entrance fee for BZ$90 (US$45/£24) per person.

Sailing ★★

The crystal-clear waters, calm seas, and excellent snorkeling spots around Caye Caulker make this an excellent place to go out for a sail. Unlike on Ambergris Caye, there's no organized bareboat charters available here, but you can go out on any number of different vessels for a half- or full-day sail, a sunset cruise, a moonlight cruise, or a combined sailing and snorkeling adventure.

A day cruise including lunch, drinks, and snorkeling gear should run between BZ$100 and BZ$220 (US$50–US$110/£27–£58) per person; a half-day tour including drinks, a snack, and snorkeling gear should cost between BZ$70 and BZ$120 (US$35–US$60/ £19–£32). Most hotels and tour operators around town can hook you up with an appropriate captain and craft. Or you can head out on the Shark-Ray Alley and Hol Chan tour with **Raggamuffin Tours** ★ (✆ **226-0348;** www.raggamuffintours.com).

Fishing

Although not nearly as developed or popular on Caye Caulker, sport fishing for tarpon, permit, and bonefish is still excellent around the caye, and on the reefs and flats. There are several dedicated fishing guides on the island, and almost every hotel, tour operator, or dive shop can hook you up with a captain and crew for some angling. If you're looking for a specific recommendation, check out Gabriel at **Gabriel's Fishing Trips** (✆ **206-0131**) or **Porfilio Guzmán** (✆ **226-0152**); both are excellent guides. You can also check in with the folks at **Angler's Abroad Fly Shop** (✆ **226-0303;** www.anglersabroad.com)

A half-day reef trolling, casting, or fly-fishing for bonefish or tarpon costs between BZ$250 and BZ$400 (US$125–US$200/£66–£106), a full day between BZ$400 and BZ$800 (US$200–US$400/£106–£212). Deep-sea trolling for larger game runs around BZ$800 to BZ$1,200 (US$400–US$600/£212–£318) for a half-day, BZ$1,600 to BZ$2,400 (US$800–US$1,200/£424–£636) for a full day. These prices are per boat for two to four fishermen and usually include drinks, tackle, and lunch.

Kitesurfing & Sailboarding

With strong, steady, but not overpowering winds, Caye Caulker is a great place to learn or practice kitesurfing. The folks at **Kitexplorer** (✆ **602-9297;** www.kitexplorer.com) rent out both kitesurfing and sailboarding equipment. They also offer an intensive 9-hour course in kitesurfing for BZ$720 (US$360/£191) that is guaranteed to get you up and skimming across the sea.

Kayaks & Other Watercraft

The calm, protected waters just offshore are wonderful for any number of watersports vehicles. Several hotels and tour operators around Caye Caulker have various types of watercraft for guest use, or general rental. Rates run around BZ$20 to BZ$30 (US$10–US$15/£5.30–£7.95) per hour for a kayak; BZ$40 to BZ$60 (US$15–US$30/£7.95–£16) per hour for a Hobie Cat or small sailboat; and BZ$60 to BZ$80 (US$30–US$40/£16–£21) per hour for a jet ski.

Fun on Dry Land

Aside from sunbathing, reading, and relaxing, there's very little to do on Caye Caulker. However, you should be sure to head south of town to the **Caye Caulker Mini-Reserve.** Located on the southern outskirts of the town, the term "mini" is certainly fitting. Nevertheless, this local endeavor features a few gentle and well-cleared paths through a small stand of littoral forest. More serious bird-watchers might want to grab a boat and a guide and head to the northern half of the island, where 40 hectares (100 acres) on the very northern tip have been declared the **Caye Caulker Forest Reserve.** As of yet, no admission fees are being charged at either of these reserves, but that could change. In all, over 130 species of resident and migrant birds have been spotted on and around Caye Caulker. Another option for bird-watchers and nature lovers is to rent a kayak for paddling around on the lagoon and mangrove side of the island.

Yoga

Located on the southwestern part of the island, **Great Island Yoga** (© **660-0411;** www.greatislandyoga.com) has a lovely ocean-facing yoga studio. While they specialize in weeklong retreats, depending upon who's teaching, you can sometimes just pop in for a class. Currently, public classes are offered January through May, on Wednesday, Friday, and Sunday at 10am, but it's always best to confirm in advance. Cost is BZ$40 (US$20/£11) per class.

Excursions on the Mainland

If you've got island fever or Caye Caulker is your only destination, and you want to see more of Belize, several tour operators on Caye Caulker offer excursions to all of the major attractions and destinations around the country, including Altun Ha, Lamanai, Xunantunich, Mountain Pine Ridge, and Tikal. You can also go cave tubing in the Caves Branch region. Most of these tours involve a flight or two in a small charter plane.

The most popular and economical tours are to the Mayan ruins of Altun Ha or Lamanai, or a spa package and lunch at Maruba Jungle Resort. Various operators offer a combined trip visiting both Altun Ha and Maruba. These trips begin with a short boat ride to the mainland, followed by a minibus ride to the selected attraction. Prices for these trips run BZ$140 to BZ$200 (US$70–US$100/£37–£53), although the spa treatments are extra.

For trips involving a flight, prices range from BZ$200 to BZ$400 (US$100–US$200/£53–£106) per person, depending on the distance traveled and number of activities and attractions crammed into 1 day. Any hotel or tour operator on the island can help you arrange any number of these tours. In most cases, these trips are subcontracted out to an operator based either in Belize City or on Ambergris Caye.

For detailed descriptions of these various destinations and attractions, see the respective regional chapters throughout this book. In addition to the dive and watersports tour operators listed above, **Tsunami Adventures** (© **226-0462;** www.tsunamiadventures.com) is good, all-purpose operator with an extensive list of offerings on and under the water, and all around the cayes and mainland, as well.

SHOPPING

In terms of shopping, you'll be amazed by the number of small gift shops and makeshift souvenir stands lining the few streets here. As on Ambergris Caye, much of the shopping on Caye Caulker is typical tourist fare. Mostly what you'll be able to buy are T-shirts and jewelry made by local artisans. **Chocolate's Boutique** ★ (© **226-0151**) has slightly

About the Water

Much of the water on Caye Caulker is collected rainwater. While it's usually safe to drink, and most locals are used to it, I advise visitors to stick to bottled water.

higher-quality goods, including reasonably priced Guatemalan and Indonesian textiles, as well as some lovely silver and stone jewelry. And yes, the Chocolate of this shop is the same Chocolate discussed in "Chocolate & the Manatee," above, although he is almost never in the shop. His wife, Annie, almost always is.

A couple of good art galleries on the island include **Caribbean Colors Art Gallery** (✆ **206-0206;** www.caribbean-colors.com), which features some interesting original artwork and hand-painted silk by artist Lee Vanderwalker-Kroll, and **Cooper's Art Gallery** ★ (✆ **226-0330;** www.debbiecooper.artspan.com), which features the work of local resident Debbie Cooper and other local artists.

As I recommend elsewhere in this book, please avoid buying black coral jewelry. Black coral is extremely beautiful, but as with every endangered resource, increased demand just leads to increased harvesting of a slow-growing coral.

WHERE TO STAY

Accommodations on Caye Caulker have improved over the years. But there are still no resorts or real luxury options to be had. In my opinion, this adds to the charm of the place. Budget and midrange lodging options are abundant, and some of these are quite comfortable.

If you plan on staying for any period of time, you should look into renting a small cottage, condo, or apartment. Look around for signs or bulletin boards, or check with Amanda at **Caye Caulker Rentals** ★ (✆/fax **226-0029;** www.cayecaulkerrentals.com). Rates begin at around BZ$100 (US$50/£27) per night, although during the high season rates go up and longer stays are often required. Another option is the fully equipped efficiency units at **Caye Caulker Condos** (✆/fax **226-0072;** www.cayecaulkercondos.com), which rent for between BZ$180 and BZ$260 (US$90–US$130/£48–£69) per night.

Expensive

Auxillou Beach Suites ★ These modern, fully equipped, one-bedroom suites are some of the best-equipped and -located rooms on Caye Caulker. Each comes with a kitchenette, a large front living room with a futon couch, an equally large bedroom, and a private balcony. The best rooms are those on the second floor, just because the seclusion and view from their oceanfront balconies are that much better. There's a roof-top terrace here with great, expansive views. These folks also rent a private house, and are related by blood to several other hotel and house rental owners around the island.

On the waterfront, in the center of town (P.O. Box 51), Caye Caulker. ✆ **226-0370.** Fax 226-0371. www.auxilloubeachsuites.com. 8 units. BZ$258 (US$129/£68) double. Rates slightly higher during peak weeks; lower during the off season. DISC, MC, V. *In room:* A/C, TV, kitchenette, coffeemaker, no phone.

Iguana Reef ★★ This is the closest thing to a resort hotel on Caye Caulker. The spacious rooms are housed in several two-story concrete block structures. Most rooms come with two queen beds, although some come with just one queen bed and a foldout futon couch. All include air-conditioning, a stocked minibar, and a programmable safe. The deluxe units have a sitting area, a stereo CD player, and a semiprivate veranda. Although there's no restaurant here, a continental breakfast is served in a pleasant open-air dining area overlooking the water. Iguana Reef, which is on the lagoon or back side of the island, has a large and comfortable sandy area for lounging, with a pier leading off this to a nice swimming spot. This is also arguably the best spot on the island to catch a sunset. The hotel also has a very inviting little pool.

Back St. (P.O. Box 31), Caye Caulker. ✆ **226-0213.** Fax 226-0087. www.iguanareefinn.com. 12 units. BZ$270–BZ$330 (US$135–US$165/£72–£87) double; BZ$750 (US$375/£199) penthouse. Rates include continental breakfast. Rates slightly higher during peak weeks; lower during the off season. DISC, MC, V. **Amenities:** Bar; small outdoor pool; tour desk; laundry service. *In room:* A/C, stocked minifridge, safe, no phone.

Moderate

In addition to the places listed below, **Popeye's Beach Resort** (✆ **226-0032;** www.popeyesbeachresort.com) is another good option in this price range, with air-conditioned rooms and an oceanfront setting.

Lazy Iguana Bed & Breakfast ★ Housed in an interesting four-story octagonal building, this little bed-and-breakfast offers comfortable rooms in a quiet setting on the back side of the island. Three of the rooms have queen beds, and one comes with two twin beds. All of the rooms are spacious and immaculate. Breakfasts always include a couple of freshly baked items, and plenty of fresh fruit and strong coffee. One of the nicest features here is the open-air fourth-floor thatched terrace, which offers excellent 360-degree views of the island, and has a couple of hammocks perfect for an afternoon siesta. Guests have free use of bicycles, and there's a small lounge with a lending library and cable television.

2 blocks north of the airstrip on the lagoon side (P.O. Box 59), Caye Caulker. ✆ **226-0350.** Fax 226-0320. www.lazyiguana.net. 4 units. BZ$210 (US$105/£56) double. Rates include full breakfast. Rates higher during peak weeks; lower during the off season. MC, V. *In room:* A/C, minifridge, free Wi-Fi, no phone.

Seaside Cabanas ★★ Rising from the ashes of a devastating fire, this hotel was built again from scratch, and is better than ever. The whole complex is set in a horseshoe around a small rectangular pool, with a broad wooden deck around it. All the rooms are spacious and painted in lively yellows and reds, and feature modern decorative touches. Four of the rooms come with private rooftop lounge areas with hammocks strung under an open-air thatch roof. These are by far my favorite rooms, but I also like no. 6, a second-floor unit with a small private balcony. There's no restaurant here, but they have a lively bar and an excellent in-house tour operation.

Front St. (P.O. Box 39), Caye Caulker. ✆ **226-0498.** Fax 226-0125. www.seasidecabanas.com. 17 units. BZ$210–BZ$260 (US$105–US$130/£56–£69) double. Rates slightly higher during peak weeks; lower during the off season. No children under 10 allowed. AE, MC, V. **Amenities:** Bar; outdoor pool; tour desk; laundry service. *In room:* A/C, TV, minifridge, no phone.

Inexpensive

There are literally scores of budget options on Caye Caulker. I list my favorite and the most dependable options below. In addition to these, **Tina's Backpacker's Hostel** (✆ **226-0351;** http://tinashostel.blogspot.com) is probably the best of the rock-bottom budget options, while **Maxhapan Cabinas** (✆ **226-0118;** maxhapan04@hotmail.com) gets high marks for its intimate vibe and personable service.

De Real Macaw (Value) This place is located just north of the center of town, across from a little sandy park and the ocean on Front Street. The hotel is its own little compound, around a central sandy garden area, with a few tall shade trees hung with hammocks. The two "beachfront" rooms are the best rooms here, but all are very clean and well kept, with tile floors, tiny television sets, and a front porch or balcony. Most of the rooms come with air-conditioning, but you'll pay a little more for it. The two-bedroom "condo" and separate beach house both come with a full kitchen, and these folks also rent out fully furnished apartments on a weekly basis, located a little bit away towards the center of town.

Front St., north of Front Bridge, Caye Caulker. ✆ **226-0459.** Fax 226-0497. www.derealmacaw.biz. 7 units. BZ$50–BZ$110 (US$25–US$55/£13–£29) double with no A/C; BZ$120–BZ$140 (US$60–US$70/£32–£37) double w/ A/C; BZ$240–BZ$260 (US$120–US$130/£64–£69) condo or beach house. Rates lower in the off season. MC, V. *In room:* TV, minifridge, safe, no phone.

Sea Beezzz (Finds) Gray buildings with white trim give this place a bit of Cape Cod styling and feel. Two of the rooms are housed off the main building and small restaurant here, while the others are in two separate duplexes in back of this. The rooms themselves are all quite simple and spartan. To make up for this, the grounds and gardens are kept in stunning shape, and you are only steps from the water. Moreover, the owners really do make you feel immediately like part of the family. The hotel has its own swimming pier built into the sea, and a broad second-floor veranda for sitting and reading or enjoying the view. Sea Beezzz's restaurant serves excellent local cuisine and fresh seafood, and the bar features tasty margaritas. The hotel is only open November through April.

Oceanfront, just south of Front Bridge (P.O. Box 812, Belize City), Caye Caulker. ✆ **631/668-9212** in the U.S., or 226-0176 in Belize. Fax 226-0276. www.geocities.com/seabeezzz. 6 units. BZ$100 (US$50/£27) double. AE, MC, V. **Amenities:** Restaurant; bar; tour desk; laundry service. *In room:* No phone.

Shirley's Guest House These picturesque white cabins with green trim are set on well-manicured grounds facing the ocean, just north of the airstrip. They're set on stilts and are shaded by coconut and casuarina palms. The setting is idyllic, safe, and quiet. The rooms have varnished floors and quilted bedspreads, and some come with a small refrigerator. Although they are a little on the expensive side for what you get, they are worth it for the location and the fairly large and comfortable rooms. Note that only adults are allowed to stay here.

Close to the airstrip on the ocean side (P.O. Box 13), Caye Caulker. ✆ **226-0145** or 600-0069. Fax 226-0264. www.shirleysguesthouse.com. 5 units (3 with private bathroom). BZ$100 (US$50/£27) double with shared bathroom; BZ$130–BZ$180 (US$65–US$90/£34–£48) double with private bathroom. Rates lower in the off season. MC, V. Children not accepted. *In room:* No phone.

Tree Tops Guest House ★ (Value) It's hard to beat this place for location and value on Caye Caulker. Set just off the ocean in the heart of town, this converted three-story home offers clean, spacious, and cool rooms. There are four rooms located on the ground floor. Each comes with tile floors, high ceilings, standing fan, cable television, and small refrigerator. Two of these share a common bathroom down the hall, but each has a vanity sink in the room itself. However, the choicest rooms here are the two top-floor suites. Each of these comes with a king bed, cable television, air-conditioning, minifridge, telephone, and private balcony. The Sunset Suite is the best of these, with the largest balcony, and views to both the lagoon and the ocean. If you opt for one of the standard rooms, however, you can still enjoy the view from the rooftop lounge area, which features several hammocks hung under a shade roof. Though the hotel is set back about 50 yards from the shore, the only things between you and the ocean are some shady coconut palms.

On the waterfront south of Front Bridge (P.O. Box 29), Caye Caulker. ✆ **226-0240.** Fax 226-0115. www.treetopsbelize.com. 6 units (4 with private bathroom). BZ$94 (US$47/£25) double with shared bathroom; BZ$120–BZ$184 (US$60–US$92/£32–£49) double with private bathroom. MC, V. *In room:* TV, minifridge, no phone.

Trends Beachfront Hotel Set right off the water and just off the main pier at Front Bridge, the rooms here are housed in a two-story wooden building painted in tropical pastel colors. The rooms are large, clean, bright, and airy, and it's hard to beat the location. There's also a separate, private bungalow, which is the closest unit to the water, and the best room in the house. These folks also run a separate hotel on Front Street a few blocks away. The rooms here are actually somewhat more modern, and most have air-conditioning; however, they lack the charm, character, and proximity to the water that you'll enjoy at the beachfront option. The Sand Box Restaurant here (p. 149) is one of the most popular on the island.

Beachfront in the center of town, Caye Caulker. ✆ **226-0094.** Fax 226-0097. www.trendsbze.com. 7 units. BZ$60–BZ$100 (US$30–US$50/£16–£27) double; BZ$120 (US$60/£32) bungalow. AE, MC, V. **Amenities:** Restaurant; bar; tour desk; laundry service. *In room:* No phone.

WHERE TO DINE

In addition to the places listed below, I've received good reports about **The Bamboo** (✆ **625-0339**), a newer beachfront restaurant serving a mix of Cajun and Caribbean-inspired fare. Also, be sure to stop in at the **Lighthouse Ice Cream Parlour** on Front Street for a cone or a scoop of some fresh, homemade ice cream.

Moderate

Agave ★★ INTERNATIONAL This is the newest entry into a seemingly crowded field of local restaurants serving up excellent fusion-inspired contemporary cuisine on little Caye Caulker. Tables are spread around a large, raised, open-air deck fronting Front Street. Inside there's a hip bar and lounge area, with a large flatscreen TV for sporting events or movies. Start things off with the excellent crab cakes, served with an orange vodka sauce, or the superb coconut shrimp bisque. For a main course, I like the fresh snapper filet with a spicy papaya glaze. There are also several nightly specials. The owner, Ricael Moran, is actually an accomplished "flair" bartender. If you ask nicely, he may put on a little show.

On Front St., near the center of town. ✆ **226-0403.** Reservations recommended during the high season. Main courses BZ$22–BZ$40 (US$11–US$20/£5.85–£11). MC, V. Daily 6–9:30pm.

Don Corleone ★★ ITALIAN Modern halogen light fixtures over the bar, combined with slow-turning ceiling fans and polished concrete floors, upon which you'll find heavy wooden tables set with linen tablecloths and fancy flatware, add up to make this the most elegant restaurant on the island. And the food easily lives up to the surroundings. The Caesar salad is excellent—and good salads are hard to come by on Caye Caulker. There are also several excellent appetizers, including the grilled portobello mushroom with mozzarella and parmegiano reggiano. A wide range of pastas, pizza, and calzones are offered, as well as some heartier main dishes. I particularly like the fresh fish filet in a spicy tomato sauce. Meat lovers can get a good cut of tenderloin with a green-pepper or mushroom sauce. The wine list is quite extensive and fairly priced.

On Front St., north of the center of town. ✆ **226-0025.** Reservations recommended during the high season. Pastas BZ$20–BZ$40 (US$10–US$20/£5.30–£11); main courses BZ$24–BZ$44 (US$12–US$22/£6.35–£12). DISC, MC, V. Thurs–Tues 7–11am, 11:30am–3pm, and 5–10pm. Closed for lunch in the low season.

Habaneros ★★★ Finds INTERNATIONAL Although the name suggests a Mexican joint, the menu here goes beyond standard Mexican fare. You can get homemade pastas and Thai coconut curries, as well as Brazilian pork. You can also get spicy fajitas made of beef, chicken, or jerk pork. I like to start things off with the Creole Voodoo Cakes, pan-sautéed seafood cakes served with a spicy dipping sauce. The nightly specials tend to be inventive takes on whatever fresh fish and seafood has been caught that day. Heavy wooden tables are spread across the pleasant, open-air, wraparound veranda of this raised-stilt wooden home right on Front Street. There's also indoor seating, but you'll really want to try to grab one of the outdoor spots. Margaritas and sangria are served by the pitcher, and there's a pretty good wine list for Caye Caulker.

On Front St., near the center of town. ✆ **226-0487.** Reservations recommended during the high season. Main courses BZ$12–BZ$42 (US$6–US$22/£3.20–£12). MC, V. Daily 5:30–10pm.

Rainbow Grill & Bar ★ SEAFOOD/INTERNATIONAL Built over the water near the center of town, this is a great place to dine to the sound of water lapping against the pilings below your feet. A dozen or so wooden tables with plastic chairs are set around the screened-in restaurant. The screen comes in handy, especially when the bugs are biting. Try to grab a table by the outer railing, closest to the water. Chicken, fish, conch, shrimp, and lobster are all offered in a variety of preparations from simply grilled or fried, to served with sauces ranging from lemon-ginger to Cajun. All are very well prepared and tasty. The lunch menu is much simpler and less expensive. I particularly like the conch fajitas.

Over the water on Front St., near the center of town. ✆ **226-0281.** Reservations recommended during the high season. Main courses BZ$12–BZ$48 (US$6–US$24/£3.20–£13); lunch BZ$8–BZ$22 (US$4–US$11/£2.10–£5.85). MC, V. Tues–Sun 11am–10pm.

Rasta Pasta Rainforest Café ★★ INTERNATIONAL This is a perennially popular place on Caye Caulker. The food is excellent, the menu eclectic, the portions huge, the prices right, and the service friendly and efficient. Appetizers include fabulous conch fritters and deep-fried crab rolls. There are several namesake pasta dishes, as well as Thai curries, and everything from chicken to conch and lobster is served grilled, blackened, or with a spicy Jamaican jerk sauce. Vegetarians are well cared for here as well, with various dishes to choose from. Whatever you do, save room for some of their B-52 Cheesecake, flavored with Bailey's and Kahlúa and baked in an Oreo cookie crust. If you like the food, be sure to pick up some of their homemade "Genesis in the Jungle" spice packages.

Front St., towards the south end of town. ✆ **206-0356.** Reservations recommended during the high season. Main courses BZ$12–BZ$30 (US$6.35–US$16). MC, V. Thurs–Tues 7am–10pm.

Sand Box Restaurant ★ SEAFOOD/INTERNATIONAL This place gets its name from its sand floor, which extends both inside and out. I prefer the outdoor tables in the shade of broad-leafed seagrape trees. Either way, you'll be able to choose from an extensive menu of Belizean and international dishes. Seafood is the strong suit here, but you can also get chicken or meat dishes. You can have your fresh fish filet served with an almond-and-garlic-butter sauce, or spicy banana chutney. Budget hounds can fill up on burgers, burritos, and quesadillas. The daily happy hour (3–6pm) is quite popular here.

Front St., on the waterfront, near the center of town. ✆ **226-0200.** Main courses BZ$8–BZ$34 (US$4–US$17/£2.10–£9). AE, MC, V. Daily 7am–9pm.

Inexpensive

In addition to the places listed below, there are several simple local restaurants serving fresh fish, seafood, and Belizean standards at very economical rates. The best of these are **Syd's Restaurant & Bar** (✆ **206-0294**) and **Marin's Restaurant & Bar** (✆ **226-0104**), both located on Middle Street, near the center of town. However, my favorite of these local joints is **Rose's Grill & Bar** (✆ **226-0085**), located on the side street, right next to Habaneros.

Perhaps the best cheap eats on Caye Caulker are the various outdoor grills that set up nightly all along Front Street, offering up chicken, shrimp, beef, and lobster (in season) at very reasonable rates.

Amor y Café ★ Value BREAKFAST This quaint and simple breakfast joint used to be Cyndi's, but is still a great place for a breakfast or early lunch. Freshly baked brownies, banana bread, and whole-wheat breads are the mainstay here, served alongside strong coffee, cappuccino, or a fresh-fruit smoothie. You can also get eggs cooked to order, or a hefty sandwich. Perhaps the best thing about Amor y Café, though, is that its few tables are set on an open-air deck overlooking Front Street, so you get to watch Caye Caulker as it slowly wakes up and gets going.

Front St., near the center of town. ✆ **601-4458.** Reservations not accepted. Main courses BZ$4–BZ$8 (US$2–US$4/£1.05–£2.10). No credit cards. Tues–Sun 7am–noon.

Glenda's Value BELIZEAN/MEXICAN This humble establishment is one of Caye Caulker's longest-standing traditions and most popular spots. The menu is written on a chalkboard on your left as you walk up to the open window into Glenda's house. Order here, and the meal will be brought to your table, but don't sit down and expect to be waited on. They specialize in simple Mexican fare, including burritos and rice and beans. Breakfasts feature eggs and johnnycakes, but the star attractions here are the fresh cinnamon rolls and freshly squeezed orange juice. There are only a few wooden tables with either plastic lawn chairs or folding metal card chairs. The best ones are on the small, screened-in porch. Come early for breakfast if you want a decent seat.

In back of Atlantic Bank, Caye Caulker. ✆ **226-2148.** Main courses BZ$.80–BZ$10 (US40¢–US$5/21p–£2.65). No credit cards. Mon–Fri 7am–3pm.

CAYE CAULKER AFTER DARK

For evening entertainment, you can stargaze, go for a night dive, or have a drink in one of the island's handful of bars. Periodically, one of the bars will crank up the music, and *voilà*—a disco. In general, the scene is so small that most folks will congregate at one or two bars. Which one or two bars is happening might shift from night to night; ask a local or two, and you'll certainly be directed to the current hot spot. My favorite bar is the open-air **I&I Bar and Cafe** ★, which features rustic wooden plank swings for most of its seating. The bar itself takes up the second and third floors of this thatch-roofed wooden structure and is located on a cross street on the southern end of town. Right in the center of town on Front Street, the **Oceanside Bar** often has either live music or karaoke and the new **Barrier Reef Sports Bar & Grill** has a raucous vibe most nights, while out by the Split, there's sometimes a crowd at the **Lazy Lizard.** Finally, you might stop in to check out the scene and the music videos projected on a large outdoor screen at **Herbal Tribe.**

Two Small Cayes on the Way

Between Belize City and the popular tourist destinations of Caye Caulker and Ambergris Caye lie scores of small islands and cayes. Of these, two are of interest to travelers, **St. George's Caye ★★** and **Caye Chapel ★★**. Each has its own charm and attractions. St. George's Caye offers easy access to Belize City and some excellent scuba diving and snorkel options. For its part, Caye Chapel is home to the only 18-hole golf course in Belize.

St. George is the closest resort caye to Belize City, just 14km (9 miles) offshore. This tiny island played a crucial role in the country's history. From 1650 until 1784, St. George's Caye was the first capital city for the early Baymen colonists, and it was also the site and namesake of the pivotal 1798 sea battle between the Baymen and a hostile Spanish fleet. Today, it is mostly a getaway for a handful of wealthy Belizeans, who have vacation cottages on the caye. There are also two small hotels here. The best of these is **St. George's Caye Lodge ★** (**✆ 877/517-9365** in the U.S. and Canada, or 220-4444 in Belize; www.gooddiving.com), a collection of wooden cabins built either facing the sea or lagoon.

There's only one option for staying on Caye Chapel, and that is the **Caye Chapel Resort ★★** (**✆ 800/901-8938** in the U.S. and Canada, or 226-8250 in Belize; www.cayechapel.com), a collection of luxury condominium units and private villas. Rates run between BZ$600 and BZ$2,400 (US$300–US$1,200/£159–£636), with unlimited golf included. While relatively flat, the par-72 course has plenty of water and sand hazards, and an unmatched number of oceanfront holes. The frequent steady trade winds here provide further challenge. There are never any crowds or waits on the course, and only a maximum of 50 overnight guests on the caye at any one time.

Any of the water taxis going to Caye Caulker or Ambergris Caye will drop off and pick up passengers at either St. Georges Caye or Caye Chapel en route. Moreover, there is an airstrip on Caye Chapel, and any of **Maya Island Air** (**✆ 223-1140;** www.mayaairways.com) or **Tropic Air** (**✆ 800/422-3435** in the U.S. or Canada, or 226-2012 in Belize; www.tropicair.com) flights to Caye Caulker or Ambergris Caye will similarly stop to drop off or pick up passengers on Caye Chapel upon demand. The fare is BZ$114 (US$57/£30) to or from Goldson International Airport, and BZ$63 (US$32/£17) each way to or from Municipal Airport. See "Essentials" in "Ambergris Caye" and "Caye Caulker," earlier in this chapter, for more details.

3 THE OUTER ATOLLS ★★★

40–80km (25–50 miles) E of Belize City

Roughly due east, out beyond the barrier reef, lie two of Belize's three open-ocean atolls, Turneffe Island Atoll and Lighthouse Reef Atoll. The reef and island rings of tranquillity in the midst of the Caribbean Sea are stunning and pristine places. The outer island atolls are popular destinations for day trips out from Belize City, Ambergris Caye, and Caye Caulker. However, if you really want to experience their unique charms, you should stay at one of the few small lodges located right on the edge of one of them, or on one of the live-aboard dive boats that ply these waters.

GETTING THERE & DEPARTING

These are remote and isolated destinations. Aside from the lodges, which all offer their own transportation, there is no regularly scheduled transportation out here. However, private water taxis and charter flights can be arranged.

BY PLANE The only airstrip located on these outer atolls is the private airstrip of the Lighthouse Reef Resort on Big Northern Caye.

BY BOAT Turneffe Island Atoll is a 1½- to 2-hour boat ride from Belize City. The lodges listed below provide their own transportation to and from Belize City as part of their vacation packages.

BY HELICOPTER The quickest and easiest way to get out to these atolls is by helicopter. **Astrum Helicopters** (**© 222-5100;** www.astrumhelicopters.com) will take you out here for BZ$2,500 (US$1,250/£663) in a helicopter that will hold four passengers, and BZ$3,750 (US$1,875/£994) in a six-passenger bird.

EXPLORING THE ATOLLS

Unlike Pacific Ocean atolls, which are often the crater rings of extinct volcanoes, these atolls were formed over millions of years by a combination of plate tectonics, rising water levels following the last ice age, and millennia of mid-ocean coral growth. Many of the atoll walls drop off steeply for over a thousand feet, while in the central lagoons, the water depths average only 3 to 12m (10–40 ft.).

Most folks come out here to do one of two things: fish or dive. Some do both. Both activities are truly world-class. In broad strokes, fishermen should head to Turneffe Island Atoll, while dedicated and serious divers would probably want to choose Lighthouse Reef Atoll, although there's great diving to be had off Turneffe.

Turneffe Island Atoll ★★

This is the largest of Belize's three ocean atolls, and the largest in the Caribbean Sea. Both the diving and the fishing here are excellent, but the fishing gets a slight nod. The extensive mangrove and saltwater flats are perfect territory for stalking permit, bonefish, snook, and tarpon. Most fishing is done with fly rods, either wading in the flats or from a poled skiff.

Turneffe Island Atoll also boasts scores of world-class wall, coral, and sponge gardens, and drift dive sites. Most of these sites are located around the southern tip of the atoll. Perhaps the most famous dive site here is **The Elbow ★★★**, a jutting coral point with steep drop-offs, huge sponges, and ample fish life. Another popular site is **Rendezvous Point ★★**, which features several grottoes that divers can swim in and out of, and there's a small modern wreck, the ***Sayonara,*** sitting in about 9.1m (30 ft.) of water.

Lighthouse Reef Atoll ★★

Boasting nearly 80km (50 miles) of wall and reef diving, including some of the best and most coveted dive sites in all of the Caribbean, this is a true scuba-diving mecca. As the atoll farthest from shore, its waters are incredibly clear and pristine. The central lagoon of this atoll is some 48km (30 miles) long and around 13km (8 miles) wide at its widest point. In the center, you'll find the world-famous **Blue Hole ★★**, a perfectly round mid-atoll sinkhole that plunges straight down to a depth of over 122m (400 ft.). You'll see postcards, photos, and T-shirts all over town showing off aerial views of this perfectly round hole in the ocean. Nearly 305m (1,000 ft.) across, the Blue Hole's eroded limestone karst walls and stalactite formations make this a unique and justifiably popular dive site. However, some of the wall and coral garden dives around the outer edges of the atoll are even better. Of these, **Half Moon Caye Wall ★★** and **North Long Caye Wall ★★** are consistently considered some of the best clear-water coral wall dives in the world.

Towards the southeastern edge of the atoll is **Half Moon Caye National Monument ★★**, a combined island and marine reserve. Half Moon Caye itself is the principal nesting ground for the beautiful and odd-looking red-footed booby. These birds are always here in massive numbers. The island is also a prime nesting site for both hawksbill and loggerhead turtles. **The Belize Audubon Society** (**© 223-5004;** www.belizeaudubon.org) has constructed a small visitor center here, and a wonderful viewing platform near the center of the island. They also allow overnight camping, with prior arrangement. The admission fee is BZ$20 (US$10/£5.30) for Half Moon Caye National Monument, and BZ$60 (US$30/£16) for entrance to the Blue Hole National Monument.

Water conditions here are amazingly consistent, with an average water temperature of around 80°F (27°C), while visibility on the outer atoll walls and reefs easily averages over 30m (100 ft.).

WHERE TO STAY & DINE ON TURNEFFE ISLAND ATOLL

Very Expensive

Turneffe Flats ★★ This is a superbly run fishing resort geared towards dedicated flat water fly-fishing. Everything here is simple, yet rustically luxurious. The rooms are all beachfront and housed in a couple of long, low buildings raised off the sandy ground just a bit on some wooden pilings. The rooms each come with one queen bed and one twin bed, large bathrooms, and a common shared veranda. Meals are served family-style in the main lodge or, weather permitting, outdoors on an open deck off the lodge. The fishing operation here is top-notch, and diving packages are offered as well. Packages are weeklong affairs, running Saturday to Saturday.

Blackbird Caye, Turneffe Island Atoll. **© 888/512-8812** or 623/298-2783 in the U.S. Fax 623/298-5008. www.tflats.com. 14 units. BZ$3,960–BZ$4,400 (US$1,980–US$2,200/£1,049–£1,166) per person per week dive package; BZ$6,460–BZ$7,500 (US$3,230–US$3,750/£1,712–£1,988) per person per week fishing package. Rates are based on double occupancy and include all meals, round-trip boat transportation from Belize City, and guided daily diving or fishing; drinks and gear rental are extra. Combination packages are available. DISC, MC, V. **Amenities:** Restaurant; bar; full-service dive and tackle shops; tour desk; laundry service. *In room:* A/C, no phone.

Turneffe Island Lodge ★★ Located on a tiny private caye at the southern tip of the Turneffe Island Atoll, this is the swankiest outfit on the outer atolls. It even features a small outdoor oceanfront pool, a rare luxury out here. You can either stay in one of the well-appointed lodge rooms, or opt for an upgrade to one of their eight private cabanas. One of my favorite features of these cabanas is the private outdoor shower. All rooms come with brightly varnished wood floors, wooden wainscoting and ceilings, and plenty of windows to take advantage of the ample sea breezes. The lodge has some excellent beaches, and several long piers built out into the ocean with thatch-roofed open-air hammock huts built at the end. Both the fishing and dive operations here are excellent.

Little Caye Bokel, Turneffe Island Atoll. ✆ **800/874-0118** in the U.S. and Canada, or 220-4142 in Belize. Fax 220-4011. www.turneffelodge.com. 20 units. BZ$5,400–BZ$7,200 (US$2,700–US$3,600/£1,431–£1,908) per person per week dive package; BZ$9,400–BZ$11,200 (US$4,700–US$5,600/£2,491–£2,968) per person per week fishing package. Rates are based on double occupancy and include all meals, round-trip boat transportation from Belize City, and guided daily diving or fishing; drinks and gear rental are extra. Combination packages are available. Rates lower in the off season. DISC, MC, V. **Amenities:** Restaurant; bar; small outdoor pool; full-service dive and tackle shops; tour desk; laundry service. *In room:* A/C, no phone.

Southern Belize

Southern Belize has only two major towns, **Dangriga** and **Punta Gorda,** and one popular beach village, **Placencia.** For years, this was the least developed region of Belize, but that's changing quickly. Placencia is arguably the hottest and fastest growing destinations in Belize. And the tiny Garífuna settlement of **Hopkins Village** is also booming. Both Placencia and Hopkins Village offer up some of the longest and finest sand beaches to be found in the country.

Southern Belize is made up of the Stann Creek and Toledo districts. It is home to the **Cockscomb Basin Wildlife Sanctuary,** a major breeding ground and reserve for the New World's largest cat, the jaguar, as well as several other lesser-known and virtually unexplored forest reserves. It is here you'll find Belize's highest mountain, **Victoria Peak,** which stands at 1,122m (3,681 ft.).

Offshore, you'll find some of Belize's most beautiful cayes and its most remote atoll, **Glover's Reef Atoll★★**. The cayes and barrier reef down here are as spectacular as those found farther north, yet far less developed and crowded. You can literally have an island to yourself down here. Much of the offshore and underwater wonders are protected in reserves, such as the **Southwater Caye Marine Reserve, Glover's Marine Reserve, Sapodilla Cayes Marine Reserve,** and **Laughing Bird Caye National Park★★**.

As historically the least developed and colonized region in Belize, the southern zone still maintains ongoing and healthy communities of traditional Mayan and Garífuna peoples. This is one of the few places on the planet where you can comfortably spend a few days in a traditional Mayan or Garífuna village and see how nice it can feel to step away from the 21st century for a bit.

1 DANGRIGA

116km (72 miles) S of Belize City; 103km (64 miles) SE of Belmopan; 77km (48 miles) N of Placencia

Dangriga, which means "sweet water" in the Garífuna language, was originally called Stann Creek, and you may still hear it referred to as such. The name Stann Creek comes from the Creole version of "Standing Creek," a description of the river's slow-moving waters. As the capital of the Stann Creek District, which is one of the main citrus-growing regions of Belize, Dangriga is an important and vibrant agricultural and fishing community. However, despite its size and almost urban feel, it lacks the seaminess that characterizes Belize City. The town fronts right on the Caribbean and has several waterfront parks, which are surrounded by simple yet attractive residential neighborhoods.

Still, Dangriga is of little interest to travelers. There are no good beaches, few good hotels, and the town can feel stiflingly hot and desolate on most days. Most travelers head farther south to either Hopkins Village, Placencia, or Punta Gorda, or out to one of the nearby offshore cayes. Dangriga is the main maritime transportation hub for trips out to Tobacco Caye, South Water Caye, and Glover's Reef Atoll. (See "What to See & Do," below, for more details.)

Dangriga is the largest city in southern Belize and the seat of the country's Garífuna culture. The Garífunas are a proud and independent people, who have managed to

The Garífuna

Throughout the 18th century, escaped and shipwrecked slaves intermarried and blended in with the native Carib Indian populations on several islands in the Lesser Antilles, but predominantly on St. Vincent. The West Africans were a mixed lot, including members of the Fon, Yoruba, Ewe, and Nago tribes. Over the years, the West African and indigenous elements blended into a new people, known first as Black Caribs and today as Garífuna or Garinagu. The Garífuna have their own language, traditions, history, and rituals, all of which blend elements of the group's two primary cultural sources. African-style drumming with complex rhythmic patterns and call-and-response singing accompany ritual possession ceremonies spoken in a language whose entomological roots are predominantly Arawak.

The Black Caribs were fierce warriors and frequently fought the larger colonial powers to maintain their freedom and independence. In 1797, despite the celebrated leadership of Joseph Chatoyer, the Garífuna were soundly defeated by the British forces, who subsequently shipped several thousand of the survivors off to exile on the island of Roatan, in then British Honduras. The Garífuna began migrating and eventually settled along the entire coast of what is present-day Honduras, Nicaragua, Guatemala, and Belize.

The Garífuna reached Belize by 1802. Since the British colonial presence was concentrated in the north, the Garífuna chose to settle in the southern parts of Belize, particularly the Stann Creek and Toledo districts. During the early part of their settlement in Belize, the Garífuna were kept at arm's length by the colonial Baymen, who were still slave owners and feared the influence of this independent free black community. Nevertheless, on November 19, 1832, the Garífuna were officially recognized as members of Belizean society and permitted to participate in the public meetings. For nearly 2 centuries now, the Garífuna have lived quiet lives of subsistence farming, fishing, and light trading with their neighbors, while steadfastly maintaining their language, heritage, and traditions.

The principal Garífuna settlements in Belize include Punta Gorda, Seine Bight, Hopkins Village, Barranco, and Dangriga, the community's unofficial capital. Each year on November 19 (and for several days around the 19th), these communities, and in particular Dangriga, come alive in a riotous celebration of the Garífuna settlement and acceptance in Belize.

maintain their unique language and culture, which dates to the 16th-century intermingling of free Africans and Carib Indians. The only time Dangriga becomes a major tourist attraction is around Garífuna Settlement Day.

ESSENTIALS

Getting There & Departing

BY PLANE There are numerous flights into and out of little Dangriga Airport (DGA) from Belize City. **Maya Island Air** (✆ **223-1140** in Belize City, or 522-2659 in Dangriga; www.mayaairways.com) has 10 flights daily between the Philip S. W. Goldson International Airport and Dangriga. The first flight leaves at 8:10am and the last flight

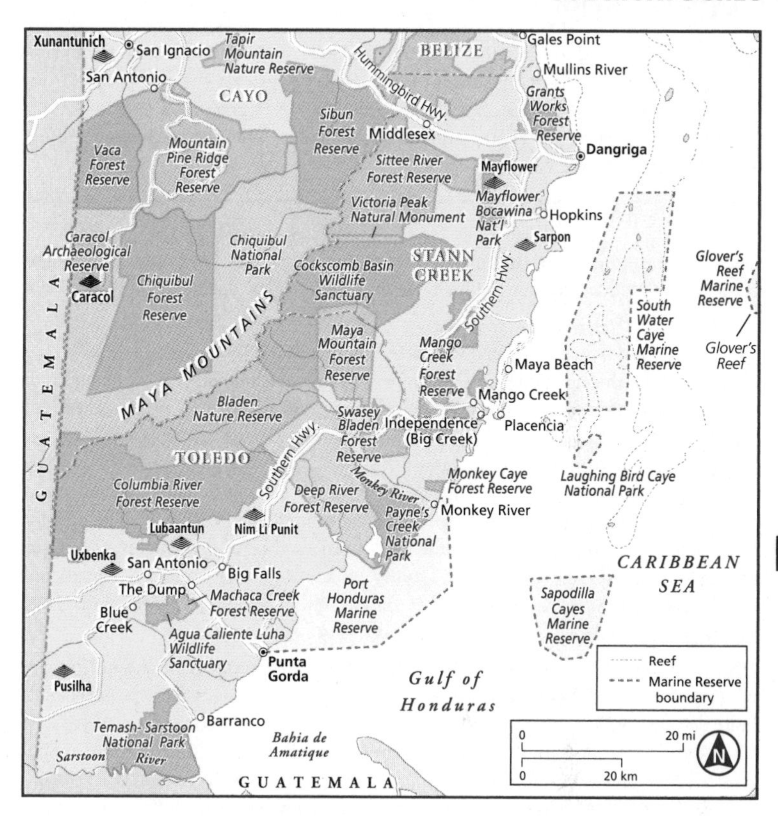

is at 5pm. Flight time is 15 minutes; the fare is BZ$109 (US$55/£29) each way. Maya Island Air also has seven daily flights between Belize City's Municipal Airport and Dangriga at 8, 9, 10, and 11am, noon, and 2:30 and 4:30pm. The fare is BZ$72 (US$36/£19) each way. These flights take 30 minutes, because they stop en route to pick up passengers at the international airport. Maya Island Air flights from Dangriga to Belize City leave between 7:25am and 4:50pm. Most of these flights stop first at the international airport and continue on to Municipal Airport.

Tropic Air (✆ **800/422-3435** in the U.S. or Canada, 226-2012 in Belize City, or 522-2129 in Dangriga; www.tropicair.com) has nine flights daily between Goldson International Airport and Dangriga, with the first flight leaving at 8:15am and the last flight at 5pm. The fare is BZ$114 (US$57/£30) each way. They also have five daily flights between Municipal Airport and Dangriga, leaving at 8:30 and 10:30am, and at 12:30, 2:30, and 4:50pm. The fare is BZ$75 (US$38/£20) each way. Tropic Air flights depart Dangriga for both of Belize City's airports daily between 7:45am and 4:45pm. Flight time runs between 15 and 30 minutes, depending on whether there is an intermediate stop.

Flights to and from Punta Gorda and Placencia on Maya Island Air and Tropic Air stop in Dangriga to pick up and drop off passengers. You can also easily book a flight

Moments Welcome

As you enter Dangriga you'll come to a traffic circle. Be sure to take a moment to check out the **Drums of My Father** monument here, a larger-than-life bronze casting of three ceremonial *dügü* drums, and the maraca-like shaker or *sísira*. This simple sculpture lets you know right away that you are entering the heartland of Garífuna society and culture.

from Dangriga to either of these onward southern destinations. On both airlines, flights are sometimes added during the high season or suspended during the low season, so check in advance.

BY CAR From Belize City, head west on Cemetery Road, which becomes the Western Highway. Take this all the way to Belmopan, where you will connect with the Hummingbird Highway heading south. Ten kilometers (6 miles) before Dangriga, the Hummingbird Highway connects with the Southern Highway. Follow the signs into Dangriga; you'll be entering from the south end of town.

Alternatively, you can take the unpaved New Belize or Manatee Road, which turns off the Western Highway just past the Belize Zoo, at around Mile Marker 30. The Manatee Road passes by the entrance road to the small Creole village of Gales Point, and rejoins the Hummingbird Highway about 17km (8½ miles) outside of Dangriga. This route is shorter as the crow flies, but in worse shape physically, so the going is slower. Either route should take around 2 to 2½ hours from Belize City.

BY BUS **James Bus Line** (✆ **702-2049**) and **National Transport** (✆ **227-2255**) have regular service throughout the day between Belize City and Dangriga, roughly every half-hour between 6:30am and 5:30pm from either the main bus terminal on West Collet Canal Street (National Transport), or the nearby Shell gas station on Cemetery Road (James). The fare is BZ$20 (US$10/£5.30). The ride takes about 3 hours.

Tip: Most of the buses take the Hummingbird Highway. A few take the coastal Manatee Road. Unless you are heading to Gales Point, I'd try to take the much more comfortable ride on the Hummingbird Highway.

BY BOAT There are no regularly scheduled boats from Belize City to Dangriga, but aside from flying, water is the most direct means of covering the 58km (36 miles) between the two cities. If you want to come by boat, head to the Marine Terminal or ask around the docks in Belize City. Expect to pay from BZ$300 to BZ$500 (US$150–US$250/£80–£133) for a boat that can carry four to eight passengers.

Getting Around

There are no official car rental agencies, but if you really search, you might be able to find an enterprising local willing to rent you a vehicle. If this is absolutely necessary, your best bet is to have your hotel try and arrange this for you.

For a taxi in Dangriga, call **Star Line Taxi Service** (✆ **621-9956**) or **Tzul's Taxi Service** (✆ **522-2438**).

Boats to Tobacco Caye leave from the Gumagurugu River or North Stann Creek in front of the Riverside Café, just below the bridge. The going rate is around BZ$30 to BZ$50 (US$15–US$25/£7.95–£13) per person one-way. Most of the boats hold between 8 and 10 people, and they leave whenever they fill up. If you already have a group together,

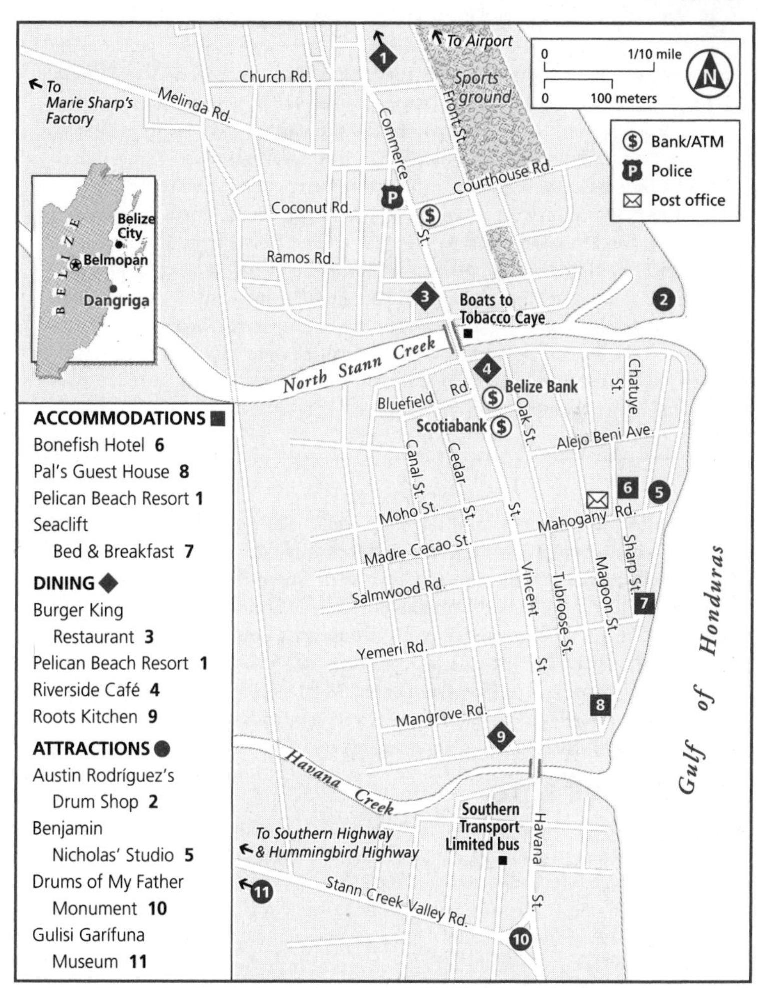

you can hire one privately, and set a definite return trip pickup time. Alternatively, you can catch a ride with the folks from **Pelican Beach Resort** (✆ **522-2044**), who run to Tobacco Caye daily and charge BZ$136 (US$68/£36) per person each way.

Orientation

The main street through Dangriga is called St. Vincent Street south of the main bridge over North Stann Creek, and Commerce Street north of it. Most of the town's businesses and attractions lie within a few blocks of this bridge in either direction. The airstrip is on the north end of town, near the Pelican Beach Resort.

FAST FACTS For the **police,** dial ✆ **911** or 522-2022; for the **fire department,** call ✆ **522-2091.** The **Dangriga Hospital** (✆ **522-2078**) is located on Courthouse Road,

If You Come to a Fork in the Road, Take Both

Given the unique sights offered by the two possible routes down to Dangriga, you might want to consider taking one route on your way south, and the other on your way back. The **Hummingbird Highway** passes through some of Belize's most picturesque countryside. The road weaves through jungle mountains and crosses clear streams and small rivers. Admire the forest-covered karst hillsides to the west, as you wind your way through mostly uninhabited country. The **Manatee Road** is a red-dirt affair, passing through the forests, lowland swamps, and mangroves that border Belize's large southern lagoon. Still, this route is not for the faint of heart. In the rainy season it can get quite muddy and slick, while in the dry season the dirt can form a hard, jarring washboard and dust can be a problem. In some places you'll have to cross single-lane, rail-less wooden plank bridges that give some drivers vertigo, even though they're not very high.

4 blocks north and 2 blocks east of the main bridge. The **post office** (✆ **522-2035**) is in the southern section of town next to the Bonefish Hotel.

Both of the principal banks in town are on St. Vincent Street: **Belize Bank,** 24 St. Vincent St. (✆ 522-2903), and **Scotiabank,** 10 St. Vincent St. (✆ 522-2031). If you need some film or developing, try either **Dangriga Photo Plus,** 64 Commerce St. (✆ 522-2394), or **Gem's Photo,** 81 St. Vincent St. (✆ 522-3859). For any contact lens or eyeglass problems, head to **Hoy Eye Center,** 18 St. Vincent St. (✆ 522-0628).

Finally, if your hotel can't or won't do it for you, take your dirty clothes to **Val's Laundry,** 1 Sharp St. (✆ **502-3324**). They charge around BZ$12 (US$6/£3.20) per load.

WHAT TO SEE & DO

The main activity in Dangriga is a slow walk up and down the main north–south thoroughfare. If you tire of watching the endless procession of people and listening to the colorful mix of English, Creole, and Garífuna, head a block or two over towards the sea and cop a seat in one of the town's oceanfront parks. If you're looking for a more active adventure, you'll have to head out of Dangriga, but your options are plentiful.

The only true attraction in the area is the quaint little **Gulisi Garífuna Museum** ★ (✆ **502-0639**). Although small, this is worth a visit. Spread around several rooms here you'll find interpretive displays of Garífuna history, culture, and daily life. Three separate documentaries are shown continually on televisions in the different rooms. There's a gift shop here, as well as paintings by prominent Garífuna artists like Benjamin Nicholas and Pen Cayetano. The museum is located 1.6km (1 mile) west of town, on the road out to the Hummingbird Highway. It is open Monday through Friday from 10am to 5pm and Saturday from 8am till noon. Admission is BZ$10 (US$5/£2.65).

If you're staying in Dangriga for any period of time, you may also want to visit any number of the relatively nearby attractions, including Guanacaste National Park, Blue Hole National Park, Caves Branch, Hopkins Village, and Cockscomb Basin Wildlife Sanctuary. For more information on the first three attractions, see chapter 10. For details about the rest, see below.

If your hotel can't arrange it for you, contact **C & G Tours and Charters** (✆ **522-3641;** www.cgtourscharters.com) to set up any number of tours and activities around Dangriga and environs.

FISHING The fishing is excellent out of Dangriga. Most folks head to the flats in search of bonefish, permit, and tarpon. Closer to shore and near the river mouths you can find snook, and beyond the barrier reef lie marlin, sailfish, tuna, wahoo, and dorado. Ask at your hotel, around the docks, or at the **Pelican Beach Resort** (✆ **522-2044**). Expect to pay between BZ$800 and BZ$2,400 (US$400–US$1,200/£212–£636) per day for a full day for several anglers aboard a modern sport-fishing boat. Alternatively, you can line up a lower-tech outing around the docks for around BZ$100 to BZ$300 (US$50–US$150/£27–£80) for a half-day.

SNORKELING & SCUBA DIVING Dangriga is the jumping-off point for some wonderful small cayes situated right on the edge of the barrier reef, as well as Glover's Reef Atoll. Most of the hotels in town can arrange for a day trip of snorkeling or scuba diving at Tobacco Caye, South Water Caye, or one of the cayes comprising Glover's Reef Atoll. Expect to pay from BZ$160 to BZ$240 (US$80–US$120/£42–£64) per person for a full-day snorkel trip out to the reef, including lunch and transportation. Add on an extra BZ$120 to BZ$160 (US$60–US$80/£32–£42) if you plan to scuba dive.

Attractions on the Hummingbird Highway

Located just off the highway in the tiny settlement of Pomona Village is one of the most important and renowned factories in all of Belize, **Marie Sharp's.** The factory is small and simple, and depending on the time of year and demand, they may be making any number of their various hot sauces, jams, and chutneys. It's best to call in advance to arrange a tour (✆ **522-2370;** www.mariesharps-bz.com). If you're lucky, you'll get to meet Marie herself. The tour is free, but you'll want to bring some money to stock up on the sauces.

Tucked a few miles off the highway is **Five Blues Lake National Park★**. The main feature of this park is a large cenote, whose various hues of blue originally gave the park its name. However, in July 2006, the cenote suddenly and rather inexplicably drained almost completely. By early 2008, the lake had recovered about 75% of its original level, and much of its former beauty. All around the park are forested lands and distinct karst hill formations, with a series of trails leading through them. The park is run by the folks from the local community of Saint Margaret's Village. The park and small village are located on Lagoon Road, just off the Hummingbird Highway around Mile Marker 32. There are about 4.8km (3 miles) of well-marked trails in the park. You can also take a refreshing dip in the lake, or rent a canoe for a leisurely paddle. Admission is BZ$8 (US$4/£2.10). Camping is allowed inside the park for BZ$6 (US$3/£1.60) per person. Some simple accommodations and restaurants are also available in Saint Margaret's Village.

FYI

North Stann Creek is also known as the Gumagurugu River in the local Garífuna language.

Gales Point & the Manatees

Gales Point is a small Creole fishing village about 40km (25 miles) north of Dangriga. It is a peaceful little village where you can get in tune with one of Belize's traditional cultures

Moments On the Road

As you drive the Hummingbird Highway, there are two interesting phenomena to be aware of. Locals swear a local mountain formation looks like a Sleeping Giant. There are several good views of the Sleeping Giant, which is best seen just slightly left of dead ahead as you drive south from Belize City, especially around the Sibun River bridge. Even more mystical and illusive—I've never been able to make it work—is the "anti-gravity" spot. Stop your car on the gentle hill around Mile Marker 26 and put it in neutral. Locals claim it is ancient earth energy that makes vehicles roll seemingly uphill. I'm guessing it's an optical illusion.

and its slower pace of life. The village stretches along a narrow peninsula that juts into the large brackish **Southern Lagoon,** which is also called Manatee Lagoon because the manatees that inhabit the water of the lagoon bring most people to Gales Point in the first place. Ask at the Manatee Lodge (see below) or around the village, and for BZ$60 to BZ$100 (US$30–US$50/£16–£27) you can hire a small boat to take you out to where the manatees usually feed. The boats generally will hold up to eight people, so the more people you can line up, the less it will cost each of you. You can also ask around in the village about renting a canoe to paddle yourself out to where the manatees feed. I prefer this option, although be sure to get a lightweight modern canoe, as the traditional carved tree-trunk dugout canoes are a bear to paddle. Canoe rentals should run you around BZ$12 (US$6/£3.20) for a half-day. Although once encouraged, swimming with the manatees is no longer allowed. The contact is potentially dangerous for manatees and humans alike, and it's best to just enjoy a pleasant sighting of these gentle water mammals. In addition to the manatees, this is a fabulous bird-watching spot, and if you're lucky you might even see a jabiru stork here.

Other possible trips from Gales Point include visits to the beach or some nearby caves and nighttime turtle walks. The beach on either side of the Manatee River is a major nesting site for the hawksbill turtle. The turtles generally lay their eggs from June to August. These tours generally cost between BZ$60 and BZ$120 (US$30–US$60) for the boat and guide.

Gales Point is one of several villages in Belize to have a community-based ecotourism homestay program (✆ **209-8031**). Rooms in local villagers' homes are very basic and often do not have running water or flush toilets. The rates run around BZ$10–BZ$16 (US$5–US$8/£2.65–£4.25) per person. You can also camp in Gales Point at **Metho's Camping** (✆ **603-6051**) for BZ$10 (US$5/£2.65) per person. By far the best lodgings in Gales Point are found at the **Manatee Lodge** (✆ **877/462-6283** in the U.S. and Canada, or 220-8040 in Belize; www.manateelodge.com), a tidy little hotel with a fabulous location at the very end of the peninsula. If you decide to eat any place other than the Manatee Lodge, check out **Gentile's Cool Spot** (no phone).

Gales Point is also home to renowned drum maker **Emmeth Young,** who runs the **Maroon Creole Drum School** (✆ **603-6051**). If you're interested in a lesson, which costs about BZ$10 (US$5/£2.65) an hour, or in making your own drum, which will take around 4 days, ask around town for Emmeth.

To drive here from Dangriga, head out of town to the Hummingbird Highway towards Belize City. At the village of Melinda, you'll see the turnoff for Manatee Road and Gales Point.

To get here by bus from Dangriga, you will have to take a Belize City–bound bus using the Manatee Road. These buses do not always enter the village of Gales Point. Ask in advance; if the bus doesn't enter the village, you will have to hike or hitchhike the final 2.4km (1½ miles) out onto the peninsula. From Belize City, you can take one of the Dangriga-bound buses using the Manatee Road. Again, ask in advance if the bus enters Gales Point village or not.

SHOPPING

As the cultural seat of the Garífuna culture, Dangriga is a great place to pick up, or just admire, local arts and crafts.

If you'd like to have a look at some Garífuna paintings, visit the studio of **Benjamin Nicholas** (**✆ 522-2785**). Using a Caribbean naïve style, Nicholas paints scenes of traditional Garífuna village life. You'll find his studio on the seafront, just north of Mahogany Street.

If the beat really gets to you, you can buy a handmade wooden drum from **Austin Rodríguez** (**✆ 502-3752**), at the **Dangriga Cultural Center** on the oceanfront on the north bank of North Stann Creek. Drums vary in size and cost between BZ$80 and BZ$300 (US$40–US$150/£21–£80). Austin's daughter runs a separate drum shop at 32 Tubroose St.

Finally, **Mercy Sabal,** 22 Magoon St. (no phone), has become quite famous for her handcrafted Garífuna dolls. These small dolls are predominantly of female figures in traditional dress, and cost between BZ$30 and BZ$80 (US$15–US$40/£7.95–£21).

Garífuna Settlement Day

Each year on November 19, Garífuna Settlement Day is celebrated in Dangriga, with Garífunas coming from around Belize and as far away as Guatemala, Honduras, Nicaragua, and New York. The celebration is a riot of street music and colorful parades. Eating, drinking, and dancing go on well into the night. The Garífuna have their own traditional music, which is based on wooden drums and choral singing. The rhythms and songs have strong African roots, and have given birth to a hybrid pop music called Punta Rock, which is probably the country's most popular music and dance form. If you plan to partake in the festivities, be sure to book far in advance, as every hotel room in Dangriga and the nearby towns and villages sells out early. For more information, contact the **National Garífuna Council of Belize** (**✆ 522-3781;** www.ngcbelize.org).

Tip: Garífuna Settlement Day isn't the only opportunity to experience the full color and vitality of traditional Garífuna culture. At the end of the Christmas and New Year season, on the weekend closest to January 6, the local Garífuna community takes to the streets to enjoy the Wanaragua or John Kunnu dancers. Wearing masks, elaborate costumes, colorful headdresses topped with macaw feathers, and vibrating arrangements of shells and vedas, Wanaragua or John Kunnu dance troupes parade through the streets of Dangriga, accompanied by the beat of traditional drummers.

Expensive

Pelican Beach Resort ★ This is a comfortable and spacious Caribbean resort and it's certainly the most upscale option right in Dangriga, although that's not necessarily saying much. The rooms range in price, location, and amenities. The best rooms have second-floor ocean views with wonderful balconies, and I think they're worth the slight splurge. Despite its age, the hotel has been well maintained through the years. There's no real beach here, but there are plenty of palm trees, lounge chairs, and hammocks spread around, as well as a long dock out into the sea, which is your best bet for swimming. There's a small gift shop featuring Garífuna crafts, Belizean books, and popular wildlife photography. The restaurant serves up excellent Belizean and Garífuna meals at reasonable rates. A variety of fishing, diving, and inland tours is available, and Pelican Beach also runs a sister cottage resort out on South Water Caye.

North end (P.O. Box 2), Dangriga. ✆ **522-2044.** Fax 522-2570. www.pelicanbeachbelize.com. 16 units. BZ$146–BZ$262 (US$73–US$131/£36–£69) double. Rates lower in the off season. AE, MC, V. Free parking. **Amenities:** Restaurant; tour desk; laundry service. *In room:* A/C (in 12 units), TV.

Moderate

Bonefish Hotel Located a block from the water and across the street from a small park, the Bonefish is a decent midrange option right in the heart of Dangriga. The carpeted guest rooms are generally quite spacious. The second-floor bar and restaurant has a view of the ocean, and serves good local fare and fresh seafood at reasonable rates. This hotel is owned and run by the same folks who have the Blue Marlin Lodge (p. 167) on South Water Caye, and is primarily used as an overnight stop for guests heading out to their island resort. However, it is also a convenient place to stay if you are headed out to any of the other hotels on Tobacco or South Water Caye.

15 Mahogany St. (P.O. Box 21), Dangriga. ✆ **800/798-1558** in the U.S., or 522-2243. Fax 522-2296. www.bluemarlinlodge.com. 7 units. BZ$150–BZ$168 (US$75–US$84/£40–£45) double. Rates include taxes and service charge. MC, V. Free parking. **Amenities:** Restaurant; tour desk; laundry service. *In room:* A/C, TV, free Wi-Fi, minifridge, no phone.

Seaclift Bed & Breakfast Set on a quiet residential block fronting a small park and then the ocean, this little converted home and nearby annex offer simple rooms in a homey environment. The furnishings and decor are rather provincial, and I think the rates are a bit steep for what you get, but there isn't much to choose from here in Dangriga, and this is a comfortable and cozy choice. I prefer the rooms in the annex building—one of these even has air-conditioning. Each building has a common veranda area overlooking the sea and shared living rooms.

1738 Southern Foreshore (P.O. Box 2), Dangriga. ✆ **522-3540.** Fax 522-3538. www.seaclift.com. 6 units. BZ$150–BZ$200 (US$75–US$100/£40–£53). Rates include full breakfast. MC, V. Free parking. **Amenities:** Tour desk; laundry service. *In room:* No phone.

Inexpensive

Pal's Guest House (Value) This budget hotel is down at the south end of town just off the water, near the mouth of Havana Creek, and is clean and quiet, although the years and constant sea breeze take their toll. The rooms with shared bathroom are particularly small and basic. If you have a bit more money to spend, you should opt for one of the second-floor beachfront rooms in a separate building, which have air-conditioning and small private balconies overlooking the sea. The owner, Augustine Flores, is friendly, knowledgeable, and an active member of the local Garífuna community.

868A Magoon St., Dangriga. ✆ **522-2365.** ✆/fax 522-2095. www.palsbelize.com. 19 units (16 with private bathroom). BZ$38 (US$19/£10) double with shared bathroom; BZ$50–BZ$72 (US$25–US$36/£13–£18) double with private bathroom. MC, V. **Amenities:** Tour desk; gift shop; laundry service. *In room:* TV, no phone.

WHERE TO DINE

When you're in Dangriga, be sure to sample some of the local Garífuna cooking. One staple you'll find at many restaurants is a bread made from cassava, also known as yuca. The best place in town to look for traditional Garífuna cooking is the down-home **Roots Kitchen** (no phone) on the north side of Havana Creek, just in from St. Vincent Street. Be sure to try the *hudut,* a dish featuring fresh fish cooked in coconut milk, accompanied by pieces of plantain and cassava.

Up and down the main street through town—St. Vincent Street and Commerce Street—you'll find numerous very basic restaurants. In addition to the restaurant listed below, **The King Burger Restaurant,** 135 Commerce St. (✆ **522-2476**), which is not affiliated with the Burger King fast-food chain, is a local favorite serving simple Belizean meals heavy on the grease. There are also several very basic Chinese restaurants along the main street.

If you're looking for a bit of a splurge and somewhat slightly more elegant ambience, the restaurant at the **Pelican Beach Resort** (✆ **522-2044**) serves well-prepared local dishes and fresh seafood.

Inexpensive

Riverside Café BELIZEAN This simple cafe and bar is funky and perennially pretty run-down. Still, it's popular with the local boatmen and one of the best places to get travel information in Dangriga. It opens early and serves food throughout the day. You can get a full meal of fried chicken, beans, and rice for BZ$8 (US$4/£2.10). Breakfasts are hearty and inexpensive. This is the place to ask about rides out to one of the nearby cayes, to set up a tour around the region, and to pick up some brochures from the wall-mounted racks. You'll find the cafe just east of St. Vincent Street on the south side of North Stann Creek.

S. Riverside Dr., Dangriga. ✆ **523-3499.** Reservations not accepted. Main courses BZ$8–BZ$20 (US$4–US$10/£2.10–£5.30). MC, V. Daily 7am–9pm.

DANGRIGA AFTER DARK

There's not much happening in Dangriga after dark. Your best bets would be to see what's happening at the Pelican Beach Resort (see "Where to Stay," above).

BEYOND DANGRIGA: OFFSHORE CAYES & GLOVER'S REEF ATOLL ★★

The Tobacco Caye range of mangrove cayes lies just 16km (10 miles) east of Dangriga. A little farther south sits South Water Caye. Beyond the barrier reef and farther out to sea is Glover's Reef Atoll.

Tobacco Caye ★★ itself is just 2 hectares (5 acres) large, with about five different lodging options set more or less side-by-side. You can walk from one end of the caye to the other in about 3 minutes, and that's at a leisurely pace.

South Water Caye ★★ is a little bit larger than Tobacco, but you can still walk from one end to the other in about 5 minutes. Nevertheless, the vibe here is slightly more spacious and luxurious than that on Tobacco Caye, although there's not anything approaching real luxury here, either.

Gentle Giants

From late March to June—especially just before, during, and after the full moons—the waters here are an excellent place to spot and dive with mammoth whale sharks, the largest fish in the sea.

Located just a stone's throw from the south end of South Water Caye, the **Smithsonian Institute of Marine Research** occupies all of the tiny Carrie Bow Caye. Your lodge can make arrangements to visit the caye, meet with resident scientists, and use their beach, which is one of the sandiest in the area.

The largest caye in the area, **Man-O-War Caye ★★**, is a bird sanctuary and major nesting site for the magnificent frigate, or man-o-war. A tour to the caye is an impressive sight, with hundreds of these large sea birds roosting on and circling above the tiny caye. As part of their mating ritual, the males inflate a huge red sack on their throats to attract a mate. In addition to the frigates, the island also is home to a large community of brown boobies.

Coco Plum Caye is another isolated and tiny caye in this area, with one small resort that features a handful of individual wooden bungalows spread around the small, sandy island. If you want to stay here, contact **Coco Plum Island Resort★** (**✆ 512/786-7309** in the U.S., or 520-2041 in Belize; www.cocoplumcay.com).

A visit to snorkel, dive, or stay out on these cayes usually involves passing through, or staying within, the **South Water Caye Marine Reserve,** which includes Tobacco Caye, Carrie Bow Caye, Cocoplum Caye, and Man-O-War Caye. Admission to the reserve costs BZ$10 (US$5/£2.65) per person per day. This fee will either be collected by your hotel, boat taxi driver, or tour operator.

To the east of these cayes, and beyond the barrier reef, lies **Glover Reef Atoll ★★★**, a stunning natural coral formation featuring an oval-shaped central lagoon nearly 35km (22 miles) long. Named after the British pirate John Glover, the steep-walled reefs here offer some of the best wall diving anywhere in the Caribbean. The entire atoll is also a marine reserve, and in 1996 it was declared a World Heritage Site by the United Nations. Inside the usually calm lagoon, patch reefs are a wonderland for snorkelers.

Finally, fishing for bonefish, permit, and tarpon is excellent throughout this area. There are no established independent operators. All the local hotels can usually arrange to set up a fishing trip, however.

Getting There

Boats to the outlying cayes leave from the south shore of the Gumagurugu River or North Stann Creek in front of the Riverside Café, just down from the bridge. The going rate is around BZ$30 to BZ$50 (US$15–US$25/£7.95–£13) per person one-way. Most of the boats hold between 8 and 10 people, and they leave whenever they fill up. If you already have a group together, you can hire one privately and set a definite return-trip pickup time. To rent a whole boat, the going rate is from BZ$400 to BZ$500 (US$200–US$250/£106–£133) round-trip for up to 10 people to Tobacco Caye. The ride takes around 30 to 40 minutes to Tobacco Caye, depending on how fast a boat you book. Add on about 20 to 40 minutes and between BZ$100 to BZ$200 (US$50–US$100/£27–£53) for either South Water Caye or Glover's Reef Atoll. Alternatively, you can catch a ride with the folks from **Pelican Beach Resort** (✆ **522-2044**), who run out to South Water Caye daily and charge BZ$136 (US$68/£36) per person each way.

Note: You really should have a reservation before heading out to one of the lodges on these cayes, as there are very limited options and they fill up fast during the high season. Try to arrange your transportation when booking a room.

Where to Stay & Dine on the Outer Cayes

All of the options listed below are self-contained lodges and resorts, meaning you will be taking all of your meals at your hotel. Fishing, diving, and multiday adventure packages are available at all of the places listed below.

In addition to the lodges listed below, **Blue Marlin Lodge** (✆ **800/798-1558** in the U.S., or 522-2243 in Belize; www.bluemarlinlodge.com) is a semiupscale outfit on South Water Caye specializing in dive and fishing packages.

However, if you want luxury out on Glover's Reef Atoll, you'll want to check in with **Isla Marisol Resort** (✆ **866/990-9904** in the U.S. and Canada; www.islamarisolresort.com), which has a collection of individual cabins on Southwest Caye.

For the more adventurous traveler, **Island Expeditions ★★** (✆ **800/667-1630,** or 604/452-3212 in the U.S.; www.islandexpeditions.com) and **Slickrock Adventures ★★** (✆ **800/390-5715,** or 435/259-4225 in the U.S.; www.slickrock.com) run various multiday kayak and dive tours to small camps and lodges on private, isolated cayes of Glover's Reef Atoll.

Glover's Atoll Resort ★ Located on the private North East Caye, this little island getaway has grown and evolved over the years. Originally a laid-back and rustic retreat on a very isolated caye, it is currently deserving of its "resort" moniker, although it still retains much of the hostel-like atmosphere and funky charm. Lodging options range from camping to dorm rooms to simple, rustic cabins with private bathrooms and kitchen facilities. My favorites are the round cabins built on stilts over the ocean. The resort also offers large, semipermanent tents, or you can pitch your own. And while they do serve meals, some of the guests actually pack in and cook their own food at the resort's communal kitchen. In addition to what you pack in, fresh fish, lobster, and conch can be purchased on the island, as can drinking water and fresh bread. Most visitors here come as part of the resort's weeklong package, which includes transportation. A meal package will run you around BZ$74 ($37/£20) per day.

Glover's Reef Atoll (P.O. Box 563, Belize City). ✆ **520-5016.** Fax 223-5424. www.glovers.com.bz. 11 units. BZ$198 (US$99/£52) per week camping; BZ$298 (US$149/£79) per week in dorm room; BZ$398–BZ$538 (US$199–US$269/£105–£143) per person per week in private cabin. Rates include round-trip transportation from Sittee River Village or Dangriga and all taxes. MC, V (add 10% surcharge). **Amenities:** Restaurant; tour desk. *In room:* No phone.

Pelican's Pouch ★★ Run by the folks at the Pelican Beach Resort in Dangriga, this isolated island getaway is one of the best-run little resorts on these little cayes. The best rooms here are the individual cabins. Set on raised stilts by the water's edge, these wooden cottages vary in size somewhat, but all are very comfortable and charming. The Egret and Heron's Hideaway are my favorites of the private cabins. The latter has a delightful private balcony set amidst and surrounded by mangroves. The rooms are housed on the second floor of a converted colonial-era convent. Each of these rooms comes with one double bed, two single beds, and a half-bathroom. A couple of communal showers are located on the ground level. The relatively small price difference makes it very worthwhile to book one of the cabins.

South Water Caye (P.O. Box 2, Dangriga). ✆ **522-2044.** Fax 522-2570. www.southwatercaye.com. 13 units (5 with shared shower). BZ$572 (US$286/£152) double room; BZ$650 (US$325/£172) double cabin. Rates include 3 meals daily and all taxes. AE, MC, V. **Amenities:** Restaurant; tour desk; laundry service. *In room:* No phone.

Reef's End Lodge Occupying the southern tip of Tobacco Caye, this rustic lodge offers several distinct rooming options. Most of the rooms here are located in a two-story converted house. Each comes with two twin beds and one full bed. The best of these are on the second floor, especially the corner units. The rooms are spartan and are geared towards students, groups, and budget travelers. The private cabins are a better bet and not significantly more expensive; however, these also feel rather spartan and rustic, although they do have air-conditioning. The best room is the honeymoon suite, which has more contemporary decor, tile floors, and loads of space. The nicest feature here is the restaurant, which is set on stilts, with a deck and some docks out over the water. These folks run the only dive operation on the island.

Tobacco Caye (P.O. Box 299, Dangriga). ✆ **522-2419.** Fax 522-2828. www.reefsendlodge.com. 11 units. BZ$130 (US$65/£34) double room; BZ$150 (US$75/£40) double cabin; BZ$390 (US$195/£103) honeymoon suite. MC, V. **Amenities:** Restaurant; dive operation; tour desk; laundry service. *In room:* No phone.

Tobacco Caye Paradise ★ **Value** This place is at the northern end of Tobacco Caye. The simple wooden cabins here are set right at the edge of the ocean, with small private verandas that, in most cases, jut out over the water. These are very basic, with just cold-water showers, minimal furnishings, and a simple floor fan. Still, their location and general vibe are just perfect. There are also five other rooms in a building slightly inland. These are certainly acceptable, but nowhere near as nice as the cabins.

Tobacco Caye. ✆ **520-2742.** bluefield@btl.net. 9 units. BZ$100 (US$50/£27) double; BZ$140 (US$70/£37) double cabin. Rates include 3 meals daily and taxes. MC, V. **Amenities:** Restaurant; tour desk; laundry service. *In room:* No phone.

EN ROUTE SOUTH: WHERE THE WILDCATS ROAM

Weighing up to 91kg (200 lb.) and measuring more than 1.8m (6 ft.) from nose to tip of tail, jaguars are king of the new-world jungle. Nocturnal predators, jaguars hunt peccaries (wild piglike animals), deer, and other small mammals. The **Cockscomb Basin Wildlife Sanctuary** ★★, established in 1990 as the world's first jaguar reserve, covers nearly 388 sq. km (150 sq. miles) of rugged forested mountains and has the greatest density of jaguars in the world. It is part of the even larger Cockscomb Basin Forest Reserve, which was created in 1984.

The forests within the preserve are home to other wildcats as well, including pumas, ocelots, and margays, all of which are very elusive, so don't get your hopes of seeing them too high. Few people do, but a good guide may be able to find you some tracks. Other mammals that you might spot if you're lucky include otters, coati-mundis, tayra, kinkajous, deer, peccaries, anteaters, and armadillos.

The largest land mammal native to Central America, Baird's tapir, is also resident. Locally known as a "mountain cow," the tapir is the national animal of Belize. A tapir can weigh up to 272kg (600 lb.) and is related to the horse, although its protruding upper lip is more like an elephant's trunk.

Much more easily spotted in the dense vegetation surrounding the preserve's trails are nearly 300 species of birds, including the scarlet macaw, the keel-billed toucan, the king vulture, and the great curassow.

Trails inside the park range from gentle and short to quite arduous and long. Many offer wonderful views of the Cockscomb Mountains and lush forested valleys. There are quite a few waterfalls and swimming holes. During the dry season, you can even climb Victoria Peak, which, at 1,122m (3,681 ft.), is the country's highest mountain. This trip takes several days and requires a permit and local guide. For more information, contact the **Belize Audubon Society** (✆ **223-5004;** www.belizeaudubon.org). Admission to the park is BZ$10 (US$5/£2.65).

Caution should be exercised when visiting the preserve. In addition to jaguars, which can be dangerous, there are also poisonous snakes, including the deadly fer-de-lance. Always wear shoes, preferably boots, when hiking the trails here.

The Belize Audubon Society co-manages this park, and even offers a few private cabins and some dormitory sleeping options inside the sanctuary. Rates run between BZ$20 and BZ$30 (US$10–US$15/£5.30–£7.95) per person for dormitory-style accommodations, or BZ$120 (US$60/£32) for one of the cabins, which can sleep up to six persons. Alternatively, you can stay down near the information center near the highway at the **Tutzil Nah Cottages** (✆ **520-3044;** www.mayacenter.com).

Cockscomb Basin Wildlife Sanctuary is located 9.7km (6 miles) inland from the Southern Highway, some 32km (20 miles) south of Dangriga. The turnoff and entrance to the sanctuary is at the roadside village of Maya Center. This is where you'll find the sanctuary's information center, and where you'll pay your BZ$10 (US$5/£2.65) entrance fee. This is also a good place to check out some of the art and craft works at the neighboring shop run by the Maya Center Women's Group and to hook up with a local guide. I've heard great reports about local guide Greg Sho, who can often be found at Greg's Bar, his other business, located right on the side of the highway before the entrance to Maya Center. Any bus heading south to Placencia and Punta Gorda will drop you off at the entrance. From here you'll have to hike the 9.7km (6 miles) or hire a local taxi for around BZ$30 (US$15/£7.95) round-trip.

A NEARBY BACK-BUSH NATURE LODGE

Nestled at the foot of the Maya Mountains is an interesting little ecolodge, **Mama Noots Jaguar Lodge** ★ (✆/fax **670-8019;** www.mamanoots.com). With a collection of comfortable rooms, as well as camping and dormitory facilities, the folks at Mama Noots are located in the heart of the **Mayflower Bocawina National Park.** The park protects the small and barely excavated Mayflower Mayan ruins, as well as vast expanses of tropical forests. There's excellent hiking and bird-watching on miles of trails leaving from the resort, including a couple of wonderful waterfalls. All of the electricity is provided by an inventive mix of solar, hydro, and wind generators. A pure mountain spring provides the water. Multiday packages with transportation provided from Dangriga are the preferred means of visiting this little lodge. Contact them for details.

2 HOPKINS VILLAGE & SITTEE RIVER VILLAGE ★★★

140km (87 miles) S of Belize City; 127km (79 miles) SE of Belmopan; 53km (33 miles) N of Placencia

The word is out on Hopkins Village, and this area is poised to boom. If you want to experience this place before it becomes another Placencia, you'd be wise to visit before too long. Hopkins Village is a midsize Garífuna community located on the shore, 24km

(15 miles) south of Dangriga. It is a picturesque village with colorfully painted raised clapboard houses. It is also my preferred destination for getting a true taste of and some direct contact with this unique culture. This is a great place to wander around talking with children, fishermen, and elderly folks hanging out in front of their homes. If you stick around long enough, you may be able to learn a bit about traditional Garífuna lifestyles. Fishing is still the main pursuit of many of the villagers, although tourism is rapidly becoming the main source of employment and income.

Hopkins Village is set on a long, narrow, curving swath of beach, which in addition to Placencia is one of the few true beaches in the country. This white-sand beach is usually quite calm and good for swimming. In recent years, several beach and dive resorts have opened on the stretch of sand south of the village, while in the village itself you'll find a hodgepodge of budget lodgings and simple restaurants. Sittee River Village is a few miles south of Hopkins and a mile or so inland, on the banks of the gently flowing Sittee River. This is a tiny little town, but it does have a hotel or two, as well as a good Internet cafe. Fishermen like the quiet riverside setting and access to both fresh- and saltwater angling.

ESSENTIALS

Getting There & Departing

BY PLANE The closest airport to Hopkins Village is in Dangriga. See "Dangriga," earlier in this chapter, for flight details. A taxi from Dangriga to Hopkins or Sittee River village should cost BZ$80 to BZ$100 (US$40–US$50/£21–£27) for up to four people. For a taxi in Dangriga, call **Star Line Taxi Service** (✆ **621-9956**) or **Tzul's Taxi Service** (✆ **522-2438**).

BY CAR From Belize City, head west on Cemetery Road, which becomes the Western Highway. Take this all the way to Belmopan, where you will connect with the Hummingbird Highway heading south. Ten kilometers (6⅓ miles) before Dangriga, the Hummingbird Highway connects with the Southern Highway. Take the Southern Highway towards Placencia and Punta Gorda. About 13km (8 miles) south of this junction, you'll see signs for the entrance to Hopkins Village. From here, it's 6.4km (4 miles) on a graded gravel road. A few miles farther south on the Southern Highway is the entrance to Sittee River Village; however, you can also enter at Hopkins and head south from there along the coast, as it's really just a small loop.

BY BUS Only a couple of the buses each day from Dangriga south make the loop through Hopkins Village and Sittee River. The ride takes between 25 and 35 minutes to Hopkins Village, with Sittee River Village just a few miles farther on the route. The fare is BZ$6 (US$3/£1.60) each way. Be sure to ask before you get on the bus if it will drop you off in the village. If not, you will be let off on the Southern Highway, at the entrance to Hopkins, but still some 6.4km (4 miles) away. If this is the case, you will hopefully have arranged pickup with your hotel in advance. Otherwise, you'll have to hitchhike in to town. The buses heading back to Dangriga or to points south can be caught in either Hopkins or Sittee River, or better yet, from the Southern Highway. See "Essentials" in section 1, earlier in this chapter, for details on bus travel between Dangriga and Belize City, and between Dangriga and points south.

Getting Around

Hopkins Village itself is very small, and you can easily walk the entire town. If you're staying south of town or in Sittee River Village, or want to explore, a bicycle is the preferred means of transportation. Most of the hotels will either lend you a bike or rent you one for a few dollars per day.

There are no official taxi services, but if you ask around town or at your hotel, you should be able to hire someone for small trips or excursions. There are also a number of freelance guides in the area who have vehicles and may be willing to provide transportation.

Orientation

The access road from the Southern Highway heads right into the heart of Hopkins Village. If you continued straight, you'd be in the Caribbean Sea. The village itself spreads out for a few hundred yards in either direction. Heading south you'll come to the larger resorts listed below. At the turnoff and entrance to Jaguar Reef Resort, the road heads back towards the highway, passing through Sittee River Village. ***Note:*** It's only a 15- to 20-minute walk from the village to any of the resorts to the south, with the exception of Kanantik, which is farther away.

FAST FACTS Both Hopkins and Sittee River villages are tiny, and there are no banks or major stores or services. There are, however, Internet cafes in both places, and you can get gas at the little marina in Hopkins.

WHAT TO SEE & DO

This is a very isolated and underdeveloped area. All of the resorts listed below specialize in scuba diving, snorkeling, and, to a lesser extent, fishing. All of them also have a long list of tour options to attractions such as Cockscomb Basin Wildlife Sanctuary, Sittee River canoeing, Blue Hole National Park, the Mayflower Mayan ruins, and cultural tours of Dangriga. If you're staying at one of the lodgings in either of the villages, you'll find numerous local operators offering snorkeling, scuba, and fishing outings, as well as all the above-mentioned tours.

If you really want to get a taste of the local culture, sign up for some classes at the **Lebeha Drumming Center★** (**© 608-3143;** www.lebeha.com), which is located on the northern edge of the village. The folks here teach traditional Garífuna drumming and dancing.

Snorkeling & Diving

Snorkeling and scuba diving are stellar all along the Belize Barrier Reef. The Tobacco Caye range lies just offshore from Hopkins Village, a simple 30- to 40-minute boat ride away, with numerous snorkeling and dive sites. Moreover, the location makes these dive resorts excellent jumping-off points for trips to Glover's Reef Atoll and even Turneffe and Lighthouse Reef atolls. All of the resorts listed below offer multiday dive packages, which are the way to go for serious divers, though we particularly recommend Hamanasi. They also all offer certification classes and advanced open-water courses. If you're not staying at one of the dedicated dive resorts, your best bet is probably to arrange to dive with them, as their equipment and dive masters are generally top-notch, and the price savings of going with a less active operator just aren't worth it. If you're feeling adventurous, for snorkeling excursions, feel free to ask around the village and head out with a local boat captain or tour guide. The lower cost and cultural richness might just make up for a slow boat, leaky mask, and loose-fitting fins.

Fishing

There's excellent bonefishing in the inland and barrier reef flats in this area. Anglers can also go for tarpon, permit, and snook, or head offshore for bigger game. Experienced guides can help you track any of the above fish, and many are taking their guests out fly-fishing for them, just to up the ante. Most of the major lodges and resorts here offer fishing packages and excursions. Well-equipped sport fishing outings cost between BZ$800 and BZ$2,400 (US$400–US$1,200/£212–£636) per day, depending on the size of the boat, number of anglers, and distance traveled. Alternatively, you can ask around Hopkins Village to line up a more low-tech outing for around BZ$100 to BZ$250 (US$50–US$150/£27–£80) for a half-day.

SHOPPING

Hopkins Village is a good place to find locally made Garífuna handcrafts. **Rudy Coleman** is a local drum maker, and his drums are excellent. Ask for Rudy around town, or at the **Lebeha Drumming Center.**

It's worth the time to check out **Joy Jah's** studio and shop, which is located near the southern edge of the village. The folks here specialize in woodcarvings and paintings done on dry coconut husks, mostly in the shape of fish. They also carry a selection of arts and crafts from around Belize.

WHERE TO STAY

There's a host of lodging options in this area, ranging from simple budget and backpacker hotels in Hopkins Village to upscale dive resorts on the beaches to the south.

Very Expensive

In addition to the places listed below, the **Belizean Dreams** and **Hopkins Bay Resort** (✆ **523-7272;** www.belizeandreams.com) are two sister condo-resort projects on either end of Hopkins Village. Both feature a series of large and luxurious fully equipped condo units spread around a grassy lawn and pool area fronting the beach.

Hamanasi ★★ This well-run dive and adventure resort offers quite comfortable rooms in an intimate setting. Diving is the main focus here, and the hotel has an excellent operation. But they also have excellent inland tour options as well. The beachfront rooms are housed in a couple of ocean-facing two-story buildings, and I definitely recommend the second-floor rooms for the improved view and privacy of your balcony. There are also a series of "treehouses," spacious individual bungalows set on stilts 3.7m (12 ft.) high in the midst of the hotel's tiny coastal forest, just a few yards behind the main operation. While these don't have an ocean view, they do offer up a lush sense of tropical isolation. There are wonderful and artistic tile and woodworking touches in all rooms, and most have quite high ceilings. Meals are served either in the main dining room or outdoors on an open-air deck. Hamanasi means "almond" in the local Garífuna language, and you'll see plenty of the namesake *hamans* trees growing around the grounds. Not a true almond, the tree does have an almond-shaped fruit.

Hopkins Village (P.O. Box 265, Dangriga). ✆ **877/552-3483** in the U.S., or 520-7073. Fax 520-7090. www.hamanasi.com. 21 units. BZ$550–BZ$750 (US$275–US$375/£146–£199) double. Published rates include taxes and service charge. Rates lower in the off season. MC, V. **Amenities:** Restaurant; bar; outdoor pool; full-service dive operation; tour desk; laundry service; free Wi-Fi; non-smoking rooms. *In room:* A/C, coffeemaker, safe, no phone.

Jaguar Reef Lodge ★★ Kids This lively resort is the largest hotel in the region, offering up the most facilities, lodging options, amenities, and tour options. The original duplex cabana rooms are set in a horseshoe facing the sea. Only a few have good ocean views, but they're still excellent rooms. Large and well lit, they feature cool tile floors, high ceilings, Guatemalan bedspreads and decorations, and thatch roofs. There are also the newer "colonial" rooms and suites; these are also very well done and comfortable. A few of these come with kitchenettes, televisions with DVD players, and other amenities that make them good for families and longer stays. The second-floor colonial suites have fabulous ocean-facing balconies. Perhaps the best rooms here are the Almond Beach villas and suites. These are all spacious, tastefully decorated, and come with a host of amenities.

In addition to the on-site activities and services, these folks have recently added a small, full-service spa. If you just want to hang around the lodge, hammocks and Adirondack chairs are set under the shade of palm trees along the lodge's white-sand beach. There's complimentary use of sea kayaks, Hobie Cats, bicycles, and snorkel gear. There are two freshwater pools as well.

Hopkins Village (P.O. Box 297, Dangriga). ✆ **800/289-5756** in the U.S., or 520-7040. Fax 520-7091. www.jaguarreef.com. 30 units. BZ$320 (US$160/£85) double; BZ$440–BZ$640 (US$220–US$320/£117–£170) suite or cabana. Rates lower in the off season, slightly higher during peak weeks. MC, V. **Amenities:** Restaurant; bar; outdoor pool; small spa; full-service dive operation; watersports equipment rental; complimentary bike and kayak use; tour desk; laundry service; free Wi-Fi. *In room:* A/C, stocked minifridge, hair dryer, safe, no phone.

Kanantik ★★ This small, all-inclusive resort is one of the more luxurious options around. Except for the purchase of a bottle of wine or some top-shelf liquor, little falls outside the all-inclusive price you pay, and this includes all your tours, scuba diving, and dive equipment or fishing gear. The rooms are all individual, hexagonal, thatch-roof cabins, set either right in front of the ocean or slightly set back in flowering gardens. Each cabin is spacious and features sapodilla wood floors, driftwood beds, either one king bed or two queen beds, and fancy stainless-steel Italian fixtures. The rooms feature a walk-in closet, and the showers are built of smooth river stones. Meals are served in a large, high-pitched dining room. The owner is Italian, and there's usually an excellent chef on hand serving up a mix of local, Italian, and other international cuisine. It is possible to bypass the all-inclusive plan, which may make sense if you don't plan on doing serious diving or fishing.

Southern Highway, Mile 18.2, south of Hopkins Village (P.O. Box 150, Dangriga). ✆ **877/759-8834** in the U.S., or 520-8048. Fax 520-8089. www.kanantik.com. 25 units. BZ$730 (US$365/£193) per person double occupancy. Rates include all meals, local drinks and soft drinks, taxes, tips, and activities. MC, V. Kanantik is located 29km (18 miles) south of Dangriga, accessed by a graded gravel road that connects with the Southern Highway. They also have their own private airstrip, and charter flights directly to the resort can be arranged. The resort is closed Sept–Oct. **Amenities:** Restaurant; bar; midsize outdoor pool w/ unheated Jacuzzi; full-service dive operation; watersports equipment; complimentary bike and kayak use; tour desk; laundry service. *In room:* A/C, no phone.

Inexpensive

In addition to the place listed below, there are literally a score (or more) of simple guesthouses and small inns. Some are run by a local renting a spare room, while others are converted houses. Most inns charge around BZ$20 to BZ$30 (US$10–US$15/£5.30–£7.95) per person. If you have the time, it might be worth your while to check out a couple before deciding where to stay.

Hopkins Inn (Value) Located right on the beach, near the center of the village, this little hotel offers clean and comfortable individual cabins at a very fair price. The cabins are all tiled, and feature wood-paneled, pitched roofs. Each has a small front porch. The two units closest to the water have the best views of the sea. A simple continental breakfast is served on your private veranda, and a host of restaurants are within easy walking distance. The owners are very friendly and knowledgeable, and can help arrange any number of tours and adventures.

Hopkins Village (P.O. Box 121, Dangriga). ✆ **523-7283.** www.hopkinsinn.com. 4 units. BZ$100–BZ$200 (US$50–US$100/£27–£53) double. Rates include continental breakfast. No credit cards. **Amenities:** Bike rental; tour desk; laundry service. *In room:* Minifridge, coffeemaker, no phone.

Jungle Jeanie's by the Sea ★ The individual wooden cabins here are set on raised stilts on the sand. Most have direct views of the ocean, although one large unit with a loft is set back slightly amongst some trees. All have a private balcony in front, as well as a small refrigerator, microwave oven, and coffeemaker. However, aside from these amenities, the furnishings and decor are quite spartan. Still, if you're looking for a comfortable cabin on the sand, just steps from the sea, this might be all you need. Some of the cabins are painted in bright primary colors, while others are simply varnished over natural wood. You'll find the hotel right on the beach, at the southern end of town.

Hopkins Village. ✆ **523-7047.** www.junglebythesea.com. 8 units. BZ$100–BZ$240 (US$50–US$120/£27–£64) double. Rates lower in the off season. MC, V. **Amenities:** Restaurant; laundry service. *In room:* Minifridge, microwave, coffeemaker, no phone.

Tipple Tree Beya (Value) This is an excellent option for budget travelers. With just two rooms in a two-story oceanfront home and one private cabin, this place has a laid-back vibe. Located at the far southern end of the village, literally where the pavement ends, Tipple Tree Beya combines the isolated feel of the more expensive beach resorts here with the convenience and proximity of the in-town options. Right in front of the hotel is an excellent stretch of beachfront. There are hammocks spread on a broad shared veranda, and rustic chairs set out on the sand. The cabin has a small kitchen area, equipped with a microwave oven, refrigerator, coffeemaker, and some basic utensils.

Hopkins Village (P.O. Box 206, Dangriga). ✆/fax **520-7006.** http://tippletree.net. 5 units (4 with private bathroom). BZ$60 (US$30/£16) double with shared bathroom; BZ$80–BZ$120 (US$40–US$60/£21–£32) double with private bathroom. MC, V. **Amenities:** Bike and kayak rental; tour desk; laundry service. *In room:* No phone.

WHERE TO DINE

Even if you're staying at one of the large resorts around here, it's worth heading into town to try a meal at one of the simple, locally run restaurants on the main street. Of these, both **Iris's Restaurant** (✆ **523-7019**) and **Innies Restaurant** (✆ **523-7026**) are perennial favorites. Both serve excellent fresh fish and seafood, and will usually have some *hudut* and other Garífuna dishes on hand. Both are very basic, inexpensive, and somewhat funky in decor and vibe. A similar option, which I prefer for its seafront location, is **Laruna Hati** (✆ **661-5753**), which is located towards the north end of the village.

For more upscale, international fare, head to the **Barracuda Bar & Grill** (✆ **523-7259**) at the Beaches and Dreams hotel, near the center of the village.

King Kassava BELIZEAN/GARIFUNA Located right at the crossroads entering Hopkins Village, this place is the town's hub on many levels. Locals stop in for a cool one or chat around the outdoor tables under steeply pitched thatch roofs. The food here is fresh and tasty, particularly the seafood. Try the Garífuna-style shrimp, in a slightly spicy red sauce over white rice. Alternately you can get some barbecued lobster in season, or whatever fish has just come in off the boats. There's a pool table in a separate room in back, and after about 9pm, the music can get turned up pretty loud.

Hopkins Village. ✆ **608-6188.** Reservations not accepted. Main courses BZ$12–BZ$28 (US$6–US$14/£3.20–£7.40). No credit cards. Daily 7am–2pm and 5–11pm.

Taste of India ★ *Finds* INDIAN With an extensive menu, fresh ingredients, and a talented chef-owner, this is my favorite restaurant in Hopkins. While the appetizer offerings are limited mostly to samosas, pakoras, and papadum, the main menu runs the gamut from curries and paneers to vindaloos and tandoor specialties. Portions are good-size, and the spiciness can be adjusted to your taste. I especially like the shrimp curry and chana saag, a spinach and chickpea combination. But the chicken tikka is also excellent. With a cement floor, exposed beams and electrical work, and rustic unmatched furnishings, the decor and ambience are rustic, to say the least. The best tables are actually outside, facing the beach.

Hopkins Village. ✆ **660-0971** or 604-0799. Reservations recommended. Main courses BZ$15–BZ$20 (US$7.50–US$10/£4–£5.30). No credit cards. Daily 5–10pm.

HOPKINS VILLAGE AFTER DARK

Aside from the various resort hotels, there is very little in the way of nightlife here—unless you can line up a night dive. Most of the resorts, however, hire local bands and dance troupes to entertain their guests. It's worth combining a dinner at one of these places with the nightly show. Aside from the bar at the King Kassava (see above), the liveliest bar on Hopkins Village's main road is **The Watering Hole,** which even has a pool table.

3 PLACENCIA ★★

241km (150 miles) S of Belize City; 161km (100 miles) SE of Belmopan; 89km (55 miles) NE of Punta Gorda

Placencia is Belize's foremost and fastest growing beach destination. Located at the southern tip of a long, narrow peninsula that is separated from the mainland by a similarly narrow lagoon, Placencia boasts nearly 26km (16 miles) of white sand fronting a calm turquoise sea and backed by palm trees. Placencia attracts everyone from hippy backpackers to avid naturalists to hard-core divers to upscale snowbirds. The whole peninsula is in the midst of an ongoing major boom, and development currently stretches from the peninsula's southern tip all the way up to Maya Beach on the northern end of the peninsula.

Placencia itself is a tiny Creole village of colorful clapboard houses mostly built on stilts. Once you settle into the slow pace and relaxed atmosphere, it's hard to move on. Placencia is *the* definition of laid-back. For years, the village's principal thoroughfare was a thin concrete sidewalk. Once listed in the *Guinness Book of World Records* as the narrowest street in the world, the sidewalk still runs through the heart of the village parallel to the sea. However, the ongoing construction and development boom have made the main road through town (called "the Back Road") actually the town's busiest thoroughfare most days.

ESSENTIALS

Getting There

BY PLANE There are numerous flights into and out of Placencia's little airport (PLJ). **Maya Island Air** (✆ **223-1140** in Belize City, or 523-3475 in Placencia; www.maya airways.com) has 10 flights daily between the Goldson International Airport in Belize

City and Placencia. The first flight leaves at 8:10am and the last flight is at 5pm. Flight time is 35 minutes, with a brief stop in Dangriga; the fare is BZ$164 (US$82/£43) each way. They also have seven daily flights between Belize City's Municipal Airport and Placencia at 8, 9, 10, and 11am, noon, and 2:30 and 4:30pm. The fare is BZ$144 (US$72/£38) each way. These flights take 50 minutes, because they stop en route to pick up and let off passengers at the international airport and in Dangriga. Maya Island Air flights from Placencia to Belize City depart throughout the day, with the first flight at 7:25am and the last flight at 4:50pm. Most of these flights stop first in Dangriga, and then at the international airport, before continuing on to Municipal Airport.

Tropic Air (© **800/422-3435** in the U.S. or Canada, 226-2012 in Belize City, or 523-3410 in Placencia; www.tropicair.com) has 11 flights daily between Goldson International Airport and Placencia, with the first flight leaving at 8:15am and the last flight at 5pm. The fare is BZ$171 (US$86/46) each way. They also have five daily flights between Municipal Airport and Placencia, leaving at 8:30 and 10:30am, and at 12:30, 2:30, and 4:50pm. The fare is BZ$144 (US$72/£38) each way. Tropic Air flights depart Placencia for Belize City's airports daily beginning at 7:25am, with the last flight of the day at 4:25pm.

Flights to and from Punta Gorda on Maya Island Air and Tropic Air stop in Placencia to pick up and drop off passengers. On both airlines, flights are sometimes added during the high season or suspended during the low season, so check in advance. Flight time runs between 25 and 50 minutes, depending on whether there is an intermediate stop or two.

BY CAR From Belize City, head west on Cemetery Road, which becomes the Western Highway. Take this all the way to Belmopan, where you will connect with the Hummingbird Highway heading south. Ten kilometers (6⅓ miles) before Dangriga, the Hummingbird Highway connects with the Southern Highway. Take the Southern Highway towards Placencia and Punta Gorda. After 37km (23 miles) on the Southern Highway, turn left onto the road to Riversdale and Placencia. From this turnoff, it's another 32km (20 miles) to Placencia. The drive from Belize City should take around 3 hours.

The road for almost the entire length of the peninsula—save for small patches of pavement—is a hard-packed red dirt, sand, and gravel affair that can often be very dusty and bumpy. They've been talking about paving it for over a decade now. Given the amount of development going on here, it seems inconceivable that this hasn't happened yet, and locals swear it might sometime soon. Currently, the road is paved from the airstrip into the center of the village.

BY BUS There is frequent bus service between all major cities in Belize and Dangriga. See "Dangriga: Getting There: By Bus" for more information. Direct buses leave Dangriga for Placencia daily at 10:30 and 11:30am, and at 4 and 5:15pm. The fare is BZ$10 (US$5/£2.65). Buses leave Placencia for Dangriga, with onward connection to Belmopan, San Ignacio, and Belize City, daily at 5:30 and 6am, and at 1:30 and 2pm. If you're heading south, you'll want to get off the bus as soon as it hits the Southern Highway and flag down the next southbound bus.

However, most independent and bus travelers will want to reach Placencia via Independence Village and Mango Creek, using the *Hokie Pokie* ferry (© **523-2376**). This short 30-minute boat ride cuts a lot of bumpy, dusty miles off the road trip. The ferry fare is BZ$12 (US$6/£3.20). All north- and southbound bus traffic along the Southern highway stops in Independence Village, near the ferry dock. Ferries to Placencia leave daily at 6:30, 7:30, 8, and 11am, at noon, and at 2:30 and 4:30pm. Return ferries from Placencia to Independence Village leave at 6:45 and 10am, and at 12:30, 2:30, 4, 5, and

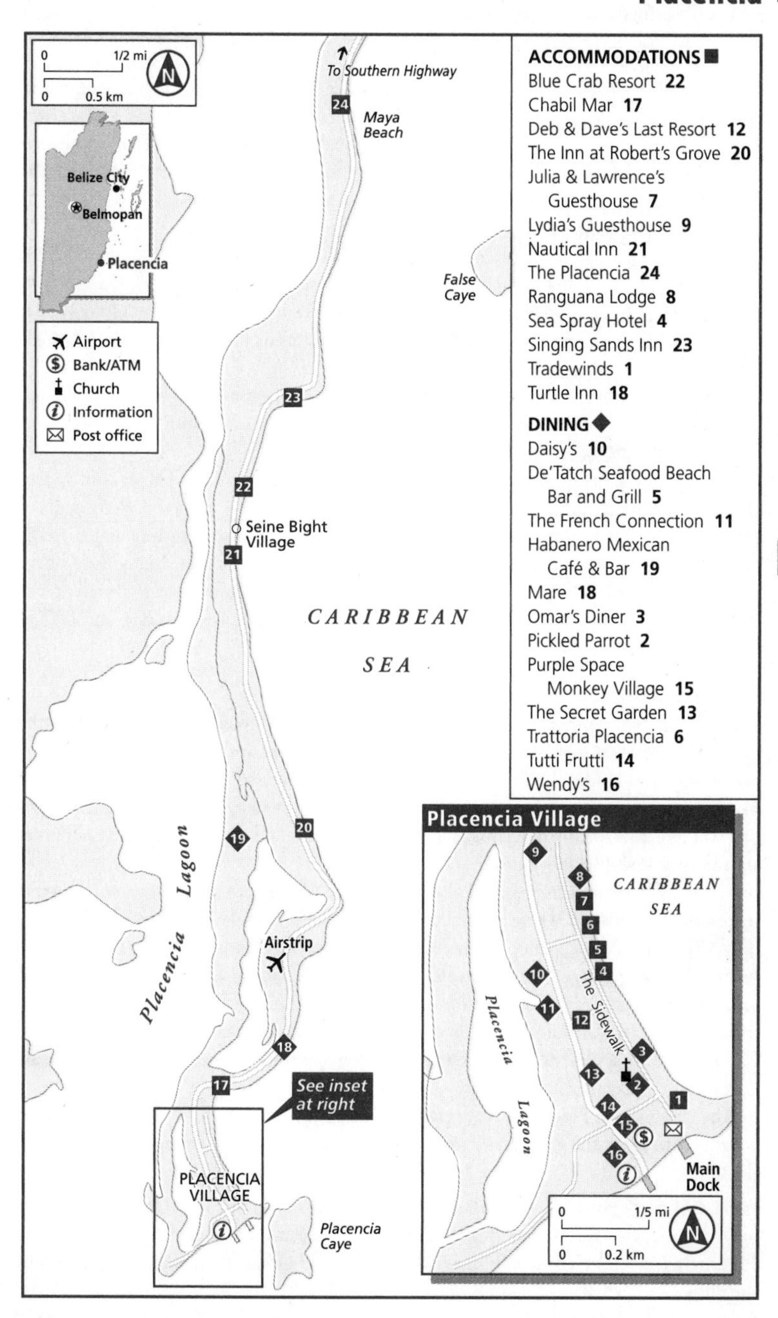
0 1/2 mi
0 0.5 km
N
Belize City
Belmopan
Placencia
Airport
Bank/ATM
Church
Information
Post office
To Southern Highway
Maya Beach
False Caye
Seine Bight Village
CARIBBEAN SEA
Placencia Lagoon
Airstrip
See inset at right
PLACENCIA VILLAGE
Placencia Caye
ACCOMMODATIONS
Blue Crab Resort 22
Chabil Mar 17
Deb & Dave's Last Resort 12
The Inn at Robert's Grove 20
Julia & Lawrence's Guesthouse 7
Lydia's Guesthouse 9
Nautical Inn 21
The Placencia 24
Ranguana Lodge 8
Sea Spray Hotel 4
Singing Sands Inn 23
Tradewinds 1
Turtle Inn 18
DINING
Daisy's 10
De'Tatch Seafood Beach Bar and Grill 5
The French Connection 11
Habanero Mexican Café & Bar 19
Mare 18
Omar's Diner 3
Pickled Parrot 2
Purple Space Monkey Village 15
The Secret Garden 13
Trattoria Placencia 6
Tutti Frutti 14
Wendy's 16
Placencia Village
CARIBBEAN SEA
Placencia Lagoon
The Sidewalk
Main Dock
0 1/5 mi
0 0.2 km

6pm. See "Punta Gorda: Getting There: By Bus" for information on buses making the run between Belize City and the southern reaches of Belize.

Getting Around

Placencia Village itself is tiny, and you can walk the entire length of the sidewalk, which covers most of the village, in about 10 to 15 minutes. If you need a taxi, call **Cobo's Taxi** (✆ **661-2370**), **J's Taxi Service** (✆ **623-4137**), **S&M Taxi** (✆ **523-3524**), or **Peninsula Star Taxi** (✆ **523-4017**). Fares within the village run around BZ$4 to BZ$6 (US$2.10–US$3.20) per person. A trip from the airstrip to the village costs BZ$12 (US$6.35) for one person, or BZ$6 (US$3.20) per person for two or more.

If you want to rent a car or golf cart while in Placencia, **Barefoot Rentals** (✆ **523-3438;** www.barefootrentals.net) is the best option, charging around BZ$130 (US$65/£34) per day for a golf cart, and between BZ$150 and BZ$180 (US$75–US$90/£40–£48) per day for an SUV. Alternately, you can rent a golf cart from **Caribbean Tours** (✆ **523-3047**) for similar rates.

If you want to explore more, a scooter is a good way to get around. Several hotels and operators in the area rent scooters. Rates run around BZ$60 (US$30/£16) for a half-day and BZ$100 (US$50/£27) for a full day.

If you want a little more exercise, a bicycle is a decent option. The terrain is flat, although it can get hot and dusty on the main road, and there aren't really any trails or off-road options. Once the road is paved, a bicycle will be an excellent way to get up the peninsula to find some deserted stretch of beach or visit Seine Bight. Many hotels have bikes either free for the guests or for rent. Several shops around town also rent out bicycles. A relatively modern bike in good shape should cost between BZ$16 and BZ$30 (US$8–US$15/£4.25–£7.95) per day.

Orientation

For most of the peninsula there is only one road. As the road reaches the end of the peninsula and the village of Placencia, it basically dead-ends at the Shell station and some boat docks. Just before this, a dirt spur turns right just beyond the soccer field and heads for a few hundred yards towards the lagoon. Once you've arrived, your main thoroughfare will hopefully be the beach and the sidewalk, both of which run parallel to each other starting near the docks and heading north.

Hotels and resorts are spread all along the length of the Placencia peninsula. To make it easier to understand where a hotel or resort is, the peninsula is broken up into three broad sections: Maya Beach, Seine Bight, and Placencia Village. Maya Beach is the northernmost section of the peninsula, and the hotels and resorts here are quite spread out, with few other services or businesses. More or less anchoring the center of the peninsula is the tiny Garífuna village of Seine Bight. Just to the north and south of Seine Bight village are several other isolated resorts. Down at the southern end of the peninsula is Placencia Village itself.

The very helpful **Placencia Information Center** (✆ **523-4045;** www.placencia.com) is located towards the end of the road, in a new mini-mall just across from the soccer field.

FAST FACTS For the local **police,** dial ✆ **911** or 503-3142; you can also reach the newly formed **tourist police** at ✆ **603-0374**. If you need any medical attention, the **Placencia Medical Center** (✆ **523-3326**) is located behind the school in the center of the village.

Seaweed Shake

It sounds weird at first, and it may not look all that inviting, but don't miss the chance to sip a seaweed shake while you're here. The basic building block of this unique concoction is a tea made from locally harvested seaweed. This is then combined in a blender with both condensed and evaporated milk, cinnamon, nutmeg, vanilla, and some ice. The drink is surprisingly refreshing and tasty. What's more, the folks here in Placencia claim that not only is it a proven aphrodisiac, but that it can also cure everything from anemia to tuberculosis.

There's a **Scotiabank** (✆ **523-3277**) on the main road near the center of the village, as well as an **Atlantic Bank** (✆ **523-3431**). Scotiabank has an ATM that accepts international cards. There's a **pharmacy** attached to Wallen's Market (✆ **523-3128**), in the center of the village. The **post office** is located above the Fishermen's Co-op, near the start of the sidewalk.

There are a couple of gas stations in Placencia. You'll find the Shell station where the road hits the end of the peninsula in the heart of the village. There's also a Texaco station at the Inn at Robert's Grove Marina.

If you need to use the Internet, there's a host of options. If you want Wi-Fi or some food or drink to go along with your surfing, I recommend the **Purple Space Monkey** (✆ **523-4094**). The **Placencia Office Supply** (✆ **523-3205**), which is on the main road and has high-speed connections, is another good option. The Live Oak Plaza is another free Wi-Fi hotspot.

FUN ON & OFF THE BEACH

You just can't help slowing down and relaxing in Placencia. Sit back, sip a seaweed shake, and forget your cares. Nobody ever seems to get up early (except maybe the fishermen), and most people spend their days camped in the sand reading books and eating seafood. The beach, although narrow in places, is arguably the best in Belize. You can walk for miles and see hardly a soul. Still, if you need more activity and adventure, there's a host of options.

Watersports Excursions

SNORKELING & SCUBA DIVING There's often decent snorkeling right off the beach, especially if you head north a mile or so. The water's clear and you'll see plenty of fish and bottom life in the sea grass and along the sand bottom.

One of the more popular snorkel excursions is to the nearby **Laughing Bird Caye** (✆ **523-3565;** www.laughingbird.org). Located just a few miles offshore from Placencia, Laughing Bird Caye is a national park. It's a tiny little island measuring roughly 11×107m (35×350 ft.). There's good snorkeling and swimming offshore, and a beautiful little beach. Many tour operators take folks here and then serve a picnic lunch on the beach.

However, if you're serious about diving or snorkeling, you'll want to get out to the **barrier reef** and its dozens of little offshore cayes. It's between 16 and 40km (10–25 miles) out to the reef here, making it a relatively quick and easy boat ride. Diving here is as spectacular as at other more popular dive destinations in Belize, and you'll often have far fewer fellow divers around.

Tips BYO

While most hotels and all of the dive shops in town have snorkeling and diving gear for rent, you might consider bringing your own. If nothing else, bring your own mask and snorkel. Fins are a lesser concern, as most operators should have fins to fit your feet. However, faces vary vastly, and a tight-fitting mask is essential to an enjoyable snorkel experience. If you plan on going out snorkeling or diving more than a few times, the investment will more than pay for itself.

The offshore **Gladden Spit ★★** site is a world-renowned spot to dive with massive whale sharks. Whale shark sightings are fairly common here from late March through June, and to a lesser extent during the months of August through October and December and January.

Most of the larger resorts have their own dive operations, and these tend to be some of the better operations on the peninsula. There is also a handful of independent operators in the village servicing folks at the rest of the hotels. If you're not staying at a hotel with a dedicated dive operation, check in with the folks at **Seahorse Dive Shop ★** (✆ **523-3166;** www.belizescuba.com).

A snorkeling trip should cost between BZ$60 and BZ$160 (US$30–US$80/£16–£42), depending on the distance traveled and whether or not lunch is included. Rates for scuba diving run between BZ$120 and BZ$300 (US$60–US$150/£32–£80) for a two-tank dive, also depending upon the length of the journey to the dive site and whether or not lunch is included. Equipment rental should cost from BZ$15 to BZ$30 (US$7.50–US$15/£4–£7.95) for a snorkeler, and BZ$30 to BZ$60 (US$15–US$30/£7.95–£16) for a scuba diver.

FISHING Fishing around here is some of the best in Belize. There's excellent bonefishing in flats in this area. Anglers can also go for tarpon, permit, and snook, or head offshore for bigger game, including grouper, yellowfin tuna, king mackerel, wahoo, mahimahi, and the occasional sail or marlin. Experienced guides can help you track any of the above fish, and many are taking their guests out fly-fishing for them as well. Most of the big lodges and resorts here offer fishing packages and excursions. Well-equipped sport-fishing outings run between BZ$1,200 and BZ$2,400 (US$600–US$1,200/£318–£636) per day, depending on the size of the boat, number of anglers, and distance traveled. However, you can hire a smaller open-air skiff perfectly suited for fly-casting for bonefish, permit, or tarpon for between BZ$400 and BZ$1,000 (US$200–US$500/£106–£265) per day.

The folks at **Kingfisher Adventures ★** (✆ **523-3323;** www.tarponcayelodge.com) are some of the more reputable fishing guides, specializing in fishing for permit and tarpon. They even have a small fishing lodge on the remote Tarpon Caye. You can also try **Trip 'N Travel** (✆ **523-3614**), another longstanding local operation with well-regarded guides.

KAYAKING Several hotels and tour operators in town rent out sea kayaks. The waters just off the beach are usually calm and perfect for kayaking. However, the lagoon is probably a better choice, offering up more interesting mangrove terrain and excellent bird-watching opportunities.

Rates for kayak rental run around BZ$10 to BZ$20 (US$5–US$10/£2.65–£5.30) per hour, or BZ$60 to BZ$80 (US$30–US$40/£16–£21) for a full day. A guided tour of the mangroves or a combined snorkeling and kayak tour offshore should cost between BZ$80 and BZ$150 (US$40–US$75/£21–£40) per person.

If you're looking for a guided tour, the best kayak operator in Placencia is **Toadal Adventure ★** (✆ **523-3207**; www.toadaladventure.com). These folks offer several different multi-day kayaking trips, both out on the ocean and on inland rivers. Custom trips can also be designed.

SAILING The crystal-clear waters, calm seas, and isolated islands surrounding Placencia make this an excellent place to go out for a sail. Your options range from crewed yachts and bareboat charters for multiday adventures to day cruises and sunset sails.

The Moorings (✆ **888/952-8420** in the U.S. and Canada, or 523-3351 in Belize; www.moorings.com) and **TMM** (✆ **800/633-0155** in the U.S., or 226-3026 in Belize; www.sailtmm.com) are two large-scale charter companies with operations in Placencia. Options include monohulls, catamarans, and trimarans of varying sizes. Given the shallow draft, increased interior space, and reduced drag, a multihull is your best bet. All of the boats are well equipped and seaworthy. Rates for a weeklong charter run between BZ$3,600 and BZ$18,000 (US$1,800–US$9,000/£954–4,770), depending on the size of the boat and whether or not you charter it bareboat or with a crew.

A day cruise, including lunch, drinks, and snorkeling gear, should cost between BZ$160 and BZ$300 (US$80–US$150/£42–£80) per person. Most hotels and tour operators around town can hook you up with a day sail or sunset cruise, or you can simply head to the docks or check in with the folks at **Next Wave Sailing** (✆ **523-3391**).

Guided Day Trips

While the ocean and outlying cayes are the focus of most activities and tours in Placencia, there are a host of other options. The most popular of these include tours to Cockscomb Basin Wildlife Sanctuary (see "Dangriga," earlier in this chapter), the Mayan ruins of Lubaantun and Nim Li Punit (see "Punta Gorda & the Toledo District," later in this chapter), and up the Monkey River. Day trips can run between BZ$100 and BZ$300 (US$50–US$150/£27–£80) per person, depending upon the distance traveled and the number of activities offered or sites visited. Almost every tour agency in town offers these trips, or ask at your hotel for a recommended guide or operator.

MONKEY RIVER ★ Perhaps the most popular "inland" trip offered out of Placencia is up the Monkey River, and most of it is actually on the water, anyway. Located about a half-hour boat ride down the coast and through the mangroves, the Monkey River area is rich in wildlife. If you're lucky, you might spot a manatee on your way down. Once traveling up the Monkey River, you should keep your eyes peeled for crocodiles, green iguana, wild deer, howler monkeys, and the occasional boa constrictor. In addition, you're likely to see scores of bird species. These tours can be done entirely in a motor launch, or may allow you to kayak on the Monkey River portion; I recommend the latter. Most tours include lunch in the quaint little Creole fishing village of Monkey River itself, as well as a short hike through a forest trail. Monkey River trips cost between BZ$90 and BZ$120 (US$45–US$60/£24–£32) per person.

Spas & Bodywork

If you're looking for a little pampering while in Placencia, there are several options. Most of the big resorts, like Turtle Inn and The Inn at Robert's Grove, have their own spas and spa services, which you may be able to book even if you're not a guest there. Alternatively,

Moments **Sidewalk Fair**

Most days, the Placencia sidewalk is a lazy affair. However, on the second weekend of February, it comes alive with the annual **Placencia Sidewalk Arts Festival.** Local artists show their wares, and a host of restaurants set up outdoor booths. There are also games, events, and raffles. For more information, contact the **Placencia Information Center** (✆ **523-4045;** www.placencia.com).

there are a couple of day spas right in the village. The **Secret Garden Day Spa** (✆ **523-3420**) is located behind Wallen's Market near the center of the village, while **Siripohn's Thai Massage & Oriental Spa** (✆ **620-8718**) is a new option located in the Placencia Village Square, next to the Tutti Frutti Ice Cream Parlor. An hour-long massage should cost you between BZ$120 and BZ$180 (US$60–US$90/£32–£48).

If you want to have an acupuncture treatment or stretch out some, head to the **Acupuncture Center** (✆ **523-3172**), which is also near Wallen's Market. These folks offer traditional acupuncture, various massage and herbal treatments, and regular yoga classes.

SHOPPING

Simple souvenir shops are abundant in Placencia. Located just off the sidewalk near the center of the village, the **Beach Bazaar ★** (✆ **523-3113**) is the best of the bunch. They've got all the traditional trinkets and souvenirs, as well as some higher-end ceramic, wood, and metal artworks.

If you're looking for some finer art, stop in at **Art 'N Soul** (✆ **503-3088**), which is on the sidewalk about 91m (300 ft.) north of the pier and features paintings and prints by local artists. While farther north, in Seine Bight, you should definitely stop in at **Lola's Art Gallery ★** (✆ **523-3342**), which features the colorful acrylic paintings of owner Lola Delgado. These paintings come in a wide range of sizes and prices.

Tip: Be on the lookout for locally produced organic chocolate. Marketed under the brand name **Goss** (www.gosschocolate.com), these milk and dark chocolate bars are sold at stores around town. If you don't pick up any here, they are also on sale at the international airport.

WHERE TO STAY

There is a host of accommodations options in and around Placencia. In general, the town's budget hotels and guesthouses are located in the village proper, either just off the sidewalk or around the soccer field. As you head north to the broader and more isolated beaches, prices tend to rise.

Very Expensive

In addition to the places listed below, **Chabil Mar** (✆ **523-3606;** www.chabilmarvillas.com) offers up luxurious, fully equipped condo units right on the beach just north of town.

The Inn at Robert's Grove ★★★ **Kids** Truly a full-service resort, the Inn at Robert's Grove features two restaurants, three pools, an in-house spa, professional dive and fishing operations, a tennis court, and a host of tour and activity options. All of the rooms are roomy, comfortable, and come with plenty of modern amenities. Rustic red-tile floors, Guatemalan textiles, and Mexican ceramic accents abound. All rooms come with a private balcony, hung with a hammock. Ceiling fans mean you can opt to forgo the air-conditioning. I'd try to land a second-floor room, as these feature higher ceilings and better views. Many of the suites come with fully equipped kitchenettes, and all have a large living room and a large balcony. There are six—count 'em—six Jacuzzis spread around the resort. The rooftop ones are particularly inviting for late-night stargazing and soaking.

Guests enjoy unlimited free use of the hotel's sea kayaks, windsurfers, Hobie Cat sailboats, tennis court, and bicycles, as well as free airport transfers. The hotel also owns and manages two small private islands, Ranagua Caye and Robert's Caye. In addition to the extensive list of tours and activities offered, guests at the inn have the option of taking a day trip to these tiny offshore cayes, or staying a night or two on one of them in a simple yet comfortable cabin.

Placencia, on the beach north of the airstrip. ✆ **800/565-9757** in the U.S., or 523-3565 in Belize. Fax 523-3567. www.robertsgrove.com. 52 units. BZ$480–BZ$520 (US$240–US$260/£127–£138) double; BZ$630–BZ$1,070 (US$315–US$535/£167–£284) suite. Rates lower in the off season; higher during peak weeks. AE, MC, V. **Amenities:** 2 restaurants; 3 bars; lounge; 3 outdoor pools; lit outdoor tennis court; exercise room; small spa; full-service dive shop; complimentary watersports equipment and bike use; tour desk; room service (7am–9pm); babysitting; laundry service; free Wi-Fi. *In room:* A/C, TV, minifridge, coffeemaker, hair dryer, safe.

The Placencia ★★ Still relatively new, this large resort and condo project claims to have the largest pool on the peninsula. The multilevel affair, with a swim-up bar and separate children's section, is the biggest I've seen here. The rooms and apartments feature marble floors throughout, as well as high-def flatscreen TVs and contemporary decor. Most of the master bedrooms come with Jacuzzi tubs. A series of three-story buildings forms a rough horseshoe shape around and behind the aforementioned pool. Oceanfront rooms are at a premium. If you can't land one of these, try for a second- or third-floor unit with a sea-facing balcony. The resort sits on an excellent long stretch of white-sand beach, with the requisite wooden dock jutting out into the sea, featuring a bar, some chaise longues, hammocks, and a swimming ladder on the end of it.

Maya Beach. ✆ **520-4110.** Fax 520-4112. www.theplacencia.com. 92 units. BZ$410–BZ$500 (US$205–US$250/£109–£133) double; BZ$540–BZ$630 (US$270–US$315/£143–£167) 2-bedroom villa. Rates higher during peak weeks. AE, MC, V. **Amenities:** 2 restaurants; 3 bars; large outdoor pool; full-service dive shop; small spa; complimentary bikes and kayaks; concierge; tour desk; room service (6:30am–10pm); babysitting; laundry service; free Wi-Fi. *In room:* A/C, TV, minibar, coffeemaker, hair dryer, safe.

Turtle Inn ★★★ (Finds) This is Francis Ford Coppola's fanciest resort in Central America. You get your choice of a one- or two-bedroom private villa here. Whichever one you choose, you're going to have plenty of space, including a large living room and a spacious bathroom that lets out onto a private interior rock garden, with its own open-air shower (the fixture is a piece of bamboo). Tons of beautiful woodwork, and a heavy dose of Asian decor and furnishings, dominate the rooms. All of the villas are set on the sand just steps from the beach, but not all have ocean views; hence the price variations. The Coppola Pavilion is a two-bedroom unit set a little off the main resort, right in front of the ocean, with its own pool and a working kitchen, wine cellar, and a steam bath/shower in each of the two bathrooms. There's a small spa on the grounds and a full-service dive operation across the street on the lagoon side of the peninsula. The resort's main restaurant, Mare (p. 186), serves excellent Italian and international fare, and there are two additional restaurant options on-site.

Placencia Village, on the beach north of the center of the village. ✆ **800/746-3743** in the U.S., or 824-4912 central reservation number in Belize, or 523-3244 at the hotel. Fax 523-3245. www.turtleinn.com. 25 units. BZ$690–BZ$930 (US$345–US$465/£183–£246) 1-bedroom double; BZ$1,000–BZ$1,250 (US$500–US$625/£265–£331) 2-bedroom double; BZ$3,600 (US$1,800/£954) Coppola Pavilion. Rates include continental breakfast. Rates lower in the off season; higher during peak weeks. AE, MC, V. **Amenities:** 3 restaurants; 2 bars; outdoor pool; full-service dive shop; watersports equipment rental; complimentary bikes and kayaks; concierge; tour desk; limited room service (6am–9pm); babysitting; laundry service; free Wi-Fi. *In room:* Minibar, coffeemaker, hair dryer, safe.

Moderate

Blue Crab Resort *Finds* There's a wonderfully relaxed and laid-back atmosphere at this small beachfront hotel north of Seine Bight village. The rooms are all simple and clean, and they're housed in several separate wooden buildings set on stilts a few feet above the sand. The newer air-conditioned rooms are all located in a fourplex building. I'd definitely try to get one that faces the beach. The two older individual cabanas are actually closer to the water, but are a bit smaller and lack air-conditioning. Of these, cabana no. 1 is your best bet, as it's closest to the sea and gets good cross-ventilation. The tiny restaurant here is locally famous for its cuisine, as the owner was born in Taiwan, and she serves up an enticing mix of Asian, international, and local fare. The hotel has quite a bit of land, extending from the ocean all the way to the lagoon, and as yet few neighbors. The folks here make the excellent organic Goss chocolate you'll see around Belize.

Seine Bight, on the beach north of the village. ✆ **523-3544.** Fax 523-3543. www.bluecrabbeach.com. 6 units. BZ$180–BZ$200 (US$90–US$100/£48–£53) double. Rates include airport transfers. Rates lower in the off season. MC, V. **Amenities:** Restaurant; tour desk. *In room:* No phone.

Nautical Inn ★ Set on the northern outskirts of the quaint little Garífuna town of Seine Bight Village, this hotel features rooms in four separate two-story octagonal buildings. The rooms are simply furnished, with rattan beds and a bright tropical decor. The showers are a tad small, but otherwise the rooms are pretty comfortable. I prefer the "deluxe" second-floor units, which have large shared balconies. A few units here are called "family rooms," and these have a microwave oven, small refrigerator, and a set of bunk beds for the kids. Diving is the main activity here, and they have an excellent operation. The second-floor restaurant has both outdoor and indoor seating, and a small bar with a captivating mermaid hanging over it.

Seine Bight Village, on the beach on the northern edge of the village. ✆ **523-3595.** Fax 523-3594. www.nauticalinnbelize.com. 12 units. BZ$232–BZ$292 (US$116–US$146/£61–£77) double. Rates lower in the off season; higher during peak periods. AE, MC, V. **Amenities:** Restaurant; outdoor pool; full-service dive shop; watersports equipment rental; bike rental; tour desk; laundry service. *In room:* A/C, TV, coffeemaker.

Ranguana Lodge *Value* The five individual cabins at this small family-run hotel are all clean and cozy. In the two older cabins, nearly everything is made of hardwood—walls, floors, ceilings, even the louvered windows. These rooms feature a full kitchenette. The three oceanfront cabins are the newest, and while they are right in front of the sea and have air-conditioning, they are a little smaller and have a little less character. All of the cabins are just steps from the ocean, and all come with a private balcony or porch area. All are painted a blinding pure white, with a different primary or Day-Glo color used for trim.

Placencia Village, on the beach in the center of the village. ✆ **523-3112.** Fax 523-3451. www.ranguanabelize.com. 5 units. BZ$160–BZ$168 (US$80–US$84/£42–£45) double. Rates include taxes. AE, MC, V. **Amenities:** Tour desk. *In room:* Minifridge, coffeemaker, no phone.

Singing Sands Inn ★ This small hotel has the lushest gardens and grounds in the area. The six individual thatch-roofed wooden cabins are simple affairs with either a queen bed or a double bed, as well as a separate twin bed or bunk beds. They are set in a row perpendicular to the beach, with cabin nos. 1 and 2 closest to the ocean. You'll still get something of an ocean view from cabin nos. 3, 4, and 5, while no. 6 is set amidst the flowers and foliage. Each has a small porch with a couple of chairs for lounging. In addition to the cabins there are a couple of larger, fully equipped apartments with kitchenettes. There's an inviting outdoor pool and a large open-air deck area facing the ocean, where meals and drinks are served, as well as a covered dining area in case it's raining. Guests have free use of sea kayaks, and there's a long dock built out into the sea with an inviting shaded palapa at the end of it. Singing Sands Inn is located on the northern end of the peninsula, on a quiet section of Maya Beach.

Maya Beach. ✆ **523-8017.** ✆/fax 520-8022. www.singingsands.com. 8 units. BZ$150–BZ$250 (US$75–US$125/£40–£66) double. Rate includes continental breakfast. Rates lower in the off season. AE, DISC, MC, V. **Amenities:** Restaurant; outdoor pool; watersports equipment rental; tour desk; laundry service. *In room:* Minifridge, no phone.

Inexpensive

If the places listed below are full, you can simply walk around the village and see what's available, or head to either **Julia & Lawrence's Guesthouse** (✆ **503-3478;** www.juliasrooms.com) or **Deb and Dave's Last Resort** (✆ **523-3207;** debanddave@btl.net), both located just off the sidewalk towards the center of the village.

Lydia's Guesthouse (Value) This is one of the longest-running and most popular budget options in Placencia, and it's fitting that this classic two-story converted home survived Hurricane Iris. The rooms are simple and clean, although a few can be a bit cramped. The shared bathrooms and showers are kept immaculate, and guests have free use of the kitchen that takes up the ground floor of the amiable Lydia Villanueva's private home next door. You'll find a convivial hostel-like atmosphere—travelers from around the world make up the guest list. There's even a good ocean view from the shared balcony on the second floor, a real steal in this price range. Lydia also rents various houses around the village for longer stays.

Placencia Village, towards the northern end of the sidewalk. ✆ **523-3117.** Fax 523-2335. lydias@btl.net. 8 units, all with shared bathroom. BZ$52 (US$26/£14) double. Rates slightly lower in the off season. MC, V. *In room:* No phone.

Sea Spray Hotel Rooms and prices vary substantially in this perennial budget and backpacker favorite. The economy rooms are a bit cramped and dark. Most rooms are in a two-story building built perpendicular to the sea. The four deluxe rooms are in a separate two-story building fronting the sea, and these come with televisions and kitchenettes, as well as comfortable private oceanview balconies. There's also a separate, fully equipped beachfront cabana, although I think the deluxe rooms are a better and more comfortable choice. The attached De'Tatch Seafood Beach Bar & Grill serves hearty local fare at very reasonable prices, and also has an Internet cafe. As at Lydia's (above), there's a convivial hostel-like atmosphere here.

Placencia Village, on the beach towards the middle of the sidewalk. ✆ **523-3148.** Fax 523-3364. www.seasprayhotel.com. 21 units. BZ$50–BZ$130 (US$25–US$65/£13–£34) double. AE, DISC, MC, V. **Amenities:** Restaurant; tour desk; laundry service. *In room:* Minifridge, no phone.

Tradewinds Finds You can't beat the setting of Tradewinds. Perched right on the ocean's edge towards the southern end of the village, the eight individual cabins here are just a few feet from the water. All are comfortable, roomy, and come with a very inviting porch, hung with a hammock overlooking the waves, where I predict you'll spend most of your time. The less expensive rooms here are set a bit farther back from the sea in a simple triplex building, although each comes with its own little veranda. Everything is painted in lively pastels, and there's a friendly, family-like vibe to the whole operation.

Placencia Village, on the beach, south end of the village. ✆ **523-3122.** Fax 523-3201. www.placencia.com. 11 units. BZ$80–BZ$140 (US$40–US$70/£21–£37) double. Rates slightly lower in the off season; higher during peak weeks. MC, V. *In room:* Minifridge, coffeemaker, no phone.

WHERE TO DINE

In addition to the places mentioned below, the restaurant at **The Inn at Robert's Grove** (p. 182) is consistently top notch. On the other end of the spectrum, **Wendy's** (✆ **523-3335**) is a popular, low-key spot serving excellent Belizean, Mexican, and international fare, located on the main road, at the southern end of town, almost by the pier.

Finally, as you wander around town in the heat of the day, be sure to stop in at **Tutti Frutti Ice Cream Shop** for some fresh, homemade ice cream or gelato. Tutti Frutti is in the on the main road in the Placencia Village Square shopping center, across from the soccer field. **Daisy's,** located on the main road near the center of town, also serves up fresh, homemade ice cream, as well as breakfasts, lunches, and dinners.

There are also several grocery stores in the village, in case you want to put together a picnic lunch.

Expensive

Mare ★★ ITALIAN/SEAFOOD This is a good place for a splurge if you're not actually staying at Turtle Inn. The lighting at night is subdued in this open-air deck area. Tables and chairs are made of heavy teak and adorned with candles and fresh flowers. The restaurant looks out over the hotel's pool and on to the sea, and the setting is also wonderful during the day for lunch. The kitchen serves up expertly prepared Italian cuisine and fresh seafood. I like to start things off with the *insalata de pesce,* which features fresh red snapper smoked on the premises. In addition to nightly specials, there are delicious thin-crust wood-oven pizzas, a selection of pastas, and several hearty main dishes. Whole freshly caught fish are roasted in the wood oven, as are lobster tails in season. Most of the herbs and vegetables served are grown right here at the hotel's organic garden. The wine list features a range of fine wines from Francis Ford Coppola's own vineyard.

At Turtle Inn, on the beach north of the center of the village. ✆ **523-3244.** www.turtleinn.com. Reservations recommended. Main courses BZ$44–BZ$88 (US$22–US$44/£12–£23). AE, MC, V. Daily 11am–3pm and 6:30–9pm.

Moderate

De'Tatch Seafood Beach Bar & Grill ★ BELIZEAN/SEAFOOD This funky open-air beachfront joint is one of the most popular spots in town. Traditional Belizean breakfasts here are hearty and inexpensive. You can get excellent seafood or shrimp burritos or tacos for lunch or dinner. There's an Internet cafe off to one side, and the sea is just steps away. The second-floor open-air deck can get hot in the daytime, but it is especially nice on starry nights.

Placencia Village, on the ocean just off the Sea Spray Hotel towards the center of the village. ✆ **503-3385.** Reservations not accepted. Breakfast and lunch main courses BZ$6–BZ$16 (US$3–US$8/£1.60–£4.25);

dinner main courses BZ$12–BZ$36 (US$6–US$18/£3.20–£9.55); lobster BZ$34–BZ$50 (US$17–US$25/£9–£13). MC, V. Thurs–Tues 7am–10pm.

The French Connection ★★★ Finds FRENCH/FUSION For a standout and memorable meal, it's hard to beat this place in Placencia. In fact, the cooking, service and ambience at this French bistro-style fusion-infused joint would stand up just about anywhere. The menu changes regularly, according to the available seasonal ingredients and the chef's whim. I recently got to start things off with a fabulous onion tartlet, topped with goat cheese, sun-dried tomatoes, and tapenade. Main-course offerings included roasted grouper in a smoked chili beurre blanc sauce, and a pinot noir–braised lamb shank. Presentations are relatively simple—no high towers—and the servings are ample. These folks have an excellent and fairly priced wine list. Owners Anna and Marcus Perigo are engaging and amiable hosts; he's from Britain and she's from Finland. At press time, the owners were constructing a new space, and by the time you read this, they should be settled into this space in the center of the village, on the lagoon side, near the police station.

Placencia Village, on the lagoon, south end of town. ✆ **523-3656.** Main courses BZ$36–BZ$40 (US$18–US$20/£9.55–£11). MC, V. Fri–Wed 6–10pm.

Habanero Mexican Café & Bar ★ MEXICAN Set on the lagoon side of the peninsula beside the marina at Robert's Grove, this restaurant serves up a mix of Tex-Mex and traditional Mexican fare. When the bugs aren't biting, you'll want to grab a table outdoors on the deck overlooking the water. This is also a great spot to catch the sunset. When the bugs are biting, you can seek refuge in the screened-in main dining room. My favorite dishes here are the garlic shrimp tacos and the spicy fish chimichanga. For those looking for a fiesta, you can order sangria and margaritas by the pitcher.

At the marina across from The Inn at Robert's Grove, north of the airstrip. ✆ **523-3665.** Reservations recommended. Main courses BZ$16–BZ$32 (US$8–US$16/£4.25–£8.50). AE, MC, V. Daily noon–10pm.

Trattoria Placencia PASTA There's not much besides pasta and some simple salads and appetizers on the menu here. But the folks here make a massive batch of fresh fettuccine daily, and they offer a long list of sauces to have with it. My favorites include the eggplant, capers, and fresh tomatoes, although the marinara sauce is also excellent and loaded with fresh shrimp, fish, conch, and lobster (in season). They also make their own pesto and have Belizean-made Italian sausage. Heavy wooden tables are spread widely on a covered porch and a screened-in dining room.

Moments Get Your Bib Out

Lobster season opens each year on June 15, and Placencia pulls out all the stops to celebrate the culinary possibilities of this underwater arthropod. In addition to concerts, games, and sidewalk booths hawking all sorts of goods and treats, you'll be able to sample everything from lobster fritters to lobster quiche to lobster bisque and beyond. If it can be made with lobster, you'll probably find it here. The Placencia Lobster Festival is held in late June each year; for more information and exact dates, contact the **Placencia Information Center** (✆ **523-4045;** www.placencia.com).

Placencia Village, on the oceanfront about midway along the sidewalk. ✆ **623-3394.** Main courses BZ$26–BZ$40 (US$13–US$20/£6.90–£11). V only. Mon–Sat 5–9:30pm.

Inexpensive

Omar's Diner *Value* BELIZEAN/MEXICAN There's no assembly-line production, Styrofoam wrappings, or U.S.-style short order cook here. Sometimes the speed of service particularly doesn't live up to diner norms. Still, this simple restaurant consistently serves up hearty and tasty local fare at great prices. Located just off the sidewalk in the center of the village, the dining room is screened in. If there's no free table, you might be able to take a seat with another fellow traveler, or at one of the large communal tables.

Placencia Village, off the sidewalk in the center of the village. ✆ **523-4094.** Breakfast and lunch main courses BZ$5–BZ$14 (US$2.50–US$7/£1.35–£3.70); dinner main courses BZ$10–BZ$24 (US$5–US$12/£2.65–£6.35); lobster BZ$30–BZ$44 (US$15–US$22/£7.95–£12). MC, V. Daily 7am–2pm and 5:30–10pm.

Pickled Parrot ★ INTERNATIONAL This popular place serves three hearty meals daily, with a menu ranging from fresh seafood and local cuisine to pizzas, burgers, and burritos. Dinner specials range from mango-rum glazed chicken to lobster curry. There's a relaxed, informal atmosphere at this open-air sand-floored restaurant, and the bar can even get rowdy at times, especially after folks have downed a few rounds of Parrot Piss, the bar's signature mixed drink. The Tuesday night dart tourney is a great place to meet and mingle with some locals.

Placencia Village. ✆ **604-0278.** www.pickledparrotbelize.com. Reservations not accepted. Breakfast and lunch main courses BZ$6–BZ$14 (US$3–US$7/£1.60–£3.70); dinner main courses BZ$16–BZ$26 (US$8–US$13/£4.25–£6.90); lobster BZ$35–BZ$50 (US$18–US$25/£9.55–£13). V only. Mon–Sat 11:30am–9:30pm; Sun 5–9pm.

Purple Space Monkey Village INTERNATIONAL Having risen from the ashes twice, once after Hurricane Iris, and then again after a devastating fire, this place remains the town's central meeting place for world travelers, expatriates and locals alike. The heavy wrought iron tables and chairs are a rainbow of primary colors. The food is well-prepared, abundant, and reasonably priced. I like to start the day with their fry jacks stuffed with eggs and cheese. The lunch menu tends towards burgers, sandwiches, wraps, and burritos, whereas their dinner menu gets more creative and extensive. Specialties here include fresh blackened fish, as well as fish, chicken, or shrimp served in a mango-teriyaki sauce. There's free Wi-Fi throughout, as well as four complimentary computer workstations and a lending library.

Placencia Village, in front of the soccer field. ✆ **523-4094.** Breakfast and lunch main courses BZ$10–BZ$15 (US$5–$7.50/£2.65–£4); dinner main courses BZ$26–BZ$40 (US$14–$21). MC, V. Daily 7am–10pm.

The Secret Garden ★ *Finds* INTERNATIONAL/COFFEE HOUSE The name of this quiet and cozy little spot is appropriate. Reached over a small yellow bridge, there are a few outdoor tables on a wood deck in a shady garden. A few more tables are located on a covered veranda, and a couple more are inside the small restaurant. Dinner choices range from shrimp in either a red or green Thai chili sauce to a grilled chicken breast in a honey-mustard sauce. There's also fresh fish, a variety of kebab options, and daily chalkboard specials. In many ways, this place is very similar to the Purple Space Monkey, including the free Wi-Fi access and lending library, but with a much mellower and more laid-back vibe.

Placencia Village, behind Wallen's Market. ✆ **523-3617.** Breakfast and lunch main courses BZ$8–BZ$17 (US$4–US$8.50/£2.10–£4.50); dinner main courses BZ$22–BZ$34 (US$11–US$17/£5.85–£9). No credit cards. Tue–Sat 7am–8:30pm; Sun 7am–2pm.

PLACENCIA AFTER DARK

Placencia is a quiet and remote beach destination, which is why my favorite late-night activity here is simply taking a stroll on the beach and stargazing. Still, there are a few bars in the village, and some of the larger resort hotels have lively nightlife scenes.

Two of the most popular spots in town are the **Barefoot Beach Bar** ★(✆ **523-3515**) and the **Tipsy Tuna Sports Bar** (✆ **523-3480**), two neighboring establishments; I prefer the relaxed vibe and outdoor setting of the Barefoot Beach Bar, while the Tipsy Tuna is more of a late-night place, with pool tables and regular live music and karaoke.

For real late night action, there's the **D'Eclipse Entertainment Club** (✆ **523-3288**), just north of the airstrip. This place is in a location where noise pollution wouldn't bother existing hotels and houses. However, it's yet to really catch on with any local or visiting crowd.

4 PUNTA GORDA & THE TOLEDO DISTRICT ★

330km (205 miles) S of Belize City; 161km (100 miles) S of Dangriga

Punta Gorda, or simply "P.G.," is Belize's southernmost town. This is the end of the road, and feels a bit like the end of the world. P.G. is a quiet place with clean, paved streets, few cars, lush vegetation, and a very slow pace. Although it is right on the Caribbean, there is no beach to speak of, and the water just off town is rather uninviting. However, there are several wonderful offshore cayes within easy reach that have excellent beaches and serve as bases for equally excellent snorkeling, scuba diving, and fishing. Inland from P.G., the surrounding scenery is as verdant as you'll find anywhere in Belize (due to nearly 508cm/200 in. of rain a year). The surrounding Toledo District is home to various Mayan ruins and numerous villages that are still peopled by Kekchi and Mopan Maya Indians, who have been migrating here from Guatemala over the last century.

Settled by Garífunas in 1823, Punta Gorda was only accessible by boat for decades, and even though the Southern Highway is now paved and easily connects the town with points north, there's still a sense of this being a distant frontier. As the administrative center for the Toledo District, Punta Gorda has an active market and bus services to the many surrounding Mayan and Garífuna villages, although connections are not very frequent. Most travelers do little more than pass through Punta Gorda on their way to or from Guatemala by way of the Puerto Barrios ferry. However, there is plenty to keep the adventurous traveler busy for several days, including fishing, scuba diving, rainforest hiking, and bird-watching.

ESSENTIALS

Getting There & Departing

BY PLANE There are several daily flights into and out of Punta Gorda's little airport (PND). **Maya Island Air** (✆ **223-1140** in Belize City, or 722-2856 in Punta Gorda; www.mayaairways.com) has four flights daily between Belize City and Punta Gorda. These flights leave from the Municipal Airport at 8:10 and 10am, and at 2:30 and 4:30pm. Most of these flights stop 15 minutes later at the Goldson International Airport to pick up passengers. The fare is BZ$182 (US$91/£48) each way from Municipal Airport, and BZ$214 (US$107/£57) each way from the international airport. When you're ready to leave, Maya Island Air flights from Punta Gorda to Belize City depart at 6:45, 9:30, and 11:30am, and at 4pm. Most of these flights stop first in Placencia and Dangriga, and then at the international airport, before continuing on to Municipal Airport.

Tropic Air (✆ **800/422-3435** in the U.S. or Canada, 226-2012 in Belize City, or 722-2008 in Punta Gorda; www.tropicair.com) has five daily flights from Municipal Airport to Punta Gorda at 8:15 and 10:20am, and at 12:20, 2:20, and 5pm. These flights stop 15 minutes later at Goldson International Airport to pick up passengers. The fare is BZ$185 (US$93/£49) each way from the Municipal Airport, and BZ$218 (US$109/£58) each way from the international airport. Tropic Air flights depart Punta Gorda for Belize City's airports daily at 6:50, 9:30, and 11:30am, and at 4pm.

Flight times run between 55 minutes and 1 hour and 20 minutes, depending on the number of stops, since most flights to and from Punta Gorda on Maya Island Air and Tropic Air stop in Placencia and Dangriga to pick up and drop off passengers. On both airlines, flights are sometimes added during the high season or suspended during the low season, so check in advance.

BY CAR It is a long way to Punta Gorda. However, the Southern Highway, which starts just outside of Dangriga, is paved the entire 161km (100 miles) to Punta Gorda, where it ends. Coming from Belize City, head first to Belmopan and turn south on the Hummingbird Highway. Just before Dangriga, the Hummingbird Highway connects with the Southern Highway, which takes you all the way to Punta Gorda. Alternatively, you can take the Manatee Road turnoff just past the Belize Zoo, although the Manatee Road is a washboard dirt-and-gravel road for most of its length. See "By Car" in "Essentials" in section 1, earlier in this chapter, for more information. It should take between 4 and 5 hours to drive between Belize City and Punta Gorda.

BY BUS **James Bus Line** (✆ **207-3937** in Belize City, or 702-2049 in Punta Gorda) and **National Transport** (✆ **227-2255**) have regular service throughout the day between Belize City and Punta Gorda. Buses leave at irregular intervals between 4:30am and 5pm, with at least 15 different buses making the run throughout the day. In Belize City, National Transport buses from the main terminal on West Collett Canal, while James buses leave from nearby, near the Shell gas station on Cemetery Road. It's worth getting an express bus, which should only take around 5½ hours. However, there are far more frequent nonexpress buses. On these, the trip takes between 6 and 7 hours. In some cases, you may have to change buses in Belmopan or Dangriga. The one-way fare is BZ$28 (US$14/£7.40).

Departing buses begin running at 3am, with the last bus leaving at 4pm. All buses, even the express buses, stop in Belmopan, Dangriga, and Independence. However, the express buses are not supposed to stop along the route to pick up and drop off passengers at intermediary points.

BY BOAT Several boats run daily between Punta Gorda and Puerto Barrios, Guatemala. If there's enough demand, the boats may stop in Livingston, Guatemala, as well. Expect to pay between BZ$30 and BZ$40 (US$15–US$20/£7.95–£11) per person. The boats leave from the main pier in Punta Gorda. **Requena's Charter Service,** 12 Front St. (✆ **722-2070;** watertaxi@btl.net), is one of the more dependable operators. When the seas are calm, the crossing takes about 1 hour. Departures for Guatemala tend to leave between 8:30 and 9am, although there are often afternoon departures as well. The boats

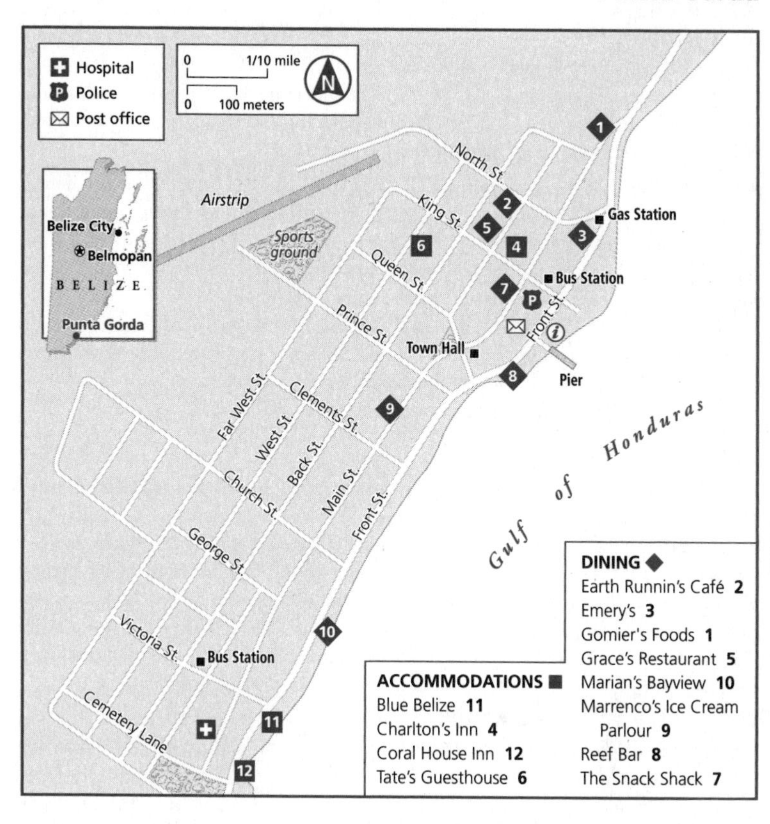

tend to return from Puerto Barrios between 2 and 4pm. You'll have to pay the BZ$7.50 (US$3.75/£2) in exit taxes. ***Note:*** When coming and going, be sure to get your passport stamped at the immigration office just up from the dock.

Getting Around

Punta Gorda is a very small and compact town, and you should be able to get around primarily on foot. If you're just too hot or tired, or you're heading farther afield, call **Galvez's Taxi Travel & Tour Service** (**© 722-2402**) or the **Roots & Herbs Taxi Service** (**© 722-2834**).

Another option for getting around is to rent a bike. Ask at your hotel, and they should be able to help you find one for rent.

Orientation

Punta Gorda is a small coastal town, and the road into town runs right along the water before angling a bit inland. There's a tiny triangular park at the center of the town. On one side is the Civic Center, or Town Hall. On one corner is a cute little clock tower, and the Belize Bank anchors another corner. Still, much of the town's activity is water-based, and many of the most important businesses, hotels, restaurants, and government offices are located on Front Street, which runs along the waterfront. The town's main pier is off the center of Front Street. On the western edge of town, only 6 blocks from the water, is P.G.'s airstrip.

The **Belize Tourist Industry Association** (✆ **722-2531**), in conjunction with local hotels and tourism operators, runs a well-staffed and helpful information center on Front just north of the main pier. This is a good place to come to find current transportation schedules, book a tour, or arrange a homestay.

FAST FACTS For the local **police,** dial ✆ **911** or 722-2022, and for the **fire department,** call ✆ **722-2032**. If you need medical attention, go to the **Punta Gorda Hospital** on Main Street, towards the southern end of town (✆ **722-2026**). The **post office** (✆ 722-2087) is on Front Street across from the main pier. **Belize Bank,** 30 Main St. (✆ 722-2324), can handle most of your banking needs.

There's a **Texaco** gas station (✆ **722-2926**) out towards the northern end of Front Street and a Shell station out by "The Dump." Finally, if your hotel can't or won't do it for you, take your dirty clothes to **Punta Gorda Laundry Services,** on Main Street across from the Belize Bank, which charges around BZ$12 (US$6/£3.20) per load.

WHAT TO SEE & DO

There's very little in the way of attractions right in town. A stroll through Punta Gorda is the best way to enjoy the Caribbean atmosphere. If you get a little antsy at such a slow pace, there are plenty of cultural wonders and natural adventures within easy reach of Punta Gorda. There are a host of tour operators and guides in P.G. Your hotel and the information center listed in "Essentials" above can probably hook you up with a good guide or adventure operator. Alternatively, you can check in with the folks at **Tide Tours** ★ (✆ **722-2129;** www.tidetours.org), a local ecotourism initiative that integrates environmentally and socially aware practices with their wide range of tour and adventure options.

REACHING THESE ATTRACTIONS Most of the villages and attractions discussed below (such as Nim Li Punit) are located along the highway and have regular bus service every day. Buses to and from the other villages and attractions generally run at least once daily. Buses tend to leave for the villages from Punta Gorda between noon and 2pm, depending upon which village or destination you are traveling to. These buses all leave from the market area in front of the Civic Center along Queen Street.

The time of departure from the villages to P.G. varies but is usually early in the morning, sometimes right around dawn. There's often only one bus per day, but some villages have two or more daily buses. Ask in P.G., or in the actual village, as schedules are subject to change. Fares run around BZ$2 to BZ$6 (US$1–US$3/55p–£1.60) per person each way.

Moments **Celebrating the Sweet**

Each year in late May, P.G. pulls out all the stops for the **Toledo Cacao Fest** (www.toledochocolate.com). The festival, which runs over a weekend, includes a wide range of events and activities, including live concerts, fireworks, cacao farm tours, and of course plenty of opportunities to taste all sorts of dishes and creations made from or with cacao and chocolate. See the above website for exact dates.

Another alternative is to hire a taxi or go on an organized trip. Ask at your hotel or the information center and you should be able to set up a trip. You can usually hire a car and driver/guide for BZ$200 to BZ$360 (US$100–US$180/£53–£95) per day. This price will usually cover a group of four.

The truly adventurous might want to tour this area by mountain bike. You can reach most of the above sites and villages in an athletic couple of hours of riding. Leave early to avoid the oppressive midday heat, and expect slow going and lots of mud in the rainy season.

Mayan Ruins

None of Belize's southern ruins is as spectacular or actively restored as the more famous sites in the northern and western parts of the country. Still, the ancient Maya did have substantial cities and trading posts all up and down the Belizean coast, and several impressive reminders can be found near Punta Gorda. Travelers interested in the ongoing Mayan tradition will find themselves in a region of numerous small Kekchi and Mopan Maya villages, many of which have taken tentative steps to enter the tourism industry with homestay programs or basic guesthouses.

LUBAANTUN The largest of the nearby Mayan ruins is **Lubaantun.** The name, which means "Place of the Fallen Stones" in Yucatec Maya, was given to the site in 1924 and it was descriptive of the state of the buildings at that time. This Late Classic Maya ruin is unusual in that the structures were built using a technique of cut-and-fitted limestone blocks rather than the usual rock-and-mortar construction technique used elsewhere by the Mayans. Set on a high ridge, the site features five plazas and two ball courts. The highest temple here rises just 15m (50 ft.) or so, and it's still mostly in ruins, with trees growing out of the rubble. Although largely unexcavated, the ancient city's center has been well cleared, and the surviving architecture and urban outline give a good sense of the former glory of this Mayan ceremonial center.

Lubaantun is perhaps most famous as the site where a crystal skull was allegedly discovered by a young Canadian woman in 1926. There's much debate as to the origin and age of the skull, which some say was planted as a surprise present for Anna Mitchell-Hedges, who just happened to discover the carved skull on her 16th birthday while accompanying her father, who just happened to be leading the archaeological expedition. Others claim that the skull was a plant that had actually been purchased in London by Mitchell-Hedges. There are also claims that the crystal skull is the work of extraterrestrials, and that it has shown remarkable healing powers. The skull is currently kept in a vault in Canada.

Lubaantun is located about 32km (20 miles) northwest from Punta Gorda, about 11km (7 miles) from the well-marked turnoff on the highway near Big Falls, and 1.6km (1 mile) from the small Mayan village of San Pedro Columbia. Admission is BZ$10 (US$5/£2.65).

Nim Li Punit ★ Nim Li Punit, meaning "Big Hat" in Kekchi Mayan, features 26 stelae, including the largest Maya carved stele in Belize, measuring almost 9m (30 ft.) tall. This stele bears the depiction of a local ruler wearing a large, broad diadem, or "big hat," hence the name of the site. Only discovered in 1976, Nim Li Punit is a relatively small site, with four compact plazas and one very well preserved ball court, with a stone marker in its center. One of the plazas served as an astronomical observation area, with a platform and stone markings indicating the point where the sun rises on the equinoxes. There are three Royal tombs that have been discovered and partially excavated, and you can peer down into two of them. However, overall, very little excavation or restoration has been undertaken. Nonetheless, the eight carved stelae, and in particular, stele 14, make this a worthwhile stop. The best-preserved stelae, including stele 14, are currently housed at the small museum and visitor center at the entrance to the site.

Nim Li Punit is set on a high hilltop, and on a clear day, you have a great view over the flat southern plains, all the way to the Caribbean Sea. It is believed that this Late Classic city had close ties to Copan, Honduras. If you can only visit one of the Mayan sites in southern Belize, I recommend Nim Li Punit over Lubaantun.

Nim Li Punit is located about 3.2km (2 miles) off the Southern Highway, near the village of Indian Creek, 40km (25 miles) north of Punta Gorda. A dirt road leads from the highway to a parking area near the visitor center. Admission is BZ$10 (US$5/£2.65).

Other minor ruins in the area include **Uxbenka** near Santa Cruz and **Pusilha** near Aguacate.

Places for a Dip

Mayan culture, past and present, may be the main attraction of Punta Gorda, but it also boasts plenty of natural attractions. In the forested hills south of San Antonio is one of the most beautiful swimming holes in all of Belize. Flowing out of a cave in a limestone mountain, the aptly named **Blue Creek★★** is a cool stream with striking deep turquoise water. Lush rainforest shades the creek, creating an idyllic place to spend an afternoon. You can cool off by swimming up into the mouth of the cave from which the stream flows. Blue Creek is also known locally as Ho Keb Ha, which means "the place where the water flows from." During the dry season, you can actually hike about 8km (5 miles) through the cave to an aboveground exit. The village of Blue Creek is reached from a turnoff about 2.4km (1½ miles) east of San Antonio. From here it's another 4km (2½ miles) south on a rough dirt road. The creek runs right through the little village, but the best swimming holes and the cave source of the creek are about a 10- to 15-minute hike upstream.

Just off the Southern Highway, near the village of Big Falls, there is a natural **hot spring** that's billed as the only such hot spring in Belize. You can have a refreshing swim in the river at the falls and then warm your muscles in the hot spring. This is a popular spot for locals on weekends.

There are also some attractive small waterfalls near the village of San Antonio, with inviting pools for a refreshing dip.

Watersports

The fishing, scuba diving, and snorkeling to be had off Punta Gorda are world-class. Kayaking on the ocean or up the Moho River is also excellent. Most tour operators and hotels in town can offer or line up a snorkel, dive trip, or fishing expedition out to the very underexplored Sapodilla Cayes.

If you want to do an extended dive trip, or some volunteer work in marine conservation, check in with the folks at **Reef Conservation International★** (**✆ 702-2117**; www.reefci.com). These folks have cabins and campsites, as well as research and dive facilities on the idyllic Frank's Caye, which is part of the Sapodilla Marine Park.

A Botanical Garden

The **Toledo Botanical Arboretum★** (**✆ 722-2470**), is a sustainable farm and botanical gardens project that accepts day visitors. In addition to a broad variety of ornamental flowers and orchids, tropical palms and bromeliads, they grow over 100 varieties of

Moments **Deer Dance**

The Mopan Mayan village of San Antonio is the site of the Deer Dance, a 9-day traditional Mayan cultural celebration, which takes place in late August and early September. Although this traditional cultural ceremony coincides with a Catholic religious holiday, the Feast of San Luis, its roots are traditional Maya.

tropical fruit, and something is always ripe for a just-picked treat. The Toledo Botanical Arboretum is close to both the Kekchi Maya village of San Pedro Columbia and the Lubaantun ruins. A 2-hour guided tour of the facility costs around BZ$10 (US$5/£2.65). Visits and transportation should be arranged in advance.

Staying in a Mayan Village

Many people who make it as far as Punta Gorda are interested in learning more about Mayan village life. Though the ruins were abandoned centuries ago, Maya Indians still live in this region. The villages of the Toledo District are populated by two main groups of Maya Indians, the Kekchi and the Mopan, who have different languages and agricultural practices. The Mopan are upland farmers, while the Kekchi farm the lowlands. Both groups are thought to have migrated into southern Belize from Guatemala less than 100 years ago. Four decades of political violence and genocide in neighboring Guatemala has bolstered this migration.

San Antonio, the largest Mopan Maya village, is in a beautiful setting on top of a hill, with an old stone church in the center of the village. Steep streets wind through the village, dotted with both clapboard houses and traditional Mayan thatched huts. In addition to the Deer Dance, the nearby village of San Pedro is also known for its annual festival on June 13th in honor of that village's patron saint. This festival includes masked dances and other Mayan rites mixed with more traditional Catholic themes and celebrations. Beyond San Antonio and San Pedro, there is a host of even smaller and more remote traditional Mayan villages.

The Maya Village Homestay Network (✆ **722-2470;** demdatsdoin@btl.net), provides accommodations directly with families in the Mayan villages. There's a BZ$10 (US$5/£2.65) registration fee for any stay, and then accommodations cost BZ$16 (US$8/£4.25) per person per night, and meals are BZ$7 (US$3.50/£1.85) per person per meal. These fees are paid directly to your host family. Accommodations during a homestay can range from a hammock to a simple bed, and almost all families have some sort of bathroom or latrine. Currently, the villages involved in the homestay program include Aguacate, Na Luum Ca, and San José.

If you opt for this program, you can expect plenty of close contact with the local villagers. You will also to be eating what the locals eat, which in most cases means plenty of beans and tortillas, as well as the occasional chicken soup, or meat dish. One of the highlights of many guests is participating in the cooking chores, and learning the simple art of tortilla making.

Staying with a Garífuna Family

Those seeking a unique Caribbean cultural experience can also look into staying with a local Garífuna family. Just 18km (11 miles) south of Punta Gorda lies the small Garífuna village of Barranco. With a little over 100 residents, Barranco is a quintessential quiet

Garífuna village. Although the road to Barranco is usually passable during the dry season, it's best to get there by boat. Ask around at the Punta Gorda pier if there's any regular ferry service. If not, you should be able to hire a ride for about BZ$80–BZ$120 (US$40–US$60/£21–£32) per boat.

SHOPPING

Wednesday and Saturday are market days around the small market square in front of the Civic Center and along the waterfront. This is a great time and place to find local and Guatemalan handcrafts, as well as fresh fruit and produce. If the outdoor market isn't happening, you can find most of the same items at either the **Southern Frontier Giftshop,** 41 Front St. (✆ **722-2870**), or the **Fajina Craft Center**★ on Front Street next to the post office (✆ **722-2470**), which is a cooperative of Mayan women from the area.

WHERE TO STAY

In addition to the places listed below, near the village of Blue Creek, **International Zoological Expeditions** (✆ **800/548-5843** in the U.S.; www.ize2belize.com) has a research station and rustic lodge where they offer educational and adventure travel tours and packages.

Very Expensive

Machaca Hill Lodge ★★ Formerly El Pescador South, this place has the plushest accommodations to be found in the Toledo district. The rooms are spread around 12 large individual bungalows, set on a high hillside of rich forest above the Río Grande. The bungalows feature cool red-tile floors, high-pitched ceilings, two queen-size beds, and a large veranda with an excellent view and inviting hammock. There are large and ample windows that let in plenty of light and cross-ventilation if you decide to opt out of the air-conditioning. Bungalow no. 11 is my favorite: A little larger, it sits on a high spot on the property and comes with one king bed. The kidney-shaped pool has a broad and inviting stone deck area around it, and it's also set on one of the highest points on the property, giving it excellent views all around. A tramway connects the lodge to the river below, where its fleet of fishing boats is docked. A meal package here runs BZ$140 (US$70/£37) per person per day. This place was originally geared towards fishermen, and you can still use this place as an excellent base for fishing. Fly-fishing for world-class permit is the principal game, although tarpon, bonefish, and snook can also be tackled.

P.O. Box 135, Punta Gorda. ✆ **722-0050.** Fax 722-0051. www.machacahill.com. 12 units. BZ$480 (US$240/£127) double. Rates lower in the off season; higher during peak periods. MC, V. **Amenities:** Restaurant; bar; lounge; outdoor pool; tour desk; laundry service. *In room:* A/C, free Wi-Fi, minibar, no phone.

Expensive

Located on a bend in the Moho River, about a 20-minute drive outside P.G., the **Cotton Tree Lodge** (✆ **670-0557;** www.cottontreelodge.com) offers up almost a dozen large, individual wood and thatch bungalows.

The Lodge at Big Falls ★ This comfortable nature lodge caters to ecotourists and those looking to explore the nearby Mayan ruins and villages, and is set on the banks of the Río Grande, just outside the village of Big Falls. The six individual octagonal cabins all overlook the river and feature high thatched ceilings, large windows providing plenty of cross-ventilation, and cool rustic tile floors. Each comes with a large covered veranda equipped with a hammock for lazing away and watching the river flow. Named after birds, my favorite cabins are Trogon, Aracari, and Tiger Heron, the closest ones to the river. Although there's electricity here, at night the light is provided by kerosene lanterns. There's a good-size outdoor pool on the broad lawn outside the main lodge, and a host of tour options is available, including lazy inner tube floats on the river right here.

Near the village of Big Falls, 29km (18 miles) north of Punta Gorda (P.O. Box 103, Punta Gorda). ✆ **671-7172.** www.thelodgeatbigfalls.com. 6 units. BZ$310 (US$155/£82) double. Rates lower in the off season. MC, V. **Amenities:** Restaurant; bar; tour desk; gift shop; laundry service. *In room:* No phone.

Moderate

In addition to the places listed below, **Blue Belize** (✆ **722-2678;** www.bluebelize.com) offers up a few fully equipped apartments facing the sea towards the southern end of town, while **Beya Suites** (✆ **722-2956;** www.beyasuites.com) is a small hotel with well-equipped, tidy rooms; an on-site restaurant; and a rooftop patio, located just across from the bay, just north of town.

Coral House Inn ★ This homey bed-and-breakfast is my favorite option right in P.G. The rooms are simple affairs, with firm beds, cable televisions, and clean, modern bathrooms. The rooms are all on the second floor, with a large shared balcony overlooking the sea. There's a refreshing lap pool set at an angle off the main building, and an artsy open-air cement door leading to a lawn and gardens that run off to the sea. The owners are a cheerful and helpful couple, and they provide free bicycles for use during your stay. These folks also rent out a separate, private little cottage. The hotel borders the town cemetery, so consider yourself forewarned if that spooks you.

151 Main St. (P.O. Box 43), Punta Gorda. ✆ **722-2878.** Fax 722-2682. www.coralhouseinn.net. 4 units. BZ$165–BZ$200 (US$83–US$100/£44–£53) double. Rates include continental breakfast. MC, V. **Amenities:** Tour desk; laundry service. *In room:* A/C, TV, free Wi-Fi, no phone.

Hickatee Cottages ★ Finds This place features a small collection of rooms set under tall trees amongst flowering gardens. Located just a mile from downtown, you'll feel a world apart nonetheless. All the rooms are quite spacious, with varnished wood floors, furniture made by Belizean Mennonites, one queen and one twin bed, a separate sitting area, and a front veranda strung with a hammock. There's a small creek running through the property, which you can explore by kayak, and you can hike some trails through thick forest and brush here. The bird-watching is excellent. If the heat of the day gets to you, there's a small but refreshing plunge pool. Meals are served in the homey main lodge. The owners, who met on the Green Tortoise bus, got off the bus to set up this little place.

Ex-Serviceman Rd. (P.O. Box 148), Punta Gorda. ✆ **662-4475.** www.hickatee.com. 4 units. BZ$140–BZ$170 (US$70–US$85/£37–£45) double. MC, V. **Amenities:** Restaurant; bar; small plunge pool; tour desk; laundry service; free Wi-Fi. *In room:* No phone.

Inexpensive

Punta Gorda has a host of budget lodgings. In addition to the place listed below, you could check out **Charlton's Inn,** 9 Main St. (✆ **722-2197**), or **Tate's Guesthouse,** 34 José María Núñez St. (✆ **722-2196**).

And, for an ecolodge experience at pretty budget prices, check out **Sun Creek Lodge** (✆ **614-2080;** www.suncreeklodge.com), a delightful collection of individual cabins, at Mile 14 on the Southern Highway.

Nature's Way Guest House Value Located 3 blocks south of the central park and across the street from the water, Nature's Way is a longtime favorite of budget travelers.

There's a variety of room, bathroom, and bed configurations, from bunk beds to a mix of twins and matrimonials. Still, everything is quite basic and rustic. Even though most rooms do not have private bathrooms, everything is kept tidy, and the shared bathrooms are large and clean. Only breakfast is served here, though it is hearty and plentiful, and the hotel is close to downtown and other dining options. The guesthouse is operated by an American named William "Chet" Schmidt, who moved down here almost 40 years ago to promote sustainable agricultural and tourism practices.

65 Front St., Punta Gorda. ✆/fax **702-2119.** 6 units (1 with private bathroom). BZ$24–BZ$36 (US$12–US$18/£6.35–£9.55) double. No credit cards. **Amenities:** Tour desk. *In room:* No phone.

WHERE TO DINE

Dining options are far from extensive in Punta Gorda. In addition to the restaurants listed below, check out **Grace's Restaurant** (✆ **702-2414**), at the corner of Main and King streets, for good local fare; or try **The Snack Shack** (✆ **702-0020**), a simple open air joint located between the post office and BTL building that's very popular for breakfast, lunch, or dinner.

Out a little bit north of town, just across from and facing the bay, **Waluco's Cool Spot** (✆ **665-3066**) is a good place for fish, pasta, or rotisserie chicken. The open-air restaurant has a great view and a friendly, casual vibe.

For a cool treat on a hot day, head to **Marrenco's Ice Cream Parlour,** 57 Main St. (✆ 722-2572).

Earth Runnins' Cafe ★ BELIZEAN/INTERNATIONAL Owned and run by the very personable Giovanni Foster, this place serves out a broad and creative menu ranging from local classics to Cajun-style blackened fish and Thai shrimp curry. Sundays are barbeque nights. The whole fish is excellent. The heavy wood tables and chairs, as well as the massive wood bar, were built by Giovanni himself. There's a stage on one side of the room, and the bar here is one of the more lively in town. The hours listed below are not strict by any means, so it always pays to check in advance to see if they'll be open.

13 Main Middle St. ✆ **702-2007.** Main courses BZ$10–BZ$18 (US$5–US$9/£2.65–£4.75). No credit cards. Wed–Sun 7:30am–2pm and 5–11pm.

Emery's BELIZEAN This is a good bet for simple, fresh local cuisine. I prefer the tables in a large, open-air, thatch-roof structure off the small wooden building that has the kitchen, bar, and small screened-in dining area. This large dining area has half-walls of bamboo and a series of floor fans cooling things off. There's a chalkboard menu with the standard fare and daily specials. Offerings range from stew chicken and stew pork to whole fried snapper and snook filets. Everything is well prepared, and the prices are right.

North St. ✆ **702-2929.** Main courses BZ$8–BZ$32 (US$4–US$16/£2.10–£8.50). No credit cards. Mon–Fri 11am–2pm and 6–10pm; Sat 6–10pm.

Gomier's Foods BELIZEAN/VEGETARIAN This should definitely be the first stop for any vegetarian or health-food nut. While the menu at this place features plenty of traditional locally prepared food and dishes, this is the only place in P.G. to find stir-fried tofu and a wide range of vegetarian entrees. Most of the herbs and vegetables are organically grown by owner Gomier himself.

At the corner of Vernon and Front sts. ✆ **722-2990.** Main courses BZ$8–BZ$20 (US$4–US$10/£2.10–£5.30). No credit cards. Mon–Fri 8am–7pm.

Marian's Bayview ★ INDIAN/BELIZEAN For years, Marian made a name for herself selling authentic East Indian food out of a simple stall at the small market in downtown Punta Gorda. Now she's got her own digs and you can actually sit at a table and enjoy your meal. Granted, the tables are rather rickety, the chairs are plastic, and the third-floor dining area has an unfinished feel to it, with bare cement on the floors and some of the walls. Still, the food is delicious. Each night, Marian makes up a limited menu that usually includes a mix of Indian and Belizean fare, and a mix of seafood and meat options.

At the corner of Vernon and Front sts. ✆ **722-0129.** Main courses BZ$8–BZ$18 (US$4–US$9/£2.10–£4.75). No credit cards. Daily 7am–3pm and 6–10pm.

Reef Bar ★ Finds INTERNATIONAL Taking over the prime location of the old Titanic Bar, this new restaurant and bar occupies an open-air, second-floor space right on the waterfront near the center of town. The menu is relatively limited, with meat and vegetarian burgers, and both meat and vegetarian lasagna, fish cakes, Thai chicken curry, and nightly fresh fish specials. Every day from 7:30am till 2pm, this place operates as the **Deja View Café,** serving up excellent breakfasts, lunches, pastries, and coffee concoctions. This place offers free Wi-Fi to go along with your coffee, drink, or meal.

At the corner of Front and Queen sts. ✆ **702-0154.** Main courses BZ$10–BZ$15 (US$5–US$7.50/£2.65–£4). MC, V. Mon–Sat 4–9pm and Sun 2–6pm.

PUNTA GORDA AFTER DARK

Overall, Punta Gorda's a pretty quiet town. The most dependable spot for any action is the **PG Sports Bar,** which only very occasionally has sporting events on the tube. Instead, this is really an all-purpose nightspot with occasional live bands, DJs, and karaoke nights. It's located on Main Street at the southern edge of the little central park. Another good spot to meet and mingle with locals is the **Bukut Bar** at Earth Runnins' (see above), which also has live music every now and again. I personally like the view and breeze at the **Reef Bar** for a quiet place to get a drink and have a conversation. Finally, you can try heading out north of town to **Waluco's,** where there are occasionally live music jam sessions, a local Punta Rock band, or a Garífuna drumming outfit.

9

Northern Belize

With few exceptions, Northern Belize is overlooked by most tourists who fly into the country and head quickly to the cayes, the Cayo District, the southern beaches, or the Mayan Mountains. Even those who enter by land from Mexico frequently make a beeline to Belize City and bypass this region. Still, northern Belize has its charms, not least of which is its undiscovered and undeveloped feel. It's here that you'll find some of the country's larger biological reserves, including the **Crooked Tree Wildlife Sanctuary,** the **Shipstern Wildlife Reserve,** and the **Río Bravo Conservation Area.** With over 430 species of birds and 250 species of orchids, this region should be especially attractive to naturalists.

The region was also an important and strategic part of the Mayan Empire, and ancient ruins abound. Most notably, it is here that you will find the **Altun Ha** and **Lamanai** ruins, two of the country's most popular and important Mayan sites. Lesser sites like **Cuello, Cerros, Santa Rita,** and **Noh Mul** are also possible stops for true aficionados. Finally, northern Belize is home to three unique and isolated lodges: **Maruba Resort Jungle Spa, Chan Chich Lodge,** and **Lamanai Outpost Lodge,** all of which are described in detail in this chapter.

For our purposes, "northern Belize" refers to the northern section of the Belize District, as well as the entire Orange Walk and Corozal districts. The land here is low and plain, with massive sugar cane, citrus, soybean, and pineapple plantations set amidst large swaths of forests; swamps; lagoons; and slow, steamy jungle rivers. Belize's Northern Highway runs from Belize City to the Mexican border, a little over 161km (100 miles) away. The road is not in good shape, and the scenery tends to be flat and monotonous. There are few people and fewer population centers. There are only two cities of any note along the way, and both are actually designated as towns, **Orange Walk Town** and **Corozal Town.** Of these, only Corozal, with its seaside setting and proximity to the Mexican border and Shipstern Wildlife Reserve, is a destination with much appeal to travelers. Orange Walk, for its part, serves mainly as a gateway to the Lamanai ruins and the Río Bravo Conservation Area.

Much of this area was originally settled by immigrants fleeing southern Mexico's Yucatán peninsula during the Caste Wars of the mid–19th century. This is undoubtedly the most Spanish region in Belize. However, it is also the region with the largest concentration of Mennonite communities. Members of this somewhat radical and oft-persecuted Christian order have thrived in this farming area. You can't miss the Mennonites in their distinctive, heavy, home-sewn garb and horse-drawn carriages.

1 ALONG THE OLD NORTHERN HIGHWAY: ALTUN HA ★ & MARUBA RESORT JUNGLE SPA ★★

The Old Northern Highway is in rough shape. The narrow, paved road is in dire need of repair; it's riddled with potholes and washed out in many sections. Still, it is the only

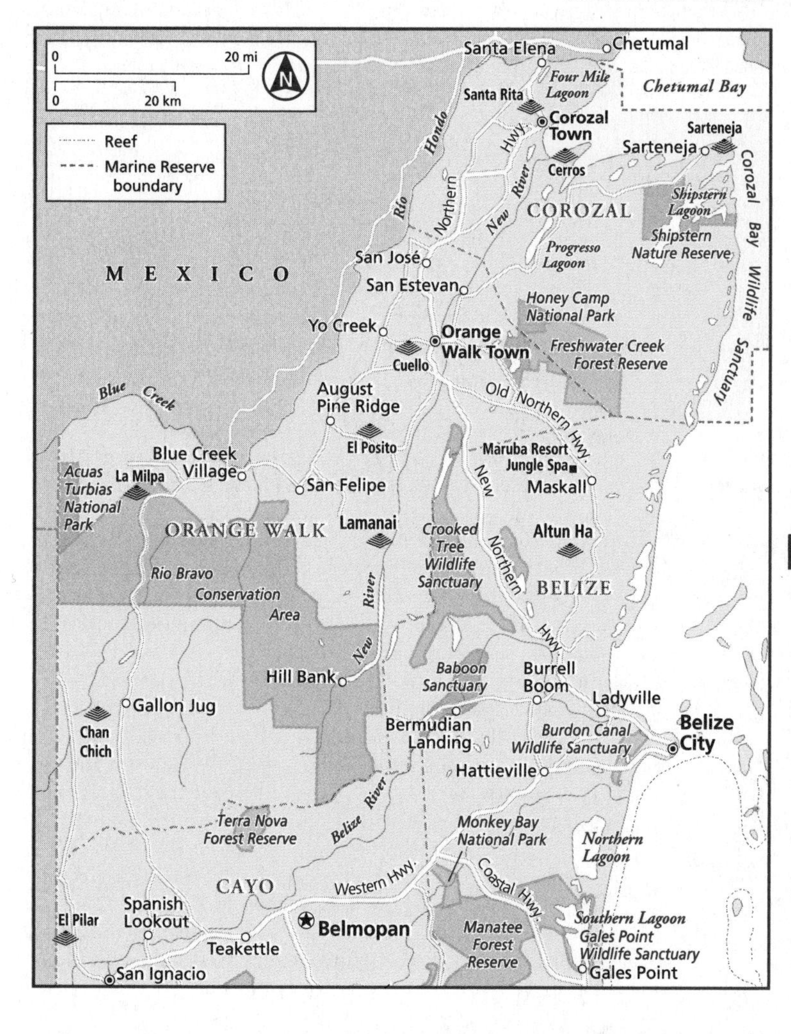

route to one major attraction and one unique resort. Aside from these two places, there's not much else along this highway, except for a few tiny communities and the occasional roadside restaurant or bar. To get here, take Freetown Road out of Belize City to connect with the Northern Highway. The turnoff to the Old Northern Highway is to the right just past Sand Hill; watch for signs for Altun Ha and Maruba Resort Jungle Spa.

ALTUN HA ★

Altun Ha is a small, well-preserved Mayan ruin. Only a few of the most imposing temples, tombs, and pyramids have been uncovered and rebuilt; hundreds more lie under the jungle foliage. Still, there are two large central plazas surrounded by midsize pyramids and mounds, as well as the beginnings of the excavation of residential areas. While nowhere near as extensive as some other sites, Altun Ha offers admirable quality and detail of excavation and restoration. Sections of different structures have been left in various states of repair and restoration, which gives a good sense of the process involved. Moreover, while the climb to the top of the tallest pyramids here is rather easy by Mayan standards, the views are still wonderful. The site was named after the village in which it's situated—Rockstone Pond, the literal Mayan translation meaning "stone water." At the back of the site, behind Plaza B, is the namesake pond. Archaeologists theorize that the pond is an example of a pre-Columbian waterworks project and a demonstration of the ingenuity of Mayan engineering.

Despite its somewhat diminutive size, Altun Ha was a major trade and ceremonial center. In its prime, during the Classic Period, Altun Ha supported a population of about 10,000. Many jade, pearl, and obsidian artifacts have been discovered here, including the unique jade-head sculpture of **Kinich Ahau** (the Mayan sun god), the largest well-carved jade from the Mayan era. Today, it's kept in a bank vault in Belmopan, out of public view, although you can see a replica at the Museum of Belize (p. 102). Some of the pieces found here show a direct link the great Mexican city of Teotihuacán.

The largest (though not the tallest) temple here is the **Temple of the Masonry Altars,** which fronts Plaza B. It has been well restored, and the pathway to the top is well maintained and even features handrails. However, if you're fairly fit and not acrophobic, I recommend you climb the almost entirely unrestored **Temple A-6,** which is truly the tallest building here. A climb to the top of Temple A-6 affords an excellent panorama of the entire site. Be careful climbing down; the Mayans were a society run by priests and holy men, not lawyers. A more litigious society would have never permitted the construction of such steep and treacherous stairways.

The site is open daily from 9am to 5pm. Admission is BZ$10 (US$5/£2.65) for adults, free for children under 12. There is no public transportation to Altun Ha, so you'll need to take a tour, a taxi, your own wheels, or hitchhike. If you're driving, Altun Ha is located about 48km (30 miles) north of Belize City on the Northern Highway. Once you're on the Old Northern Highway, it's 18km (11 miles) to the Altun Ha road. From the highway, it's another bumpy 3.6km (2¼ miles) to the ruins.

Half-day tours to Altun Ha from Belize City cost between BZ$80 and BZ$160 (US$40–US$80/£21–£42). Full-day tours can be combined with visits to Crooked Tree Wildlife Sanctuary (see "En Route North: Crooked Tree Wildlife Sanctuary," below) or the Community Baboon Sanctuary (see "What to See & Do" in chapter 6) and should run between BZ$150 and BZ$280 (US$75–US$140/£38–£70). Many of the tours include lunch and an optional spa treatment at Maruba Resort Jungle Spa.

AN ISOLATED JUNGLE SPA

Maruba Resort Jungle Spa ★★ Finds Decadent, sensual, and exotic are the words most often used to describe this small resort, and for good reason. The whole place is an imaginative jungle fantasy where health, hedonism, and happiness are the primary goals. The accommodations are a collection of uniquely designed and decorated rooms and private villas, set in a patch of densely planted gardens and forest. Artistic touches abound and range from the many interesting architectural details to the eclectic mix of decorations and furnishings from Africa, Asia, the Caribbean, the Middle East, and, of course, Belize. The best rooms here are the private suites. Of these, the Chapel Suite is my favorite, with a large, enclosed private sitting area featuring a floor of loose stones, a two-person hot mineral bath with Jacuzzi jets, and heavy wooden Indonesian chaise

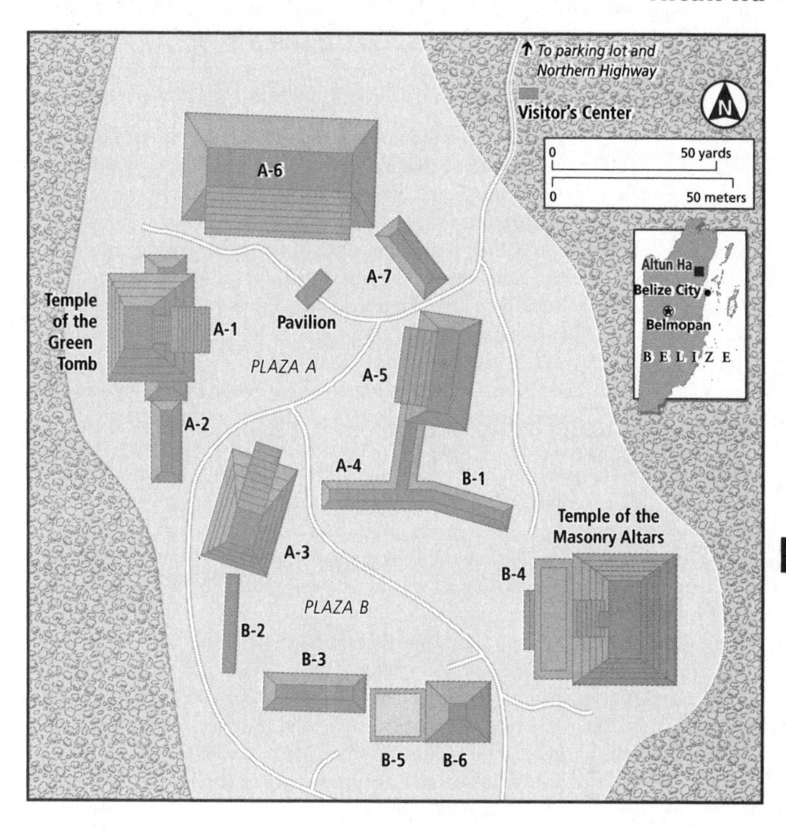

lounges. The standard rooms are certainly up to snuff, but I think it's worth the splurge for one of the suites.

There are two outdoor pools here, as well as a separate hot mineral pool. The spa facilities and services are wonderfully done and reasonably priced. The Mood Mud Massage is their signature offering, and I highly recommend it. The food at the restaurant here is excellent, featuring a creative mix of international and fusion cuisine. This place is very popular with day-trippers from the cayes and Belize City, as well as cruise-ship passengers. Luckily, one of the pools is reserved for hotel guests, and once the day tours clear out, you'll have the place to yourself. In addition to the spa treatments, a host of tours, activities, and adventures is offered here. If you're in the mood for some serious imbibing, don't miss a taste of their home-brewed Viper Rum and Scorpion Stinger.

Old Northern Hwy., Mile Marker 40½, Maskall Village. ✆ **800/627-8227** in the U.S., or 225-5555 in Belize. Fax 225-5506. www.maruba-belize.com. 18 units. BZ$450 (US$225/£119) double; BZ$540 (US$270/£143) junior suite; BZ$900–BZ$1,400 (US$450–US$700/£239–£371) suite. Rates include full breakfast. AE, MC, V. **Amenities:** Restaurant; bar; lounge; 2 outdoor pools; spa; tour desk; car-rental desk; laundry service. *In room:* A/C, hair dryer, no phone.

2 EN ROUTE NORTH: CROOKED TREE WILDLIFE SANCTUARY ★

53km (33 miles) NW of Belize City

Crooked Tree Wildlife Sanctuary is a swampy lowland that is home to over 260 resident species of birds and serves as a resting spot for scores of migratory species. During a visit here you are sure to spot any number of interesting water birds, including kites, hawks, ducks, grebes, pelicans, ospreys, egrets, and herons. However, the preserve was established primarily to protect Belize's main nesting site of the endangered jabiru stork, the largest bird in the Western Hemisphere. The jabirus arrive every November and pass the winter in these warm lowland climes. The jabiru is an impressive bird, standing nearly 1.5m (5 ft.) tall, with a wingspan that can reach up to 3.7m (12 ft.). Crooked Tree has rapidly become known as an excellent place to spot other endangered wildlife as well. Crocodiles, iguanas, coati-mundi, and howler monkeys are all frequently sighted. There are six major lagoons here connected by a series of creeks, rivers, and wetlands.

The small Creole village of Crooked Tree is the gateway to this wildlife sanctuary. The village is reputed to be some 300 years old, and one of the oldest ongoing settlements in Belize. If you poke around, in addition to the sanctuary's visitor center, you'll find the church, school, soccer field, a few general stores, and a couple of simple guest houses.

The best way to explore the preserve is by dugout canoe. Ask in town or at the visitor center and administrative building for a local who will paddle you around in a dugout for a few hours. The going rate is around BZ$20 to BZ$30 (US$10–US$15/£5.30–£7.95) per person for a 2- to 3-hour paddle tour of the lagoons. Or, if you're in the mood for a little exercise, Bird's Eye View Lodge (see below) offers canoe rental for BZ$10 (US$5/£2.65) per person per hour. If you're looking for a good local bird guide, contact **Sam Tillet** (✆ **220-7026;** www.crookedtreebelize.com), who also runs a simple guest house. All visitors must first register at the visitor center and pay the BZ$8 (US$4/£2.10) admission fee. The Crooked Tree Wildlife Sanctuary was set up and is still administered by the **Belize Audubon Society** (✆ **223-5004;** www.belizeaudubon.org).

If you'd like to spend the night, accommodations can be arranged with a local family for around BZ$30 to BZ$60 (US$15–US$30/£7.95–£16), double occupancy. Meals should run you an additional BZ$24 to BZ$50 (US$12–US$25/£6.35–£13) per person per day. Or, if you want to stay in a comfortable lodge right on the edge of a lagoon, check out the **Bird's Eye View Lodge★** (✆ **225-7027;** www.birdseyeviewlodge.com), where a double costs between BZ$120 and BZ$200 (US$60–US$100/£32–£53).

Going Nuts

Crooked Tree is also home to a thriving cashew industry. Each year during the first weekend of May, Crooked Tree village hosts its annual Cashew Festival. In addition to letting you sample raw and roasted nuts, this is a great chance to taste some cashew wine, cashew jelly, and a whole plethora of dishes cooked around or including the local nut.

Crooked Tree is located 53km (33 miles) northwest of Belize City. If you are driving, head up the Northern Highway and watch for the turnoff to Crooked Tree. From the turnoff, it's another 4.8km (3 miles) on a well-graded dirt road.

Jex & Sons (✆ **225-7017**) direct buses leave for Crooked Tree Village Monday through Saturday from a bus terminal on Regent Street West in Belize City at 10:55am; and Monday through Friday from a terminal at Pound Yard Bridge at 4:30 and 5:15pm, and they leave Crooked Tree for Belize City at 6:30 and 7am. The fare is BZ$6 (US$3/£1.60) each way. Alternately, you can take any bus heading to Orange Walk Town, Corozal, or the northern border and ask to be dropped off at the entrance to Crooked Tree. From here you'll have to walk or hitchhike, or get really lucky and find a cab patrolling around. If you're staying at a hotel in the village, they will usually pick you up.

Half-day tours to Crooked Tree from Belize City or the northern cayes cost between BZ$80 and BZ$120 (US$40–US$60/£21–£32). A full-day trip combining Crooked Tree and Altun Ha, including transportation, guide, and lunch, should cost between BZ$160 and BZ$280 (US$80–US$140/£42–£74).

3 ORANGE WALK TOWN

89km (55 miles) N of Belize City; 50km (31 miles) S of Corozal

Between Belize City and Corozal Town, the only settlement of any size is Orange Walk Town, a bustling agricultural and business community with a population of some 18,000. This is the heart of Belize's sugar cane industry, and some locals still call the town "Sugar City." Originally called Holpatin by the ancient Maya, the town's riverside location has ensured its status as a trade center for over 2,000 years. The town's current name comes from the many citrus groves once planted alongside the New River here. Orange Walk Town's residents are a very heterogeneous mix of mestizos, Mayans, Chinese, and Black Creoles. There's not too much of interest to travelers in the town, but this is the gateway to several of the surrounding attractions of note, including the Lamanai ruins and the Río Bravo Conservation Area to the west.

ESSENTIALS

Getting There & Departing

BY PLANE Although there's a small airstrip here, no regularly scheduled commuter traffic arrives in Orange Walk Town. The closest active airports are those in Corozal Town (see "Corozal Town," later in this chapter), and the Philip S. W. Goldson International Airport outside of Belize City (see chapter 6).

BY CAR Orange Walk is on the Northern Highway about 89km (55 miles) from Belize City. Take Freetown Road out of Belize City to connect with the Northern Highway. The highway is also known in this area as the Belize-Corozal Road, and Queen Victoria

Fun Facts **What's in a Name?**

"Orange walk" is the Creole term for "orange orchard" or "orange grove," just as "sugar walk" would be the Creole version of "sugar plantation."

Avenue right in the heart of town. After passing through the small downtown section of Orange Walk Town, the highway continues on north to Corozal.

There's a tollbooth where the Northern Highway crosses the New River a few miles south of Orange Walk Town. The fee is BZ$1 (US50¢/27p) per car.

BY BUS Buses (✆ **227-2255** in Belize City, or 302-2858 in Orange Walk Town) leave throughout the day, roughly every half-hour between 5:30am and 7:30pm. Morning buses leave from the main bus terminal on West Collet Canal Street. Catch any bus going to Corozal Town or Chetumal. The Orange Walk Town bus station is right on the Northern Highway in the center of town near Town Hall. You can pick up a return bus here to Belize City, or continue onward to Corozal. Buses can be either direct or local, and they vary in age and comfort. You'll pay more for a comfortable direct or express bus. The fare is BZ$5 to BZ$8 (US$2.50–US$4/£1.30–£2.10) between Belize City and Orange Walk Town, and BZ$6 to BZ$10 (US$3–US$5/£1.60–£2.65) between Orange Walk Town and Corozal Town.

Mennonites in Belize

Mennonites are a Protestant branch of the 16th-century Anabaptist movement, which also gave birth to the Amish and Hutterites. Believing that the New Testament is the sole word of God and that children should not be baptized, the Mennonites also believe that true Christians should not hold political or public office or serve in the military. Modern Mennonites are somewhat split as to the use of electricity and the internal combustion engine.

Mennonites get their name from Menno Simons, a Dutch Catholic priest who converted to Anabaptism and went on to lead the budding movement. From the start, the Anabaptists were severely persecuted and repeatedly forced into exile. Mennonites first migrated to Belize from Mexico in 1958. While the initial wave of immigrants was small, the Mennonites quickly settled in, buying large tracts of land and establishing very successful dairy farming and agricultural enterprises. The early Mennonite settlers were successful in negotiating certain strategic concessions and guarantees from the government, including that of religious freedom and exemption from military service and some forms of taxation.

While there are Mennonites throughout Belize, the Orange Walk District and northern Belize have one of the highest concentrations in the country, with large communities in Shipyard, Blue Creek Village, Little Belize, and Spanish Lookout. Most Mennonites, even in Belize, speak an archaic form of German. They are easily recognized, with their fair skin and blond hair, especially when they're traveling in their low-riding, horse-drawn carriages. The women often wear puffy cloth bonnets and simple cotton dresses, while the men sport broad-rimmed straw hats, dark jeans, and distinctive full beards with no moustache.

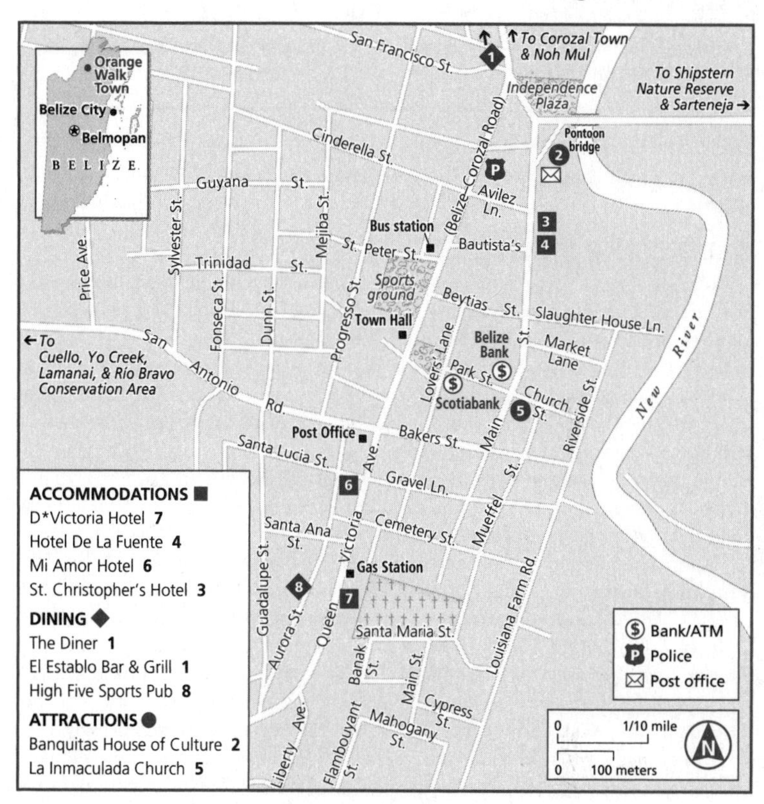

Getting Around

Orange Walk is pretty compact, and the city center is just a few blocks wide in either direction. Still, a few taxis can be had around town. If you can't flag one down, call ✆ **322-2050,** or head to the little park across from Town Hall.

Orientation

The Northern Highway runs right through the heart of Orange Walk Town. However, there is also a bypass that skirts the city proper, for those in a rush to get to Corozal. Several gas stations are located on the outskirts of either end of town. As you're traveling north, the New River and "downtown" district will be to your right, while the Town Hall and Sports Ground are right on the highway, on your left.

FAST FACTS If you need to call the **police,** dial ✆ **911** or 322-2022; for the **fire department,** dial ✆ **322-2090;** and for medical emergencies, call the **Orange Walk Hospital** at ✆ **322-2072.**

There's a **Belize Bank** (✆ **322-2019**) at the corner of Main and Park streets, and a **Scotia Bank** (✆ **322-0866**) down the block on the corner of Park Street and Lover's Lane. The **Post Office** (✆ **322-2345**) is located on the north end of Main Street. If you

Fun Fact

The original Mayan name for the New River, Dzuilhuinicob, translates roughly as "River of Strange People."

need film or developing, head to **Belicolor Photo Services,** 22 Lover's Lane (✆ **322-2819**).

SEEING THE SIGHTS

If you're staying in Orange Walk Town, you might want to visit the **Banquitas House of Culture,** at Main Street and Banquitas Plaza (✆ **322-0517**), which is set just off the river on some expansive and manicured grounds. The House of Culture itself features a small collection of artifacts and historic displays from the Mayan, logging, and colonial eras. There's also a small amphitheater here that very occasionally may have live music, theater, or dance. In the center of town you'll find **La Inmaculada Church,** one of the few colonial Spanish churches in the country.

You might also want to stop at **Godoy's Orchid Garden,** 4 Trial Farm Rd. (✆ **322-2969**). Commercial growers and exporters, the Godoy family also offers visitors a stunning and informative tour of their extensive collection.

Two of the most popular tours out of Orange Walk Town are to **Crooked Tree Wildlife Sanctuary** (see "En Route North: Crooked Tree Wildlife Sanctuary," earlier in this chapter) and the **Lamanai ruins** (see "The Submerged Crocodile: Lamanai," below).

If you're looking for some nearby outdoor adventure and a refreshing dip, head to **Honey Camp Lagoon,** which features an unlikely sandy beach ringed by palm trees next to a spring-fed freshwater swimming hole. Honey Camp Lagoon is located about a 20-minute drive south from Orange Walk Town, via the Old Northern Highway.

If your hotel can't hook you up and you want a local guide for any of the aforementioned tours or trips to any of the nearby ruins or up to Lamanai (see below), call **J. Avila & Sons River Tours,** 42 Riverside St. (✆ **322-3068**), or **Jungle River Tours ★**, 20 Lovers Lane (✆ **302-2293**), which is run by the very personable and knowledgeable Wilfrido Novelo.

A Couple of Minor Mayan Sites Nearby

CUELLO This small site is located just over 4.8km (3 miles) from Orange Walk Town, near the Cuello Rum Distillery. It is named after the family that owns the land and distillery, and permission to visit the site must be obtained in advance. While very small and little excavated, Cuello is nonetheless one of the oldest-known Mayan sites in Belize, showing evidence of occupation as far back as 2600 B.C., in the early Pre-Classic Period.

There are two main plazas on the site, surrounded by small temples and ceremonial structures. Very little has been excavated and restored so far. Evidence exists that this minor ceremonial city was razed on more than one occasion during distinct warring periods.

Permission to visit Cuello can be obtained by stopping at the rum distillery at the entrance to the site, or by calling in advance (✆ **322-2183**). If you ask, you will probably be able to get a quick tour of the distillery as well. You might also be able to arrange for a guided tour by asking around Orange Walk Town. To get here, take the San Antonio Road out of Orange Walk Town towards Yo Creek.

NOH MUL Noh Mul means "great mound," and this site boasts the largest Mayan structure in the Orange Walk District. Noh Mul was active in two distinct periods, the late Pre-Classic era from around 350 B.C. to A.D. 250, and during the late Classic era from A.D. 600 to 900. At the time, it was a major ceremonial center and supported a massive residential community that extended for nearly 21 sq. km (8 sq, miles). One of the more interesting features here is the fact that the two major ceremonial plazas are connected by a raised walkway, or *sacbe.* Crude excavation techniques, pillaging, and local agriculture have combined to limit the amount of restoration and conservation in evidence at Noh Mul.

Noh Mul is located about 1.6km (1 mile) west of the small village of San Pablo, which itself is about 14km (9 miles) north of Orange Walk Town. Any nonexpress bus running the northern line to Corozal and Chetumal can drop you off at San Pablo. However, your best bet for visiting Noh Mul is to try to arrange a tour in advance in Orange Walk Town or Belize City. You should have permission to visit Noh Mul; to get permission in San Pablo, check in with **Esteban Itzab** (no phone), whose house is located across from the water tower in the heart of the village. There are no facilities on-site, so bring some food and water with you.

WHERE TO STAY & DINE

There are few good dining options in Orange Walk Town. Your best bet is **El Establo Bar & Grill,** Northern Highway (✆ **322-0094**), a tidy roadside joint on the main highway just north of town. Another good option is **The Diner,** 37 Clark St. (✆ **302-2131**), which actually serves slightly more adventurous and varied dishes than its simple name implies.

For a taste of Orange Walk Town's nightlife, see if there's anything happening at either the **D*Victoria Hotel** (✆ **322-2518**) or the somewhat seedier **Mi Amor Hotel,** 19 Belize-Corozal Rd. (✆ **322-2031**). Alternately, head to the south end of town and check out the **High Five Sports Pub,** 8 Aurora Avenue (✆ **322-0552**).

Inexpensive

In addition to the places listed below, the **D*Victoria Hotel** (✆ **322-2518;** fax 322-2847; www.dvictoriabelize.com) is a longstanding option, and the only hotel in town with a pool. However, I think both of the other two hotels listed here are better choices.

Hotel De La Fuente ★ This newer two-story hotel is easily the best option in Orange Walk Town. Located just north of St. Christopher, this place offers more amenities than any other hotel in town. Even the budget rooms here feature televisions, air-conditioning, free DSL connection ports, minifridges, and in-room coffeemakers. The pricier rooms are larger and have microwave ovens. Still, before you think I sound too glowing, remember this is a small, isolated town with few attractions and little competition. Even with the above recommendation intact, note that the rooms feel rather bare and spartan.

14 Main St., Orange Walk. ✆/fax **322-2290.** Fax 322-3651. www.hoteldelafuente.com. 12 units. BZ$70–BZ$140 (US$35–US$70/£19–£37) double. MC, V. **Amenities:** Tour desk; laundry service. *In room:* A/C, TV, dataport, minifridge, coffeemaker.

St. Christopher's Hotel Named after the patron saint of world wanderers, this is a dependable option in Orange Walk Town. It's a better bet than the D*Victoria, although St. Christopher's is not nearly as well known and it lacks a swimming pool. The rooms and bathrooms are spacious, clean, and comfortable, and the hotel is on a quiet street, right across from the New River. Most of the rooms here have air-conditioning, although a few less expensive rooms come with just fans.

10 Main St., Orange Walk. ✆/fax **302-1064** or 322-2420. www.stchristophershotelbze.com. 25 units. BZ$60–BZ$100 (US$30–US$50/£16–£27) double. MC, V. **Amenities:** Restaurant; tour desk; laundry service. *In room:* TV, no phone.

4 THE SUBMERGED CROCODILE: LAMANAI ★★

Lamanai is one of the more interesting and picturesque Maya ruins to visit in Belize. Set on the edge of the New River Lagoon, it is one of the largest Maya sites in Belize and features three large pyramids, a couple of residential areas, restored stelae, and open plazas, as well as a small and unique ball court that featured a large round stone set flush in its center. In addition, nearby are the ruins of two churches built by the Spanish during the 16th century; just off these ruins are the rusting remains of an abandoned sugar mill, which was set up and settled by U.S. Confederate soldiers who chose exile after the Civil War.

Lamanai was occupied continuously from around 1500 B.C. until the Spanish arrived in the 16th century, and it supported non-Maya populations into the 19th century. Because it was still occupied by the Maya when the Spanish arrived, Lamanai is one of the few sites to retain its traditional name. Lamanai translates as "submerged crocodile" in Mayan; one of the principal rulers here was Lord Smoking Shell, who claimed he was the descendant of the spirit of a crocodile. Numerous crocodile images have been found in the stelae, carvings, and pottery here. And there are still plenty of live crocs in the lagoon.

Lamanai was an important and powerful Pre-Classic trading city. As at Altun Ha, relics here can be traced to various cities throughout the early Mayan, Aztec, and Olmec worlds. It's a steep and scary climb to the top of the **High Temple,** but the view over the treetops and the lagoon is well worth it. The site's most striking feature just may be the **Mask Temple,** which features a series of 3.7m-high (12-ft.) stone-and-mortar faces set into its sides. One of these faces is quite well restored and shows a distinct Olmec influence.

While many of the temples and ruins here have been cleared and restored to varying degrees, they are still surrounded by dense rainforest. The trails leading between temples offer excellent bird- and wildlife-watching opportunities.

There's a modern visitor center and museum here. The collection, though small, is quite interesting as it shows chronologically the distinct styles and influences present over the long history at Lamanai.

Lamanai is open daily from 8am to 4pm. Admission is BZ$10 (US$5/£2.65). Although you can drive or fly here, the most common and scenic way to reach Lamanai is via boat up the New River. A host of different boats leave from docks just south of Orange Walk. The trip on the river is an hour of naturalist heaven as you cruise between narrow and densely forested banks and alongside flooded marshes and wetlands. Eventually, the river opens on to the New River Lagoon, with the ancient Mayan city perched strategically atop some small limestone cliffs.

Most of the year it's possible to drive to Lamanai if you have a four-wheel-drive vehicle. During the heavy part of the rainy season, the road may become impassable. To

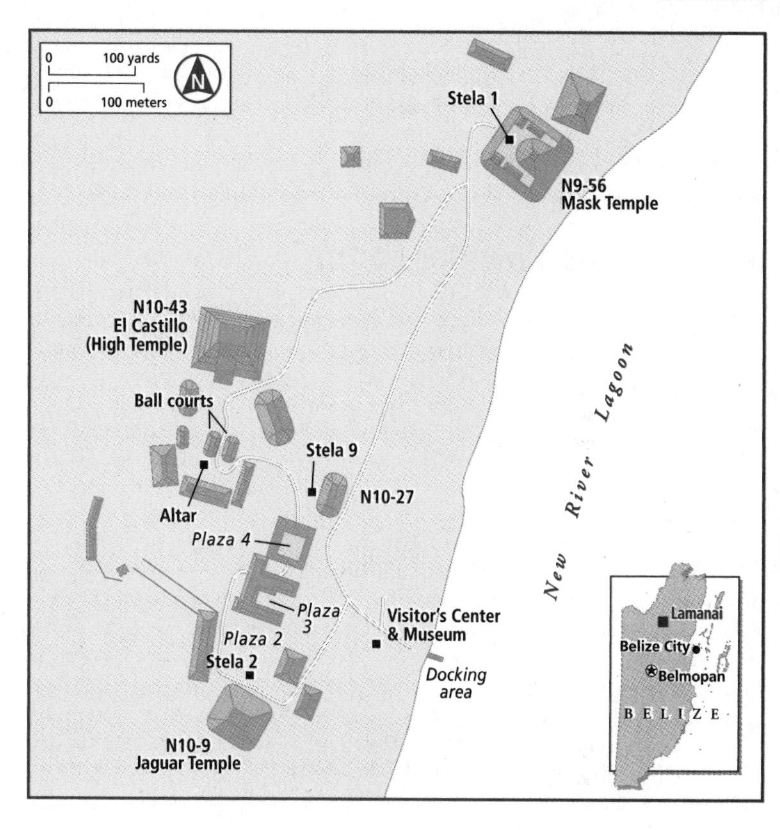

drive here, take the Northern Highway into Orange Walk Town. Turn left near the center of town onto San Antonio Road. Follow signs to Yo Creek and San Felipe. There's an intersection at San Felipe; follow the signs to Indian Church and Lamanai. The total distance from Orange Walk Town is just about 48km (30 miles), but it will take you at least an hour to drive there on the rough dirt road. There's also a small airstrip in the neighboring village of Indian Church, and charter flights can be arranged through Lamanai Outpost Lodge.

While most folks either go on a guided tour or have a reservation at the Lamanai Outpost Lodge (see review below), you can drive yourself to the boat docks, just south of the Toll Hill Bridge over the New River a few miles before Orange Walk, and pick up a boat there. Expect to pay around BZ$70 (US$35/£19) per person for a boat to take you upriver to the ruins and back. The boats tend to leave for Lamanai between 8 and 10am, returning between 2 and 5pm. Many are booked in advance by large tour groups, although it's almost always possible to find a few spaces available with a boat departing in short order. Parking is safe near the docks, and the boat companies will usually watch your car for free or a nominal fee. If you want to set up the trip in advance, I recommend you book with **Jungle River Tours** ★, 20 Lovers Lane (✆ **302-2293**).

Take Your Time

With the rise in cruise-ship traffic, many of the new operators run massive speedboats between Orange Walk and Lamanai. Not only are these noisier and more impersonal, but they also remove almost all of the opportunity to enjoy the bird- and wildlife-viewing along the way. Be sure to try to book a smaller, slightly slower boat—you'll enjoy the trip much more.

A NEIGHBORING NATURE LODGE

Lamanai Outpost Lodge ★★ Finds This rustic yet very comfortable lodge is set on a gentle hillside on the banks of the New River, just about 1.6km (1 mile) from the Lamanai ruins. The rooms here are all quite spacious and made of heavy local hardwoods, with high thatch roofs and ceilings. A ceiling fan is all you have—and all you will need—to cool things off. All the rooms have a private or semiprivate balcony or veranda; most of these come with a hammock all ready for your afternoon siesta. There's also a separate open-air palapa strung with a series of hammocks, if your room is unequipped. While all the rooms are very similar in comfort and design, you'll want to ask for a riverfront room to be able to catch the sunrise from your front porch.

A wide range of tours and activities is available here, and the guides are excellent. The family-style meals (included in the rates) are hearty and well prepared, and the long communal tables encourage guests and groups to mix it up, although some smaller tables are also available for honeymooners, families, and others wanting privacy. Down by the river there's a swimming and sunbathing dock. There are also canoes here that guests can take out on the New River at any time.

Indian Church Village, on the New River (P.O. Box 63, Orange Walk). ✆ **888/733-7864** in the U.S., or 672-2000 in Belize. Fax 212/500-3366 in the U.S. www.lamanai.com. 17 units. BZ$390 (US$195/£103) double. Rates include tax. Rates lower in the off season. Multiday packages available. AE, MC, V. **Amenities:** Restaurant; bar; lounge; tour desk; laundry service; nonsmoking rooms. *In room:* No phone.

5 GOING WEST: RIO BRAVO CONSERVATION AREA, LA MILPA & CHAN CHICH ★★

The far western section of Orange Walk District is a wild area of virgin forest, remote farmlands, and underexplored Mayan ruins. It is also home to one of the country's premier and most unique nature lodges, Chan Chich Lodge.

RIO BRAVO CONSERVATION AREA ★

Administered by the nonprofit **Programme for Belize,** this 105,218-hectare (260,000-acre) tract is a mix of virgin forest, sustainable-yield managed forest, and recovering reforestation areas. The goal of the project is to combine sustainable management techniques with educational and tourism uses in a model that can prove the practical benefits of forest preservation and conservation. The land is home to nearly 400 bird species and over 200 species of tropical trees. It also supports a healthy population of most of the new-world cat species, and is one of the best areas in the Americas for spotting a jaguar—although these sightings are far from common or easy to come by.

La Milpa ★

Located inside the Río Bravo Conservation Area, La Milpa is the third largest Mayan site in Belize, behind Caracol and Lamanai. Enshrouded in jungle and just barely beginning to be excavated, La Milpa is a great site for budding archaeologists and those looking for a sense of what it must have been like to discover and begin uncovering an ancient Mayan city. Set on a high ridge, La Milpa was once a great ceremonial city. So far, at least one **Great Plaza,** numerous smaller plazas and courtyards, and two ball courts have been uncovered. The main plaza is one of the largest such public spaces yet discovered in the Mayan world. Polychrome pottery from various periods as well as numerous carved stelae have been uncovered. In 1996, excavation of a royal tomb here revealed a male skeleton buried with an elaborate and beautiful jeweled necklace. Ongoing archaeological research is being led by Boston University, in conjunction with the National Geographic Society and Programme for Belize.

A visit to La Milpa ruins is usually combined with a stay at **La Milpa Field Station** (see below), although it is possible to do it as a day trip from Orange Walk or on your way driving to or from Chan Chich Lodge. In any event, you will need permission and a reserved guide arranged in advance by calling the **Programme for Belize** (✆ **227-5616;** www.pfbelize.org).

WHERE TO STAY

Inside Rio Bravo

La Milpa Field Station Run by the Programme for Belize, this simple lodge is located in the heart of the wild Río Bravo Conservation Area and just 4.8km (3 miles) from La Milpa ruins. This working biological and archaeological field station also offers rooms, meals, and tours for travelers, students, and volunteers. The private thatch-roof cabins, while still relatively rustic, do feature private bathrooms and a sense of being at a more typical nature lodge. For their part, the dormitory rooms and shared bathrooms are kept quite clean, and would certainly please even the most discerning backpacker or budget traveler. The dorm rooms and shared bathrooms use solar power and high-tech composting toilets. Guided tours are always available, and educational packages, sometimes including fieldwork, are often offered.

La Milpa section of Río Bravo Conservation Area, Orange Walk district. ✆ **227-5616.** Fax 227-5635. www.pfbelize.org. 8 double-room cabins, 30 dormitory beds. BZ$280 (US$140/£74) per person for cabins; BZ$258 (US$129/£68) per person for dormitories. Rates, based on double occupancy, include 3 meals, taxes, and 2 guided tours daily. MC, V. **Amenities:** Restaurant; lounge; tour desk; laundry service; nonsmoking rooms. *In room:* No phone.

Ruins of Your Own

Chan Chich Lodge ★★ Finds Set in the central plaza of a small Mayan ceremonial city, Chan Chich is one of the most unique jungle lodges in Mesoamerica. The low hills that surround 12 individual bungalows are all unexcavated pyramids and temples. The rooms feature high-pitched thatch roofs and wraparound wooden decks, and are all spacious, clean, and quite comfortable. Most come with two queen beds, made up with heavy comforters and lots of pillows. My only complaint is that given the restricted size of the central plaza, most of the bungalows are quite close to each other. The deluxe bungalows are slightly larger, especially in the bathroom area, and feature king-size beds and some Japanese-style decor. There's also a luxurious two-bedroom villa, with its own Jacuzzi and expansive living areas, well suited for families.

Barry Bowen, Belikin Beer, Coca-Cola & Chan Chich

Building a modern nature lodge in the central plaza of an ancient Mayan ceremonial city is bound to be controversial. Some see it as a desecration and outrage. However, most recognize that the construction and operation of Chan Chich Lodge has served as a wonderful safeguard against looters, and a strong tool for raising awareness and money to support conservation and excavation efforts.

First discovered in 1938 by J. Eric Thompson, the site was originally named Kaxil Uinic, before being renamed by Barry Bowen in 1987. Bowen, owner of the Belikin Beer company and exclusive distributor for Coca-Cola in Belize, had bought over 303,514 hectares (750,000 acres) of land (about one-sixth of the country) in western Orange Walk District in 1984. When Bowen and his workers rediscovered Chan Chich, the site had been severely looted, and many of the mounds and temples showed signs of active looting trenches.

Chan Chich sits on some 101,171 hectares (250,000 acres) of private reserve, and is bordered to the north by the 106,028 hectares (262,000 acres) of the Río Bravo Conservation Area. Since Bowen bought the land, a total hunting ban has been enacted, and if these protected lands are connected to the Kalakmul Reserve in Mexico and the Maya Biosphere Reserve in Guatemala, they may one day form a major Mesoamerican environmental and archaeological mega-reserve spanning three countries.

Behind one of the overgrown temple mounds, there's a screened-in pool and Jacuzzi area with its own bar. Some 14km (9 miles) of well-groomed trails lead off from the central plaza, and a host of guided tours and hikes is available. Wildlife viewing here is excellent, with over 350 bird species identified nearby. They also claim to average 50 to 80 daylight jaguar sightings per year. You can go horseback riding, visit nearby agricultural communities, or canoe and swim at Laguna Verde. Day trips to Lamanai, La Milpa, and other Mayan sites can also be arranged. The food here is excellent, which is a good thing, since you have no other options.

Gallon Jug, Orange Walk District (mailing address: P.O. Box 37, Belize City). ✆ **800/343-8009** in the U.S., or ✆/fax 223-4419 in Belize. www.chanchich.com. 13 units. BZ$500–BZ$600 (US$250–US$300/£133–£159) double; BZ$1,790 (US$895/£474) villa. Rates lower in the off season. A meal package will run you an extra BZ$140 (US$70/£37) per day. Multiday packages are available. AE, MC, V. You can either drive here or take a charter flight to nearby Gallon Jug; if you choose the charter, Chan Chich can arrange the flight and pick you up at the airport. If you choose to drive, it takes about 4 hr. from Belize City, much of it on dirt roads, so a 4-wheel-drive vehicle is recommended. If you are driving here, you will need permission to pass through the Programme for Belize's lands; call the lodge in advance to arrange this. **Amenities:** Restaurant; bar; lounge; small pool; Jacuzzi; tour desk; laundry service; nonsmoking rooms. *In room:* Coffeemaker, no phone.

6 COROZAL TOWN

13km (8 miles) N of Belize City; 50km (31 miles) N of Orange Walk Town; 13km (8 miles) S of the Mexican border

Corozal is a quiet seaside town, located just south of the Río Hondo (Hondo River), which forms the border between Mexico and Belize. Set on a crystal-clear bay, Corozal was an important point on the early Mayan trading routes, and the evidence remains in the ruins of **Cerros** and **Santa Rita.** During the mid-1800s the modern town was settled with a large population of refugees from Mexico's Caste War. In 1955, Hurricane Janet paid a visit and left few of the town's wooden buildings standing. The rebuilding relied heavily on cement and cinderblock construction. Today, Corozal is home to a growing expatriate community. While not part of the traditional tourist circuit, Corozal Town makes a good base for fishing excursions in the calm bay; bird- and wildlife-viewing tours into nearby **Shipstern Nature Reserve;** shopping trips to neighboring **Chetumal, Mexico;** and explorations of the aforementioned Mayan ruins. New attractions in this area are a couple of swank casinos and shopping centers located just on the Belizean side of the Mexico–Belize border.

ESSENTIALS

Getting There & Departing

BY PLANE Most flights to and from Corozal Airport connect through San Pedro Airport on Ambergris Caye. There are numerous flights connecting San Pedro to both of Belize City's airports, as well as other destinations around the country.

Maya Island Air (✆ **223-1140** in Belize City, or 422-2333 in Corozal; www.mayaairways.com) has daily flights between Corozal and San Pedro, leaving San Pedro at 7 and 10am, and at 2, and 4:30pm, and returning at 7:30 and 10:30am, and at 2:30 and 5pm. Flight duration is 25 minutes. The fare is BZ$82 (US$41/£22) each way.

Tropic Air (✆ **800/422-3435** in the U.S. or Canada, 226-2012 in Belize City, or 422-0356 in Corozal; www.tropicair.com) has direct flights between Belize City's two airports and Corozal, leaving every 2 hours between 7:30am and 5:30pm. The flight originates at the Municipal Airport and stops briefly to pick up passengers at the international airport. Return flights follow the same schedule. Tropic Air also has daily flights departing from San Pedro at 7, 9, and 11am, and at 3 and 5pm. The flights return to San Pedro at 7:30, 9:30, and 11:30am, and at 3:30 and 5:30pm. Flight duration runs between 25 and 40 minutes depending upon the number of intermediary stops. The fare is BZ$86 (US$43/£23) each way for any of the above segments.

See chapters 6 and 7 for more information on flights between San Pedro and Belize City, and other destinations around the country.

BY CAR Corozal Town is the last town on the Northern Highway before you reach the Mexican border. Take Freetown Road out of Belize City to connect with the Northern Highway. If you're driving in from Mexico, you'll reach a fork in the road 4.8km (3 miles) from the border; bear left and follow the signs to reach Corozal Town.

BY BUS Buses (✆ **227-2255** in Belize City, or 402-3034 in Corozal) leave Belize City for Corozal and the Mexican border throughout the day, roughly every half-hour between 5:30am and 7:30pm from the main terminal on West Collet Canal Street. Catch any bus going to Corozal Town or Chetumal. The Corozal Town bus station is located 2 blocks west of the small central plaza and Town Hall. You can pick up a return bus here to Belize City, or onward to the Mexican border and Chetumal. The fare is BZ$16 to BZ$20 (US$8–US$10/£4.25–£5.30) between Belize City and Corozal Town, BZ$6 to BZ$10 (US$3–US$5/£1.60–£2.65) between Orange Walk Town and Corozal Town, and around BZ$6 (US$3/£1.60) between Chetumal and Corozal Town.

BY BOAT The ***Thunderbolt*** (✆ **226-2904** in San Pedro or 422-0026) has two daily boats running between San Pedro on Ambergris Caye and Corozal. The boats leave each destination at 7am and 3pm, and cross paths about mid-way. The trip takes around 90 minutes. Fare is BZ$50 (US$25/£13) one-way.

Getting Around

Corozal Town is very compact, and it's easy to walk anywhere in the entire downtown and waterfront areas. However, if it's just too hot, you're too tired, or you're heading farther afield, you can have your hotel call a taxi. Or try **Corozal Taxi Association** (✆ **422-2642**) or **Venus Taxi Service** (✆ **422-3626**).

If you're looking to rent a car up here, contact **Corozal Car Rentals** (✆ **422-3339;** www.corozalcars.com).

Orientation

Corozal is located right on a beautiful section of Corozal Bay. The town is laid out more or less in a grid, with avenues running roughly north–south and streets running east–west. The avenues run up numerically in order beginning with the waterfront 1st Avenue. The streets run in parallel but separate numerical order north and south from the town's central plaza, so that 3rd Street North and 3rd Street South are two distinct roads, one located 3 blocks north of the central plaza, the other 3 blocks south. The Northern Highway from Belize City and Orange Walk enters the town from the south. If you bear right and stay close to the water, you will be on 1st Avenue. If you bear left, you will be on 7th Avenue, the town's busiest thoroughfare, which skirts the western edge of downtown before passing the bus terminal and continuing on to Chetumal and the Mexican border.

The **post office** (✆ **422-2462**) and Town Hall front the small central plaza. Most banks and businesses are within a 2-block radius in either direction.

FAST FACTS If you need to call the **police,** dial ✆ **911** or 422-2202; for the **fire department,** dial ✆ **422-2105;** and for medical emergencies, call the **Corozal Hospital** at ✆ **422-2076.**

There are several banks in Corozal Town: **Atlantic Bank,** 1 Park St. (✆ **422-3473**); **Scotiabank,** 4th Avenue (✆ **422-2322**); and **Belize Bank,** 5th Avenue and 1st Street South (✆ **422-2087**). All of these change U.S. dollars, Belize dollars, and Mexican pesos, as well as provide cash advances on your credit card.

If your hotel doesn't have a tour desk or good connections, and you want to visit any of the sites mentioned below or take an organized tour in this region, call **Belize VIP Transfer & Tours** (✆ **422-2725;** www.belizetransfers.com).

WHAT TO SEE & DO

There isn't much to see or do in Corozal Town. It's mostly just a stopping point for weary travelers. However, it sits on the shores of a pretty, quiet bay with amazing turquoise-blue water that is officially the **Bay of Chetumal,** but locally dubbed **Corozal Bay.** If you want to split hairs, the small bay just off Corozal Town could be considered a separate entity from the larger Bay of Chetumal that it sits in.

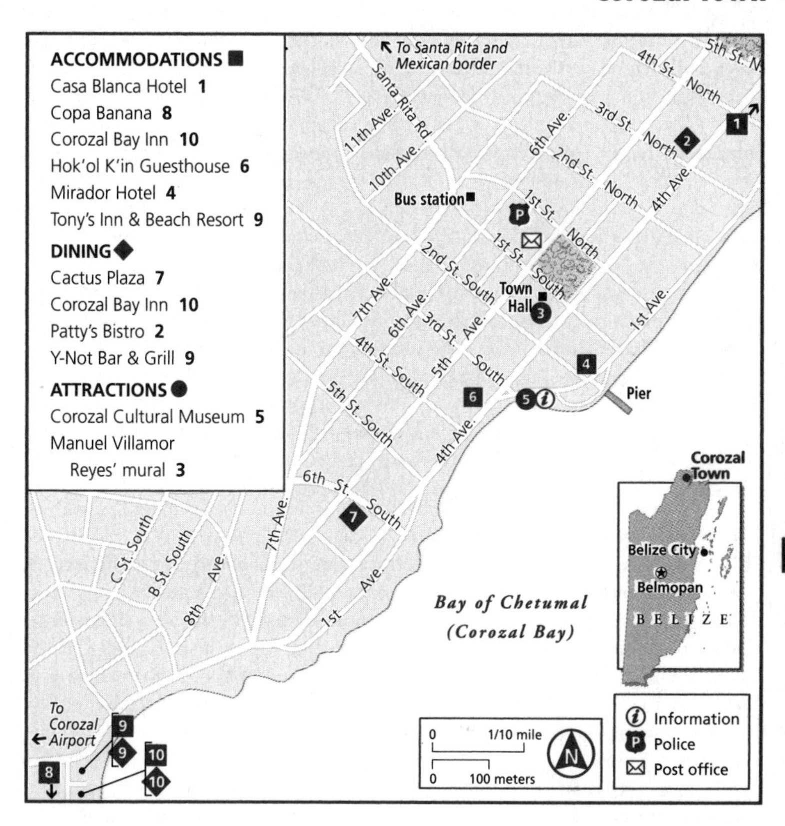

If you've just come from Mexico, you can take a day or two to walk around town and marvel at the difference between Mexican culture and Belizean culture. The countries are so close and yet worlds apart. Belize is truly a Caribbean country, with frame houses built on high stilts to provide coolness, protection from floods, and shade for sitting.

The heart of Corozal Town is the small plaza between 1st Street North and 1st Street South and 4th and 5th avenues. This is a good place to grab a bench and watch the locals go about their daily business. If you're hanging out here, it's worth a quick visit to the **Town Hall** to see the historical **mural** painted by Belizean-Mexican artist Manuel Villamor Reyes. The mural covers the local history from the Mayan era to the days of sugar cane plantations. However, if you want a really inviting park bench, I recommend heading a couple of blocks east to tiny parks and public lands you'll find all along the bayfront. Just off the town's central waterfront area, there's the little **Corozal House of Culture** (**✆ 422-3176**). While it's far from impressive, you can glean a little bit of the area's history by touring its simple exhibits. Originally built in 1886 as the town's Custom's House, the museum has a collection of Mayan artifacts, as well as natural history exhibits and photos, documents, and relics from the town's more recent history. The House of Culture is open daily from 8am to 5pm; admission is BZ$10 (US$5/£2.65).

Mayan Ruins

If you haven't yet had your fill of Mayan ruins, there are a couple to visit in the area. If you look across the water from the shore in Corozal Town, you can see **Cerros** or **Cerro Maya** on the far side of the Bay of Chetumal. "Cerro" means hill in Spanish, and the site is that little bump in the forest you can see across the bay. (Up close it seems much larger.) Cerros was an important coastal trading center during the late Pre-Classic Period. Some of the remains of this city are now under the waters of the bay, but there's still a 21m-tall (70-ft.) **pyramid** built right on the water's edge that you can climb for a wonderful view of the bay. Ask around town to find someone willing to take you by boat to the ruins. Or you can drive, by heading out of town to the south and catching the free ferry across the New River; this will connect you with the road to Cerros.

Right on the outskirts of town you'll find some of the remains of another ancient city many believe was the Mayan trading center of **Chactemal (Chetumal).** It is currently called **Santa Rita.** Corozal Town is actually built on the ruins of Santa Rita, which was an important late Post-Classic Mayan town and was still occupied at the time of the Spanish Conquest. The only excavated building is a small temple across the street from the Coca-Cola bottling plant. To reach it, head north past the bus station and about a kilometer (1/2 mile) later, at the sharp curve to the right, take the road straight ahead that leads up a hill. You'll see the building 1 block over to the right.

Two Nearby Nature Reserves

Bird-watchers and naturalists will want to visit the nearby **Shipstern Nature Reserve** ★ (www.shipstern.org). The reserve's 8,903 hectares (22,000 acres) protect a variety of distinct ecosystems and a wealth of flora and fauna. Managed by the Swiss International Tropical Conservation Foundation, Shipstern Nature Reserve is home to over 250 bird species, and its mangroves, lagoons, and flat wetlands are excellent bird-watching sites. The massive network of lagoons and wetlands is home to manatees and Morelet's crocodiles. The reserve also has lowland tropical dry forest unique to Belize, as well as a butterfly breeding project. The reserve is open daily from 8am to 4pm. Admission is BZ$10 (US$5/£2.65) per person and includes a short guided hike. It is possible to spend the night in some simple accommodations or pitch a tent inside of Shipstern Nature Reserve; rates are around BZ$30–BZ$40 (US$15–US$20/£7.95–£11) per person for a room and BZ$10 (US$5/£2.65) per person for camping. There's no restaurant here, but kitchen facilities are available at the rooms. To make a reservation, call the ranger station at ✆ **423-2247.**

Tip: The wetlands here are a major insect breeding ground. This is a bonanza for the birds and bats, but you might want to bring along plenty of insect repellent, and probably lightweight long-sleeved shirts and pants.

Five kilometers (3.1 miles) beyond Shipstern Nature Reserve, on the edge of the peninsula, lies the tiny lobster and fishing community of **Sarteneja.** In Sarteneja, the best place to stay is **Fernando's Seaside Guesthouse** (✆ **423-2085;** www.cybercayecaulker.com/sarteneja.html). Fernando is an excellent guide, and he can arrange everything from fishing or snorkeling trips to Mayan ruin excursions and night tours of the Shipstern Nature Reserve.

To drive to Shipstern Nature Reserve and Sarteneja, you used to have to first drive down to Orange Walk Town and take the Sarteneja Highway through San Estevan and Little Belize. There is now another route that cuts some time and distance off this trip.

Crossing into Mexico

While Corozal Town is a sleepy little burg with a village feel to it, Chetumal, its nearby Mexican neighbor, is a bustling little border city, with a lively shopping and nightlife scene. Chetumal is also the gateway to the beaches and Mayan ruins of the Yucatán Peninsula.

Chetumal is the capital of Quintana Roo, the Mexican state that makes up much of the Yucatán Peninsula and is home to the resort towns of Cancún, Cozumel, Playa del Carmen, and Isla Mujeres, as well as the Mayan sites of Tulúm and Cobá.

Most Belizeans come to Chetumal to take advantage of the town's "free zone," an area with scores of duty-free shops, modern multiplex cinemas, restaurants, and even a couple of casinos. You can also visit the **Museo de la Cultura Maya★**, Avenida de los Héroes, between avenidas Colón and Ghandi (✆ **983/832-6838**), which offers a much more extensive museum representation of Mayan history, art, and archaeology than you will find anywhere in Belize. The museum is open Tuesday through Sunday from 9am to 7pm (it stays open 1 hr. later Fri–Sat). Admission is around US$4 (£2.10).

Just 40km (25 miles) north of Chetumal lies the beautiful **Bacalar Lagoon.** This natural area is also known as Las Lagunas de los Siete Colores (The Lagoons of Seven Colors), and is a good place to have lunch and admire the views.

Frequent buses run between Corozal and Chetumal. The ride takes about 1 hour, including the formalities of the border crossing. The actual border is at the Belizean city of Santa Elena on the Hondo River, 13km (8 miles) north of Corozal Town. You don't need a visa in advance, but you will have to pay BZ$38 (US$19/£10) in departure fees. The bus fare runs around BZ$12 (US$6/£3.20) one-way.

Alternatively, you can head to Chetumal by boat, a quick 10-minute hop away. If you depart Belize by boat, your departure fee is just BZ$7.50 (US$3.75/£2).

Tip: Your best bet for changing money from U.S. or Belize dollars into Mexican pesos are the money-changers on the Belize side. Alternatively, there's widespread compatibility between ATMs in Chetumal and other Mexican destinations and most PLUS and Cirrus debit and credit cards.

For more on the area, pick up a copy of *Frommer's Cancún, Cozumel & the Yucatán* or *Frommer's Mexico.*

Heading south out of Corozal, stick close to the bay. Just outside of Corozal, take the small barge ferry over the New River, which then connects to the roads to Copper Bank, Progresso, and Shipstern and on to Sarteneja.

Several buses daily connect Shipstern Nature Reserve and Sarteneja to Orange Walk, Corozal Town, Chetumal, and Belize City. Alternatively, you can hitch a ride on the *Thunderbolt* (see "By Boat" under "Essentials," above) heading to San Pedro, or hire a boat on the docks in Corozal for around BZ$160 (US$80/£42). The price is for the entire boat, and most can carry as many as 10 passengers.

Tropic Air (✆ **800/422-3435** in the U.S. or Canada, 226-2012 in Belize City, or 422-0356 in Corozal; www.tropicair.com) will land its regularly scheduled 7am and 5pm flights between San Pedro and Corozal at an airstrip in Sarteneja, if there is demand. The fare is BZ$86 (US$43/£23) each way.

The **Bacalar Chico National Park & Marine Reserve** lies about an hour's boat ride away from Corozal Town. This is a great spot for snorkeling and wildlife viewing. Ask around town or at the docks; you should be able to hire a boat for around BZ$240 (US$120/£64), and the snorkeling equipment and a bag lunch will probably run an extra BZ$30 to BZ$50 (US$15–US$25/£7.95–£13) per person. For more information on Bacalar Chico National Park & Marine Reserve, see chapter 7.

WHERE TO STAY

Moderate

Casa Blanca Hotel This is a good place to come if you really want to get away from it all. Casa Blanca is located in Consejo Village, a small retirement and vacation community located on Corozal Bay about 11km (7 miles) north of Corozal Town. All of the rooms are located on the second floor. I like no. 10, which is a large end room. The doors are all hand-carved with Mayan motifs in local mahogany. The restaurant serves good American, Belizean, and international fare. The best things here are a couple of large thatch palapas built fronting a long dock that juts out into the bay. Here you'll find hammocks and tables and chairs; either option is well suited for hanging out in the cool shade and reading a book or watching the water.

Consejo Village (P.O. Box 212), Corozal District. ✆ **423-1018.** Fax 423-1003. www.casablancabelize.com. 10 units. BZ$150–BZ$300 (US$75–US$150/£40–£80) double. AE, MC, V. **Amenities:** Restaurant; tour desk; laundry service. *In room:* A/C, TV, coffeemaker, no phone.

Tony's Inn & Beach Resort This beachfront hotel has long been the lodging and meeting-place of choice in Corozal, but it's definitely got some competition these days. The rooms are all housed in a two-story L-shaped building and feature clean tile floors, either one king bed or two double beds, a small sitting area, and 27-inch television sets. Still, they have a bit of a forlorn and spartan feel to them. The second-floor rooms are all nonsmoking and have a shared veranda overlooking a grassy garden area. As at the neighboring Corozal Bay Inn, there's a sandy area by the water's edge here that can sort of be considered a beach, although the best swimming is off the end of the private pier. The Y-Not Bar & Grill (p. 222) serves lunch and dinner, and breakfast is served in a dining room just off the hotel lobby.

Corozal Bay Rd. (P.O. Box 12), Corozal Town. ✆ **800/447-2931** in the U.S. and Canada, or 442-2055. Fax 422-2829. www.tonysinn.com. 24 units. BZ$170 (US$85/£45) double. Rates slightly lower in the off season. AE, MC, V. **Amenities:** Restaurant; bar; tour desk; laundry service. *In room:* A/C, TV, free Wi-Fi, hair dryer.

Inexpensive

Copa Banana (Value) The five suites here are actually located in two side-by-side residential-style homes. Each has a full-service communal kitchen for guest use, and if you take two or three (or five) rooms, you can have one or both of the houses to yourself. Rooms are clean, bright, and spacious and come with either one queen bed or two twin beds. Several have sea views, although the hotel is located across a small street and vacant lot from the water. Both houses have large living rooms, and one has a dining room if you decide to cook dinner. Guests have free use of the hotel's bicycles, which is a nice plus. All rooms and buildings are nonsmoking.

409 Corozal Bay Rd. (P.O. Box 226), Corozal Town. ✆ **422-0284.** Fax 422-2710. www.copabanana.bz. 5 units. BZ$110 (US$55/£29) double. MC, V. **Amenities:** Complimentary bike use. *In room:* A/C, TV, free Wi-Fi, no phone.

Corozal Bay Inn ★ This is my top choice in Corozal Town. Ten individual thatch-roof cabins are spread around the grounds of this seaside hotel. If you're looking for amenities, this is the place to stay in Corozal. Each room has two double beds under mosquito netting, as well as a 27-inch flatscreen TV, and the entire grounds are wired for Wi-Fi. The bathrooms are large, and each room comes with small refrigerator and a hand-painted Mexican ceramic sink in a nook off the main bedroom. The Corozal Bay Inn boasts Corozal's only swimming pool, and they also have a broad sandy area that they call their beach, although on the water's edge it's held in by a sea wall, and the best salt-water swimming is at the end of their 183m (600-ft.) pier. The restaurant here is very good, and often crowded.

Corozal Bay Rd. (P.O. Box 1), Corozal Town. ✆ **442-2691.** Fax 800/836-9188 in the U.S. and Canada. www.corozalbayinn.com. 10 units. BZ$120–BZ$180 (US$60–US$90/£32–£42) double. Rates lower in the off season. AE, MC, V. **Amenities:** Restaurant; outdoor pool; tour desk; laundry service. *In room:* A/C, TV, free Wi-Fi, minifridge, coffeemaker, hair dryer, no phone.

Hok'ol K'in Guesthouse There are a handful of budget hotels in Corozal Town, but this is definitely the best of the bunch. The rooms here are located in a two-story building located right across the street from the bay and its little seaside promenade. Rooms are simple and most are a bit cramped, but everything's kept sparkling clean. Those on the second floor have small private balconies, most with pretty sea views. Some of the rooms have air-conditioning, although you'll pay extra for it. The restaurant here serves good American and Belizean fare at reasonable prices.

89 4th Ave. (P.O. Box 145), Corozal Town. ✆ **442-3329.** Fax 422-3569. www.corozal.net. 11 units. BZ$60–BZ$110 (US$30–US$55/£16–£29) double. MC, V. **Amenities:** Restaurant; tour desk; laundry service. *In room:* TV, free Wi-Fi, no phone.

Mirador Hotel ★ This new hotel has a commanding location, fronting Corozal Bay in the heart of Corozal Town. The imposing four-story concrete building, with a curved facade, seems a bit out of place. Rooms are spotless and simply appointed. About half the rooms face town, so be sure to request an oceanview or corner-view room. The best feature here is the large rooftop terrace, with a covered area hung with a couple of hammocks. The hotel's restaurant serves local and Chinese fare.

2nd Street South and 4th Avenue, Corozal Town. ✆ **442-0189.** www.mirador.bz. 24 units. BZ$70–BZ$80 (US$35–US$40/£19–£21) double; BZ$100–BZ$180 (US$50–US$90/£27–£48) double with A/C. AE, MC, V (5% surcharge). **Amenities:** Restaurant; tour desk; room service (7am–9pm); laundry service. *In room:* TV, free Wi-Fi.

Safety Note

Be sure to see the section directly following this one, "Staying Healthy: Protecting Yourself Against Natural Hazards," before setting out on any adventure; it includes useful information on hiking, camping, and ocean safety. Even if you just plan to lie on the beach, be sure to check out the box called "Don't Get Burned: Smart Tanning Tips" on page 48 to learn how to protect yourself against the sun's harmful rays—a must for everyone in Hawaii.

WHERE TO DINE

In addition to the places listed below, the restaurant at the **Corozal Bay Inn** is also quite good, and a popular hangout for the local expatriate community.

Moderate

Y-Not Bar & Grill ★ BELIZEAN/INTERNATIONAL This open-air joint is the principal restaurant and bar at Tony's Inn & Beach Resort. It has a lovely setting on the water's edge under a high-pitched thatch roof. There's a loft area with seating in the main restaurant, but my favorite tables on a warm starry night are located on an uncovered little wooden deck built right over the water. Start things off with some conch fritters or coconut-battered shrimp. The chicken and beef fajitas are the most popular items here, but if you want something more substantial, try a T-bone or rack of barbecue ribs. There's also always plenty of fresh seafood, simply prepared.

At Tony's Inn & Beach Resort (p. 220), Corozal Bay Rd. ✆ **422-2055.** Main courses BZ$10–BZ$36 (US$5–US$18/£2.65–£9.55). AE, MC, V. Daily 11am–11pm.

Inexpensive

Cactus Plaza (Value) MEXICAN Serving basic Mexican fare in a pleasant open-air setting, this is perennially one of the most popular restaurants in Corozal Town. The menu here is simple: Get some tacos, tostados, or *salbutes* (a round disc of fried corn meal, somewhat thicker than a traditional tortilla, usually topped with some shredded chicken, refried beans, or a cabbage salad), and maybe a side of rice and beans. My favorite seats are on the canvas shaded rooftop patio, although you can also grab a seat at the small counter or at heavy tables on the ground floor. On weekend nights, the bar here is pretty lively.

6 6th St. S. ✆ **422-0394.** Reservations not accepted. Main courses BZ$2–BZ$10 (US$1–US$5/53p–£2.65). MC, V. Tues–Sun 11:30am–10pm.

Patty's Bistro ★ (Value) BELIZEAN/INTERNATIONAL This quaint little joint is a local favorite for lunch, but is also open for dinner and does a brisk business in takeout as well. The menu here ranges from Belizean staples like stew chicken and *escabeche* (a local chicken soup) to coconut curry shrimp and beef burritos. Brave souls might start things off with the cow-foot soup, but I prefer the shrimp and conch ceviche. There are daily chalkboard specials. Be sure to sign one of the graffiti-filled walls before you leave.

13 4th Ave. ✆ **402-0174.** Reservations not accepted. Main courses BZ$8–BZ$20 (US$4–US$10/£2.10–£5.30). MC, V. Daily 11am–9pm.

COROZAL TOWN AFTER DARK

Corozal Town is a pretty quiet place. If you're looking for anything resembling action, forget about it. If you want to meet some locals, fellow travelers, or expatriates, head to the bars at either **Tony's Inn & Beach Resort** (p. 220) or the **Corozal Bay Inn** (p. 221). They're side by side, so if one's not happening, you can just walk next door. On Friday and Saturday nights, you can also try the bar at **Cactus Plaza** (above).

If you're in the mood to try your luck, head north of town to the free zone and hit the tables at the **Princess Casino** (✆ **423-7652**) or the **Golden Princess Casino** (✆ **423-7680**).

The Cayo District & Western Belize

Western Belize, from the capital city of Belmopan to the Guatemalan border, is a land of rolling hills, dense jungles, abundant waterfalls, clear rivers, extensive caves, and numerous Maya ruins. This region was the heart of the Belizean Maya world, with the major ruins of Caracol, Xunantunich, and El Pilar, as well as lesser sites like Cahal Pech. At the height of the Classic Maya Period, there were more residents in this area than in all of modern Belize.

Today, the area around Belmopan and extending throughout the Cayo District is the heart of Belize's ecotourism industry. There are a host of national parks and protected areas, including the **Guanacaste** and **Blue Hole National parks,** the **Mountain Pine Ridge Forest Reserve,** and the **Chiquibil National Park.** The pine forests and rainforests here are great for hiking and bird-watching; the rivers are excellent for canoeing, kayaking, and inner tubing; and the dirt roads are perfect for horseback riding and mountain biking.

The cave systems of the Cayo District were sacred to the ancient Maya, and many of them are open for exploration by budding and experienced spelunkers alike. Some of the more popular underground attractions include **Actun Tunichil Muknal, Barton Creek Cave, Chechem Ha, Crystal Cave,** and the **Río Frío Cave.** Of particular interest is the **Caves Branch River,** which provides the unique opportunity to float on an inner tube, kayak, or canoe through a series of caves.

The Western Highway runs through the heart of the Cayo District all the way to the Guatemalan border, and serves as the gateway to side trips into Guatemala's Petén Province and the majestic Mayan ruins of **Tikal** (see chapter 11).

1 BELMOPAN

84km (52 miles) W of Belize City; 32km (20 miles) E of San Ignacio; 161km (100 miles) NW of Placencia

Belmopan is a desultorily planned city and the official capital of Belize. After Hurricane Hattie devastated Belize City in 1961—not the first time a storm leveled or flooded the city—government officials figured enough was enough and decided to move the country's capital safely inland. A host of government buildings, including the National Assembly, is laid out according to a master plan, surrounded by residential areas, with everything connected by a ring road. Unfortunately, the planners who designed it didn't count on the people's resistance to moving here. Belmopan is an example of what happens when you build it and no one comes. In fact, many government workers make the daily commute from either Belize City or San Ignacio—both are easy rides on well-paved roads.

Unless you are coming to Belize on government business, you will probably want to avoid Belmopan entirely. However, if you are traveling around by bus, you will at least pass through it. If you get into town late at night, don't despair—you can easily spend the night and make an early onward connection in the morning. The area around Belmopan is chock-full of natural wonders, including **Guanacaste** and **Blue Hole National parks,** as well as the **Caves Branch River** and its network of hollowed-out limestone caves. There are also several very comfortable and interesting nature lodges in close proximity to Belmopan.

ESSENTIALS

Getting There & Departing

BY PLANE Belmopan has a small airport (BCV), but none of the local commuter airlines have regularly scheduled flights here. There is really little reason to fly into Belmopan, as it's such a short and easy drive from Belize City.

BY CAR From Belize City, take Cemetery Road to the Western Highway. At Mile 50 you'll see the well-marked turnoff for the Hummingbird Highway and Belmopan. Turn left here and follow signs to Belmopan, about 3.2km (2 miles) beyond the turnoff. It should take about 1 hour to drive from Belize City to Belmopan.

BY BUS Belmopan has very frequent bus service from Belize City. Nearly all buses heading west and south from Belize City stop in Belmopan. Buses to Belmopan leave roughly every half-hour from the main bus station on West Collet Canal Street between 5am and 7pm. Return buses to Belize City leave the main bus station in Belmopan about every half-hour between 5am and 7pm. The fare each way is BZ$6 (US$3/£1.60). The trip takes 1½ hours. From Belmopan, there are also frequent onward connections to Dangriga, Placencia, Punta Gorda, and other points south, as well as to San Ignacio, Benque Viejo, and the Guatemalan border.

Getting Around

Belmopan is an extremely compact little city. You can easily walk to most places around the central hub. If you need a taxi, there are always taxis near the bus station and central market. Alternatively, you can call **Elvi's Taxi Service** (**© 802-3732**). A taxi ride anywhere in town should cost around BZ$8 (US$4/£2.10).

Orientation

Belmopan is a planned city with a ring road and broad streets. The city itself is located just off the Hummingbird (Southern) Highway, 3.2km (2 miles) south of the Western Highway. The bus station and small central market area are the heart of the town, and you will hit them soon after heading in off the highway. Within a 2-block radius, you'll find a couple of banks, two gas stations, and a few small strip malls. At the center of the city's radius, just off the market and bus station, is Independence Plaza, which houses the post office and prime minister's office. Sidewalks cut through Independence Plaza in various directions, making most of downtown Belmopan easily accessible by foot.

FAST FACTS Both of the principal banks in town, **Scotiabank,** Ring Road (**© 822-1412**), and **Belize Bank,** 60 Market Sq. (**© 822-2341**), are located close to the central market and bus station.

For the **police,** dial **© 911,** or 822-2220; for the **fire department,** dial **© 822-2311.** The **Belmopan Hospital** (**© 822-2264**) is located on Constitution Drive, a block north of its intersection with the North Ring Road.

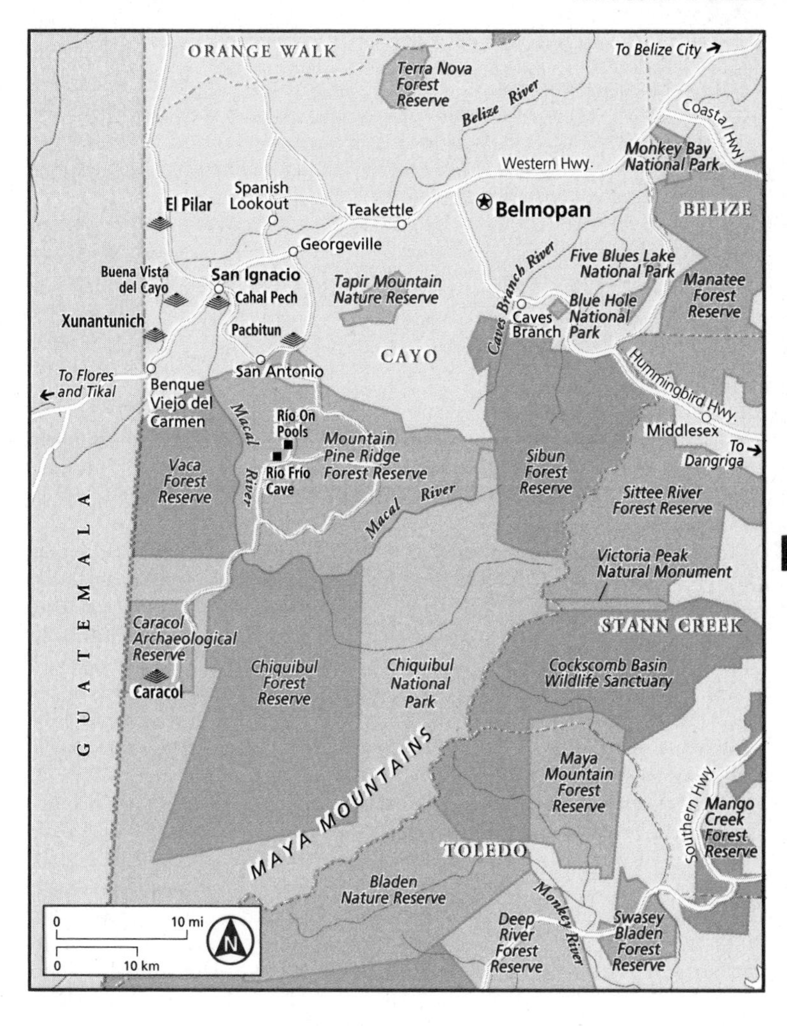

The **Market Square Drug Store** (✆ **822-0045**) is a well-stocked pharmacy located just off the Market Square.

WHAT TO SEE & DO

Perhaps the biggest attraction close to Belmopan is the **Belize Zoo,** Western Highway, Mile Marker 29 (✆ **220-8004;** www.belizezoo.org). For more information on visiting the zoo, see p. 105.

If you're spending any time in Belmopan, it pays to see if anything is happening at the **George Price Centre for Peace & Development** (✆ **822-1054;** www.gpcbelize.com). Primarily geared towards providing the local community with a library, classes, computer facilities, and meeting facilities, this place often hosts traveling art and museum exhibits, as well as movie showings, concerts, dance recitals, and theater performances.

The Underworld

The ancient Maya believed that caves were a mystical portal between the world of the living and the underworld of spirits and the dead. From their earliest days, there is evidence that the Mayans made extensive use of caves for ritual purposes, as well as for more mundane and rudimentary things such as keeping dry, storing grains, and gathering water. They called this mystical realm **Xibalba.**

Belize is literally riddled with caves. In almost every explored cave to date, some evidence of use by the Mayans has been uncovered. Fire pits, campsites, burial mounds, and ritual altars have all been found. Numerous pieces of pottery and abundant bones and artifacts have also been encountered. Belize offers many unique and easily accessible opportunities to explore this fascinating world, on foot, by kayak or canoe, or by floating on an inner tube. Don't miss it.

Caves Branch River Cave System ★★★

The Caves Branch River is a gently flowing body of water coming down off the Mountain Pine Ridge. It really should be called a creek in most places. However, what makes the Caves Branch River unique is the fact that it flows in and out of a series of long limestone caves that are easily navigable on inner tubes and in kayaks.

There are two major entry points along the river for visits to the Caves Branch caves: One is at **Ian Anderson's Caves Branch** jungle lodge (p. 231), and the other is just above **Jaguar Paw,** a luxury hotel built on the banks of the river (p. 232). In general terms, travelers looking for more adventurous and gritty trips into the caves should head to Ian Anderson's place; those seeking a more luxurious excursion into the underworld should head to Jaguar Paw. Still, for anyone looking for some serious cave adventures and explorations, both of the aforementioned lodges offer a host of guided tours to much less commonly explored caves, including the fabulous **Crystal Cave ★★★**, located just off the Jaguar Paw grounds.

By far, most visitors go either directly through Jaguar Paw or use the same section of the river. There's a government-operated parking area (BZ$4/US$2/£1.05) about a kilometer (1/2 mile) downriver from Jaguar Paw and a host of operators running the tubing tour from here. Either way, you will have to hike upstream to a put-in. Depending on the tour you choose and the amount of hiking you want to do, you will eventually climb into your inner tube and begin a slow float through anywhere from one to four caves. You will be equipped with a headlamp, and little else. If your group is small enough, I recommend you coordinate and all shut off your headlamps for a period of time. It's quite a spooky sensation to be floating in total darkness, wondering where the walls and ceilings are and whether or not you'll ever emerge into daylight again.

Most of the caves here contain Mayan pottery and artifacts, although you won't see them on the majority of tube trips, unless your guide stops for a short hike.

Cave tubing tours cost between BZ$60 and BZ$220 (US$30–US$110/£16–£58), depending on the length of the tour. The most inexpensive way to go is to drive yourself to the government parking area below Jaguar Paw and hire one of the local guides there for around BZ$30 to BZ$60 (US$15–US$30/£7.95–£16). However, you'll generally get better guides, better service, and better equipment if you go with one of the more established operators.

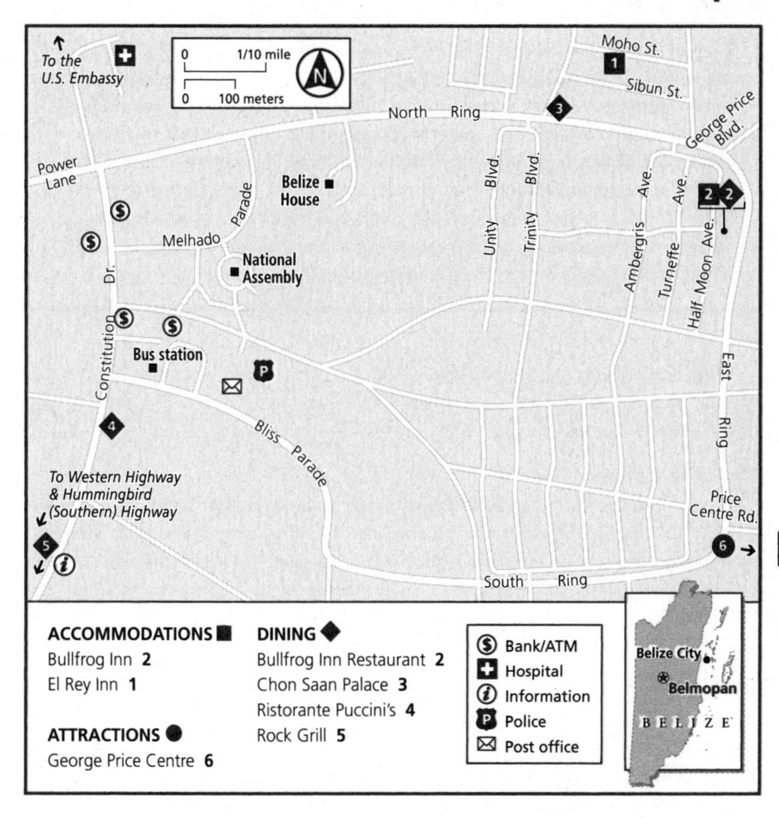

Actun Tunichil Muknal ★★

Actun Tunichil Muknal means "Cave of the Crystal Sepulcher," and the site was featured in the 1993 National Geographic Explorer film *Journey Through the Underworld.* This is one of the most adventurous and rewarding caves you can visit in Belize. The trip involves a 45-minute hike through dense forest to the entrance of the cave. A midsize stream flows out of the beautiful entrance. From here you wade, crawl, and scramble, often up to your waist in water. There are some tight squeezes. Inside, you'll come to several ceremonial and sacrificial chambers. Fourteen skeletons and burial sites have been found inside here, as well as numerous pieces of pottery and ceramic shards. There are even two rare slate stelae, believed to have been used by Mayan religious and political leaders for ritual bloodletting ceremonies. Many of the skulls, skeletons, and pieces of pottery have been encased in calcium, creating an eerie effect, while others are very well maintained, making it hard to imagine that they are over a thousand years old. Moreover, given its remote location and relatively recent discovery, Actun Tunichil Muknal has been spared much of the serious looting that has plagued many other Mayan cave sites. Only licensed guides can take visitors into this cave. Most hotels and tour agencies in the Cayo District can arrange these tours.

For the Most Enjoyable Experience

The Caves Branch River cave system is a very popular tourist attraction, and it can get crowded at times, especially in the three caves closest to Jaguar Paw and the public entrance. When the cruise-ship groups are in the caves, it's downright overcrowded. Whatever tour operator you use, try to time it so that you avoid other large groups if possible. I also highly recommend hiking the extra 15 minutes or so upstream to get to the fourth cave. However, if you choose to do the tour with Ian Anderson's Caves Branch outfit, you are assured of avoiding the crowds. Also, wear plenty of insect repellent, as the mosquitoes can be fierce here (only on the hike—once you're in the caves there are none).

Note: You will get wet on this trip. Make sure your guide has a dry bag for your camera, and be sure to pack a change of clothing for when you get back to your transportation.

Zip Line Canopy Tour ★

The folks at **Jaguar Paw** (**© 820-2023;** www.jaguarpaw.com) have set up an "Aerial Trek Canopy Tour," in which visitors get to strap on a climbing harness and glide along steel cables, or zip-lines, from one treetop platform to another, above and through the forest canopy. There are a total of eight different platforms. At its highest, you are some 24m (80 ft.) above the forest floor. The two-hour trip costs BZ$110 (US$55/£29) per person, and can easily be combined with their cave tubing excursion (see above) for a full-day adventure outing.

National Parks

Guanacaste National Park ★, a 20-hectare (50-acre) park located where the Hummingbird Highway turns off of the Western Highway, about 3.2km (2 miles) north of Belmopan, is an excellent introduction to tropical forests. The park is named for a huge old guanacaste (or tubroos) tree that is found within the park. Guanacaste trees were traditionally preferred for building dugout canoes, but this particular tree, which is about 100 years old, was spared the boat-builders' ax because it has a crooked and divided trunk that makes it unacceptable for canoe building. More than 35 species of epiphytes (plants that grow on other plants), including orchids, bromeliads, ferns, mosses, lichens, and philodendrons, cover its trunk and branches.

There are nearly 3.2km (2 miles) of well-marked and well-maintained trails in the park, with several benches for sitting and observing wildlife. The park is bordered on the west by Roaring Creek and on the north by the Belize River. Among the animals you might see are more than 120 species of birds, large iguanas, armadillos, kinkajous, deer, agoutis (large rodents that are a favorite game meat in Belize), and jaguarundis (small jungle cats). Bring along a bathing suit in case you want to take a refreshing dip in the Belize River. This park is administered by the **Belize Audubon Society** (**© 223-5004;** www.belizeaudubon.org) and is open daily from 8am to 5pm. Admission is BZ$5 (US$2.50/£1.35).

The Maya Mountains are primarily limestone and laced with caves, which is why this region of Belize is also known as Cave Branch. About 19km (12 miles) south of Belmopan on the Hummingbird Highway, you'll find **Blue Hole National Park ★**. The first signs you see of the park will be the parking area, visitor center, and trail entrance to **St. Herman's Cave,** although I recommend you continue on to the park's principal entrance. A little farther on down the Hummingbird Highway you'll come to a principal entrance to **Blue Hole National Park.** The park gets its name from a crystal-clear pool, or cenote, formed in a collapsed cavern. A short, well-marked trail leads to the main attraction here. Dense jungle surrounds a small, natural pool of deep turquoise. A limestone cliff rises up from the edge of the pool on two sides. The water flows for only about 30m (100 ft.) on the surface before disappearing into a cave and flowing on underground to the Sibun River. This is a great place for a quick dip on a hot day because the water is refreshingly cool and clear. It can get crowded here on weekends, but early in the morning during the week, you may have the place almost to yourself. You can clearly see fish swimming around the edges of the Blue Hole. A 2.4km (1 1/2-mile) trail connects the Blue Hole pool with St. Herman's Cave. This trail passes through lush and beautiful primary and secondary tropical forests that are rich in flora and fauna. Over 200 species of birds have been recorded here. Be sure to wear plenty of insect repellent or long-sleeved clothing, as the mosquitoes can be fierce. ***Tip:*** If you're only interested in the pool, be sure to continue on the Hummingbird Highway, and don't park at the St. Herman's Cave entrance.

In March 2008, two massive rocks collapsed the ceiling near the entrance to St. Herman's cave. At present, the cave is closed, and at press time it's unclear if and when it will be reopened. If it is reopened, it's less than .8km (1/2-mile) hike from the road to one of the largest and most easily accessible caves in Belize. You'll need a good flashlight and sturdy shoes to explore this undeveloped .8km-long (1/2-mile) cave.

With a guide hired at the park entrance, you can explore the **Crystalline Cave** here. This cave system goes on for miles and features beautiful geological structures and formations, Mayan relics, and some calcified skeletons. The park, which is administered by the **Belize Audubon Society** (**© 223-5004;** www.belizeaudubon.org), is open daily from 8am to 5pm, and admission is BZ$8 (US$4/£2.10). A self-guided trail map and a brochure about the park are available at the small visitor center. And if the park ranger is available, he'll usually throw in a brief guided tour for free. You'll have to pay an additional BZ$30 (US$15/£7.95) for a 10 1/2- to 2-hour guided tour of the Crystalline Cave.

A Private Park & Educational Center

Located just inland from Mile Marker 31 on the Western Highway is **Monkey Bay Wildlife Sanctuary** (**© 820-3032;** www.monkeybaybelize.org), a private reserve and environmental education center comprising some 433 hectares (1,070 acres) of varied natural habitat. There's a visitor center, and a range of tours is offered. This place specializes in hosting student groups, but anyone can visit for the day, or even stay in accommodations that range from somewhat plush private rooms to a dormitory-style bunkhouse to camping. In all cases, be forewarned: The showers are cold water only, and the bathrooms are outdoor latrines. Tours include guided hikes, bird-watching expeditions, cave explorations, and canoe outings on the Sibun River. With the recent declaration of the neighboring 911-hectare (2,250-acre) **Monkey Bay Nature Reserve,** this has become a considerably large protected area, with over 250 recorded bird species.

While walk-ins can often be accommodated, it's best to contact them in advance before coming for any tour or stay. Rates run around BZ$12 (US$6/£3.20) per person for camping; BZ$30 (US$15/£7.95) per person for a dorm bunk and shared bathroom; and BZ$87 (US$44/£23) for a double room with private bath. Meals cost between

BZ$16 and BZ$20 (US$8–US$10/£4.25–£5.30). A guided 3-hour paddle on the Sibun River costs BZ$60 (US$30/£16) per person.

WHERE TO STAY

In Belmopan

Moderate

In addition to the places listed below, you could also try the **Belmopan Bed & Breakfast** (✆ **822-0176;** www.belmopanbedandbreakfast.com), which is located at 8 Trio St. and rents two neat rooms in a residential home with a swimming pool.

Bullfrog Inn This is the most modern and comfortable hotel in Belmopan. Rooms are spacious, and come with one king bed or two queen beds, air-conditioning, and cable television. Most rooms have a small private balcony with a wrought-iron railing overlooking a small patch of grass and the ring road. This place is justifiably popular with business travelers, as it's really the only game in town. The restaurant here is one of the more dependable in town, and the bar can actually get hopping.

25 Half Moon Ave. (P.O. Box 28), Belmopan. ✆ **822-3425.** Fax 822-3155. www.bullfroginn.com. 25 units. BZ$170 (US$85/£45) double. MC, V. **Amenities:** Restaurant; bar; tour desk; laundry service. *In room:* A/C, TV.

Inexpensive

El Rey Inn If you're looking for a clean, inexpensive place to spend the night, try this small hotel located in a residential neighborhood just off the north ring road. The rooms are fairly basic, but the rates are some of the best in Belmopan. This little hotel has a simple restaurant serving reasonably priced meals, and a host of tours can be arranged. El Rey Inn is about a 10-minute hike or a short taxi ride from the bus station.

23 Moho St., Belmopan. ✆ **822-3438.** Fax 822-2682. hibiscus@btl.net. 12 units. BZ$50–BZ$80 (US$25–$40/£13–£21) double. MC, V. **Amenities:** Restaurant; tour desk; laundry service. *In room:* No phone.

WHERE TO DINE

In addition to the place listed below, Belmopan now has a branch of the ever popular and ever expanding local Chinese franchise, **Chon Saan Palace,** 7069 George Price Blvd. (✆ **822-3366**), where you can get a host of well-prepared Cantonese and Szechwan favorites. The restaurant at the **Bullfrog Inn,** 25 Half Moon Ave. (✆ **822-3425**), which serves a mix of local and international cuisine, is another of the better restaurants in the city proper. Budget travelers and those looking for some local flavor should probably grab food from the various vendors and stalls at the central market. But this option is not for those with delicate digestive tracts.

Some of your best options lie just outside of the city, about 26km (16 miles) east along the Western Highway at Mile Marker 32, where you'll find a pair of popular roadside restaurants and bars: **Cheers** (✆ **822-2065**) and **Amigos** (✆ **820-2014**). Both are large and lively spots serving local fare, grilled meats, seafood, and typical bar food like nachos and burgers.

Ristorante Puccini's ITALIAN/INTERNATIONAL This unremarkable looking and rather rundown little restaurant has a wide-ranging menu and serves some of the best food in Belmopan. There's a broad selection of pasta dishes, and all are well prepared and served al dente. If you venture away from their Italian selections, the tequila lime chicken is a good choice. Otherwise, you can also get everything from fajitas to veal piccata to a hefty rib-eye steak. If the heat is a problem, grab a table in the air-conditioned dining room, but at night, or when it's cool out, I recommend one of the outdoor tables.

Constitution Dr., Belmopan. ✆ **822-1366.** BZ$12–BZ$24 (US$6–US$12/£3.20–£6.35). MC, V. Daily 11:30am–2pm and 5–10pm.

BELMOPAN AFTER DARK

There's really very little in the way of nightlife in and around Belmopan. The most happening spot in town is the new **Rock Grill** (✆ **822-1963**) located just off Constitution Drive, behind Dave's Furniture. The **Bullfrog Inn** (see above) is another of the city's more popular watering holes, and they frequently have raucous karaoke nights. The restaurants out on the Western Highway mentioned above are another good bet for an evening out.

LODGES NEAR BELMOPAN

While Belmopan itself is of very little interest to most travelers, several of the country's best and most interesting nature lodges are located within close proximity to the capital city. All of the places below have their unique charms.

Banana Bank Lodge ★ Kids Owners John and Carolyn Carr moved to Belize from the United States over 27 years ago. Carolyn is an artist and John is a cowboy from Montana. Together, they operate one of the oldest cattle ranches in Belize and one of the original ecolodges in the country. There are a variety of options, from two-bedroom cabanas that are well suited to families to lodge rooms to the large Chateau Brio suites. Three of these suites have full kitchenettes. I find the furnishings and decor touches a bit too provincial and quaint for my taste, but this is offset by beautiful stained-glass pieces and interesting architectural touches. The rooms and suites have air-conditioning, while the cabanas only come with fans. Tasty meals are served family style in a large dining room with a high, peaked thatch roof, where guests are encouraged to join other guests at larger tables.

The lodge is set on a high hill above the Belize River. Horseback riding is the most popular attraction here, but canoeing, visits to Maya ruins, and other day and overnight trips can all be arranged. On the grounds, you can visit Carolyn's studio and get close to the Carrs' pet jaguar, Tika. Cruise-ship passengers come here frequently for day trips, and it can get a little crowded and hectic when they're around.

Western Hwy., Mile Marker 47 (P.O. Box 48, Belmopan). ✆ **820-2020.** Fax 820-2026. www.bananabank.com. 14 units. BZ$260–BZ$350 (US$130–US$175/£69–£93) double. Rates include full breakfast. AE, MC, V. **Amenities:** Restaurant; bar; large outdoor pool; tour desk; laundry service; nonsmoking rooms; free Wi-Fi. *In room:* No phone.

Ian Anderson's Caves Branch ★★ Finds Originally a rustic camp for hard-core adventure travelers, this place has expanded, and while they still focus on some seriously rugged adventure travel, they've also added some comfortable accommodations. Set on the banks of the Caves Branch River amidst dense forest, you'll find a widespread collection of individual cabins, suites, bunkhouses, and camping. By far the most luxurious options here are the jungle suites and bungalows, and these are in fact quite plush for jungle lodgings. The latter feature red-tile floors, large verandas, and a beautiful shower with a large screened window opening up to the forest. Folks choosing to camp or stay in the jungle cabanas or bunkhouse share common bathroom and shower areas. These open-air showers are quite fun, as the showerheads are just old buckets with nail holes perforating them. Perhaps my favorite accommodations here are the "treehouse" suites, overlooking the river. A wide range of cave explorations, hiking, mountain biking, and kayaking tours are offered here, including overnight cave tours and jungle treks. Meals are served buffet style, and a full meal plan here costs BZ$84 (US$42/£22) per day.

Hummingbird Hwy., Mile Marker 41½ (P.O. Box 356, Belmopan). ✆ **822-2800.** www.cavesbranch.com. 20 units. BZ$10 (US$5/£2.65) per person camping; BZ$30 (US$15/£7.95) per person bunkhouse; BZ$196 (US$98/£52) double cabana; BZ$276–BZ$390 (US$138–US$195/£73–£103) double suite or bungalow. No credit cards. **Amenities:** Restaurant; bar; tour desk; laundry service; nonsmoking rooms. *In room:* No phone.

Jaguar Paw ★ With bold architectural and decor touches, and a prime location amidst dense forests at the heart of the Caves Branch river and cave network, Jaguar Paw is one of the more unique lodges in Belize. The rooms here are housed in a series of fourplex buildings spread through the lush grounds. While each room is identical in size, they are radically different in decor, each sporting a unique motif. My favorites include the Africa, Aboriginal, and Shell rooms. Honeymooners or couples looking for some "jungle fever" should request the Bordello room. All of the rooms are plenty spacious and have a small front porch area.

This hotel's greatest attraction is its location on the banks of the Caves Branch River, from which the popular cave tubing trips leave, and just a 5-minute walk from the entrance to the very impressive Crystal Cave. The owners were instrumental in the exploration of the surrounding cave system, and their dedication to the exploration and preservation is very apparent. Since most of the cruise ships use Jaguar Paw for their cave tubing excursions, guests here can usually avoid the crowds by coordinating with the hotel and going before or after the masses hit the river. These folks also have a zip-line canopy tour on site.

Western Hwy., Mile Marker 37 (P.O. Box 1832, Belmopan). ✆ **877/624-3770** in the U.S. and Canada, or 820-2023 in Belize. Fax 820-2024. www.jaguarpaw.com. 16 units. BZ$370 (US$185/£98) double. Rates lower in the off season. AE, MC, V. **Amenities:** Restaurant; bar; outdoor pool; tour desk; laundry service. *In room:* A/C, no phone.

Pook's Hill ★ **Finds** This isolated little jungle resort is set on the grounds of a small Maya ruin in the midst of a lush forest and a 121-hectare (300-acre) private reserve. The individual thatch-roof cabins are set on a hillside just off the ancient central plaza and are named after local fauna. Those highest up the hill have the best views of the surrounding forest, but they're a little bit smaller and slightly less luxurious than the newer units a little lower down. My favorite cabin is Kinkajou, which is tiled with river stones. Two cabins are located below the main lodge and across a small creek; they are built on raised stilts 3.7m (12 ft.) above the ground. These two cabins have large decks and are great for bird-watching.

A host of activities and tours is offered, including horseback riding, mountain biking, cave tubing, and guided hikes and bird-watching tours. Pook's Hill is within hiking distance of the Actun Tunichil Muknal cave, and day trips are offered here. Meals are served in a screened-in common dining area. Above the dining area is the open-air lounge and bar, which is lit by kerosene lanterns at night, and buzzes with hummingbirds during the day. A meal plan here costs BZ$88 (US$44/£23) per person per day.

Western Hwy., Mile Marker 52½ (P.O. Box 14, Belmopan). ✆/fax **820-2017.** www.pookshillbelize.com. 11 units. BZ$370–BZ$430 (US$185–US$215/£98–£114) double. Rates lower in the off season. MC, V. Turn south off Western Hwy. at Mile Marker 52½ at Teakettle Village. Follow signs on the dirt roads 9.7km (6 miles) until you reach the lodge. **Amenities:** Restaurant; bar; tour desk; laundry service. *In room:* No phone.

2 SAN IGNACIO ★★

116km (72 miles) W of Belize City; 32km (20 miles) W of Belmopan; 13km (9 miles) E of the Guatemalan border

In the foothills of the mountains close to the Guatemalan border lie the sister towns of Santa Elena and San Ignacio, which are set on either side of the beautiful Macal River. For all intents and purposes, San Ignacio is the more important town, both in general terms and particularly for travelers. Just north of town, the Macal and Mopan rivers converge to form the Belize River. San Ignacio is the business and administrative center for the Cayo District, a region of cattle ranches and dense forests, of clear rivers and Mayan ruins. It is also the second largest metropolitan center in the country. Still, you won't find any urban blight here. If you've come from Guatemala, you'll sense immediately that you are now in a Caribbean country. If you've come up from the coast, you might be surprised by how cool it can get up here in the mountains. Despite the similarity in the sound of their names, the Cayo District and the cayes are worlds apart. While the cayes cater to those looking for fun in the sun, Cayo caters to those interested in nature, outdoor adventures, and Mayan ruins. This area makes a great first stop in Belize; you can get in a lot of activity before heading to the beach to relax.

ESSENTIALS

Getting There & Departing

BY PLANE While there is an airstrip in San Ignacio (SQS), none of the local commuter airlines has regular service here.

BY CAR Take the Western Highway from Belize City. It's a straight shot all the way to San Ignacio. You'll come to the small town of Santa Elena first. Across the Macal River lies San Ignacio. If you're heading to San Ignacio and points west, a well-marked detour will lead you through the town of Santa Elena to a Balley bridge that enters San Ignacio towards the north end of town. The more prominent and impressive Hawksworth Bridge is solely for traffic heading east out of San Ignacio towards Santa Elena, Belmopan, and Belize City.

BY BUS San Ignacio has very frequent bus service from Belize City. Buses to San Ignacio leave roughly every half-hour from the main bus station on West Collet Canal Street between 5am and 8pm. Return buses to Belize City leave the main bus station in San Ignacio roughly every half-hour between 4am and 6pm. The fare is BZ$10 (US$5/£2.65). The trip takes 2½ hours. Most of the western-bound buses continue on beyond San Ignacio to Benque Viejo and the Guatemalan border.

Getting Around

The downtown center of San Ignacio is quite compact and easily navigated by foot. If you want to visit any of the major attractions listed below, you'll probably have to find transportation. Frequent buses (see above) will take you to the entrances to most of the hotels listed below on Benque Viejo Road, as well as within walking distance of the Xunantunich ruins. Infrequent buses (ask around town or at the bus station; ✆ **824-3360**) do service the Mountain Pine Ridge area. However, if you don't have your own vehicle, you will probably need to take some taxis or go on organized tours.

For Short

The name "Cayo" is used to refer to both the Cayo District as well as to the city of San Ignacio.

As in the rest of Belize, roads are minimal, and almost everything can be found on or just off the Western Highway, or the road through Mountain Pine Ridge. Numerous buses ply the main road between Belmopan and San Ignacio, continuing on to the border town of Benque Viejo del Carmen. If you want to drive yourself, particularly anywhere off the main highway, a four-wheel-drive vehicle is recommended.

You can rent a car from **Cayo Rentals** (✆ **824-2222;** www.cayoautorentals.com) or **Matus Car Rental** (✆ **824-2005;** www.matuscarrental.com). A small four-wheel-drive vehicle here should run you around BZ$150–BZ$200 (US$75–US$100/£40–£53) per day.

If you need a cab, call the **Cayo Taxi Association** (✆ **824-2196**) or **San Ignacio Taxi Stand** (✆ **824-2155**). Taxi fares around the Cayo District should run you as follows: BZ$6 (US$3/£1.60) around town, BZ$18 (US$9/£4.75) between San Ignacio and Bullet Tree Falls, and BZ$55 (US$23/£12) between San Ignacio and Chaa Creek or duPlooy's. Collective taxis run regularly between downtown San Ignacio and the border at Benque Viejo; the fare is BZ$6 (US$3.20) per person.

Orientation

San Ignacio is on the banks of the Macal River, on the western side of an old metal bridge across from its sister city of Santa Elena. Across the single-lane Hawksworth Bridge is a traffic circle and a Shell gas station. Downtown San Ignacio is to the north on Burns Avenue, and the San Ignacio Hotel is located south up a steep hill on Buena Vista Road. Most of the hotels and restaurants in town are on or within a block of Burns Avenue. The road to Benque Viejo del Carmen, Xunantunich ruins, and the Guatemalan border branches off Buena Vista Road. This is actually a continuation of the Western Highway.

FAST FACTS There are several banks located right in the heart of downtown San Ignacio: **Atlantic Bank,** at Burns Avenue and Columbus Park (✆ **824-2347**); **Scotiabank,** at Burns Avenue and Riverside Street (✆ **824-4190**); and **Belize Bank,** 16 Burns Ave. (✆ **824-2031**).

To reach the **police,** dial ✆ **911** or 824-2022; for the **fire department,** dial ✆ **824-2095.** The **San Ignacio Hospital** is located on Simpson Street, on the western side of town (✆ **824-2066**). The **post office** (✆ **824-2049**) is located on Hudson Street, near the corner of Waight's Avenue.

For film or developing, head to **Belicolor Photo Service** on Hudson Street (✆ **824-3549**). If you need eyeglass repair or help, head to the **Hoy Eye Center,** 4 Far West St. (✆ **824-4101**). The succinctly named **The Pharmacy** (✆ **824-2510**) is located on West Street. If you need laundry done and your hotel doesn't offer the service or charges too much, you can drop off your dirty clothes at **Martha's Guesthouse,** 10 West St. (✆ **804-3647**), for same-day service at about BZ$12 (US$6/£3.20) per load.

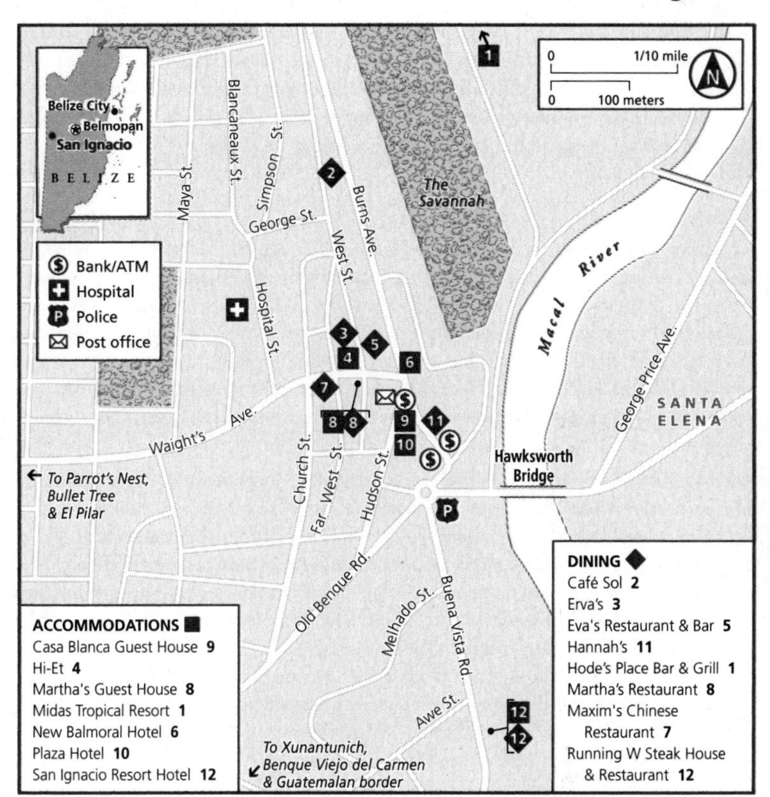

If you need to log on, head to **Eva's Restaurant,** 22 Burns Ave. (✆ **804-2267**); or the **Café Sol,** Far West St. (✆ **824-2166**). Both offer a few computers with high-speed Internet connections. Eva's is one of the most popular restaurants and meeting places in town, while the Café Sol also offers free Wi-Fi.

WHAT TO SEE & DO

The Cayo District is Belize's prime inland tourist destination. There's a lot to see and do in this area, from visiting Mayan ruins and caves to engaging in a broad range of adventure activities. In addition to the tours, activities, and attractions listed below, all of the listings in the Mountain Pine Ridge section (later in this chapter), and in the Belmopan section (earlier in this chapter) are easily accessible from San Ignacio.

Some of the tours, activities, and attractions listed below can be done on your own, but others will require a guide or adventure tour operator. Most hotels in the area either have their own tour operations or can arrange to hook you up with a reputable local operator. In addition, there are several long-standing tour agencies based in San Ignacio.

Some of the best of these include **Belize Eco Tours** (✆ **824-4290;** www.belize-ecotours.com), **Cayo Adventure Tours** (✆ **824-3246;** www.cayoadventure.com), **Pacz Tours** ★★ (✆ **824-2477;** www.pacztours.net), and **Yute Expeditions** ★★ (✆ **824-2076;** www.inlandbelize.com). All of these companies offer virtually all of the options listed in this chapter and more, including multiday tours, treks, and adventures.

In addition, serious bird-watchers might want to give a call to **Birds Without Borders** (✆ **824-4416**), or sign up for a tour with **Birding in Belize** (✆ **610-5593;** www.birdinginbelize.com).

Mayan Ruins

The Cayo District is in the heart of the Mayan highlands, with several major ruins and cave systems used by the ancient residents of this region. The most impressive are **Xunantunich** ★★ (on Benque Viejo Rd.), **El Pilar** ★★ (near Bullet Tree Falls Village), and **Caracol** ★★ (deep in the Mountain Pine Ridge area; see "Mountain Pine Ridge & Caracol," later in this chapter), but true Maya-philes can keep busy visiting a host of sites in this area. Close by, in Guatemala, lies **Tikal** ★★★, perhaps one of the best excavated and most impressive Mayan cities in Mesoamerica. See chapter 11 for complete coverage.

CAHAL PECH High on a hill to the southwest of downtown San Ignacio are the Mayan ruins of **Cahal Pech.** Although compact, there are actually seven plazas here, as well as numerous residences, temples, and a couple of ball courts. Formerly the home of Mayan royals, this site has received some meticulous restoration. The restoration created a bit of controversy in town because parts of the ruins were restored to an approximation of the way they were supposed to have looked when they were first built, which is a bit more polished and modern-looking than most people like their ruins. However, the setting is beautiful, with tall old trees shading the site's main plaza and pyramid. ***Tip:*** Be sure to climb the small B4 pyramid, on your left near the entrance to the site. Though diminutive, it offers excellent views of the Macal River.

The name Cahal Pech means the "Place of the Family of Pech" (*Pech* means "tick" in Mayan). The name was given to the site in the 1950s when there were quite a few ticks in the area. The ruins date back to between 650 and 900, though many think that the site was used prior to this time as well.

At the entrance, you'll find a small museum that displays a collection of artifacts recovered from the site and provides insight into the Cahal Pech social structure. It also has a small model of the old city, as well as a skeleton recovered from one of the graves here.

Admission to the museum and ruins is BZ$10 (US$5/£2.65), and the site is open daily from 8am to 5pm. Be sure to ask for a copy of the informative guide to the site. To reach Cahal Pech, walk or drive up toward the San Ignacio Resort Hotel (p. 241), continuing on around the curve for a few hundred yards until you pass the soccer field. Turn left here and climb the hill towards the ruins. The entrance to the ruins is beyond a large thatched building that houses the Cahal Pech disco. It's about a 20-minute walk.

XUNANTUNICH ★★ Although you may have trouble pronouncing it (say "Zoo-nahn-too-*neetch*"), Xunantunich is an impressive, well excavated, and easily accessible Mayan site. The name translates as "Maiden of the Rocks." The main pyramid here, El Castillo, rises to 39m (127 ft.) and is clearly visible from the Western Highway as you approach. It's a steep climb, but the view from the top is amazing—don't miss it. You'll

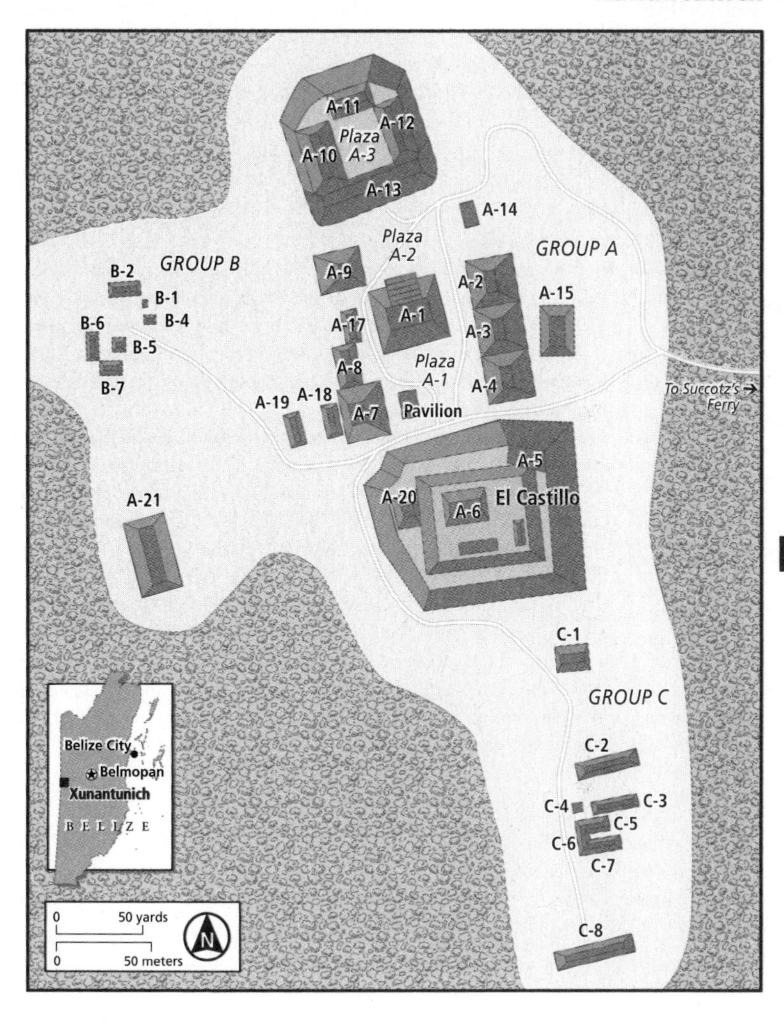

be able to make out the twin border towns of Benque Viejo, Belize, and Melchor de Menchos, Guatemala. On the east side of the pyramid, near the top, is a remarkably well-preserved stucco frieze.

Down below in the temple forecourt, archaeologists found three magnificent stelae portraying rulers of the region. These have been moved to the protection of the small, on-site museum, yet the years and ravages of weather have made most of the carvings difficult to decipher. Xunantunich was a thriving Mayan city about the same time as Altun Ha, in the Classic Period, about 600 to 900.

The visitor center at the entrance contains a beautiful scale model of the old city, as well as a replica of the original frieze. Open daily from 8am to 4pm, the site charges an admission of BZ$10 (US$5/£2.65). Xunantunich is located 10km (6½ miles) past San Ignacio on the road to Benque Viejo. To reach the ruins, you must cross the Mopan River aboard a tiny hand-cranked car-ferry in the village of San José Succotz. You may be able to watch colorfully dressed women washing clothes in the river as you are cranked across by the ferryman. After crossing the river, it is a short, but dusty and vigorous, uphill walk to the ruins. If you've got your own vehicle, you can take it across on the ferry and drive right to the ruins. To get here by bus, take any bus bound for Benque Viejo and get off in San José Succotz.

CHECHEM HA ★ This ancient Mayan burial cave was discovered by accident when a local hunter, Antonio Morales, went chasing after his errant dog. When the cave was explored, a cache of Mayan artifacts, including many large, fully preserved pots, was discovered. Archaeologists estimate the relics could have been placed here over 2,000 years ago. This cave is one of only two in the area with an elaborate altar used for ceremonial purposes by the religious and ruling classes.

The cave is located 16km (10 miles) south of Benque Viejo, on a dirt road that is recommended only for four-wheel-drive vehicles. Chechem Ha, which means "Cave of Poisonwood Water," is privately owned by the Morales family, and admission is only allowed with a prearranged guided tour. Ideally, you should make a reservation in advance, although it's often hard to contact and confirm with the Morales family; their phone number is ✆ **820-4063.** If you receive no response, you can usually drive out to the entrance any morning and arrange the tour directly with the Morales family beforehand. The cost of a 45-minute tour is BZ$60 (US$30/£16) for up to three people, if you book directly. Local hotels and tour companies also offer this trip, but charge a little bit more. You can also visit Chechem Ha on an organized tour with one of the local agencies working with the Morales family. Almost every hotel and tour agency in the area can arrange this for you, although they tend to charge a little bit more for their efforts.

A short hike from the entrance, the Chechem Ha Falls make a refreshing spot to wash and cool off after clambering around inside the caves. Also close to Chechem Ha is **Vaca Falls,** a beautiful and remote waterfall that's often combined with a visit to the cave, though it's a destination in its own right.

River Tours

For much of Belize's history, the rivers were the main highways. The Maya used them for trading, and British loggers used them to move mahogany and logwood. If you're interested, you can explore the Cayo District's two rivers—the Macal and Mopan—by canoe, kayak, and inner tube. Throughout most of the year, the waters in these rivers are easily navigable both up- and downstream. However, during the rainy season, things can change drastically—and fast. I've heard of a few flash floods, and even one story of water nearly reaching the road on the Hawksworth Bridge.

Still, for the most part, trips are leisurely, with plenty of places to stop for a quick swim or land excursion. During the rainy season (July–Sept), white-water kayaking is available, although it's not very consistent. Inflatable kayaks are a much more common and dependable option, not requiring nearly as much technical proficiency or water.

Most tours put in upstream on the Macal River somewhere around Chaa Creek (p. 245) or duPlooy's (p. 247) and then float leisurely downstream. The trip can take anywhere from 1 to 3 hours, depending on how much time you spend paddling, floating,

River Race

While it's still possible to navigate the Belize River all the way to Belize City—the Macal and Mopan rivers join and become the Belize River—this is not generally something tourists get to do. Still, each year in early March, scores of three-person canoe teams undertake the long 290km (180-mile) paddle from San Ignacio to Belize City in the **Ruta Maya Belize River Challenge.** Teams gather in San Ignacio below the Hawksworth Bridge on March 5, and thousands of people line the banks of the river for the start. The finish line, fittingly enough, is the Swing Bridge in Belize City. It takes between 3 and 4 days to complete the course, with the teams scheduled to arrive in Belize City on or around Baron Bliss Day, on March 9.

or stopping to hike or swim. Both of these hotels offer this service, as well as a host of operators in San Ignacio. For its part, the Mopan River is more easily accessible in many ways, since Benque Viejo Road borders it in many places. The Mopan is well suited for inflatable kayaks and inner tubes.

In addition to most of the tour operators listed above, you can contact **Toni's River Adventures** (✆ **824-3292**) or **David's Adventure Tours** (✆ **824-3674**). If you want to go inner tubing, contact the folks at the **Trek Stop** (✆ **823-2265;** www.thetrekstop.com).

Both of Cayo's principal rivers are great for swimming. On the Macal River you can join the locals right in town where the river is treated as a free laundry, car wash, horse and dog wash, and swimming hole. However, you'll do better to head upstream. The farther upstream you head, the more isolated and clear the swimming holes become.

Another alternative is to head downriver about 2.4km (1½ miles) to a spot called **Branch Mouth,** where the different-colored waters of the Macal and Mopan rivers converge. Branch Mouth is a favorite picnic spot, with shady old trees clinging to the riverbanks. There's even a rope swing from one of the trees. The road is dusty, so you'll be especially happy to go for a swim here. Farther upstream, on both the Macal and Mopan rivers, are numerous swimming holes.

Other Adventure Activities & Natural wonders

BELIZE BOTANIC GARDENS ★★ Located next to duPlooy's (p. 247) and run by the same family, the Belize Botanic Gardens (✆ **824-3101;** www.belizebotanic.org) is a sprawling collection of local and imported tropical fauna. They have an excellent mix of fruit trees, palms, bromeliads, and bamboos, all well laid out whether you are taking a self-guided or guided tour. The orchid house is not to be missed, with its beautiful collection of orchids and sculpted waterfall wall. The gardens are open daily from 7am to 5pm. Admission is BZ$10 (US$5/£2.65). Guided tours cost BZ$20 (US$10/£5.30) per person, including the entrance fee. You can also buy a helpful self-guided tour booklet for BZ$15 (US$7.50/£4), and even take a leisurely horse and buggy ride through the lovely gardens for BZ$20 (US$10/£5.30) per person.

BARTON CREEK CAVE ★ This is one of the area's easier and more relaxing caves to explore. The trip is conducted entirely by canoe, and while there are a few tight squeezes and areas with low ceilings, in general you won't get as wet (you'll stay dry, in fact) or claustrophobic here as you will at many of the other caves in Belize. Located beside a small Mennonite community, Barton Creek is navigable for nearly a mile inside the cave. Along the way, by the light of headlamps and strong flashlights, you'll see wonderful natural formations, a large gallery, and numerous Mayan artifacts, including several skeletons, believed to be the remains of ritual sacrifices. One skull sits so prominently atop a natural bridge that it's likely that a local tour operator moved it there to heighten the dramatic effect. You can climb along the dry edges of the cave in certain parts.

There's a BZ$10 (US$5/£2.65) fee to visit the site, but that doesn't include the canoe trip or transportation. If you drive there yourself, you can hire a canoe that holds two passengers, plus the guide, for around BZ$30 to BZ$40 (US$15–US$20/£7.95–£11). Tours out of San Ignacio average around BZ$60 to BZ$120 (US$30–US$60/£16–£32) per person, not including the entrance fee. Barton Creek Cave is located just off the Pine Ridge Road, about 6.4km (4 miles) from the Western Highway. Visits to Barton Creek Cave are often combined with a stop at the Green Hills Butterfly Ranch (see "Mountain Pine Ridge & Caracol," later in this chapter).

HORSEBACK RIDING If you enjoy horseback riding, there's some wonderful terrain in this area. Rides can be combined with visits to jungle waterfalls and swimming holes, as well as nearby Mayan ruins. Most of the hotels in the area offer horseback riding tours.

Alternatively, you can contact the folks at **Mountain Equestrian Trails** (✆ **669-1124;** www.metbelize.com), who have one of the better stables and horse riding operations in the Cayo District. Also, keep in mind that most lodges in the area offer horseback riding, so ask at your hotel or lodge first.

THE RAINFOREST MEDICINE TRAIL ★ Located directly between the Chaa Creek and the Macal River Jungle Camp, this is the former Ix Chel Farm, which was set up by Drs. Rosita Arvigo and Greg Shropshire. Rosita studied traditional herbal medicine with Don Elijio Panti, a local Mayan medicine man and a folk hero in Belize. Panti died in February 1996 at the estimated age of 104. Here on the farm, they built a trail through the forest to share with visitors the fascinating medicinal values of many of the tropical forest's plants.

The farm boasts a small gift shop that features local crafts, T-shirts, and several relevant books, including a couple by Arvigo. You'll also find Ix Chel's line of herbal concentrates, salves, and teas called Rainforest Remedies.

Self-guided visits to the Medicine Trail, along with a tour of Chaa Creek's Natural History Museum, and a visit to their Blue Morpho Butterfly Breeding project cost BZ$18 (US$9/£4.75). You can easily spend 3 hours visiting all three attractions. Guided tours of the Medicine trail are also available. Call ✆ **824-2037** for reservations.

MOUNTAIN BIKING If your preferred activity is mountain biking, you can go on an organized tour or rent bikes in San Ignacio. From San Ignacio, a great ride is out to El Pilar ruins. You can also ride out to Xunantunich; however, that ride is mostly on the main highway. Mountain bikes are available for rent at various hotels and tour agencies around San Ignacio and should cost around BZ$4 to BZ$8 (US$2–US$4/£1.05–£2.10) per hour, or BZ$30 to BZ$60 (US$15–US$30/£7.95–£16) per day.

Be careful, the hills here are steep, and the heat and humidity can be overwhelming. Take (and drink) lots of water, and try to avoid pedaling during the middle of the day.

A SPA If you want some serious pampering, or a soothing massage after some hard-core adventure, head to the **Spa at Chaa Creek** ★★ (✆ **824-2037;** www.chaacreek.com). A wide range of treatments is offered, including a hydrating manicure (BZ$56/US$28/£15), a variety of facials (BZ$140–BZ$190/US$70–US$95/£37–£50), and a range of full-body massage treatments (BZ$170–BZ$220/US$85–US$110/£45–£58). Full-day and multiday spa packages are also available. The spa itself is quite lovely, set on a high hill above the Chaa Creek hotel (p. 245), and the equipment and facilities are top-notch. It's usually open daily 8am to 4pm.

TROPICAL WINGS NATURE CENTER ★ Located just off the main road, at Mile Marker 71½ near the village of San José Succotz, is this small attraction. You'll find an enclosed butterfly garden with scores of brightly colored and varied species flitting about. There's also a butterfly breeding center, as well as an open-air medicinal plant nature trail. Hummingbird feeders ensure that you'll be buzzed by these frenetic, flighty creatures. This place is open daily from 9am to 5pm; admission is BZ$6 (US$3/£1.60). Call ✆ **823-2265** for more information.

SHOPPING

Orange Gift Shop & Gallery is probably the best-stocked gift shop in this region, if not the whole country, and can be found at **Caesar's Place** (✆ **824-2341;** www.orangegifts.com) about 11km (7 miles) east of San Ignacio. However, I find the prices a bit high, and similar goods can be found less expensively at other shops. A good alternative in town is **Arts & Crafts of Central America,** 24 Burns Ave. (✆ **824-2253**).

Throughout Belize, and especially in Cayo, you will see slate carvings of Mayan hieroglyphs. If you're in the area, it's worth a visit to one of the sources, the **García Sisters** ★★. This family of artisans runs an interesting little museum-cum-craft shop (p. 254). It's located outside of San Antonio village on the road to Mountain Pine Ridge (see "Mountain Pine Ridge & Caracol," later in this chapter, for more information).

WHERE TO STAY

Expensive

San Ignacio Resort Hotel ★★ This small, full-service resort is easily the most comfortable and luxurious option in town. Set on a high ridge above the Macal River, it has magnificent views of the lazy river below and surrounding forests. The rooms are all spacious, modern, and smartly designed. The standard rooms all come with a private balcony or patio letting out on to gardens. I actually prefer them to the Regal suites, which are somewhat larger but lack the balcony. The plushest room here is a large second-floor master suite, with a private Jacuzzi tub on its large balcony.

The hotel has a pool, a lit tennis court, and convention and conference facilities. There are jungle trails, a small iguana farm, a riverside beach and swimming hole, and a medicinal plant trail. A host of guided hikes and tours are offered, both on the grounds and farther afield. There's also a modest gift shop and a good restaurant and bar with great views from its terrace. There is a small casino, as well as the popular Stork Club bar and lounge (p. 245), both of which are equally popular with locals and guests.

18 Buena Vista St. (P.O. Box 33), San Ignacio, Cayo. ✆ **800/822-3274** in the U.S., or 824-2125. Fax 824-3362. www.sanignaciobelize.com. 24 units. BZ$260 double (US$130/£69) double; BZ$330 (US$165/£87) Regal suite; BZ$600 (US$300/£159) master suite. Rates slightly lower in the off season. AE, MC, V. **Amenities:** 2 restaurants; bar; lounge; casino; midsize outdoor pool; lit tennis court; tour desk; laundry service. *In room:* A/C, TV, hair dryer.

Moderate

In addition to the place listed below, **The Rolson Hotel** (✆ **824-2730;** www.rolsons.com) offers clean, business-class-style rooms, with televisions, air-conditioning, and free Wi-Fi.

Cahal Pech Village Resort (Value) Set on a hillside on the outskirts of town, this hotel has a wonderful view of San Ignacio and is a stone's throw away from the Cahal Pech ruins. Accommodations can be had either in the main building or in one of the thatch-roof individual bungalows. All are clean, spacious, well maintained, and feature carved Mayan wall hangings and colorful Guatemalan bedspreads. Most have air-conditioning. The rooms have larger bathrooms, and they are higher up and thus have better views from their private balconies—particularly the rooms on the third floor. On the other hand, the bungalows offer up a greater sense of privacy, and are set amidst well-tended gardens on the hillside below the main building. There's a large, open-air restaurant on the second floor of the main building, where guests gather for meals and to trade travel tales. The newest addition here is a two-tiered midsize outdoor pool set on a high spot near the main building with a great view over the town and valley.

Cahal Pech Hill, San Ignacio, Cayo District. ✆ **888/790-5264** in the U.S. and Canada, or 824-3740 in Belize. Fax 824-2225. www.cahalpech.com. 42 units. BZ$158 (US$84) double room; BZ$198–BZ$238 (US$99–US$119/£52–£63) double bungalow. MC, V. **Amenities:** Restaurant; bar; lounge; outdoor pool; mountain-bike rental; tour desk; laundry service; free Wi-Fi. *In room:* TV, no phone.

Inexpensive

San Ignacio is a very popular budget travel destination, and there are plenty of good options in town. During the high season, reservations are recommended for the more popular places. At other times, backpackers might prefer to arrive in town early enough to visit a few places, and see which place gives the best bang for the buck. Of the backpacker-geared options, I like the **Hi-Et,** 12 West St. (✆ **824-2828**), with its hostel-like vibe and playful name. Those looking for accommodations with the trappings of a business-class hotel but at budget prices could also check out the **New Balmoral Hotel,** 17 Burns Ave. (✆ **804-3502**), or the **Plaza Hotel,** 4A Burns Ave. (✆ **824-3332**).

Cosmos Camping (✆ **824-2116;** cosmoscamping@btl.net) is a campground on the road leading out toward Branch Mouth and Las Casitas, where you can pitch your tent for BZ$10 (US$5/£2.65) per day. There are showers and communal bathrooms that are kept clean, and the river is just across a field. This place is about a 15-minute hike from downtown San Ignacio, doable for a backpacker. They also have some simple cabins here as well. Still, I prefer the camping options farther outside of town, including Clarissa Falls Cottages and the Trek Stop, or Midas Tropical Resort, which is on the same road before Cosmos. See below for more information on all of these options.

Casa Blanca Guest House This centrally located hotel has won a loyal following in a short period of time. The rooms are all located on the second floor of a building set in the heart of the city's commercial core. The compact rooms all come with a television, ceiling fan, private bathroom, and air-conditioning, although you'll have to pay more for the A/C. There's a large common sitting area and a communal kitchen where you're always likely to bump into fellow travelers. There's also a small common balcony overlooking the hustle and bustle of Burns Avenue.

10 Burns Ave., San Ignacio, Cayo District. ✆/fax **824-2080.** www.casablancaguesthouse.com. 8 units. BZ$60–BZ$100 (US$30–US$50/£16–£27) double. MC, V. **Amenities:** Laundry service. *In room:* A/C, TV, no phone.

Martha's Guest House This cozy guesthouse is located in the heart of San Ignacio, above a popular little restaurant. The vibe here is somewhere between that of a homestay and a youth hostel. All of the rooms are immaculate. The more expensive rooms are larger and have minifridges and coffeemakers. There are also a couple of common lounge and balcony areas, where guests can hang out and read a book or chat. The fourth-floor First Lady suite is huge, and it features a large balcony with wonderful views of the town. It also comes with its own kitchenette, making it a good option for families. These folks also have a separate option a few blocks away that they are calling The Inn at Martha's, with fully equipped studio apartments.

10 West St. (P.O. Box 140), San Ignacio, Cayo District. ✆ **804-3647.** Fax 804-2917. www.marthasbelize.com. 10 units. BZ$80–BZ$110 (US$40–US$55/£21–£29) double; BZ$120–BZ$160 (US$60–US$80/£32–£42) suite. AE, MC, V. **Amenities:** Restaurant; bar; 2 lounges; tour desk; laundry service. *In room:* TV, no phone.

Midas Tropical Resort Value Though Midas is just a short walk from downtown San Ignacio, it feels a world away. The rooms are an excellent value when stacked up against other in-town options. The round Mayan-style cottages have thatch roofs and screen walls, and there are also some wood cabins on raised stilts with corrugated roofs. All are comfortable, clean, and spacious, with ceiling fans and plenty of screened windows for ventilation. The wooden cabins come with their own private verandas, which I like. Most of the rooms have cable television. The hotel has ample grounds with plenty of shady trees. Camping here will run you BZ$10 (US$5/£2.65) per person. The Macal River is only a stroll away down a grassy lane, and you can spend the day lounging on the little beach on the riverbank. If you don't want to swim in the river, these folks offer use of a pool at their in-town sister, Venus Hotel. To reach Midas, walk north out of town on Savannah Street, which is 1 block east of Burns Avenue. The hotel is only about .8km (1/2 mile) from the center of town.

Branch Mouth Rd., San Ignacio, Cayo District. ✆ **824-3172.** Fax 824-3845. www.midasbelize.com. 13 units. BZ$78 (US$49/£26) double; BZ$158 (US$79/£42) suite. Rates lower in the off season. MC, V. **Amenities:** Restaurant; tour desk; laundry service; free Wi-Fi. *In room:* No phone.

WHERE TO DINE

Moderate

Running W Steak House & Restaurant ★★ STEAKHOUSE/BELIZEAN This restaurant is located in the San Ignacio Resort Hotel and is affiliated with Belize's largest beef and cattle operation, its namesake. Try the Mayan Steak, marinated strips of tenderloin grilled and served with fresh tortillas. If you want something more traditional, order the 16-ounce porterhouse. There are also fish and chicken dishes, as well as some Belizean standards. The dining room is large and comfortable, with plenty of varnished wood. A few wrought-iron tables line an outdoor patio and make a great place to have lunch with a jungle view, or dinner under the stars.

18 Buena Vista St., in the San Ignacio Resort Hotel. ✆ **824-2034.** Reservations recommended. Main courses BZ$16–BZ$50 (US$8–US$25/£4.25–£13). AE, MC, V. Daily 7am–11pm.

Inexpensive

In addition to the places listed below, **Maxim's Chinese Restaurant,** 23 Far West St. (✆ **824-2283**), is the place to go for Chinese food. You might also want to take the adventure of finding **Sanny's Grill,** 23rd Street (✆ **824-2988**), which is tucked away in a residential neighborhood, but serves up excellent seafood and grilled meats. For inexpensive eats in a large outdoor setting, you can try **Hode's Place Bar & Grill** (✆ **804-2522**), located out on the northern end of town.

Café Sol ★ Finds INTERNATIONAL/VEGETARIAN This simple, downtown restaurant and coffeehouse features an eclectic menu ranging from a Thai noodle salad to jerk chicken to soy burgers. You can also get burritos and quesadillas, and a range of pasta dishes, as well as hearty sandwiches on freshly baked focaccia. Be sure to check the chalkboard for the daily specials. I like the tables on the covered front porch. You can also head inside, where you'll also find a small Internet cafe and a helpful corkboard with a variety of tour and hotel brochures and information. This is a great place for everything from breakfast to a coffee break to a filling meal.

Far West St. ✆ **824-2166.** Main courses BZ$12–BZ$20 (US$6–US$10/£3. .20–£5.30). MC, V. Tues–Sat 7am–9pm; Sun 7am–2:30pm.

Erva's BELIZEAN/MEXICAN There are scores of places in San Ignacio serving local cuisine, but this place is a local favorite. Erva is an excellent cook and congenial hostess. In addition to traditional Belizean and Mexican standards, you can get pizza and some seafood dishes here. Still, it's the stew chicken and rice and beans that brings folks in the door, and keeps them (and me) coming back for more. Erva's is located on the ground floor of the Pacz Hotel.

4 Far West St. ✆ **824-2821.** Main courses BZ$8–BZ$18 (US$4–US$9/£2.10–£4.75). MC, V. Daily 7am–10pm.

Eva's Restaurant & Bar Finds BELIZEAN/INTERNATIONAL Above and beyond dishing up good economical meals, Eva's serves as San Ignacio's central meeting place and unofficial tourist bureau. Hotel and tour advertisements cover the walls here, and brochures are abundant. The social scene is the main draw here, but you can get hearty servings of well-prepared Belizean and Mexican standards. If you want to get a group of people together to rent a taxi or canoe or to defray the costs of a tour, this is a good place to find other like-minded folks.

22 Burns Ave. ✆ **804-2267.** Main courses BZ$6–BZ$18 (US$3–US$9/£1.60–£4.75). MC, V. Daily 7am–midnight.

Hannah's ★ INDIAN/PAN-ASIAN Don't be put off by the humble state of this small restaurant, with simple furniture and half walls with steel grating substituting for windows. The menu is massive, with a host of curries and vindaloos and other Indian staples, mixed with a hefty dose of Chinese and Thai cuisine. Heck, you can even get burgers, burritos, Belizean fare, and big breakfasts here. Still, I recommend you come for the Indian and Thai cooking. The chef here is not shy to spice things up. The vindaloos and other spicy dishes can blow your head off if you're not accustomed to authentic cooking. This is a great restaurant for vegetarians, with ample options to choose from.

5 Burns Avenue. ✆ **824-3014.** Main courses BZ$16–BZ$44 (US$8–US$22/£4.25–£12). MC, V. Daily 6am–9pm.

Martha's Restaurant & Pizza House BELIZEAN/PIZZA The restaurant at this popular budget hotel is equally popular. The homemade pizzas are excellent. You have your choice of a variety of toppings, and you can build your own pizza. You can also get everything from burgers to burritos to vegetarian entrees, as well as local Mayan specialties like chaya tamales, made from cornmeal and a locally grown green. This is a great place for breakfast, including the typical Belizean breakfast of fry jacks, eggs, and beans, as well as excellent huevos rancheros and strong coffee. Try to grab one of the outdoor tables, and be sure to thank Martha herself.

10 West St. ✆ **804-3647.** Main courses BZ$16–BZ$40 (US$8–US$20/£4.25–£11). MC, V. Daily 7am–10pm.

SAN IGNACIO AFTER DARK

San Ignacio is a pretty sleepy town. Many travelers end up at **Eva's Restaurant & Bar** (see "Where to Dine," above), trading tales and planning adventures with new friends. Several bars are around the downtown area, though. Most nights, but especially on weekends, the most happening spot in town can be found up the hill at **The Stork Club** (✆ **824-2034**), which is located in the San Ignacio Resort Hotel. This place has karaoke on Thursday nights, and live bands often on the weekends. Another raucous place for late-night revelry and dancing is the **Rhumba Room** (no phone), which is on the outskirts of town, on the road heading to Benque. On the north end of town, **Hode's Place Bar & Grill** (✆ **804-2522**) is a massive spot that is very popular with locals. They have a tiny casino, as well as a large video arcade, and a pool and foosball tables. Alternatively, you can find out if there's live music at **Caesar's Place** (✆ **824-2341**), which is the home turf of the Mango Jam band, a local jazz outfit. Caesar's is located out on the Western Highway, about 11km (7 miles) east of San Ignacio.

If you're the gambling type, you'll want to head to the **Princess Casino** (✆ **824-4099**), which is also located at the San Ignacio Resort Hotel. I'd definitely choose this one over the very little casino at **Hode's Place** (✆ **804-2522**).

NEARBY LODGES & RETREATS

On the Road to Benque Viejo & the Guatemalan Border

While San Ignacio is the regional hub and does make a good base for side trips, the real attractions in western Belize are up the rivers and in the forests. Within a few miles of San Ignacio are several lodges set somewhat off the beaten path, where you can canoe down clear rivers past 1.2m (4-ft.) iguanas sunning themselves on the rocks; ride horses to Mayan ruins; hike jungle trails, and spot scores of beautiful birds and, occasionally, other wild animals. Out on the road to Caracol and Mountain Pine Ridge, there are more of these lodges. Except for the true budget traveler, I highly recommend that you stay at one of the lodges listed below while you're in the area. A few of the lodges can be reached by public bus from San Ignacio, though you may have up to a 20-minute walk after getting off the bus, so consider taking a taxi or arranging pickup in town. All the lodges offer a wide range of active adventures and tours to all the principal sites in the area.

Very Expensive

In addition to the places listed below, **Ka'ana** (✆ **824-3350;** www.kaanabelize.com) is a new, high-end resort hotel, with a series of rooms and private cottages with modern perks like flatscreen televisions and iPod docking stations. While **Ek' Tun** ★★ (✆ **820-3002;** www.ektunbelize.com) is a unique, isolated, and gorgeous retreat with just two individual cottages set on the banks of the Macal River, it can only be reached by boat.

Chaa Creek ★★★ (Finds) This is the premier lodging choice in this neck of the woods, and one of the nicest hotels in the country. Much loving care has gone into creating the beautiful grounds and cottages here. Located on a high, steep bank over the

Moments Los Finados

On November 2, the residents of Benque Viejo del Carmen celebrate **Los Finados,** a local version of El Día de los Muertos (The Day of the Dead), or All Souls' Day. Families visit the local cemetery, where graves are spruced up and adorned with flowers and votive candles. Many families set up a makeshift altar for their dead at home or on the front lawn. *Bollos* are prepared of cornmeal dough stuffed with chicken and a local purple bean, the *ixpelon.* Local children make jack-o-lanterns out of hollowed-out squash or even grapefruit. At night the cemetery is alight with the flicker from hundreds of candles.

Macal River, this is one of the lodges in the Cayo District, and it's only improved with age. All of the thatched-roof cottages are artistically decorated with local and Guatemalan textiles and handcrafts. Each comes with a quiet porch or balcony area set amid the flowering gardens. My favorite rooms are the large treetop suites, which feature a queen bed, a sunken living-room area, and a wraparound deck fitted with a sunken Jacuzzi.

By the time this book goes to press, there will be a new, outdoor pool and a new dining room. The lodge also has a lovely full-service spa, as well as an informative, but small, natural history museum, horse stables, and a Blue Morpho butterfly breeding project. Chaa Creek has also taken over the former Panti Medicine trail and the neighboring Ixchel Farm, which you can explore with a guide or with a self-guided trail map. Canoes and mountain bikes are available, and horseback rides can always be arranged. Over 250 bird species have been spotted within an 8km (5-mile) radius of the lodge. The guides here are well trained and knowledgeable. Mick and Lucy Fleming, who originally began farming this land in 1977, are the engaging hosts, and much of the food served in the restaurant is organically grown on the hotel's own farm.

Off the road to Benque Viejo (P.O. Box 53, San Ignacio), Cayo District. ✆ **824-2037** reservations office, or 820-4010 at the lodge. Fax 824-2501. www.chaacreek.com. 23 units. BZ$600 (US$300/£160) double; BZ$700–BZ$1,150 (US$350–US$575/£186–£305) suite or villa. AE, MC, V. To reach Chaa Creek, drive 5 miles (8km) west from San Ignacio and watch for the sign on your left. It's another couple of miles down a rough dirt road from the main highway. **Amenities:** Restaurant; bar; lounge; midsize outdoor pool; small, well-equipped spa; bike rental; tour desk; laundry service; free Wi-Fi; nonsmoking rooms. *In room:* No phone.

Mopan River Resort ★★ This lovely resort is set right on the banks of the Mopan River just across from the border town of Benque Viejo. In fact, you must reach the resort by crossing the river in the resort's little diesel-powered ferry. The individual bungalows are spread along the hotel's lush property lining the banks of the river, so all have a view of the flowing water. The bungalows are spacious, with high-pitched thatch roofs, varnished wood floors and walls, and plenty of dresser and closet space. I find the bathrooms a tad small and not quite up to the luxurious standards set throughout the rest of the operation. Quite a few of the units come with two twin beds, so if you want a true king-size bed, be sure to specify.

The resort is all-inclusive. Aside from a very limited number of entrance and border crossing fees (if you go to Tikal), and call liquor or wine, you should have virtually no out-of-pocket expenses beyond the hotel rates, which include all food, drinks, tips, tours, taxes, and transfers to and from the international airport. Still, this is not the place for independent and spontaneous travelers. Tours are scheduled on a fixed rotating basis. So, if you absolutely must visit Tikal, make sure it's on the rotation during your days there. Dinners are usually served buffet-style. Breakfasts are a la carte, and lunches are often packed lunches served during the day's tour or activity.

Riverside North, Benque Viejo del Carmen, Cayo District. ✆ **823-2047.** Fax 823-3272. www.mopanriverresort.com. 12 units. BZ$1,314–BZ$1,446 (US$657–US$723/£348–£383) per person for a 3-night package, double occupancy. Rates are all-inclusive. Rates higher during peak periods. The resort is closed July 1–Oct 27. Minimum 3-night stay. DISC, MC, V. **Amenities:** Restaurant; bar; lounge; outdoor pool; tour desk; laundry service; nonsmoking rooms. *In room:* A/C, TV, minibar, coffeemaker, hair dryer, safe, no phone.

Expensive

duPlooy's ★ This family-run lodge overlooks the Macal River, with jungle-covered limestone cliffs opposite. This stunning location, combined with personalized attention, makes duPlooy's one of Cayo's most popular jungle lodges. My favorite rooms here are the spacious bungalows, which come with a king-size bed, futon couch, and large wooden veranda. Another option is the Belize River House, two separate multiroom suites that can be rented separately, or as one huge unit sleeping up to 14 people. The lodge's open-air bar features a spacious deck overlooking the river. There's a beach on the river, as well as several trails through the forest. Horses and canoes are available for rent. One of the nicest features here, though, is an elevated walkway running at the level of the forest canopy, which connects much of the complex and also juts out into the forest, offering up wonderful opportunities for bird-watching. The neighboring **Belize Botanic Gardens ★★** provides even greater bird-watching opportunities, in addition to an abundance of tropical flora.

Off the road to Benque Viejo (P.O. Box 180, San Ignacio), Cayo District. ✆ **824-3101.** Fax 824-3301. www.duplooys.com. 19 units. BZ$360–BZ$450 (US$180–US$225/£95–£119) double; BZ$520–BZ$580 (US$260–US$290/£138–£154) casita or suite. Rates include breakfast. AE, MC, V. To get here, head out of town on the road to Benque Viejo; the turnoff for duPlooy's is the same as that for Chaa Creek, and it is well marked. DuPlooy's is a bit farther on the same dirt road, but be sure to take the right fork and follow the signs. **Amenities:** Restaurant; bar; lounge; small spa; tour desk; laundry service. *In room:* No phone.

Moderate

Black Rock Jungle River Lodge ★ Finds So, you *really* want to get away from it all? Well, this is the place. To reach Black Rock, you travel 9.7km (6 miles) down a dirt road and 1.6km (1 mile) alongside the Macal River. The setting, on a high bluff overlooking the Macal River, is one of the nicest in the area. Swimming and inner tubing on the river from the lodge are excellent. The deluxe cabanas are truly beautiful, with stone floors, two queen beds, plenty of large screened windows, and views of the valley and river below from a private veranda. The standard cabanas and shared bathroom units are quite comfortable and beautifully situated as well. Meals are served in the large open-air dining room and main lodge area, which also has a fabulous view of the river below and forests all around. A full meal plan here will run you BZ$84 (US$42/£22) per day. A host of tours and activities is offered, and the staff is very friendly and attentive.

Off the road to Benque Viejo (P.O. Box 48, San Ignacio), Cayo District. ✆ **824-2529** reservations office, or 820-3929 at the lodge. www.blackrocklodge.com. 14 units (1 with shared bathroom). BZ$140 (US$70/£37) double with shared bathroom; BZ$220–BZ$350 (US$110–US$175/£58–£93) double. Rates lower in the off season; higher during peak periods. MC, V. If you're driving, take the turnoff for Chaa Creek and duPlooy's, and then follow the signs to Black Rock. **Amenities:** Restaurant; tour desk; laundry service. *In room:* No phone.

Clarissa Falls Resort Clarissa Falls, which are really more rapids than waterfalls, and the jade-green waters of the Mopan River are the backdrop for this resort. Situated on a 324-hectare (800-acre) working cattle ranch, the resort boasts a range of accommodations from deluxe suites to individual cabins to campsites. The thatch-roof cabins are fairly basic, with cement floors, bamboo walls, simple beds, and little else. However, the spartan decor is more than compensated by the beautiful surroundings. The suites are nicely done and feature a full kitchen and dining area.

The open-air restaurant here serves excellent Belizean and Mexican cuisine for very reasonable prices, and sits atop a small Mayan ruin. Owner Chena Gálvez is extremely personable, and staff members can help arrange boats and inner-tube rentals; horseback riding is also available. If you'd like to just visit for the day, you can swim in the river and picnic for BZ$2 (US$1/53p), which is a very popular activity on weekends (if you crave peace and tranquillity, visit on a weekday).

Benque Viejo Rd., Mile Marker 70½ (P.O. Box 44, San Ignacio), Cayo District. ✆/fax **824-3916.** www.clarissafalls.com. 12 units. BZ$150 (US$75/£37) double; BZ$350 (US$175/£93) suite; BZ$15 (US$7.50/£4) per person to camp. MC, V. Clarissa Falls Resort is about 1.6km (1 mile) down a dirt road, off the highway about 6km (4 miles) west of San Ignacio. The bus to Benque Viejo will drop you at the turnoff. **Amenities:** Restaurant; tour desk; laundry service. *In room:* No phone.

Macal River Jungle Camp (Finds) Run by the folks at Chaa Creek, this deluxe campsite is a great choice for those who want to be close to nature, but like to have a few frills and easy accessibility. These spacious units are all set on raised platforms among the forest trees. Each comes with two to four single beds, as well as a couple of kerosene lanterns. There's a small sitting area or front porch, with an oil lamp and a couple of chairs. Meals are served in a central open thatched-roof structure, which also has some hammocks for hanging out. The communal bath and shower areas are clean and well maintained. The river is down a short path from the campsite; Rainforest Medicine Trail and Chaa Creek are nearby. Guests at the tent camp can rent canoes, head over for meals a la carte, or sign up for any tours offered at Chaa Creek. Overall, this is a pretty plush camping experience, but you may be asked to help wash your own dishes.

Off the road to Benque Viejo (P.O. Box 53, San Ignacio), Cayo District. ✆ **824-2037** reservations office, or 820-4010 at the lodge. Fax 824-2501. www.belizecamp.com. 10 tents. BZ$110 (US$55/£29) per person. Rates include breakfast and dinner. Rates slightly lower during the off season. AE, MC, V. **Amenities:** Restaurant; tour desk; laundry service. *In room:* No phone.

Inexpensive

The Trek Stop This rustic little outpost is geared towards backpackers and adventure travelers. The accommodations here are spread around a broad garden and backed by dense forest, and they range from campsites to simple cabins to a couple of newer cabins with private bathrooms. Most of the wooden cabins are quite small, but they do come with a private little front porch, where you can sit and read. Guests can either eat at the little restaurant here, or cook their own food in the communal kitchen. A wide range of tours and activities is offered, and inner tubing on the Mopan River is one of their specialties. They also have a 9-hole Frisbee golf course, which is free for guests and costs BZ$6 (US$3/£1.60) per person for visitors. This place is very close to the ferry over to Xunantunich. The Trek Stop is located next to the Tropical Wings Nature Center, just off the main road about 9.7km (6 miles) west of San Ignacio.

Benque Viejo Rd., Mile Marker 71½, San José Succotz, Cayo District. ✆ **823-2265.** www.thetrekstop.com. 10 units (8 with shared bathroom). BZ$76 (US$38/£20) double cabin; BZ$48–BZ$56 (US$24–US$28/£13–£15) double with shared bath; BZ$10 (US$5/£2.65) per person camping. MC, V. **Amenities:** Restaurant; mountain-bike rental; tour desk; laundry service; free Wi-Fi. *In room:* No phone.

On the Road to Bullet Tree Falls

El Pilar ★★ (✆ **824-3612;** www.marc.ucsb.edu/elpilar) was discovered in the 1970s, but real excavation and exploration didn't begin for another 20 years, and in fact it's still in its nascent stages. The site sits on a high hill some 274m (900 ft.) above the Mopan River and is one of the largest Mayan settlements in Belize. Some say it even rivals Caracol. This ancient ceremonial city featured over 25 known plazas and covered some 40 hectares (100 acres), straddling the Belize and Guatemala border. The site is quite large, but most visitors concentrate on Xaman Pilar (North Pilar) and Nohol Pilar (South Pilar). Pilar Poniente (West Pilar) is in Guatemala, a little less than a mile away. There are several well-marked and well-maintained trails through the site. While you can explore El Pilar by yourself—you can even download a very informative trail map from the above website—I still recommend hiring a local guide. Plan on spending at least 3 hours here, though you could easily spend a full day or two exploring this site. The sunsets from Plaza Ixim looking west to Pilar Poniente and the forested hills of Guatemala are spectacular.

El Pilar is located about 19km (12 miles) north of San Ignacio, past the village of Bullet Tree Falls. In addition to driving your own vehicle, several tour agencies in San Ignacio offer horseback or mountain-bike tours out to El Pilar.

A Place to Stay in Bullet Tree Falls

In addition to the place listed below, folks love **Cohune Palms River Cabanas** (✆ **824-0166;** www.cohunepalms.com), which has a collection of thatch-roofed cabins on the banks of the Mopan River. **Casa del Caballo Blanco** (✆ **707/974-4942** in the U.S.; www.casacaballoblanco.com) is the new kid in town, with neat, cozy rooms, just on the outskirts of downtown.

Parrot's Nest Located 4.8km (3 miles) outside of San Ignacio and operated by Fred Prost, who once ran the popular Seaside Guest House in Belize City, the Parrot's Nest features some of the more unique rooms in the Cayo District. Set on a 2-hectare (5-acre) tropical plant farm on the banks of the Mopan River, this simple lodge consists of a few rustic wooden cabins. Two of these are set high on stilts, amongst the branches of a huge guanacaste tree. Only one of the units has a private bathroom, but the shared showers and toilets are kept immaculate. A host of tours and activities can be arranged. You can also take an inner tube right from the lodge and spend some time floating on the river.

Bullet Tree Falls (P.O. Box 198, San Ignacio), Cayo District. ✆ **820-4058.** www.parrot-nest.com. 6 units (5 with shared bathroom). BZ$80–BZ$90 (US$40–US$45/£21–£24) double. MC, V. To get here, take Waight's Ave. west out of the center of San Ignacio. This turns into Bullet Tree Falls Rd. If you arrange it in advance, the owners will often provide pickup, or a taxi should cost you around BZ$20 (US$10/£5). **Amenities:** Restaurant; mountain-bike rental; tour desk; laundry service. *In room:* No phone.

3 MOUNTAIN PINE RIDGE & CARACOL ★★

111km (69 miles) W of Belize City

South of San Ignacio and the Western Highway lies the Mountain Pine Ridge region of Belize. Few people think of pine trees when thinking about the tropics—but you'll see plenty of them in these rugged mountains. This area is a natural wonderland of spectacular waterfalls, wild orchids, parrots, keel-billed toucans, and other exotic flora and fauna. **Mountain Pine Ridge Forest Reserve, Hidden Valley Falls** (also called Thousand Foot Falls), **Five Sisters Falls,** and the **Río on Pools** and **Río Frío Caves** are all located in this area.

Continuing on through the Mountain Pine Ridge, you'll eventually come to **Caracol,** which is the largest of the Belizean Mayan ruins. Caracol was a major Classic Mayan center, rivaling and frequently battling nearby Tikal. Excavation is still in its infancy here, but the site is nonetheless impressive. At nearly 42m (140 ft.), the main pyramid at Caracol remains the tallest man-made structure in Belize.

In 2000 and 2001 a pine beetle infestation ravaged the forests of the Mountain Pine Ridge reserve, killing as much as 60% of the total forest and leaving broad swaths totally barren with little more than rotting trunks sticking straight up for miles. The forests here have recovered well. Still, you will still notice some of the effects of this plague in different parts of the Mountain Pine Ridge area.

ESSENTIALS

Getting There & Departing

BY PLANE The nearest airport to this region is in San Ignacio. Although it gets no regularly scheduled commuter traffic, there is a private airstrip at Blancaneaux Lodge (p. 254) for charter flights to that hotel.

BY CAR If you're driving to the Mountain Pine Ridge area from Belize City along the Western Highway, the first turnoff is at Georgeville, around Mile Marker 61. This is the quickest route if you're going deep into the Mountain Pine Ridge area and to Caracol. There's another turnoff in the town of Santa Elena that will take you through Cristo Rey and San Antonio villages, as well as to some of the lodges listed below. Whichever of these routes you take, the roads merge around Mile Marker 10, where you will come to the entrance to the Mountain Pine Ridge Forest Reserve. The guard will ask you where you are going, and if you have a reservation, but there is no fee to enter the reserve.

These roads can get pretty muddy and slick in the wet season and are bumpy and rugged in the dry season, so I strongly recommend you have a four-wheel-drive vehicle, if nothing else for the extra clearance it will provide. Even though the distances seem relatively slight in terms of mileage, the going can be slow, so allow plenty of driving time if you plan on visiting this area.

Tip: The difference in time and distance between these two turnoffs is negligible, as they meet up about 14km (9 miles) in from the Western Highway (19km/12 miles if you're coming via Cristo Rey Village and San Antonio Village).

BY BUS There is no regular direct bus service to the Mountain Pine Ridge area from Belize City.

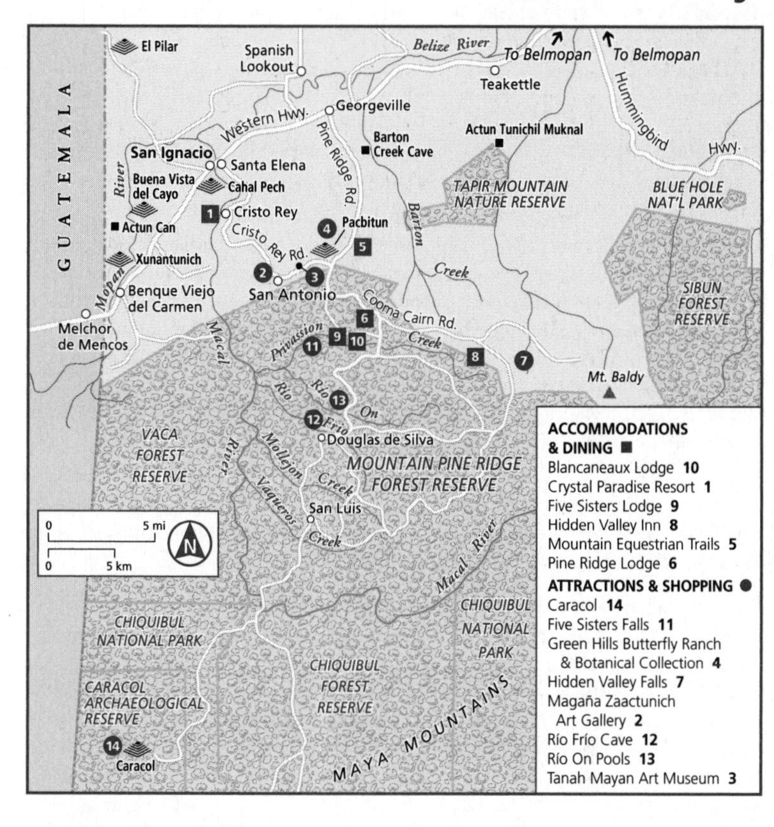

Getting Around

Your best bet for getting around this area is to have your own vehicle. Short of that, you can rely on your hotel or organized tours. Taxis can be called from San Ignacio and Santa Elena. For a cab, call **Cayo Taxi Association** at © **824-2196.** A cab from San Ignacio to any of the hotels in this area cost around BZ$80 to BZ$120 (US$40–US$60/£21–£32), and a cab from Philip S. W. Goldson International Airport in Belize City to a hotel in this area costs between BZ$240 and BZ$300 (US$120–US$150/£64–£80).

Orientation

Once the two entrance roads join up, there is basically one "major" road leading through the Mountain Pine Forest Reserve and on out to the Caracol ruins. This rough dirt road is alternately known as the Pine Ridge Road or the Chiquibil Road. Caracol, the Río on Pools, Río Frío Cave, and Five Sister Falls, are located either right on or just off this road. Various spurs and assorted lesser roads head off towards some of the other attractions and destinations listed below. Everything is fairly well marked and signposted.

There are no major settlements in this area. The only town of any size and note is San Antonio Village, a quaint little Maya village.

WHAT TO SEE & DO

The easiest way to visit Mountain Pine Ridge and its many attractions is on a guided tour out of San Ignacio or one of the nearby lodges. These tours average between BZ$50 and BZ$100 (US$25–US$50/£13–£27) per person for a half-day tour of Mountain Pine Ridge and a visit to one of the waterfalls, and about BZ$180 to BZ$280 (US$90–US$140/£48–£74) for a full-day guided trip to Caracol with lunch. If you're staying in Mountain Pine Ridge, just arrange the tour with your hotel. If you're in San Ignacio, check in with **Cayo Adventure Tours** (✆ **824-3246;** www.cayoadventure.com) or **Yute Expeditions** ★ (✆ **824-2076;** www.inlandbelize.com).

HORSEBACK RIDING The terrain here is wonderful for horseback riding. Most horseback tours will take you to one or more of the major attractions in this area, or at least to some quiet swimming hole or isolated waterfall. Most of the hotels out here offer horseback riding tours. Alternatively, you can contact the folks at **Mountain Equestrian Trails** (✆ **669-1124;** www.metbelize.com), who have one of the better stables and horse riding operations in the Cayo District. A half-day trip including lunch costs BZ$122 (US$61/£32) per person; a full-day trip costs BZ$166 (US$83/£44).

MOUNTAIN BIKING This region lends itself equally well to mountain biking. The same trails and dirt roads that are used by cars and horses are especially well suited for fat-tire explorations. Most of the hotels in the region have bikes for rent or free for guests. If not, you'll probably have to have them arrange it for you, or contact an agency in San Ignacio (see "San Ignacio," earlier in this chapter).

Will Natural Wonders Never Cease?

WATERFALLS Waterfalls are abundant in this region. Perhaps my favorite are the falls found at the **Río on Pools** ★★. This is a series of falls and pools somewhat reminiscent of Ocho Ríos in Jamaica. There's a little entrance hut and parking lot when you enter the area. From here, some concrete steps lead straight down a very steep hill to the base of the falls. While the views and swimming are fine at the bottom, it's a very strenuous hike back up, and I personally think you'll find better pools and views by hiking a few minutes upstream. Here you'll find numerous pools and rapids flowing between big rocks. Many of these rocks are perfect for sunbathing. This place can get crowded on weekends, when locals come for family picnics and getaways. The Río on Pools are located at around Mile Marker 18½ of the Pine Ridge Road. There is no entrance fee.

You can also visit the **Five Sister Falls** ★★, a lovely series of cascading falls that divides into five distinct side-by-side cascades just above the riverside beach and bar area of the Five Sisters Lodge (p. 254). If you are not staying at the lodge, you may visit the falls for BZ$5 (US$2.50/£1.35). For an extra charge of BZ$6 (US$3/£1.60), a funicular will take you to and from the base of the falls, where the hotel has a little beach area and several natural swimming holes. There are some nature trails you can hike, and a small snack bar, restrooms, and changing facilities. You'll even find a wonderful open-air thatch palapa on the banks of the river strung with hammocks—a compelling spot for an afternoon siesta.

RIO FRIO CAVE This high, vaulted cave is about 183m (600 ft.) long and open at both ends, with a lazy creek flowing through it. There's a path leading through the cave, and several hiking trails through the forests surrounding it. This is a good cave for those who might normally find the thought of spelunking too claustrophobic for comfort. The views looking out from within the cave are gorgeous. Along the neighboring trails you

Fun Facts **Sky Scraper**

The largest pyramid at Caracol, **Caana** or "Sky Palace," stands some 41m (136 ft.) high, and is the tallest Maya building in Belize, and still the tallest man-made structure in the country (the Radisson Fort George in Belize City is the only modern structure that even comes close).

will find other caves that you can venture into. However, be careful and be sure to have a good flashlight. To reach the Río Frío Cave, drive the Pine Ridge Road to Douglas Da Silva Village at about Mile Marker 24. Do not follow the turnoff for Caracol, but head into the little village. Here you will see signs for the turnoff to the cave. The cave is about 1.6km (1 mile) outside the village. There's a small parking area very close to the mouth of the cave and a couple of picnic tables and benches along the river. No admission is charged to visit here.

BUTTERFLIES The **Green Hills Butterfly Ranch & Botanical Collection** (**© 820-4017;** www.green-hills.net) is a lovely little project affording you the chance to see numerous butterfly species and a range of tropical flora. These folks raise dozens of local species of butterflies, and visitors get to see them up close and personal. This place is located at around Mile Marker 8 of the Pine Ridge Road, across from Mountain Equestrian Trails. Guided tours (BZ$10/US$5/£2.65) are offered daily, between 8am and 3:30pm. Reservations are recommended.

Caracol ★★

Caracol (www.caracol.org) is the largest known Mayan archaeological site in Belize, and one of the great Mayan city-states of the Classic era (A.D. 250–950). At one point, Caracol supported a population of over 150,000. Caracol, which means "shell" in Spanish, gets its name from the large number of snail shells found here during early explorations. So far three main plazas with numerous structures and two ball courts have been excavated.

Caracol has revealed a wealth of informative carved glyphs that have allowed archaeologists to fill in much of the history of this once powerful city-state. Glyphs here claim Caracol defeats of rivals Tikal in A.D. 562 and Naranjo in 631. One of the earliest temples here was built in A.D. 70, and the Caracol royal family has been officially chronicled since 331. The last recorded date on a glyph is 859, and archaeologists conclude that by 1050 Caracol had been completely abandoned.

Caracol is located deep within the Chiquibil Forest Reserve. The ruins are not nearly as well cleared nor excavated as Tikal or Xunantunich. However, this is part of the site's charm. There is great bird-watching and the chance to see other wild fauna out here. Moreover, the area has been declared the **Caracol Archaeological Reserve,** and excavation and restoration are ongoing. A visit to Caracol is often combined with a stop at the Río on Pools, or one or more of the other attractions in the Mountain Pine Ridge area.

Caracol is open daily from 8am to 4pm; admission is BZ$15 (US$7.50/£4). There's a small visitor center at the entrance, and a guide can sometimes be hired here, although most visitors come with their own guide as part of an organized tour. Caracol is about 80km (50 miles) along a dirt road from the Western Highway. Actually, the final 16km (10 miles) into the park are paved. Plan on the drive taking about 2 hours, a little more if the road is in bad shape.

If you're in the area, be sure to stop at the **Tanah Mayan Art Museum★** (✆ **824-3310;** daily 8am–5pm), run by the García Sisters, some of the premier artisans working in carved slate. While it's a stretch to call their little shop and showroom a museum, you will find a nice collection of the García sisters' carvings, as well as other Maya artifacts and handicrafts. This place is located at about Mile Marker 8 of the Cristo Rey Road, about a mile before you reach the village of San Antonio. Inside the village, you should stop at the **Magaña Zaactunich Art Gallery** (no phone), which carries a range of local craftworks and specializes in woodcarvings.

WHERE TO STAY & DINE

Very Expensive

Blancaneaux Lodge ★★★ Finds This remote lodge was built with style and grace, which is fitting, as the owner is director Francis Ford Coppola. The lodge is set on a steep, pine-forested hillside, overlooking the Privassion River and a series of gentle falls. The individual cabanas here are all comfortable and intimate, with wood floors, a private balcony or deck, and a mix of furnishings and decorations from around the world that blend together in a sort of chic world fusion. Most of these cabanas are "riverfront" units, although a couple are termed "garden view." My favorite cabanas are the riverfront "honeymoon" units, which have private plunge pools. Most of the villas are two-bedroom, two-bathroom affairs. The best feature of these is their large, open-air central living area, which flows into a forest- and river-view deck. Villa 7 is Coppola's private villa whenever he visits, and it features some of the director's photo memorabilia, as well as a painting by his daughter and fellow director Sofia Coppola. You can rent it whenever he's not around, and it also comes with a private plunge pool and a personal butler. The newest additions here are a midsize pool up near the main lodge and the luxurious private "Enchanted Cottage" a short distance from everything else, which has a great view, an infinity pool, and personal butler service, as well.

The main restaurant serves excellent Italian and international cuisine, and there's a separate, more intimate restaurant specializing in Guatemalan cuisine. A wide range of tours and activities is offered. There's a small spa here, with a large horseshoe-shaped Jacuzzi, and a wooden massage room set on the banks of the river. The masseuses are from Thailand and provide Thai massage, alongside a host of other treatments.

Mountain Pine Ridge Reserve (P.O. Box B, Central Farm), Cayo District. ✆ **800/746-3743** in the U.S., 824-4912 reservations office in Belize, or 824-3878 at the lodge. Fax 824-3919. www.blancaneaux.com. 20 units. BZ$520–BZ$990 (US$260–US$495/£138–£262) double cabin; BZ$1,000–BZ$1,350 (US$500–US$675/£265–£358) 2-bdrm villa; BZ$2,000 (US$1,000/£530). Rates include continental breakfast. Rates lower in the off season; higher during peak weeks. AE, MC, V. Blancaneaux has its own airstrip, and charter flights from Belize City can be arranged. **Amenities:** Restaurant; bar; lounge; outdoor pool; small spa; bike rental; horse stables; tour desk; laundry service. *In room:* Free Wi-Fi, safe, no phone.

Expensive

Five Sisters Lodge ★ This hotel is located in the heart of the Mountain Pine Ridge Reserve, about 61m (200 ft.) above its namesake Five Sisters Falls, a beautiful and rambling series of waterfalls and swimming holes. The individual cottages have palmetto stick walls, thatched roofs, and beds hung with mosquito netting. Some have polished wood floors, while others feature cool Mexican tiles. All have a mix of local and Guatemalan furnishings and decor, as well as a screened-in veranda hung with a hammock. The

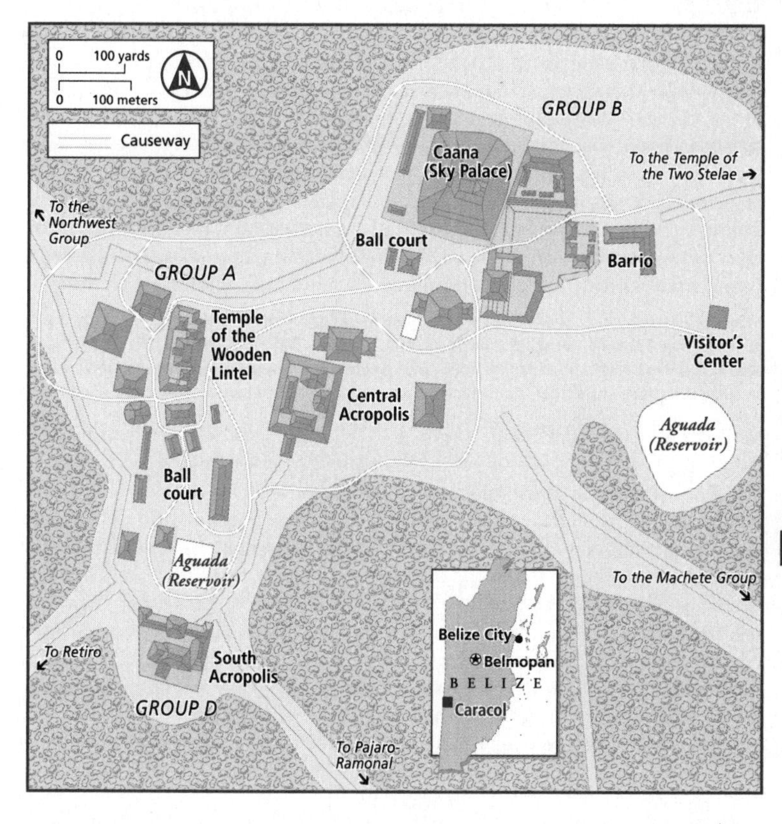

junior suites feature excellent waterfall views, king-size beds, and large tubs. The standard rooms are comfortable enough, but most lack a view or balcony. The best room here, although it's a good distance from the main lodge, is the Riverside Villa, a luxurious cabin set down by the river and falls.

Even if you don't stay in the Riverside Villa, you'll certainly want to check out the river and falls. It's 290 steps, almost straight down, to the water and the base of the falls. Luckily, you don't have to hoof it, unless you want to, since they have a little funicular. Down there, you'll find a snack bar, a small riverside beach, an open-air rancho strung with hammocks, and countless secluded swimming holes just a short walk up or down the river.

Mountain Pine Ridge (P.O. Box 173, San Ignacio), Cayo District. ✆ **800/447-2931** in the U.S., or 820-4005. Fax 820-4024. www.fivesisterslodge.com. 19 units. BZ$210–BZ$290 (US$105–US$145/£56–£77) double; BZ$300 (US$150/£80) junior suite; BZ$500 (US$250/£133) Riverside Villa. Rates include continental breakfast. Rates lower in the off season. AE, MC, V. **Amenities:** Restaurant; bar; lounge; tour desk; laundry service. *In room:* No phone.

Hidden Valley Inn ★★ This isolated mountain resort has a beautiful setting on over 2,833 hectares (7,000 acres) of private land. The individual bungalows are all plenty roomy, and come with either one queen bed or two twin beds, as well as cool red-tile floors, high ceilings, a couple of plush sitting chairs, and a working fireplace. The outdoor pool and Jacuzzi are surrounded by a beautiful slate deck. This is the closest hotel to the Hidden Valley, or Thousand Foot Falls, the tallest waterfall in Belize, a semi-strenuous 2-hour hike from the hotel. However, there are actually several other, much more easily accessible, jungle waterfalls and swimming holes right on the property. The property also boasts an extensive network of trails, and the bird-watching is excellent. This is a great place to explore by mountain bike, and the hotel provides them free for guest use. A meal plan will run you BZ$120 (US$60/£32) per person per day. The coffee you're served at breakfast is grown right here, as are many of the fruits and vegetables.

Mountain Pine Ridge (P.O. Box 170, Belmopan), Cayo District. ✆ **866/443-3364** in the U.S., or 822-3320 in Belize. Fax 822-3334. www.hiddenvalleyinn.com. 12 units. BZ$388 (US$194/£103) double. Rates slightly lower in the off season; higher during peak periods. MC, V. **Amenities:** Restaurant; bar; lounge; small outdoor pool; Jacuzzi; free mountain-bike use; tour desk; laundry service. *In room:* No phone.

Mountain Equestrian Trails (MET) ★ This lodge is set in a very lush patch of forest, and the folks here are some of the best horse- and adventure-tour operators in the area. The rooms are decidedly rustic and a bit pricey for what you get. Housed in a series of duplex buildings, all feature high thatched roofs, cool tile floors, queen beds hung with mosquito netting, and plenty of windows for cross-ventilation. The rooms do feature colorful Guatemalan bedspreads and indigenous arts and crafts on the walls. There's no electricity in the rooms, and kerosene lanterns provide light. A much better bargain are the large safari-style tents, which feature two little single beds, a nightstand to hold your lantern, and a small throw rug. A large open-air palapa serves as the lodge's restaurant, bar, and meeting area. While horses and horseback riding tours are the principal draw here, a whole range of tours and activities is offered. The owners at MET helped create the private Slate Creek Preserve, a 1,214-hectare (3,000-acre) tract of land bordering the Mountain Pine Ridge Preserve. A meal package here costs BZ$78 (US$39/£21) per person per day.

Pine Ridge Rd., Cayo District. ✆ **800/838-3918** in the U.S., or 669-1124. Fax 822-3361. www.metbelize.com. 10 units. BZ$264 (US$132/£70) double. Rates lower in the off season. AE, MC, V. **Amenities:** Restaurant; bar; tour desk; laundry service. *In room:* No phone.

Moderate

Crystal Paradise Resort The nicest thing about this little family-run resort is probably the Tut Family that runs it. Most of the rooms are in thatch-roof duplex buildings, with tile floors, ceiling fans, and private verandas. The best rooms face the Macal River Valley, with beautiful views of the surrounding forests. They've been doing a lot of new building and renovation here in recent years, and the work shows. One recent addition is a bird-watching platform built to blend in with the forest canopy. A host of tours is offered, and the in-house guides—most of them family members—are excellent. The restaurant serves wonderful Belizean cuisine, and there's always a convivial vibe in the open-air dining room, bar, and lounge areas. This place is located on the road to Mountain Pine Ridge, near the tiny Cristo Rey Village.

Cristo Rey Village (P.O. Box 126), Cayo District. ✆/fax **824-2772** reservations office or 820-4014 at the lodge. www.crystalparadise.com. 17 units. BZ$170–BZ$250 (US$85–US$125/£45–£66) double. Rates include breakfast and dinner. AE, MC, V. **Amenities:** Restaurant; bar; lounge; tour desk; laundry service. *In room:* No phone.

Pine Ridge Lodge This rustic little lodge is located in the heart of the Mountain Pine Ridge area, close to all attractions. Most of the rooms are in duplex units, with polished concrete floors, simple wooden furniture, and local and Guatemalan crafts and textiles completing the decor. Light in the rooms is provided by kerosene lanterns, and the showers are heated by on-demand butane heaters. The grounds are loaded with a wide variety of orchids and attract an equally wide variety of bird species. The lodge is set on the banks of a small creek, and the best rooms are close to and overlooking this creek. There's also a small waterfall an easy hike from the lodge. Meals are served family-style in the small screened-in dining room and bar area.

Mountain Pine Ridge (P.O. Box 128, San Ignacio), Cayo District. ✆ **800/316-0706** in the U.S., or 606-4557. www.pineridgelodge.com. 6 units. BZ$198 (US$99/£52) double. Rates lower in the off season. Rates include continental breakfast. No credit cards. **Amenities:** Restaurant; bar; tour desk; laundry service. *In room:* No phone.

11

Tikal & Guatemala's Petén

Occupying the entire northeastern section of Guatemala, the Petén is Guatemala's largest and least populated province. Most of the Petén is forest—thick tropical rainforest. It is a lush and wild landscape that contains some of Mesoamerica's richest archaeological treasures. In 1990, the government of Guatemala officially established the **Maya Biosphere Reserve,** a tract of 1 million hectares (2.5 million acres) that includes most of the Petén Province. Moreover, the Maya Biosphere Reserve adjoins the neighboring **Calakmul Biosphere Reserve** in Mexico and the **Río Bravo Conservation Area** in Belize, comprising a joint protected area of over 2 million hectares (5 million acres).

The Petén Province is home to perhaps the most impressive and best preserved of the ancient Mayan ceremonial cities, **Tikal.** It is also home to numerous other lesser, and less excavated, sites. In addition, the area is a rich and rewarding destination for bird-watchers and ecotourists. Given the close proximity of Tikal to the Belize border (and the long distance between Guatemala City and the Petén), it is in some ways more convenient to visit Tikal from Belize than it is from Guatemala. This chapter will give you all the necessary information to plan a visit to this fascinating destination, whether you want to take a quick 1-day tour of the ruins at Tikal or a multiday adventure exploring the region.

1 TIKAL ★★★

100km (62 miles) NW of the Belize border; 65km (40 miles) N of Flores

Tikal is the greatest of the surviving Classic Maya cities. It is estimated that Tikal once supported a population of about 100,000 people. Archaeologists have identified over 3,000 structures, and in its heyday, the city probably covered as much as 65 sq. km (25 sq. miles). Tikal is far more extensively excavated than any ruins in Belize, and unlike the grand cities and excavations in Mexico, Tikal rises out of dense jungle. The pyramids here are some of the most perfect examples of ceremonial architecture in the Maya world. Standing atop Temple IV, you are high above the rainforest canopy. The peaks of several temples poke through the dense vegetation. Toucans and parrots fly about, and the loudest noise you'll hear is the guttural call of howler monkeys.

Tikal is within easy reach of Belize's western border, and scores of organized tour groups and independent travelers from Belize visit the site every day.

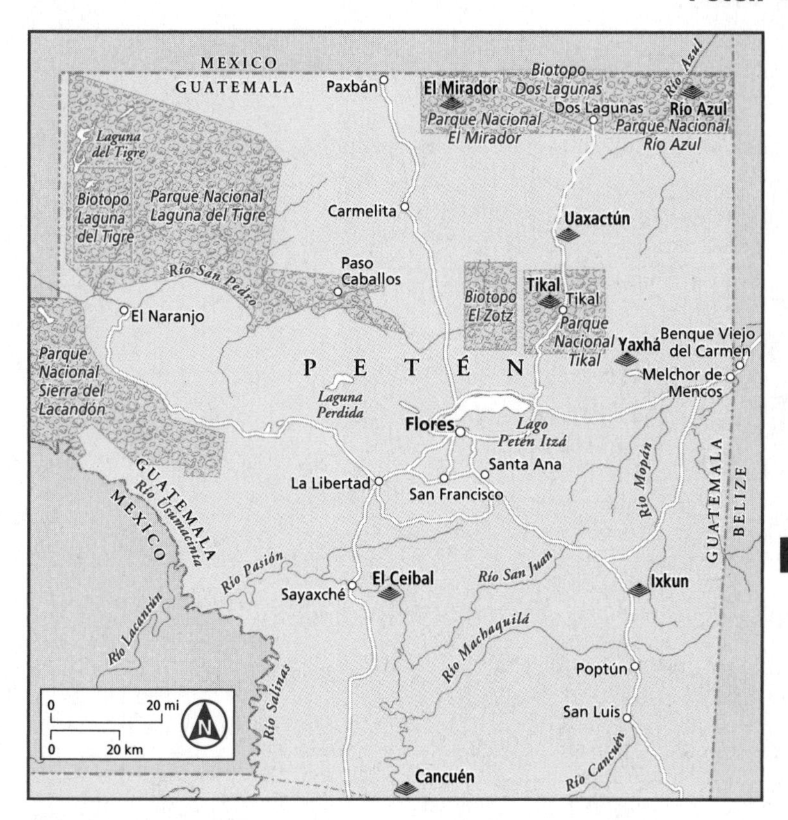

ESSENTIALS

Getting There & Departing

BY PLANE It is no longer possible to fly directly from Belize to Tikal. In 2007, for reasons related to airport and airline technical standards, Guatemala suspended the permission for **Maya Island Air** (✆ **223-1140;** www.mayaairways.com) and **Tropic Air** (✆ **800/422-3435** in the U.S. or Canada; www.tropicair.com) flights to land at the Maya International Airport (airport code: FRS) just outside of Flores. In the past, both airlines had regular daily service, and it's worth checking before you go if the service has resumed.

BY CAR Driving from Belize City, take the Western Highway to San Ignacio, and continue on to the border town of Benque Viejo del Carmen. From Benque, follow the signs to the border at a bridge over the Mopan River, a little over 1.6km (1 mile) out of town.

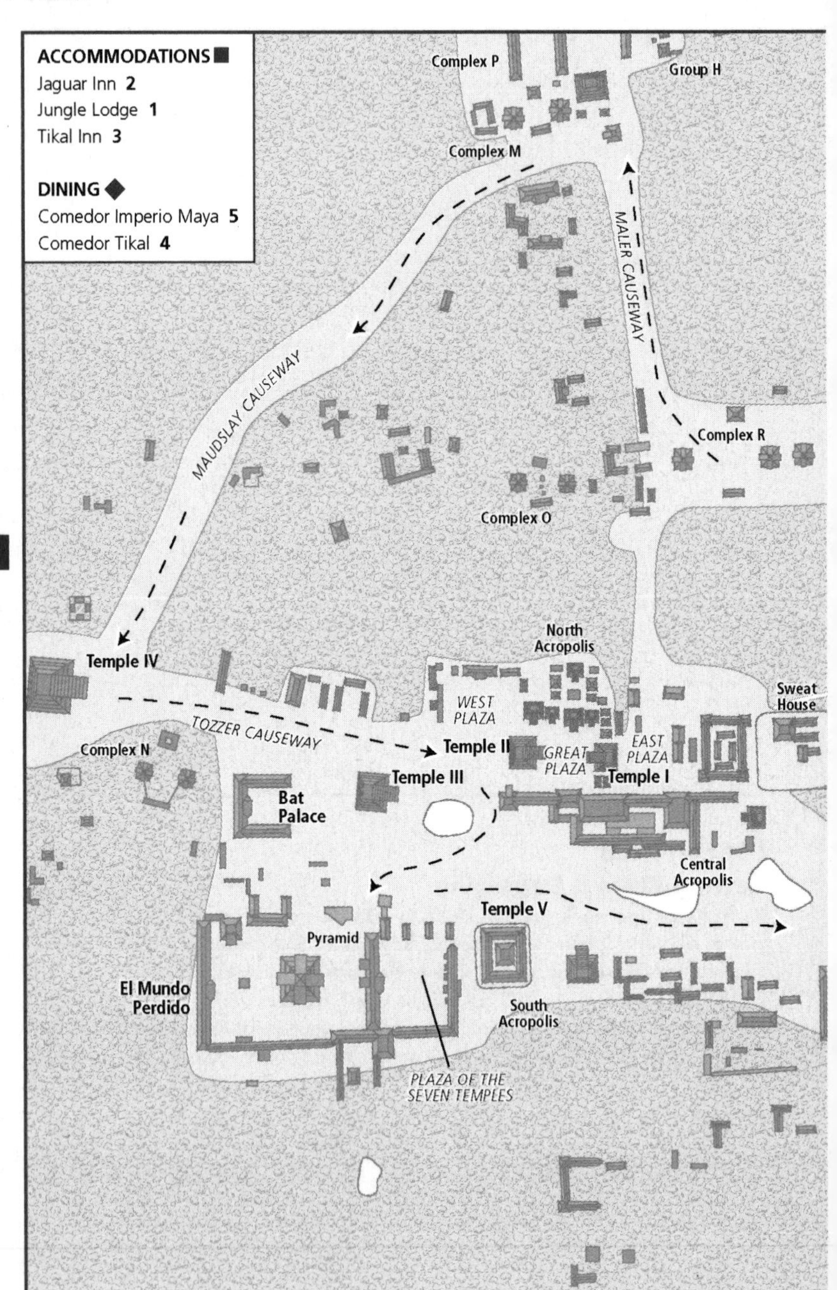
ACCOMMODATIONS
Jaguar Inn 2
Jungle Lodge 1
Tikal Inn 3
DINING
Comedor Imperio Maya 5
Comedor Tikal 4
Complex P
Group H
Complex M
MALER CAUSEWAY
MAUDSLAY CAUSEWAY
Complex R
Complex O
North Acropolis
Temple IV
Sweat House
WEST PLAZA
TOZZER CAUSEWAY
Temple II
GREAT PLAZA
EAST PLAZA
Temple I
Complex N
Temple III
Bat Palace
Central Acropolis
Temple V
Pyramid
El Mundo Perdido
South Acropolis
PLAZA OF THE SEVEN TEMPLES

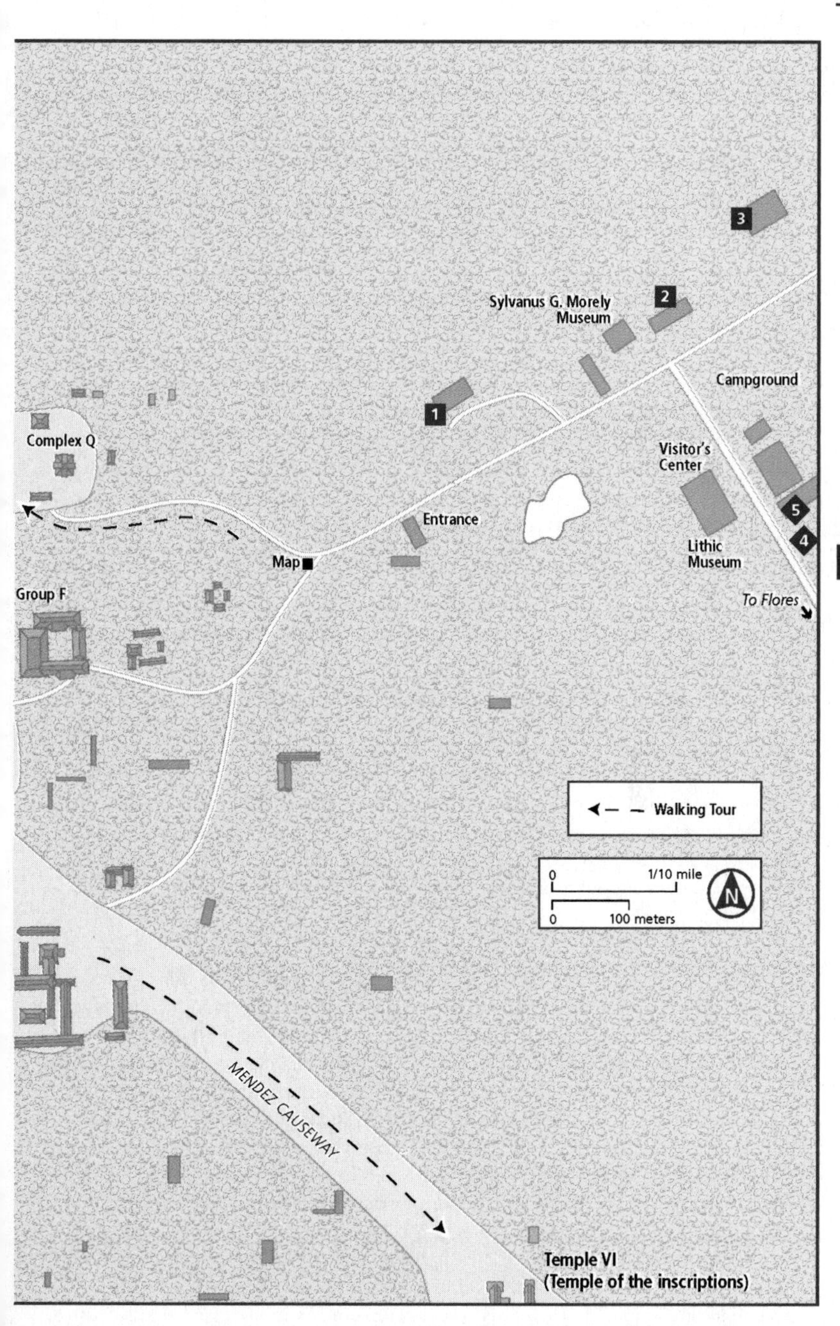
3
2
Sylvanus G. Morely
Museum
Campground
1
Complex Q
Visitor's
Center
5
4
Entrance
Lithic
Museum
Map
Group F
To Flores
Walking Tour
0
1/10 mile
0
100 meters
N
MENDEZ CAUSEWAY
Temple VI
(Temple of the inscriptions)

Telephone Tip

Guatemala's country code is **502** (Belize's is 501). Guatemala uses an 8-digit phone numbering system. Nonetheless, to avoid confusion between Belizean and Guatemalan telephone numbers, we have included the country code in the Guatemalan numbers, whereas in this section and throughout the book, we've omitted the Belizean country code in phone number listings.

The border crossing and formalities are very similar to those described below in "By Bus." You will be corralled by touts on the Guatemalan side offering all sorts of aid and services, and demanding all sorts of fees and duties. By law you are supposed to have your tires fumigated. This should only cost a U.S. dollar or two. You should not have to pay any additional fees. Whether you are driving your own car or a rental car, be sure to have all your current registration, title, and insurance papers.

Once across the border, follow signs out of Melchor de Mencos towards Flores and Tikal. It's about a 1-hour drive to the crossroads at Ixlú, also known as El Cruce. If you are going to El Remate or Tikal, you will turn right here. If you are going to Flores or Santa Elena, you will continue on straight. From Ixlú, it's about 25 to 30 minutes either way to Santa Elena/Flores or the ruins at Tikal. The entrance to Tikal National Park is located 18km (11 miles) south of the visitor center and true entrance to the ruins and its network of trails. Here you will have to pay the Q150 (US$20/£11) entrance fee. The entrance is open daily from 6am to 6pm. If you arrive after 3pm, tell them you plan to visit the ruins the following day, and they will stamp your ticket to that effect. If you plan to spend more than a day here staying at one of the hotels or campsites near the ruins, advise them and try to pay your entrance fee for subsequent days in advance, as sometimes they send people all the way back to the entrance gate to buy a subsequent day's ticket.

If you're traveling in a rental car, be sure that the company you rented from in Belize allows the car to cross into Guatemala. **Crystal Auto Rental** (✆ **0800/777-7777** in Belize; www.crystal-belize.com) does.

Beware: It is strongly advised that you do not travel at night. It is a sad fact that armed groups occasionally set up roadblocks along these isolated yet frequently trafficked roads.

BY BUS If you're traveling from Belize City by bus, you can take one of two daily buses. These buses run between Belize City and Santa Elena, not the Tikal ruins. If you're coming from Belize City, you'll have to get further transportation to visit Tikal. The buses leave at 9:30am and 2:30pm from right in front of the Marine Terminal in downtown Belize City. The fare is BZ$40 (US$20/£11) one-way. The trip takes around 6 hours. The return buses leave Flores/Santa Elena at 5 and 7:30am. Two separate bus lines make this trip run by the **Línea Dorada** (✆ **502/7926-0070;** www.tikalmayanworld.com) and **San Juan Travel** (✆ **502/7926-0042;** sanjuantravel@hotmail.com.gt). Both can be contacted in Belize at ✆ 223-0457 and 223-1235, respectively.

Alternatively, you can take one of the many buses from Belize City (or from San Ignacio) to the Guatemalan border. Buses to San Ignacio leave roughly every half-hour from the main bus station on West Collet Canal Street between 5am and 8pm. Return buses to Belize City leave the main bus station in San Ignacio roughly every half-hour between 4am and 6pm. The fare is BZ$10 (US$5/£2.65). The trip takes 2½ hours. Most

Safety in Guatemala

Over the past 50 years Guatemala has had an ongoing history of political and civil violence and repression. Crime, both petty and violent, is a problem throughout Guatemala. The Guatemalan police and judiciary are underfunded, understaffed, and largely ineffectual. Decades of civil war, genocide, and paramilitary activity in addition to historic poverty and underdevelopment have created a dangerous climate where lawlessness is rampant. Foreign nationals—as well as everyday Guatemalans—are the targets of robberies, kidnapping, murders, and rapes. The U.S. State Department strongly cautions visitors to Guatemala and keeps a relatively up-to-date analysis of the situation at **http://travel.state.gov**.

Luckily, the Petén District, where Tikal is located, is a largely isolated and forgotten section of eastern Guatemala. The most common attacks against tourists visiting Tikal occur on the road between the Belizean border and Flores. Taxis, local buses, and air-conditioned minivans have all been targeted. These highway robberies tend to occur in waves, and are by far the exception and not the norm. In almost all known cases, the attacks are armed but nonviolent robberies. If you plan to visit Tikal for a few days as a side trip from Belize, it is often a good idea to find a hotel safe in Belize that will guard any valuables you do not need with you while in Guatemala.

Still, hundreds of tourists visit Tikal and Flores every day, and the vast majority of them have no problems whatsoever. Be sure to take all necessary precautions. Never travel alone or at night, and stick to the most popular and populous tourist destinations and attractions. If you are driving, only stop for people holding guns; do not try to run blockades. Common wisdom cautions against using the low-fare Guatemalan buses and tour agencies; however, high-end tour groups in fancy air-conditioned microbuses do attract the attention of organized criminal gangs. Some tour groups travel with armed guards. This may or may not increase your sense of security and your actual security, to boot. (As far as I'm concerned, the jury is out on that one.) If you are confronted with any sort of criminal attempt, do not resist, as a simple mugging can easily end up turning into murder.

In 2005, the Guatemalan Tourist Institute (INGUAT) and National Police beefed up the special police force, POLITUR, created to patrol tourist destinations and deal directly with tourists. You will hopefully see them present in most major tourist destinations, including Tikal and Flores. You can also call ASISTUR, a tourist assistance service of INGUAT, by dialing ✆ **1500** from any phone in the country.

of the western-bound buses continue on beyond San Ignacio to Benque Viejo and the Guatemalan border. Some of these leave you in Benque Viejo, while others go all the way to the border crossing, a little over 1.6km (1 mile) away. There are numerous taxis at the Benque Viejo bus station that will take you to the border for BZ$6 (US$3/£1.60).

 **Shameless Plug**

If you're going on to Guatemala for any extended time or travel, you'll want to pick up a copy of *Frommer's Guatemala*.

On the Belize side, you will have to fill out a departure card, have your passport stamped, and pay the departure tax of BZ$30 (US$15/£7.95), plus the BZ$7.50 (US$3.75/£1.90) PACT tax. Just over the bridge lies the Guatemalan border town of Melchor de Mencos. When you pass through Guatemalan immigration, you will be provided with a tourist card good for up to 90 days. Theoretically this card is free. However, border formalities in Guatemala are often open to corruption, with border officials and local touts looking to glean some extra money. Moreover, Guatemalan border formalities change from time to time, and there is a running dispute between Guatemala and Belize (Guatemala claims that all of Belize is actually part of Guatemala, dating back to the mid–19th c.), so it always pays to check with the Guatemalan Embassy in your home country if you are certain you will be traveling there. The border crossing can take from 20 minutes to over an hour, depending on the crowds.

Once finished with the border formalities, it is a simple matter to find onward transportation to Tikal or Flores and Santa Elena. The least expensive means of transport is the local bus; however, none of the local buses go directly to Tikal. Instead, they head to Flores and Santa Elena, but they will drop you off at Ixlú (El Cruce), where you can flag down one of the many minivans and collective taxis going from Flores and Santa Elena to the ruins. Be forewarned that while local buses are very inexpensive (around Q3–Q7/US50¢–US$1/25p–50p), they can be overcrowded and very slow. They stop almost constantly along the way to pick up and discharge passengers and their cargo. I recommend you take one of these buses only if you're more interested in the local color and adventure of the trip than in a speedy arrival at the ruins.

A much better bet is to take one of the collective taxis or minivans that leave right from Melchor de Mencos. Most of these wait just outside the border station and leave as soon as they fill up. Some go to Flores and Santa Elena, while others go directly to Tikal. Most charge just Q60 to Q100 (US$8.15–US$14/£4.25–£7.10) per person.

Finally, if there are no collective taxis or minivans available, you can hire a taxi that will carry up to six people for between Q375 and Q560 (US$51–US$76/£27–£40).

Tip: If you are only going for the day, try to arrange a round-trip fare with your taxi or minivan driver, with a specific departure time from Tikal. Usually, it's best to leave Tikal by 4pm, so as to drive during daylight and arrive at the border with plenty of time.

BY ORGANIZED TOUR Organized day trips leave daily for Tikal from Belize City, San Ignacio, San Pedro, Caye Caulker, and Placencia. Costs for these all-inclusive trips are approximately BZ$200 and BZ$400 (US$100–US$200/£53–£106) by land (from Belize City, or any of the other major tourist destinations in Belize), depending on group size. Budget an additional BZ$100 to BZ$300 (US$50–US$150/£27–£80) per person per day for multiday excursions. In Belize City, call **Discovery Expeditions** (© **223-0748;** www.discoverybelize.com) or **S & L Travel and Tours** (© **227-7593;** www.sltravelbelize.com). In San Ignacio, you can call **Pacz Tours ★★** (© **824-2477;** www.pacztours.net) or **Yute Expeditions ★★** (© **824-2076;** www.inlandbelize.com).

Getting Around

BY TAXI OR MINIVAN Minivans and collective taxis leave throughout the day plying the route between Tikal and Santa Elena/Flores. Minivans and collective taxis charge between Q25 and Q50 (US$3.40–US$6.80/£1.75–£3.55) per person each way. From Santa Elena, you can catch a bus back to the border. A private cab from Tikal to Santa Elena/Flores will run around Q300 to Q400 (US$41–US$54/£21–£28) each way. Between Tikal and El Remate, the fare is about Q200 (US$27/£14).

BY CAR There are several local car rental agencies at the airport. Of these, a good choice is **Tabarini Rent A Car** (✆ **502/7926-0253;** www.tabarini.com). All rent small jeeps and SUVs. Do get a four-wheel-drive vehicle; even though you may never need the traction or off-road ability, the extra clearance will come in handy. Rates run from Q300 to Q410 (US$41–US$56/£21–£29) per day.

Orientation

There is no village or town inside Tikal National Park. After having paid your Q150 (US$20/£11) admission at the entrance booth 18km (11 miles) south of the ruins, you will eventually come to the large central parking area and visitor center. This is where you will find the three hotels and campsite reviewed in "Where to Stay," later in this chapter, as well as the two museums and a collection of simple restaurants. The ruins themselves are about a 15- to 20-minute walk through the forest from the trail entrance here.

You'll spot a post office and telegraph office on the left as you arrive at the parking area. You'll find a public phone in the Stelae Museum. There is no bank or ATM here in Tikal, and most of the little restaurants and gift stands only accept quetzales. Moreover, while some of the hotels here do accept credit cards, the phone connections are spotty, and they sometimes have problems getting the authorizations. It's best to bring quetzales to pay for your entire stay. Also, be sure to bring plenty of insect repellent with you—the bugs here are rapacious.

Tikal National Park is open daily from 6am to 6pm. If you'd like to stay in the park until 8pm (for sunset and nocturnal wildlife viewing), get your admission ticket stamped at the office behind the Stelae Museum. If you arrive after 3pm, your admission is good for the following day as well. If you are staying multiple days, you must pay the admission fee each day. The best times to visit the ruins are in early morning and late afternoon, which are the least crowded and coolest times of day.

FAST FACTS There are no banks, medical facilities, laundromats, or other major services available at Tikal. All of these can be found in Flores and Santa Elena, some 64km (40 miles) away; see section 3, later in this chapter.

Money

The Guatemalan monetary unit is the quetzal. In August 2008, the exchange rate was 7.38 quetzales to the U.S. dollar, and 14.09 quetzales to the British pound. If you're coming from Belize, your best bets for changing dollars into quetzales are at the border or at the numerous banks in Santa Elena and Flores (see "Flores & Santa Elena," later in this chapter). Most of the hotels and restaurants in Tikal, in fact, will exchange dollars for quetzales, although they may give you a slightly less favorable rate than you would get at a bank.

A Familiar Site

Tikal provides such a stunning and unique landscape that it was chosen for an exterior shot in George Lucas's *Star Wars,* as well as the site of a famous series of Nike commercials.

EXPLORING TIKAL

Tikal, one of the largest Mayan cities ever uncovered and the most spectacular ruins in Guatemala, ranks with Mexico's Chichén Itzá in pre-Columbian splendor. However, unlike at Chichén Itzá, the ruins of Tikal are set in the middle of a vast jungle through which you must hike from temple to temple. The many miles of trails through the park provide numerous opportunities to spot interesting birds such as toucans and parrots and such wild animals as coati-mundis, spider monkeys, howler monkeys, and deer. Together, the ruins and the abundance of wildlife make a trip to Tikal an absolute must for anyone interested in Mayan history, bird-watching, or wildlife viewing.

Tikal was a massive ceremonial metropolis. So far, archaeologists have mapped about 3,000 constructions, 10,000 earlier foundations beneath surviving structures, 250 stone monuments (stelae and altars), and thousands of art objects found in tombs and cached offerings. There is evidence of continuous construction at Tikal from 200 B.C. through the 9th century A.D., with some suggestion of occupation as early as 600 B.C. The Maya reached their zenith in art and architecture during the Classic Period, which began about A.D. 250 and ended abruptly about 900, when for some reason Tikal and all other major Mayan centers were abandoned. Most of the visible structures at Tikal date from the Late Classic Period, from 600 to 900.

No one's sure just what role Tikal played in the history of the Maya: Was it mostly a ceremonial center for priests, artisans, and the elite? Or was it a city of industry and commerce as well? In the 16 sq. km (6 sq. miles) of Tikal that have been mapped and excavated, only a few of the buildings were domestic structures; most were temples, palaces, ceremonial platforms, and shrines. Workers are excavating the innumerable mounds on the periphery of the mapped area and have been finding modest houses of stone and plaster with thatched roofs. Just how far these settlements extended beyond the ceremonial center and how many people lived within the domain of Tikal is still to be determined. At its height, Tikal may have covered as much as 65 sq. km (25 sq. miles).

Making the Most of Your Visit

Tikal is such an immense site that you really need several days to see it thoroughly. But you can visit many of the greatest temples and palaces in 1 day. To do it properly, as a first-time visitor, you should probably hire a guide. Guides are available at the visitor center and charge around Q150 (US$20/£11) for a half-day tour of the ruins. In addition, most hotels and all tour agencies in the region offer guided tours for a similar price.

A Walking Tour

To orient yourself, begin your tour of Tikal at the visitor center and neighboring Stelae Museum. Here you'll find some informative exhibits and relics, as well as an impressive relief map of the site. See "The Museums" below for more information on the stelae.

A full tour of Tikal will require an extensive amount of walking, as much as 9.7km (6 miles). The itinerary described here will take you to most of the major temples and plazas, and can be accomplished in about 3 to 4 hours. If your time is really limited, you should follow the signs and head straight to the Great Plaza. If you have a full day, consider this route:

Walking along the road that goes west from the museum toward the ruins, turn right at the first intersection to get to **twin complexes Q** and **R.** Seven of these twin complexes are known at Tikal, but their exact purpose is still a mystery. Each complex has two pyramids facing east and west; at the north is an unroofed enclosure entered by a vaulted doorway and containing a single stele and altar; at the south is a small palacelike structure. Of the two pyramids here, one has been restored and one has been left as it was found, and the latter will give you an idea of just how overgrown and ensconced in the jungle these structures had become.

At the end of the Twin Complexes is a wide road called the **Maler Causeway.** Turn right (north) onto this causeway to get to **Complex P,** another twin complex, a 15-minute walk. Some restoration has been done at Complex P, but the most interesting points are the replicas of a stele (no. 20) and altar (no. 8) in the north enclosure. Look for the beautiful glyphs next to the carving of a warrior on the stele, all in very good condition. The altar shows a captive bound to a carved-stone altar, his hands tied behind his back—a common scene in carvings at Tikal. Both these monuments date from about A.D. 751.

From Complex P, head south on the **Maudslay Causeway** to **Complex N,** which is the site of **Temple IV, the Temple of the Two-Headed Serpent ★★★**. Finished around A.D. 740, Temple IV is the tallest structure in Tikal and is 65m (212 ft.) from the base of its platform to the top. The first glimpse you get of the temple from the Maudslay Causeway is awesome, for the temple has not been restored, and all but the temple proper (the enclosure) and its roof comb are covered in foliage. The stairway is occluded by earth and roots, but there is a system of steep stairways (actually rough-hewn wooden ladders set against the steep sides of the pyramid) to the top of the temple. The view of the setting and layout of Tikal—and all of the Great Plaza—is magnificent. From the platform of the temple, you can see in all directions and get an idea of the extent of the Petén jungle, an ocean of lush greenery. **Temple III (Temple of the Great Priest)** is in the foreground to the east; **temples I** and **II** are farther on at the Great Plaza. To the right of these are the **South Acropolis** and **Temple V.**

Temple IV, and all the other temples at Tikal, are built on this plan: A pyramid is built first, and on top of it is built a platform; the temple proper rests on this platform and is composed of one to three rooms, usually long and narrow and not for habitation but rather for priestly rites. Most temples had beautifully carved wooden lintels above the doorways. The one from Temple IV is now in the Völkerkunde Museum in Basel, Switzerland.

From Temple IV, walk east along the **Tozzer Causeway** to get to the **Great Plaza,** about a 10-minute walk. Along the way you'll pass the twin-pyramid Complex N, the **Bat Palace,** and Temple III. Take a look at the altar and stele in the complex's northern enclosure—two of the finest monuments at Tikal—and also the altar in front of Temple III, showing the head of a deity resting on a plate. By the way, the crisscross pattern shown here represents a woven mat, a symbol of authority to the Mayas.

The Great Plaza ★★★

Entering the Great Plaza from the Tozzer Causeway, you'll be struck by the towering stone structure that is Temple II, seen from the back. It measures 38m (125 ft.) tall now, although it is thought to have been 43m (140 ft.) high when the roof comb was intact. Also called the Temple of the Masks, from a large face carved in the roof comb, the temple dates from about A.D. 700. Walk around this temple to enter the plaza proper.

Directly across from Temple II you'll see Temple I (Temple of the Great Jaguar), the most striking structure in Tikal. Standing 44m (145 ft.) tall, the temple proper has three narrow rooms with high corbeled vaults (the Mayan "arch") and carved wooden lintels made of zapote wood, which is rot-resistant. One of the lintels has been removed for preservation in the Guatemala National Museum of Archaeology and Ethnology in Guatemala City. The whole structure is made of limestone, as are most others at Tikal. It was within this pyramid that one of the richest tombs in Tikal was discovered. Believed to be the tomb of Tikal ruler Hasaw Chan K'awil, when archaeologists uncovered it in 1962, they found the former ruler's skeleton surrounded by some 180 pieces of jade, 90 bone artifacts carved with hieroglyphic inscriptions, numerous pearls, and objects in alabaster and shell. ***Note:*** Tourists can no longer scale temples I or III. However, those in need of serious cardio workouts will get their fill climbing some of the other temples.

The **North Acropolis** (north side of the Great Plaza) is a maze of structures from various periods covering an area of 8.5 hectares (21 acres). Standing today 9m (30 ft.) above the limestone bedrock, it contains vestiges of more than a hundred different constructions dating from 200 B.C. to A.D. 800. At the front-center of the acropolis (at the top of the stairs up from the Great Plaza) is a temple numbered **5D-33.** Although much of the 8th-century temple was destroyed during the excavations to get to the Early Classic temple (A.D. 300) underneath, it's still a fascinating building. Toward the rear of it is a tunnel leading to the stairway of the **Early Classic** temple, embellished with two 3m-high (10-ft.) plaster polychrome masks of a god—don't miss these.

Directly across the plaza from the North Acropolis is the **Central Acropolis,** which covers about 1.6 hectares (4 acres). It's a maze of courtyards and palaces on several levels, all connected by an intricate system of passageways. Some of the palaces had five floors, connected by exterior stairways, and each floor had as many as nine rooms arranged like a maze.

Before you leave the Great Plaza, be sure to examine some of the 70 beautiful stelae and altars right in the plaza. You can see the full development of Mayan art in them, for they date from the Early Classic Period right through to the Late Classic Period. There are three major stylistic groups: the stelae with wraparound carving on the front and sides with text on the back; those with a figure carved on the front and text in glyphs on the back; and those with a simple carved figure on the front, text in hieroglyphs on the sides,

Tips Beat the Crowds

Tikal fills up with tour buses most days, with the hours between 10am and 2pm being the busiest period. I prefer visiting the Great Plaza either before or after the main crowds have left. Feel free to reverse the order of this walking tour if it will help you avoid the masses.

Moments Sunrise, Sunset

Tikal is a magical and mystical place. Many claim that this magic and mystique is only heightened around sunrise and sunset. Sunsets are easier to catch and a more dependable show. Sunrises tend to be more a case of the sun eventually burning through the morning mist than of any impressive orb emerging. However, afternoons can often be clear, especially during the dry season, allowing for excellent sunset viewing from the tops of the main temples here. If you're staying right at the ruins, your chances are better of catching either or both of these occasions. In fact, visitors staying inside the park are often admitted to Tikal as early as 5am. Aside from this, the most dependable way to catch the sunrise is to sign up with **San Juan Travel** (✆ **502/7926-0042**) for their daily tour leaving Flores at 3:30am. San Juan has special permission to enter the park early, and they promise to get you to the top of Temple IV in plenty of time for Apollo's appearance. The cost is Q60 (US$8.15/£4.25) per person, and once at Tikal, you can take any of San Juan's regularly scheduled return vans back to Flores.

For do-it-yourselfers, minivans and collective taxis leave Flores and El Remate early enough to get you to the Tikal entrance gate at 6am when it opens. This will generally enable you to get to the top of one of the main temples by 6:30am, which is usually still early enough to catch the sun burning through the mist just over the rainforest canopy.

Tip: For either the sunrise or sunset tour, it's a very good idea to bring along a flashlight.

and a plain back. The oldest stele is no. 29 (now in the Tikal Museum—see "The Museums," below), dating from A.D. 292; the most recent is no. 11 in the Great Plaza, dating from A.D. 869.

If you head south from Temple II, you will come to the area known as **El Mundo Perdido (The Lost World).** This plaza contains the **Great Pyramid,** which stands 35m (114 ft.) high and is the oldest excavated building in Tikal. This pyramid is one of the most popular spots for watching the sunset. If you've timed it right, you might be able to hang out here and watch the show; otherwise, make a mental note to get your bearings and come back later, if possible. Directly east of the Great Pyramid is the **Plaza of the Seven Temples,** which dates to the Late Classic Period. Bordering this plaza on the east side is an unexcavated pyramid, and behind this is Temple V. This entire area is known as the **South Acropolis.** You can climb Temple V, but be forewarned, the climb, both up and down a very steep and rather rickety wooden stairway, is somewhat harrowing. The view from above is beautiful. However, the steep pitch of the pyramid's original stairway is almost as scary as the climb.

If you cross through the South Acropolis to the east and then turn north in the general direction of the Great Plaza, you will come to the East Plaza. From here you can walk southeast on the Mendez Causeway to **Temple VI (Temple of the Inscriptions),** which contains a nearly illegible line of hieroglyphics that are the most extensive in Tikal. It's

Moments Seeing the Forest from the Trees

Just outside the entrance to Tikal National Park is the **Canopy Tour Tikal** (✆ **502/7926-4270;** www.canopytikal.com). A series of treetop platforms is connected by heavy wire cables, so that more adventurous travelers can zip from platform to platform via a harness-and-pulley system. Canopy Tour Tikal actually has two separate zip-line tours to choose from, a somewhat slower tour for wary souls and a faster system for adrenaline junkies. They also have a series of trails and hanging suspension bridges through the thick rain forest here. This attraction is open daily from 7am to 5pm, and the cost is Q224 (US$30/£16) per person, including shuttle transportation to or from Tikal or El Remate. For transport to and from Santa Elena or Flores, add on an extra Q37 (US$5/£2.60).

worth coming out this way just for the chance to spot some wild animals, which seem to be fairly common in this remote corner of the park.

The Museums

The most formal museum here has been officially christened the **Sylvanus G. Morely Museum,** but is also known as the **Tikal** or **Ceramic Museum.** This museum contains a good collection of pottery, mosaic masks, incense burners, etched bone, and stelae that are chronologically displayed—beginning with Pre-Classic objects on up to Late Classic pieces. Of note are the delicate 7.6 to 13cm (3- to 5-in.) mosaic masks made of jade, turquoise, shell, and stucco. There is a beautiful cylindrical jar from about A.D. 700 depicting a male and female seated in a typical Mayan pose. The drawing is of fine quality, and the slip colors are red, brown, and black. Also on exhibit are a number of jade pendants, beads, and earplugs as well as the famous **stele no. 31,** which has all four sides carved. On the two sides are spear throwers, each wearing a large feathered headdress and carrying a shield in his left hand; on the front is a complicated carving of an individual carrying a head in his left arm and a chair in his right. It is considered one of the finest stele examples from the Early Classic Period. Another fine attraction here is the reconstruction of the tomb of Hasaw Chan K'awil, who was also known as Ah Cacao, or "Lord Chocolate." The museum is located between the Jungle Lodge and the Jaguar Inn.

The second museum is known as the **Lithic** or **Stelae Museum** and is in the large visitor center, which is on your left as you arrive at the parking area coming from Flores. This spacious display area contains a superb collection of stelae from around the ruins. Just outside the front door of the museum is the scaled relief map (mentioned above) that will give you an excellent perspective on the relationships among the different ruins here at Tikal. Both museums are open daily from 9am to 5pm. A Q20 (US$2.70/£1.40) admission will get you into both.

Tip: Only visit the museums if you have extra time, or a very specific interest in either the stelae or ceramic works. The ruins themselves are by far a much more interesting attraction.

WHERE TO STAY

There are only three hotels and a campground at the little Tikal village near the entrance to the ruins. Unless you have more than 2 days to spend exploring the region, I personally highly recommend staying near the ruins, as it allows you to enter early and stay late. It also allows you to avoid the Great Plaza and North Acropolis during the peak period of the day, when they are swarmed with day-trippers.

Although the ruins are officially open from 6am to 6pm, those staying at the site can usually finagle their way in even earlier. Better yet, those staying at the site can have their admission ticket stamped, allowing them to stay inside the park until 8pm. When the moon is full or close to full, that's enough time to catch both the sunset and moonrise from the top of one of the temples here.

Note: Rooms are often difficult to get at the park, and making reservations is essential during the high season. However, communication with the hotels here is difficult and undependable, and many reserve all of their high-season bookings for groups and prepaid package tours. Overbooking on behalf of these hotels is also not uncommon. Demand is high, and rooms are very limited here. If you're just going for a couple of nights, go with an organized tour to save yourself some hassle; if you plan to spend more time in the area or don't mind spending a night in Flores or Santa Elena if necessary, you can probably make your arrangements in Tikal.

All of the hotels below get their electricity from generators, and usually only run these generators for limited periods throughout the day.

Expensive

Jungle Lodge ★ Also known as Posada de la Selva, this is the biggest and most comfortable hotel right at the park. However, at times there can be a cattle-car feel to the operation. The majority of the rooms, and the best rooms, are housed in duplex bungalows, with high ceilings, white-tile floors, two double beds with mosquito netting, and a ceiling fan. Each has its own little porch with a couple of chairs, which are great places to sit and read a book, or do some bird-watching. The bungalows are connected by stone paths through lush gardens. Two newer junior suites feature king-size beds, a large Jacuzzi-style tub (but without jets), and private patios in both the front and back of the room. There are also 12 older rooms with polished cement floors and shared bathroom facilities. These are certainly comfortable enough, but not nearly as plush. It's hot and steamy here in the jungle, so you'll be thankful you can cool off in the hotel's pool, which is built on a rise and shaped like a Mayan pyramid.

Tikal village, Petén. ✆ **502/7861-0447** or 502/2476-8775. Fax 502/7861-0448. www.junglelodge.guate.com. 50 units (38 with private bathroom). Q1,120 (US$152/£79) bungalow; Q305 (US$41/£22) double with shared bathroom. MC, V. **Amenities:** Restaurant; bar; small outdoor pool; tour desk; laundry service. *In room:* No phone.

Tikal Inn Set back amid the trees, the Tikal Inn is the farthest hotel from the entrance to the ruins as you walk down the old airstrip. The best rooms here are the individual bungalows, which feature high thatch roofs, tile floors, local furniture and textiles, and rustic wood trim. The smaller rooms in the main building have cement floors. All of the rooms are airy and cool, but feel pretty spartan. As at the Jungle Lodge, there's a refreshing pool here, and these folks even have a small Internet cafe. Meals are served family-style, and the food is a definite step up from the fare served at the *comedores* near the campground.

Tikal village, Petén. ✆ **502/7926-1917,** or ✆/fax 502/7926-0065. www.tikalinn.com. 29 units. Q1,045 (US$142/£74) double. Rate includes breakfast and dinner. MC, V. **Amenities:** Restaurant; bar; small outdoor pool; tour desk; laundry service. *In room:* No phone.

Inexpensive

Jaguar Inn *Value* This is the most humble and economical of the hotels right at the park. Still, the rooms are all quite clean, spacious, and well kept. Most come with two queen beds and a small veranda strung with a hammock. The best rooms are a couple of large, second-floor affairs. However, I also like bungalow no. 10, with its king-size bed and private veranda. If you're on a tight budget, you can also camp here, or rent one of their hammocks with mosquito netting and a locker for Q40 (US$5.35/£2.70) per person. These folks even offer free Wi-Fi, while the generator's running.

Tikal village, Petén. ✆ **502/7926-0002** reservations in Santa Elena, or 502/7783-3647 at the lodge. Fax 502/7926-2413. www.jaguartikal.com. 14 units. Q448 (US$61/£32) double. Rates lower in the off season. AE, MC, V. **Amenities:** Restaurant; tour desk; laundry service; Wi-Fi. *In room:* No phone.

Camping

Just off the main parking lot at the site is a nice lawn with some trees for shade, marked and designated as the camping area. You can also set up your tent on some concrete pads, under an open-air thatch palapa roof. The camping area has simple shared shower and toilet facilities, and a communal cooking area. The campground (no phone) charges Q30 to Q45 (US$4.05–US$6.10/£2.15–£3.20) for the privilege of putting up a tent and using the facilities. You can also rent hammocks and pitch them under open-air palapas for an additional Q30 (US$4.05/£2.15).

Tip: If you plan on sleeping in a hammock, or even taking an afternoon siesta, you should really try to get a mosquito net that fits over the hammock. Most of the places that rent and sell hammocks in this area have these nets.

WHERE TO DINE

Most folks who stay near the ruins take all their meals at their hotel. If you're looking for variety or staying at the campsite, there are several little restaurants *(comedores)* between the main camping area and parking lot and the gate at the beginning of the road to Flores. As you arrive at Tikal from Flores, you'll see them on the right side; **Comedor Imperio Maya, Comedor La Jungla,** and **Comedor Tikal** are the best of the bunch. All are rustic and pleasant, and all serve hefty plates of fairly tasty food at low prices. You can get a large serving of roast chicken, with rice, beans, and fresh tortillas, along with a drink, for around Q40 (US$5.40/£2.85).

Within the area of the ruins, you'll find picnic tables beneath shelters and itinerant soft-drink peddlers, but no snack stands. If you want to spend all day at the ruins without having to walk back to the parking area for lunch, take sandwiches. Most of the hotels here and in Flores, as well as the *comedores,* will make you a bag lunch to take into the park.

TIKAL AFTER DARK

Aside from hanging around at your hotel bar or at one of the simple *comedores,* or swinging in a hammock at the campsite, the best nighttime activity here is to visit the ruins by moonlight. Those staying near the entrance to the ruins can have their admission ticket validated to allow them to roam the park until 8pm, and in some cases even later, depending on the disposition of the guards. If the moon is waxing, full, or just beyond full, you're in for a real treat. ***Tip:*** Before venturing into the park at night, be sure to ask around as to the current level of safety inside the park after dark.

2 EL REMATE ★★

32km (20 miles) E of Flores; 32km (20 miles) S of Tikal; 60km (37 miles) W of Melchor de Mencos

El Remate is a small village on the eastern shores of Lake Petén Itzá that is a popular spot in which to stay while visiting Tikal. It's located about midway between Flores and Tikal, which means that staying here cuts travel time between your hotel and the ruins. El Remate is much more tranquil and pristine than Flores or Santa Elena. Currently, a handful of budget lodgings can be found in the tiny village here, while a more upscale options can be found on the shores of the lake heading north out of the village.

ESSENTIALS

Getting There & Departing

BY MINIVAN Scheduled and independent minivans ply the route between Santa Elena/Flores and Tikal throughout the day. Any of these will drop you off in El Remate. For more information on these, see "Getting Around" in section 1 and below. Fares from Flores to El Remate run around Q25 and Q50 (US$3.40–US$6.80/£1.80–£3.55) per person each way.

BY CAR El Remate is located about 1.6km (1 mile) north of Ixlú (El Cruce). The road is paved and in good shape all the way from the Belize-Guatemala border 60km (37 miles) away.

Getting Around

El Remate is a tiny village, and you can easily walk anywhere in town. Some of the hotels listed below are located 1.6km (1 mile) or so north of the village, on the road that circles Lake Petén Itzá. If you're in El Remate, you'll most likely want to go to Tikal, visit Santa Elena and Flores, or explore the region.

BY TAXI Taxis charge between Q200 to Q300 (US$27–US$41/£14–£21) for the one-way trip between El Remate and Tikal, and around Q150 to Q200 (US$20–US$27/£11–£14) for the trip between El Remate and Santa Elena and Flores. The higher rates are for a minivan that can hold anywhere from six to eight passengers. A taxi is your best option if you decide to explore the area around the lake. There are often taxis hanging around the small village. If not, your hotel can call one for you. Be sure to have your hotel set a fair price, or be prepared to bargain, as the first price you are quoted is almost assuredly above the going rate and subject to some negotiation.

BY MINIVAN If you don't have a car, the best way to get around is by minivan. Scheduled and unscheduled minivans ply the route between Flores and Tikal throughout the day. All of these pass through El Remate, dropping off and picking up passengers. You can get a minivan at almost any hotel in El Remate, or walk a few hundred yards out to the main road to Tikal and flag one down. The ride takes about a half-hour to either Tikal or Flores, and the one-way fare is from Q20 to Q50 (US$2.70–US$6.80/£1.40–£3.55) per person.

WHAT TO SEE & DO

The village of El Remate itself is very small and provincial, with little of interest to tourists. Most people use El Remate as a base for explorations of the ruins at Tikal. However, as small lodges and isolated resorts start to pop up here, many tour and activity options will follow.

Just west of El Remate is the **Biotopo Cerro Cahuí,** a small nature reserve with some trails and good wildlife-viewing opportunities. Over 180 species of birds have been spotted here. A couple of loop trails climb uphill from the entrance and at various points offer excellent views of the lake. I recommend visiting this park with a guide, as a spate of robberies and attacks against tourists closed it for a period several years ago. The reserve is open daily from 8am to 4pm, and admission is Q25 (US$3.40/£1.75).

One of the most popular activities in El Remate is **renting a canoe or kayak** for paddling around on the lake. Most of the hotels in town either rent kayaks or canoes, or can arrange one for you. Rates run around Q10 to Q20 (US$1.35–US$2.70/70p–£1.40) per hour, or around Q75 (US$10/£5.30) per day.

Similarly, most of the hotels in town either rent or provide **mountain bikes** for their guests, or can arrange for their rental. The dirt road that circles Lake Petén Itzá is excellent for a mountain-bike ride. Rates are about Q35 to Q80 (US$4.75–US$11/£2.50–£5.70) per day.

Finally, the village of El Remate is gaining some local renown for its woodcarving. You'll see several roadside stands set up on the route between Ixlú and El Remate, and onwards to Tikal. If you ask around El Remate, you might even be able to visit one or more of the artisans.

WHERE TO STAY & DINE

Most folks take their meals at their hotels. You'll find some simple restaurants *(comedores)* in the center of the village. The best of these is probably **El Muelle** (**© 502/5514-9785**), which has a great view of the lake, as well as a swimming pool, which you can use if you eat here. If you're looking for something different, try the restaurant at the **Hotel Mon Ami** (**© 502/7928-8413;** www.hotelmonami.com), which features a mix of Guatemalan, French, and Italian fare.

Expensive

La Lancha Resort ★★ This is filmmaker Francis Ford Coppola's Guatemalan piece of his mini-hotel chain in the Mundo Maya. The main lodge has a commanding view of the lake and features a soaring, open-air, A-frame thatch roof oriented towards the view. Below the lodge is a kidney-shaped pool. A steep trail leads down to the shore of the lake, where you'll find a swimming area and some canoes and kayaks. The rooms are all duplex bungalows. The six "lake view" units are quite spacious, while the "jungle view" rooms are more compact. All are tastefully and artistically decorated and very comfortable. All feature a shared wooden veranda, and you can probably figure out the view from the room names. Plans here include the addition of some independent suites with private plunge pools.

Lago Petén Itzá, Petén. © **800/746-3743** in the U.S., or ©/fax 502/7928-8331 in Guatemala. www.lalanchavillage.com. 10 units. Q1,007–Q1,567 (US$136–US$212/£71–£111) double. Rates lower in the off season; higher during peak periods. AE, MC, V. **Amenities:** Restaurant; bar; outdoor pool; bike rental; tour desk; laundry service. *In room:* A/C, no phone.

Moments **Watch Out for Crocs**

If you're out on the lake during the daytime, scan the shoreline northwest of El Remate and try to pick out the **"Sleeping Crocodile,"** a silhouette formed by the shape of the forested hills as they descend towards the lake. If you can't pick it out, ask a local for help.

Moderate

La Mansión del Pájaro Serpiente ★ Finds Set off the main road to Tikal, on a hillside overlooking the lake, this place has both standard and deluxe bungalows, beautiful gardens, and a friendly atmosphere. The bungalows feature beautiful stone and woodworking details, with local textile and crafts filling out the decor. The deluxe rooms feature televisions and air-conditioning. Several rooms are quite large and should be classified as junior suites, as they also have a separate sitting area just off the bedroom. The "honeymoon suite" comes with its own plunge pool and is high up the hill, with a great view. The midsize free-form pool is set amidst lush gardens, and almost feels like a natural pond in the jungle. The open-air restaurant has a great view of the lake and specializes in local cuisine. The owners raise peacocks, and there are always several wandering around the grounds.

El Remate, Petén. ✆/fax **502/7926-8498** or 502/5702-9434. 11 units. Q330 ($45/£23) double; Q410 (US$56/£29) deluxe double. MC, V. **Amenities:** Restaurant; bar; outdoor pool; tour desk; laundry service. *In room:* No phone.

Inexpensive

In addition to the places listed below, a few very inexpensive options, catering to the backpacker crowd, are right in El Remate. I recommend simply walking around to see which one best suits your fancy and budget. One good option is **Hotel Mon Ami** (✆ **502/7928-8413;** www.hotelmonami.com).

Hotel Gringo Perdido Three kilometers (1¾ miles) north of El Remate on the dirt road that circles Lake Petén Itzá, you'll find one of Guatemala's original jungle lodges. This little offbeat paradise is arranged along the lakeshore, with shady rustic hillside gardens, a little restaurant, a quiet camping area, and rooms ranging from a rustic dormitory to some almost plush private bungalows. The whole thing seems to blend into and get swallowed up by the rainforest. The Gringo Perdido, which means "the lost American," offers good swimming in the lake, 3.2km (2 miles) of nature trails, and tranquillity. This little lodge borders the Biotopo Cerro Cahuí. On my last visit, these folks had begun building eight upscale rooms, which should be ready by the time you read this.

3.2km (2 miles) west of El Remate, Petén. ✆ **502/2334-2305** or 502/5804-8639. www.hotelgringo perdido.com. 23 units (6 with shared bathroom). Q373 (US$51/£26) double with shared bath; Q522 (US$70/£37) per person with private bath. Rates include breakfast and dinner. Q37 (US$5/£2.60) per person to camp, with meals extra. V only (with 8% surcharge). **Amenities:** Restaurant; tour desk; laundry service. *In room:* No phone.

La Casa de Don David Hotel Value This hotel's rooms are located in a series of buildings arrayed around a large and lush garden area. All are clean and simple. There's an open-air octagonal hammock hut for reading and resting, and you can catch a glimpse of Lake Petén from here. Most of the rooms have air-conditioning, and you'll pay slightly more for these. My favorite room is no. 13, which is a corner unit with a private hammock on its front porch. The hotel offers bicycles free for guest use. David Kuhn and his wife Rosita have lived in this area for almost 30 years, and they are a wealth of information and advice. David was the original *gringo perdido* of the nearby nature lodge (see above), but left there to open this delightful little place.

El Remate, Petén. ✆ **502/5306-2190** or 502/7928-8469. www.lacasadedondavid.com. 15 units. Q270–Q388 (US$36–US$53/£19–£28) double. Rates include 1 meal (breakfast, lunch, or dinner). MC, V. **Amenities:** Restaurant; tour desk; laundry service. *In room:* No phone.

EL REMATE AFTER DARK

El Remate is a quiet village. Most visitors head to the small bar at their hotel or hostel to chat with fellow travelers, or they take tours. One popular tour offered at night involves journeying to the lake to see crocodiles. This 2-hour tour involves a ride in a small motor launch with a high-powered flashlight or headlamp. The guide will scan the shore and inlets for the red reflection of the crocodiles' eyes. If you're lucky, they won't submerge as you slowly approach. All of the hotels in town can arrange this tour. The cost is between Q75 and Q150 (US$10–US$20/£5.30–£11).

3 FLORES & SANTA ELENA ★

64km (40 miles) SW of Tikal; 135km (84 miles) NW of the Belizean border; 451km (280 miles) NE of Guatemala City

Since accommodations in Tikal are limited, most travelers either choose to (or must) overnight in the sister cities of Flores and Santa Elena. Still, this is not necessarily such a bad thing. Flores itself is a picturesque little town built on an island in the middle of Lake Petén Itzá. A narrow causeway connects Flores to Santa Elena. There's a lot more to do and see in Flores and Santa Elena than there is closer to Tikal, and a far wider range of hotels and restaurants to choose from.

Seen from the air, Flores appears almost perfectly round. This quiet town, with its colonial-style buildings and cobblestone streets, is one of the most fascinating in Guatemala. Though most people spend time here only en route to or from the Tikal ruins, Flores is well worth exploring for a day or two. A walk around the circumference of the island presents a sort of Venetian experience. Buildings come right down to the water's edge. In fact, since the lake's water level has risen over the years, some of the outlying streets and alleys are flooded. Dugout canoes, kayaks, and motor launches sit at makeshift docks all around the circumference of the island.

Santa Elena, Flores's mainland counterpart, on the other hand, is a ramshackle, modern boomtown with little at all to recommend it. However, Santa Elena is where you'll find the airport, the bus stations, a host of hotels, and a good view of Flores. Just to the west of Santa Elena is the town of San Benito, a rough-and-tumble area with little appeal to visitors. The name Flores is often used as a bucket term encompassing the island of Flores itself, along with Santa Elena and San Benito.

Flores is the unofficial capital of the Petén region of Guatemala. El Petén has always been a remote region, and it was here, on the banks of Lake Petén Itzá, that the Itzá people, descendents of the Mayas, resisted Spanish conquest until the end of the 17th century. Hernán Cortés had visited the Itzá city of Tayasal, which once stood on the far side of the lake, in 1525 but had not tried to conquer the Itzás, who had a reputation for

ACCOMMODATIONS ■
Casa Elena **14**
Hotel Del Patio **15**
Hotel Isla de Flores **6**
Hotel Petén **2**
Hotel Petén Espléndido **12**
Hotel Santana **1**
La Casona de la Isla **4**
La Casona del Lago **13**

DINING & NIGHTLIFE ◆
AAdictos **10**
Bar Raices **11**
Café Archeologico Yax-há **7**
Capitan Tortuga **3**
El Mirador Restaurant **12**
La Luna **5**
Las Puertas **9**
Maya Princesa **16**
Pizzería Picasso **8**

ATTRACTIONS ●
Aktun Kan **17**

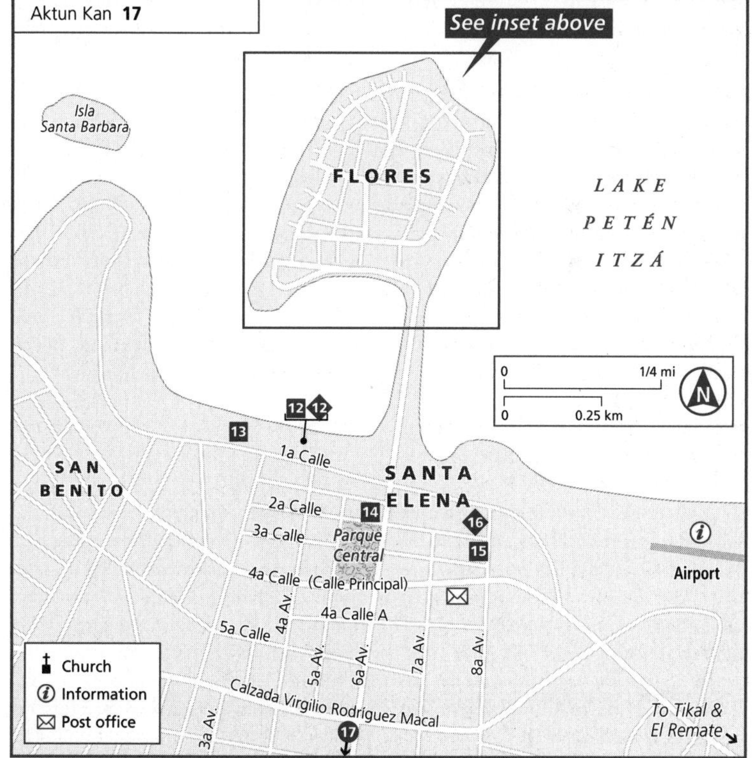

being fierce warriors. However, in 1697, the Spanish finally conquered the Itzás, and Tayasal became the last Indian city to fall under Spanish rule. Two years after taking Tayasal, the Spanish moved to Flores, an island that could easily be defended. They renamed this island Nuestra Señora de los Remedios y San Pablo de los Itzaes and between 1700 and 1701 built a fort here. In 1831, the island was once again renamed, this time being given the name Flores in honor of a Guatemalan patriot.

One of the most curious pieces of local history is the story of a sick horse left in Tayasal by Cortés when he passed through the area. The Itzás had never seen horses before and as soon as Cortés left, they began worshipping the horse. When the horse died, a stone statue of it was made, and the worship continued until Spanish missionaries arrived in Tayasal 100 years later. The missionaries, appalled by this idolatry, proceeded to pitch the blasphemous statue into the lake. To this day the legendary horse statue has never been discovered, though searches continue to be launched from time to time.

ESSENTIALS

Getting There & Departing

BY CAR To get here from Belize, see "By Car" under "Essentials" in section 1, earlier in this chapter.

The road between Tikal and Flores is a good, paved road, and the trip takes around an hour by car. To get to either of the sister towns from Tikal, head south out of the ruins and turn right at Ixlú (El Cruce). Continue on past the airport. You will come to Santa Elena first. Stay on the main avenue into town and head towards the lake, where you will find the causeway over to Flores.

BY BUS For information on getting to Flores and Santa Elena by bus from Belize, see "By Bus" under "Essentials" in section 1, earlier in this chapter. See "Getting Around," below, for details on getting from Santa Elena and Flores to the ruins.

There are several companies operating first-class buses to Guatemala City. **ADN** (**✆ 502/7924-8131;** www.adnautobusesdelnorte.com), **Línea Dorada** (**✆ 502/7926-0070;** www.tikalmayanworld.com), and **Transportes Fuentes del Norte** (**✆ 502/7926-0517**) all operate out of the main bus terminal in Santa Elena, located about 8 blocks south of downtown along 6a Avenida.

The trip to Guatemala City takes about 8 to 10 hours, and first-class fares run around Q180 to Q225 (US$24–US$30/£13–£16). Línea Dorada and ADN have more modern and comfortable buses.

Getting Around

If you're in Santa Elena or Flores, you'll most likely want to go to Tikal or explore the region around Lake Petén.

BY MINIVAN If you don't have a car, the best way to get around this area is by minivan. Minivans from Flores and Santa Elena to Tikal leave roughly every hour between 5am and 10am, and less frequently thereafter. These minivans leave from Tikal for the return trip roughly every hour from noon to 6pm. Every hotel in Flores and Santa Elena can arrange a minivan pickup for you. The trip usually takes an hour and costs Q25 to Q50 (US$3.40–US$6.75/£1.75–£3.55) per person each way. You can buy a round-trip fare at a slight savings; however, this commits you to a specific minivan company, and I've found I prefer paying a little extra to have more flexibility in grabbing my return ride when I'm ready to leave.

BY TAXI Taxis charge between Q300 to Q400 (US$40–US$54/£21–£28) for the one-way trip between Flores or Santa Elena and Tikal. Between Flores or Santa Elena and El Remate, the fare is around Q150 to Q200 (US$20–US$27/£11–£14). The higher rate is for a minivan that can hold anywhere from six to eight passengers. A taxi is your best option if you decide to explore the area around the lake. Be sure to bargain, as the first price you are quoted is almost certainly above the going rate and subject to some negotiation.

BY CAR If you have your own car, the road between Santa Elena and Flores and Tikal is paved, well marked, and heavily traveled. It's about 32km (20 miles) from Flores to Ixlú (El Cruce), and another 32km (20 miles) on to the park and ruins of Tikal.

For information on renting a car, see "Getting Around" in section 1, earlier in this chapter.

BY BUS Very inexpensive local bus service connects Flores and Santa Elena to Tikal and several neighboring communities. However, this service is infrequent, slow, and often uncomfortably overcrowded. Línea Dorado (see above) has three daily buses from Santa Elena to Tikal leaving at 5 and 8:30am and at 3:30pm. The return buses leave Tikal at 2 and 5pm. Ask at your hotel or around town for current schedules, as they change periodically. The trip takes 2 hours; the one-way fare is Q22 (US$3/£1.55).

Orientation

The town primarily known as Flores actually consists of three smaller towns that have merged. Flores proper sits on a small island out in Lake Petén Itzá, and is connected to the mainland by a long causeway. On the mainland are Santa Elena (nearest the airport) and San Benito (closer to the bus terminal and market). Whether you arrive by air or by bus from Guatemala City or Belize, you will come into town from the east. The road in from the airport leads straight through Santa Elena to the market and bus terminal, while the causeway to Flores is a turn to the right in the middle of Santa Elena. While there are a host of budget lodgings in San Benito, especially around the bus terminal, I strongly advise most travelers to stick to Santa Elena and Flores proper.

FAST FACTS You'll find numerous banks in downtown Flores and Santa Elena. Most have ATMs, and many of these will work with your debit or credit card. Check with your home bank and the PLUS or Cirrus systems in advance to confirm. All will exchange money. Most of the hotels and restaurants in Flores and Santa Elena will also exchange dollars for quetzales, although they may give you a slightly less favorable rate than you would get at a bank.

The **Flores post office** is on the Avenida Barrios, one block south of the Parque Central, or Central Park, which is in front of the church. **Santa Elena's post office** is on Calle 4 and Avenida 7. Both are open Monday through Friday from 8am to 5pm. To contact the **local police,** dial **© 502/7926-1365.**

There is an information booth run by the Guatemalan Tourist Board, **Inguat** (**© 502/7926-0533;** www.visitguatemala.com) at the Flores airport, and another one in downtown Flores (**© 502/5116-3182**) on Avenida Flores, on the north side of the Central Park. Both can help provide basic maps to the region and ruins, as well as brochures for local hotels and tour agencies.

WHAT TO SEE & DO

Flores is a wonderful town to explore by walking. The whole island is only about 5 blocks wide in any direction. At the center is a small central park or plaza, anchored by the town's Catholic church. Be sure to take a peek inside to check out the beautiful stained glass windows. After first exploring the island on foot, you should have a look at the island from the perspective of a boat.

One of the most popular things to do in Flores is take a **tour of the lake ★**. You will be inundated with offers for boat tours. Ask at your hotel or one of the local tour agencies, or talk to the numerous freelancers approaching you on the street. Be sure to inspect the craft beforehand, if possible, and make sure you feel comfortable with its lake-worthiness. Also, make sure your guide is bilingual. These tours last anywhere from 1 to 3 hours, and usually include stops at La Guitarra Island (Guitar Island), which features a picnic and swimming area, as well as at the mostly unexcavated ruins of Tayasal. Here, be sure to climb **El Mirador ★**, a lakeside pyramid that offers a fabulous view of Flores. Many of these tours also stop at the small **Petencito Zoo** and **ARCAS** (www.arcasguatemala.com), a conservation organization and animal rehabilitation center that has some interpretive trails and displays of rescued animals either in recuperation or unable to be released. These tours cost between Q75 and Q187 (US$10–US$25/£5.30–£13) per person, depending on the length of the tour and the size of your group. Don't be afraid to bargain. Entrance to the zoo is an extra Q20 (US$2.70/£1.45).

You can also explore the lake on your own in a kayak or canoe. These are also rented all around Flores. Again, ask at your hotel or at one of the local tour agencies. Rates for kayaks and canoes run around Q15 (US$2.05/£1.05) per hour. Be careful paddling around the lake; when the winds pick up, especially in the afternoons, it can get quite choppy and challenging.

If you're a spelunker, you might want to explore **Aktun Kan (Cave of the Serpent),** a large cavern just outside of Santa Elena. The cave takes its name from a legend about a giant snake living there. But don't worry, it's only a legend. Yet another legend has it that this cave is connected to a cave beneath the church on Flores. To reach the cave, either walk south out of Santa Elena on the road that crosses the causeway from Flores, or ask a taxi to take you out there. The fare should be around Q150 (US$20/£11) round-trip. Although there are lights in the cave (admission Q20/US$2.70/£1.45), be sure to bring a flashlight for a little extra illumination.

A host of local tour operators here can arrange any of the tours listed above, as well as guided tours to Tikal and the ruins listed below. The best of these are **Martsam Travel ★★** (✆ **866/832-2776** in the U.S. and Canada, or 502/7867-5093 in Guatemala; www.martsam.com) and **San Juan Travel** (✆ **502/7926-0042;** sanjuantravel@hotmail.com.gt).

Yaxhá, El Ceibal & Other Nearby Ruins

If your life's passion is Mayan ruins or you simply crave more adventure than you have had so far on your visit to El Petén, you should think about visiting some of the more remote ruins of this region. In addition to exploring seldom-visited Mayan ruins, you'll be traveling through uninhabited jungles where you'll likely encounter a great deal of wildlife, which might include coati-mundis, howler and spider monkeys, anteaters, tapirs, and possibly even jaguars.

Thanks to the publicity and infrastructure bestowed upon this site by the TV show *Survivor: Guatemala,* **Yaxhá ★★** is now one of the prime archeological sites to visit in Guatemala. In fact, this is the third largest Mayan ceremonial city in Guatemala—behind Tikal and El Mirador. Be sure to climb **Temple 216 ★★★**, located in the East Acropolis. This is the tallest structure here, and provides excellent views of lakes Yaxhá and Sacnab, as well as the surrounding rainforests. The sunsets here rival those in Tikal. Yaxhá is one of the few Mayan cities to retain its traditional Mayan name, which translates as "green waters." You can combine a visit to Yaxhá with a trip to the ruins of **Topoxté,** which are located on a small island in Lake Yaxhá. This small yet intriguing site is thought to have been a residential city for local elites. However, it was also a fortified city where Mayan warriors put up a valiant defense against Spanish forces. ***Note:*** You'll probably be warned, and see the signs, but just in case, do not swim in Lake Yaxhá, as it is home to a robust population of crocodiles. Many organized tours here also include a stop at the nearby minor ruins of Nakum, which are currently being excavated. However, this makes for a long day. The turn-off for the 11km (7-mile) dirt road into the site is located about 32km (20 miles) east of Ixlú, or El Cruce. The Q80 (US$11/£5.70) admission grants you access to Yaxhá, Topoxté, and Nakum. If you want to stay at Yaxhá, camping is allowed at a well-tended campsite down by the lakeshore.

Another popular site is **El Ceibal ★**, which offers one of the most scenic routes along the way. To reach El Ceibal, you first head the 64km (40 miles) from Flores to Sayaxché, which is a good-size town for El Petén (it even has a few basic hotels). From Sayaxché, you must hire a boat to carry you 18km (11 miles) up the Río de la Pasión. El Ceibal is a Late Classic–era ruin known for having the only circular temple in all of El Petén. There are also several well-preserved stelae arranged around one small temple structure on the central plaza, as well as a ball court. Many of the designs at El Ceibal indicate that the city had extensive contact with cities in the Yucatán, but whether this contact was due to trade or to warfare is unclear. Your best bet for visiting El Ceibal is to book the excursion with one of the tour agencies in Flores or Santa Elena. Full-day trips run around Q447 to Q671 (US$60–US$91/£32–£48). Overnight trips can also be arranged, combining a visit to El Ceibal with even more obscure Mayan sites like Aguateca and Petexbatún. If you get to Sayaxché on your own, look for **Viajes Don Pedro** (**© 502/7928-6109**). These folks run regular boats to El Ceibal and charge around Q300 (US$41/£21) per person round-trip. However, if you have a group, be sure to try to negotiate a flat rate for the boat, which should carry anywhere from four to eight people. If you want to stay in this area, check out **Chiminos Island Lodge ★** (**© 502/2335-3506;** www.chiminosisland.com), which has six rustic yet luxurious cabins in the rainforest on a small island in the waters of the Petexbatún Lagoon.

Uaxactún (pronounced "Wah-shahk-*toon*") is another Mayan ceremonial center located 24km (15 miles) north of Tikal. Though many of the pyramids and temples here have been uncovered, they have not been restored nearly as extensively as those at Tikal. One of the most interesting finds at Uaxactún is what is believed to be the oldest known astrological observatory yet discovered in the Mayan world. In Group E, on the eastern side of these ruins, you can watch a sunrise from the observatory temple that lines up precisely with other temples on the equinoxes and solstices. Your best bet for visiting Uaxactún is to book the excursion with one of the tour agencies in Flores or Santa Elena. Full-day trips cost about Q375 to Q600 (US$50–US$81/£27–£43), and can be combined with a stop at Tikal, although I think that's trying to cram too much into a single day. If you have your own four-wheel-drive vehicle, you can drive here yourself. The ruins at Uaxactún are open daily from 6am to 6pm, and no admission is charged. However, you must reach it by passing through Tikal National Park, and so you must pay the Tikal entrance fee of Q150 (US$20/£11). Moreover, be forewarned that the dirt road between Tikal and Uaxactún is sometimes not passable during the rainy season. Be sure to ask locally about current conditions before heading off.

Finally, truly adventurous travelers can book a multi-day jungle trek to **El Mirador ★★**, the largest Mayan ceremonial city in Guatemala. Barely excavated, El Mirador features the tallest pyramidal structure in the known Mayan world, La Danta, which reaches some 79m (260 ft.) in height. The trip here involves at least 5 days of hiking and jungle camping. **Martsam Travel ★★** (✆ **866/832-2776** in the U.S. and Canada, or 502/7867-5093 in Guatemala; www.martsam.com) is the best operator to contact for one of these trips.

Studying Spanish

Eco Escuela de Español ★ (✆ **502/5940-1235;** www.ecoescuelaespanol.org) runs a community-based language school program in the small village of San Andrés, on the shore of Lake Petén Itzá. The program costs just US$150 (£80) per week, including lodging and three meals daily with a local family, as well as 4 hours of daily class time, usually one-on-one. The setting allows for intensive language instruction, as well as many chances to really interact with the local culture and natural surroundings.

If you want to stick closer to the action in town, check in with the **Dos Mundos Spanish Academy** (✆ **502/5830-2060;** www.flores-spanish.com), which offers a wide range of course and accommodations options.

WHERE TO STAY

Moderate

Hotel Petén Espléndido This modern upscale hotel is located in Santa Elena just off the causeway on the shore of Lake Petén Itzá, with a great view of Flores. The rooms feature contemporary decor and more modern amenities than you'll find anywhere else in town. The bathrooms are even equipped with telephones, and four rooms are truly fitted out for travelers with disabilities. The best rooms are the second-floor rooms with balconies directly fronting the lake. If you don't get one of these, the hotel's waterfront restaurant has a great view and serves good international and local cuisine. There's a relaxing and refreshing pool area, with a separate Jacuzzi. This place offers a free airport shuttle, as well as free paddleboats for use on the lake, and has a helpful tour desk and concierge.

1a Calle 5-01, Zona 1, Santa Elena, Flores, Petén. ✆ **502/2360-8140** reservations number in Guatemala City, or 502/7926-0880 at the hotel. Fax 502/7926-0866. www.petenesplendido.com. 62 units. Q670–Q820 (US$90–US$111/£48–£58) double. AE, DC, MC, V. **Amenities:** Restaurant; outdoor pool and Jacuzzi; watersports equipment rental; concierge; tour desk; car-rental desk; limited room service (6:30am–11:30pm); laundry service. *In room:* A/C, TV, dataport, hair dryer, safe.

La Casona del Lago ★★ This is the newest and most luxurious hotel in the area, run by a small local chain, although it's also the only one not on the island of Flores proper. (Don't confuse this with La Casona de la Isla, which is part of the same chain and in Flores.) Still, this hotel is located right on the shores of the lake, with excellent views of its waters and picturesque island city. The three-story building is built in an L-shape, around a central pool and Jacuzzi area, and painted a bright primary blue, with sparkling white trim. Rooms are spacious, with two double beds, white-tile floors, a couple of sitting chairs, and a separate desk area, and they feature a host of modern amenities, including 21-inch televisions.

1a Calle, Zona 1, Santa Elena, Flores, Petén. ✆/fax **502/7952-8700.** www.hotelesdepeten.com. 32 units. Q640–Q709 ($87–$96/£45–£50) double. Rates higher during peak periods. AE, DC, MC, V. **Amenities:** Restaurant; outdoor pool and Jacuzzi; tour desk; laundry service; free Wi-Fi. *In room:* A/C, TV, dataport, hair dryer.

Inexpensive

Casa Elena ★ Value This neat little hotel in downtown Santa Elena offers well-kept rooms at a fair price. Most of the rooms are a bit small, and their televisions are tiny. At the center of the hotel is a pretty little pool and lovely interior courtyard with shady palm trees. The pool even has a water slide, which is a big hit with children. The hotel is kept immaculate, and there's a friendly air to the whole operation. You'll find a simple restaurant on the grounds, as well as an inviting second-floor bar. For a good view, head up to the unfinished rooftop terrace.

Av. 6 and Calle 2, Santa Elena, Petén. ✆ **502/7926-2235.** Fax 502/7926-0097. www.casaelena.com. 28 units. Q224–Q335 (US$30–US$45/£16–£24) double. AE, MC, V. **Amenities:** Restaurant; outdoor pool; tour desk; limited room service (7am–10pm); laundry service. *In room:* A/C, TV.

Hotel Del Patio This hotel's central courtyard, with its tall fountain flowing into a cloverleaf pool, is classic colonial Guatemala. The rooms are simple, clean, and comfortable, although the decor is definitely dated. I'd opt for a second-floor unit, just so you can admire the courtyard from above as you enter and exit your room. A midsize kidney-shaped pool and tiny gym, as well as a good international restaurant, round out the amenities.

Calle 8 and Av. 2, Santa Elena, Petén. ✆ **502/7926-0104** or 502/2337-4402. Fax 502/7926-1229. www.caminoreal.com.gt. 21 units. Q187–Q300 (US$25–US$41/£13–£21) double. Rate includes breakfast. AE, MC, V. **Amenities:** Restaurant; bar; pool; small gym; tour desk; limited room service (6:30am–10pm); laundry service. *In room:* A/C, TV.

Hotel Isla de Flores ★ This four-story hotel in downtown Flores is intimate and charming. The decor and architecture feature a mix of modern and colonial elements. The rooms are compact, but clean and comfortable. Most come with two double beds, a good-size television with a variety of cable channels, and a tiny balcony. The rooms on the higher floors have good views over the town and lake. A couple of rooms are set up for larger groups or families, and a couple have no balcony or view to speak of. White wicker furniture is spread around the lobby and restaurant areas. This place has a helpful tour desk, and it is run by the same folks who have the Jungle Lodge inside Tikal National Park.

Av. La Reforma, Flores, Petén. ✆ **502/7926-0614** or 502/2476-8775. Fax 502/2476-0294. www.hotelisladeflores.com. 18 units. Q410 (US$56/£29) double. Rate includes breakfast. AE, MC, V. **Amenities:** Restaurant; bar; tour desk; laundry service. *In room:* A/C, TV.

Hotel Petén From the street, this hotel looks very modest. Walk through the doorway, though, and you'll find a small courtyard with tropical plants, a tiny semi-indoor pool, and a nice brick-and-stucco building of several floors. The rooms are all well kept. The best rooms are those on the top two floors with private balconies and an excellent view of the lake. In fact, only five rooms here don't have a lake view, so when you reserve or check in, be sure you get one that does. There's a popular restaurant on the ground floor. These folks also have an in-house tour company, and a couple of other nearby hotels, if this one is full.

Calle Centroamérica, Flores, Petén. ✆/fax **502/7867-5203.** www.hotelesdepeten.com. 21 units. Q343–Q380 ($46–$51/£24–£27) double. AE, DC, MC, V. **Amenities:** Restaurant; pool; Jacuzzi; tour desk; laundry service. *In room:* A/C, TV.

Hotel Santana ★ Value This is a great choice if you're looking to snag a lakefront room with a balcony and a view, all at a very good price. Most of the rooms here fit the criteria I just mentioned, and those on the third and fourth floors have the best views—still, be sure you get a lake-view room, and not one of the less desirable interior affairs. The rooms here are all cool, clean, and fairly spacious, and a definite cut above the rest of the options on the island of Flores in this price range. The large open-air dining room is a delightful place to sit and enjoy the lakeside setting as well. There's a small kidney-shaped pool, with a built-in waterfall and swim-up bar, in a little courtyard to the side.

Calle 30 de Junio, Flores, Petén. ✆/fax **502/7867-5123** or 502/7867-5193. www.santanapeten.com. 35 units. Q300–Q450 (US$41–US$61/£21–£32) double. AE, MC, V. **Amenities:** Restaurant; outdoor pool; tour desk; laundry service. *In room:* A/C, TV, safe.

La Casona de la Isla La Casona de la Isla shows the same attention to service as the other properties run by this local hotel group. The guest rooms here are all fairly small and lack much in the way of style, but they do have tile floors, ceiling fans, and air-conditioning—although some of these A/C units can be rather old and noisy. Most come with a private balcony, and almost all of these have good views of the lake. The hotel is built in an L-shape around a stone terrace with lush gardens and a small swimming pool featuring a sculpted stone waterfall and separate Jacuzzi. Its restaurant serves good Guatemalan and international fare in a small dining room off the lobby, and there's a back patio bar with an excellent view overlooking the lake.

Calle 30 de Junio, Flores, Petén. ✆ **502/7867-5163.** www.hotelesdepeten.com. 26 units. Q373–Q410 (US$51–US$56/£26–£29) double. AE, DC, MC, V. **Amenities:** Restaurant; bar; outdoor pool and Jacuzzi; tour desk; laundry service. *In room:* A/C, TV.

WHERE TO DINE

There are tons of places to eat around Flores and Santa Elena. Most are simple affairs serving local and Mexican cuisine, and geared towards locals and the backpacker crowd. Most of the hotels listed above have restaurants, and most of these are quite dependable. **El Mirador Restaurant** at the Hotel Petén Espléndido (p. 282) serves good but far from spectacular international fare; however, the setting is certainly the most elegant you'll find in this neck of the woods.

In addition to the places listed below, **Pizzeria Picasso** (✆ **502/7867-5198;** Calle 15 de Setiembre, across from El Tucán) serves pretty good wood-oven pizza and a variety of pastas, while **Café Arqueológico Yaxhá** (✆ **502/5830-2060;** www.cafeyaxha.com; Calle 15 de Setiembre, across from El Tucán) is a relaxed and welcoming new place that serves local fare, including dishes based on pre-Colombian recipes and ingredients, as well as coffee drinks and fresh fruit smoothies.

Capitán Tortuga ★ INTERNATIONAL This popular restaurant has a long and wide-ranging menu. You can get everything from pizzas to barbecue ribs to vegetarian shish kabobs. They also have a wide range of coffee and espresso drinks, as well as ice creams and freshly baked desserts. The large main dining room sits under a high thatch room. However, I prefer the tables on the small outdoor patio that fronts the lake, or those in the second-floor, open-air dining room reached from a stairway out back. Service can be slow at times, but if you're with a group or sharing a drink with fellow travelers, you might not mind.

Calle 30 de Junio, next to La Casona de la Isla, Flores. ✆ **502/7867-5089.** Main courses Q30–Q110 (US$4.05–US$15/£2.10–£7.80). MC, V. Daily 11:30am–11pm.

La Luna ★★ *Finds* INTERNATIONAL This hip little restaurant is the most creative and refined option in Flores. The menu ranges from steak in pepper sauce to lobster tails, with a host of fish and chicken—and even some vegetarian—options in between. I recommend starting things off with some stuffed peppers or a falafel side. There are three separate dining areas, and all are artistically decorated. My favorite room features a faux ceiba tree in the center and a wild sculpture on one wall made of wood and mirrors.

Calle 30 de Junio, across from La Casona de la Isla, Flores. ✆ **502/7926-3346.** Main courses Q40–Q130 (US$5.40–US$18/£2.85–£9.20). MC, V. Tues–Sun 11am–11pm.

FLORES & SANTA ELENA AFTER DARK

Most folks simply frequent the bar at their hotel, or stick around after dinner at one of the local restaurants. There are several bars along Calle Sur fronting the lake just over the bridge as you enter Flores. Of these, **AAdictos** is one of the liveliest. For a view of the lake and a happening party scene, you can head to **Bar Raíces,** at the far western end of Calle Sur. Another good option, near the center of the island, is **Las Puertas,** which has been playing a mix of house and chill dance tunes in a hip little space, and sometimes has live music; it's located at the corner of Calle Centroamérica and Avenida Santa Ana.

Finally, if you're in a gambling mood, you can head to the **Maya Princess** (✆ **502/7924-8764**) located on 2a Calle 7-00, Zona 1, in Santa Elena. This place has a wide range of electronic gaming machines; nightly bingo; and a swank, Las Vegas–style ambience.

Appendix A: Fast Facts, Toll-Free Numbers & Websites

1 FAST FACTS

AMERICAN EXPRESS American Express Travel Services is represented in Belize City by **Belize Global Travel Services Ltd.,** 41 Albert St. (✆ **227-7185;** www.belizeglobal.bz), which can issue traveler's checks and replacement cards, and provide other standard services. They are open Monday through Friday from 8am to noon and 1 to 5pm, and on Saturday from 8am to noon. To report a lost or stolen Amex credit card or traveler's checks within Belize, call the local number above, or call collect to ✆ **336/393-1111** in the U.S.

AREA CODES There are no area codes in Belize. All local phone numbers are seven-digit numbers.

ATM NETWORKS/CASHPOINTS See "Money & Costs," p. 43.

BUSINESS HOURS Banks are generally open Monday through Friday from 8am to 4:30pm. However, in many small towns, villages, and tourist destinations, bank hours may be limited. In very few instances, banks have begun opening on Saturday. Belizean businesses tend to be open Monday through Friday from 8am to noon, and from 1 to 5pm. Some businesses do not close for lunch, and some open on Saturday. Most bars are open until 1 or 2am, although some go later.

CAR RENTALS See "Getting There & Getting Around" in chapter 3 and "Toll-Free Numbers & Websites," later in this chapter.

DRINKING LAWS The legal drinking age in Belize is 18 years old, although it is often not enforced. Beer, wine, and liquor are all sold in most supermarkets and small convenience stores from Monday through Saturday. No liquor is sold on Good Friday or Easter Sunday. On Election Day, no liquor can be sold until 6pm.

DRIVING RULES See "Getting There & Getting Around," p. 39.

DRUGSTORES There are a handful of pharmacies around Belize City, and in most of the major towns and tourist destinations. Perhaps the best-stocked pharmacy in the country can be found at **Belize Medical Associates,** 5791 St. Thomas Kings Park, Belize City (✆ **223-0303;** www.belizemedical.com).

ELECTRICITY Electricity is 110-volt AC, and most outlets are either two- or three-prong U.S.-style outlets.

If you wish to access the Internet with your own computer, bring a **connection kit** of the right power and phone adapters, a spare phone cord, and a spare Ethernet network cable—or find out whether your hotel supplies them to guests.

EMBASSIES & CONSULATES The **United States Embassy** is located in Belmopan on Floral Park Road (✆ **822-4011;** http://belize.usembassy.gov). The **British High Commission** is located in

Belmopan, at Embassy Square (✆ **822-2146**). You can contact the **Canadian Honorary Consul** in Belize City at 80 Princess Margaret Drive (✆ **223-1060**).

EMERGENCIES In case of any emergency, dial ✆ **90** from anywhere in Belize. This will connect you to the police. In most cases, ✆ **911** will also work. I've listed the various numbers for fire departments, ambulances, and hospitals in the "Fast Facts" sections throughout the book.

GASOLINE (PETROL) Gasoline is sold as "unleaded" and "super." Both are unleaded; super is just higher octane. Diesel is available at most gas stations as well. At press time, a liter of super cost around BZ$10 (US$5/£2.50).

HOLIDAYS For more information on holidays, see "Belize Calendar of Events," in chapter 3.

HOSPITALS **Belize Medical Associates,** 5791 St. Thomas Kings Park, Belize City (✆ **223-0303;** www.belizemedical.com), is a modern, 24-hour private hospital, with emergency care and numerous private-practice physicians. The country's main public hospital, the **Karl Heusner Memorial Hospital,** Princess Margaret Drive, Belize City (✆ **223-1548**), is also open 24 hours and has a wide range of facilities and services.

INSURANCE **Medical Insurance** For travel overseas, most U.S. health plans (including Medicare and Medicaid) do not provide coverage, and the ones that do often require you to pay for services upfront and they reimburse you only after you return home.

As a safety net, you may want to buy travel medical insurance, particularly if you're traveling to a remote or high-risk area where emergency evacuation might be necessary. If you require additional medical insurance, try **MEDEX Assistance** (✆ **410/453-6300;** www.medexassist.com) or **Travel Assistance International** (✆ **800/821-2828;** www.travelassistance.com; for general information on services, call the company's **Worldwide Assistance Services, Inc.,** at ✆ **800/777-8710**).

Canadians should check with their provincial health plan offices or call **Health Canada** (✆ **866/225-0709;** www.hc-sc.gc.ca) to find out the extent of their coverage and what documentation and receipts they must take home in case they are treated overseas.

Travelers from the U.K. should carry their European Health Insurance Card (EHIC), which replaced the E111 form as proof of entitlement to free/reduced cost medical treatment abroad (✆ **0845-606-2030;** www.ehic.org.uk). Note, however, that the EHIC only covers "necessary medical treatment," and for repatriation costs, lost money, baggage, or cancellation, travel insurance from a reputable company should always be sought (www.travelinsuranceweb.com).

Travel Insurance The cost of travel insurance varies widely, depending on the destination, the cost and length of your trip, your age and health, and the type of trip you're taking, but expect to pay between 5% and 8% of the vacation itself. You can get estimates from various providers through **InsureMyTrip.com.** Enter your trip cost and dates, your age, and other information, for prices from more than a dozen companies.

U.K. citizens and their families who make more than one trip abroad per year may find that an annual travel insurance policy works out to be cheaper. Check **www.moneysupermarket.com**, which compares prices across a wide range of providers for single- and multi-trip policies.

Most big travel agents offer their own insurance and will probably try to sell you their package when you book a holiday. Think before you sign. **Britain's Consumers' Association** recommends that you insist on seeing the policy and reading the fine print before buying travel insurance. **The Association of British Insurers** (✆ **020/7600-3333;** www.abi.org.uk) gives advice by phone and publishes *Holiday Insurance,* a free guide to policy provisions and prices. You might also shop around for better deals: Try **Columbus Direct** (✆ **0870/033-9988;** www.columbusdirect.net).

Trip Cancellation Insurance Trip-cancellation insurance will help retrieve your money if you have to back out of a trip or depart early, or if your travel supplier goes bankrupt. Trip cancellation traditionally covers such events as sickness, natural disasters, and State Department advisories. The latest news in trip-cancellation insurance is the availability of **expanded hurricane coverage** and the **"any-reason"** cancellation coverage—which costs more but covers cancellations made for any reason. You won't get back 100% of your prepaid trip cost, but you'll be refunded a substantial portion. **TravelSafe** (✆ **888/885-7233;** www.travelsafe.com) offers both types of coverage. Expedia also offers any-reason cancellation coverage for its air-hotel packages. For details, contact one of the following recommended insurers: **Access America** (✆ 866/807-3982; www.accessamerica.com); **Travel Guard International** (✆ 800/826-4919; www.travelguard.com); **Travel Insured International** (✆ 800/243-3174; www.travelinsured.com); and **Travelex Insurance Services** (✆ 888/457-4602; www.travelex-insurance.com).

INTERNET ACCESS Cybercafes can be found at most major tourist destinations around Belize. Wi-Fi is also increasingly common, and many hotels are offering it for free. Rates at cybercafes run between BZ$2 and BZ$10 (US$1–US$5/55p–£2.65) per hour. Alternatively, **BTL** (✆ **0800/112-4636;** www.btl.net), the state Internet monopoly, sells prepaid cards in BZ$10 (US$5/£2.65), BZ$25 (US$13/£6.90), and BZ$50 (US$25/£13) denominations for connecting your laptop to the Web via a local phone call.

LANGUAGE English is the official language of Belize, and it is almost universally spoken. However, Belize is a very polyglot country, and you are likely to hear and come across Spanish, Creole, and Garífuna. For some help in communicating in Spanish and Creole, see appendix B.

LAUNDROMATS Most folks rely on their hotel's laundry and dry-cleaning services, although these can be expensive. Where they exist, I've listed laundromats and laundry options in the "Fast Facts" sections of the destination chapters.

LEGAL AID If you need legal help, your best bet is to first contact your local embassy or consulate. See "Embassies & Consulates" above for contact details. Alternatively, ask at your hotel for an appropriate recommendation.

LOST & FOUND Be sure to tell all of your credit card companies the minute you discover your wallet has been lost or stolen and file a report at the nearest police precinct. Your credit card company or insurer may require a police report number or record of the loss. Most credit card companies have an emergency toll-free number to call if your card is lost or stolen; they may be able to wire you a cash advance immediately or deliver an emergency credit card in a day or two. It's a good idea to write this number down and carry it someplace separate from your wallet or credit cards. **Visa**'s emergency number is ✆ **800/847-2911** toll-free in the U.S., or call 410/581-9994 collect from Belize. **American Express** cardholders and traveler's check holders should call ✆ **800/221-7282** toll-free in the U.S., or ✆ 336/393-1111 collect from Belize. **MasterCard** holders should call ✆ **800/307-7309** toll-free in the U.S., or 636/722-7111 collect from Belize.

If you need emergency cash over the weekend when all banks and American Express offices are closed, you can have money wired to you via **Western Union** (✆ **800/325-6000** in the U.S. and Canada, or **227-0014** in Belize; www.westernunion.com), although the service charges are substantial.

MAIL Most hotels will post a letter for you, and there are post offices in the major towns. It costs BZ$.80 (US40¢/21p) to send a letter to the United States, and BZ$1 (US50¢/27p) to send a letter to Europe. Postcards to the same destinations cost BZ$.40 (US20¢/11p) and BZ$.50 (US25¢/13p) respectively.

If your postal needs are urgent, or you want to send anything of value, several international courier and express-mail services have offices in Belize City, including **DHL,** 38 New Rd. (✆ **223-1070;** www.dhl.com); **FedEx,** 1 Mapp St. (✆ **224-5221;** www.fedex.com); and **Mail Boxes Etc.,** 166 N. Front St. (✆ **227-6046;** www.mbe.com). All can arrange pick up and delivery services to any hotel in town, and sometimes in the different outlying districts.

MEASUREMENTS English measurements are the norm in Belize, although the metric system is making slight inroads. See the chart on the inside front cover of this book for details on converting metric measurements to nonmetric equivalents.

NEWSPAPERS & MAGAZINES Belize has no daily newspaper. There are four primary weeklies and bi-weeklies, ***Amandala*** (www.amandala.com.bz), the ***Reporter*** (www.reporter.bz), ***Belize Times*** (www.belizetimes.bz), and the ***Guardian*** (www.guardian.bz). All come out on Friday, with the bi-weeklies also having a Tuesday edition. All are relatively similar in terms of content, although with some differing (and usually obvious) political leanings and loyalties.

PASSPORTS The websites listed below provide downloadable passport applications as well as the current fees for processing applications. For an up-to-date, country-by-country listing of passport requirements around the world, go to the "International Travel" tab of the U.S. State Department at **http://travel.state.gov**. Allow plenty of time before your trip to apply for a passport; processing normally takes 4 to 6 weeks (3 weeks for expedited service) but can take longer during busy periods (especially spring). And keep in mind that if you need a passport in a hurry, you'll pay a higher processing fee.

For Residents of Australia You can pick up an application from your local post office or any branch of Passports Australia, but you must schedule an interview at the passport office to present your application materials. Call the **Australian Passport Information Service** at ✆ **131-232,** or visit the government website at www.passports.gov.au.

For Residents of Canada Passport applications are available at travel agencies throughout Canada or from the central **Passport Office,** Department of Foreign Affairs and International Trade, Ottawa, ON K1A 0G3 (✆ **800/567-6868;** www.ppt.gc.ca). ***Note:*** Canadian children who travel must have their own passport. However, if you hold a valid Canadian passport issued before December 11, 2001, that bears the name of your child, the passport remains valid for you and your child until it expires.

For Residents of Ireland You can apply for a 10-year passport at the **Passport Office,** Setanta Centre, Molesworth Street, Dublin 2 (✆ **01/671-1633;** www.irlgov.ie/iveagh). Those under age 18 and over 65 must apply for a 3-year passport. You can also apply at 1A South Mall, Cork (✆ **21/494-4700**) or at most main post offices.

For Residents of New Zealand You can pick up a passport application at any New Zealand Passports Office or download it from their website. Contact the

Passports Office at ✆ **0800/225-050** in New Zealand or 04/474-8100, or log on to www.passports.govt.nz.

For Residents of the United Kingdom To pick up an application for a standard 10-year passport (5-year passport for children under 16), visit your nearest passport office, major post office, or travel agency, or contact the **United Kingdom Passport Service** at ✆ **0870/521-0410** or search its website at www.ukpa.gov.uk.

PHOTOGRAPHIC NEEDS While I recommend bringing as much film as you foresee needing and waiting until you return to develop it, you can buy and develop film at most popular tourist destinations (but it's more expensive in Belize).

POLICE The police in Belize are generally rather helpful; there is a dedicated tourism police force in Belize City. Dial ✆ **90** or **911** in an emergency. You can also dial ✆ **227-2222.**

SMOKING Belize has yet to pass any no-smoking legislation, and aside from a handful of hotels that are entirely nonsmoking, few others have true nonsmoking rooms or floors. Similarly, many restaurants don't have a nonsmoking section. Luckily, so much dining in Belize is alfresco that this may not be a problem, especially if you can snag an upwind seat.

TAXES There is a US$35 (£19) departure tax that must be paid in cash at the airport upon departure. There is a 9% hotel tax added on to all hotel bills, and there is a 10% GST tax on all goods and services. A 10% service charge is sometimes added on to restaurant bills. Take this into account when deciding how much to tip.

TELEPHONES Belize has a standardized seven-digit phone numbering system. There are no city or area codes to dial from within Belize; use the country code, 501 (not to be confused with the area code for the state of Arkansas), only when dialing a Belizean number from outside Belize.

For directory assistance: Dial ✆ **113** if you're looking for a number inside Belize, and for numbers to all other countries dial ✆ **115** and (for a charge) an operator will connect you to an international directory assistance operator.

For operator assistance: If you need operator assistance in making a call, dial ✆ **115,** whether you're trying to make a local or an international call.

Toll-free numbers: Numbers beginning with 0800 and 800 within Belize country are toll-free, but calling a 1-800 number in the States from Belize is not toll-free. In fact, it costs the same as an overseas call.

TIME Belize is on Central Standard Time, 6 hours behind Greenwich Mean Time. Belize does not observe daylight saving time.

TIPPING Most Belizeans don't tip. Many restaurants add a 10% service charge. However, if the service is particularly good, or if the service charge is not included, tipping is appropriate.

TOILETS There are very few public toilets or restrooms in Belize. About the only ones I know of are located at the little cruise-ship tourist village on Fort Street in the Fort George section of Belize City. However, most hotels and restaurants will let tourists use their facilities.

USEFUL PHONE NUMBERS **Time, date, and temperature,** ✆ 121; **U.S. Dept. of State Travel Advisory,** ✆ 202/647-5225 (manned 24 hr.); **U.S. Passport Agency,** ✆ 202/647-0518; **U.S. Centers for Disease Control International Traveler's Hot Line,** ✆ 404/332-4559.

WATER The water in most major cities and tourist destinations in Belize is ostensibly safe to drink. However, many travelers react adversely to water in foreign countries, and it is probably best to drink bottled water throughout your visit to Belize.

2 TOLL-FREE NUMBERS & WEBSITES

MAJOR U.S. AIRLINES

American Airlines
✆ 800/433-7300 (in U.S. and Canada)
✆ 020/7365-0777 (in U.K.)
www.aa.com

Continental Airlines
✆ 800/523-3273 (in U.S. and Canada)
✆ 084/5607-6760 (in U.K.)
www.continental.com

Delta Air Lines
✆ 800/221-1212 (in U.S. and Canada)
✆ 084/5600-0950 (in U.K.)
www.delta.com

United Airlines
✆ 800/864-8331 (in U.S. and Canada)
✆ 084/5844-4777 (in U.K.)
www.united.com

US Airways
✆ 800/428-4322 (in U.S. and Canada)
✆ 084/5600-3300 (in U.K.)
www.usairways.com

MAJOR INTERNATIONAL AIRLINES

Air France
✆ 800/237-2747 (in U.S.)
✆ 800/375-8723 (in U.S. and Canada)
✆ 087/0142-4343 (in U.K.)
www.airfrance.com

Air New Zealand
✆ 800/262-1234 (in U.S.)
✆ 800/663-5494 (in Canada)
✆ 0800/028-4149 (in U.K.)
www.airnewzealand.com

Alitalia
✆ 800/223-5730 (in U.S.)
✆ 800/361-8336 (in Canada)
✆ 087/0608-6003 (in U.K.)
www.alitalia.com

American Airlines
✆ 800/433-7300 (in U.S. and Canada)
✆ 020/7365-0777 (in U.K.)
www.aa.com

British Airways
✆ 800/247-9297 (in U.S. and Canada)
✆ 087/0850-9850 (in U.K.)
www.british-airways.com

Caribbean Airlines (formerly BWIA)
✆ 800/920-4225 (in U.S. and Canada)
✆ 084/5362 4225 (in U.K.)
www.caribbean-airlines.com

Continental Airlines
✆ 800/523-3273 (in U.S. and Canada)
✆ 084/5607-6760 (in U.K.)
www.continental.com

Cubana
✆ 888/667-1222 (in Canada)
✆ 020/7538-5933 (in U.K.)
www.cubana.cu

Delta Air Lines
✆ 800/221-1212 (in U.S. and Canada)
✆ 084/5600-0950 (in U.K.)
www.delta.com

Iberia Airlines
✆ 800/722-4642 (in U.S. and Canada)
✆ 087/0609-0500 (in U.K.)
www.iberia.com

Japan Airlines
✆ 012/025-5931 (international)
www.jal.co.jp

Korean Air
✆ 800/438-5000 (in U.S. and Canada)
✆ 0800/413-000 (in U.K.)
www.koreanair.com

Lan Airlines
✆ 866/435-9526 (in U.S.)
✆ 305/670-9999 (in other countries)
www.lanchile.com

Lufthansa
✆ 800/399-5838 (in U.S.)
✆ 800/563-5954 (in Canada)
✆ 087/0837-7747 (in U.K.)
www.lufthansa.com

Philippine Airlines
✆ 800/I-FLY-PAL (800/435-9725) (in U.S. and Canada)
✆ 632/855-8888 (in Philippines)
www.philippineairlines.com

Qantas Airways
✆ 800/227-4500 (in U.S.)
✆ 084/5774-7767 (in U.K. and Canada)
✆ 13-13-13 (in Australia)
www.qantas.com

South African Airways
✆ 271/1978-5313 (international)
✆ 0861/FLY-SAA (086/135-9122) (in South Africa)
www.flysaa.com

Swiss Air
✆ 877/359-7947 (in U.S. and Canada)
✆ 084/5601-0956 (in U.K.)
www.swiss.com

TACA
✆ 800/535-8780 (in U.S.)
✆ 800/722-TACA (8222) (in Canada)
✆ 087/0241-0340 (in U.K.)
✆ 503/2267-8222 (in El Salvador)
www.taca.com

United Airlines
✆ 800/864-8331 (in U.S. and Canada)
✆ 084/5844-4777 (in U.K.)
www.united.com

US Airways
✆ 800/428-4322 (in U.S. and Canada)
✆ 084/5600-3300 (in U.K.)
www.usairways.com

CAR-RENTAL AGENCIES

Avis
✆ 800/331-1212 (in U.S. and Canada)
✆ 084/4581-8181 (in U.K.)
www.avis.com

Budget
✆ 800/527-0700 (in U.S.)
✆ 087/0156-5656 (in U.K.)
✆ 800/268-8900 (in Canada)
www.budget.com

Hertz
✆ 800/645-3131
✆ 800/654-3001 (for international reservations)
www.hertz.com

Thrifty
✆ 800/367-2277
✆ 918/669-2168 (international)
www.thrifty.com

MAJOR HOTEL & MOTEL CHAINS

Best Western International
✆ 800/780-7234 (in U.S. and Canada)
✆ 0800/393-130 (in U.K.)
www.bestwestern.com

Radisson Hotels & Resorts
✆ 888/201-1718 (in U.S. and Canada)
✆ 0800/374-411 (in U.K.)
www.radisson.com

Appendix B: Useful Terms & Phrases

English is the official language of Belize, but the country is one of the most polyglot places on the planet. In addition to English, many Belizeans speak Spanish, and amongst some members of the population, this is the primary language. You will find Spanish prevalent in the northern and western regions, near the borders with Mexico and Guatemala, but given Belize's long history of immigration, Spanish speakers can be found throughout the country. In fact, conversations amongst Belizeans are often a mix of English and Spanish ("Spanglish"), with a fair amount of Creole thrown in for good measure.

Creole, or Kriol, is the local patois, a colorful, rhythmic, and often difficult-to-understand dialect. Although based almost entirely on English, it takes some getting used to before most Westerners can grasp the pronunciations and sentence structures that distinguish Belizean Kriol. While this was originally the language of former black slaves and their descendants, today most Belizeans understand and speak Kriol, and they will often use it amongst themselves in the presence of foreigners if they don't want to be understood.

In addition to English, Spanish, and Kriol, Belize's Garífuna (or Garinagu) people have their own distinct language, while the various Maya tribes still speak primarily their native languages.

1 SPANISH TERMS

BASIC PHRASES

English	Spanish	Pronunciation
Good morning	**Buenos días**	*Bweh*-nohss *dee*-ahss
Good afternoon/ evening	**Buenas tardes**	*Bweh*-nahss *tahr*-dehs
Good night	**Buenas noches**	*Bweh*-nahss *noh*-chehs
How are you?	**¿Cómo está usted?**	*Koh*-moh eh-*stah* oo-*stehd*
Very well	**Muy bien**	Mwee byehn
Thank you	**Gracias**	*Grah*-syahss
Good-bye	**Adios**	Ad-*dyohss*
Please	**Por favor**	Pohr fah-*vohr*
Yes	**Sí**	See
No	**No**	Noh
Excuse me (to get by someone)	**Perdóneme**	Pehr-*doh*-neh-meh

English	Spanish	Pronunciation
Excuse me (to begin a question)	**Disculpe**	Dee-*skool*-peh
Give me	**Deme**	*Deh*-meh
Where is . . . ?	**¿Dónde está . . . ?**	*Dohn*-deh eh-*stah*
the station	**la estación**	la eh-*stah*-syohn
the bus stop	**la parada**	la pah-*rah*-dah
a hotel	**un hotel**	oon oh-*tehl*
a restaurant	**un restaurante**	oon reh-stow-*rahn*-teh
the toilet	**el servicio**	el ser-*bee*-syoh
To the right	**A la derecha**	Ah lah deh-*reh*-chah
To the left	**A la izquierda**	Ah lah ee-*skyehr*-dah
Straight ahead	**Adelante**	Ah-deh-*lahn*-teh
I would like . . .	**Quiero . . .**	*Kyeh*-roh
to eat	**comer**	ko-*mehr*
a room	**una habitación**	*oo*-nah ah-bee-tah-*syohn*
How much is it?	**¿Cuánto?**	*Kwahn*-toh
The check	**La cuenta**	La *kwen*-tah
When?	**¿Cuándo?**	*Kwahn*-doh
What?	**¿Qué?**	Keh
What time is it?	**¿Qué hora es?**	Keh *oh*-rah ehss
Yesterday	**Ayer**	Ah-*yehr*
Today	**Hoy**	Oy
Tomorrow	**Mañana**	Mah-*nyah*-nah
Breakfast	**Desayuno**	Deh-sah-*yoo*-noh
Lunch	**Almuerzo**	Ahl-*mwehr*-soh
Dinner	**Cena**	*Ceh*-nah
Do you speak English?	**¿Habla usted inglés?**	*Ah*-blah oo-*stehd* een-*glehss*
Is there anyone here who speaks English?	**¿Hay alguien aquí que hable inglés?**	Eye *ahl*-gyehn ah-*kee* keh *ah*-bleh een-*glehss*
I speak a little Spanish.	**Hablo un poco de español.**	*Ah*-bloh oon *poh*-koh deh eh-spah-*nyohl*
I don't understand Spanish very well.	**No (lo) entiendo muy bien el español.**	Noh (loh) ehn-*tyehn*-doh mwee byehn el eh-spah-*nyohl*

1 **uno** (*oo*-noh)
2 **dos** (dohss)
3 **tres** (trehss)
4 **cuatro** (*kwah*-troh)
5 **cinco** (*seen*-koh)
6 **seis** (sayss)
7 **siete** (*syeh*-teh)
8 **ocho** (*oh*-choh)
9 **nueve** (*nweh*-beh)
10 **diez** (dyehss)
11 **once** (*ohn*-seh)
12 **doce** (*doh*-seh)
13 **trece** (*treh*-seh)
14 **catorce** (kah-*tohr*-seh)
15 **quince** (*keen*-seh)
16 **dieciséis** (dyeh-see-*sayss*)
17 **diecisiete** (dyeh-see-*syeh*-teh)
18 **dieciocho** (dyeh-*syoh*-choh)
19 **diecinueve** (dyeh-see-*nweh*-beh)
20 **veinte** (*bayn*-teh)
30 **treinta** (*trayn*-tah)
40 **cuarenta** (kwah-*rehn*-tah)
50 **cincuenta** (seen-*kwehn*-tah)
60 **sesenta** (seh-*sehn*-tah)
70 **setenta** (seh-*tehn*-tah)
80 **ochenta** (oh-*chehn*-tah)
90 **noventa** (noh-*behn*-tah)
100 **cien** (syehn)
1,000 **mil** (meel)

DAYS OF THE WEEK

Monday	**lunes** (*loo*-nehss)
Tuesday	**martes** (*mahr*-tehss)
Wednesday	**miércoles** (*myehr*-koh-lehs)
Thursday	**jueves** (*wheh*-behss)
Friday	**viernes** (*byehr*-nehss)
Saturday	**sábado** (*sah*-bah-doh)
Sunday	**domingo** (doh-*meen*-goh)

MENU TERMS

FISH

Atún Tuna
Calamares Squid
Camarones Shrimp
Cangrejo Crab
Ceviche Marinated seafood salad
Dorado Dolphin, or mahimahi
Langosta Lobster
Langostinos Prawns
Lenguado Sole
Mejillones Mussels
Mero Grouper
Ostras Oysters
Pargo Snapper
Pulpo Octopus
Tiburón Shark

MEATS

Bistec Beefsteak
Cerdo Pork
Chicharrones Fried pork rinds
Chuleta Cutlet
Conejo Rabbit
Cordero Lamb
Costillas Ribs
Jamón Ham
Lengua Tongue
Pato Duck
Pavo Turkey
Pollo Chicken

VEGETABLES

Aceitunas Olives
Alcachofa Artichoke
Berenjena Eggplant
Cebolla Onion
Elote Corn on the cob
Ensalada Salad
Espárragos Asparagus
Espinacas Spinach
Palmito Heart of palm
Papa Potato
Pepino Cucumber
Remolacha Beet
Repollo Cabbage
Tomate Tomato
Vainica String beans
Yuca Cassava, or manioc
Zanahoria Carrot

FRUITS

Aguacate Avocado
Carambola Star fruit
Cereza Cherry
Ciruela Plum
Fresa Strawberry
Limón Lemon or lime
Mango Mango
Manzana Apple
Melocotón Peach
Mora Raspberry
Naranja Orange
Pera Pear
Piña Pineapple
Plátano Banana
Sandía Watermelon
Toronja Grapefruit
Uvas Grapes

BASICS

Aceite Oil
Ajo Garlic
Azúcar Sugar
Frito Fried
Mantequilla Butter
Miel Honey
Mostaza Mustard
Natilla Sour cream
Pan Bread
Pimienta Pepper
Queso Cheese
Sal Salt
Tamal Filled cornmeal pastry
Tortilla Flat corn pancake

2 CREOLE TERMS

Creole, or Kriol, is largely based on English, although it does incorporate words and syntax from various African languages as well. Once you get the hang of certain pronunciations and syntactical phrasings, however, it's actually quite easy to understand. Almost any Kriol speaker will understand you if you speak in English. However, they'll be really impressed if you start inserting various Kriol words and phrases into your conversations.

BASIC WORDS

Agen Again
Aks To ask
An And
Bak Back
Bwai Boy
Chinchi A very small amount
Daata Daughter
Da At, on, in, to
Da Is, am, are
Da It is
Deh/di Am, is, are (located); for instance, "Ih deh pahn di boat" means "He/she is on the boat"
Dehn Them

Di The
Doe Door
Fi To
Fo For
Ih He, she, it
Kunku Small
Nize Noise
Noh Isn't it so?
Shudda Should have
Tideh Today
Uman Woman
Unu You all
Vex/bex Angry
Waata Water
Wudda Would have
Yaiy Eye
Yaiy waata Tears, literally "eye water"
Yerriso Gossip

MENU ITEMS

Bail op Traditional dish made with cassava, cocoa, sweet potatoes, plantains, boil cake, and fish or pig's tail
Bambam Traditional dish made with cassava
Bami Cassava bread
Chimoaleh Traditional dish of blackened chicken soup and rice; *chimole* in Spanish
Dukunu Dish of mashed and steamed corn, wrapped in a leaf, similar to a *tamal*
Eskabaycheh Pickled onion soup with chicken or fish; derived from the Spanish word *escabeche* ("pickled")
Garnache Fried tortilla topped with beans and rice
Janny kake Traditional fried or baked bread, served at breakfast
Konks Conch
Panades Traditional dish of finely chopped fish wrapped in a tortilla
Recado Red *achiote* paste
Reyeno Soup made with chicken, pork, and boiled eggs
Rise and beanz Rice and beans with coconut milk
Rompopo Alcoholic drink similar to eggnog
Strech-mi-gots Traditional taffy
Tablayta Coconut candy

WILDLIFE

Bilam Small river fish
Chaaly prise Large rat
Gaalin Heron
Gibnut Paca
Gwaana Iguana
Hooyu Owl
Jankro Vulture
Janny fidla Fiddler crab
Kwash Coati, coati-mundi
Taapong Tarpon
Tuba River fish
Waari Wild pig or peccary
Waata daag River otter
Weewi ants Leaf-cutter ant
Wowla Boa constrictor, also used to refer to a type of basket used for processing cassava for bread

FOLKLORE & TRADITIONAL TERMS

Anansi/Hanaasi Popular character in local folklore, portrayed as the trickster and hero of local tales
Bram A dance party held at Christmas; a type of dance at parties
Brokdong/Brukdown Traditional folk music, from "break down"
Gombeh Typical hand drum made with goat skin
Punta Sensual and vigorous dance, also refers to its accompanying music
Sambai Full-moon fertility dance
Tata Duhendeh Mythical forest gnome, with no thumbs and backwards feet
Wine op A lively, hip-swinging dance

Appendix C: Belizean Wildlife

with assistance from E. Z. Weaver

For such a tiny country, Belize is incredibly rich in biodiversity. Whether you come to Belize to check a hundred or so species off your lifetime list, or just to check out of the rat race for a week or so, you'll be surrounded by a rich and varied collection of flora and fauna. The information below is meant to be a selective introduction.

In many instances, the prime viewing recommendations should be taken with a firm dose of reality. Most casual visitors and even many dedicated naturalists will never see a wildcat or kinkajou in the wild. However, anyone working with a good guide should be able to see a broad selection of Belize's impressive flora and fauna.

See "The Lay of the Land" in chapter 2 for more information, as well as "Tips on Health, Safety & Etiquette in the Wilderness" in chapter 5 for additional tips on enjoying Belize's flora and fauna.

1 FAUNA

MAMMALS

Belize has some 150 identified species of mammals, ranging from the majestic jaguar to the rowdy howler monkey. Note that the dolphin and manatee have been included in the "Sea Life" section, later in this appendix.

Jaguar

Jaguar *(Panthera onca)* This cat measures from 1.1 to 1.8m (3½–6 ft.) plus tail, and is distinguished by its tan/yellowish fur with black spots. As jaguars are protected by Belize's hunting ordinances, the country maintains one of the healthiest populations in Central America. **Prime Viewing:** Although they exist throughout mainland Belize, jaguars are extremely hard to see in the wild. The best places to spot them are in the Cockscomb Basin Wildlife Sanctuary and Río Bravo Conservation Area.

Puma

Puma *(Puma concolor)* Nearly 1.5m (5 ft.) long when fully grown, these feline predators are the largest unspotted cats in the region. Also known as a mountain lion, the puma is brownish, reddish-brown, or tawny in color with a white throat. **Prime Viewing:** Southeastern, western, and southern Belize in the lowland forests and semi-open areas.

Jaguarundi

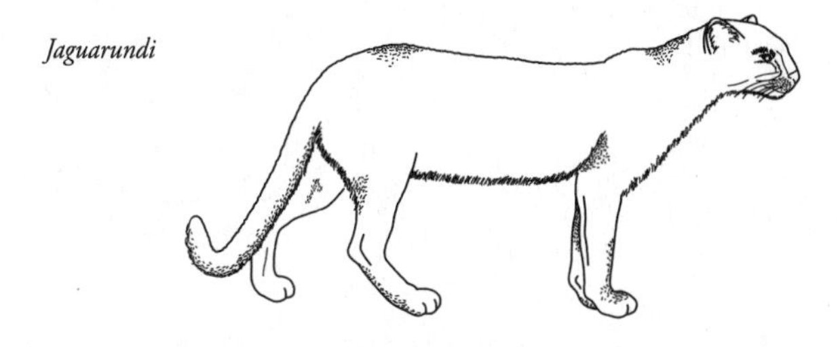

Jaguarundi *(Herpailurus yaguarondi)* This smallish to midsize cat, with a solid black, brown, or reddish coat, can occasionally be spotted in a clearing or climbing trees. **Prime Viewing:** Wet and dry forests throughout Belize.

Ocelot

Ocelot *(Leopardus pardalis)* The tail of the tiger cat (as it's called in Belize) is longer than its rear leg, which makes for easy identification. Ocelots are mostly nocturnal, and during the daytime they sleep in trees. **Prime Viewing:** Dense forests in all regions of Belize.

Margay

Margay *(Leopardus wiedii)* An endangered species, it's one of the smaller wild cats of the region and (like its cousin, the ocelot), is often found in trees. **Prime Viewing:** Forests in all regions of Belize.

Gibnut

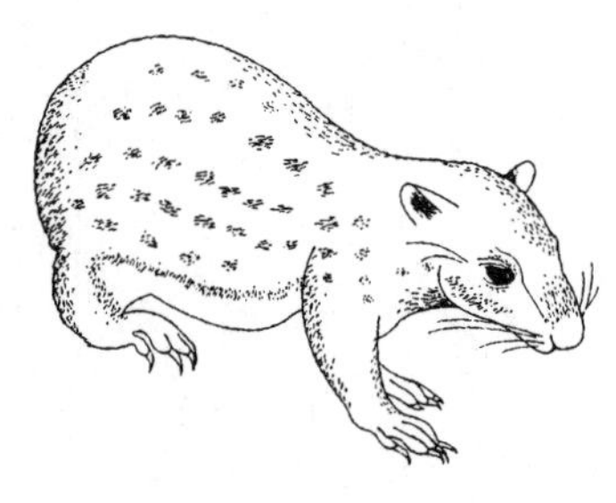

Gibnut *(Agouti paca)* This nocturnal rodent (also called a paca) inhabits the forest floor, feeding on fallen fruit, leaves, and some tubers dug from the ground. **Prime Viewing:** Most often found near water throughout many habitats of Belize, from river valleys to swamps to dense tropical forest. However, you're almost as likely to see gibnut on a restaurant menu as in the wild.

Neotropical Otter

Neotropical Otter *(Lutra longicaudis)* The neotropical otter goes by many nicknames in Belize, including *perro de agua* (water dog) and *lobito de río* (little river wolf). **Prime Viewing:** In rivers and streams throughout the country.

Baird's Tapir

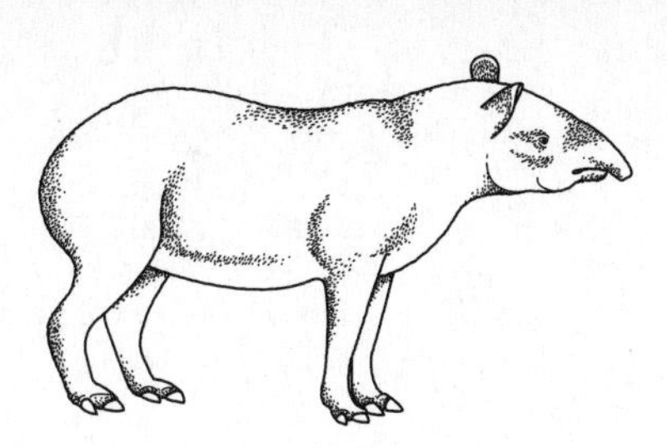

Baird's Tapir *(Tapirus bairdii)* Known as the "mountain cow" in Belize, the tapir is active mostly at night, foraging along riverbanks, streams, and forest clearings. **Prime Viewing:** The Stann Creek and Toledo districts of southern Belize and the Cayo District of western Belize.

Coatimundi

Coatimundi *(Nasua narica)* This raccoonlike mammal is one of few with the ability to adapt to habitat disturbances. During the night, they tend to hunt along open trails; during the day, they stay hidden within the deeper bush. **Prime Viewing:** Found in a variety of habitats in Belize, from dry scrub to dense forests, on the mainland as well as some coastal islands.

Collared Peccary

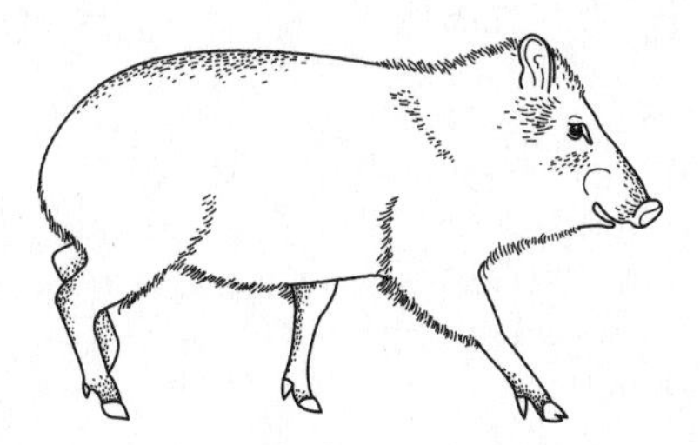

Collared Peccary *(Tayassu tajacu)* These black or brown piglike animals travel in small groups (larger where populations are still numerous) and have a strong musk odor. **Prime Viewing:** Throughout dry and moist forests in most of Belize.

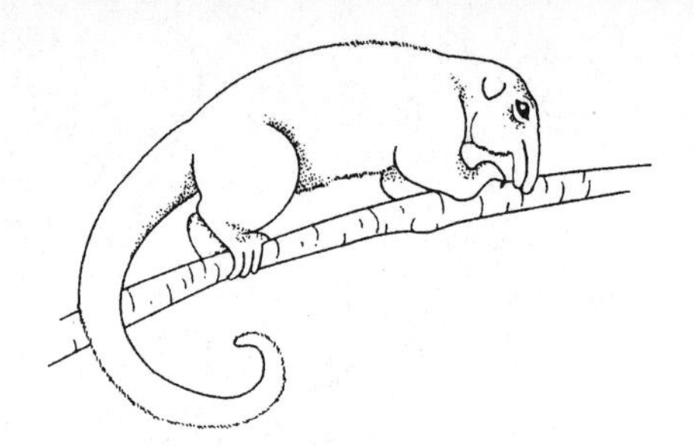
Anteater

Anteater *(Cyclopes didactylus)* Also known as the pygmy anteater, this nocturnal creature grows up to 18cm (7 in.), not counting its thick tail (which is as long as or longer than its body). **Prime Viewing:** Wet forests in all regions of Belize.

Armadillo

Armadillo *(Dasypus novemcinctus)* Also known as the dilly in Belize, these prehistoric-looking animals are nocturnal and terrestrial. **Prime Viewing:** All regions.

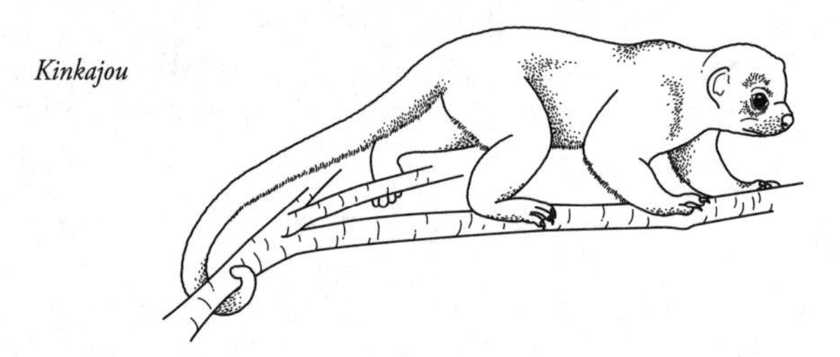
Kinkajou

Kinkajou *(Potos flavus)* The nocturnal, tree-dwelling kinkajou is appropriately nicknamed "nightwalker" in Belize. **Prime Viewing:** Strictly nocturnal and extremely hard to see, the kinkajou nevertheless is found in forests throughout Belize.

Spider Monkey

Spider Monkey *(Ateles geoffroyi)* A large monkey (64cm/25 in.) with brown or silvery fur, this creature is often hunted for its meat and is listed as endangered in some countries. **Prime Viewing:** The Orange Walk (northwestern), Cayo (western), and Toledo (southern) districts of Belize.

Howler Monkey

Howler Monkey *Alouatta pigra* Known locally as a baboon, this highly social creature grows to 56cm (22 in.) in size. As the species travel only from tree to tree (limiting their presence to dense jungle canopy), a community-based conservation organization protects the land along the Belize River for the howler monkey, ensuring that their food trees are not destroyed to make way for pasture. **Prime Viewing:** In the lowland forests that encompass Belize's mainland. Sightings are pretty much guaranteed at the Community Baboon Sanctuary (see "What to See & Do" in chapter 6).

Red Brocket Deer

Red Brocket Deer *(Mazama americana)* Also known as the antelope in Belize, these small animals measure 1 to 1.4m (3½–4½ ft.). Small, straight antlers distinguish the male. **Prime Viewing:** Southern and southeastern Belize and some coastal islands.

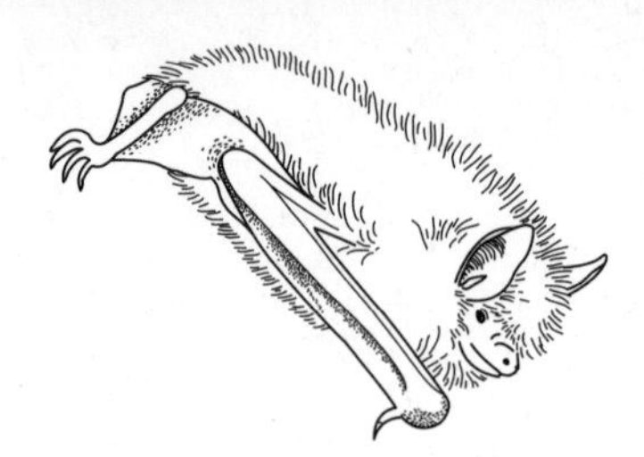
Hairy-Legged Bat

Hairy-Legged Bat *(Myotis keaysi)* The hairy-legged bat grows to a whopping 5.1cm (2 in.) in length, not including the length of its tail. **Prime Viewing:** All regions of Belize, in forests, rock crevices, gardens, and buildings.

BIRDS

Belize has at least 618 identified species of resident and migrant birds. The variety of habitats and compact nature of the country make this a major bird-watching destination.

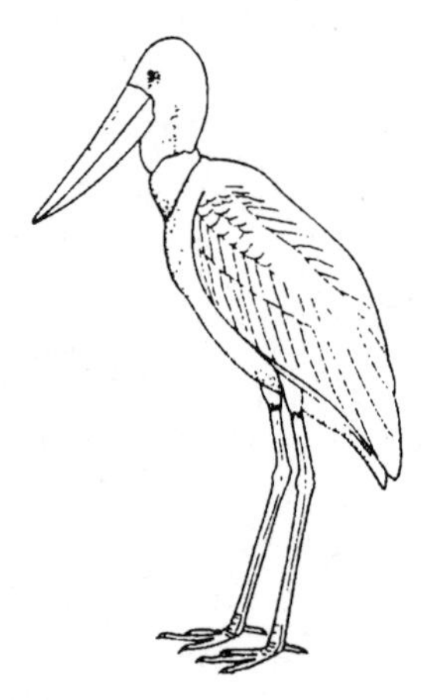
Jabiru Stork

Jabiru Stork *(Jabiru mycteria)* One of the largest birds in the world and an endangered species, the jabiru stands 1.5m (5 ft.) tall, with a wingspan of 2.4m (8 ft.) and a .3m-long (1 ft.) bill. The birds arrive in Belize from Mexico in November and fly north with the first rains in June or July. **Prime Viewing:** The Crooked Tree Wildlife Sanctuary, located 53km (33 miles) north of Belize City, has the largest population in the country. (See "En Route North: Crooked Tree Wildlife Sanctuary" in chapter 9.)

Keel-Billed Toucan

Keel-Billed Toucan *(Ramphastos solfurantus)* The canoe-shape bill and brightly colored feathers make the national bird of Belize almost instantly recognizable. The toucan is about 51cm (20 in.) in length. **Prime Viewing:** Throughout the country's lowland forests, nesting in the holes of tree trunks.

Scarlet Macaw

Scarlet Macaw *(Ara macao)* Over most of its range, the scarlet macaw is endangered. However, in 1996, a new population of over 100 birds was "discovered" south of the Cockscomb Basin Wildlife Sanctuary. **Prime Viewing:** The wet lowland forests of the Toledo District in southern Belize.

Ocellated Turkey

Ocellated Turkey *(Agriocharis ocellata)* This colorful bird has a thin, light blue head and neck with orange-yellow knoblike wattles on the top that the bird will proudly display. The wings and tail are rounded with shimmering metallic bronze primaries and metallic emerald-green shoulders; the feathers are a dark, shiny brown, barred with a metallic shimmering green that looks black in poor light. **Prime Viewing:** Northern and western Belize.

Frigate Bird

Frigate Bird *(Fregata magnificens)* The frigate bird is a naturally agile flier and it swoops (unlike other birds, it doesn't dive or swim) to pluck food from the water's surface—or more commonly, it steals catch from the mouths of other birds. **Prime Viewing:** All coastal regions of Belize. Man-O-War Caye is a protected nesting site for this bird (see "Dangriga" in chapter 8).

Red-Footed Booby

Red-Footed Booby *(Sula sula rubripes)* This unique bird experiences many color changes during its life. Adult boobies have a blue-gray bill and eye ring, and pink skin about the bill base. The head and neck are washed with yellow, and the white body holds black primary and secondary feathers. The feet and legs of the aptly named species are all red. **Prime Viewing:** Half Moon Caye National Monument, Belize's first national park, is now the protected home for over 4,000 red-footed boobies (see "The Outer Atolls" in chapter 7), but these birds can be found in all coastal regions of Belize.

Montezuma's Oropendola

Montezuma's Oropendola *(Pasrocolius montezuma)* Also called "yellowtails" in Belize, these birds have a black head and chest, a yellow-edged tail, a large black bill with an orange tip, and a blue patch under the eye. **Prime Viewing:** Throughout Belize.

Osprey

Osprey *(Pandion haliatus)* These large (.6m/2 ft., with a 1.8m/6-ft. wingspan), brownish birds with white heads are also known as "fishing eagles." In flight, the osprey's wings "bend" backward. **Prime Viewing:** Throughout Belize, although predominantly near the coasts, flying or perched in trees near water.

Roseate Spoonbill

Roseate Spoonbill *(Ajaia ajaja)* This large water bird is pink or light red in color, with a large spoon-shape bill. They were almost made extinct in the United States because their pink wings were sought for feather fans. **Prime Viewing:** Along the coast and in the wetlands of northern Belize.

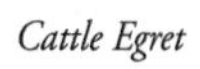

Cattle Egret

Cattle Egret *(Bubulcus ibis)* The cattle egret changes color during breeding: A yellowish buff color appears on the head, chest, and back, and a reddish hue emerges on the bill and legs. They are often seen following behind tractors, because these stir up insects. **Prime Viewing:** Throughout the country. As the name implies, almost always found accompanying livestock.

Pygmy Owl

Pygmy Owl *(Glaucidium brasilianum)* This small (about 38cm/15 in.) grayish brown or reddish brown owl is also known as the *lechucita listada* ("little striped screech owl"). Unlike most owls, they are most active during the day. **Prime Viewing:** Throughout Belize.

Boat-Billed Heron

Boat-Billed Heron *(Cochlearius cochlearius)* This midsize heron (about 51cm/20 in.) has a large black head, a large broad bill, and a rusty brown color. **Prime Viewing:** Throughout the country, near marshes, swamps, rivers, and mangroves.

Laughing Falcon

Laughing Falcon *Herpetotheres cachinnans* This largish (56cm/22 in.) bird of prey is also known as the *vaquero* (cowboy) in Belize. The laughing falcon's wingspan reaches an impressive 94cm (37 in.). **Prime Viewing:** Throughout the country.

SEA LIFE

Boasting the longest continuous barrier reef in the Americas, Belize has a rich diversity of underwater flora and fauna. Any visitor to Belize's beach or island resorts should take some time to peek at the various undersea wonders of the ocean and barrier reef, whether it be by snorkeling, scuba diving, or riding in a glass-bottomed boat.

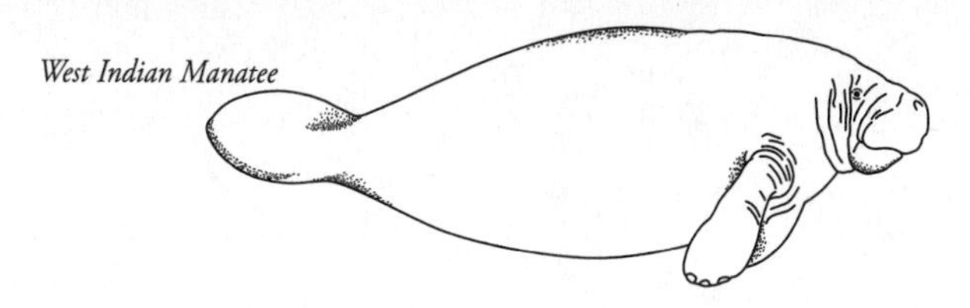

West Indian Manatee

West Indian Manatee *(Trichechus manatus)* Manatees in Belize are Antillean manatees, a subspecies of the West Indian manatee. Belize is home to the largest known concentration of Antillean manatees in the wider Caribbean. These "sea cows" can reach lengths of 3 to 4m (10–13 ft.) and weigh 499 to 1,588kg (1,100–3,500 lb.). **Prime Viewing:** Coastal mangroves, and particularly in the Gales Point Lagoon.

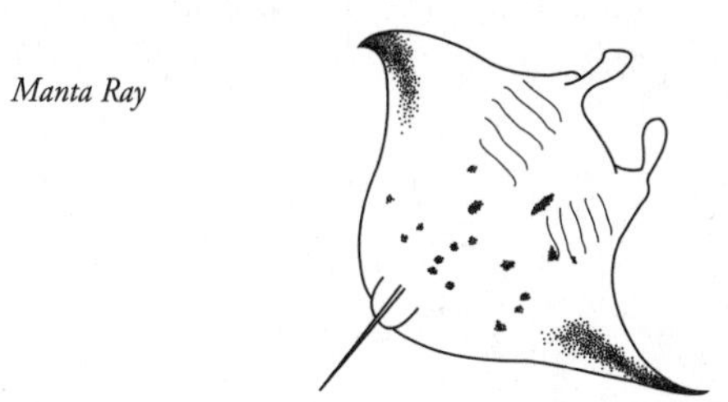

Manta Ray

Manta Ray *(Manta birostris)* Manta rays are the largest type of rays, with a wingspan that can reach 6m (20 ft.) and a body weight known to exceed 1,361kg (3,000 lb.). Despite their daunting appearance, manta rays are quite gentle. If you are snorkeling or diving, watch for one of these extraordinary and graceful creatures. **Prime Viewing:** All along the barrier reef, particularly in deeper water, or alongside steep walls and drop-offs.

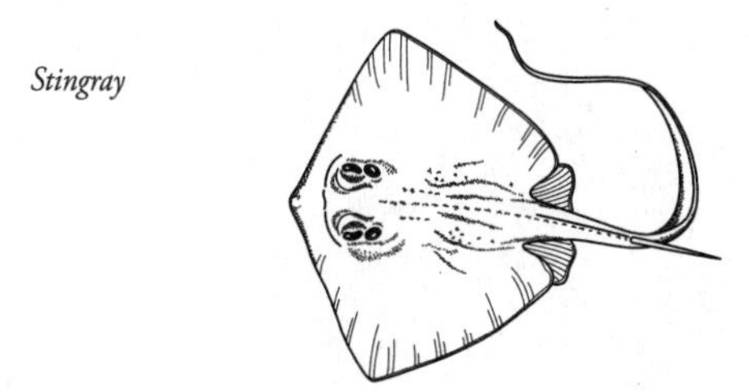

Stingray

Stingray *(Dasyatis americana)* True to their name, these rays can give you a painful shock if you touch the venomous spine at the base of their tails. Be careful when wading in sandy areas, where they prefer to bury themselves. **Prime Viewing:** All along the coast and barrier reef, especially in shallow sand or grassy areas.

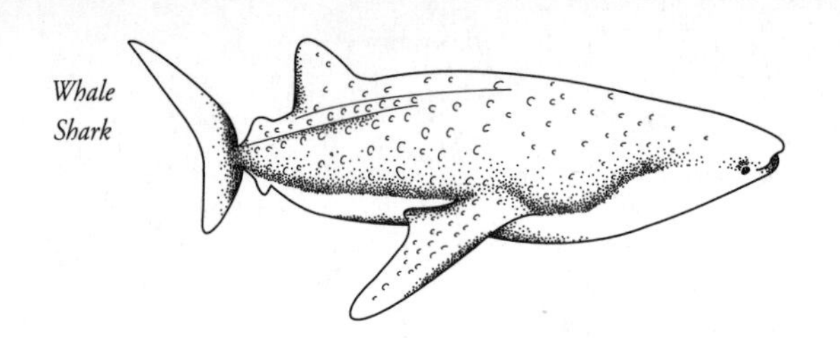
Whale Shark

Whale Shark *(Rhincodon typus)* Although the whale shark grows to lengths of 14m (45 ft.) or more, its gentle nature makes swimming with them a special treat for divers and snorkelers. Although 3 or 4 days before and after the full and new moons in April and May are the best times to interact with the sharks, they are often sighted in the summer months as well. **Prime Viewing:** Gladden Spit, off Placencia (see "Placencia" in chapter 8).

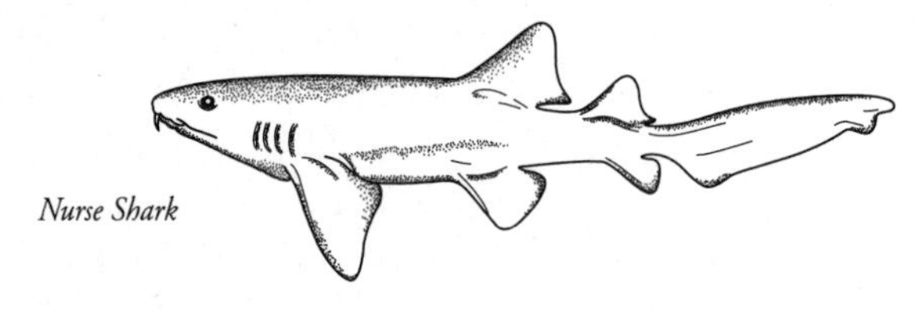
Nurse Shark

Nurse Shark *(Ginglymostoma cirratum)* The most frequently spotted shark in Belizean waters, this species spends most of its time resting on the ocean floor. Reaching lengths of 4.3m (14 ft.), their heads are larger than those of most sharks, and they appear to be missing the bottom half of their tail. **Prime Viewing:** All along the coast and barrier reef.

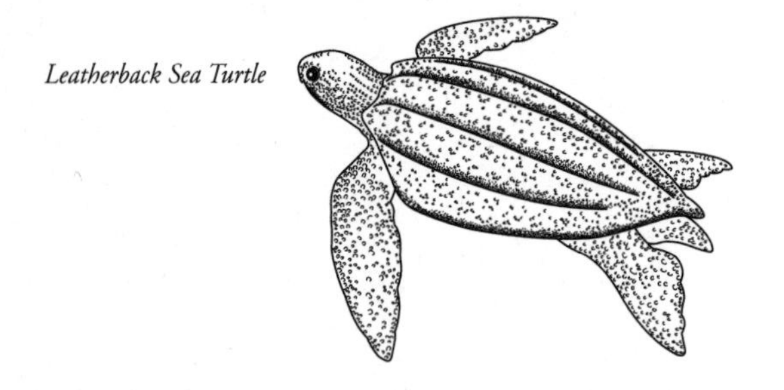
Leatherback Sea Turtle

Leatherback Sea Turtle *(Dermochelys coriacea)* The world's largest sea turtle (reaching nearly 2.4m/8 ft. in length and weighing more than 544kg/1,200 lb.), it's now an endangered species. **Prime Viewing:** Sightings are exceedingly rare, so it's highly unlikely that you'll spot them nesting on the coast of Belize, but you might get lucky and spot them in the sea.

Hawksbill Sea Turtle

Hawksbill Sea Turtle *(Eretmochelys imbricata)* The hawksbill turtle is a shy, tropical, reef-dwelling species that feeds primarily on sponges. Registered on the endangered species list, commercial exploitation exacerbates the species' continued decline. **Prime Viewing:** All along the coast and barrier reef.

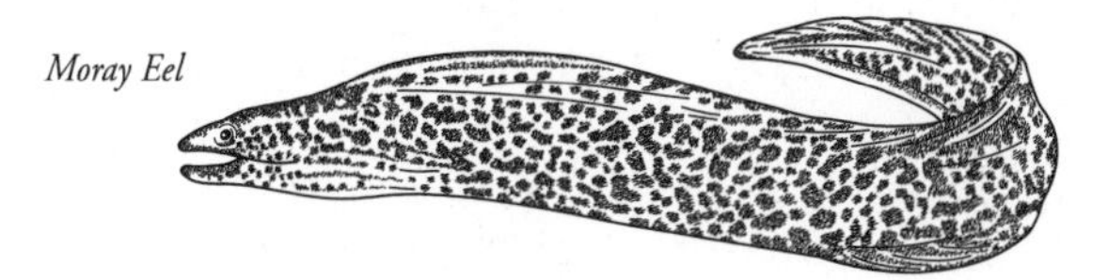

Moray Eel

Moray Eel *(Gymnothorax moringa)* Distinguished by a swaying serpent-head and teeth-filled jaw that continually opens and closes, the moray eel is most commonly seen with only its head appearing from behind rocks. At night, however, it leaves its home along the reef to hunt for small fish, crustaceans, shrimp, and octopus. **Prime Viewing:** Saltwater areas along the coast, usually near coral reefs or kelp forests.

Barracuda

Barracuda *(Sphyraena barracuda)* The barracuda is a slender fish with two dorsal fins and a large mouth. Juvenile barracudas often swim near the shore, so exercise caution, as attacks on humans occasionally occur. **Prime Viewing:** All along the coast and barrier reef.

Bottle-Nosed Dolphin

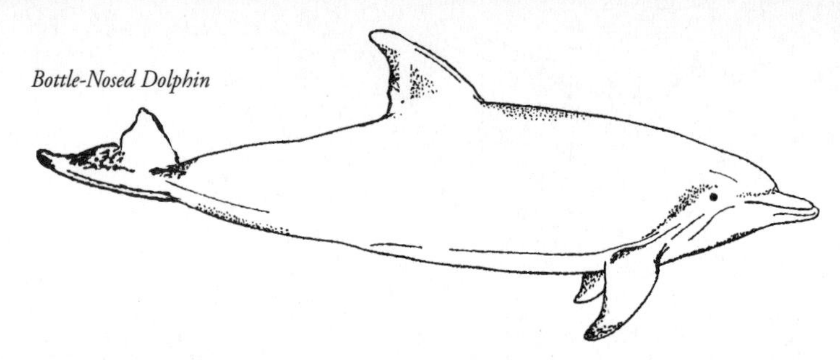

Bottle-Nosed Dolphin *(Tursiops truncates)* Their wide back fin, dark-gray back, and light-gray sides identify bottle-nosed dolphins. Dolphins grow to lengths of 3.6m (12 ft.) and weigh up to 635kg (1,400 lb.). **Prime Viewing:** Along the coast and barrier reef.

Loggerhead Sponge

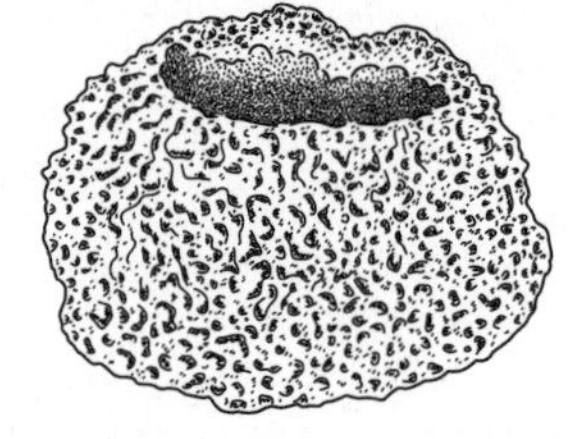

Loggerhead Sponge *(Spheciospongia vesparia)* This barrel sponge is a large, stubby, purplish creature. Its large, central depression often plays host to small fish; shrimp and other sea life dwell in its canals. **Prime Viewing:** All along the barrier reef.

Elkhorn Coral

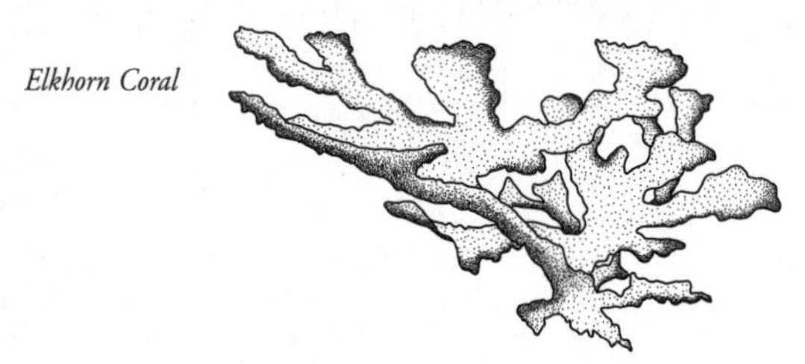

Elkhorn Coral *(Acropora palmata)* Elkhorn coral was formerly the dominant species in shallow water throughout the Caribbean, forming extensive thickets in areas of heavy surf. Since 1980, populations have collapsed from disease outbreaks, with losses compounded locally by hurricanes, increased predation, and bleaching. **Prime Viewing:** Along the barrier reef.

Brain Coral

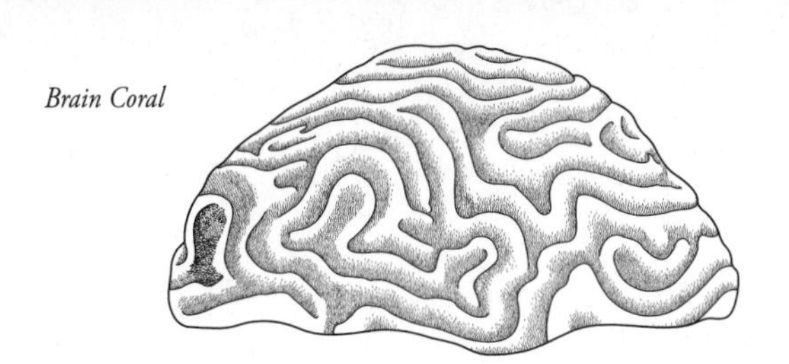

Brain Coral *(Diploria strigosa)* Named for its striking physical similarity to a human brain, brain coral has been growing continuously in the waters off Belize for at least a century, though it's vulnerable to hurricanes. **Prime Viewing:** All along the barrier reef.

Porous Coral *(Porites)* The branches of this pink coral have a fuzzy appearance during the day, when its polyps are extended. **Prime Viewing:** All along the barrier reef.

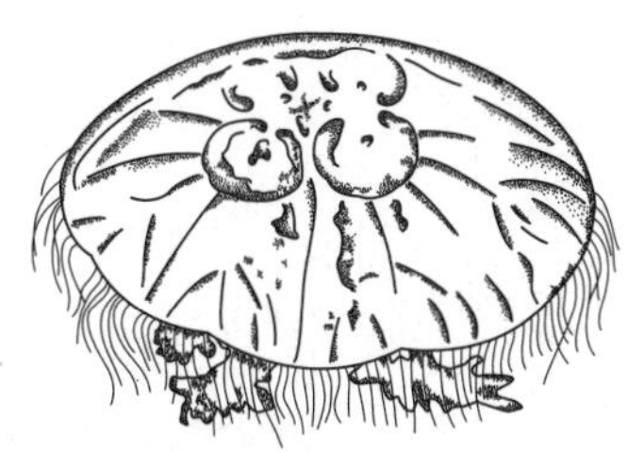

Moon Jelly *(Aurelia aurita)* Like most jellies, the moon jelly is almost transparent. That four-leaf-clover-like area on its top is its reproductive organs. **Prime Viewing:** All along the coast and barrier reef.

AMPHIBIANS

Frogs, toads, and salamanders are actually some of the most beguiling, beautiful, and easy-to-spot residents of tropical forests.

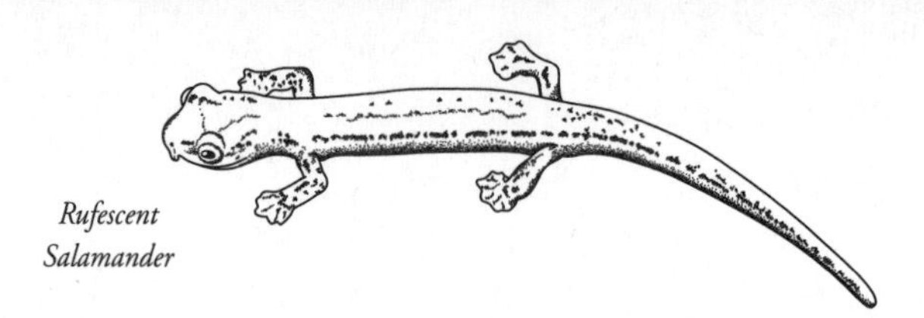

Rufescent Salamander

Rufescent Salamander *(Bolitoglossa rufescens)* This very small (3.8cm/1½-in.), brown amphibian is also known as the "northern banana salamander," which is fitting since it can often be found in banana leaves. **Prime Viewing:** Forest floors and creek beds, particularly in the Stann Creek, Toledo, and Cayo districts.

Red-Eyed Tree Frog

Red-Eyed Tree Frog *(Agalychnis callidryas)* This colorful 7.6cm (3-in.) frog usually has a pale or dark green back, sometimes with white or yellow spots, with blue-purple patches and vertical bars on the body, orange hands and feet, and deep red eyes. **Prime Viewing:** This nocturnal frog can be found in forests throughout Belize. It is often best to look on the undersides of broad-leafed plants.

Maya Rain Frog

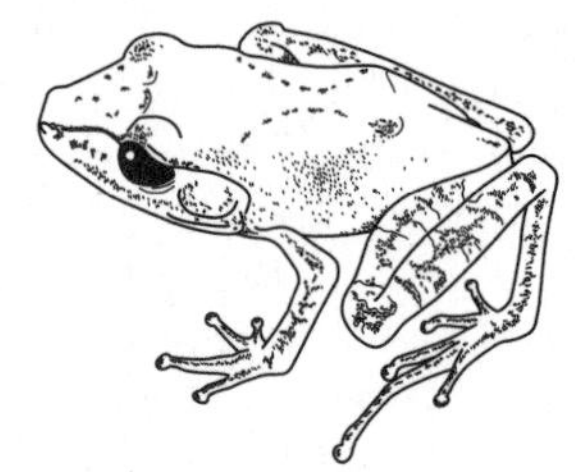

Maya Rain Frog *(Eleutherodactyulus chac)* This small, skinny frog is usually brown or yellowish, with webbed toes and red eyes. **Prime Viewing:** Forests in southeastern, southern, and western Belize.

Marine Toad

Marine Toad *(Bufo marinus)* This 20cm (8-in.), wart-covered toad is also known as *sapo grande,* or "giant toad." The females are mottled in color, while the males are uniformly brown. **Prime Viewing:** This terrestrial frog can be found in forests throughout Belize.

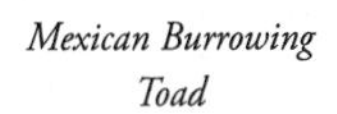

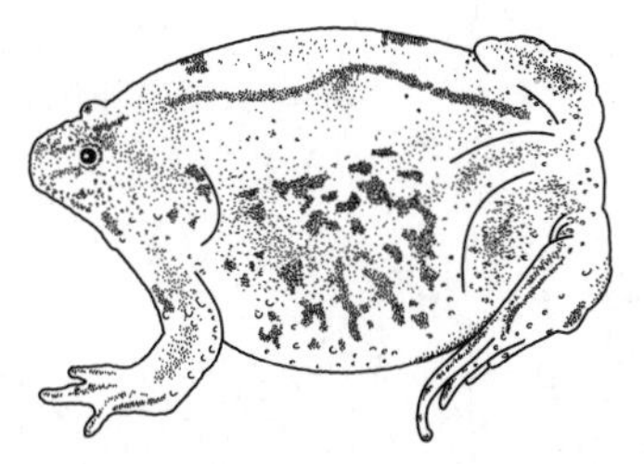

Mexican Burrowing Toad

Mexican Burrowing Toad *(Rhinophrynus dorsalis)* This bloblike, 7.6cm (3-in.) toad will inflate like a blowfish when frightened. It often has a single red, orange, or yellow line down the center of its brown or black back. **Prime Viewing:** This terrestrial frog can be found throughout Belize.

REPTILES

Belize's reptile species range from the frightening and justly feared fer-de-lance pit viper and American crocodile to a wide variety of turtles and lizards. (Note that the sea turtle is included in the "Sea Life" section, above.)

Snapping Turtle

Snapping Turtle *(Chelydra serpentina)* This turtle's back is brown, olive, or black, and marked with three ridges of sharp bumps—which might explain why it's also known as *tortuga lagarto* ("alligator turtle") in Belize. **Prime Viewing:** In ponds and streams throughout Belize.

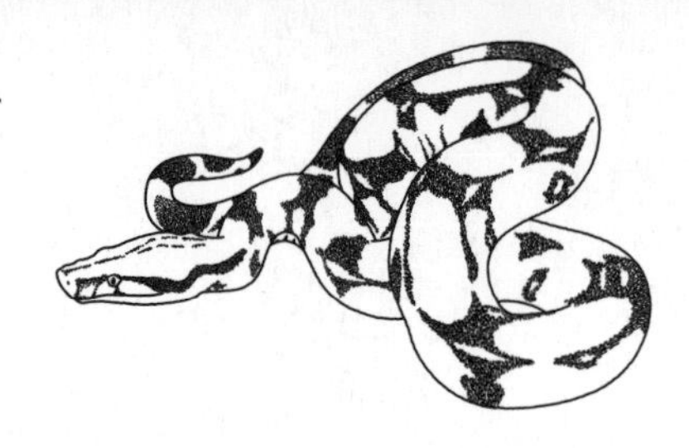
Boa Constrictor

Boa Constrictor *(Boa constrictor)* Adult boa constrictors average about 1.8 to 3m (6–10 ft.) in length and weigh over 27kg (60 lb.). Their coloration camouflages them, but look for varying patterns of cream, brown, tan, gray, and black with ovals and diamonds. **Prime Viewing:** In forests and mangroves countrywide, including on some of the offshore cayes.

Fer-de-Lance

Fer-de-Lance *(Bothrops asper)* Also known as a tommygoff in Belize, this venomous and aggressive snake can grow to 2.4m (8 ft.) in length. Beige, brown, or black triangles flank either side of the snake's head, while the area under the head is a vivid yellow. **Prime Viewing:** All regions. This snake is arboreal as a youngster and becomes terrestrial as it grows larger and older.

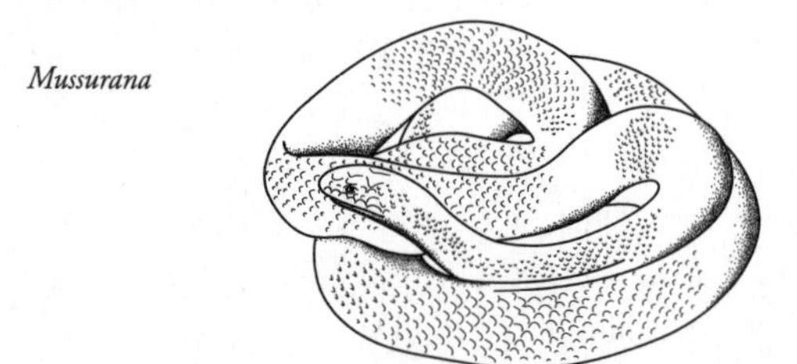
Mussurana

Mussurana *(Clelia clelia)* This bluish-black, brown, or grayish snake grows to 2.4m (8 ft.) in length. While slightly venomous, this snake is a rear-fanged snake and of little danger to humans. In fact, it is prized and protected by locals, since its primary prey happens to be much more venomous pit vipers, like the fer-de-lance. **Prime Viewing:** Forests in central, southeastern, and western Belize.

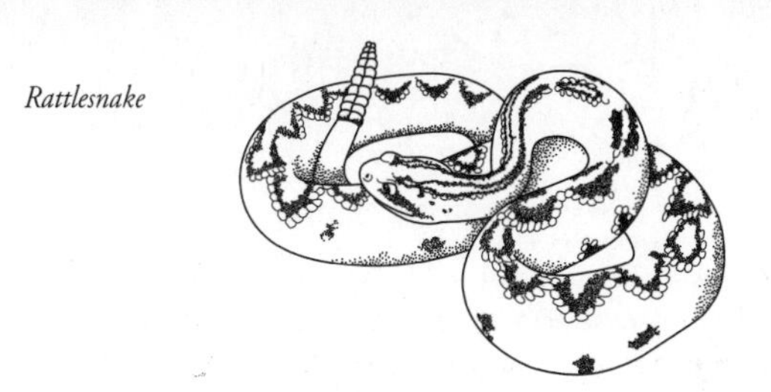

Rattlesnake

Rattlesnake *(Crotalus durissus)* Look out for its triangular head, 1.8m (6-ft.) length, the ridge running along the middle of its back, and (of course) its rattling tail. **Prime Viewing:** Throughout the country

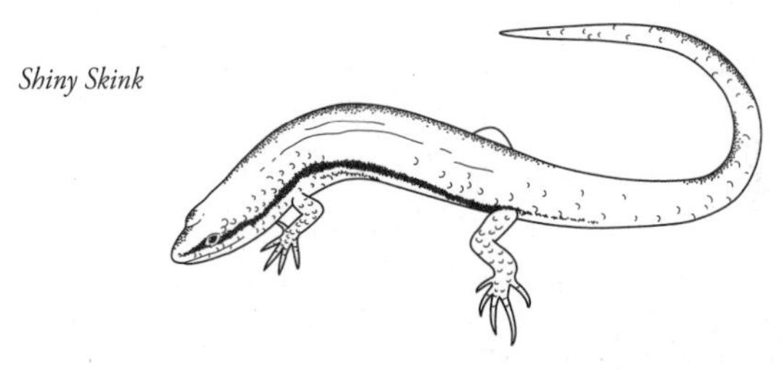

Shiny Skink

Shiny Skink *(Mabuya brachypoda)* This midsize (7.6cm/3 in.) brown lizard with a narrow head and short legs is also known as "snake waiting boy." **Prime Viewing:** Throughout the country.

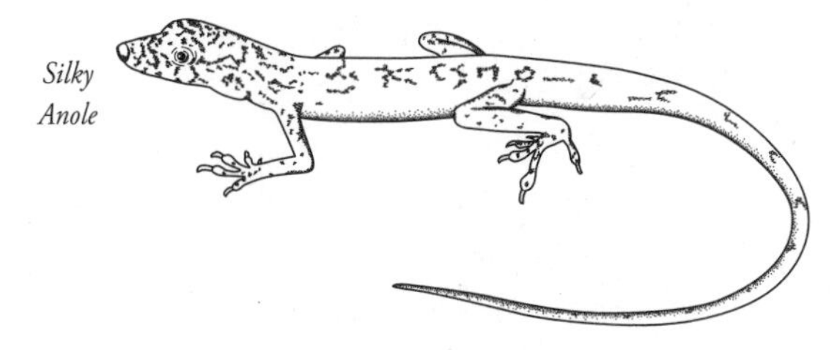

Silky Anole

Silky Anole *(Anolis sericeus)* This small (5.1cm/2-in.) gray lizard can be hard to spot, as it often aligns itself on a blade of grass when startled. **Prime Viewing:** On the ground and forest floors throughout the country.

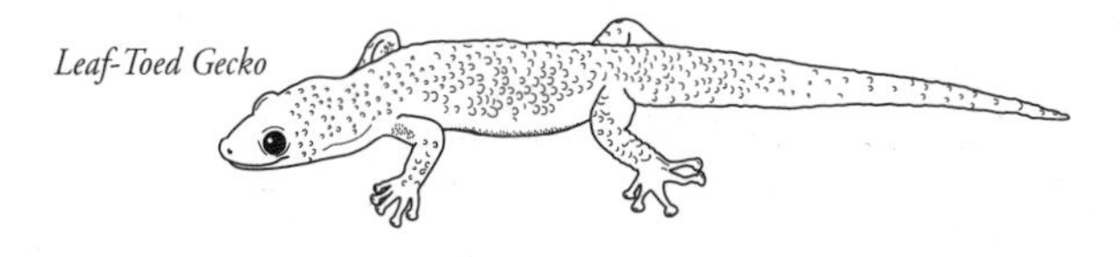

Leaf-Toed Gecko

Leaf-Toed Gecko *(Phyllodactylus tuberculosus)* You'll have no problem spotting this 6.4cm (2½-in.) gecko on rocks and on the ground—it loves to be around buildings and other areas of human activity. **Prime Viewing:** Central, southeastern, and western Belize.

Smooth Gecko

Smooth Gecko *(Thecadactylus rapicaudus)* This gecko's autonomous tail detaches from its body and acts as a diversion to a potential predator; it grows back later in a lighter shade. **Prime Viewing:** In northwestern, western, and southern Belize, especially where humans can be found.

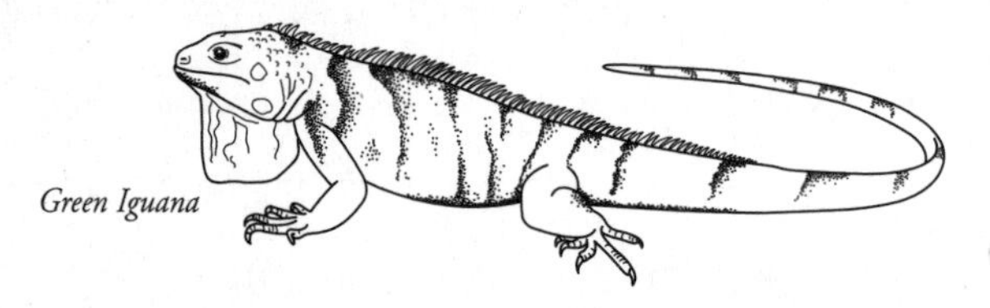
Green Iguana

Green Iguana *(Iguana iguana)* Green iguanas, not surprisingly, are green in color, but vary in shades ranging from bright green to a dull grayish-green. The iguana will often perch on a branch overhanging a river and plunge into the water when threatened. **Prime Viewing:** All regions of the country, living along the rivers and streams. Often seen sunning on exposed rocks or tree limbs.

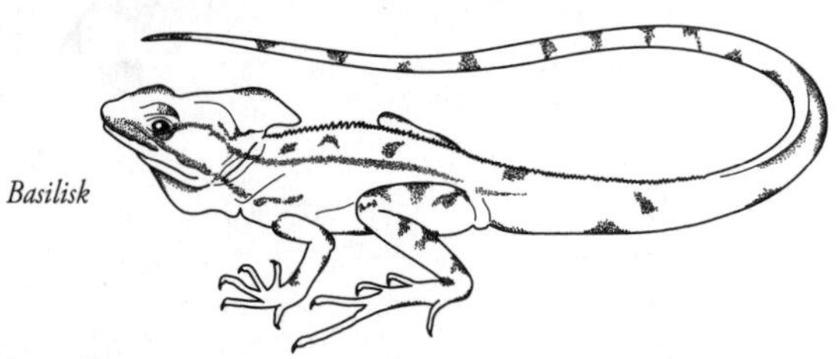
Basilisk

Basilisk *(Basiliscus vittatus)* The basilisk can run across the surface of water for short distances by using its hind legs and holding its body almost upright; thus, the reptile is also known as "the Jesus Christ lizard." **Prime Viewing:** In trees, rocks, and forest floor, especially near water in tropical rainforests.

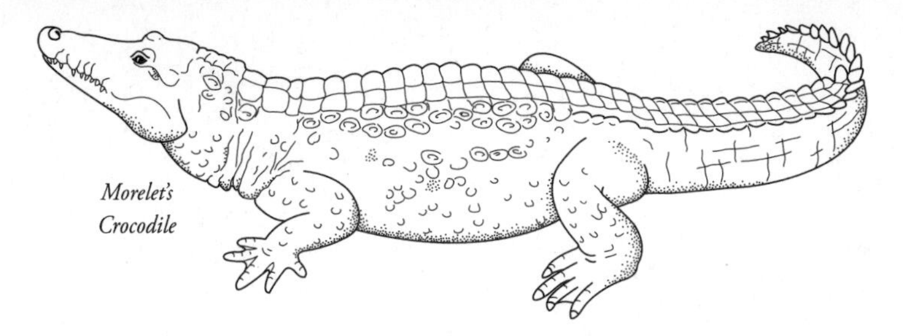

Morelet's Crocodile

Morelet's Crocodile *(Crocodylus moreleti)* This reptile can grow to a length of 4m (13 ft.), although the average specimen measures less than 2.4m (8 ft.). Adults are brown or blackish in color, while young Morelet's crocodiles are olive or yellowish, with dark bands on their bodies and tails. **Prime Viewing:** Northern and central coastal Belize, in most of the freshwater lowland interior rivers, lagoons, and ponds.

American Crocodile

American Crocodile *(Crocodylus acutus)* This endangered species is distinguished from the Morelet's crocodile by their generally larger size and narrower snout. While they can reach lengths of 6.4m (21 ft.), the majority are much smaller, usually less than 4m (13 ft.). **Prime Viewing:** Near swamps, mangrove swamps, estuaries, large rivers, coastal lowlands, and islands.

2 FLORA

TREES

Despite the cliché to the contrary, it's often a good thing to be able to identify specific trees within a forest. We've included illustrations of the leaves, flowers, seeds, or fruits to get you started.

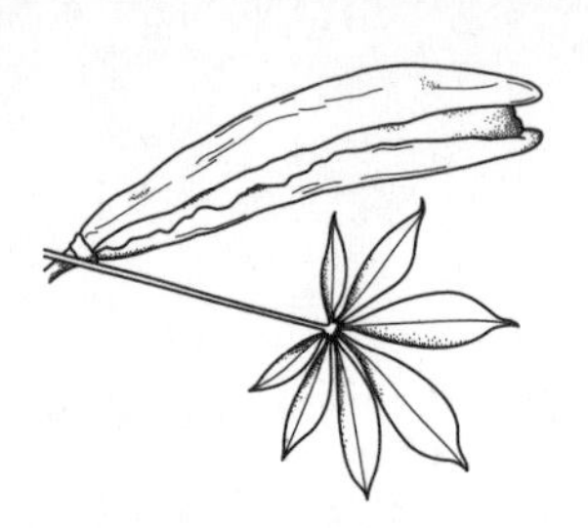

Ceiba

Ceiba *(Ceiba pentandra)* Also known as the kapok tree, ceiba trees are typically emergent (their large umbrella-shape canopies emerge above the forest canopy), making the species among the tallest trees in the tropical forest. Reaching as high as 61m (200 ft.), their thick columnar trunks often have large buttresses. Ceiba trees may flower as little as once every 5 years, especially in wetter forests. **Prime Viewing:** Countrywide.

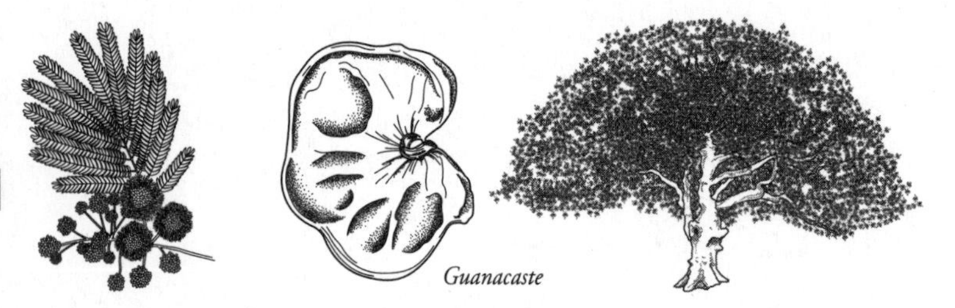

Guanacaste

Guanacaste *(Enterolobium cyclocarpum)* The guanacaste, or tubroos, tree is one of the largest trees found in Central America. It can reach a total elevation of over 40m (130 ft.), its straight trunk comprising 9.1 to 12m (30–40 ft.) of the height (the trunk's diameter measures more than 1.8m/6 ft.). **Prime Viewing:** Countrywide. A particularly impressive specimen gives its name to Guanacaste National Park (see "Belmopan" in chapter 10).

Gumbo Limbo

Gumbo Limbo *(Bursera simaruba)* The bark of the gumbo limbo is perhaps its most distinguishing feature: A paper-thin outer layer is red when peeled off the tree, revealing a bright green bark underneath. The bark is reportedly used as a remedy for gum disease; and gumbo-limbo bark tea allegedly alleviates high blood pressure. Another remarkable property of this tree is its ability to root from its cut branches. When a branch is cut and planted right end up, roots will develop and leaves will sprout, forming a new tree within a few years' time. **Prime Viewing:** Primary and secondary forests, countrywide.

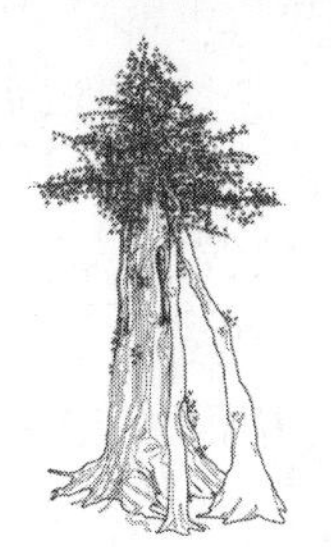

Strangler Fig

Strangler Fig *(Ficus aurea)* This parasitic tree gets its name from the fact that it envelops and eventually strangles its host tree. The strangler fig actually begins as an epiphyte, whose seeds are deposited high in a tree's canopy by bats, birds, or monkeys. The young strangler then sends long roots down to the earth. The sap of the strangler fig is used to relieve burns. **Prime Viewing:** Primary and secondary forests, countrywide.

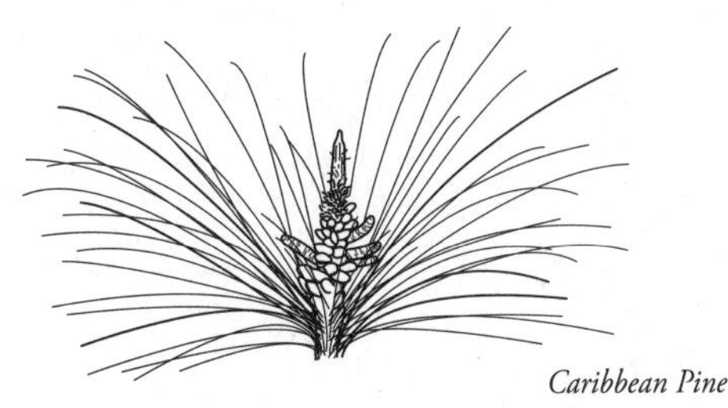

Caribbean Pine

Caribbean Pine *(Pinus caribaea)* This fast-growing pine species is the defining tree of the Mountain Pine Ridge area of western Belize. The tree is actually fire resistant, and benefits from controlled burns. The resin is used as an adhesive and insect repellent. **Prime Viewing:** Mountain Pine Ridge Forest Reserve (see chapter 10).

Mahogany

Mahogany *(Swietenia macrophylla)* The national tree of Belize, the mahogany tree can grow to heights of over 30m (100 ft.). Mahogany wood is heavy and strong, and resists rot and termites. From its wood, artisans and carpenters craft the world's finest furniture. **Prime Viewing:** Primary and secondary rainforests, countrywide.

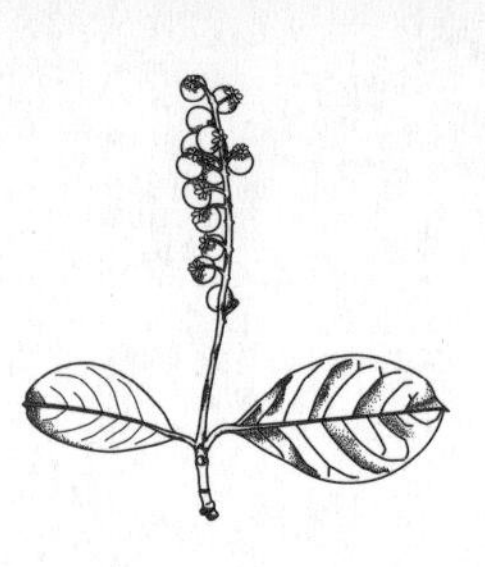

Craboo

Craboo *(Byrsonima crassifolia)* The craboo's flowers are beautiful orange and yellow racemes about 15cm (6 in.) long. The tree also bears a small orange-yellow berry, whose flavor varies from bland to sweet, acidic, or even cheeselike. The flowers usually bloom around April, with fruits gathered around June. Hurricane Iris destroyed many Belizean craboo trees in 2001. **Prime Viewing:** Countrywide.

FLOWERS

Belize has over 4,000 species of flowering plants, including some 250 orchid species.

Black Orchid

Black Orchid *(Encyclia cochleatum)* The black orchid is the national flower of Belize. The plant's most distinguishing feature is its lip, which resembles the shape of a clamshell valve. The flower is a deep blackish color with purple veins, and its leaves are a greenish-yellow with purple spots. The black orchid is sometimes likened to an octopus because of its straggling "tentacles" and its ability to thrive in a damp environment. **Prime Viewing:** Countrywide, particularly in moist environments.

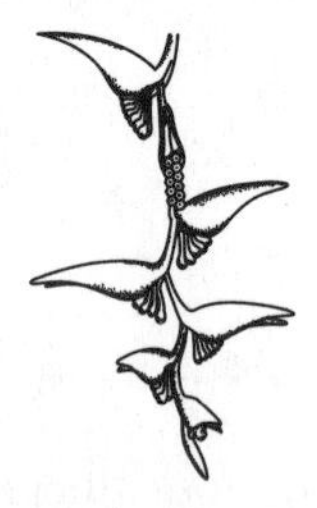
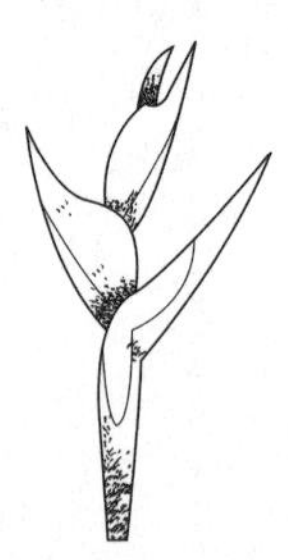

Heliconia

Heliconia *(Heliconia collinsiana)* There are over 250 species of tropical heliconia. The flowers of this species are darkish pink in color, and the underside of the plants' large leaves are coated in white wax. **Prime Viewing:** In the Toledo and Stann Creek districts.

Hot Lips

Hot Lips *(Psychotria poeppigiana)* Also called "devil's ear" in Belize, its small white flowers (inside the red "lips") attract a variety of butterflies and hummingbirds. **Prime Viewing:** In the undergrowth of dense forests, countrywide.

INDEX

See also Accommodations and Restaurant indexes, below.

General Index

Accommodations

Restaurants

Frommer's® Complete Travel Guides

Alaska
Amalfi Coast
American Southwest
Amsterdam
Argentina
Arizona
Atlanta
Australia
Austria
Bahamas
Barcelona
Beijing
Belgium, Holland & Luxembourg
Belize
Bermuda
Boston
Brazil
British Columbia & the Canadian Rockies
Brussels & Bruges
Budapest & the Best of Hungary
Buenos Aires
Calgary
California
Canada
Cancún, Cozumel & the Yucatán
Cape Cod, Nantucket & Martha's Vineyard
Caribbean
Caribbean Ports of Call
Carolinas & Georgia
Chicago
Chile & Easter Island
China
Colorado
Costa Rica
Croatia
Cuba
Denmark
Denver, Boulder & Colorado Springs
Eastern Europe
Ecuador & the Galapagos Islands
Edinburgh & Glasgow
England
Europe
Europe by Rail
Florence, Tuscany & Umbria
Florida
France
Germany
Greece
Greek Islands
Guatemala
Hawaii
Hong Kong
Honolulu, Waikiki & Oahu
India
Ireland
Israel
Italy
Jamaica
Japan
Kauai
Las Vegas
London
Los Angeles
Los Cabos & Baja
Madrid
Maine Coast
Maryland & Delaware
Maui
Mexico
Montana & Wyoming
Montréal & Québec City
Morocco
Moscow & St. Petersburg
Munich & the Bavarian Alps
Nashville & Memphis
New England
Newfoundland & Labrador
New Mexico
New Orleans
New York City
New York State
New Zealand
Northern Italy
Norway
Nova Scotia, New Brunswick & Prince Edward Island
Oregon
Paris
Peru
Philadelphia & the Amish Country
Portugal
Prague & the Best of the Czech Republic
Provence & the Riviera
Puerto Rico
Rome
San Antonio & Austin
San Diego
San Francisco
Santa Fe, Taos & Albuquerque
Scandinavia
Scotland
Seattle
Seville, Granada & the Best of Andalusia
Shanghai
Sicily
Singapore & Malaysia
South Africa
South America
South Florida
South Korea
South Pacific
Southeast Asia
Spain
Sweden
Switzerland
Tahiti & French Polynesia
Texas
Thailand
Tokyo
Toronto
Turkey
USA
Utah
Vancouver & Victoria
Vermont, New Hampshire & Maine
Vienna & the Danube Valley
Vietnam
Virgin Islands
Virginia
Walt Disney World® & Orlando
Washington, D.C.
Washington State

Frommer's® Day by Day Guides

Amsterdam
Barcelona
Beijing
Boston
Cancun & the Yucatan
Chicago
Florence & Tuscany
Hong Kong
Honolulu & Oahu
London
Maui
Montréal
Napa & Sonoma
New York City
Paris
Provence & the Riviera
Rome
San Francisco
Venice
Washington D.C.

Pauline Frommer's Guides: See More. Spend Less.

Alaska
Hawaii
Italy
Las Vegas
London
New York City
Paris
Walt Disney World®
Washington D.C.

Frommer's® Portable Guides

Acapulco, Ixtapa & Zihuatanejo
Amsterdam
Aruba, Bonaire & Curacao
Australia's Great Barrier Reef
Bahamas
Big Island of Hawaii
Boston
California Wine Country
Cancún
Cayman Islands
Charleston
Chicago
Dominican Republic
Florence
Las Vegas
Las Vegas for Non-Gamblers
London
Maui
Nantucket & Martha's Vineyard
New Orleans
New York City
Paris
Portland
Puerto Rico
Puerto Vallarta, Manzanillo & Guadalajara
Rio de Janeiro
San Diego
San Francisco
Savannah
St. Martin, Sint Maarten, Anguila & St. Bart's
Turks & Caicos
Vancouver
Venice
Virgin Islands
Washington, D.C.
Whistler

Frommer's® Cruise Guides

Alaska Cruises & Ports of Call
Cruises & Ports of Call
European Cruises & Ports of Call

Frommer's® National Park Guides

Algonquin Provincial Park
Banff & Jasper
Grand Canyon
National Parks of the American West
Rocky Mountain
Yellowstone & Grand Teton
Yosemite and Sequoia & Kings Canyon
Zion & Bryce Canyon

Frommer's® With Kids Guides

Chicago
Hawaii
Las Vegas
London
National Parks
New York City
San Francisco
Toronto
Walt Disney World® & Orlando
Washington, D.C.

Frommer's® PhraseFinder Dictionary Guides

Chinese
French
German
Italian
Japanese
Spanish

Suzy Gershman's Born to Shop Guides

France
Hong Kong, Shanghai & Beijing
Italy
London
New York
Paris
San Francisco
Where to Buy the Best of Everything.

Frommer's® Best-Loved Driving Tours

Britain
California
France
Germany
Ireland
Italy
New England
Northern Italy
Scotland
Spain
Tuscany & Umbria

The Unofficial Guides®

Adventure Travel in Alaska
Beyond Disney
California with Kids
Central Italy
Chicago
Cruises
Disneyland®
England
Hawaii
Ireland
Las Vegas
London
Maui
Mexico's Best Beach Resorts
Mini Mickey
New Orleans
New York City
Paris
San Francisco
South Florida including Miami & the Keys
Walt Disney World®
Walt Disney World® for Grown-ups
Walt Disney World® with Kids
Washington, D.C.

Special-Interest Titles

Athens Past & Present
Best Places to Raise Your Family
Cities Ranked & Rated
500 Places to Take Your Kids Before They Grow Up
Frommer's Best Day Trips from London
Frommer's Best RV & Tent Campgrounds in the U.S.A.
Frommer's Exploring America by RV
Frommer's NYC Free & Dirt Cheap
Frommer's Road Atlas Europe
Frommer's Road Atlas Ireland
Retirement Places Rated